Intermediate
Microeconomics

PEARSON CUSTOM PUBLISHING

Intermediate Microeconomics

ALWAYS LEARNING

PEARSON

Harlow, England • London • New York • Boston • San Francisco • Toronto • Sydney • Auckland • Singapore • Hong Kong
Tokyo • Seoul • Taipei • New Delhi • Cape Town • Sao Paulo • Mexico City • Madrid • Amsterdam • Munich • Paris • Milan

Pearson Education Limited
Edinburgh Gate
Harlow
Essex CM20 2JE

And associated companies throughout the world

Visit us on the World Wide Web at:
www.pearsoned.co.uk

This Custom Book Edition © John D. Hey 2012
Published by Pearson Education Limited 2012

Compiled from:

Intermediate Microeconomics
by John D. Hey

ISBN 978 1 78016 013 9

Printed and bound in Great Britain by Ashford Colour Press Ltd.

To my first grandchild, Jack

Errata

(the line numbering does not include counting the running head)

1. Page 74, line 31: '80' should be '180'
2. Page 74, line 32: '70' should be '160'
3. Page 100, line 26 (not counting the '6.10 Mathematical Appendix'):

   $'dq_2 / dq_1 = -aq_2 / [(1 - q_1)q_1]'$ should be $'dq_2 / dq_1 = -aq_2 / [(1 - a)q_1]'$

4. Page 184, line 43: 'consuming' should be 'producing'
5. Page 185, line 2: 'consumes' should be 'produces'
6. Page 187, line 11, '0.24' should be '0.28'
7. Page 190, line 22 (not counting the heading 'Application...?'):
   '100' should be '12'
8. Page 191, line 13: '(0,6)' should be '(6,0)'
9. Page 195, line 16 (counting the heading 'Competitive Trading'): '5.1' should be '15.1'
10. The website on page 6 has been omitted. It should be http://www-users.york.ac.uk/~jdh1/micro%202/.

Brief table of contents

Detailed table of contents

Part 2   Economies with Production   137

Part 3   Applications and Implications of the Basic Tools   217

Preface

About the Book

Intended audience: This text is designed and developed for students who have studied the principles of economics to take them through to the next level in their study of microeconomics. Students who already have some knowledge of economics when starting university will also find this a useful introduction to microeconomics at level 1. The book offers a grounding in the key principles of microeconomics; it supplies the bedrock of core concepts for further study in an economics degree programme.

Relates economics to people in the real world: The author aims to show how economics relates to people. Economic activity stems from the need for different people to trade different resources. This premise is illustrated throughout the book through numerous examples, making the text interesting and relevant to the experience of the student.

Economic methods, with or without maths: The insightful combination of numerous diagrams and figures, and simple mathematics, offers a step-by-step example-led presentation. This enables students to get to grips with the fundamentals, without advanced economic or mathematical competence. Appendices of relevant maths and calculus are supplied for those who wish to study the mathematical background in more detail.

Learning and Assessment Material: Each part begins with a summary outlining what is to follow and providing a clear structure to the student. Chapter introductions and summaries help students to check that they have grasped the key ideas. End of chapter Applications including games and group tasks focus on the applied nature of the topics covered. Exam questions also allow the student to test understanding as they progress and prepare for exams and assessments.

Online Learning Centre: This website resource accompanying the book offers separate sections for both the lecturer and the student. The Lecturer Centre provides PowerPoints, Theoretical Exercises, Lecturer Manual, and Extra Exam Questions. The Student Centre offers Multiple Choice Questions, Test Exercises, and an Ask the Author section.

Message from the author

The first English edition of this book was written in the Clinica Santa Lucia in Rome in 2002, and published by McGraw-Hill in 2003, with the valuable assistance of Julian Partridge, Caroline Howell and a number of referees. An Italian edition was published in 2007 by Aracne Editrice and was co-authored by myself and Carmelo Petraglia. The present edition, which is the same as the first English edition, owes its existence to Heidi Varley.

John Hey
York
June 2011

How to use this Book and the Website

This edition of the book is being published by Pearson Custom Publishing specifically for students on the module of Microeconomics 2 at the University of York. These students will have access to my site http://www-users. york.ac.uk/~jdh1/micro 2/index.htm which contains a wealth of related material. The book and the site should be used in tandem.

The site contains links to the following resources:
- my personal website and those of the tutorial assistants
- the chapters in the book
- the exercises that are used in tutorials
- Dreamweaver animated presentations of each chapter/lecture
- PowerPoint presentations that are used in the lectures to supplement the lecture material
- The raw Maple files that were used to construct the lectures and the book
- information about the examinations
- the timetable of the lectures and the tutorials

I elaborate on each of these below and suggest a study strategy.

A recommended study strategy

First buy the book. You should work constantly (a little bit at a time) and not intermittently. You should work chapter by chapter. Do note that for each chapter in the book, there is one lecture, one PowerPoint presentation, one animated Dreamweaver web page, and one raw Maple file. The latter is only for the real enthusiasts; if you are not (or do not become) an enthusiast then you do not need to look at the raw Maple files. The lectures, the PowerPoints and the Dreamweaver web pages are synchronised – and are giving the same message in different ways. You will find a lot of repetition – or, perhaps better, reinforcement.

The whole idea of the book is to teach a methodology; you are not expected to remember detail. What is the methodology? This is related to what economists do: essentially we propose theories to describe economic behaviour; if the theories are valid (or approximately so) we can then use them to predict behaviour and to make policy recommendations (to governments, local authorities, businesses and individuals). This book is about microeconomics so we are restricting our predictions and our policy recommendations to those at the micro level (though we should note that much of modern macro theory is built on top of microfoundations). While the module is largely theoretical, the methodology is built on the interaction between theories and evidence. We start with theories; we then get empirical data to see if the theory works or not; often the theories involve parameters which are context specific; we have to estimate these parameters; we can then see how well the theories 'explain' the empirical facts and can then use the theories to predict behaviour. Obviously no theory can 'explain' behaviour exactly and there is always a random component; we thus want to see how much of the empirical evidence is 'explained' by our theory and whether we should abandon the theory and generate a more general one which may be able to 'explain' the facts significantly better. (Note that I put the word 'explain' in quotation marks because we can never be sure, even if a theory fits the data exactly, that the theory is actually a description, an explanation, of behaviour.) This methodology is shown in Chapter 16. Here we use as an illustration the question: "what will be the effect on the welfare of the consumers, the profits of the food producers, and the tax revenue of the government, of a tax on food in the UK?". In order to answer the question we need to know a number of things: how the imposition of a tax on food will affect the demand for food; how the imposition of a tax on food will affect the supply of food; how the imposition of a tax on food will affect the price of food; how the welfare of the consumers will be affected; how the profits of the supplies will be affected; and how much tax revenue will be raised by the government.

In order to do this we need to study demand and welfare (this we do in Part 1); we need to study supply and profits (this we do in Part 2); and exchange (this we do in both Parts 1 and 2).

Our theories start simple – in an abstract and simplified world. We then steadily complicate the theories – hopefully making them more realistic – as we move through the book. In a book at this level, we cannot hope to cover the whole field of microeconomics – but we hope that we give an overview of the method: propose a theory; test it empirically; if the theory fits the data sufficiently well, stop there; otherwise propose a more general, hopefully more realistic, theory.

I should now return to advice on studying. Do not remember detail: when you are employed, you can always go to Google for information about detail. Do however remember broad principles – and try and realise the way that economists view and model the world. If you want an expression that distinguishes economists from human beings, then the following encapsulates it all: "life is a trade-off problem". Or "on the one hand this, on the other hand that". We strive to get the optimal balance between things: for consumers between beer and bread; for firms between labour and capital; for governments between this person and that.

Back to studying: liaise your study with the lectures. First, before the lecture, smell the relevant chapter; read it quickly and superficially; concentrate on the assumptions and the conclusions; scan the 'Summary' at the end of the chapter; try and understand new terms and their definitions. Then go to the lecture; do not take detailed notes but simply note any terms and concepts that are not clear to you. After the lecture, re-read the chapter in more detail; concentrate again on the general principles and not on the detail. You might like to go at this stage to the Lecture (Dreamweaver) presentations on the site: http://www-users.york.ac.uk/~jdh1/micro%202/lectures/me??.htm, where ?? is the number of the chapter. This is an html version of the Maple presentations that I will use during the lecture. I supplement this from time to time with Power-Point presentations which are really only a very superficial and incomplete summary of the material in the chapters; you should realise that these are meant for pedagogical use solely in a lecture context, and are in no way a substitute for the chapters in the book. Read again the 'Summary' of the chapter and then try and respond to the 'Review Questions' at the end of the chapter. Fifteen of the 34 chapters also have an 'Application' at the end; these are designed to show you how the theory might be applied to answer questions in the (simplified) real world. You will not be examined on these applications but they will show you how the theory might be used.

The Maple files that I will use during the lectures are only for the aficionados. The material in them is exactly the same as in the Lecture (Dreamweaver) files. However, if you want to look at these, and understand things more deeply, you are very welcome to do so. If you are familiar with Maple you could change the code (in the program sub-directory) and play around with different parameters and functional forms. All the computers on campus have Maple 14 potentially available and you can load them on to the machine, though I understand that those for public use are 'cleaned' daily – so you will have to reload Maple every time you login afresh on those machines.

I should also say a word about mathematics. You will see from the book that I try to avoid the use of mathematics where possible. I illustrate everything graphically. If you have problems with graphs then you will have problems with the book, and you should try and bring yourself up to speed with graphs as soon as possible. But graphs are not mathematics – they are merely one way of expressing things, a visual way. I use coloured graphs to make them simpler (so do not try and read the book, or anything else connected with the book, on a Kindle, or printed in black and white). This book uses four colours to make the point. If this is the last module of microeconomics that you are going to study, you will not need mathematics any further. However, if you are going on to do Micro 3, for example, or any other module that builds on Micro 2, then you will, at some stage, need some maths. That is why I have inserted a 'Mathematical Appendix' at the end of some of the chapters. If you like maths you will enjoy these appendices, and if you are taking your study of microeconomics further, you will need these appendices. If you are not taking microeconomics further, you can probably happily ignore these appendices.

You will notice that there is a lot of repetition in the material on the site. This is partly because I am lazy (or, rather, efficient as we economists like to say) but it is more to do with reinforcement: so much of the material on individuals is remarkably similar to the material on firms – one can exploit and learn from the parallels; also I use the same graphs in different contexts – because the concepts are similar. You can learn a lot, and save energy, by exploiting these parallels.

There are also the tutorials. They are on the site. I will brief the tutors about how they should conduct the tutorials. You should participate wholeheartedly and not be intellectually arrogant. You will notice that there is a mix of things to do in the tutorials: some are straightforward exercises; some are games; some are competitions; you can even do experiments. I try to avoid maths wherever possible: there is one that looks mathematical but it is more about manipulation and interpretation rather than mathematical technique. Before the tutorial finishes do ensure that the tutor has clarified anything that confuses you. Tutorials are for you to learn – and are not things to survive and endure. If necessary, fix an appointment with your tutor to clear up any residual misunderstandings.

Finally a word about the examination. As I write these words I have not yet finally decided on the format of the examinations. I intend, however, given the large number of students on the module, and the nature of the subject, to have examinations that are not only marked by the computer, but also generated by the computer. I am NOT going to extract multiple choice questions at random from a large data bank of such questions, but I am planning to extend what I did when I taught in Italy (I have taught there for some eleven years). In Italy there is an enormous number of students, and there are lots of examination sessions every year (when I taught in Bari there were eleven sessions every year, and when I went to complain to the Dean of the Faculty he said "John, you should be happy – there used to be twelve!"). I wrote a computer program which generated sets of exercises – not mathematical ones but ones that could be solved with graphs and economic intuition. The great joy of my system was that each exercise (on any particular topic) was different from any past ones, so that memorising answers did not work for the students – they had to work out the solution to each problem afresh and from first principles. So my examinations tested understanding and application of general principles. You can get some feel for the type of questions by going to my Italian website, but I intend to make it more sophisticated and extensive before implementing it here at York. Incidentally the 'exam questions' at the end of the book are not an indication of what the exams in the future will be like.

I really do hope you enjoy the module and the book. Economics is great fun and very useful. I hope that I can communicate these two things through the module and the book.

John D Hey
York
June 2011

Acknowledgements

Our thanks go to the following reviewers for their comments at various stages in the text's development:

Fredrik Andersson	Lund University, Sweden
Margaret Bray	London School of Economics and Political Science
Martin Dufwenberg	Stockholm University, Sweden
Pablo Garcia	University of Newcastle upon Tyne
Robert Scott Gassler	Vrije University, The Netherlands
Henrick Jaldell	Karlstad University, Sweden
Tim James	Sheffield University
Todd Kaplan	University of Exeter
Francis Kiraly	Keele University
Alistair Munro	University of East Anglia
Silvia Palano	University of Oxford
Gioia Pescetto	University of Durham
Renee Prendergast	Queen's University, Belfast
Bettina Rockenbach	University of Erfurt, Germany
Cillian Ryan	The University of Birmingham
Michael Ryan	University of Hull
Sigbjorn Sodal	Agder University College, Norway
Thibaud Verge	University of Bristol
Robert E. Wright	University of Stirling

Guided tour

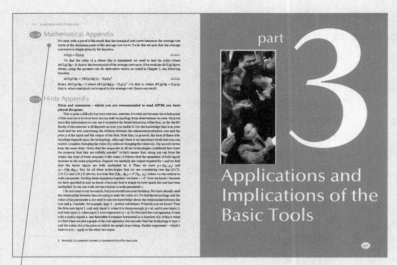

Part Openers

There are four Part Openers, which introduce the topics and themes covered throughout the four Parts of the text.

Mathematical Appendix

These sections at the end of the chapters provide formal mathematical derivations for those who wish to use them. They are not necessary to understand the economics of the text, but rather are for those who are interested in using the mathematics.

Important Concepts/Ideas

These are highlighted throughout each chapter and provide key points for ease of reference.

Introduction

Each chapter opens with an Introduction, which sets the scene for the reader and introduces them to the issues that will be addressed in the chapter.

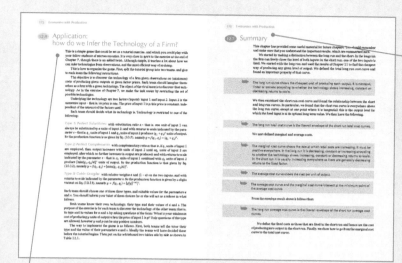

End of Chapter Summary

This briefly reviews and reinforces the main topics you will have covered in each chapter, to ensure you have acquired a solid understanding of the key topics.

Applications

Relevant chapters end with an Application that aims to illustrate the main themes of the chapter, allowing you to visualize how the theory applies in real life.

Figures and Tables

Each chapter provides a number of figures and tables to help you to visualize the various economic models, and to illustrate and summarize important concepts.

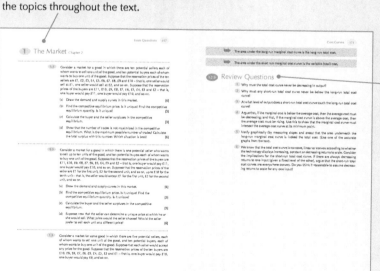

Exam Questions and Exercises

This appendix provides a multitude of questions you can use to practise for your exams. They may be used as helpful revision questions, or to check your progress as you cover the topics throughout the text.

Review Questions

These questions encourage you to review and apply the knowledge you have acquired from each chapter, and can be undertaken to test your understanding.

Introduction

1.1 People are Different

I should begin by explaining the theme of this book. It is very simple but also quite profound, and relates to the question as to why there is economic activity. To answer it we need to first ask: 'what is economic activity?'. It is simply the exchange of goods and services between individuals. And why is there such activity? Because *people are different*. If, on the contrary, all people were identical in terms of their preferences and their endowments then (except in certain exceptional cases – some examples are given in the text) there will no opportunity for trade or exchange between individuals. However if *people are different* – either in their preferences or in their endowments – then in general (though there are some exceptional cases – examples are given in the text) there will be the opportunity for some exchange between individuals that makes all people involved in the trade better off; that is, they would voluntarily take part in the exchange. I think this result is simultaneously very profound and rather trivial, but understanding why it is true is crucial to becoming an economist. In the pages that follow I will explain it and illustrate it in a variety of contexts, ranging from simple exchange of goods, to the exchange of goods through time, to the exchange of risk, and so on.

I should explain in a little more detail why I define economic activity as exchange. Certain examples are obvious. When I go to the supermarket to buy something, I am exchanging some of my money for the items I have bought, and the supermarket is exchanging the items that I have bought for money. Both of us do it because we are better off as a consequence. Similarly, when I work for someone I am exchanging my labour for the wage, and the person who is employing me is exchanging money for my labour. Again, both of us do it because we are better off as a consequence.

There are two sides to any exchange: each of us is giving one thing in exchange for another. In capitalist economies one of the two things is usually money, but that does not have to be the case; one of the things could be tokens or payments in kind. Often one of the two things is a physical good like a television set or beer, but that does not have to be the case; one of the things could be a service. For example, when you buy a ticket for a concert you are exchanging money for the music in the concert. One of the things being exchanged could be a financial asset – a stock or a share – which may give money at some time in the future. In this way you are exchanging money at one point in time for money at other points in time. One of the things being exchanged could be insurance – which is a promise to pay some money if some event happens. For many exchanges there are usually well-defined markets in which the exchanges take place, but this does not necessarily have to be the case. In such cases it may be true that one side of the exchange is giving something to the other side without getting anything in return. The thing being given may be something good – for example, when you see some pretty flowers in some garden and get pleasure out of them; or it may be something bad – for example, when someone is making a loud noise when you are trying to sleep. As we shall see, situations in which there is no well-defined market for the item being exchanged create problems, but we will still be able to say something useful about the nature of the exchange. There are other contexts in which one side of the market is implicit rather than explicit; when you do a favour for someone there is often an implicit understanding that the favour will be repaid in the future. In many contexts there is usually some kind of implicit understanding between the two sides to the exchange, simply because it is often not possible to specify all the details of the exchange completely and explicitly. But let us worry about these awkward cases later, and begin by considering the more straightforward ones.

The crucial point is the following: economic activity stems from the fact that *people are different*. It follows that, in general, the exchange of goods and services between individuals can be good for everyone involved in the exchange. The obvious next question is: 'what is the best way of organizing such an exchange?' In one sense most of the book is addressed to answering this question. We shall see that economists can say something, but cannot say everything. This is a consequence of the fact that economists cannot really say anything about distributional issues. To understand what is meant by this, we should take a step back and ask ourselves how we might measure the gains from exchange. We have already established that, in general, there are mutual advantages from exchange: in the sale and purchase of a good, both the buyer and the seller are better off as a consequence of the sale. Obviously the gains from the sale to the buyer and the seller depend upon a number of things, including the price at which the good is sold; the higher the sale price, the higher the gain to the seller and the lower the gain to the buyer. As we shall see, there are ways of measuring the gains from exchange. We can therefore calculate the gains accruing to the various participants in the exchange for any given exchange mechanism.

An 'exchange mechanism' is simply some way of organizing the exchange; if we look at what happens in the real world we see that there is a whole variety of different exchange mechanisms, ranging from auctions, through tenders to supermarkets. We can then ask: 'which is the best exchange mechanism?' Obviously the answer to this depends upon what we mean by best. One possibility is that we mean that the total gains from the exchange are maximized. Economists can give an answer to this question. However if we are worried as to whether the distribution of the gains is optimal in some sense, economists have difficulties unless they are told how to trade-off one set of surpluses against another.

One of the things that economists can do is to measure the gains from exchange and hence determine which exchange mechanisms are better in terms of the total gains realized from the exchanges in the market. So economists can advise governments on: what may be the best way to sell rights to mobile telephone companies; the best way to organize the buying and selling of goods and services; the best way to intervene when one side of the market becomes too powerful; and so on. But economists can do much more. How much more will become clearer as the book proceeds, but we can give some examples here.

We restrict attention in these examples to exchanges in which one of the things being exchanged is money. So one side of the exchange is using money to buy the good or service (or whatever it is that is being exchanged), while the other side is selling the good or service for money. Consider first the buyer. We can see that the willingness of the buyer to buy obviously depends upon the price of the good in the exchange; in general the higher the price, the less of the good that the buyer would want to buy. What determines the demand of the buyer? Clearly the price, as we have already discussed, and obviously the income of the buyer. The availability of other goods similar to the one involved in this particular exchange is important also; if there are lots of close substitutes, then the price that the individual will be willing to pay will not depart much from the prices of these substitutes; and particularly important are the preferences of the buyer. These preferences are fundamental and they generally differ from individual to individual. Indeed the preferences may well determine what goods the buyer thinks are close substitutes. For example, I find it almost impossible to distinguish between different kinds of lager – to me, all lagers taste almost the same. Yet I know there are other people who think Stella is wonderful while Harp is terrible (while others think the opposite). A more subtle determinant is the existence of complements to the good being exchanged. There are smokers who think that a cigarette is the perfect complement to a beer: when drinking a beer in a pub, they consider a cigarette is the perfect accompaniment and they would not smoke unless they were drinking. For such people the price of cigarettes is going to affect their demand for beer; for non-smokers the price of cigarettes is completely irrelevant.

As we will see later in the book, if we know the preferences of an individual and his or her income, we can determine how much the individual (as a buyer) would demand at any given price of the good, and indeed whether the individual would in fact be a buyer at some price. This latter is an important point: whether we are buyers or sellers of a good or service will depend upon how much of the good or service we currently have, and the price at which we could buy or sell it. Suppose, for example, you already own a TV set in your house. If the price of a second TV set were sufficiently low, you might buy a second TV (to put in the bedroom or even the bathroom), while if someone offered you a sufficiently high price for the TV set you already own, you might be tempted to sell.

In general, the quantity of a good that an individual will be willing to sell depends on the quantity that he or she already has and the price being offered. It obviously depends also on the income of the individual and, most crucially, on the individual's preferences. For example, whether the individual has other goods which he or she regards as close substitutes for the good in question, as well as goods which are highly complementary to it, will influence the quantity that he or she is willing to sell. As we will see later in the book, if we know the preferences of an individual and his or her income, we can determine how much the individual (as a seller) would sell at any given price of the good, and indeed whether the individual would be a seller at some price.

You could argue that we are unlikely to know the preferences of any individual, and until we do all the above is quite irrelevant. True – but there are ways of identifying the preferences. We could ask the individual. A more feasible alternative is to follow the methodology used by all scientists. This involves the economist first observing the individual, using those observations to infer the preferences of the individual, and then using those inferred preferences to predict the demand and supply of the individual. The economist can use this methodology to predict the demand and supply for a group of individuals, or indeed a whole economy. You might argue that this methodology appears somewhat circular and does not get us anywhere. But it does: we only need to observe the individual in a subset of circumstances to predict his or her behaviour in others. This is exactly what is done when predicting where the earth will be in relation to the sun at some time in the future: the astronomer has observed the way the earth and the sun have moved together in the past, has used these observations to construct a theory of the relationship between the sun and the earth, and uses this theory to predict the future relationship. The theory that we will construct later in this book, concerning the effect of preferences on demand and supply, is equivalent to the theory of gravity which explains the relative movements of the sun and the earth.

In many exchanges one side of the exchange is a firm not an individual, and some of the above needs to be modified appropriately. A firm is different from an individual in that typically it is involved in a process of transformation – it buys some inputs (factors) and transforms them through some production process into outputs which it then sells. If you like, the production process technology of the firm replaces the preferences of the individual in the previous discussion. As we shall show, the quantity that a firm is willing to produce and sell depends on the price of that output, the prices of all the inputs into the production process, and on the technology of the firm. If we know the technology of the firm we can predict the supply of the firm at any price. If we do not know the technology, we use either of the techniques discussed above: we either ask the firm or we infer the technology by observing the firm. Once again the economist uses the methodology of the scientist. Note carefully: this scientific methodology requires the construction of a theory based on reasonable assumptions (just like the astronomer), which is then tested and used for prediction.

Once we know how demand and supply are determined, we can begin our analysis of the best exchange mechanism. We can also offer advice to governments or other policy makers if they are not happy with an existing exchange mechanism. For example, if we see a market in which there is just one seller, and it is this one seller who is choosing the price, we can ask whether this is a good thing and, if it is not, we can suggest ways round the problem. You will probably have noticed that many governments are enthusiastically in favour of competition, though from time to time they permit the existence (if perhaps a controlled existence) of monopoly – a single agent on one side of the market. We show why later in the book.

There are other things that the economist can do, as will become apparent as the book proceeds; it would be premature to discuss them here. I hope that I have convinced you that what the economist does is important and that the methodology of the economist is close to that of the natural scientist. It is for that reason that we will be constructing theories to describe behaviour throughout the book.

One final thing: why *micro*economics? Many microeconomic texts start with some statement saying that microeconomics is what *little* economists do. But this is neither funny nor true. The essential point about microeconomics is that it starts at the level of the individual – the individual person or the individual firm – an entity with a supposed unitary objective. It starts at the most basic level and builds up from there. As we shall show in Chapter 17, we can aggregate our findings so that they apply to a group of any size, or indeed to an economy. When we get to the level of the economy we have entered the realm of *macro*economics. But note: this is built on the *micro*-foundation that this book has provided.

1.2 The Underlying Philosophy

The writing of this book has been guided by an underlying philosophy which has two components: one concerning what should be included and in what order; and the second concerning how it should be presented.

The ordering of the material differs from other texts, and is determined by the considerations which underlie the discussion above. The book starts with an example of exchange and its efficiency. It goes on to discuss preferences and how they determine supply and demand; this enables a deeper discussion to take place of the benefits of exchange and the relative advantages of different exchange mechanisms. There follows a brief interlude on welfare issues before the book turns to a treatment of the firm. There is then an empirical interlude which is followed by a part generalizing and applying the methods of the early part. Finally, there is an extended treatment of 'what might go wrong'. What this means will become clearer as the book proceeds, but it covers some of the issues that have been discussed in Section 1.1 – the lack of a market or a single seller; it also considers further difficult cases of exchange.

More generally, the book is concerned with what is traditionally referred to as intermediate microeconomics. The word 'intermediate' refers partly to the level of sophistication of the assumed readers, but mainly to the level of sophistication of the results contained within the book. It is normally assumed that the readers already have some basic knowledge of economics in that they have already studied a one-year introductory course covering the whole of economics. This is not to say that the book cannot be tackled unless one has studied such an introductory course; on the contrary, the material in this book should be accessible even to those who have made no such preliminary study.

More importantly, the word intermediate refers to the level of sophistication of the results presented. Here some caution is needed relating to the level of sophistication of the techniques needed to derive the results. This is one key area which distinguishes this text from its competitors, and which relates to the use of mathematics within economics. I myself am a firm believer that, to be truly able to apply economics to real-world problems, at some stage one has to learn the appropriate associated mathematical techniques, including reasonably sophisticated calculus, and associated statistical techniques including econometrics. But I am also a firm believer that one can understand the key economic concepts without the use of such mathematical techniques. Indeed, in a world where the level of mathematical understanding of the typical undergraduate student is shrinking at a frightening pace I believe that, unless properly taught, the use of mathematics in intermediate microeconomics courses can seriously impede the learning of economics by the typical economics student. However, and fortunately, at the same time advances in computing techniques have taken place in recent years which mean that advantage can be taken of such advances in the teaching of economics, in such a way that students do not need to have a deep understanding of mathematics to understand the key points of economics advanced in this book. Although one could argue the contrary, the key concepts that economists (as distinct from non-economists) understand, and hence which make them economists – such as the fact that all interesting problems involve some kind of trade-off and hence a relative evaluation of gains and losses (or benefits and costs) – can, in my opinion, be taught without the use of sophisticated mathematical techniques by the student. This is not to say that one does not need such techniques; rather, that they do not need to be exercised (or understood) by the students themselves. In this book I, or more correctly my computer-based mathematical software, does the mathematical analysis. So the mathematics is there; it is just that the reader does not have to do it, or understand it.

The price (for there is always a trade-off) is that the analysis in this book is almost 100 per cent graphical – I assume that the reader can read graphs and understands what they mean. I also assume, very particularly and importantly, that the reader can compute the slope of a line, and hence the slope of a curve at a particular point (the slope of the tangent to that curve at that point), and can compute (at least in principle) the magnitude of any area within a graph. To give readers confidence in their ability to do this, and hence in their ability to understand key concepts of economics, I deliberately and consistently draw precise graphs wherein such slopes and areas can be calculated accurately by the reader. I draw my own graphs (or more precisely, my mathematical software does if for me under my instructions) rather than let some artist, who knows no economics, draw them for me.

The fact that I have accurately drawn the various graphs is important in the sense that the reader can physically verify the various examples presented in the text. For some readers such a process of verification is important; it helps build up their confidence. For other readers it is general principles that are important – that is, the general method how one goes from one kind of analysis to another. For me, both are important: as far as general understanding is concerned, the first is important; as far as applying the material in a particular case, the second is important. While economists like to make their analysis as general as possible, almost always they have to make some assumption about particular functional forms.

The book differs from some other competitors also in that it always keeps in mind how the material is to be applied. I do not do theory just for theory's sake, but for the purpose of applying the material in practice. At the same time the book is essentially a book about theory, so such references are relatively minor; however the whole of Chapter 16 is devoted to such issues.

1.3 Associated Material

This book is self-contained and can be used by itself. There is, however, an associated web site. This is accessible at the address:

http://www.mcgraw-hill.co.uk/textbooks/hey

This web site contains a wealth of useful material. The lecturers' site contains a set of Maple lecture files, one for each chapter of the book; and the readers' site contains *html* output from these Maple files which can be used as lecture handouts. The graphs in this book are a subset of the graphs in the Maple lecture files[1]. The readers' site contains an interactive exercise section, guiding the students through the exercises without directly giving them the answers. The lecturers' site contains a set of tutorial exercises and a set of exam questions.

1.4 Mathematical Pre-requisites

As I have already noted, readers are not required to have a sophisticated knowledge of mathematics in order to understand this book. However, some mathematical terminology is used as well as some mathematical concepts. I discuss these in this section.

There are students who like mathematics, and lecturers who think that students ought to be able to use mathematics. For them, the book would be incomplete without some formal derivations. After much thought, I have decided to include these derivations in an appendix to most chapters. If you like mathematics, you will like these appendices; if you do not, I would advise you that it is not necessary to understand the mathematics in the appendices in order to understand the economics of the book. Do keep this in mind as you read the book. I conclude this section with a discussion of the mathematical concepts and terminology used in the book.

I start with the idea of variables and constants. Rather obviously, a variable is something that varies, or may take different values, while a constant is something that remains constant. Sometimes I use the word parameter to describe something that is constant.

---

1. The lecture files are available on the lecturer's website.

The next key concept is that of a *relationship* between variables. In this book, relationships usually describe how one variable depends upon another. Mathematically we use the expression *function* to express and describe a relationship. The graph of a function shows the relationship in graphical terms.

Let me give an example. Suppose a car is moving at a constant 30 kilometres per hour. This is a constant, a parameter. What is the relationship between the time that the car has been travelling and the distance it has travelled in that time? If it has been travelling for one hour it will have travelled 30 kilometres; if it has been travelling for two hours it will have travelled 60 kilometres; and so on. There is a clear relationship between the time that it has been travelling and the distance travelled. We can describe this in mathematical terms as follows. First, we give names to the two variables involved: the time that it has been moving and the distance covered. Let us call the first t (for time) and the second d (for distance). These are variables because they can take a whole range of values. These values refer to the units in which the variables are measured. Let us take the units of time to be hours and the units of distance to be kilometres. So, for example, $t = 3$ means the car has been travelling for 3 hours, and $d = 25$ means that it has travelled 25 kilometres. How can we express the relationship between d and t if the car is travelling at a constant 30 kilometres per hour?

In our two examples above, we have that if $t = 1$ then $d = 30$, and if $t = 2$ then $d = 60$. It should be obvious that d is always 30 times t – precisely because the car is moving at a constant 30 kilometres per hour. The relationship between d and t can be expressed in the following way:

$$d = 30t$$

(1.1)

This equation represents the relationship between d and t; Eq. (1.1) is a function between d and t. We can show this relationship graphically. In Fig. 1.1 we put the variable t on the horizontal axis and the variable d on the vertical axis. The line represents the relationship. Note that on the line, when $t = 1$ $d = 30$, and when $t = 2$ $d = 60$, and so on. The line does indeed correctly represent the relationship between the time travelled and the distance travelled. Incidentally, when we have a graph in which the variables on the axes are t and d (as in this example), we will refer to the graph as being drawn 'in (t, d) space'. This is simply a shorthand way of referring to the variables on the axes.

Note that, in this example, we could describe d as the *dependent* variable as its value depends upon the value of t, which we could call the *independent* variable. Normally the independent variable is put on the horizontal axis and the dependent variable on the vertical axis, but this does not need to be the case. We could show the relationship between t and d as in Fig 1.2, which is the inverse of Fig. 1.1.

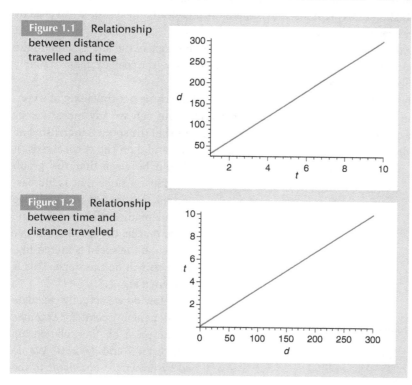

Figure 1.1 Relationship between distance travelled and time

Figure 1.2 Relationship between time and distance travelled

Once again, the line represents the relationship. Note that, on the line, when $t = 1$ then $d = 30$, and when $t = 2$ then $d = 60$, and so on. The line does indeed correctly represent the relationship between the time elapsed and the distance travelled. But the graph does not tell us which variable is dependent and which is independent; we have to understand that from elsewhere.

We can see in this example that the graph of the relationship is a straight line. Accordingly, we say that the function given in Eq. (1.1) is a *linear function*. The general case is presented in Eq. (1.2), in which a and b are constants or parameters and x and y are variables:

$$y = a + bx \qquad\qquad (1.2)$$

You should note that when x is zero then $y = a$, and that for every increase of one unit in x, the variable y increases by b. Note therefore that the graph of this relationship, when plotted with x on the vertical axis and y on the horizontal, is a straight line which cuts the vertical axis when $y = a$. We naturally call a the *intercept* of the line with the y axis.

The next important mathematical concept is that of the *slope* of a straight line. This measures how much the line rises when we move rightwards. More precisely, it measures how much the variable on the vertical axis increases if we increase the variable on the horizontal axis by one. If we look at Fig. 1.1, we see that, for every extra hour elapsed, the distance travelled increases by 30. The slope is 30 or, more properly, 30 kilometres per hour (for every extra hour elapsed, the distance travelled increases by 30 kilometres.) You will notice something about this slope – it is precisely equal to the speed of the car! This is no coincidence, as you will discover if you draw the graph of the relationship between d and t at a constant 60 kilometres per hour, or at a constant 100 kilometres per hour, or whatever. In our 30 kilometres per hour example, the slope of the relationship between t on the horizontal axis and d on the vertical axis is precisely 30 (kilometres per hour) because the car is going at 30 kilometres per hour, and is therefore increasing the distance travelled by 30 kilometres for every extra hour elapsed.

In the general linear case, as specified by Eq. (1.2), the slope of the line is equal to the parameter b. Notice that the slope is equal to the coefficient of x. The coefficient of x is simply the constant which multiplies x in Eq. (1.2).

What happens to the relationship between d and t if the car is not travelling at a constant speed? The relationship is clearly no longer linear, but can we say more? Let us suppose that the car is accelerating all the time. This means that the speed is increasing all the time. If we draw a graph with t on the horizontal axis and d on the vertical axis, it should be clear that the graph will have a slope that is increasing all the time. Why? Well, we have already established that the slope reveals the speed of the car and so, if the speed is increasing, then so will be the slope. This is shown in Fig. 1.3.

How do we actually calculate the slope at any point, for example, at the point on this relationship where $t = 5$ and $d = 250$? We do so by drawing the *tangent* to the

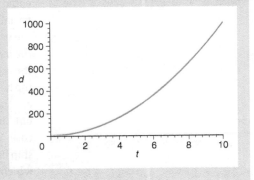

Figure 1.3 Relationship between distance and time if accelerating

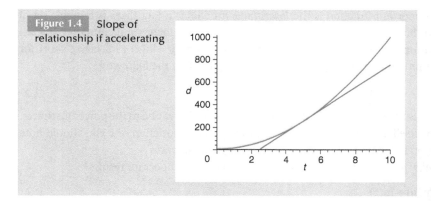

Figure 1.4 Slope of relationship if accelerating

curve at this point. The tangent[2] is a straight line which touches the curve at the point ($t = 5$, $d = 250$) and therefore has the same slope as the curve at that point; see Fig. 1.4. We can calculate the slope of this tangent; it is 100 because along the tangent, for each increase of t by one unit, the value of d increases by 100. You should check this out.

A relationship in which the slope is constant, as we have already noted, is called a linear relationship; one in which the slope is increasing all the time we call a *convex* relationship, and one in which the slope is decreasing all the time we call a *concave* relationship. Note that if the slope is decreasing all the time it may eventually become negative. A straight line which slopes downwards, rather than upwards as in the graphs above, has a constant negative slope, telling us how much the variable on the vertical axis decreases when the variable on the horizontal axis increases by one.

Mathematically, if some variable y is a function of some other variable x, denoted by $y = f(x)$, then the slope of the function is called the *derivative* of y with respect to x. Mathematicians use the notation dy/dx to indicate the derivative of y with respect to x.

There are some particular functions, in addition to the linear function, that we will be using in this book. It is not really important that you understand all the details but I should warn you in advance that these functions may appear. One is the *power* function where the relationship is given by the function

$$y = ax^b \tag{1.3}$$

In Eq. (1.3) the a and b are constants (or parameters). This says that y is equal to a times x raised to the power b; this latter means x multiplied by itself b times[3]. If the parameters a and b are both positive then y is an increasing function of x. If the parameter b is greater than one, the relationship is convex, if b is equal to one, then the relationship is linear, and if b is less than one the relationship is concave. You are not expected to be able to prove these results, but you could take some particular values for a and b and verify that they are true.

A particularly important function is the *exponential* function given by

$$y = ae^{bx} \tag{1.4}$$

The letter e is a very important constant (2.718281828 ...). This has some magical properties that are difficult to explain without some rather complicated maths. One of these properties is that the slope of the function $y = e^x$ is also equal to e^x. Note that Eq. (1.4) says that y is equal to a multiplied by e raised to the power of b multiplied by x – that is, e multiplied by itself bx times.

---

2. The crucial point about the tangent is that it touches the curve at just one point. If we take a line slightly higher it intersects the curve at two points; if we take a line slightly lower it does not touch the curve at all. The important property of the tangent to the curve at some point is that it touches the curve at that point and therefore has the same slope as the curve at that point.

3. If b is an integer, this is clear – for example x^2 is simply x times x, x^3 is simply x times x times x, and so on. If b is not an integer, we need to define x^b rather more precisely.

Another important function is the *logarithmic* function. In fact there is a whole set of these functions but I will consider just one, called the natural logarithmic function. If y is a natural logarithm of x then we denote the relationship by $y = \ln(x)$ ('ln' being short for natural logarithm) and the relationship is defined implicitly by the following

$$y = \ln(x) \qquad \text{if and only if} \qquad x = e^y \tag{1.5}$$

This says that y is the natural logarithm of x if and only if x is e raised to the power y, (that is, e multiplied by itself y times). If we draw the graph of y as a function of x you should note that the function is concave – the slope is decreasing as x increases.

Because $e^y e^z = e^{(y+z)}$ and $(e^y)^z = e^{yz}$ we get the following important results[4]

$$\ln(yz) = \ln(y) + \ln(z) \tag{1.6}$$

$$\ln(y^z) = z \ln(y) \tag{1.7}$$

We will be making use of these in later chapters of the book. If you like mathematics you could try and verify these results. Otherwise you should just accept them – your future understanding will not depend on knowing how to prove them.

The last few equations have been a bit tough – and a bit peripheral. Let us return to some simpler and more important material. Frequently throughout this book we will want to find the point at which something is maximized (like profits) or minimized (like costs). Usually what is being maximized or minimized is a function of some variable under the control of someone. We then ask: what is the best value of this control variable in the sense of maximizing or minimizing the item of interest? Graphically it is simple. Consider Fig. 1.5. Can you indicate graphically the point on the graph where the value of y is maximized?

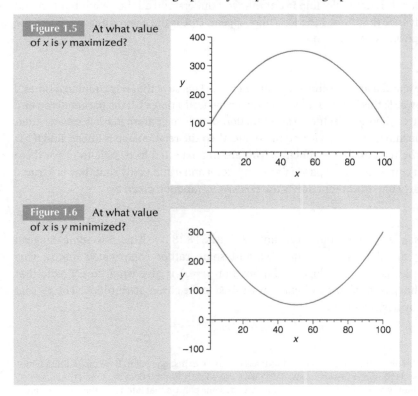

Figure 1.5 At what value of x is y maximized?

Figure 1.6 At what value of x is y minimized?

Graphically it is easy – it is simply at the top of the hill. What do you notice about the top of the hill? Yes, it is flat – the slope at the top is zero. This is how we identify the point where y (the dependent variable) is maximized. What about the opposite? Consider Fig. 1.6. Can you indicate graphically the point on the graph where the value of y is minimized?

Graphically, again it is easy; it is simply at the bottom of the valley. What do you notice about this point? Yes, once again the graph is flat at that point; the slope of the function at the bottom is zero. This is how we identify the point where y (the dependent variable) is minimized.

This is all very well and good, but there is one remaining problem. We note that we have

---

4.   Indeed, this is also true if we replace e by any other constant.

exactly the same condition at the top and at the bottom, at a maximum or at a minimum; namely, that the slope is zero. How do we distinguish between them? Simply as follows: when you arrive at the top of a hill, you know that the slope up to that point was positive (you were going up) but decreasing; whereas after, when you start going down the hill, the slope is negative. The opposite is the case at the bottom of the valley. So the difference is clear; at a maximum the slope is zero and it is decreasing; at a minimum the slope is zero and it is increasing. Mathematicians call the first of these conditions (slope = 0) the *first-order* condition and the second (whether the slope is decreasing – a maximum; or increasing – a minimum) the *second-order* condition. Now you know how simple these two terms are, there is no need to be worried about the mathematics!

So far we have been discussing situations in which one variable is dependent on one other variable. We shall encounter cases in which one variable is dependent on several other variables. Let us first consider the case when there are just two other variables. Suppose the dependent variable is called y and the independent variables are called x_1 and x_2. We can write the relationship in the following form.

$$y = f(x_1, x_2) \tag{1.8}$$

Eq. (1.8) simply says what we have already said in words: that y is a function of x_1 and x_2. An example is the demand for some good or service by some individual; as we have already discussed, this is usually a function of the price of the good and the income of the individual. A graph of this relationship would be a graph in three dimensions, which of course we are all familiar with as the world has three physical dimensions (up and down, north and south, and east and west). We have the same condition for the maximum or the minimum of y with respect to x_1 and x_2; the slope in every direction should be zero. Just imagine that you are at the top or at the bottom of a hill; at the exact point at which you are standing, the hill is flat in every direction. In particular, if we move eastwards or westwards the slope is zero, and if we move northwards or southwards the slope is zero. There are also corresponding second-order conditions to distinguish between when we are at the top of a hill and when we are at the bottom.

We can generalize this to the situation in which one variable is dependent upon lots of other variables. Suppose the dependent variable is called y and the independent variables are called $x_1, x_2, ..., x_n$; there are n of them. We can write the relationship in the following form

$$y = f(x_1, x_2, ..., x_n) \tag{1.9}$$

Eq. (1.9) simply says what we have already said in words: that y is a function of $x_1, x_2, ..., x_n$. A graph of this relationship would be a graph in $(n + 1)$ dimensions, which is rather difficult to visualize but exists in the world of mathematics. We have the same condition as before for the maximum or the minimum of y with respect to $x_1, x_2, ..., x_n$; the slope in every direction should be zero. There are also corresponding second-order conditions.

We can use these properties to find the maximum or minimum of some function subject to some constraints. We do not need much material at this stage and indeed, if you are not familiar with mathematics, it will not mean much to you. But I am introducing it so that you will know what I am talking about when I refer to it in the future. More detail is given in the mathematical appendix. We consider here just a simple case where there are two independent variables x_1 and x_2, which are subject to some constraint. We can write the relationship between y and x_1 and x_2 in the form of Eq. (1.8) above, and we can write the constraint in the form:

$$g(x_1, x_2) = 0 \tag{1.10}$$

This simply says that there is some function which x_1 and x_2 must satisfy. To maximize (or minimize) y with respect to x_1 and x_2, subject to the constraint (1.10), we use a clever trick invented by the mathematician Lagrange. He suggested forming a new function L defined by

$$L = f(x_1, x_2) + \lambda g(x_1, x_2) \tag{1.11}$$

We then maximize (or minimize) L with respect to x_1, x_2 and λ. Maximization (or minimization) with respect to λ automatically guarantees that the constraint is met. Why? Because Eq. (1.11) is linear in λ, and therefore its slope in the λ direction is simply its coefficient $g(x_1, x_2)$. Putting this equal to zero guarantees that the constraint is met. Clever! We will occasionally be using this technique to prove results that will be useful, but it is not necessary that you understand the technique. What is important is that you recognize it when it appears (it is called the Langrange multiplier technique), and have faith that it really does work.

There is one final thing that we ought to discuss because we will use it frequently throughout the book. It is the concept of an area. How to calculate areas in general is quite difficult unless we can use some mathematics, but there are two cases that are easy to consider. One is the area of a rectangle and the other is the area of a triangle. If a rectangle (a four-sided figure in which adjacent sides are at right-angles to each other) has sides measuring a and b, then its area is simply ab or a times b. This is also the area of a parallelogram (a four-sided figure in which opposite sides are parallel – that is, have the same slope) with base a and height b. From this we can see that the area of a triangle with base a and height b is one-half of a times b (since a triangle is simply one-half of a parallelogram).

Mathematically, an area under a function is the integral of that function. We shall discuss this intuitively in Chapters 12 and 13. In the meantime it is not important that you know what the integral of a function is.

1.5 Summary and Preview

Perhaps the most important thing to get from this chapter is the notion that economics exists, and economic activity exists, because *people are different*. If people were not different then usually mutually advantageous trade would not exist, and there would be no need for economic activity. However if people differ, either in their tastes or their endowments, then there usually exists the possibility of mutually advantageous trade in which all parties to the trade end up better off than before.

The whole point of the study of economics is to see how this possibility for mutually advantageous trade can best be implemented. This partly involves how best to organize the process of exchange – how to bring people together who might benefit from exchange and how best to organize their exchange, how to stop people being exploited, etc. This involves working out how, and how much, people gain from exchange – how we can measure that, both at an individual level and at a market level.

We also need to be able to predict what people will do in certain situations. These situations may be completely new situations in that we do not know anything to begin with. Or they may be changes from some situations in which we already know something about the behaviour of the people, or in which we may not know what they are doing already, but we want to predict how their behaviour changes in some way – for example, how their demand changes if their income changes or if the price of some good changes.

We may also want to predict what effect this change has on the welfare of individuals, who may already have been indulging in economic activity but the change affects what activity they can do. Or it may let them start indulging in some new activity and we may wish to measure what effect this has on them.

1.6 Review Questions

1   Why is economic activity caused by the fact that *people are different*?

2   Do you think that there could be economic activity even if people were identical? (Be careful – this is a difficult question. For a possible answer you could look at the end of Chapter 25.)

3   Consider any exchange activity and describe the two sides to the exchange. Why is there such an exchange?

1.7 Mathematical Appendix

In the text we have done almost as much as we need. Most of the material is accessible graphically and usually you will not need to do any mathematics. But if you like to do mathematics, then the following additional notes may be helpful.

We have defined a function as a relationship between one variable and another. Let us call them y and x and suppose that y is a function of x, which we can write $y = f(x)$ where $f(.)$ is some function. As already noted, the slope of the graph of y against x (plotted with x on the horizontal axis and y on the vertical axis) measures the rate at which y increases when x increases. Mathematically the slope is defined as the derivative of y with respect to x, and this is denoted by dy/dx. Formally, this is defined as the limit of the slope of the line joining (x, y) and $(x + \Delta x, y + \Delta y)$. That is,

$$dy/dx = \lim[f(x + \Delta x) - f(x)]/\Delta x \text{ as } \Delta x \text{ approaches zero} \tag{A1.1}$$

There are various standard results concerning the derivates of certain functions which we may use, and which it will be useful to remember. I collect them here for reference.

$$\text{if } f(x) = ax^b \qquad \text{then} \qquad dy/dx = abx^{(b-1)} \tag{A1.2}$$

$$\text{if } f(x) = ae^{bx} \qquad \text{then} \qquad dy/dx = abe^{bx} \tag{A1.3}$$

$$\text{if } f(x) = \ln(x) \qquad \text{then} \qquad dy/dx = 1/x \tag{A1.4}$$

There are some other rules concerning derivatives that we will find useful. These are as follows, and are referred to as the product and quotient rules:

$$\text{If } y = f(x)g(x) \qquad \text{then} \qquad dy/dx = [df(x)/dx]g(x) + f(x)[dg(x)/dx] \tag{A1.5}$$

$$\text{If } y = f(x)/g(x) \qquad \text{then} \qquad dy/dx = [df(x)/dx]/g(x) - f(x)[dg(x)/dx]/[g(x)]^2 \tag{A1.6}$$

We can also find the slope of the slope, which indicates the rate of increase of the slope. Mathematically it is the derivative of the derivative, or the second derivative of the original variable. It is denoted by d^2y/dx^2 and is found by taking the derivate of the derivative. We can find higher order derivates but we will not be using them in this book.

Let us now formally define the conditions for a maximum or a minimum of some function; first, where y is a function of just one other variable. Translating into mathematical language what we have already shown, we have the following conditions, first for a maximum and then for a minimum:

$$dy/dx = 0 \qquad \text{and} \qquad d^2y/dx^2 < 0 \tag{A1.7}$$

$$dy/dx = 0 \qquad \text{and} \qquad d^2y/dx^2 > 0 \tag{A1.8}$$

In each equation, the first term is the first-order condition and the second the second-order condition. There are the obvious generalizations of the first-order condition when y is dependent on n variables $x_1, x_2, ..., x_n$; namely that dy/dx_i should be zero for all $i = 1, 2, ..., n$.

For a constrained maximization of the kind discussed in the text, the solution to the problem of the maximization (or minimization) of $y = f(x_1, x_2)$ subject to the constraint $g(x_1, x_2) = 0$ is found by forming the lagrangian function $L = f(x_1, x_2) + \lambda g(x_1, x_2)$ and maximizing L with respect to x_1, x_2 and λ. The appropriate first-order conditions are $dL/dx_1 = 0$, $dL/dx_2 = 0$ and $dL/d\lambda = 0$. There are corresponding second-order conditions, but we can usually tell whether we are at a minimum or a maximum from the context.

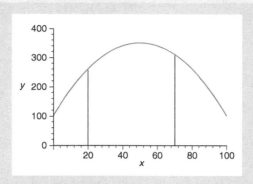

Figure A1.1   Area under a graph

Finally we should define mathematically the area under some function $f(.)$ between two values; this is given by the (definite) integral of the function between the two values. For example, suppose the function in Fig. A1.1 is $y = f(x)$ and that we want to find the area under it between $x = 20$ and $x = 70$; then we find the definite integral of $f(x)$ from 20 to 70. We write this as

$$\int_{20}^{70} f(x)\mathrm{d}x \tag{A1.9}$$

More generally, the area under a function $f(.)$ between the values $x = x_1$ and $x = x_2$ is written as

$$\int_{x_1}^{x_2} f(x)\mathrm{d}x \tag{A1.10}$$

To find an integral, we use the fact that differentiation (the process of finding a derivative) is the reverse of the process of integration (that of finding an integral). That is,

$$\text{if } g(x) = \mathrm{d}f(x)/\mathrm{d}x \quad \text{then } f(x) = \int g(x)\mathrm{d}x \text{ (plus a constant}^5) \tag{A1.11}$$

It therefore follows, from equations (A1.2) to (A1.4) above, that

$$\text{If } g(x) = ax^b \quad \text{then } \int g(x)\mathrm{d}x = ax^{b+1}/(b+1) \text{ (plus a constant)} \tag{A1.12}$$

$$\text{If } g(x) = ae^{bx} \quad \text{then } \int g(x)\mathrm{d}x = ae^{bx}/b \text{ (plus a constant)} \tag{A1.13}$$

$$\text{If } g(x) = 1/x \quad \text{then } \int g(x)\mathrm{d}x = \ln(x) \text{ (plus a constant)} \tag{A1.14}$$

---

5. The constant is known as the constant of integration, and depends upon the range over which the integral is being evaluated.

1

Economies without Production

1.1 Summary

Part 1 looks at exchange in a competitive world without production, using both conventional supply and demand analysis for a single market, and the Edgeworth box analysis for the economy as a whole. The part starts in a discrete world where only integer units of a good can be bought and sold, with reservation prices which, under certain rather special conditions, encapsulate preferences. The derivation of demand and supply from these given reservation prices is rather obvious and so is the calculation of surpluses in this simple world. The buyer surplus is the area between the price paid and the demand curve, while the seller surplus is the area between the price received and the supply curve. We discuss various forms of trade under these conditions and show the properties of competitive trade as measured in terms of surpluses. We then generalize, first to continuous goods with the same specialized preferences that implicitly imply reservation prices for each unit of the good, and then to more general preferences. We next talk about preferences more generally and show how demand can be derived from them. We go on to show how all of this can be turned round so that we can infer preferences from demand, and hence use this information to prescribe and predict. The part then looks at exchange in a simple 2-person 2-good world without production, using Edgeworth box analysis; it discusses the concept of efficient trade, using the concept of the contract curve, and shows that competitive trade is efficient, whilst monopolistic and monopsonistic trade are not. The part closes with a discussion of welfare and some consideration of how a particular point on the contract curve might be chosen.

1.2 Detail

Part 2 yields the basic material to:

- derive supply and demand curves and show that the area between the price paid and the demand curve is the buyer surplus, and the area between the price received and the supply curve is the seller surplus;
- hence show that total surplus is maximized in the competitive equilibrium;
- derive an Edgeworth box and use it to show that there are always potential gains from trade if people are different in either preferences or endowments;
- hence demonstrate that efficient trade takes place along the contract curve;
- and finally, show that the competitive equilibrium is efficient whilst the other equilibria are not.

In this part we have both supply and demand but without conveying the impression that households are on the demand side and firms on the supply side. Both positive and normative material are included here; by positive material we mean material relating to how people do behave, and by normative material we mean material relating to how people should behave. We will expand on these issues later.

Chapter 2 Gains from Exchange: This chapter presents the basic story of how and when exchange between individuals might be fruitful, taking as the starting point a market for some good in which there are many buyers and sellers all with given reservation prices, various possible ways of trading, and the gains from each of them. This obviously takes a number of things as given, but it demonstrates some key results. The chapter shows that competitive exchange is efficient – in the sense of maximization of the total surplus – but monopoly and monopsony are not.

Chapter 3 Discrete Goods: Reservation Prices, Demand and Supply, and Surpluses: Using very simple indifference curve analysis for a good and money with quasi-linear preferences, which we define and discuss, we define the concept of a reservation price and show where it comes from, noting that reservation prices are constant with quasi-linear preferences. The chapter derives demand and supply schedules in a simple world with one good and money. We show that, in general, if the individual is endowed with both money and the good he or she will be a supplier of the good at sufficiently high prices and a demander at sufficiently low prices. Further, we show that the natural measure of surplus or profit from a trade is equal to the area between the price paid and the demand curve for a demander, and the area between the price received and the supply curve for a supplier.

Chapter 4 Continuous Goods: Demand and Supply, and Surpluses: We repeat the analysis of Chapter 3 but here with continuous goods, again using indifference maps in (money, good) space, and again using quasi-linear preferences to begin with. We derive demand and supply curves and demonstrate the surplus property with continuous goods. Then we generalize the analysis to non-quasi-linear preferences, and incidentally show that the concept of a reservation price needs to be generalized and qualified.

Chapter 5 Preferences: We examine the general case of preferences over two goods. We discuss how we can describe preferences with indifference curves, and how we can represent them with utility functions. We show that the utility function representation is not unique which means, *inter alia*, that we cannot measure happiness or compare it across individuals. The chapter contains a number of examples of different kinds of preferences which vary according to the relationship and substitutability between the two goods. The examples include: perfect substitutes, perfect complements, Cobb–Douglas, Stone–Geary and quasi-linear.

Chapter 6 Supply and Demand with Income in the Form of Endowments: This chapter derives the relevant demand or supply functions for given preferences, and discusses the relationship between the preferences and the implied demand and supply schedules. The chapter emphasizes the point that we can infer (at least partially) preferences from demand, and consequently use this knowledge to predict future behaviour using observations of past behaviour.

Chapter 7 Demand with Income in the Form of Money: This chapter slightly generalizes the material of the preceding chapters and provides the derivation of demand or supply functions when income is received in the form of money rather than in the form of endowments of the two goods. We once again emphasize the relationship between demand and supply functions and the form of an individual's preferences. This is essentially a simple generalization of the material in the previous chapter.

Chapter 8 Exchange: This chapter introduces the Edgeworth box and uses it to show that mutually beneficial exchange is usually possible if tastes or endowments are different. We define and derive the contract curve and show that competitive equilibrium is on the contract curve whereas, for example, monopoly or monopsony equilibrium is not. The chapter explores the consequences and relates the important results to those of Chapter 2.

Chapter 9 Welfare: We discuss how society may chose between the various possibilities open to it – that is, how it might choose between the various points along the contract curve. Some elementary social choice theory is introduced here, but only as much as is necessary to demonstrate that economic arguments alone are not sufficient to select a point from the contract curve, and consequently political judgements are necessary as the choice involves different income distributions. We mention briefly the first and second theorems of welfare economics, which are useful if one wants to take the study of welfare issues further.

Gains from Exchange

2.1 Introduction

This chapter, although introductory, achieves a lot. It shows how exchange can be mutually beneficial and it provides a way of measuring the gains from exchange. Building on this, the chapter shows how different ways of organizing exchange can yield different gains. We show that there is a maximum total gain that can be achieved in a market, and we ask what market organization yields this maximum. This enables us to talk about the efficiency of a market mechanism, and enables us to identify which market organizations may be efficient and which may not be efficient. When I teach this material, I always implement a particular form of organization during the lecture so that students can experience at first-hand the advantages and disadvantages of a particular mechanism – although of course there are plenty of examples in the real world.

2.2 A Hypothetical Market

Let us consider a hypothetical market for some good. The good is of a particular type: one which can be bought and sold only in integer units; that is, people can buy and sell only 0, 1, 2, ... units of the good. It is therefore what we call a *discrete* good. In the real world there are many obvious examples – cars, televisions, etc. The contrary case, which we shall study later, is that of a *continuous* good – one that can be bought and sold in any amounts; examples include many real-world goods such as petrol, wood, sand and so on.

Let us make the market really simple by assuming that each potential market participant wants to buy or sell at most one unit of the good: each potential buyer wants to buy at most one unit of the good; and each potential seller wants to sell at most one unit of the good. Note the terminology: potential buyers and potential sellers – in general whether they are actual buyers or sellers depends on whether they can find a price at which they are willing to buy or sell. This, in turn, depends upon the market organization, and on how much they value the good.

At this stage we need to introduce an important concept which will be defined more formally in Chapter 3: that of the *reservation price* which the seller or buyer has for the unit of the good that they are potentially willing to sell or buy. Let us begin with a typical potential buyer. The buyer will have a maximum price which he or she is willing to pay to buy one unit of the good. This maximum price is such that, at that price, the individual is *indifferent* between buying and not buying. If the potential buyer is asked to pay more than this maximum price, he or she will strictly prefer not to buy; if the potential buyer is asked to pay less than this maximum price, he or she will strictly prefer to buy. This maximum price is referred to as the buyer's *reservation price* for the one unit of the good which he or she is considering buying, For example, suppose a potential buyer's reservation price is £40. This means that the potential buyer would buy at any price up to and including £40, but would not buy at any price above £40.

Let us assume that every potential buyer has a unique reservation price for the one unit of the good that they potentially want to buy. Moreover, in keeping with the spirit of this book, and particularly the notion that *people are different*, let us assume that, in general, different buyers have different reservation prices – though of course this does not preclude the possibility that some buyers may have the same reservation prices.

Let us now consider a typical potential seller. There will be a minimum price that he or she is willing to accept to sell the one unit of the good. This minimum price is such that, at that price, the individual is indifferent between selling and not selling. If the potential seller is asked to accept less than this minimum price, he or she will strictly prefer not to sell; if asked to accept more than this minimum price, he or she will strictly prefer to sell. This minimum price is referred to as the seller's reservation price for the one unit of the good that he or she is considering selling, For example, suppose that a potential seller's reservation price is £70. This means that the potential seller would sell at any price down to and including £70, but would not sell at any price below £70.

Let us assume that every potential seller has a unique reservation price for the one unit of the good that they potentially want to sell. Moreover, in keeping with the spirit of this book, and particularly the notion that *people are different*, let us assume that, in general, different sellers have different reservation prices; though, of course, this does not preclude the possibility that some sellers have the same reservation prices.

Now let us consider the gains from trade – the gains from exchange. What will happen in this market is that, depending upon the type of market organization, there will be a number of trades or exchanges, in each of which some buyer will buy from some seller; this will be at some price between the reservation price of the buyer and the reservation price of the seller[1]. The gains that each makes from the trade depend upon the price at which the exchange takes place and their respective reservation prices.

Consider first the buyer. If a buyer pays a price exactly equal to the reservation price then, because this price is the maximum that he or she would pay, and therefore the price at which he or she is indifferent between buying and not buying, clearly the buyer has not gained from the trade and we can say that his or her surplus from the trade is zero. However if he or she pays a price less than the reservation price, we can argue that the surplus from the trade is equal to the difference between the price that he or she would have paid (that is, the reservation price) and the price that actually was paid. If we denote an individual's reservation price by r and the actual price paid by p, then the surplus gained by the buyer is given by Eq. (2.1)

$$\text{buyer's surplus} = r - p \qquad (2.1)$$

Consider now a seller for whom very similar arguments apply. If a seller accepts a price exactly equal to the reservation price then, because this price is the minimum that would be

---

1. By definition, the buyer is not willing to pay more than his or her reservation price, and the seller is not willing to accept any less than his or her reservation price.

acceptable, and therefore is the price at which he or she is indifferent between selling and not selling, clearly the seller has not gained from the trade; hence we can say that the surplus from the trade is zero. But if the seller accepts a price greater than his or her reservation price, we can argue that the surplus from the trade is equal to the difference between the price that was actually accepted and the price that he or she would have accepted (that is, the reservation price). If we denote an individual's reservation price by r and the actual price paid by p, then the surplus gained by the seller is simply given by:

$$\text{seller's surplus} = p - r \tag{2.2}$$

Note the similarity and differences between these two expressions; they differ because a buyer is better off the less he or she pays, while a seller is better off the more he or she accepts. For example, suppose that a buyer with a reservation price of £70 buys at a price of £60 from a seller with a reservation price of £40. The buyer has a surplus of £10 and the seller has a surplus of £20.

The reservation prices of buyers and sellers determine the possibilities for exchange in the market. For example, if all the buyers' reservation prices are lower than all the sellers' reservation prices there would be no mutually advantageous trades; no buyer could find a seller who was willing to sell at a price acceptable to both. However if there was some overlap between the buyers' reservation prices and the sellers' reservation prices, then some trade should be possible. What actually happens will depend upon the particular form of market organization. Below we consider a particular form.

In my lectures I always implement a particular organization – the crucial point of which is to get everyone thinking about different ways of organizing the exchanges. At the beginning of this lecture I give each student a slip of paper on which is written something like the following. Either:

'YOU ARE A BUYER OF THE GOOD. You want to buy one unit of the good. Your reservation price is £40; that is, you are willing to pay any amount up to and including £40 to buy one unit of the good.' Or:

'YOU ARE A SELLER OF THE GOOD. You want to sell one unit of the good. Your reservation price is £70; that is, you are willing to sell your unit of the good at any price greater than or equal to £70.' Or:

'You are neither a buyer nor a seller of the good.'[2].

I tell the students that what is written on the slip of paper is private information and they should not reveal the information to anyone else. I also tell them that they should imagine that what is going to happen is a real experiment in which they can earn real money. The money that they earn will depend upon whether they trade or not, the price at which they trade, and upon their reservation price. They know that different people have, in general, different reservation prices. I may or may not tell them the actual values of the reservation prices[3]. I have on the overhead projector a slide on which, after trades have been agreed, students can fill in the names of the participants to the trade, their reservation prices,

---

2. Alternatively we could specify these non-participants as either buyers with a reservation price of £0 (that is, they would not pay anything for the good) or as sellers with a reservation price of infinity (that is, there is no price at which they would part with the good.)

3. Note that in a real market they would be unlikely to know the values of the reservation prices of the other agents in the market.

the price of the trade, and hence their implied profits or surpluses. I tell the students that in a real experiment they would be paid in cash the surpluses that they made from the trade, so everyone should behave in a way that maximizes their surplus.

Then, usually, I just tell them to get on with it without explicitly imposing any market organization. Obviously there is an implicit organization; the actual trades will be the outcome of a series of bilateral negotiations between buyers and sellers. I tell the students that, when they have agreed to an exchange, they should write the details of the trade on the slide. I then leave them to it.

As you might imagine, the result is chaotic. First, there is a period of silence. Then all hell breaks loose as students try to find someone with whom to trade. There are some quick trades and students start writing on the slide. A queue builds up to write on the slide. When the slide is full – though before all possible trades are consummated – I usually call a halt to the proceedings. At this stage the first bit of the slide generally looks something like that which appears in Table 2.1.

Table 2.1   Illustrative market: reservation prices, traded prices and surpluses

Buyer	Seller	Buyer's reservation price	Seller's reservation price	Price agreed	Buyer's profit/ surplus	Seller's profit/ surplus
Mike	Sandra	60	40	50	10	10
Julie	Tania	100	20	90	10	70
Fred	James	90	10	10	80	0
Katie	John	40	40	40	0	0
Susan	Felicity	40	50	55	−15	5
Donald	Fabrizio	80	40	60	20	20
Kevin	Susan	40	20	40	0	20

I then invite comments. Usually a number of observations are made, for example:

● there is a variety of different prices at which trade takes place; in the example above, the agreed prices vary between 10 and 90;

● some trades split the surplus equally – for example, the trade between Donald and Fabrizio;

● some trades yield a much higher surplus to the seller (Julie and Tania) or to the buyer (Fred and James);

● some trades imply a loss to one of the participants (for example, Susan in the trade between her and Felicity).

I then ask whether they think this organization is good or not. At this point a number of comments are made: is it fair and/or efficient to have trades at different prices? Is it fair and/or efficient to have different surpluses for different people? Is it fair and/or efficient that people make losses?

This latter point can easily be covered; Susan made a mistake, which was the fault of the individual not of the system. When this is pointed out to Susan, she is embarrassed and admits that it was a mistake and she would not do it again.

The other points are less easily dealt with. It is not clear at this stage how we might discuss the efficiency of the market organization, nor how we might decide whether something is fair or not. To try to understand these points, let us analyse in detail what would happen under some particular organization – one that is reasonably common in the real world. In this particular organization there is a unique price at which trades can take place, thus eliminating a possible source of unfairness – different prices for the same kind of trade (remember: the good is homogeneous); and we ask the question: 'is there a unique price at which the number of units that people want to sell is equal to the number of units that people want to buy?'. We might be tempted to call such a price – if one exists – some kind of equilibrium price for the market. We will discuss later whether such a terminology might be justified.

To ascertain whether such an equilibrium price exists or not, we need to find the aggregate demand at any price – that is, the number of units that would be demanded at any price; and the aggregate supply at any price – that is, the number of units that would be offered at any price. This we do in the next two sections.

2.3 Demand

Let us start with individuals and then aggregate. We will consider first a potential buyer with a reservation price of £40. This individual would buy one unit of the good at any price up to and including £40, but would buy zero units if the price exceeded £40. We thus have the demand curve for this individual pictured in Fig. 2.1. For reasons that may not become clear until later, we put the price on the vertical axis and the quantity demanded on the horizontal axis. Recall that we said that it is not necessarily the dependent variable that goes on the vertical axis. Indeed in this case the dependent variable is the quantity demanded, which is on the horizontal axis, while the independent variable is the price of the good which is on the vertical axis. It is the context that tells us which is the dependent variable and which is the independent variable. So Fig. 2.1 should be read as telling us the demand at each possible price.

This graph is easily read. If the price exceeds £40 then the demand is zero; if the price is less than £40, the demand is one unit. Note that it is a step function, with a (single) step at the (single) reservation price of the individual.

Figure 2.1 Demand curve for a buyer with a reservation price of £40

We will later want to discuss the efficiency of the market mechanism. To this end, it is useful to represent graphically the surplus or profit (these words are used interchangeably at the moment) made by this potential buyer. We have already discussed this – the surplus is simply the difference between the price paid and the buyer's reservation price. Let us take a particular example; suppose this buyer buys at a price of £30. Then his or her surplus is £10, which is the difference between the reservation price of the individual (£40) and the price paid (£30). Examine Fig. 2.2.

The surplus is £10 – the vertical difference between the price paid and the buyer's reservation

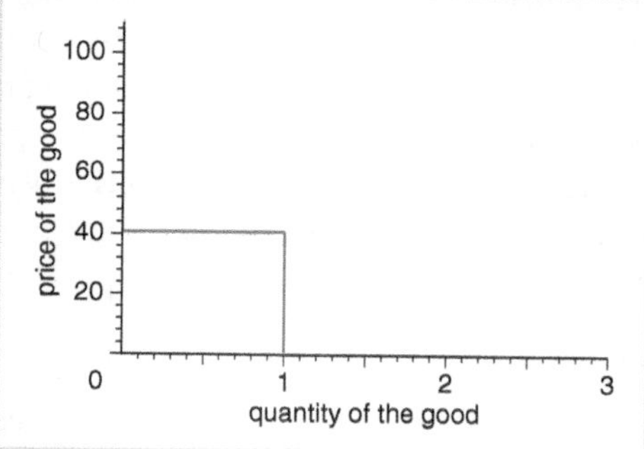

Figure 2.2 Surplus for a buyer at a market price of £30 and reservation price of £40

price. Now note that the horizontal distance between the vertical axis and the demand curve for prices below £40 is one (unit of the good). It follows that the area between the price paid and the demand curve is exactly equal to £10 – the surplus of the individual when buying at a price of £30. We now have an extremely important result.

> The buyer surplus is exactly equal to the area between the price paid and the demand curve.

We shall come across this result, and prove it more formally later, over and over again in this book. It is vitally important.

A digression on units is useful at this stage. Consider the units of the variables we are using. The variable on the horizontal axis is the quantity of the good; its units depend upon what the good is. Suppose it is television sets; then the units of the variable on the horizontal axis are television sets. What about the variable on the vertical axis? This is the price of the good. What are its units? Be careful – it is not just pounds; it is pounds per television set – an amount of money for each television set[4]. We can now calculate the units of the area between the price paid and the demand curve – they are the units of the variable on the horizontal axis multiplied by the units of the variable on the vertical axis; that is, television sets multiplied by pounds per television set – that is, simply pounds. So the area we have identified is measured in pounds; it is an amount of money, which is exactly what we use to measure the buyer's surplus.

That was one buyer. What happens if we take more than one? Let us take just two – the one above who has a reservation price of £40 and a second one with a reservation price of £60. For this second buyer demand is zero at any price greater than £60, and is equal to one for any price up to and including £60. His or her demand curve looks exactly the same as that in Fig. 2.1 except that the step occurs at a price of £60 (the reservation price) rather than at £40 (the first individual's reservation price). As before, the buyer's surplus is measured by the area between the price paid and the demand curve.

What happens if we combine them? One will not buy at a price above £40; the other will not buy at a price above £60. So neither will buy at a price above £60; only one (the buyer with a reservation price of £60) will buy at a price between £40 and £60; and both will buy at a price below £40. The demand curve for these two buyers together is in Fig. 2.3.

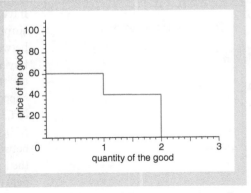

Figure 2.3   Demand curve for two buyers with reservation prices of £40 and £60

Note that this demand curve has the correct properties. At a price above £60 the combined demand is zero; at a price between £40 and £60 the combined demand is one; and at a price below £40 the combined demand is two. Once again it takes the form of a step function with a step at each reservation price.

We can also see that our result about the surplus remains

4.   This is always true. For example, when we say that the price of beer is £2.20 we mean £2.20 per pint – we always have to specify how much of the good we are buying for any particular price.

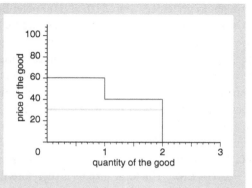

Figure 2.4 Surplus for two buyers with reservation prices of £40 and £60 at a market price of £30

true. Suppose both individuals buy at a price of £30; what surpluses do they make? The buyer with a reservation price of £40 makes a surplus of £10 and the buyer with a reservation price of £60 makes a surplus of £30. The combined surplus is (£10 + £30) = £40. Graphically this is shown in Fig 2.4.

Consider the area between the price of £30 and the demand curve. This area can be considered as the sum of two rectangles – one with a height of £30 and width one; the second with a height of £10 and a width one. So the total area is equal to (£30 + £10) = £40, exactly equal to the combined surplus of the two individuals when buying at a price of £30 as previously calculated. So once again, even though we are now dealing with more than one individual, we have the important result that:

 The buyer surplus is exactly equal to the area between the price paid and the demand curve.

This extension from one individual to more than one will be shown more formally later in the book. If you are mathematically inclined you may regard it as rather obvious, but it is more important at this stage that you have an intuitive understanding of why it is true. The numerical example above should make things clear; for the time being understanding that is sufficient.

If we now look at the demand curve for all the buyers together – that is, the aggregate demand curve – one thing should be clear; it must take the form of a step function with a step at every reservation price. The precise form of the curve will depend upon the distribution of the reservation prices over the set of all buyers, and until we specify that we cannot construct the aggregate demand curve. Suppose we know the following: there 100 buyers, of whom there are 10 with a reservation price of £100, 10 with a reservation price of £90, 10 with a reservation price of £80, 10 with a reservation price of £70, 10 with a reservation price of £60, 10 with a reservation price of £50, 10 with a reservation price of £40, 10 with a reservation price of £30, 10 with a reservation price of £20 and 10 with a reservation price of £10. The aggregate demand curve thus takes the form of a step function with steps of 10 units at £100, £90, £80, £70, £60, £50, £40, £30, £20 and £10. It is shown in Fig. 2.5.

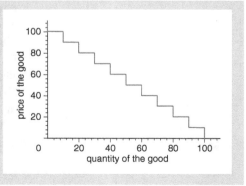

Figure 2.5 Aggregate demand curve

Check that you understand this. No buyer has a reservation price above £100 so no-one is willing to pay more than £100; demand is zero at all prices above £100. Between £90 and £100 there are the 10 buyers with reservation prices of £100, all of whom would be willing to buy one unit at a price between £90 and £100; so aggregate demand in this range is 10 units; and so on. By the time we get to prices less than £10, all 100 potential buyers would be willing to buy one unit so the aggregate demand at all prices less than £10 is 100.

Note that we still have the same property about the aggregate surplus. Consider any price, for example, a price of £67. The total demand at that price is 40: those 10 buyers with a reservation price of £100; those 10 buyers with a reservation price of £90; those 10 buyers with a reservation price of £80; and those 10 buyers with a reservation price of £70[5]. How much surplus does each of these make at a price of £67? Those 10 with a reservation price of £100 each have a surplus of £33 (= £100 − £67); those 10 with a reservation price of £90 each have a surplus of £23 (= £90 − £67); those 10 with a reservation price of £80 each have a surplus of £13 (= £80 − £67); and those 10 with a reservation price of £70 each have a surplus of £3 (= £70 − £67). The total surplus is therefore £330 (= 10 × £33) plus £230 (= 10 × £23) plus £130 (= 10 × £13) plus £30 (= 10 × £3), which is equal to £720. This is precisely equal to the area between the price of £67 and the aggregate demand curve in Fig. 2.5; you should check this and make sure that you understand why it is true. So once again we have the important result:

 The buyer surplus is exactly equal to the area between the price paid and the demand curve.

2.4 Supply

Let us now repeat the analysis on the supply side. Once again we will start with individuals and then aggregate. Consider first a potential seller with a reservation price of £70. This individual would sell one unit of the good at any price down to and including £70, but would sell zero units if the price was less than £70. Fig. 2.6 shows the supply curve for this individual. Note again that the price is on the vertical axis while the quantity supplied is on the horizontal axis.

This graph is easily read: if the price is less than £70 the supply is zero; if the price is greater than £70 the supply is one unit. Note that it is a step function with a single step at the single reservation price of the individual.

We shall later want to discuss the efficiency of the market mechanism. To this end, it is useful to represent graphically the surplus or profit (the words continue to be used interchangeably at the moment) made by this potential seller. We have already discussed this; the surplus is simply the difference between the reservation price of the seller and the price received. Let us take a particular example: suppose this seller sells at a price of £80. Then the surplus is simply £10, the difference between the individual's reservation price of £70 and the price received (£80). Graphically it is shown in Fig. 2.7.

The surplus is £10 – the vertical difference between the price

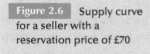

Figure 2.6 Supply curve for a seller with a reservation price of £70

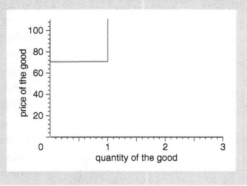

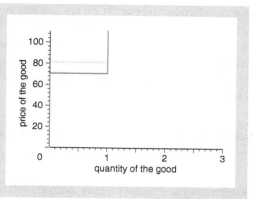

Figure 2.7 Surplus for a seller at a market price of £80 and reservation price of £70

received and the reservation price of the individual. Now note that the horizontal distance between the vertical axis and the supply curve, for prices above £70, is one unit of the good. It follows that the area between the price paid and the supply curve is exactly equal to £10 – the surplus of the individual when selling at a price of £80. We have another extremely important result.

 The seller surplus is exactly equal to the area between the price received and the supply curve.

We shall come across this result, and prove it more formally later, over and over again. It is vitally important.

That was one seller. What happens if we take more than one? Let us take just two – the one above who has a reservation price of £70, and a second one with a reservation price of £50. For this second seller his supply is zero at any price less than £50, and is equal to one for any price £50 or above. His or her supply curve looks exactly the same as Fig. 2.6, except that the step is at a price of £50 (his or her reservation price) rather than at £70 (the first seller's reservation price). As before, the surplus is measured by the area between the price received and the supply curve.

What about the two together? One will not sell at a price below £70; the other will not sell at a price below £50. So neither will sell at a price below £50; only the seller with a reservation price of £50 will sell at a price between £50 and £70; and both will sell at a price above £70. The

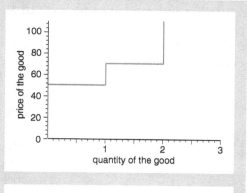

Figure 2.8 Supply curve for two sellers with reservation prices of £50 and £70

supply curve for these two sellers together is therefore that in Fig. 2.8. Note that the supply curve has the correct properties. At a price below £50 the combined supply is zero; at a price between £50 and £70 the combined supply is one; and at a price above £70 the combined supply is two. Once again it takes the form of a step function with a step at each reservation price.

Figure 2.9 Surplus for two sellers with reservation prices of £50 and £70 at a market price of £80

We also see that our result about the surplus remains true. Suppose both individuals sell at a price of £80. What surpluses do they make? The seller with a reservation price of £70 makes a surplus of £10 and the seller with a reservation price of £50 makes a surplus of £30; so the combined surplus is (£10 + £30) = £40. Graphically this is pictured in Fig. 2.9.

Consider the area between the price of £80 and the supply curve. This area can be considered as the sum of two rectangles – one of them of height £30 and width one, and the second of height £10 and width one – so the total area is equal to (£30 + £10) = £40, exactly equal to the combined surplus of the two individuals when selling at a price of £80. So, once again, even though we are now dealing with more than one individual we have the important result that:

 The seller surplus is exactly equal to the area between the price received and the supply curve.

This extension from one individual to more than one will be shown more formally later. If you are mathematically inclined you may regard it as obvious; but it is more important at this stage that you have an intuitive understanding of why it is true. The numerical example above should make things clear; for the time being understanding that is sufficient.

If we now look at the supply curve for all the sellers together – that is, the aggregate supply curve – one thing should be clear; it must take the form of a step function with a step at every reservation price. The precise form depends upon the distribution of the reservation prices over the set of all sellers, and until we specify that we cannot construct the aggregate supply curve. Suppose we know the following: there 100 sellers, of whom 10 have a reservation price of £10, 10 have a reservation price of £20, 10 have a reservation price of £30, 10 have a reservation price of £40, 10 have a reservation price of £50, 10 have a reservation price of £60, 10 have a reservation price of £70, 10 have a reservation price of £80, 10 have a reservation price of £90, and 10 have a reservation price of £100[6]. The aggregate supply curve thus takes the form of a step function with steps (of 10 units – because there are 10 sellers associated with each reservation price) at £10, £20, £30, £40, £50, £60, £70, £80, £90 and £100. It is shown in Fig. 2.10.

Check that you understand this. No seller has a reservation price below £10 – no-one is willing to accept less than £10 – so the supply is zero at all prices below £10. Between £10 and £20 there are 10 sellers with reservation prices of £10, all of whom would be willing to sell one unit at a price between £10 and £20; so the aggregate supply in this range is 10 units; and so on. By the time we get to prices greater than £100, all 100 potential sellers would be willing to sell one unit, so the aggregate supply for all prices greater than £100 is 100.

Figure 2.10 Aggregate supply curve

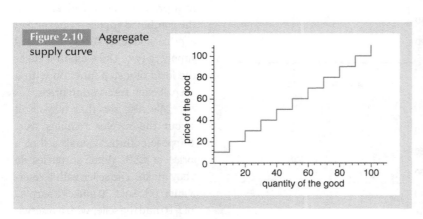

Note that we still have the same property about the aggregate surplus. Consider any price, for example, a price of £47. The total supply at that price is 40 – those 10 sellers with a reservation price of £10, those 10 sellers with a reservation price of £20, those 10 sellers with a reservation price of £30, and those 10 sellers with a reservation price of £40[7]. How much surplus does each of these make at a price of £47? Those 10

6. Note that we have chosen these values to make the market symmetrical in a sense that will be obvious from the figures that follow, but clearly this does not need to be the case.
7. Note that no seller with a reservation price greater than £47 would be willing to sell at a price of £47.

with a reservation price of £10 each have a surplus of £37 (= £47 − £10), those 10 with a reservation price of £20 each have a surplus of £27 (= £47 − £20), those 10 with a reservation price of £30 each have a surplus of £17 (= £47 − £30), and those 10 with a reservation price of £40 each have a surplus of £7 (= £47 − £40). The total surplus is thus £370 (= 10 × £37) plus £270 (= 10 × £27) plus £170 (= 10 × £17) plus £70 (= 10 × £7), which is equal to £880. This is precisely equal to the area between the price of £47 and the aggregate supply curve. You should check this and make sure that you understand why it is true. So once again we have the important result.

> The seller surplus is exactly equal to the area between the price received and the supply curve.

2.5 The Market as a Whole

Consider now the whole market; let us put together the aggregate demand and supply curves. We get the picture drawn in Fig. 2.11.

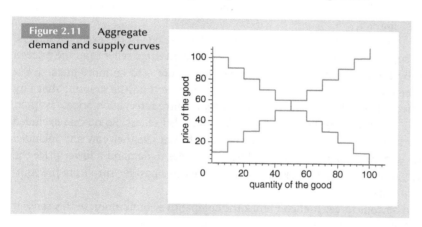

Figure 2.11 Aggregate demand and supply curves

We now ask the question: 'is there a price at which aggregate demand equals aggregate supply?'. The answer should be obvious; at any price between[8] £50 and £60 the aggregate demand and supply are both equal to 50. Which buyers would buy? Those 50 with reservation prices of £100, £90, £80, £70 and £60. Which sellers would sell? Those 50 with reservation prices equal to £10, £20, £30, £40 and £50. If any single price between £50 and £60 prevailed then we would have 50 trades – between those 50 buyers with reservation prices of £100, £90, £80, £70 and £60 and those 50 sellers with reservation prices of £10, £20, £30, £40 and £50. Obviously the precise surpluses will depend upon the exact price between £50 and £60; but it is clear that the combined surpluses of the buyers and the sellers must be equal to the area between the demand and supply curves to the left of the equilibrium quantity 50. Simple arithmetic reveals that this area is equal to £(900 + 700 + 500 + 300 + 100) = £2500.

---

8. We need to be a little careful. Clearly for any price strictly between £50 and £60 the statement is true. For prices exactly equal to £50 or £60 the statement *could* be true. Consider a price of exactly £60. The demand is somewhere between 40 and 50 – the reason being is that the 10 buyers with a reservation price of £60 are indifferent – we really do not know whether they will buy at the price of £60 or not. Similarly for the sellers – the supply is somewhere between 50 and 60 – the reason being is that the 10 sellers with a reservation price of £60 are indifferent – we really do not know whether they will sell at a price of £60 or not. However in the case when the indifferent buyers do enter the market and when the indifferent sellers do not enter the market, a price of £60 yields a situation in which demand and supply are equal. A similar situation occurs for a price exactly equal to £50.

If we consider particular prices we can calculate the surpluses for buyers and sellers separately. Take a price of £50[9]. The buyer surplus is £(500 + 400 + 300 + 200 + 100) = £1500 and the seller surplus is £(400 + 300 + 200 + 100 + 0) = £1000. The total surplus is indeed £2500. Alternatively take a price of £60[10]. Here the buyer surplus is £(400 + 300 + 200 + 100 + 0) = £1000 and the seller surplus £(500 + 400 + 300 + 200 + 100) = £1500, giving once again a total surplus of £2500.

This form of organization – in which some single price at which aggregate supply is equal to aggregate demand is imposed on the market, and in which agents take this price as given and trade accordingly – is called (for reasons which at this stage may not be obvious but which will be explained later) a *competitive equilibrium*. We might be tempted to ask 'in what sense is it an equilibrium?'. Consider what happens if such an equilibrium is proposed. For simplicity consider a proposal in the context of our particular example – for example, a price of £55. If this proposal were implemented, then the traders would be the buyers with reservation prices of £100, £90, £80, £70 and £60, making respective surpluses of £45, £35, £25, £15 and £5; and also sellers with reservation prices of £10, £20, £30, £40 and £50, making respective surpluses of £45, £35, £25, £15 and £5. Note that the buyers with reservation prices of £50, £40, £30, £20 and £10 would not trade as their surpluses from this market would be zero. Similarly, sellers with reservation prices of £60, £70, £80, £90 and £100 would not trade as their surpluses would be zero. In a sense we could say that the buyers who are not willing to pay 'very much', and the sellers who want 'too much', are excluded from the market.

Who could argue against such a proposal? Consider first one of the excluded buyers. Could he or she suggest a price which would be more attractive to a seller than the price of £55 suggested by the competitive equilibrium? Obviously not – to be more attractive it would have to be greater than £55, yet such a price is more than the amount that any excluded buyer would be willing to pay (recall that they all have reservation prices less than or equal to £50). A similar argument applies to the excluded sellers. So no-one excluded from the competitive equilibrium can 'break' the equilibrium. Neither can any included trader. Consider one of the included buyers; if he or she tries to demand a lower price the sellers will simply disagree, so the buyer has a choice between a positive surplus in the equilibrium or zero surplus.

There are no obvious forces that can break the competitive equilibrium; in this sense it really is equilibrium. Moreover aggregate demand is equal to aggregate supply at the equilibrium price, so there is no excess demand which might manifest itself in an upward pressure on price, and there is no excess supply which might manifest itself in a downward pressure on price[11]. This competitive equilibrium has important properties, the most crucial of which is the following:

The total surplus (buyer surplus plus seller surplus) is maximized in the competitive equilibrium.

At this stage I cannot offer a general proof of this statement, as such a proof requires a comparison of the competitive equilibrium with all other possible forms of market organization.

---

9. Strictly speaking, in the light of the discussion in footnote 8 we should consider a price greater than £50 – for example £50 plus ε of a penny. This makes the results that follow slightly inaccurate, though the error approaches zero as ε approaches zero.
10. See footnotes 8 and 9.
11. This is the same point as made in the previous paragraph.

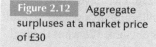

Figure 2.12 Aggregate surpluses at a market price of £30

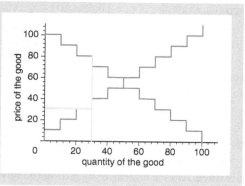

However I can give some examples. To begin with, it is easy to show that total surplus is higher in the competitive equilibrium (when demand and supply are equal) than for any other single price. Consider a non-equilibrium price, for example £30, which is lower than the competitive range. The effect of this is shown in Fig. 2.12.

At a price of £30 the aggregate supply is between 20 and 30; the sellers with reservation prices of £10 and £20 will definitely want to sell and those with reservation prices of £30 will be indifferent between selling and not selling. At a price of £30, aggregate demand is between 70 and 80, depending on whether those with a reservation price of £30 buy or not. Whether they do or not, it is clear that aggregate demand exceeds aggregate supply; there has to be rationing. The number of units exchanged depends upon the sellers with a reservation price of £30 – those that are indifferent between selling and not selling. Let us assume that they do sell and hence the quantity exchanged is 30. Let us suppose moreover (to strengthen the argument that follows) that the 30 units are sold to the buyers with the highest reservation prices[12] – those of £100, £90 and £80. Then the buyers' total surplus is £(700 + 600 + 500) = £1800, which is larger than in any competitive equilibrium, while the sellers' total surplus is £(200 + 100 + 0) = £300, which is lower than in any competitive equilibrium. Note that the distribution of the surpluses is different from the competitive equilibrium, and the total surplus (£1800 + £300) = £2100 is lower than in the competitive equilibrium. There is a loss of total surplus caused by the fact that the quantity exchanged is reduced relative to the competitive equilibrium.

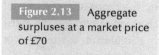

Figure 2.13 Aggregate surpluses at a market price of £70

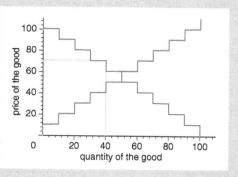

The same is true if too high a price is chosen. Consider a price of £70 and suppose that the marginal buyers (those who are indifferent between buying and not buying) actually do buy. This situation is depicted in Fig. 2.13.

The quantity exchanged will be 40 units and there is excess supply because the price is too high. The buyers' total surplus is £(300 + 200 + 100 + 0) = £600, lower than in any competitive equilibrium; the sellers' total surplus[13] is £(600 + 500 + 400 + 300) = £1800, higher than in any competitive equilibrium. The total surplus is £600 + £1800 = £2400 – once again it is lower than in the competitive equilibrium. The 'missing' £100 is the little square to the right of a quantity of 40; it is missing because the quantity traded is smaller (the price is too high) than in the competitive equilibrium.

---

12. This need not be the case of course as there is rationing. Also the buyers with reservation prices equal to £70, £60 and £50 would buy at this price. But if they do the buying, the buyers' surplus would be lower.

13. Assuming that the sellers with the lowest reservation prices do the selling.

We have given two examples of non-competitive outcomes, and we have shown that in both of these the total surplus is less than in the competitive equilibrium. In a sense the result that the competitive equilibrium maximizes the total surplus is obvious. We want the high-reservation-price buyers to trade, and the low-reservation-price sellers to trade, and we need equal quantities of each; a person cannot trade unless there is someone with whom they can trade. This almost defines the competitive equilibrium.

Of course, we might be interested in other things. For example, we might be interested in maximizing the number of trades. If we are constrained to having a unique price, then obviously this gives us once again the competitive outcome. But if we can have different prices for different trades then we might be able to increase the number of trades. In our example, we could have 100 trades. How? By letting the buyers with a particular reservation price (say $£x$) buy from those sellers with the same reservation price at a price of $£x$. Clearly the surplus from each trade, and hence the total surplus, is zero, but 100 trades can take place in this way.

There are obviously lots of different ways that trading can be organized. We could ask one side of the market to organize some kind of collective optimal price. We could have some kind of auction mechanism in which buyers make bids for the good and sellers make asks. We could use the mechanism of the lecture – just leave the participants to find their own 'best' trades.

We might think the latter is not a particularly good mechanism; from the experience of countless lectures we see that it leads to trade at lots of different prices and hence, perhaps, to the possibility that trades which might take place under different mechanisms might not take place under this. The problem with this mechanism is that traders have very little information on which to base their activity; therefore they may well behave in a way that does not maximize their surplus.

In contrast, for the competitive equilibrium all traders have to decide whether or not it is in their interests to trade at the equilibrium price; this is a very simple decision to take. Of course finding the equilibrium price is not an easy task; but once one is found we know that the resulting equilibrium has certain nice properties, including maximization of the total surplus. In one sense we can refer to this as saying that the mechanism maximizes the gains from trade: given the set of reservation prices, the competitive equilibrium is such that it maximizes the gains from trading the good. This mechanism extracts the maximum possible surplus. This seems to be an important and useful property. We shall discuss it more fully after we have explored other mechanisms in later chapters. We call a mechanism which extracts the maximum possible surplus *efficient*. Mechanisms – such as some of those we have seen – which involve a non-equilibrium price extract a lower total surplus and are therefore inefficient. We should note, however, that there is another dimension we should consider, and that is the distribution of the total surplus. Some mechanisms (for example, those involving a lower price) give more of the surplus to the buyers; some give more to the sellers. How we might compare these depends on how we view the buyers vis-à-vis the sellers. This might involve some political judgement, and therefore may take us beyond the scope of economics.

2.6 Summary

We have covered a lot of material in this chapter. We have introduced and defined the reservation price for a buyer and for a seller. We have the following definitions.

> For a buyer of a good the reservation price is the maximum amount that he or she would pay to buy the good.

> For a seller of a good the reservation price is the minimum amount that he or she would accept to sell the good.

We have also shown, for a discrete good, how the resulting demand and supply curves depend upon the reservation prices of the good. We have the following results.

> The aggregate demand curve is a step function with a step at every reservation price.

> The aggregate supply curve is a step function with a step at every reservation price.

We have shown that the gains from trade, as measured for buyers by the difference between the price paid and the reservation price and, for sellers, by the difference between the price received and the reservation price, can be measured graphically as follows.

> The buyer surplus is the area between the price paid and the demand curve.

> The seller surplus is the area between the price received and the supply curve.

Finally we considered different trading mechanisms, concentrating particular attention on the competitive equilibrium mechanism, defined as follows.

> A competitive equilibrium is a state in which there is a single price at which trades can take place – taken as given by all competitors – for which the aggregate demand equals the aggregate supply.

We have seen that the competitive equilibrium is efficient in the sense that

> In a competitive equilibrium the total surplus from trade is maximized.

Of course this tells us nothing about the fairness of the equilibrium (whether the distribution of the surplus is good in any sense), but this may be something on which economists cannot pass judgement.

2.7 Review Questions

1 If the price paid by a buyer decreases, what happens to his or her surplus?

2 How might the surplus which a seller receives increase?

3 If the price in the market is lower than the competitive price, what happens to the quantity exchanged and the surpluses gained by the two sides of the market?

4 In the competitive equilibrium, what is the surplus of buyers whose reservation price is lower than the competitive price, and what is the surplus of sellers whose reservation price is higher than the competitive price? Do these agents trade? Is that fair? (The latter is a difficult question as the answer depends on what we mean by fair.)

5 Should we be interested in the number of trades *per se*?

2.8 Application: are Trade Unions Good for the Workers?

We are in a position to use the analysis of this chapter to investigate an important question about the influence of trade unions on the welfare of workers. We should emphasize that this is a very simplistic analysis, but it does show how our analytical framework is useful in exploring important and contentious issues.

We take a simple example where a firm is considering whether to hire extra workers in a particular week, for a one-off project. We assume that, because of this one-off nature, the wages paid to these extra workers are not constrained by the wages paid to existing workers. We will assume that the firm has calculated the effect on profits of taking on extra workers for this week. Suppose that the firm has calculated that taking on one extra worker will increase profits by £650; taking on a second extra worker will increase profits by a further £550; taking on a third extra worker will increase profits by a further £450; taking on a fourth extra worker will increase profits by a further £350; taking on a fifth extra worker will increase profits by a further £250; taking on a sixth extra worker will increase profits by a further £150; and taking on a seventh extra worker will increase profits by a further £50. It therefore follows that, as a demander of labour which we assume is homogeneous, the firm has a step demand function with steps at £650, £550, £450, £350, £250, £150 and £50; that is, with reservation prices of these amounts. The firm's demand function for labour is thus as shown in Fig. 2.14.

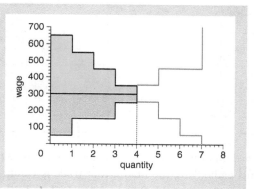

Figure 2.14 Labour demand, supply and surpluses under competition

Suppose that there are seven potential employees in the market, who differ in their enthusiasm to be employed for this week. One individual (individual A) is particularly keen and would work for any wage rate at or above £50; A's reservation price is £50 for this week. Two other individuals (B and C) are less keen; they require a minimum wage of £150. Two others (D and E) are even less keen; they have reservation wages of £250 and £350 respectively. Finally F and G would only work for this week if they got at least £450. It follows that the supply of labour curve is a step function with steps (of one) at £50, (of two) at £150, (of one) at £250, (of one) at £350 and (of two) at £450. These are the reservation prices of the sellers of labour in this market. We should note that these reservation prices take everything into account including, if it exists, the pleasure or displeasure implied by being employed *per se*. The implied supply of labour curve is the upward-sloping step function in Fig. 2.14.

What will happen in this market situation? As ever, it depends upon the market institution by which trades take place. For example if we assume a competitive market in which a single wage is chosen, at which the supply of labour is equal to the demand for labour, we get the situation illustrated in Fig. 2.14 in which the wage rate is somewhere between £250 and £350 and four workers are employed. In the figure we have taken the mid-point (£300), but we should emphasize that any wage between £250 and £350 is an equilibrium wage. We should note that £250 and £350 could also be equilibria depending upon whether the indifferent worker works or not, and on whether the firm employs a worker on whom the marginal profit is zero.

We have indicated the surpluses generated in one of these competitive equilibrium – that at the mid-price of £300. Notice that the total surplus is the same at any other competitive price, although its distribution differs. The firm makes a profit of £350 (= £650 – £300) on the first of these workers, a profit of £250 (= £550 – £300) on the second, a profit of £150 (= £450 – £300) on the third and a profit of £50 (= £350 – £300) on the fourth; a total profit of £800. This is the shaded area between the wage of £300 and the demand curve in Fig. 2.14. The surplus of individual A is £250 (= £300 – £50), that of individuals B and C £150 each (= £300 – £150), whilst that of D is £50 (= £300 – £250). The total surplus that the employed workers receive is therefore £600. This is the shaded area between the wage of £300 and the supply curve. In this competitive equilibrium, individuals E, F and G do not work and therefore receive no surplus. They are unemployed because they will only work for a wage higher than the competitive equilibrium wage.

If the market mechanism is not the competitive one, the outcome may be different and the realized surpluses may be different. Consider an institution in which a single price is chosen. We can calculate the employment and the resulting surpluses for each possible price. Table 2.2 shows the implications for certain key wage rates.

Table 2.2   Labour market with workers' and firms' surpluses

Wage	Labour employed	Workers' surplus	Firm's surplus (or profit)	Total surplus
> £650	0	0	0	0
£650	1	600	0	600
£550	2	900	100	1000
£450	3	1000	300	1300
£350	4	800	600	1400
£250	4	400	1000	1400
£150	3	100	1200	1300
£50	1	0	600	600
< £50	0	0	0	0

We have assumed that the employment of labour is always equal to the smaller of demand and supply, thus embodying the notion that trade is voluntary. Note that we have also assumed in constructing the table that any marginal trade (that is, one in which the resulting surplus is zero) that has a partner actually does take place. If it does not, the table needs to be recalculated at certain wage rates. We further assumed that, if the supply of labour exceeds the demand, then the workers with the lowest reservation prices are employed so the realized surplus is maximized.

We note that the total surplus is maximized when the wage rate is equal to between £250 and £350; that is, when we have a competitive wage rate so that the demand and supply are equal.

If the firm could choose a single wage rate, what would it choose? A rate equal to £150, where its profit is maximized. In this situation just three workers would be employed and they would each receive a wage of between £100 and £200 less than the competitive wage. The workers would lose out if the firm could choose the wage.

Suppose now that there is a trade union representing the workers – one that is sufficiently strong as to be able to impose the (unique) wage rate it prefers. What wage would it choose? If it wants to maximize the surplus going to the workers then, looking at Table 2.2 we see that it would be a wage rate of £450 – at which rate just three workers would be employed. Fig. 2.15 illustrates this case. In drawing this figure, we have assumed (as we

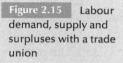

Figure 2.15 Labour demand, supply and surpluses with a trade union

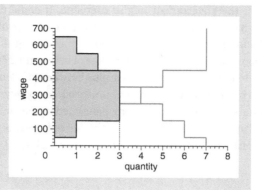

have already noted) that the firm actually employs the third worker, even though it is indifferent to so doing.

In this situation just three workers are employed (A, B and C) – rather than four (A, B, C and D) in the competitive equilibrium. However the wage rate going to those that are employed is higher than in the competitive equilibrium. But D loses out; under the competitive equilibrium D would receive a surplus of £50, but with the trade union he or she is unemployed and gets a surplus of zero. In maximizing its surplus, the trade union is able to obtain a higher wage than occurs in the competitive situation, but at the necessary expense of having a reduced employment of its members. This is the inevitable trade-off: given the downward-sloping demand for labour, the wage can be increased only at the expense of employment unless the firm can be forced to employ workers on which it is making a loss.

It looks as if the benefits of having a trade union are ambiguous: those workers who remain employed under the trade union have a higher wage and are therefore better off; those workers who become unemployed because of the trade union are worse off. However, we note something important: the surplus of the workers *in total* is improved. Examine Table 2.3, ignoring for the moment the bottom row.

Table 2.3 Labour market surplus with and without a trade union

Worker	A	B	C	D	E	F	G	All
Surplus under competition	£250	£150	£150	£50	£0	£0	£0	£600
Surplus with the union	£400	£300	£300	£0	£0	£0	£0	£1000
Surplus with discrimination	£600	£400	£300	£100	£0	£0	£0	£1400

This confirms that A, B and C are better off with the union and that D is worse off. But observe: the workers collectively are better off with the union; their surplus is higher. The union could then impose a levy on the workers who remain employed to compensate the worker(s) who become unemployed. All the workers would then be better off! This is an important result, but you should ask yourself: is this what trade unions really do?

Actually, if the trade union is sufficiently powerful there is something even cleverer that it can do. It can insist[14] that A is employed at a wage of £650; B is employed at a wage of £550; C is employed at a wage of £450; and D is employed at a wage of £350. The surpluses going to the workers would then be those in the bottom row of Table 2.3. The total surplus going to the workers would be £1400 – exactly equal to the total surplus (to both workers and the firm) under competition. The surplus of the firm would be zero. By discriminating the wage paid to different workers, the union has managed to extract all of the surplus in the market. It could then distribute some of the surplus generated to the unemployed workers.

---

14. You should ask yourself: why these particular wages? Because these are the reservation wages of the firm. And why these particular individuals? Because they have the lowest reservation wages.

At this point the government might intervene. It could do so by taxing some of the surplus away or it could intervene directly in the market. One obvious thing it could do is to impose a particular wage. If it was interested in maximizing the total surplus generated in the market, it could impose a competitive wage of between £250 and £350. This might not lead to some desired distribution of the surplus between the workers and the firm, but that could be realized by an appropriate income and profit tax policy. In this way the government could not only maximize the surplus being generated in the market, but it could also ensure its appropriate distribution. Of course to do this it needs to know the competitive price. This is where economists can help (see Chapter 16 in particular).

Discrete Goods

Reservation Prices, Demand and Supply, and Surpluses

3.1 Introduction

We continue to work with a discrete good – that is, one that can be bought and sold only in integer units. In this chapter we explain where the reservation prices which we assumed in Chapter 2 come from, and we generalize the analysis of Chapter 2 so that the individual may buy or sell more than one unit of the good and may, depending upon the price of the good, be either a buyer or a seller of the good. We explain the circumstances under which the individual is a buyer and under which he or she is a seller. Finally, we show more formally that the buyer surplus is the area between the price paid and the demand curve, and the seller surplus is the area between the price received and the supply curve. These results are of particular importance in practice, since we might have an estimate of the supply and demand curves and want to calculate the effects of some proposed policy measure.

3.2 The Initial Position

We are interested in a particular individual's demand and supply for some specific good. I am going to use a graphical analysis, and I put the quantity of the good on the horizontal axis. In addition to the particular good in which we are interested, we suppose that the individual has money to spend on other goods; I put the quantity of money that the individual has on the vertical axis. Take the units of money to be pounds. Let us assume that the individual starts with an initial endowment of some units of the good (this could be zero) and some amount of money (this could also be zero). In the example that follows it is assumed that the individual starts with 3 units of the good and 30 units of money – that is, £30. This initial endowment point is indicated in Fig. 3.1 by the letter 'X'.

The individual starts at point X. Perhaps through trade he or

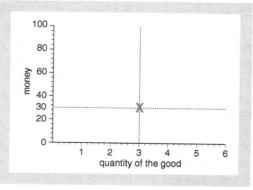

Figure 3.1 Initial endowment point

she can move to some other point in the space. Let us see what we can say about other points as compared to the point X. You will see that in the graph the space has been divided into four quadrants based on the point X. It should be clear that any point in the north-east quadrant must be preferred by the individual to the point X (assuming that he or she likes the good and likes money), as all points in this north-east quadrant have more of at least one unit of money or the good. Similarly we can say that the individual prefers point X to all the points in the south-west quadrant, as point X gives him or her more of at least one of money or the good than any point in that quadrant. What about the remaining two quadrants? In each of these, the individual has either more money and less of the good, or less money and more of the good, than at point X. So, unless we know more about the individual's preferences, we cannot say whether he or she prefers point X or some point in the two remaining quadrants.

3.3 Indifference

Let us suppose that we know something about the preferences of the individual as far as this good is concerned. In particular, let us suppose that we know that the individual would pay at most £5 to buy one extra unit of the good; that is, we know that the reservation price for the first extra unit of the good is £5. What does this tell us? The individual starts at the point (3, 30), that is with three units of the good and £30. If he or she were to spend £5 acquiring one extra unit of the good, this would cause a move to the point (4, 25), with one extra unit of the good and £5 less in money. If this £5 is the maximum that he or she would pay, we can conclude that the individual is indifferent between the points (3, 30) and (4, 25). In graphical terms, he or she is indifferent between point X and the point labelled '4' in Fig. 3.2.

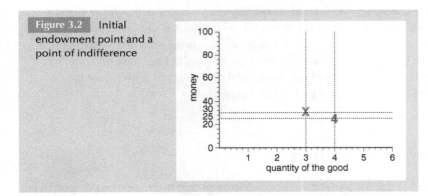

Figure 3.2 Initial endowment point and a point of indifference

We should be clear that we understand what is meant by this; indifference is an extremely important property to economists, but its meaning is not always obvious. When we say that the individual is indifferent between the point X and the point 4, we mean that the individual does not care whether he or she is at point X (with 3 units of the good and 30 units of money) or at point 4 (with 4 units of the good and 25 units of money). In fact, because of this indifference, the individual would be perfectly happy if someone else (or some machine) decided whether he was at point X or at point 4. Furthermore an implication of this indifference is that, if the individual was offered a choice between point X and some point better than point 4 (for example, point (4, 26) – check that you are clear that this is better than point 4), then he or she would choose the point better than point 4. Furthermore if offered a choice between point X and a point worse than point 4 – for example, the point (4, 24) – the individual would choose point X.

So far we have assumed that we know that the individual's reservation value for the first extra unit of the good is £5; that is, £5 is the maximum amount of money he or she would pay to have 4 units instead of 3 units of the good. Obviously this £5 depends upon the preferences of the individual and how he or she feels about the good *vis-à-vis* money.

Suppose we know some more; for instance that, after acquiring this first extra unit, the individual would pay at most £3 to acquire a second extra unit, and would then pay at most £2 to acquire a third extra unit of the good. This tells us that the individual's reservation price for the second extra unit is £3 and the reservation price for the third extra unit is £2. This information also tells us that the individual is indifferent between the points (3, 30) and (4, 25) because his or her reservation price for the first unit is £5, the point (5, 22) because the reservation price for the second unit is £3, and the point (6, 20) because the reservation price for the third unit is £2.

We might also have information about the individual's preferences in the other direction. Recall that the individual starts at the point (3, 30) with three units of the good and 30 units in money. Suppose we are told that the individual would sell one of the three units of the good if he or she was given sufficient extra money, and we are told that 10 units of money are the least that would be acceptable to sell one of the three units of the good. This information tells us that the individual is indifferent between the initial point (3, 30) and the point (2, 40) where there is one less unit of the good but £10 more in money. Finally let us suppose that we know that the individual would sell a second unit of the good, but only for a minimum compensation of 30 units of money. This tells us that the individual is indifferent between point X (3, 30), the point (2, 40) and the point (1, 70). In Fig. 3.3 we show all this graphically, with the individual indifferent between point X and the points 1, 2, 4, 5 and 6.

If we join all these points together we get what is called an indifference curve – the individual is indifferent between all the points along it[1]. This is shown in Fig. 3.4. Moreover it follows from what has gone before that the individual prefers any point above and to the right of this indifference curve to any point on it; and he or she prefers any point on it to any point below and to the left of it.

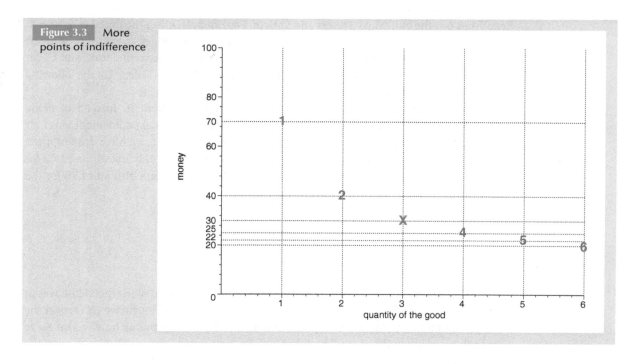

Figure 3.3 More points of indifference

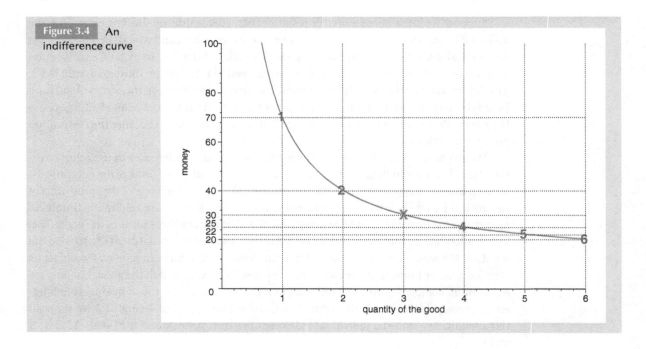

Figure 3.4 An indifference curve

3.4 Reservation Prices

In order to construct this indifference curve, we started with the knowledge of the individual's reservation prices. We can work in the other direction. Given the indifference curve, we can work out the individual's reservation prices. For example, given the initial endowment point (3, 30), the individual would be a buyer at sufficiently low prices; specifically, he or she has the following reservation prices £5 for the first unit; £3 for the second unit; and £2 for the third unit. For sufficiently high prices the individual would be a seller with the following reservation prices: £10 for the first unit and £30 for the second.

These reservation prices depend on the initial endowment. If, instead of being endowed with three units of the good and £30 of money, the initial endowment was four units and £25 (notice that this is on the indifference curve which we have drawn), then the reservation prices would be the following: as a buyer, £3 for the first unit and £2 for the second unit; as a seller, £5 for the first unit, £10 for the second unit and £30 for the third unit.

3.5 Indifference Curves

In the above analysis we assumed that the initial endowment point of the individual was at (3, 30) – that is, with 3 units of the good and £30 in money. Obviously we can repeat the analysis for any initial endowment point, and we can therefore derive an indifference curve through any point in the space. The shape of these indifference curves will depend upon the individual's preferences, although they will always be downward-sloping because we have assumed that the individual likes both the good and money. However, if we make a particular assumption about these preferences we can derive any other indifference curve from the one that we have already derived. As will be realized, this is a strong assumption; in future chapters we will weaken it, but it will prove useful to us throughout this chapter and the next. This assumption is the following[2]:

 The individual's reservation prices for the good depend upon the number of units of the good in his or her possession but do not depend upon the amount of money that the individual has.

What does this imply? Consider the individual's indifference curve through an initial endowment point (3, 40); this differs from that considered previously in that the initial endowment of income is £10 higher. If we assume that the reservation prices are the same as when the initial endowment point was (3, 30), we can draw a second indifference curve through the new initial point. This is shown in Fig. 3.5

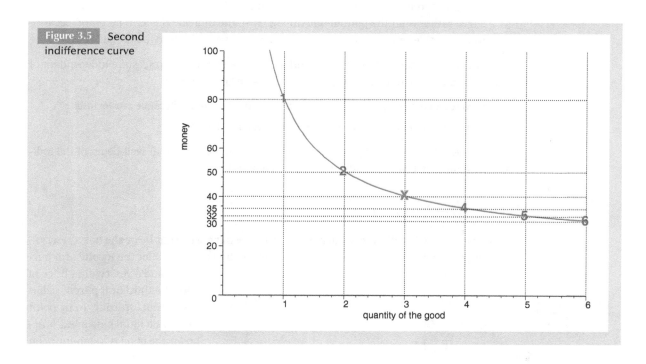

Figure 3.5 Second indifference curve

Note that moving from point X to point 4 in this figure involves giving up £5 in exchange for an extra unit of the good – just as before. The reservation prices implied by the indifference curve in Fig. 3.5 are exactly the same as those implied by the indifference curve in Fig. 3.4.

If we compare Figs. 3.4 and 3.5, we see that the indifference curve in Fig. 3.5 is parallel in a vertical direction to that in Fig. 3.4. In other words, the vertical distance between the two curves is everywhere equal to £10.

---

2. For reasons which will become clear later, this is referred to as the assumption that the individual's preferences are *quasi-linear*.

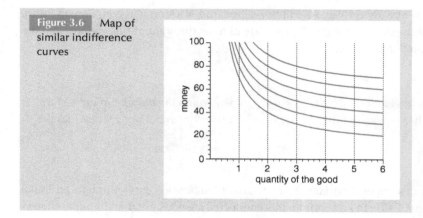

Figure 3.6 Map of similar indifference curves

Let us assume that the indifference curves always have this property. Then, if we draw indifference curves through the points $(3, 30)$, $(3, 40)$, $(3, 50)$, $(3, 60)$, $(3, 70)$ and $(3, 80)$, we have a map of indifference curves which is pictured in Fig. 3.6.

Each curve is a constant distance away from any other in a vertical direction; the indifference curves are parallel in a vertical direction. We can conclude a number of things from this:

- the higher the indifference curve on which the individual is, the happier he or she is;

- we can measure how much happier he or she is by the vertical distance between the relevant two indifference curves. For example, if he or she is on the top indifference curve rather than the bottom one (in Fig. 3.6), the individual is £50 better off because the top indifference curve is everywhere £50 above the bottom indifference curve[3].

Obviously, maintaining the assumption that the reservation prices are independent of the initial endowment of money, all the above can be generalized:

- through every point in the space in Fig. 3.6 there is an indifference curve; and

- all the indifference curves are parallel in a vertical direction.

This implies that the vertical distance is a measure of the change in well-being of the individual in moving from one indifference curve to another.

3.6 Implied Demand Curve

What is the individual's implied demand curve? We have seen that he or she has a reservation price of £5 for the first unit purchased, a reservation price of £3 for the second unit purchased, and a reservation price of £2 for the third unit purchased. It

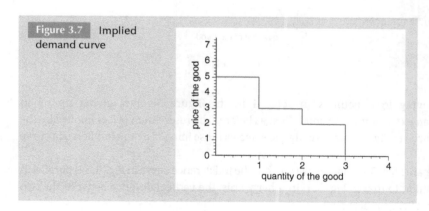

Figure 3.7 Implied demand curve

follows that, starting from point X, the individual's demand function for the good is a step-function with steps at the prices £5, £3 and £2. The demand curve is shown in Fig. 3.7, which has the quantity of the good on the horizontal axis and the price of the good on the vertical axis. (Note that this is a different space from that used in the previous figures.)

---

3. Check that you are happy with this. One point on the top indifference curve is $(3, 80)$ and one point on the bottom indifference curve is $(3, 30)$. How much better off is the individual at $(3, 80)$ as compared with $(3, 30)$? That is, how much better off is the individual with 3 units of the good and £80 as compared with having 3 units of the good and £30? Surely £50.

We check that this demand curve has the correct properties. It indicates that, at any price greater than £5, the individual would not demand any units of the good. At a price between £5 and £3 (the reservation prices for the first and second units purchased), demand would be one unit. At a price between £3 and £2 (the reservation prices for the second and third units purchased), demand would be two units. At a price less than £2 (the reservation price for the third unit) the demand would be three units; I am ignoring the possibility of more than 3 units being purchased. The demand function is a step-function with a step at every reservation price.

Let us consider some particular examples. We shall also work out the gains from trade in these examples and show that our general result, that the surplus is equal to the area between the price paid and the demand curve, is true in this context. Consider a price of £4. If the individual is offered the opportunity to buy or sell the good at a fixed price of £4 per unit, what would he or she do? To answer this, let us consider the opportunities offered by the existence of this price, which is indicated by point 1 in Fig. 3.8.

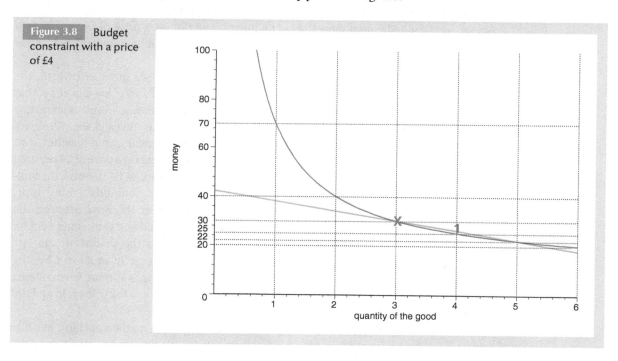

Figure 3.8 Budget constraint with a price of £4

The individual starts at point X with three units of the good and £30. Given a price of £4 per unit, we can work out where he or she could move to with different trades. For example, if he or she buys just one unit at a price of £4 per unit, he or she will move from point (3, 30) to point (4, 26) – there will be one more unit of the good but £4 less in money; if two units are bought, he or she moves from (3, 30) to (5, 22) – the two units purchased costing £8; if three units are purchased, then he or she moves from (3, 30) to (6, 18); and so on. Alternatively the individual could sell. If one unit is sold at price of £4 per unit, he or she moves from (3, 30) to (2, 34); if two units are sold at a price of £4 the move is from (3, 30) to (1, 38); and so on. So a price of £4 per unit offers the individual the opportunity to either stay at (3, 30) or move to any one of the points (0, 42), (1, 38), (2, 34), (4, 26), (5, 22) or (6, 18). If we join these points up we get the straight line through point X in Fig. 3.8. Note that this line has a slope (– £4) equal to (minus) the price of the good, since each unit bought decreases the money holdings by the price and since each unit sold increases the money holdings by the price. This line is called the individual's *budget constraint*; it shows the possibilities offered to the individual by a price of £4 per unit.

The budget constraint shows the opportunities open to the individual. What does he or she do? In principal it is easy to answer this: choose the point on it which is highest in terms of the indifference map; that is, he or she chooses the point which is highest in a vertical direction from the indifference curve passing through the initial point. From Fig. 3.8 it is clear that all the points to the left of point X lie below the initial indifference curve so the individual would be worse off moving to the left, that is, by selling. The reason is simple; the price is too low. Furthermore we know the point (5, 22) is on the original indifference curve and that the point (6, 18) lies below it. This leaves the point (4, 26), which is clearly on a higher indifference curve than originally. In fact we can work out that it must be on an indifference curve £1 higher as the point (4, 25) lies on the original curve and the point (4, 26) is £1 higher in a vertical direction from (4, 25).

It follows that, of all the points with integer values for the quantity of the good on the budget constraint for a price of £4 per unit, the best is unambiguously the point (4, 26). Accordingly the individual moves there by buying one unit at a price of £4 and is, as a consequence, £1 better off [4]. This £1 is the surplus the individual has when offered a price of £4 for the good.

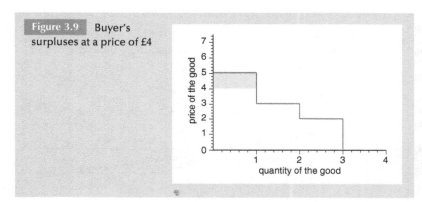

Figure 3.9 Buyer's surpluses at a price of £4

If we now return to the demand curve, we can show that our previous result about this surplus is still valid. Fig. 3.9 shows the demand curve together with the surplus at a price of £4 per unit. At a price of £4 per unit the individual demands one unit. Moreover the area between the price paid and the demand curve, which is the shaded area in Fig. 3.9, is exactly equal to £1 – the individual's surplus when offered a price of £4. Our result that the surplus is equal to the area between the price paid and the demand curve remains true.

This result is both profound and trivial (trivial if you are a mathematician), but it is important. Fully understanding why it is true may take a little time. In the meantime I am happy if you are satisfied that it works in these numerical examples. To reinforce your understanding let me give two more examples. After you have studied these you could try some examples of your own.

Consider now a lower price – say a price of £2.50 per unit. Fig. 3.10 shows the budget constraint implied by this price; it is the straight line passing through the initial point. Note that it passes through the following points: (0, 37.5) where the individual sells all three units; (1, 35) where the individual sells 2 units; (2, 32.5) where the individual sells one unit; (3, 30) where the individual neither buys or sells; (4, 27.5) where the individual buys one unit; (5, 25) where the individual buys 2 units; and (6, 22.5) where the individual buys 3 units. Note also that this budget line has a slope equal to −£2.50.

---

4. This improvement can be seen another way. At a price of £4 the individual buys one unit – for which the reservation price is £5. He or she was willing to pay up to £5 for this unit, but paid only £4 and is therefore £1 better off as a consequence.

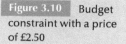

Figure 3.10 Budget constraint with a price of £2.50

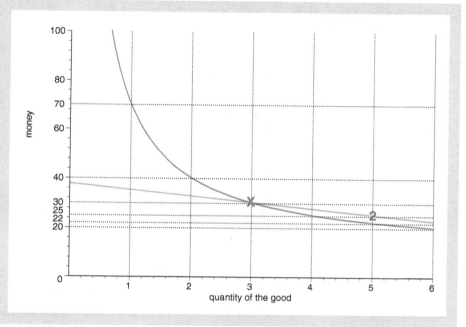

Once again it is clear that the individual is worse off if he or she sells any units. At (4, 27.5) he or she is £2.50 better off than originally because the original indifference curve passes through (4, 25). At (5, 25) he is £3 better off than originally since the original indifference curve passes through (3, 22). At (6, 22.5) he or she is £2.50 better off than originally as the original indifference curve passes through (6, 20). Clearly the individual is best off at (5, 25) – that is, by buying 2 units – and there he or she is better off by £3. The surplus from the trade is £3. Let us now return to the demand curve which is shown in Fig. 3.11, this time with the price of £2.50 per unit.

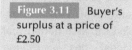

Figure 3.11 Buyer's surplus at a price of £2.50

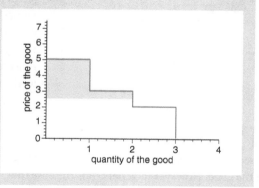

Figure 3.11 shows that demand at the price of £2.50 is 2 units of the good. The surplus is the area between the price line at £2.50 and the demand curve, which is the shaded area between the two lines. The area equals £2.50 + £0.50 = £3, exactly as we derived it earlier. The result is once again confirmed.

Finally, let us consider a price of £1.80 per unit. The implied budget constraint is the straight line in Fig. 3.12, with a slope equal to – £1.80. Where is the best point on this budget constraint? You should be able to verify that it is at (6, 24.6), to which the individual moves by buying 3 units at a cost of £5.40 and at which the individual is £4.60 better off than originally. His or her surplus from the trade is £4.60.

Once again we confirm this result by means of the demand function in Fig. 3.13. At a price of £1.80 per unit demand is three and the surplus is the shaded area, which is equal to (£3.20 + £1.20 + £0.20) = £4.60; this is identical to the surplus of £4.60 made by the individual when offered a price of £1.80.

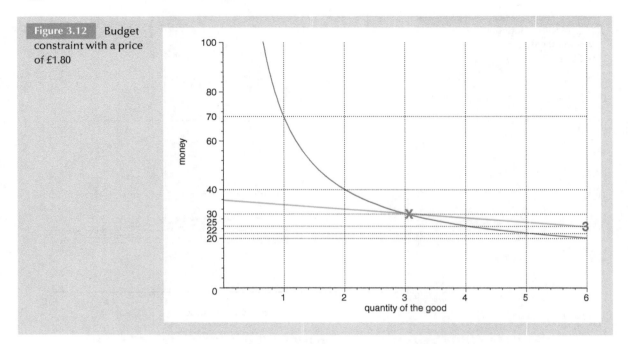

Figure 3.12   Budget constraint with a price of £1.80

The crucial point about all the above is that we have verified the result that

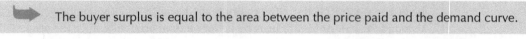

The buyer surplus is equal to the area between the price paid and the demand curve.

Figure 3.13   Buyer's surplus at a price of £1.80

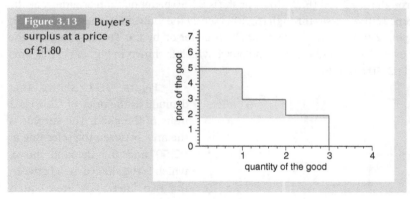

It should be noted that this result relies on the assumption that we made earlier, that the indifference curves are parallel in a vertical direction; that is, the reservation prices are independent of the initial money endowment. This assumption is called the assumption that the individual has *quasi-linear preferences*. We shall discuss this further in Section 3.8.

3.7   Implied Supply Curve

In the previous section we took as examples prices sufficiently low that the individual chose to be a buyer of the good. However in general it is the case that, if the individual is endowed with some units of the good, there will exist prices sufficiently high to induce the individual to be a seller. In fact we know this already because we know that the individual will sell one of the units of the good at a reservation price of £10, and will sell a second at a reservation price of £30. The implied supply curve is readily derived and is shown in Fig. 3.14.

We check that this has the correct properties. It says that at any price less than £10, the individual would not sell any units of the good; at a price between £10 and £30, the reservation prices for the first and second units sold, the supply would be one unit; at a price greater than £30, the reservation price for the second unit, the supply would be two units (I am ignoring the possibility of more than two units being sold). The supply function is a step-function with a step at every reservation price.

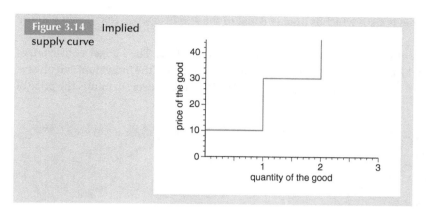

Figure 3.14 Implied supply curve

As in the case of demand, let us consider some particular examples. Consider first a price of £20 per unit. The budget constraint is shown in Fig. 3.15 as the straight line passing through the initial point X. It has a slope equal to −£20 that is, equal to (minus) the price of the good. Where is the best point on this budget constraint? Obviously the individual does not want to buy the good; he or she does not want to move to the right of the initial point because the position there is worse in the sense that he or she is on a lower indifference curve than originally. Nor will the individual want to sell two or more units. Indeed it is clear that the best point, restricting ourselves as ever to integer values of the good, is (2, 50), to which the individual moves by selling one unit of the good. At the point (2, 50) he or she is better off than originally, by £10; the location is on an indifference

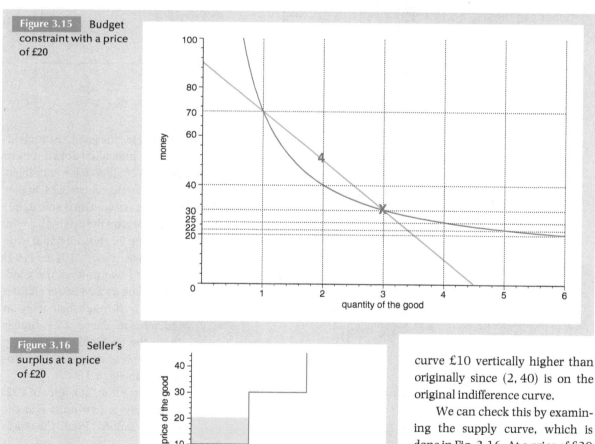

Figure 3.15 Budget constraint with a price of £20

Figure 3.16 Seller's surplus at a price of £20

curve £10 vertically higher than originally since (2, 40) is on the original indifference curve.

We can check this by examining the supply curve, which is done in Fig. 3.16. At a price of £20 the supply is one, and the surplus is the shaded area between the price received and the supply curve in Fig. 3.16. It can easily be seen that this area is £10, which is exactly equal to the surplus gained from trading at the price of £20[5].

Let us present one final example: consider a price of £32. The budget constraint is shown in Fig. 3.17 passing through the initial endowment point (the individual can always choose to remain there), and with a slope of −£32; it is equal, as ever, to minus the price of the good.

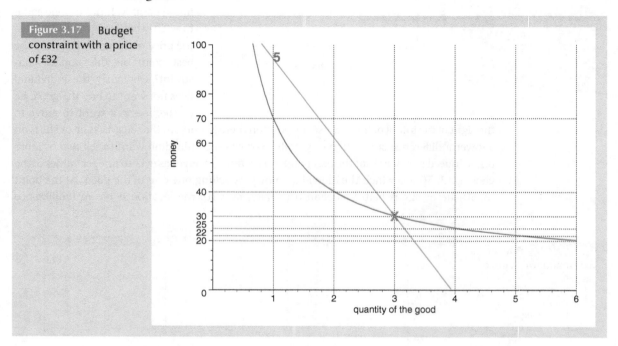

Figure 3.17 Budget constraint with a price of £32

Given the budget constraint and the restriction to integer values for the good, the individual can move to (0, 126), (1, 94), (2, 62), or stay at (3, 30) (the individual does not have enough money to buy even one unit of the good). The point (0, 126) is on a lower indifference curve than the original. The point (1, 94) is on an indifference curve £24 higher than the original one since (1, 70) is on the original indifference curve. The point (2, 62) is on an indifference curve £22 higher than the original as (2, 40) is on the original. So the

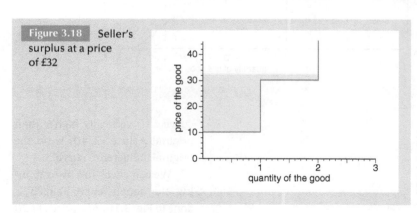

Figure 3.18 Seller's surplus at a price of £32

best thing for the individual to do is to move from (3, 30) to (1, 94) by selling two units of the good, and ending up £24 better off than originally through being on an indifference curve £24 higher than the original. The supply curve representing this new situation is in Fig. 3.18.

We see that, at a price of £32, the supply is two units and the surplus gained from the trade

5. Another way of checking the surplus calculation is to note that the individual's reservation price for the first unit sold is £10; and hence there is a surplus of £10 if the individual sells that first unit for £20.

is the shaded area in Fig. 3.18, which is equal to £22 + £2 = £24, exactly the same as we have already demonstrated.

The crucial point about all the above is that we have verified the result that

> The seller surplus is equal to the area between the price received and the supply curve.

Once again it should be noted that this result relies on the assumption we made earlier that the preferences of the individual are quasi-linear – that is, the indifference curves are parallel in a vertical direction. We shall discuss this further in the following section.

3.8 Comments

First I should comment on the fact that this whole chapter has used a specific example. You might be wondering why I have done this and how much of the detail you need to understand and remember. The reason that I have used a specific example throughout is so that the various results that I have been claiming can easily be confirmed; the calculations involved are simple arithmetic operations. So one reason for using a specific example is to build up your confidence in the various results that I am claiming, some of which can only be proved formally with rather complex mathematics. However I do not want you to get bogged down with detail, and I certainly do not want you to memorize any details of the special example that I have used. What I want you to concentrate your attention on are the methods and the principles which I have used. I hope that you get the following out of this chapter.

- Quasi-linear preferences (parallel-in-a-vertical-direction indifference curves) are important because they enable us to measure how much better or worse off an individual is if he or she moves from one point in the space to another; this, in turn, enables us to measure the surplus gained when buying or selling.

- The budget constraint in (q, m) space must have a slope equal to minus the price of the good.

- The best place for the individual to be, given a particular budget constraint, is as high as possible vertically relative to the original indifference curve, taking into account the restriction to integer values for the quantities.

- By using this procedure, we can find the best strategy for the individual at any price; we can compute the gross demand for the good at any price.

- If this gross demand is greater than the initial endowment, then the individual wants to buy more of the good – his or her net demand is positive. By plotting these net demands against the price we get the person's demand curve and, if we look at the area between the price paid and the demand curve, we find the surplus made as a result of the purchase; that is, we find out how much better off he or she is as a consequence of the purchase.

- If this gross demand is less than the initial endowment, then the individual wants to sell some of the good – his or her net supply is positive. By plotting these net supplies against the price we get the supply curve, and the area between the price received and the supply curve represents the surplus made as a result of the sale; that is, we find out how much better off he or she is following the sale. These results concerning the surpluses should be fairly obvious in the context used here (the integer-only context).

We have shown that the two key results concerning the buyer and seller surplus are true in the context of this chapter. This chapter is special in two key respects: first, the good is discrete; and second, I have assumed that the preferences are such that the indifference curves are parallel in a vertical direction. The two key results do not depend on the discrete nature of the good, as I will show in the next chapter, but they do depend crucially on the assumption about the indifference curves. We have already seen that this parallel property is known in the literature as the assumption that the preferences are quasi-linear[6]. The important intuitive point is that it means that reservation prices for the good do not depend upon the amount of money that an individual has. Is this true for you? Suppose you have no units of some good. Ask yourself whether the amount you are willing to pay to possess one unit of the good depends upon how much money you have. If it does, you do not have quasi-linear preferences; if it does not, you may have.

You should understand why this assumption is important. The consequences of indifference curves being parallel in a vertical direction is that, if at some quantity of the good one curve is £10 higher than another, then it will be £10 higher at any quantity of the good. This means that we can unambiguously say that the individual is £10 better off if he or she is on the higher curve than on the lower curve; we have an unambiguous measure of how much better off the individual is. If indifference curves are not parallel, we do not have such an unambiguous measure. We will explore the implications of this in later chapters.

I have spent some considerable time deriving and discussing the key results about the measurement of the surplus. Perhaps you are asking why? These key results are important for a number of reasons, not least when we want to assess the impact of some policy change. Often such a change in policy will have an impact on the price in some market, and we may want to calculate the effect on the welfare of the participants in that market. If the price goes up it makes the buyers worse off and the sellers better off. We can calculate how much better off and worse off using the key results. The loss of the buyer surplus is the area between the demand curve and the old and new prices. Similarly, the increase in the seller surplus is the area between the supply curve and the old and new prices. Often we can make estimates of demand and supply curves (see Chapter 16), and hence we can estimate the losses and gains in the surpluses. This helps us to decide whether to implement a policy change or not.

6. The reason for this is that the equation of an indifference curve in (q, m) space (where q denotes the quantity of the good and m denotes the quantity of money) is given by an equation of the form $m + f(q) = $ constant, where $f(.)$ is some decreasing function. That is, the indifference curves are partly linear (in m) and partly non-linear.

3.9 Summary

We have restricted attention in this chapter to the case of a discrete good – one that can be bought and sold only in integer units. Moreover, for most of the chapter we have assumed that the preferences take the particular form of quasi-linear preferences. But, independent of these two restrictions, we have defined the key concept of an indifference curve as being:

 An indifference curve is a locus of points about which the individual feels indifferent.

We have defined what we mean by a budget constraint and shown that it has the following important property:

 The slope of the budget constraint in (quantity of the good, money) space is equal to minus the price of the good.

In addition, we have shown how to derive demand and supply curves from indifference curves. In particular we have shown that:

 The demand function takes the form of a step-function with a step at every reservation price.

 The supply function takes the form of a step-function with a step at every reservation price.

 The individual is a buyer for sufficiently low prices and a seller for sufficiently high prices.

We have also verified two key results from Chapter 2, namely:

 The buyer surplus is the area between the price paid and the demand curve.

 The seller surplus is the area between the price received and the supply curve.

Finally we recall the definition of quasi-linear preferences:

 With quasi-linear preferences, the indifference curves are parallel in a vertical direction and the reservation prices are independent of the amount of money held by the individual.

3.10 Review Questions

1. What are the implications for the indifference curves of an individual if he or she has quasi-linear preferences?

2. Can you think of a good for which your preferences are quasi-linear – that is, one for which the reservation prices which you would pay, or accept, are independent of the amount of money income that you have?

3. If not, do you think that the reservation prices increase or decrease with your income? What would that imply about the shapes of your indifference curves?

4. If indifference curves are not parallel, there is no longer a unique measure of how much better off the individual is when he or she moves from one point to another; can you think of any approximate measures? (This is a difficult question and one which you might not be able to answer until Chapter 19.)

3.11 Mathematical Appendix

Let me repeat the warning I gave earlier: if you have followed and are happy with the results presented in the text, and do not like mathematics, then you do not need to read or understand this appendix. But if you like mathematics and are curious about the proof, you might find this appendix interesting. At a first glance it looks quite complicated, but when you understand what is going on it is really quite simple.

The general proofs of the propositions in the text are straightforward. Assume quasi-linear preferences and that the individual starts with Q units of the good and M of money. We will consider only the situation when the price is sufficiently low for the individual to act as a buyer. The case when the price is high enough for the individual to act as a seller follows precisely the same line of argument.

Let us suppose that an individual's reservation prices as a buyer are $r_1, r_2, ...,$ and so on. That is, the individual would pay at most r_1 for the first extra unit of the good, r_2 for the second extra unit, and so on. Let p denote the price of the good. Assume that p is less than r_1, so the individual will buy at least one extra unit of the good. If p is greater that r_1 the individual will not be a buyer; the price is too high to buy even one unit of the good.

The individual starts with an endowment of (Q, M), that is Q units of the good and M of money. If a purchase is made of one unit of the good at a price of p, he or she will have $(Q + 1, M - p)$ – that is, one more unit of the good and p less in money; if two units of the good are purchased, then he or she will have $(Q + 2, M - 2p)$, or two units more of the good and $2p$ less of money; and so on. We show this in tabular form in Table A3.1.

Table A3.1   Calculation of an individual's optimal demand

Quantity of the good	Quantity of money on original indifference curve	Quantity of money at a price of p	How much better off is the individual? This is given by the difference between the third and the second columns	Change in the fourth column from previous row
(1)	(2)	(3)	(4)	(5)
Q	M	M	0	–
$Q+1$	$M - r_1$	$M - p$	$r_1 - p$	$r_1 - p$
$Q+2$	$M - r_1 - r_2$	$M - 2p$	$r_1 + r_2 - 2p$	$r_2 - p$
...		...		
$Q+i$	$M - r_1 - r_2 - ... - r_i$	$M - ip$	$r_1 + r_2 + ... + r_i - ip$	$r_i - p$
$Q+i+1$	$M - r_1 - r_2 - ... - r_{i+1}$	$M - (i+1)p$	$r_1 + r_2 + ... + r_{i+1} - (i+1)p$	$r_{i+1} - p$
...				
$Q+n$	$M - r_1 - r_2 - ... - r_n$	$M - np$	$r_1 + r_2 + ... + r_n - np$	$r_n - p$

Column 1 in Table A3.1 shows the quantity of the good possessed after any purchase $(Q, Q + 1, Q + 2,)$ etc. Column 2 indicates the quantity of money on the original indifference curve at the various amounts of the good.

The first row indicates the starting position; if the individual stays there he or she is no better off than originally; this implies a zero in column 4, which is the difference between columns 2 and 3.

The second row of the table indicates what happens if the individual buys one unit of the good at a price of p; he or she will then have $(Q + 1)$ units of the good and $(M − p)$ in money. How much better off would the individual be in this situation? With quasi-linear preferences we can measure this by measuring how much vertically higher the individual is than initially. We can calculate this exactly as we know where the original indifference curve is at a quantity of $(Q + 1)$; it is at a quantity of money $(m − r_1)$. Why? Because r_1 is the reservation price for the first extra unit bought, and is therefore the maximum that the individual would pay to have $(Q + 1)$ units of the good. With the price of p, the individual could be at $(Q + 1, Q − p)$ which is higher by $(r_1 − p)$ than the original indifference curve. So the individual is $(r_1 − p)$ better off than originally by buying one unit at a price of p. We put this in column 4 of the table. This of course is what we have claimed in the text. Note that we have assumed that p is less than r_1, so this is a positive improvement.

Row 3 of the table indicates what would happen if the individual bought two extra units. He or she would then have $(Q + 2)$ of the good and $(M − 2p)$ in money. How much higher is this than the original indifference curve? We know that this curve passes through the point $(Q + 2, M − r_1 − r_2)$ because r_1 and r_2 are the reservation prices for the first two units of the good. Hence the individual would be $(M − 2p) − (M − r_1 − r_2)$ higher than originally – that is, an amount $(r_1 + r_2 − 2p)$ better off than originally. We can continue in this way, and can therefore get the general case which is presented in the final row of the table. Here the individual buys n extra units and ends up $(r_1 + r_2 + ... + r_n − np)$ better off.

The question now is: what is the best option for the individual to take? Obviously this depends upon the price and his or her reservation prices. We know that in general these reservation prices are decreasing – that is, the individual would be happy to pay more for the first extra unit than for the second, and more for the second than for the third, and so on. In general, therefore, $r_1 > r_2 > ... > r_n$. It therefore follows that $(r_i − p)$ must be decreasing, and will become negative at some point. Let us define i as the number such that $(r_i − p)$ is positive and that $(r_{i+1} − p)$ is negative; obviously this particular value of i depends upon the value of p. Now look at column 4 of Table A3.1. From the first row to the second row of column 4 the difference is $(r_1 − p)$; from the second row to the third row the difference is $(r_2 − p)$; in general the difference between the ith row and the $(i + 1)^{th}$ row is $(r_{i+1} − p)$. We place these differences in column 5 of the table. Now the entries in column 4 are increasing until we get to the ith row, with i as defined above. It follows that the best thing that the individual can do is to buy i units of the good, as this maximizes how much better off he or she is. So, at a price p such that $(r_i − p)$ is positive and $(r_{i+1} − p)$ is negative, the optimal demand is i units of the good. This states that the price p is such that the individual would be willing to buy up to and including i units of the good, but would be unwilling to buy the $(i + 1)^{th}$ unit, because the price is higher than his or her reservation price for the $(i + 1)^{th}$ unit. The condition that $(r_i − p)$ is positive and that $(r_{i+1} − p)$ is negative can be written as $r_i > p > r_{i+1}$; hence we have the result that, for a price in this range, the optimal demand is i units of the good. Furthermore we can see from Table A3.1 that the surplus of the individual at such a price is $(r_1 + r_2 + ... + r_i − ip)$; he or she is that much better off than in the original position.

This is all we need. For any price p we can find the corresponding i and hence find the demand. It immediately follows that the demand is one unit for $r_1 > p > r_2$; two units for $r_2 > p > r_3$; three units for $r_3 > p > r_4$; and, in general, is i units for $r_i > p > r_{i+1}$. It is therefore a step function as we stated previously, with steps at the reservation prices. Moreover the surplus at a price of p such that $r_i > p > r_{i+1}$ is exactly $(r_1 + r_2 + ... + r_i − ip)$, as claimed in the text. This is precisely the area between the price of p and the step demand function we have derived – the sum of i rectangles each of width one unit.

Continuous Goods

chapter 4

Demand and Supply, and Surpluses

4.1 Introduction

The only difference between the previous chapter and this one is that in this chapter we have a good which can be bought and sold in any amounts, not just discrete amounts. This changes the details of the previous chapter somewhat, but the broad principles remain the same. To stress the similarities between this chapter and the previous one we deliberately start with the same example; an individual with the same preferences as in the previous chapter, but now the preferences refer to a continuous good.

4.2 The Initial Position

We are interested in an individual's demand and supply for some particular good. As before we will use a graphical analysis in which the quantity of the good is on the horizontal axis. In addition to the particular good, the individual has money to spend on other goods, and we put the quantity of money which the individual has on the vertical axis. This, we assume, is meas-

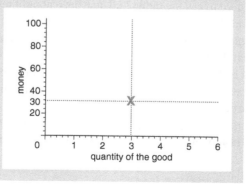

Figure 4.1 The initial endowment point (again)

ured in pounds. Let us assume that the individual starts with an initial endowment of some units of the good (this could be zero), and some amount of money (this could also be zero). In the example that follows it is assumed that the individual starts with three units of the good and 30 units of money – that is, £30. This initial endowment point is indicated in Fig 4.1 by the letter 'X'.

4.3 An Indifference Curve

As before, we assume that we know something about the individual's preferences; in this case that he or she would pay up to a maximum of £5 to have one extra unit of the good, pay up to a maximum of £3 for a second extra unit, and up to a maximum of £2 for a third extra unit of the good. Moreover we assume that we know that the individual would sell one unit of the good if he or she was paid at least £10, and would then sell a second unit if paid at least

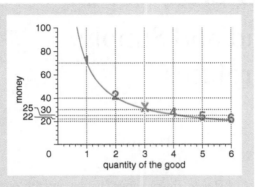

Figure 4.2 The original indifference curve (again)

£30. This information, which is exactly the same as was assumed in Chapter 3 [1], enables us to conclude that the individual is indifferent between the points 1, 2, X, 4, 5 and 6 in Fig. 4.2.

There must be points of indifference in between these six points. If we join together all these points of indifference, as we have done in the figure, we obtain what is called an indifference curve through the initial point X. In the case of a continuous good all the points on the indifference curve have meaning; the individual is indifferent between all points on the curve. If offered a choice between any two randomly chosen points on the curve, the individual would reply that he or she does not mind which he or she has; and would not mind if someone else did the choosing.

We can say something stronger: it follows from what has gone before that the individual prefers any point above and to the right of the indifference curve to any point on it; and will prefer any point on it to any point below and to the left of it.

4.4 Indifference Curves

We have found one indifference curve – that passing through the initial point X – by using information about the individual's preferences as expressed through reservation prices. Clearly this method can be used to construct an indifference curve through any point in the (quantity of the good, money) space that we are using. There exists an indifference curve through every point in this space. Clearly the form of these curves depends upon the individual's preferences – his or her feelings about the good *vis-à-vis* money. In general, to find them we would need to ask the individual questions about these preferences over the entire space. However in this chapter, as in Chapter 3, we make a simplifying assumption which enables us to immediately discover all the indifference curves of the individual. The assumption is simply that the reservation prices are independent of the amount of money the individual has. This is the same assumption that we made in Chapter 3, and it enables us to conclude that the indifference curves are parallel in a vertical direction. Fig. 4.3 shows six such curves, one being the original from Fig. 4.2.

Recall that this assumption regarding the indifference curves enables us to say how much better off the individual is at one point in the space as compared to a second point. For

---

1. To make what follows easier to assimilate.

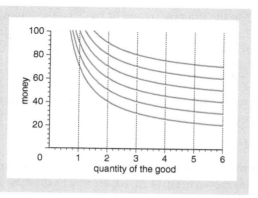

Figure 4.3 The map of parallel indifference curves (again)

example, take any point on the top indifference curve and compare it with any point on the bottom indifference curve. The individual is indifferent between the first of these and the point (3, 80); the individual is indifferent between the second of these and the point (3, 30). Now compare (3, 80) with (3, 30); the first point is clearly £50 better than the second, so the individual is £50 better off. And what is this £50? It is the vertical distance between the top curve and the bottom one; crucially, this vertical difference is constant because the indifference curves are parallel in a vertical direction.[2]

4.5 Implied Demand

As in Chapter 3 we can find the individual's demand at any price. We take the same examples as we did in Chapter 3, but note that in this chapter the good is continuous and the individual is no longer constrained to integer

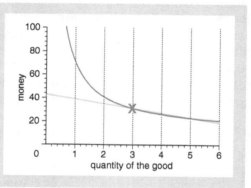

Figure 4.4 The budget constraint at a price of £4 (again)

demands. Consider first a price of £4 per unit. The budget constraint for this is shown in Fig. 4.4.

As before, at a price of £4 per unit, the individual can sell all three units and move from (3, 30) to (0, 42), or sell two units and move to (1, 38), or sell one unit and move to (2, 34); he or she can stay at point X, or can buy one unit and move to (4, 26), or buy two units and move to (5, 22), or can buy three units and move to (6, 18). If we join the points (0, 42), (1, 38), (2, 34), (3, 30), (4, 26), (5, 22) and (6, 18) together, we get the budget constraint facing the individual at a price of £4 per unit. This is the straight line passing through the point X in Fig. 4.4. Note that this has a slope equal to − £4; that is, minus the price of the good.

Of course with a continuous good the individual is not constrained to buying or selling integer amounts of the good. He or she could buy 2.5 units; this would cost £10 at a price per unit equal to £4, and would move the individual from (3, 30) to (5.5, 20). This point is on the budget constraint which we have already drawn.

Can we be more general? Let us suppose that the individual wants q units of the good and m units of money. This combination would cost $(pq + m)$ at a price p for the good (note that the price of money is obviously one). To finance this purchase, the individual can use the initial endowment of the good and of money. If we denote the initial endowment of the

---

2. This means that we can make the comparison at any quantity of the good. For example, we could compare (4, 75) with (4, 25), or (5, 72) with (5, 22), or (6, 70) with (6, 20), and so on; the monetary amount differs by £50 at each quantity of the good.

good by Q ($Q = 3$ in the example we are using), and the initial endowment of money by M (note that M is 30 in the example we are using), then the value of the initial endowment is equal to $(pQ + M)$. So we can write the budget constraint as in Eq. (4.1).

$$pq + m = pQ + M \qquad (4.1)$$

In English, this reads that the cost of purchases should be equal to the value of the initial endowment. Alternatively we can write the budget constraint (4.1) in the form

$$p(q - Q) = M - m \qquad (4.2)$$

This may be the most appropriate form to use when the individual is a buyer of the good. We can also write it as shown in Eq. (4.3), which may be the most appropriate format when the individual is a seller.

$$p(Q - q) = m - M \qquad (4.3)$$

Consider the 'buyer' form in Eq. (4.2). If the individual chooses to buy some (more) of the good, then $q > Q$ and the left-hand side of Eq. (4.2) is positive. It represents the cost of buying the extra units. This purchase has to be financed; the equation tells us that this is financed by running down money holdings from M to m. Now consider the 'seller' form, that is, Eq. (4.3). If the individual chooses to sell some of the good, then $Q > q$ and the left-hand side of Eq. (4.3) is positive. It represents the money raised by selling some units. This money increases the individual's money holdings from M to m, as Eq. (4.3) tells us.

Eqs. (4.1), (4.2) and (4.3) are of course all the same. They each represent a straight line in (q, m) space (the equations are linear in q and m) passing through point X; you should substitute $q = Q$ and $m = M$ in the equation and see that these values satisfy the equation. The line has a slope equal to $-p$ (the price of the good). To see this latter point, write the equation as $m = (pQ + M) - pq$, which is an equation linear in m and q with the coefficient on q equal to $-p$.

Which is the best point for the individual on this budget constraint? To make the question, and perhaps the answer, easier to see, let us eliminate the vertical lines at the integer values as the individual is no longer constrained to buying and selling integer values. We now have Fig. 4.5, which is Fig. 4.4 without the vertical lines.

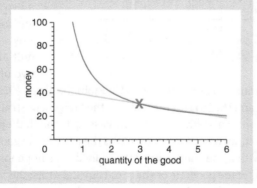

Figure 4.5 Budget constraint (continuous) at a price of £4

Now it is a bit difficult to see where the best point is from this figure, although perhaps it is apparent that it must be somewhere between three and five units of the good; that is, the individual should buy between zero and two units. We can tell this because we know that the budget constraint intersects the original indifference curve at the points (3, 30) and (5, 22), from which is follows that the budget constraint is above the original indifference curve between $q = 3$ and $q = 5$. To find precisely the best point is a bit difficult in practice without mathematics, but you should be able to state precisely what it is that we are looking for. In essence we are looking for the point on the budget constraint which is highest vertically relative to the original indifference curve. That is, it lies on the highest (new) indifference curve possible; in other words, it is such that the vertical distance between the budget line and the original indifference curve is maximized.

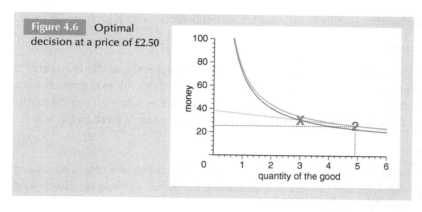

Figure 4.6 Optimal decision at a price of £2.50

Luckily we have some mathematical software which can do the calculation for us[3]. It finds that at the point $(3.87, 26.52)$, which is on the budget constraint, the vertical distance is maximized and is equal to £1.02. So the best thing for the individual to do is to move from $(3, 30)$ to $(3.87, 26.52)$ by buying 0.87 units of the good, thereby making him or herself better off by £1.02.

Before turning to the demand curve, let us take another two examples. First, with a price of £2.5 the budget constraint has a slope of $-£2.50$ and is given in Fig. 4.6. Once again the software calculates the best point; that is, the point on the budget constraint (the straight line through the initial point X) such that the vertical distance between the point and the original indifference curve is maximized. From the figure we can see roughly where it is; my software finds the point exactly. It is $(4.9, 25.25)$, and it is reached from $(3, 30)$ by buying 1.9 units at a total cost of £4.75 (the price is £2.50 per unit), thus reducing money holdings by £4.75 from £30 to £25.25. The point $(4.9, 25.25)$ is £4.62 higher than the original indifference curve; that is, the optimal point (labelled 2 in the Fig. 4.6) is £4.62 above the original indifference curve.

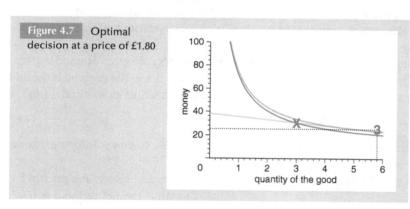

Figure 4.7 Optimal decision at a price of £1.80

Our final example (as in Chapter 3) is with a price of £1.80. The budget constraint has a slope of $-£1.80$ and is shown in Fig. 4.7. The optimal point (again found by the software) is labelled 3 in Fig. 4.7. It occurs at the point $(5.77, 25.01)$ and is £4.62 above the initial indifference curve. At a price of £1.80 per unit the individual buys 2.77 extra units of the good costing £4.99, and ends up £4.62 better off than originally.

We have found three points on the demand curve. To find more we can proceed in the same way, or we can try and find a general solution. To the latter end we need a little mathematics. This we put in the mathematical appendix to this chapter. If you do not like maths, you do not need to check the appendix, although you should understand both the statement of the problem and the statement and interpretation of the solution. What is important is not the mathematics but the economics. Here we sketch the outline of the solution; we present the details in the appendix.

To find the demand curve we need to specify the problem being solved. The budget constraint is given in this instance by $pq + m = 3p + 30$ (remember $Q = 3$ and $M = 30$). What we are trying to do is to reach the highest possible indifference curve – that is, maximize the vertical distance between the point chosen and the original indifference curve. Now in the

---

3. A general proof can be found in the mathematical appendix to this chapter.

graphs which we have been using in this chapter, an indifference curve is given by Eq. (4.4).

$$m - 60/q = \text{constant} \tag{4.4}$$

Rather trivially, the larger the value of the constant, the higher the indifference curve[4]. So, the formal statement of our problem is that we want to find the values of q and m such that $m - 60/q$ is maximized, subject to the constraint that $pq + m = 3p + 30$. As the mathematical appendix shows, the solution to this maximization problem is given by Eq. 4.5.

$$q = \sqrt{(60/p)} \tag{4.5}$$

This reads that the optimal choice of the quantity of the good is the square root of 60 divided by p. Note that as p increases the quantity demanded decreases; demand is a decreasing function of the price of the good.

We should be aware that this gives the *gross* demand, in the sense of the optimal amount of the good consumed. If we want to talk about *net* demand or *net* supply, we need to compare optimal gross demand with the original endowment of the good. First we note that the optimal q is less than, equal to or greater than the original endowment if and only if $\sqrt{(60/p)}$ is less than, equal to or greater than three; that is, if and only if $60/p$ is less than, equal to or greater than nine; that is, if and only if $p/60$ is greater than, equal to or less than $\frac{1}{9}$; that is, if and only if p is greater than, equal to or less than $60/9 = 6\frac{2}{3}$. We shall use this value several times in the course of this chapter.

It follows that the individual will be a net buyer of the good if p is sufficiently low (less than $6\frac{2}{3}$), and will be a net seller if p is sufficiently high (greater than $6\frac{2}{3}$). He or she will neither buy or sell, but will remain at the initial point when p is equal to $6\frac{2}{3}$. Later we shall need to ask why this critical number is $6\frac{2}{3}$, and how is it connected with the individual's preferences; you may like to start thinking about this now.

The individual is a net buyer when p is less than $6\frac{2}{3}$. In this case gross demand is given by Eq. (4.5) above, and this expression is strictly greater than three. Net demand is the difference between gross demand and the initial endowment, and is thus given by Eq. (4.6).

$$q = \sqrt{(60/p)} - 3 \tag{4.6}$$

Note that this function is decreasing in price; the demand curve is downward-sloping. I draw this net demand curve in Fig. 4.8.

Inserted in Fig. 4.8 is one of the examples that we have studied before; at a price of £4 per unit the net demand is 0.87 units of the good. You might like to check the other two examples yourself.

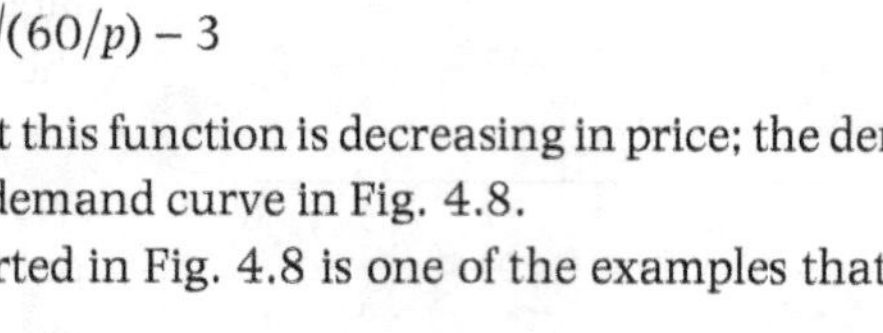

The final thing we should check is our result about surpluses. You will recall that, for a buyer, the surplus is given by the area between the price paid and the demand curve. We can calculate the area approximately from Fig. 4.8; at a price of £4 the surplus is

Figure 4.8   Implied demand curve (continuous)

4. In Fig. 4.3 above, the value of the constant for the lowest indifference curve is 10 (note that a point on the curve is $q = 3$ and $m = 30$), so the equation of the lowest indifference curve is $m - 60/q = 10$. For the highest indifference curve the value of the constant is 60, so its equation is $m - 60/q = 60$.

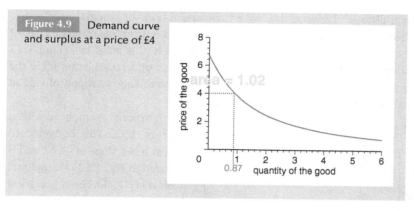

Figure 4.9 Demand curve and surplus at a price of £4

the area between the price of £4 and the demand curve. It is approximately a triangle with base 0.87 and height $2\frac{2}{3}$, and is therefore approximately equal to $(0.5 \times 0.87 \times 2.67) = 1.16$, although we know that the actual area must be a little less than this because the true area is somewhat smaller than that of the triangle we have just calculated. In fact we already know what the true value is from our calculations above – it is £1.02. If we calculate the area exactly, which you could do manually or mathematically[5], we can easily verify that it is exactly £1.02.

You might like to check yourself the other two results we have about surpluses as a buyer.

4.6 Implied Supply

We have already implicitly found the implied supply. We discovered that the individual will be a seller if the price is sufficiently high, and we have found what is meant by 'sufficiently high' in this context: it means a price greater than $6\frac{2}{3}$. From Eq. (4.5) above we know that, if the price exceeds $6\frac{2}{3}$, the desired position has a quantity of the good less than the initial holding; that is, the individual will want to sell some of the initial holding. The net supply is

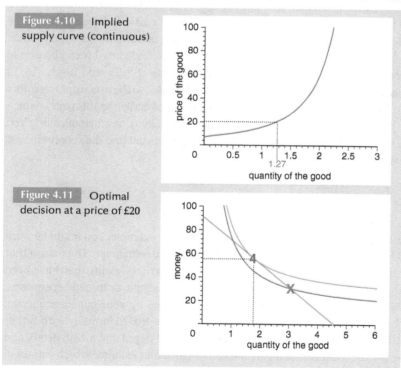

Figure 4.10 Implied supply curve (continuous)

Figure 4.11 Optimal decision at a price of £20

the difference between the initial holding (in this case three units) and that given by Eq. (4.5). The net supply function relevant for $p > 6\frac{2}{3}$ is therefore given by Eq. (4.7).

$$q = 3 - \sqrt{(60/p)} \qquad (4.7)$$

Note that this is an increasing function of price, that is, the supply curve is upward-sloping. It is shown in Fig. 4.10.

A particular example is given in Fig. 4.10 with a price of £20. Let us go back to the indifference curve analysis and look at the example in detail; this is shown in Fig. 4.11.

With a price of £20 per unit, the budget constraint has a slope of −£20. The optimal point is marked 4 in Fig. 4.11; this is

5. A formal derivation is provided in the mathematical appendix.

where the vertical distance between the budget constraint and the original indifference curve is maximized. The point is precisely at (1.73, 55.4), and is a vertical distance £10.72 above the original indifference curve. The individual moves to this point by selling 1.27 units, thereby raising £25.40 in money and, in so doing, ends up £10.72 better off in the sense of being on an indifference curve £10.72 above the original. This net supply of 1.27 at a price of £20 is shown on the supply curve in Fig. 4.10.

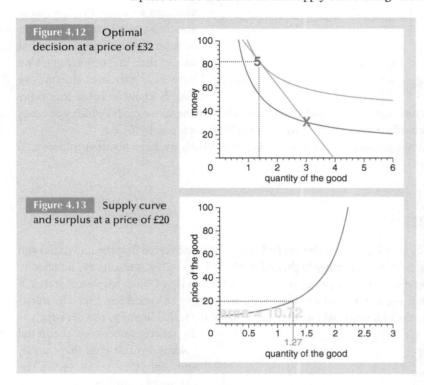

Figure 4.12 Optimal decision at a price of £32

Figure 4.13 Supply curve and surplus at a price of £20

A second example is with a price of £32. The budget constraint has a slope of −£32 and is pictured in Fig. 4.12. The optimal point is (1.37, 82.16); it is marked 5 in Fig. 4.12, and is reached by selling 1.63 units and raising £52.16 in money. Point 5 is £28.36 above the initial indifference curve.

The result about surpluses – the seller surplus is the area between the price received and the supply curve – can now be verified. Consider, for example, a price of £20. We know that the net supply at that price is 1.27. This is seen from the supply curve in Fig. 4.13.

To obtain the surplus, we need to calculate the area between the price of £20 and the supply curve. From the figure this can be seen to be somewhat greater than the area of a triangle with a base of 1.27 and height 13.33 (= 20 − 6.67). This triangle has an area 0.5 × 1.27 × 13.33 = 8.47, so the true surplus is rather more than this. In fact it is 10.72 – the true surplus as calculated earlier on this page – which you could verify by calculating the area exactly either manually or mathematically[6]. You might also like to check that the area between a price of £32 per unit and the supply curve is equal to £28.36, which we have shown above.

4.7 Comments

The whole of this chapter has been built around one particular example. You might be wondering why, and how much detail you need to understand and remember. The reason that we have used a specific example throughout is so that the various results that have been claimed can easily be confirmed; the calculations involved are simple arithmetic operations. So one reason for using a specific example is to help you build up your confidence in the various results that I am claiming, some of which can only be proved formally with rather complex mathematics. But it is important that you do not get bogged down with detail, and you certainly do not need to memorize any details of the particular example which was used.

6. A formal proof is provided in the mathematical appendix.

What you should concentrate on are the methods that have been used. You should get the following out of this chapter.

- Quasi-linear preferences (parallel-in-a-vertical-direction indifference curves) are important because they enable us to measure how much better or worse off an individual is if he or she moves from one point in the space to another; this, in turn, enables us to measure the surplus gained when buying or selling.

- The budget constraint in (q, m) space must have slope equal to minus the price of the good.

- The best place for the individual, given a particular budget constraint, is to be as high as possible relative to the original indifference curve.

- By using this procedure we can find the best strategy for the individual at any price; we can calculate the gross demand for the good at any price.

- If gross demand is greater than the initial endowment the individual will want to buy more of the good; net demand is positive. By plotting these net demands against the price we get the demand curve, and if we look at the area between the price paid and the demand curve we find the surplus made by the individual as a result of the purchase; that is, we find out how much better off he or she is as a consequence of the purchase.

- If gross demand is less than the initial endowment the individual wants to sell some of the good; net supply is positive. By plotting these net supplies against the price we get the supply curve, and if we look at the area between the price received and the supply curve we find the surplus made by the individual as a result of the sale; that is, we find out how much better off he or she is as a consequence of the sale.

I should admit that the two results about the surpluses may at first appear a bit magical – a bit mysterious. To fully understand them you may need to know some mathematics, but I am happy if you see the results are true in our specific example, and if you are happy to take my word for it that they are true more generally.

You might like to explore things a bit yourself, starting with some other (quasi-linear) preferences. These are really easy to construct; as there is basically just one indifference curve, all the rest are just parallel shifts. If you do not like maths, you can simply do it all graphically; just draw one curve wherever you wish, then copy it and reproduce it over and over again parallel to itself. Then try reproducing what I have done in this chapter, for these (your) preferences.

I shall finish by asking you where the '$6\frac{2}{3}$' comes from. Recall that this is the price at which the individual switches from being a buyer to being a seller. At this price, the individual will want to stay at the initial point. Under what circumstances is this the case? The answer is: when the budget constraint is everywhere (except obviously at the initial point) below the original indifference curve. This can only happen if the budget constraint is tangential to the original indifference curve at the initial point. This implies that the slope of the budget line is equal to the slope of the original indifference curve at the initial point. But we know that the slope of the budget line is equal to minus the price. So the condition for no trade is simply that (minus) the price of the good is equal to the slope of the original indifference curve at the initial point. You might like to verify that this slope is indeed equal to $-6\frac{2}{3}$.

Incidentally you may now have realized why quasi-linear preferences are given that name. If you look back at Eq. (4.4), which gives the equation of indifference curves used in this chapter as $m - 60/q$ = constant, you will see that it is linear in m but non-linear in q. Any indifference curve of this form has the property that the reservation prices are independent of income.

4.8 Summary

In essence all we have done in this chapter is extend the material of Chapter 3 to the case of a continuous good: one which can be bought and sold in any quantity. As such, virtually all the summary points from Chapter 3 remain relevant. These include the indifference curve:

 An indifference curve is a locus of points about which the individual feels indifferent.

We defined what we mean by a budget constraint and show that it has the following important property.

 The slope of the budget constraint in (quantity of the good, money) space is simply equal to minus the price of the good.

Moreover we have shown how to derive demand and supply curves from indifference curves and, in particular, we have shown the following characteristics.

 The demand function is generally a downward-sloping function.

 The supply function is generally an upward-sloping function.

 The individual is a buyer for sufficiently low prices and a seller for sufficiently high prices.

We have verified two key results from Chapter 2.

 The buyer surplus is the area between the price paid and the demand curve.

 The seller surplus is the area between the price received and the supply curve.

Finally we recall the definition of quasi-linear preferences.

 With quasi-linear preferences, the indifference curves are parallel in a vertical direction and the reservation prices are independent of the amount of money held by the individual.

4.9 Review Questions

1. What property must the reservation prices have if the demand curve is everywhere downward-sloping and the supply curve everywhere upward-sloping?

2 Can indifference curves cross?

3 If the price paid by a buyer decreases what happens to his or her surplus? If the price received by a seller increases what happens to his or her surplus?

4 What determines whether an individual is a buyer or a seller of a good of which he or she already owns a certain quantity?

4.10   Mathematical Appendix

Once again this appendix is for completeness. We provide a proof of the derivation of the demand and supply curves, and a proof of the propositions concerning the area between the price and the demand and supply curves. If you like mathematics you may enjoy this appendix; if you do not, you do not need to read it.

We start by presenting a proof of the proposition that the gross demand of the individual, with the preferences used in this chapter, is given by the expression in Eq. (4.5). Recall that the problem was to find the value of p which places the individual on the highest indifference curve, given the constraint implied by the budget. The budget constraint is given by $pq + m = 3p + 30$, from Eq. (4.1); it passes through the point $(Q, M) = (3, 30)$. The equation of an indifference curve is given by $m - 60/q = $ constant in Eq. (4.4), where the larger the value of the constant the higher is the indifference curve.

Method 1 – solution by substitution: There are two main ways to solve this constrained maximization problem but perhaps the simplest is to substitute the constraint in the objective function. More precisely, from the constraint we know that $m = 3p + 30 - pq$; if we use this to eliminate the m from the objective function (the indifference curve), we need to find the value of q which maximizes the following.

$$E = 3p + 30 - pq - 60/q \qquad (A4.1)$$

To find this value of q, we need to find where the derivative of E with respect to q is zero (that is, the value of q which gets us to the top of the hill). The derivative of the above expression with respect to q is $-p + 60/q^2$, and thus we get the following condition for the optimal choice of q:

$$dE/dq = -p + 60/q^2 = 0 \qquad (A4.2)$$

Solving Eq. (A4.2) yields Eq. (A4.3), which is the required equation.

$$q = \sqrt{(60/p)} \qquad (A4.3)$$

Method 2: solution by the method of Lagrange: This was outlined in Chapter 1. We form the Lagrangian function which is the objective minus λ times the constraint.

$$L = (m - 60/q) - \lambda(pq + m - 3p - 30) \qquad (A4.4)$$

We next maximize Eq. (A4.4) with respect to m, q and λ to give the following three equations

$$dL/dm = 1 - \lambda = 0 \qquad (A4.5)$$

from which $\lambda = 1$

$$dL/dq = 60/q^2 - \lambda p = 0 \qquad (A4.6)$$

from which $q^2 = 60/\lambda p$, from which, using Eq. (A4.5), $q^2 = 60/p$, from which Eq. (4.5) is readily obtained.

$$dL/d\lambda = 0 \qquad (A4.7)$$

This implies the budget constraint $pq + m - 3p - 30$, from which we find the value of m.
Precisely,

$$m = 3p + 30 - pq$$
$$= 3p + 30 - p\sqrt{(60/p)}$$
$$= 3p + 30 - \sqrt{(60p)}$$

Summarizing: the individual starts at the point $(3, 30)$ and ends at the point $(\sqrt{(60/p)}, 3p + 30 - \sqrt{(60p)})$.

To verify the results concerning the areas between the price paid and the demand and supply curves, we need to use the technique of integration. In general, the area between some price p and a demand curve given by some function $q = f(p)$ is the integral of the function $q = f(p)$ between the given price p and the price at which the demand becomes zero.

In the case where the demand function is that implied by the preferences used in this chapter, the area below the curve is the integral of the function $q = \sqrt{(60/p)} - 3$, over the range from the specified price p to $p = 6.67$ (the price at which demand falls to zero). The integral of $q = \sqrt{(60/p)} - 3$ is $2\sqrt{(60p)} - 3p$. Substituting $p = 6.67$ into $2\sqrt{(60p)} - 3p$ gives a value 20. Thus the area below the demand curve between some specified price p and $p = 6.67$ is given by the following expression:

$$\text{area between price } p \text{ and demand curve} = 20 - 2\sqrt{(60p)} + 3p \tag{A4.8}$$

If $p = 4$, this is 1.02 as stated on page 63.

We can do similar calculations for the seller surplus. In general, the area between some specified price and a supply curve given by some function $q = f(p)$ is the integral of $q = f(p)$ between the price at which supply is zero and the specified price.

Where the supply function is implied by the preferences in this chapter, the area is the integral of the function $q = 3 - \sqrt{(60/p)}$ from $p = 6.67$ (this is the price at which supply becomes zero) to that specified price. The integral of $3 - \sqrt{(60/p)}$ is $3p - 2\sqrt{(60p)}$, and evaluated between $p = 6.67$ and some specified price p is $20 - 2\sqrt{(60p)} + 3p$. This is exactly the same expression as before. Thus we have

$$\text{area between price } p \text{ and supply curve} = 20 - 2\sqrt{(60p)} + 3p \tag{A4.9}$$

If $p = 20$ this gives 10.72, as stated on page 66.

Finally we need to prove that these areas are in fact the surpluses. As we have seen, the individual starts at the point $(3, 30)$ and moves to the point $(\sqrt{(60/p)}, 3p + 30 - \sqrt{(60p)})$. The equation of an indifference curve in this chapter is given by Eq. (4.4) $m - 60/q = \text{constant}$, where the value of the constant tells us how well off the individual is; the higher the constant, the better off is the individual. Initially the individual has $q = 3$ and $m = 30$, so the value of the constant equals $30 - 60/3 = 10$.

After moving to the optimal position given by $(\sqrt{(60/p)}, 3p + 30 - \sqrt{(60p)})$, the value of the constant is equal to $3p + 30 - \sqrt{(60p)} - 60/(\sqrt{(60/p)}) = 3p + 30 - 2\sqrt{(60p)}$. This is exactly $20 - 2\sqrt{(60p)} + 3p$ more than initially. And this is precisely equal to the areas which we have calculated above.

You might like to see a more general treatment. The general case of quasi-linear preferences is when the utility function has the form

$$U(q, m) = u(q) + m \tag{A4.10}$$

It follows that the equation of an indifference curve is given by

$$u(q) + m = \text{constant} \tag{A4.11}$$

Using either method to find the optimal point on the budget constraint $pq + m = pQ + M$, Eq. (4.1), where Q is the endowment of the good and M the endowment of money, the optimal choice of q is where

$$u'(q) = p \tag{A4.12}$$

$u'(q)$ is the derivative of u with respect to q. Thus the demand curve for the good is given implicitly by Eq. (A4.12). Note that this does not depend upon M, so money is irrelevant to the demand, as we already know with this kind of preferences.

Preferences

5.1 Introduction

In Chapters 3 and 4 we considered a particular type of preference in which all the indifference curves are parallel to each other and each indifference curve is convex. The first of these assumptions implies that the individual's reservation prices are independent of the amount of money with which he or she starts. The second assumption implies that the individual has lower and lower reservation prices for additional units of the good as more units are aquired; that is, the more someone has of the good, the less he or she is willing to pay for additional units. Whether these assumptions are reasonable or not depends upon the individual, the good, and how the individual feels about the good *vis-à-vis* money; that is, it depends upon the individual's preferences with respect to the good. As economists we cannot say that a particular kind of preference is reasonable or not; we must simply take the preferences as given.

This chapter recognizes that the assumptions made in Chapters 3 and 4 may be reasonable for some people – they may accurately describe some people's preferences – but they may not be reasonable for others. The chapter considers other possibilities as far as preferences are concerned.

We also take the opportunity to slightly generalize what we are doing. So far we have been working with one good and money; we put the quantity of the good on the horizontal axis and the quantity of money on the vertical axis. We used p to denote the price of the good; the price of money is rather obviously one (to buy one lira costs one lira).

In this chapter we shall work with two goods: good 1 and good 2. We will put the quantity of good 1, which we will denote by q_1, on the horizontal axis and the quantity of good 2, which we will denote by q_2, on the vertical axis. Later we shall use p_1 and p_2 to denote the respective prices of the two goods. The material of Chapters 3 and 4 is simply a special case of this, when good 2 is money and hence $p_2 = 1$. So in an obvious sense this chapter generalizes the material of Chapters 3 and 4. We assume that both goods are genuinely goods in the sense that the individual would always happily accept more of each.

5.2   Perfect Substitutes

It may be the case that the individual considers the two goods as identical; he or she regards any one unit of the first good as identical to any one unit of the other good; in other words the individual cannot tell any difference between the two goods. For me this is true for any two kinds of lager; I like lager, but I really cannot tell (and really do not care whether there is) any difference between Lager Number 1 and Lager Number 2. If these are goods 1 and 2, then my indifference curves resembles those in Fig. 5.1.

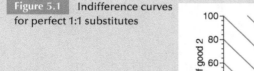

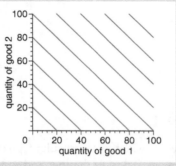

Figure 5.1   Indifference curves for perfect 1:1 substitutes

Suppose the quantity units are litres. Consider, for example, the third highest indifference curve in Fig. 5.1, joining the points (60, 0) and (0, 60). What do you notice about this curve? Simply that $q_1 + q_2 = 60$ at every point along it; indeed this is the equation of the line. What does this mean? It means that the total quantity of Lager Number 1 and Lager Number 2 is equal to 60. What is not important is how this total is composed – how it is split between Lager Number 1 and Lager Number 2. This embodies the notion that I regard the two goods as perfect substitutes.

Another way of seeing this is to note that everywhere the slope of every indifference curve is equal to −1. What does this mean? The reservation price everywhere for one litre of Lager Number 1 is one litre of Lager Number 2; to take one more litre of Lager Number 1, the individual is prepared to pay at most one litre of Lager Number 2. Whatever way we look at it, it is clear that the indifference curves in Fig. 5.1 are telling us that the individual regards the two goods as identical; also that he or she regards the two goods as perfect 1:1 substitutes, that any and everywhere he or she would happily substitute one unit of one good with one unit of the other.

It will be useful for future reference to note the equation defining an indifference curve in the case of perfect 1:1 substitutes. If we look at any curve in Fig. 5.1, it is apparent that the sum of q_1 plus q_2 is constant along any one of these curves: along the top one the sum is 80; along the next to the top the sum is 70; ...; along the bottom curve the sum is 20. So an indifference curve of this particular type is defined by Eq. (5.1).

$$q_1 + q_2 = \text{constant} \tag{5.1}$$

Note that the higher the constant, the higher the level of happiness of the individual; being on the top indifference curve with 80 litres of lager is better than being on the second highest with 70 litres of lager; ...; is better than being on the lowest with 20 litres of lager. So we can define perfect 1:1 substitutes as having indifference curves defined by Eq. (5.1). The only problem with this definition is that it is not unique; if $(q_1 + q_2)$ is constant, then so is $(q_1 + q_2)^2$ and also $(q_1 + q_2)^3$, and indeed so is $f(q_1 + q_2)$ where $f(.)$ is any increasing function. So we have to be careful: Eq. (5.1) above defines perfect 1:1 substitutes but is not the only definition. This, as we shall see later, creates a little difficulty if we want to define a utility function, but it is not an insuperable problem.

Of course it could be the case that the individual regards the two goods as perfect substitutes but not 1:1. Take an example which I find in Italy: there they have large bottles of

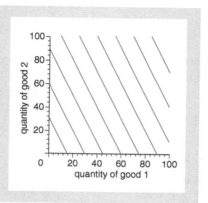

Figure 5.2   Indifference curves for perfect 1:2 substitutes

Peroni beer and small bottles. The large bottles contain 660 ml of beer, the small bottles 330 ml. The beer is the same. For me, two small bottles of beer is exactly the same as one large bottle of beer – I really do not mind which I have. So, if we take good 1 to be large bottles with the quantity being the number that I have; and we take good 2 to be small bottles with the quantity being the number that I have, then my indifference curves will look like those in Fig. 5.2.

Consider, for example, the third highest indifference curve in Fig. 5.2 – the line joining (45, 0) to (0, 90). At one extreme, the point (45, 0), I have 45 large bottles and no small bottles; at the other extreme, the point (0, 90), I have 90 small bottles and no large bottles. If I regard one large bottle as the same as two small bottles, then these two extremes are identical. Now consider an intermediate point, one-third of the way from (45, 0) to (0, 90) – that is the point (30, 30) – where I have 30 large and 30 small bottles. Given that I consider one large bottle as always the same as two small bottles, this is again exactly equivalent to 45 large bottles (and no small) or 90 small bottles (and no large).

So, if an individual regards the two goods as perfect 1:2 substitutes, his or her indifference curves look like those in Fig. 5.2. Moreover we could describe these indifference curves by the equation:

$$q_1 + q_2/2 = \text{constant} \tag{5.2}$$

Note that the higher the constant, the higher the indifference curve. Note also the obvious sense of Eq. (5.2); it is simply counting the number of big-bottle-equivalents – one big bottle is one big bottle and one small bottle is half a big bottle. You should also note the slope of the indifference curves; from Fig. 5.2 or from Eq. (5.2) we can see that the slope of all the indifference curves anywhere is equal to –2. The rate of substitution is 1:2 – that is, one big bottle can everywhere be substituted by two small bottles. This (magnitude of the) slope has a name: economists call it the *marginal rate of substitution* (abbreviated to MRS); – it indicates the rate at which good 1 can be substituted by good 2[1]. For perfect substitutes this MRS is everywhere constant.

We can generalize. We can conceive of goods for which some individual regards as perfect 1:*a* substitutes; that is, for which 1 unit of good one is everywhere substitutable with *a* units of good 2. Clearly for such preferences, the indifference curves are everywhere straight lines with slope –*a*. The MRS is everywhere *a*. Moreover such indifference curves can be described by the following equation.

$$q_1 + q_2/a = \text{constant} \tag{5.3}$$

We note, once again, that this is a description, but it is not a unique description.

---

1. We should be a little careful – the indifference curves everywhere are downward-sloping – that is, they have a negative slope. The MRS is the magnitude of the slope; and therefore is the negative value of the slope.

5.3 Perfect Complements

Perfect substitutes are one extreme – the individual regards the goods as perfectly inter-changeable. The other extreme is perfect complements. In this type of preference the individual considers that the goods should be consumed together. One example is perfect 1-with-1 complements for which the individual regards it as crucial that every one unit of good 1 is consumed with one unit of good 2; and moreover he or she regards having more of one good without having more of the other as being pointless. If the individual regards the two goods as having this kind of relationship, then the indifference curves resemble those in Fig. 5.3.

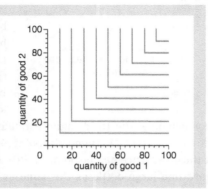

Figure 5.3   Indifference curves for perfect 1-with-1 complements

Consider, for example, the third indifference curve counting from the bottom left corner. It has a corner point at (30, 30) where the individual has 30 units of each good. From this corner point the indifference curve is horizontal to the right and vertical above. What does this mean? First, consider the horizontal segment to the right. It says that the individual is indifferent between the point (30, 30) and the points to the right, for example, (40, 30), (50, 30), (60, 30), (70, 30), (80, 30), (90, 30), (100, 30), and more generally $(q_1, 30)$ for any q_1 greater than 30. This simply says that increasing the quantity of good 1 without increasing the quantity of good 2 does not make the individual any better off; having an extra unit of good 1 without any extra units of good 2 is of no value to the individual. Now consider the points vertically above corner point (30, 30); they all lie on the same indifference curve so the individual is indifferent between point (30, 30) and the points above, namely (30, 40), (30, 50), (30, 60), (30, 70), (30, 80), (30, 90) and (30, 100), and more generally the point $(30, q_2)$ for any value of q_2 greater than 30. This simply says that increasing the quantity of good 2 without increasing the quantity of good 1 does not make the individual any better off; having an extra unit of good 2 without any extra units of good 1 is of no value to the individual.

The usual example associated with this kind of preferences is left and right shoes; good 1 represents left shoes and good 2 right shoes. Assuming that the individual has two feet, he or she wants one left shoe to go with each right shoe, and *vice versa*. So the preferences are perfect 1-with-1 complements. An equation which describes these indifference curves is given in Eq. (5.4).

$$\min(q_1, q_2) = \text{constant} \tag{5.4}$$

We can check: at every point along the third indifference curve in Fig. 5.3 we have the minimum of q_1 and q_2 is equal to 30. Obviously the larger the constant, the higher is the indifference curve. But there are other ways to describe such indifference curves; Eq. (5.4) is not the only way.

Preferences can be perfect complements but not necessarily 1-with-1. For example it might be that the individual considers the two goods as perfect 1-with-2 complements; that is, for each unit of good 1 the individual requires two units of good 2 and *vice versa*. In this case the indifference map would be as drawn in Fig. 5.4. Notice that at the corner points the

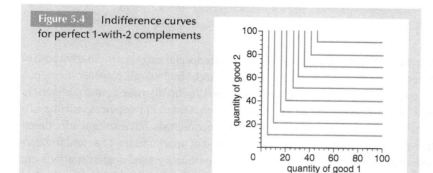

Figure 5.4   Indifference curves for perfect 1-with-2 complements

quantity of good 2 is always double the quantity of good 1. An equation which describes indifference curves for this kind of preferences is Eq. (5.5)

$$\min(q_1, q_2/2) = \text{constant} \quad (5.5)$$

Obviously we can generalize further; thus we can have perfect 1-with-a complements; one unit of good 1 needs to be always combined with a units of good 2, and *vice versa*. For this kind of preferences the indifference curves can be specified by Eq. (5.6)

$$\min(q_1, q_2/a) = \text{constant} \quad (5.6)$$

Once again, we note that this representation is not unique.

5.4 Concave Preferences

The two cases that we have considered so far in this chapter can be considered as two extremes of the convex preferences case when the indifference curves are convex. The alternative, which we introduce if only to dismiss it as being relatively unrealistic when ordinary goods are being considered, is that of concave preferences. In the latter the indifference curves are concave; you should be able to work out what such preferences imply. Consider the individual's reservation prices; because the indifference curves are concave this implies that the more units of the good that the individual has, the more he or she is willing to pay for additional units. Rather than fall as the number of units held increases, the reservation price will rise; the individual is willing to pay increasingly more for extra units. Because this obviously works in both directions, it implies that the individual prefers to consume either one good or the other rather than the two together. The individual prefers the extremes – consuming all of one good or the other – to the average (consuming both together). An extreme example of this concave preferences case is in Fig. 5.5.

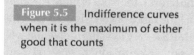

Figure 5.5   Indifference curves when it is the maximum of either good that counts

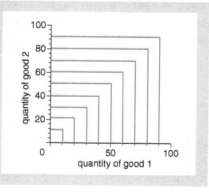

The title of Fig. 5.5 shows what is important with such preferences – the maximum of either good. Note that, given a quantity Q of one good, increasing the quantity of the other from zero to Q has no effect on the individual. But you should be careful in interpreting this figure; both goods are still desirable. It is just that the desirability depends upon the quantity being at least as large as the quantity of the other good. These preferences can be represented by the following equation; obviously the higher the value of the constant, the better.

$$\max(q_1, q_2) = \text{constant} \quad (5.7)$$

5.5   Cobb–Douglas Preferences

The cases which we have considered so far are all rather special cases, particularly those of perfect substitutes and perfect complements. In reality most individuals consider most situations to be somewhere in between these two extremes. We can discover actual preferences in a number of ways, and we can build up pictures of what actual preferences look like. To enable generalizations to be made (see Chapter 16), economists have sought functional forms for indifference curves which are reasonably good approximations to actual indifference curves. Two functional forms which seem to be reasonably good approximations are the Cobb–Douglas preferences and the Stone–Geary preferences. We shall consider the first of these in this section and the second in the next; we should note that the second is a relatively simple generalization of the first.

Obviously the extent to which Cobb–Douglas preferences (named after its originators) can adequately describe, or can reasonably approximate to, a person's actual preferences is an empirical question, and one which we shall examine in Chapter 16. For the time being we shall describe these preferences; we shall explore the implications later. A Cobb–Douglas indifference curve has the following functional relationship.

$$q_1^a q_2^{1-a} = \text{constant} \tag{5.8}$$

In Eq. (5.8), a is a given parameter which affects the shape of the indifference curves, as we shall see below. Alternatively, taking the logarithm of Eq. (5.8)[2], a Cobb–Douglas indifference curve can be set out in the following form.

$$a \ln(q_1) + (1 - a)\ln(q_2) = \text{constant} \tag{5.9}$$

Equations (5.8) and (5.9) say the same thing – they can be used interchangeably – since, if something is constant, then so is its logarithm.

What does the implied indifference map look like? Well, it obviously depends upon the parameter a which effectively determines the relative importance of the two goods in the individual's preferences. Let us start with the symmetric case where $a = 0.5$; (note this implies $(1 - a) = 0.5$). The indifference map is in Fig. 5.6.

Note the symmetry about the line $q_1 = q_2$. Note also how the marginal rate of substitution (MRS) changes. If q_1 is low but q_2 is high (the top left of the figure), the MRS is high; the individual is willing to give up a lot of good 2 in order to get a little more of good 1. Conversely if q_1 is high but q_2 is low (the bottom right of the figure), the MRS is very low; the individual will not give up much of good 2 in order to get more of good 1. When q_1 and q_2 are approximately equal, then the MRS is close to unity and the individual is willing to give up approximately one unit of good 2 in order to get one more unit of good 1 (and *vice versa*). Note crucially that the indifference curves are not parallel in any direction, so reservation prices are not independent of the quantity of good 2;

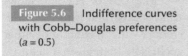

Figure 5.6   Indifference curves with Cobb–Douglas preferences $(a = 0.5)$

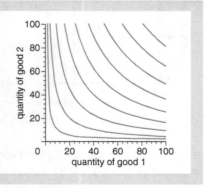

2. Recall the rules for the manipulation of logarithms given in Chapter 1.

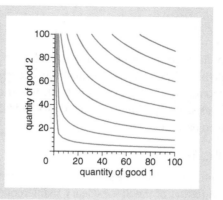

Figure 5.7 Indifference curves with Cobb–Douglas preferences ($a = 0.3$)

Cobb–Douglas preferences are not quasi-linear. Nor is the MRS constant, as in the case of perfect substitutes, nor are the indifference curves in the shape of an L as in the case of perfect complements. The case of Cobb–Douglas preferences is somewhere between the two extremes of perfect substitutes and perfect complements.

We now consider a non-symmetrical case with $a = 0.3$; the indifference map is shown in Fig. 5.7. Note that if $a = 0.3$ it follows that $(1 - a) = 0.7$, so the equation for the indifference curves is given, from Eq. (5.8), by the following

$$q_1^{0.3} q_2^{0.7} = \text{constant} \tag{5.10}$$

You might like to think of this as putting more weight on the quantity of good 2 consumed. Now look at the indifference map in Fig. 5.7. We note a number of things: first, it is not symmetric; second, at any point in the space the indifference curves are flatter (the magnitude of the slope is smaller) than in the case of symmetrical Cobb–Douglas considered earlier. For example it is clear that along the line $q_1 = q_2$ the slope has a magnitude less than one[3]. So when the individual has the same amount of both goods he or she is willing to give up less than one

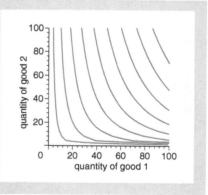

Figure 5.8 Indifference curves with Cobb–Douglas preferences ($a = 0.7$)

unit (in fact 0.3/0.7 of a unit) of good 2 in order to have an extra unit of good 1. This embodies the idea that this individual puts relatively more weight on good 2 than on good 1.

A contrary case, when more weight is put on good 1, occurs when $a = 0.7$; the indifference map for this situation is pictured in Fig. 5.8. This is just the reverse of the $a = 0.3$ case.

Now it may be the case that an individual's preferences are such that they can be reasonably well approximated by a Cobb–Douglas preference function for some appropriate value of the parameter a. However it may equally well be the case that for no value of a does the Cobb–Douglas preferences represent actual preferences. In such a case we need to seek a more general specification of preferences. There are many that economists use, but most of these are too complicated to be included in this book. However I do include one more which is a rather simple extension of the Cobb–Douglas preferences that we have already considered. This generalization is known as Stone–Geary preferences (once again named after its originators), which we discuss in the next section.

---

3. In fact, the slope here is −0.3/0.7 or, more generally, the slope is given by $a/(1 - a)$.

5.6 Stone–Geary Preferences

Stone–Geary preferences are an extension of Cobb–Douglas preferences. The extension is simple; the individual has to consume subsistence levels of the two goods before allocating the residual income between the two goods. Denote the subsistence levels by s_1 and s_2 for goods 1 and 2 respectively. Then a Stone–Geary indifference curve is given by Eq. (5.11), where a is a given parameter.

$$(q_1 - s_1)^a (q_2 - s_2)^{1-a} = \text{constant} \tag{5.11}$$

Clearly the parameter a affects the shape of the indifference curves as we shall see below. An alternative formulation of the Stone–Geary indifference curves is obtained by taking logarithms of Eq. (5.11)[4], which produces the following.

$$a \ln(q_1 - s_1) + (1 - a)\ln(q_2 - s_2) = \text{constant} \tag{5.12}$$

Note the difference between Eqs. (5.8) and (5.11), and the difference between Eqs. (5.9) and (5.12): the inclusion of the subsistence terms s_1 and s_2. You might like to think of these preferences as simply Cobb–Douglas preferences expressed relative to s_1 and s_2 rather than relative to the usual origin. This will be obvious from Figs. 5.9 and 5.10. Note that Cobb–Douglas is a special case of Stone–Geary when s_1 and s_2 are both equal to zero.

I will give some examples. In all of these I make the subsistence terms s_1 and s_2 equal to 10 and 20 respectively. In the first example the parameter $a = 0.5$, so it is a sort of symmetric case; but only with respect to the subsistence levels s_1 and s_2. This should be apparent from the indifference map in Fig. 5.9.

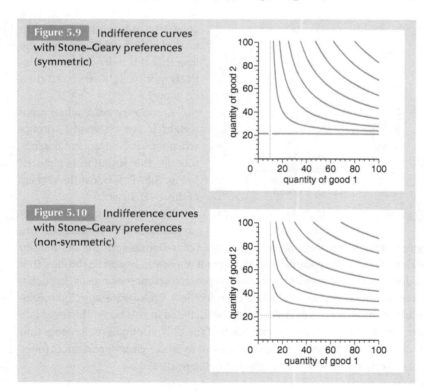

Figure 5.9 Indifference curves with Stone–Geary preferences (symmetric)

Figure 5.10 Indifference curves with Stone–Geary preferences (non-symmetric)

The subsistence levels are the vertical line (at $q_1 = 10$) and the horizontal line (at $q_2 = 20$). You will see that the indifference curves are not defined for values of q_1 below its subsistence level, or for values of q_2 below its subsistence level. Note also that the symmetry of the indifference map is relative to the subsistence levels, not to the normal axes.

A non-symmetric example with the same subsistence levels is given by letting $a = 0.3$. This has the indifference map shown in Fig. 5.10. Note the similarities with and the differences from the Cobb–Douglas case, with the same parameter $a = 0.3$ used in Fig. 5.7.

Sometimes we find that preferences can be better approximated with a Stone–Geary function; sometimes not. If not,

---

4. Recall the rules for the manipulation of logarithms in Chapter 1.

we have to search further. For reasons that will be discussed in Chapter 16, economists prefer to approximate preferences (and indeed anything) with a function that contains just a few parameters rather than attempt to describe preferences precisely. To this end, economists have found a number of functional forms which are good approximations of many of the preferences that exist in society. We cannot go into detail as some of these forms are mathematically rather complicated. In a sense this does not matter; what I want to convince you of is the following:

- Different people may have different preferences over goods.
- Some may think of goods as perfect substitutes or perfect complements.
- Some may have concave preferences.
- Some may have Cobb–Douglas or Stone–Geary preferences.
- If people have different preferences they will in general have different demand and supply functions for goods; this should be obvious now, but we shall see it formally later.
- If we know their preferences we can predict their demand (see Chapter 16).
- If we can observe their demand we can infer their preferences and hence predict their future demand (as we shall do later).

In the next two chapters we will find the demand functions for the preferences which we have examined in this chapter. Because of the technical difficulty, and the fact that this book cannot contain everything, I shall not present demand functions for other kinds of preferences. In a sense this does not matter as you can look up the results in a more advanced text. But, more importantly, it should not matter because this book is designed to teach you methods rather than details. If you follow the points listed above, you are well on the way to becoming an economist.

5.7 Representing Preferences with Utility Functions

You might be asking whether there is some mathematical way to describe preferences. So far we have used a graphical method involving indifference curves which have various properties.

- First, along a particular indifference curve we know that the individual is indifferent – he or she is equally happy at all points along it.
- Second, if we compare the happiness of the individual at any point on one indifference curve with his or her happiness at any point on a lower indifference curve, then we can say that the individual prefers to be at – is happier at – the first of these two points.

Can we specify a happiness or utility function defined over (q_1, q_2) space which reflects these properties? That is, can we specify a utility function $U(q_1, q_2)$ such that this remains constant along an indifference curve and increases as we move to higher and higher indifference curves?

Clearly we can. Suppose, for example, that a particular preference is such that an indifference curve is defined by the function Eq. (5.13)

$$f(q_1, q_2) = constant \tag{5.13}$$

In Eq. (5.13) we take it that the value of the constant rises as we move from a lower to a higher indifference curve. Then we simply define our utility function in the following manner.

$$U(q_1, q_2) = f(q_1, q_2) \tag{5.14}$$

Let us take perfect 1:1 substitutes as an example. In this case the indifference curve is defined by $q_1 + q_2 = $ constant (see Eq. (5.1)), so we simply define the individual's utility function as

$$U(q_1, q_2) = q_1 + q_2 \tag{5.15}$$

This has all the right properties. The implied utility is constant along a particular indifference curve, and it rises as we move up the indifference curves. Referring to Fig. 5.1, we see that utility equals 20 at all points on the first indifference curve, 40 at all points on the second indifference curve, ..., equals 180 at all points on the last indifference curve.

That works fine. But then so does any increasing transformation. Instead of Eq. (5.15), consider the the following:

$$U(q_1, q_2) = 2(q_1 + q_2) \tag{5.16}$$

This also has all the right properties. The implied utility is constant along a particular indifference curve and it rises as we move up the indifference curves. Referring to Fig. 5.1, we see that utility equals 40 at all points on the first indifference curve, 80 at all points on the second indifference curve, ..., equals 360 at all points on the last indifference curve. So that works too. So does Eq. (5.17)

$$U(q_1, q_2) = (q_1 + q_2)^2 \tag{5.17}$$

This too has all the correct properties. The implied utility is constant along a particular indifference curve and it rises as we move up the indifference curves. Referring to Fig. 5.1, we see that utility is equals 400 at all points on the first indifference curve, 1600 at all points on the second indifference curve, ..., equals 32 400 at all points on the last indifference curve.

It follows that, whereas Eq. (5.15) correctly describes the individual's preferences, it is not unique; any increasing transformation also describes the preferences. But is this a problem or a strength? If we look at the different representations above, we see that each representation simply attaches different numbers to each indifference curve. So, if we take the bottom indifference curve in Fig. 5.1, we see that the first representation attaches to it the number 20, the second representation the number 40, and the third representation the number 400. This seems to be telling us that any old number can be attached to the indifference curve; the actual number is unimportant. Recall what this number is meant to tell us – the happiness or the utility of the individual at a point. So we are being told that we cannot attach a meaningful number to such a concept. Should that surprise us? Clearly not. It would be amazing if we could say that Julie has a happiness measurement of 10 today and that David has a happiness measurement of 20 and is therefore happier than Julie; but our analysis is telling us that this is not possible. This is not surprising; indeed it is something of a relief.

So our conclusion is as follows: we can represent preferences through utility functions but these representations are not unique, and therefore no meaning can be attributed to the utility numbers that emerge. For the record, there follows a list of possible utility representations for the preferences which we have considered in this chapter:

perfect 1:1 substitutes:	$U(q_1, q_2) = q_1 + q_2$	from Eq. (5.1)
perfect 1:2 substitutes:	$U(q_1, q_2) = q_1 + q_2/2$	from Eq. (5.2)
perfect 1:a substitutes:	$U(q_1, q_2) = q_1 + q_2/a$	from Eq. (5.3)
perfect 1-with-1 complements:	$U(q_1, q_2) = \min(q_1, q_2)$	from Eq. (5.4)
perfect 1-with-2 complements:	$U(q_1, q_2) = \min(q_1, q_2/2)$	from Eq. (5.5)
perfect 1-with-a complements:	$U(q_1, q_2) = \min(q_1, q_2/a)$	from Eq. (5.6)
concave preferences	$U(q_1, q_2) = \max(q_1, q_2)$	from Eq. (5.7)

Cobb–Douglas with parameter a: $U(q_1, q_2) = q_1^a q_2^{1-a}$ from Eq. (5.8)

or: $U(q_1, q_2) = a \ln(q_1) + (1 - a)\ln(q_2)$ from Eq. (5.9)

Stone–Geary with parameter a
and subsistence levels of
consumption s_1 and s_2: $U(q_1, q_2) = (q_1 - s_1)^a (q_2 - s_2)^{1-a}$ from Eq. (5.11)

or: $U(q_1, q_2) = a \ln(q_1 - s_1) + (1 - a)\ln(q_2 - s_2)$

from Eq. (5.12)

5.8 Summary

In a sense this chapter has been a preparatory chapter for future reference. We have not really done any kind of analysis; we have simply defined things for future use. However in addition to the various definitions, you should have got the following out of the chapter.

 The shape of indifference curves depends upon the preferences of the individual.

There are two broad classes: convex and concave.

 Indifference curves are convex if the individual likes to consume the two goods together. They are concave if the individual prefers to consume them separately.

Two special cases include perfect substitutes and perfect complements.

 Indifference curves are linear if the individual regards the two goods as perfect substitutes. They are L-shaped if the individual regards the two goods as perfect complements.

We studied two more general cases:

 Two important special cases of convex preferences are Cobb–Douglas and Stone–Geary.

And we discovered, perhaps not to our surprise, that

 Preferences can be represented by utility functions but these utility functions are not unique.

5.9 Review Questions

1. Suppose one of the two goods is a *bad* (that is, the individual does not like it and the more that he or she has, the less happy he or she is). What do you think this implies about the shape of the indifference curves? Distinguish between two cases: when the individual is forced to consume the goods whether he or she likes them or not; and when the individual can costlessly throw away any of the goods that he or she does not like.

2. Consider any two goods that you consume. Try and decide what kind of preferences you have for these two goods. Might the indifference curves be concave? What would this imply about whether you like to consume them together or separately?

3. Why might it be the case that two different individuals have different preferences over the same two goods? (Because *people are different*.)

5.10 Application: what if the Individual can become Satiated?

In this chapter we have assumed throughout that both the goods we have been studying are always considered by the individual to be goods rather than bads; that the individual always will prefer more of each. You may have been wondering what happens if one or both of the goods is a bad, or becomes a bad at some stage. Suppose, for example, that the individual could have too much of one or both goods; that is, he or she becomes sated with a good and thereafter it becomes a bad. How does this affect our graphical representation of preferences? As we shall see, much depends on whether the individual has to consume the goods even when they are considered as bads. (For example, as we shall see in Chapter 32, I was forced in Bari to 'consume' the loud music provided by my neighbours.) We shall first assume that the individual is indeed forced to consume the bads; then we discuss how our analysis changes if that is not the case.

We consider here just one possibility; that the individual likes both goods up to a consumption level of 50, but if he or she has to consume more than 50 units of a good, then that good becomes a bad. In such a situation his or her indifference curves resemble those in Fig. 5.11.

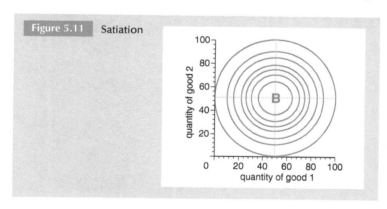

Figure 5.11   Satiation

We can divide Fig. 5.11 up into four quadrants.

- In the south-west quadrant the indifference curves have the usual downward-sloping convex shape; the individual still considers both goods as goods since the consumption level of each is less than 50.

- In the south-east, however, the curves are upward-sloping. This is a consequence of the fact that, in this quadrant, he or she has too much of good 1; the individual is sated with good 1. The upward-sloping shape of the indifference curves indicates the fact that the individual would be happy to give up some units of good 2, which he or she still considers as a good, in return for consuming less of good 1 which he or she now considers a bad. Alternatively, he or she would only consume more of the bad if he or she were compensated by consuming more of the good.

- The same is true *mutatis mutandis* in the north-west quadrant.

- In the north-east quadrant the indifference curves once again resume their downward-sloping form, because in this quadrant both goods are bads. If the individual has less of one bad then, to keep him or her indifferent, he or she has to have more of the other. Interestingly the shape is now concave – you might like to think why.

The point labelled 'B' in the Fig. 5.11 could be considered the individual's *bliss point*; up to this point he or she gets happier and happier; after it, he or she gets more and more unhappy.

If the individual is not forced to consume the goods when they become bads, the indifference curves in the south-east quadrant will become horizontal and those in the north-west quadrant will become vertical. Where do you think the 'indifference curves' are in the north-east quadrant?[5]

The final thing you might think about, particularly when you are reading the next two chapters, is how the existence of bads may affect the individual's behaviour when deciding how to allocate his or her income.

5. This is an unfair question: if the individual can refrain from consuming more than he or she wants, then all the points in the north-east quadrant are indifferent to the bliss point.

Supply and Demand with Income in the Form of Endowments

6.1 Introduction

This chapter and the next contain almost identical analyses concerning the supply and demand implied by different kinds of preferences, though they differ in one crucial respect. In this chapter it is assumed that the individual receives an income in the form of an endowment (of the two goods considered in the analysis); in the next chapter it is assumed that the individual receives an income in the form of money. Otherwise the analyses are almost identical. The reasons why there are separate chapters are two-fold: first, the material of this chapter follows naturally the discussion in Chapters 3 and 4 in which the individual's income was in the form of endowments; second, the case discussed in this chapter is, in a sense that may not become obvious until later, a more general case which can be applied elsewhere. In fact it is used repeatedly throughout the book, in particular in Part 3. It follows that Chapter 7 is in one sense a special case of this chapter – so when you have mastered this chapter it will be easier for you to master the contents of Chapter 7.

In this chapter it is assumed that the individual has an income in the form of an endowment of each of the two goods. By this we mean that, at the start of the day, the individual has in his or her possession a quantity of each of the two goods, though the quantity of one or the other could be zero. There is no money in this chapter; the only thing the individual can do is to exchange one of the goods which he or she possesses for more of the other. This is a useful framework and we shall exploit it often in the chapters that follow. Given this starting point the chapter then explores, for different kinds of preferences, what is the best thing for the individual to do at any given price. Should he or she buy good 1 and sell good 2? Should he or she sell good 1 and buy good 2? Should he or she do nothing? And if he or she should buy or sell, how much?

We then explore how these optimal demands and supplies depend upon the key exogenous variables. By exogenous variable we mean a variable that is outside the control of the individual – that he or she has to take it as given. In this instance the key exogenous variables are the prices of the two goods and the endowments of the two goods. We examine how demand and supply depend on these variables. Economists call these kind of exercises comparative static exercises. In the particular case when we find the relationship between demand or supply of some good and the price of that good, such a relationship is usually called the demand or supply curve of that good. However we should note that this terminology is somewhat misleading; in general, the demand or supply of some good depends upon both the price of that good and also the price of the other good, as well as the endowments of the two goods.

In this chapter we look at demand and supply for a variety of preferences. Some results you should remember; these will be pointed out to you. But it is more important that you understand the general methodology that is used. After reading this chapter you should be able to apply this methodology to other kinds of preferences – at least in principle – though you might find the mathematical detail a little difficult.

6.2 The Budget Constraint with Income in the Form of Endowments

We continue to use the framework adopted in Chapter 5. We are considering an individual's preferences and choice over two goods, good 1 and good 2. We put the quantity of good 1, which I denote by q_1, on the horizontal axis and the quantity of good 2, which I denote by q_2, on the vertical axis. We use p_1 and p_2 to denote the respective prices of the two goods.

In this chapter we assume that the individual gets his or her income in the form of endowments of the two goods; a quantity e_1 (which could be zero) of good 1 and a quantity e_2 (which could be zero) of good 2. (Obviously one or other of these two endowments must be non-zero, otherwise there would be nothing to discuss!)

We presume that the prices of the two goods are *exogenous* to the individual – he or she simply takes them as given. Given any prices, the individual has various trading opportunities as defined by his or her budget constraint. What form does this take? Obviously it must pass through the initial endowment point as the individual can always choose to do nothing. What else? Well, we can argue that the budget constraint must be such that the cost of the bundle consumed is equal to the value of the initial endowment. That is, the following condition must hold:

$$p_1 q_1 + p_2 q_2 = p_1 e_1 + p_2 e_2 \tag{6.1}$$

The left-hand side of Eq. (6.1) is simply the cost of the consumed bundle; the right-hand side is the value of the initial endowment. This is the individual's budget constraint. We note that in (q_1, q_2) space this is simply a straight line passing through the initial point (e_1, e_2) and having a slope equal to $-p_1/p_2$.

There are other ways we can write this budget constraint which might be more understandable; suppose we view the individual as starting at the point (e_1, e_2), and moving from there to the point (q_1, q_2) by either buying good 1 and selling good 2, or selling good 1 and buying good 2. If the individual chooses to buy (more of) good 1, then q_1 must be bigger than e_1 and q_2 smaller than e_2. Let us therefore write Eq. (6.1) in the following form:

$$p_1(q_1 - e_1) = p_2(e_2 - q_2) \tag{6.2}$$

The left-hand side of Eq. (6.2) is simply the cost of buying the extra units of good 1. This purchase has to be financed; this is achieved by selling $(e_2 - q_2)$ units of good 2, which raises enough revenue to finance the purchase.

Alternatively, the individual may choose to sell some of good 1 and buy some more of good 2. In this case q_1 is less than e_1 and q_2 is greater than e_2. To reflect this, let us re-write Eq. (6.1) in a different format:

$$p_1(e_1 - q_1) = p_2(q_2 - e_2) \tag{6.3}$$

The left-hand side of Eq. (6.3) is the money raised by selling $(e_1 - q_1)$ units of good 1 at a price p_1, while the right-hand side is the cost of financing the purchase of $(q_2 - e_2)$ extra units of good 2 at a price of p_2. These two expressions must be equal.

Equations (6.1), (6.2) and (6.3) are of course all the same. They each represent a straight line in (q_1, q_2) space (the equations are linear in q_1 and q_2), passing through the endowment point X (substitute $q_1 = e_1$ and $q_2 = e_2$ in the equation and see that these values satisfy the equation), with a slope equal to $-p_1/p_2$ (the price of good 1 relative to the price of good 2). To see the latter point, we can write Eq. (6.1) in the following form:

$$q_2 = (p_1 e_1 + p_2 e_2)/p_2 - (p_1/p_2)q_1 \tag{6.4}$$

This is an equation linear in q_1 and q_2 with the coefficient on q_1 equal to $-p_1/p_2$.

You should note carefully that the budget line must pass through the initial endowment point; the individual can always choose to do nothing and stay at that initial point. This fact has important consequences – not the least of which is the budget constraint rotates around the initial point when either p_1 or p_2 change. More precisely, if either p_1 rises or p_2 falls, the magnitude of the slope will increase so that the budget line rotates clockwise around the original point. If the individual is buying good 1 and selling good 2, such a rotation will make the individual worse off because the price of the good that he or she is buying goes up, or the price of the good being sold goes down. Whereas if the individual is selling good 1 and buying good 2, such a rotation would make the individual better off because the price of the good that is being sold goes up, or the price of the good that he or she is buying goes down. We shall explore such cases in what follows.

Given any endowment and any prices, what is optimal for the individual to do depends on the preferences of the individual. In what follows we shall take different preferences and work out the implications. In particular, we shall consider Cobb–Douglas preferences, Stone–Geary preferences, then perfect substitutes and finally perfect complements. What you should get out of this is the concept that preferences determine demands.

6.3 Choice with Cobb–Douglas Preferences

While much of our analysis will be graphical we shall find it useful to start this section with a little mathematics. This can be ignored if you do not like mathematics as we shall later verify the results with particular numerical examples. In any case the results will be explained to you; what is more important is that you understand the explanation, and you appreciate that these particular demands are a consequence of the particular preferences.

You will recall that Cobb–Douglas preferences can be represented by the following utility function.

$$U(q_1, q_2) = q_1^a q_2^{1-a} \tag{6.5}$$

This can be expressed in the following format:

$$U(q_1, q_2) = a \ln(q_1) + (1 - a)\ln(q_2) \tag{6.6}$$

For any given budget constraint, the individual wants to find the point on the constraint which lies on the highest possible indifference curve – that is, where the utility is maximized. The budget constraint is given by Eq. (6.1); the utility function by Eq. (6.6). So the individual's problem is to find the point (q_1, q_2) which maximizes $a \ln(q_1) + (1 - a)\ln(q_2)$ subject to the constraint $p_1 q_1 + p_2 q_2 = p_1 e_1 + p_2 e_2$.

Now there are various ways that one can solve this constrained maximization problem. One way is provided in the mathematical appendix to this chapter. As will be seen there, the solution to the problem of maximizing $U(q_1, q_2)$ subject to the budget constraint $p_1 q_1 + p_2 q_2 = p_1 e_1 + p_2 e_2$ is given by the following equations:

$$q_1 = a(p_1 e_1 + p_2 e_2)/p_1$$
$$q_2 = (1-a)(p_1 e_1 + p_2 e_2)/p_2 \tag{6.7}$$

These expressions are the demand functions for the two goods. They are vitally important expressions – you should remember them. They are probably easier to remember in the following form:

$$p_1 q_1 = a(p_1 e_1 + p_2 e_2)$$
$$p_2 q_2 = (1-a)(p_1 e_1 + p_2 e_2) \tag{6.8}$$

Note that $(p_1 e_1 + p_2 e_2)$ is simply the value of the initial endowment – the individual's income if you like. So the first of Eq. (6.8) says that the amount which the individual spends on good 1 $(p_1 q_1)$ is a constant fraction a of his or her income, while the second says that the amount spent on good 2 $(p_2 q_2)$ is a constant fraction $(1-a)$ of his or her income.

So the story with Cobb–Douglas preferences is clear and simple; the individual takes his or her income $(p_1 e_1 + p_2 e_2)$ and divides it up into two unequal (unless $a = 0.5$) parts. He or she spends a fraction a on good 1 and a fraction $(1-a)$ on good 2; hence the amount spent on each good is a constant fraction of the income. This implies that the quantity purchased depends upon the price of the good.

So if the value of a is 0.25, the individual spends one-quarter of his or her income on good 1 and a three-quarters of the income on good 2. If the value of income is £100, then £25 is spent on good 1 and £75 on good 2. The actual quantity purchased depends on the prices of the goods. If he or she spends £25 on good 1 and its price is £5 per unit then 5 units can be bought; if the price is £2 per unit, 12.5 units can be bought; and so on.

There is one complication that may cause confusion. When income is in the form of endowments, the value of the income is affected by the prices. So a price change affects both the value of the income and also the purchasing power of any given sum of money. As an example, let us continue to work with $a = 0.25$. Take $e_1 = 15$ and $e_2 = 25$. At prices $p_1 = p_2 = £1$ the value of this endowment is £40, and our Cobb–Douglas individual with $a = 0.25$ spends a quarter of this (£10) on good 1 and three-quarters (£30) on good 2. At prices $p_1 = p_2 = £1$ this means he or she can buy 10 units of good 1 and 30 units of good 2. Now suppose that the price of good 2 rises to $p_2 = £2$ while the price of good 1 remains unchanged. The value of the endowment (the income of the individual) will increase to £65 ($= 15 \times £1 + 25 \times £2$). The Cobb–Douglas individual will continue to spend a quarter of income on good 1 and three-quarters on good 2, so he or she will spend £16.25 on good 1 and £48.75 on good 2. With the £16.25 he or she can buy 16.25 units of good 1, while the £48.75 will buy 24.375 units of good 2 (recall that the price of good 2 is now £2). So the effect of the rise in price of good 2 from £1 to £2 is twofold: it will increase the gross demand for good 1 from 10 to 16.25 because the value of the income has risen; and it will decrease the gross demand for good 2 from 30 to 24.375, which is a combined effect of a rise in income coupled with a fall in the purchasing power of money for good 2.

So with Cobb–Douglas preferences it is easy to compute the (gross) demand for either good. We work out the value of the income; we then allocate a fraction a to good 1 and a fraction $(1-a)$ to good 2; and then we work out how many units of the two goods this allows the individual to buy. You might like to ask yourself whether this represents your behaviour.

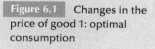

Figure 6.1 Changes in the price of good 1: optimal consumption

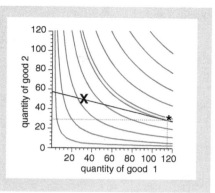

Do you allocate fixed fractions of your income to different expenditure categories? Perhaps you do!

Let us now turn to a graphical analysis of a particular case. This ties things up with what we did in Chapter 4. Moreover it provides graphical proof that Eq. (6.7) works. I give one example in the text; you can easily provide further examples. In this example I take the case of an individual with symmetric Cobb–Douglas preferences (that is, $a = 0.5$). I assume that he or she has an endowment of 30 units of good 1 and 50 units of good 2 ($e_1 = 30$ and $e_2 = 50$). Fig. 6.1 shows the indifference curves and the endowment point marked X.

What he or she should do depends upon the prices of the goods. We will start[1] with a particular case in which $p_1 = \frac{1}{4}$ and $p_2 = 1$. You should be able to work out that the budget line, as ever, passes through the initial endowment point X, and has slope $= -p_1/p_2 = -\frac{1}{4}/1 = -\frac{1}{4}$. This budget line is shown in Fig. 6.1.

Let us check that the budget constraint is correct. Clearly it passes through the initial endowment point. At prices $p_1 = \frac{1}{4}$ and $p_2 = 1$ the value of the initial endowment ($e_1 = 30$, $e_2 = 50$), is $(\frac{1}{4} \times 30 + 1 \times 50) = 57.5$. If the individual wanted, he or she could spend the whole of this endowment on good 2; this would enable him or her to reach the point (0, 57.5), consuming none of good 1 and 57.5 units of good 2. This is the point where the budget constraint intersects the vertical axis. Alternatively, if the individual wanted he or she could spend the entire income of 57.5 on good 1; at a price equal to $\frac{1}{4}$ this would enable him or her to reach the point (230, 0) and consume 230 units of good 1 and none of good 2. The point (230, 0) is where the budget constraint intersects the horizontal axis; you could check this by extending the constraint.

Given this budget constraint, the best thing that the individual can do is to move to the point that is on the highest possible indifference curve. This is shown in Fig. 6.1 at the point indicated with an asterisk; the highest reachable indifference curve is also indicated. Note an important and perhaps rather obvious property; the budget constraint is tangential to the highest indifference curve at the optimal (asterisked) point.

We know the optimal point. We know that, in this symmetric case ($a = 0.5$), the individual spends half the income on good 1 and half on good 2. The income is 57.5. So the individual spends 28.75 on good 1 and 28.75 on good 2. With 28.75 to spend on good 1 at a price of $\frac{1}{4}$ the individual can afford 115 units of good 1; with 28.75 to spend on good 2 at a price of 1 the individual can afford 28.75 units of good 2. This (115, 28.75) is the asterisked point in Fig. 6.1. It is the individual's optimal consumption.

To get to (115, 28.75) from the initial endowment point (30, 50), what does the individual do? He or she must sell $(50 - 28.75) = 21.25$ units of good 2, thereby raising 21.25 in money since the price of good 2 is one; this is spent on good 1, thereby buying 85 more units of good 1 at a price $\frac{1}{4}$ and increasing the holdings of good 1 from 30 to 115. The net demand for good 1 is 85 and the net supply of good 2 is 21.25. This is shown in the first column of Table 6.1.

---

1. Later I will change the price of good 1, which is why the figure has the title it has.

Table 6.1   Calculation of net demand for goods 1 and 2 (p_2 is fixed at 1)

Price of good 1	$\frac{1}{4}$	$\frac{1}{3}$	$\frac{1}{2}$	1	2	3	4
p_1/p_2 (relative price)	$\frac{1}{4}$	$\frac{1}{3}$	$\frac{1}{2}$	1	2	3	4
Value of endowment	57.5	60	65	80	110	140	170
Amount spent on good 1	28.75	30	32.5	40	55	70	85
Amount spent on good 2	28.75	30	32.5	40	55	70	85
Gross demand for good 1	115	90	65	40	27.5	23.33	21.25
Gross demand for good 2	28.75	30	32.5	40	55	70	85
Net demand for good 1*	85	60	35	10	−2.5	−6.67	−8.75
Net demand for good 2*	−21.25	−20	−17.5	−10	5	20	35

* If negative, indicates a net supply. Note in this table $p_2 = 1$, $e_1 = 30$ and $e_2 = 50$.

We have found what the individual should do for a particular set of prices and endowments. For other prices and endowments we simply repeat the procedure. We can therefore discover what happens to demand and supply as some variable changes. There are several variables that could change – specifically, the prices of the two goods and the individual's endowment of the two goods.

Let us begin by exploring how the demands and supplies change when the price of good 1 changes. During this exercise we keep the price of good 2 and the endowments fixed; specifically $p_2 = 1$ and $e_1 = 30$ and $e_2 = 50$ throughout. Let us take 6 more values of p_1 – namely $\frac{1}{3}$, $\frac{1}{2}$, 1, 2, 3 and 4. You should check all these out yourself. I will check just one – that with $p_1 = \frac{1}{3}$.

If $p_1 = \frac{1}{3}$, the value of the endowment is $(\frac{1}{3} \times 30) + (1 \times 50) = 60$. If this were all spent on good 2 it would buy 60 units of good 2; if it were all spent on good 1 it would produce 180 units of good 1. So the budget line goes from (180, 0) to (0, 60), passing through (30, 50) on the way. You could insert this on Fig. 6.1.

Where is the optimal point? The value of the endowment is 60. Our symmetric individual spends half of this on good 1 thus demanding 90 units of good 1, and the other half on good 2 thus demanding 30 units of good 2. With initial holdings of 30 and 50, this leads to net demands of 60 and −20 on goods 1 and 2 respectively. You should verify the other entries in the table.

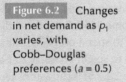

Figure 6.2   Changes in net demand as p_1 varies, with Cobb–Douglas preferences ($a = 0.5$)

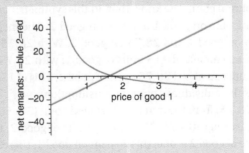

We have found how the demand and supply for the two goods depend upon the price of good 1. We can take the figures from Table 6.1, specifically the first row and the final two rows, and plot them separately. This I do in Fig. 6.2, where I put the price of good 1 on the horizontal axis and the net demands and supplies on the vertical axis.

The net demand for good 1 is the curve that starts out positive and then becomes negative. The net demand for good 2 is the straight line that starts negative and then becomes positive. You will notice that when one is positive the other is negative. So if the price of good 1 is sufficiently low (between 0 and $\frac{5}{3}$), the individual is a net buyer of good 1 and a net seller of good 2. When the price of good 1 is sufficiently high, the individual becomes a net seller of good 1 and a net buyer of good 2. You might ask: what is the significance of the price of $\frac{5}{3}$? Well, it is the price at which the individual wants to be neither a buyer nor a seller; he or she just wants to stay in the initial position. This is optimal if and only if the budget constraint is everywhere (except at the initial point, of course) below the original indifference curve. That is true if the budget constraint is tangential to the original indifference curve at the initial point. So it follows[2] that the slope of the original indifference curve at the initial point is $-\frac{5}{3}$.

Fig. 6.2 shows two things which are generally – but not always – true:

● the demand for a good falls as its price rises; and
● the demand for a good rises as the price of the other good rises.

Demand is switched away from the increasingly relatively expensive good towards the other good.

We know the general form of the gross demands; these were given in Eq. (6.7). If we substitute into Eq. (6.7) the particular values relevant to this example, namely $e_1 = 30$, $e_2 = 50$ and $p_2 = 1$, we can derive the net demand functions relevant to this case. For good 1 net demand is given by gross demand $q_1 = a(p_1 e_1 + p_2 e_2)/p_1$ minus the initial endowment e_1; so net demand for good 1 is given by $[0.5(p_1 30 + 50)/p_1 - 30]$ or $(25/p_1 - 15)$. This is the equation plotted in Fig. 6.2; for low p_1 it starts out positive; it becomes zero when $p_1 = \frac{25}{15} = \frac{5}{3}$, and then becomes and stays negative. The net demand for good 2 is given by the gross demand $q_2 = (1 - a)(p_1 e_1 + p_2 e_2)/p_2$ minus the initial endowment e_2. So net demand for good 2 is given by $[0.5(p_1 30 + 50) - 50]$ or $(15p_1 - 25)$. Note that this is linear in p_1 as is obvious from Fig. 6.2. It starts out negative for low p_1, becomes zero when $p_1 = \frac{25}{15} = \frac{5}{3}$, and then it becomes and stays positive.

We have now completed our first comparative static exercise; we have studied how net demands depend upon the price of good 1. Other comparative static exercises can be carried out in the same way. These include changes in the price of good 2, and changes in the endowments of the two goods.

The effect of changes in p_2 should be easy to predict. Why? Because what is crucial is the slope of the budget constraint which we know is $-p_1/p_2$. It is not the absolute value of either price that matters but the relative price. In Table 6.1, p_2 was always equal to 1 and

Table 6.2   Calculation of the net demand for goods 1 and 2 (p_1 is fixed at 1)

Price of good 2	$\frac{1}{4}$	$\frac{1}{3}$	$\frac{1}{2}$	1	2	3	4
p_1/p_2 (relative price)	4	3	2	1	$\frac{1}{2}$	$\frac{1}{3}$	$\frac{1}{4}$
Value of endowment	42.5	46.67	55	80	130	180	230
Amount spent on good 1	21.25	23.33	27.5	40	65	90	115
Amount spent on good 2	21.25	23.33	27.5	40	65	90	115
Gross demand for good 1	21.25	23.33	27.5	40	65	90	115
Gross demand for good 2	85	70	55	40	32.5	30	28.75
Net demand for good 1*	−8.75	−6.67	−2.5	10	35	60	85
Net demand for good 2*	35	20	5	−10	−17.5	−20	−21.25

* If negative indicates a net supply. Note in this table $p_1 = 1$, $e_1 = 30$ and $e_2 = 50$.

2. There is a general property of Cobb–Douglas indifference curves that is useful to know. The marginal rate of substitution (the negative of the slope of the indifference curve) is $aq_2/[(1 - a)q_1]$. For a proof, see the mathematical appendix.

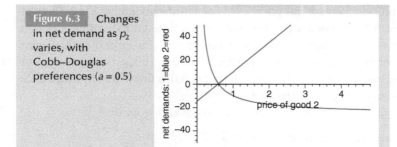

Figure 6.3 Changes in net demand as p_2 varies, with Cobb–Douglas preferences ($a = 0.5$)

we let p_1 take the values $\frac{1}{4}, \frac{1}{3}, \frac{1}{2}, 1, 2, 3,$ and 4; so the values of the relative price $-p_1/p_2$ were $\frac{1}{4}, \frac{1}{3}, \frac{1}{2}, 1, 2, 3,$ and 4. Now, suppose instead we keep the value of p_1 fixed at 1 and we want to let p_2 take the values $\frac{1}{4}, \frac{1}{3}, \frac{1}{2}, 1, 2, 3,$ and 4; for these prices, the values taken by the relative price $-p_1/p_2$ are $4, 3, 2, 1, \frac{1}{2}, \frac{1}{3}$ and $\frac{1}{4}$. So we can easily calculate the comparative static effects of changes in p_2 for given values of p_1, e_1 and e_2. We obtain Table 6.2 from Table 6.1, adjusting the price of good 2 and the relative price as described, whilst keeping p_1 constant.

Note the implications: in particular, the final two rows of this table are the same as the final two rows of the first table because we have exactly the same relative prices – except in the reverse order. If we plot the final two rows of this table against the first row we obtain Fig. 6.3, which is the equivalent of Fig. 6.2.

You should note that the variable on the horizontal axis is how the price of good 2. Note also that the curve in Fig. 6.3 represents the net demand for good 2; it starts out positive for low p_2, becomes zero when $p_2 = \frac{3}{5}$ (what is the significance of this?) and then becomes and stays negative. The straight line is the net demand for good 1 which starts out negative, is zero at a price of $\frac{3}{5}$, and then becomes and stays positive.

The final comparative static exercise which we perform with these preferences is that of varying one of the endowments – specifically we vary e_1. At the same time we keep prices constant, and for simplicity we make the prices equal so that the budget line has a slope -1. We also keep the endowment of good 2 fixed at 50. We vary e_1, starting with a value of 10. This situation is pictured in Fig. 6.4.

You can probably see where the optimal point is. As everything is symmetrical, the optimal point is too; it is indicated with an asterisk and is at (30, 30). The net demands are 20 for good 1 and −20 for good 2. What do you think happens when we increase e_1 to 20? The optimal point becomes (35, 35) and net demands are 15 for good 1 (slightly less than before because the initial endowment of good 1 has increased) and −15 for good 2. If we continue to increase e_1 in this way, the gross demand for good 1 will continue to increase because the individual is getting better off, but net demand will continue to fall. By the time that e_1 has reached 50 (the same as e_2) the net demand for good 1 has sunk to zero. Thereafter it becomes negative. This is illustrated in Fig. 6.5. The line that starts out positive is the net demand for good 1; the other is the net demand for good 2.

We have now done three comparative static exercises. You should be able

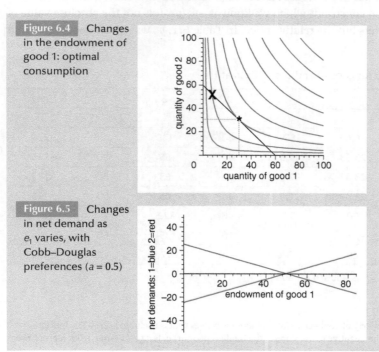

Figure 6.4 Changes in the endowment of good 1: optimal consumption

Figure 6.5 Changes in net demand as e_1 varies, with Cobb–Douglas preferences ($a = 0.5$)

to do a fourth (changes in the endowment of good 2 with fixed prices and fixed endowment of good 1) for yourself.

We do not want to get involved in too much detail. What is important is not that you understand the detail, but the principles involved in finding the optimal position and hence seeing how the individual responds to changes in the exogenous variables. Also of importance is that you have some feeling of how the shape of the various demand functions in Figs 6.2, 6.3 and 6.5 are influenced by the underlying preferences, as manifested in the indifference curves. To reinforce the feeling, let me use some slightly different preferences – non-symmetrical Cobb–Douglas – and see how one of the figures differs. Let $a = 0.3$ so that $(1 - a) = 0.7$. The new indifference map is shown in Fig. 6.6.

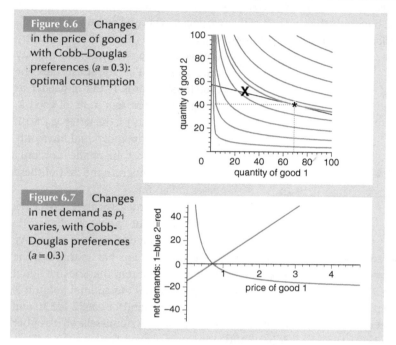

Figure 6.6 Changes in the price of good 1 with Cobb–Douglas preferences ($a = 0.3$): optimal consumption

Figure 6.7 Changes in net demand as p_1 varies, with Cobb–Douglas preferences ($a = 0.3$)

We can derive the relationship between net demands and the price of good 1 from the indifference map in Fig. 6.6 or from Eq. (6.8), as depicted in Fig. 6.7.

Compare Fig. 6.7 with Fig. 6.2. You will see differences in the slopes and the point at which the individual switches from being a buyer of one good to being a seller of it. Clearly the preferences determine the demand functions.

6.4 Choice with Stone–Geary Preferences

To reinforce this latter point let us turn to Stone–Geary preferences. As before we will find it simplest to begin with a mathematical derivation of the demand functions. Now you may think this will be rather difficult, but it turns out that we can use a simple trick. Recall that with Stone–Geary preferences the individual has subsistence levels of the two goods, but the indifference curves, relative to these subsistence levels, are Cobb–Douglas. So, recalling that a Cobb–Douglas individual spends a constant fraction a of his or her income on good 1 and a constant fraction $(1 - a)$ on good 2, we can argue the following: first, a Stone–Geary person buys a quantity s_1 of good 1 and a quantity s_2 of good 2; secondly, he or she spends a constant fraction a of the residual income on good 1 and a constant fraction $(1 - a)$ on good 2. This leads us to the following gross demand functions:

$$q_1 = s_1 + a(p_1 e_1 + p_2 e_2 - p_1 s_1 - p_2 s_2)/p_1$$

$$q_2 = s_2 + (1 - a)(p_1 e_1 + p_2 e_2 - p_1 s_1 - p_2 s_2)/p_2 \qquad (6.9)$$

You should compare these with the Cobb–Douglas demands in Eq. (6.7). They have different properties; this implies that, if we know the demand functions, we may be able to infer the underlying preferences.

6.5 Choice with Perfect Substitute Preferences

If the individual regards the two goods as perfect substitutes the decision problem becomes simple; the individual buys only the cheapest of the two goods, where cheapest is defined relative to his or her preferences. For 1:1 substitutes it is clear: if $p_1 < p_2$ the individual will buy only good 1; if $p_2 < p_1$ he or she will buy only good 2. For 1:a substitutes the individual regards 1 unit of good 1 as being equivalent to a units of good 2. The former costs p_1; the latter ap_2. So, if $p_1 < ap_2$ then the individual buys only good 1; if $ap_2 < p_1$ he or she buys only good 2. We illustrate the first of these cases in Fig. 6.8.

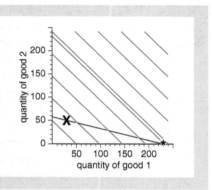

Figure 6.8 Changes in the price of good 1 with perfect 1:1 substitutes: optimal consumption

In this example we have perfect 1:1 substitutes. The price of good 2 is assumed to be one and the respective endowments are 30 and 50. The price of good 1 is $\frac{1}{4}$ – the budget line passes through the initial endowment point (X), and has a slope equal to $-\frac{1}{4}$. The maximum that the individual can buy of good 2 is 57.5, and of good 1 is 230. The figure shows the optimal point; it is when the individual spends all his income on good 1. His gross demand for good 1 is 230 and for good 2 is 0; The net demands therefore are 200 and −50. The individual sells all his or her 50 units of good 2 and with the proceeds buys 200 more units of good 1.

Clearly the same kind of solution is valid whenever $p_1 < p_2$. When they are equal the budget constraint coincides with an indifference curve so any point along the budget constraint is optimal. When $p_2 < p_1$ the situation changes and the individual sells all the endowment of good 1 and with the proceeds buys good 2. This is shown in Table 6.3.

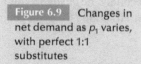

Table 6.3   Calculation of net demand for goods 1 and 2 (perfect substitute preferences)

Price of good 1	$\frac{1}{4}$	$\frac{1}{3}$	$\frac{1}{2}$	1	2	3	4
Gross demand for good 1	230	180	130	*	0	0	0
Gross demand for good 2	0	0	0	*	110	140	170
Net demand for good 1	200	150	100	*	−30	−30	−30
Net demand for good 2	−50	−50	−50	*	60	90	120

* Any amount satisfying the budget constraint. Note, in this table $p_2 = 1$, $e_1 = 30$ and $e_2 = 50$.

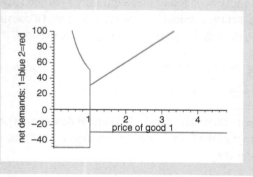

Figure 6.9 Changes in net demand as p_1 varies, with perfect 1:1 substitutes

Notice how the gross demand switches from good 1 to good 2 as the price of good 1 rises above one. If we graph the final two rows of Table 6.3 against the first row, we get the net demand functions for the two goods as functions of the price of good 1, as shown in Fig. 6.9.

This may figure look a bit odd, but you should study it carefully.

It says that at any price between zero and one the individual will sell all 50 units of good 2 and with the proceeds buy as much of good 1 as possible. For prices above one, the individual will sell all 30 units of good 1 and with the proceeds buys as much as possible of good 2. Mathematically the gross demands are presented in Eq. (6.10).

$$\text{if } p_1 < p_2 \quad q_1 = (p_1 e_1 + p_2 e_2)/p_1 \quad q_2 = 0$$
$$\text{if } p_2 < p_1 \quad q_2 = (p_1 e_1 + p_2 e_2)/p_2 \quad q_1 = 0 \tag{6.10}$$

The net demands are found by subtracting the initial holdings and are therefore as shown in Eq. (6.11).

$$\text{if } p_1 < p_2 \quad \text{net } q_1 = (p_1 e_1 + p_2 e_2)/p_1 - e_1 \quad \text{net } q_2 = -e_2$$
$$\text{if } p_2 < p_1 \quad \text{net } q_2 = (p_1 e_1 + p_2 e_2)/p_2 - e_2 \quad \text{net } q_1 = -e_1 \tag{6.11}$$

For perfect 1:a substitutes we have the following generalization for gross demands.

$$\text{if } p_1 < ap_2 \quad q_1 = (p_1 e_1 + p_2 e_2)/p_1 \quad q_2 = 0$$
$$\text{if } ap_2 < p_1 \quad q_2 = (p_1 e_1 + p_2 e_2)/p_2 \quad q_1 = 0 \tag{6.12}$$

The derivation of the net demands is left for you.

One thing should be obvious – there is a startling difference between the demand functions with Cobb–Douglas preferences and those with perfect substitute preferences; just compare Figs 6.2 and 6.9.

6.6 Choice with Perfect Complement Preferences

This is a relatively easy case as the individual has to buy the two goods in fixed proportions. Why? Just examine the optimization problem with 1-with-1 perfect complements which is shown in Fig. 6.10.

Where is the optimal point? It is always at a corner. So the optimal solution is simply where the budget constraint and the line joining the corners intersect. In the case of 1-with-1 perfect complements the line joining the corners has equation $q_1 = q_2$, whereas the budget constraint has the equation $p_1 q_1 + p_2 q_2 = p_1 e_1 + p_2 e_2$. Solving these two equations simultaneously, we get the following gross demands:

$$q_1 = q_2 = (p_1 e_1 + p_2 e_2)/(p_1 + p_2) \tag{6.13}$$

The net demands are easily found by subtracting e_1 from q_1 and e_2 from q_2.

We illustrate the implications for the net demands in the above example, where $e_1 = 30$, $e_2 = 50$, and $p_2 = 1$. We plot the net demands as functions of the price of good 1 in Fig. 6.11. Notice that the individual is always a net demander of good 1 and a net supplier of good 2. Why is this?

Figure 6.10 Changes in the price of good 1 with perfect 1-with-1 complements: optimum consumption

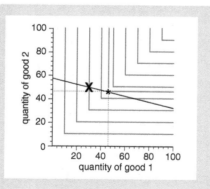

Figure 6.11 Changes in net demand as p_1 varies, with perfect 1-with-1 complements

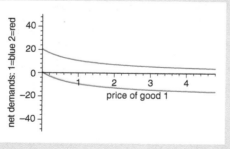

For perfect 1-with-a complements, the line joining the angles has the equation $q_2 = aq_1$, and so the optimal gross demands are the intersection of this line and the budget constraint. This gives us the following gross demands.

$$q_1 = (p_1 e_1 + p_2 e_2)/(p_1 + ap_2)$$
$$q_2 = a(p_1 e_1 + p_2 e_2)/(p_1 + ap_2) \tag{6.14}$$

It is up to you to find the net demands.

6.7 Comments

The main point has already been made – the demands depend upon the preferences. If we compare figures 6.2, 6.7, 6.9 and 6.11 this is very clear. The point is important, not least because it enables us to infer preferences from observations. We might want to do this, for example, if we have some observations on an individual's demand and want to make predictions about future demand. First, we use the observations on demand to tell us something about preferences; then we use the information on preferences to predict future demand. This is standard economic, or scientific, methodology.

6.8 Summary

You may already have realized that we can distinguish between some of the preferences we have studied here quite easily.

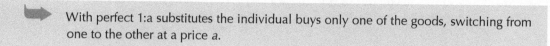

With perfect 1:a substitutes the individual buys only one of the goods, switching from one to the other at a price a.

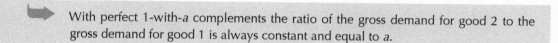

With perfect 1-with-a complements the ratio of the gross demand for good 2 to the gross demand for good 1 is always constant and equal to a.

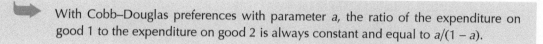

With Cobb–Douglas preferences with parameter a, the ratio of the expenditure on good 1 to the expenditure on good 2 is always constant and equal to $a/(1 - a)$.

You might like to see if you can discover a similar kind of rule for Stone–Geary preferences.

6.9 Review Questions

1. Suppose an individual has perfect 1:a substitute preferences over two goods. What happens to his or her demands for the two goods when the price of good 1 rises with the price of good 2 fixed at 1 and the endowments of the two goods fixed? At what price does the demand for good 1 become zero?

2. Suppose an individual's preferences are either perfect substitutes or perfect complements or Cobb–Douglas; what happens to the demands for the two goods when the endowments increase in the same proportion?

3. How do the results of this chapter help us to infer preferences from observations on demand? (We will answer this question at the end of the next chapter.)

6.10 Mathematical Appendix

We derive the Cobb–Douglas demands. It will be recalled that the problem is to find the solution to the constrained maximization:

$$\text{maximize} \qquad U(q_1, q_2) = a \ln(q_1) + (1 - a)\ln(q_2) \tag{6.6}$$

$$\text{subject to} \qquad p_1 q_1 + p_2 q_2 = p_1 e_1 + p_2 e_2 \tag{6.1}$$

The easiest way is to set up the Lagrangian function, which is the objective minus λ times the constraint.

$$L = a \ln(q_1) + (1 - a)\ln(q_2) - \lambda(p_1 q_1 + p_2 q_2 - p_1 e_1 - p_2 e_2) \tag{A6.1}$$

We need to maximize L with respect to q_1, q_2 and λ. Optimality conditions are in Eqs (A6.2).

$$dL/dq_1 = a/q_1 - \lambda p_1 = 0$$
$$dL/dq_2 = (1 - a)/q_2 - \lambda p_2 = 0 \tag{A6.2}$$
$$dL/d\lambda = p_1 q_1 + p_2 q_2 - p_1 e_1 - p_2 e_2 = 0$$

From the first of these we have $p_1 q_1 = a/\lambda$, and from the second $p_2 q_2 = (1 - a)/\lambda$. Substituting these into the third condition of Eq (A6.2) produces $1/\lambda = p_1 e_1 + p_2 e_2$. This is now substituted in turn into the first two equations of Eq. (A6.2) to obtain

$$q_1 = a(p_1 e_1 + p_2 e_2)/p_1$$
$$q_2 = (1 - a)(p_1 e_1 + p_2 e_2)/p_2 \tag{A6.3}$$

These are Eqs (6.7) in the text.

An alternative proof uses the fact that, at the optimal point, the slope of the indifference curve is equal to the slope of the budget line. We know the latter is $-p_1/p_2$ and the former is minus the MRS. We can work this out from the equation of an indifference curve, which is given by

$$a \ln = a \ln(q_1) + (1 - a)\ln(q_2) = \text{constant}$$

If we differentiate this equation we get

$$adq_1/q_1 + (1 - a)dq_2/q_2 = 0$$

From this it follows that the slope of the indifference curve

$$dq_2/dq_1 = -aq_2/[(1 - q_1)q_1]$$

Imposing the condition that, at the optimal point, the slopes of the budget line and the indifference curve are equal, we obtain

$$-p_1/p_2 = -aq_2/[(1 - a)q_1]$$

It follows that

$$p_1/p_2 = aq_2/[(1 - a)q_1]$$

Combining this with the budget constraint gives Cobb–Douglas demand functions as in Eq. (A6.3).

Demand with Income in the Form of Money

7.1 Introduction

In one sense this is a partial repeat of Chapter 6. There is only one important difference; the individual gets his or her income in the form of money rather than in the form of an endowment of the two goods. You should be able to anticipate most of the results. This will build your confidence and, as we will see, it is useful to have two separate chapters. We shall make use of them both in the future.

7.2 The Budget Constraint with Income in the Form of Money

We continue to use the framework adopted in Chapter 5 and used in Chapter 6. We are considering an individual's preferences and choice over two goods, good 1 and good 2. We put the quantity of good 1, which is denoted by q_1, on the horizontal axis and the quantity of good 2, denoted by q_2, on the vertical axis. We use p_1 and p_2 to denote the respective prices of the two goods.

In this chapter we assume that the individual gets his or her income in the form of money, the quantity of which is denoted by m. This quantity does not depend upon the prices of the two goods, though obviously the purchasing power of the income does. This income determines the budget constraint of the individual which is given by the following expression

$$p_1 q_1 + p_2 q_2 = m \tag{7.1}$$

This says that the cost of purchases must equal the value of the income; the individual must be able to finance his or her purchases.

The budget constraint (7.1) is a straight line in (q_1, q_2) space with slope $-p_1/p_2$. This expression for the slope will be familiar. If the individual spends nothing on good 2 he or she can buy a total of m/p_1 units of good 1. If nothing is spent on good 1, a total of m/p_2 units of good 2 can be bought. So the budget constraint goes from $(0, m/p_1)$ to $(m/p_2, 0)$. Given any budget constraint and any set of preferences, the individual's optimal point is the point on that budget constraint which is on the highest attainable indifference curve. In the remainder of this chapter we will consider some particular preferences.

7.3 Choice with Cobb–Douglas Preferences

We can make use of previous results. We already know from Chapter 6 that an individual with Cobb–Douglas preferences and a value a for the parameter will spend a fraction a of his or her income on good 1 and a fraction $(1 - a)$ on good 2. Therefore the demands for goods 1 and 2 (both net and gross because he does not start with any endowments of the goods), are given by

$$q_1 = am/p_1$$
$$q_2 = (1 - a)m/p_2 \tag{7.2}$$

These results are particularly simple and elegant and you should remember them. They imply that:

- the effect of the good's own price on the demand is simple – demand always adjusts so that the amount spent remains constant;
- changes in the price of the other goods have no effect;
- the effect of income is particularly simple since q_i is linearly related to m – so that when income doubles so does demand.

The two price effects are shown in Fig. 7.1, which is for an individual with symmetric Cobb–Douglas preferences. In this example income is 100 and the price of good 2 is always equal to unity. The price of good 1 is on the horizontal axis, and the demands for the two goods on the vertical axis. The horizontal line is the demand for good 2; this is always 50 irrespective of the price of good 1. The curve represents the demand for good 1. it shows that, as the price of good 1 rises, demand for it falls. At a price of one demand is 50, so the amount spent is 50 – equal to half the income; at a price of two the demand is 25 so the amount spent is 50 – equal to half the income; at a price of five the demand is 10, so the amount spent is 50 – equal to half the income; and so on.

The effect of changes in the money income on net demands is particularly simple and is illustrated in Fig. 7.2. Note that this is the graph for the demand for good 1; that for good 2 coincides with it since this is the symmetric case.

If we take a non-symmetric

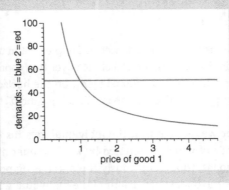

Figure 7.1   Changes in demand as p_1 varies, with Cobb-Douglas preferences ($a = 0.5$)

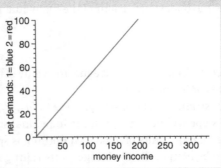

Figure 7.2   Changes in net demand as income varies, with Cobb-Douglas preferences ($a = 0.5$)

Cobb–Douglas case we get something different. Perhaps you can work out what the value of a is in the case which is illustrated in Fig. 7.3. (We continue to assume that money income is 100 and the price of good 2 is one.)

The horizontal line is the demand for good 2; the curve is the demand for good 1. You should be able to work out that the value of a is 0.3: the individual always spends 30 on good 1 and 70 on good 2. But what about the following case (Fig. 7.4), where both prices are equal to one? The upper line is for good 2; the lower for good 1. Once again $a = 0.3$.

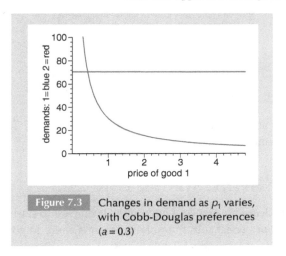

Figure 7.3   Changes in demand as p_1 varies, with Cobb-Douglas preferences ($a = 0.3$)

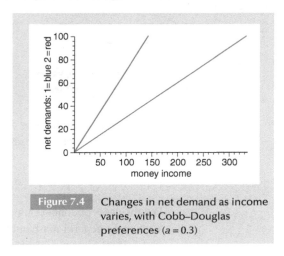

Figure 7.4   Changes in net demand as income varies, with Cobb–Douglas preferences ($a = 0.3$)

7.4 Choice with Stone–Geary Preferences

We can make the obvious extension. Stone–Geary preferences are just like Cobb–Douglas preferences relative to the subsistence levels. So we get the usual story; first the individual buys the subsistence levels of the two goods, then he or she spends a fraction a of the residual income on good 1 and a fraction $(1 - a)$ on good 2. After buying the subsistence levels s_1 and s_2 the residual income is $(m - p_1 s_1 - p_2 s_2)$. So the demands are the following:

$$q_1 = s_1 + a(m - p_1 s_1 - p_2 s_2)/p_1$$
$$q_2 = s_2 + (1 - a)(m - p_1 s_1 - p_2 s_2)/p_2 \qquad (7.3)$$

Notice that these differ quite markedly from the Cobb–Douglas demand functions:

● Changes in the good's own price are not compensated in such a way as to keep spending constant;

● the demand for a good is affected by the price of the other good;

● the demand remains a linear function of the price, but it no longer passes through the origin.

If we take an example we can see the implications. Consider the case we used in the Cobb–Douglas section with $a = 0.5$, income 100, the price of good 2 was held at one, and the price of good 1 was allowed to vary. We obtained the results shown in Fig. 7.1. For Stone–Geary preferences with $s_1 = 10$ and $s_2 = 20$ we have the situation which is illustrated in Fig. 7.5. You should note the differences between the two sets of results.

Now, if we vary money income keeping both prices fixed at one throughout, we have a very different situation regarding net demands; this is pictured in Fig. 7.6. Note that the curves do not start until income is sufficiently high to buy the subsistence levels of both goods; you will recall that indifference curves are not defined unless both subsistence levels

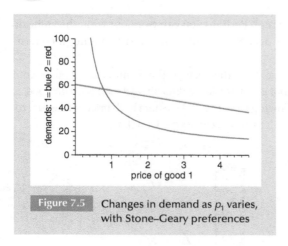

Figure 7.5 Changes in demand as p_1 varies, with Stone–Geary preferences

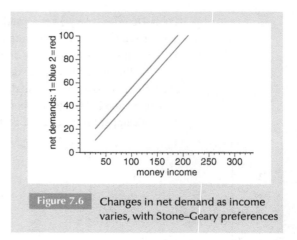

Figure 7.6 Changes in net demand as income varies, with Stone–Geary preferences

are attained. At an income of 30, 10 units are bought of good 1 (s_1) and 20 units of good 2 (s_2). Thereafter demand rises linearly with income.

7.5 Choice with Perfect Substitute Preferences

For the cases of Cobb–Douglas and Stone–Geary preferences I have found it simplest to start with some general mathematical results. For perfect substitutes, however, it is easier to go back to first principles. Consider the following case: perfect 1:1 substitutes; income 100; price of good 2 equal to one; price of good 1 varies, starting at $\frac{1}{4}$. What does the individual do?

The budget constraint has an intercept 400 on the horizontal axis and an intercept 100 on the vertical axis. Since the individual regards the two goods as perfect substitutes, and given that good 1 is cheaper, it is obviously better to consume only good 1. Demand for good 1 is thus 400 and that for good 2 is zero, as shown in Fig. 7.7 by an asterisk.

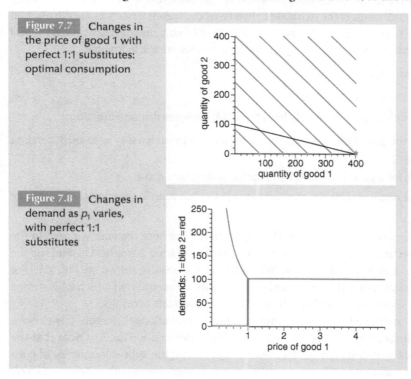

Figure 7.7 Changes in the price of good 1 with perfect 1:1 substitutes: optimal consumption

Figure 7.8 Changes in demand as p_1 varies, with perfect 1:1 substitutes

The same is true if $p_1 = \frac{1}{3}$, when the budget line goes from (300, 0) to (0, 100) and for $p_1 = \frac{1}{2}$, when the budget line connects (200, 0) to (0, 100). When $p_1 = 1$, the budget line goes from (100, 0) to (0, 100) and it coincides with an indifference curve; thus all points along it are equally attractive. When $p_2 = 2$, the budget line goes from (50, 0) to (100, 0) and it now becomes more attractive to buy only good 2 and none of good 1. The same is obviously true for any higher price. We thus get the demand curves for good 1 and good 2 as a function of the price of good 1 which are shown in Fig. 7.8.

Note that the demand for good 1 is the curve which starts out high at the left and sinks to

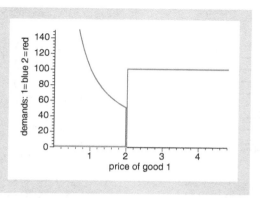

Figure 7.9 Changes in demand as p_1 varies, with perfect 1:2 substitutes

100 as the price approaches one, after which it becomes zero. Up to a price of one, the demand is simply what can be bought with an income of 100 at that price – so it is 100 divided by the price. The other line is the demand for good 2. This is zero until the price of good 1 reaches one, after which point the demand for good 2 is always 100 because that is the fixed amount that the individual can buy at a price of one when income is 100.

With perfect 1:2 substitutes the picture is similar, but there are some important differences – not least that demand switches from good 1 to good 2 at a price of two instead of one; see Fig. 7.9.

For the record, we write here the optimal demands in the general case of perfect $1:a$ substitutes:

$$\text{if} \quad p_1 < ap_2 \quad \text{then} \quad q_1 = m/p_1 \quad \text{and} \quad q_2 = 0$$
$$\text{if} \quad ap_2 < p_1 \quad \text{then} \quad q_2 = m/p_2 \quad \text{and} \quad q_1 = 0 \tag{7.4}$$

7.6 Choice with Perfect Complement Preferences

As in the last chapter, optimal demands with perfect complement preferences have the property that the ratio of the quantity of good 1 purchased to the quantity of good 2 purchased is constant. The optimal point is always at a corner. So, as before, the demands are given by the intersection of the budget constraint and the line joining the corners. For perfect 1-with-a complements the line joining the corners has the equation $q_2 = aq_1$, while the budget constraint has the equation $p_1q_1 + p_2q_2 = m$. So optimal demands are given by:

$$q_1 = m/(p_1 + ap_2)$$
$$q_2 = am/(p_1 + ap_2) \tag{7.5}$$

7.7 Choice with Quasi-linear Preferences

Let us finally return to the case with which we started this book – quasi-linear preferences. You will recall that the indifference curves are parallel[1]. Fig. 7.10 shows such a map of indifference curves together with a budget constraint.

You should ask yourself what happens to the optimal demands when income increases while prices remain fixed. Obviously the budget line moves parallel to itself; the slope, which is equal to the price of good 1 relative to the price of good 2, does not change if prices are fixed. So, what happens to the optimal point? It must move vertically upwards. This means that the optimal demand for good 1 is fixed and does not depend upon the amount of income

---

1. Here and elsewhere in a vertical direction. But they could instead be parallel in a horizontal direction, in which case goods 1 and 2 must be reversed in what follows.

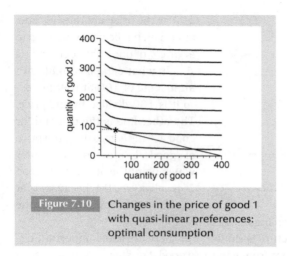

Figure 7.10   Changes in the price of good 1 with quasi-linear preferences: optimal consumption

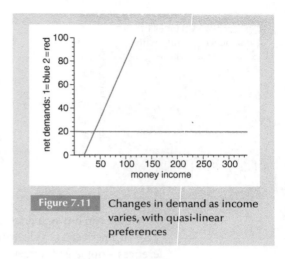

Figure 7.11   Changes in demand as income varies, with quasi-linear preferences

the individual has. This is shown in Fig. 7.11. Rather obviously, the horizontal line is the demand for good 1 as a function of income, while the upward-sloping line is the demand for good 2.

7.8   Comments

This chapter has in some ways been a bit of revision. In essence we have been reviewing the material of Chapter 6 with a slight change; income was in the form of money rather than endowments. This means that, when a price changes, the budget constraint rotates around the intercept on the horizontal axis (if it is p_2 that has changed) or on the vertical axis (if it is p_1 that has changed), rather than around the initial endowment point. Moreover all demands in this chapter are both gross and net demands because the individual does not start with any endowment of either good.

7.9 Summary

The main points are the same as those in Chapter 6; different preferences imply different demands. We can distinguish between some of the preferences we have studied using the following.

 With perfect 1:a substitutes the individual buys only one of the goods, switching from one to the other at a price a.

 With perfect 1-with-a complements, the ratio of the gross demand for good 2 to the gross demand for good 1 is always constant and equal to a.

 With Cobb–Douglas preferences with parameter a, the ratio of the expenditure on good 1 to the expenditure on good 2 is always constant and equal to $a/(1 - a)$.

Do you yet have any feeling about Stone–Geary? And what about quasi-linear preferences?

7.10 Review Questions

1. If your preferences are Cobb–Douglas with parameter a, then the results of this chapter indicate that you will spend a fraction a of your money income on good 1, and a fraction $(1 - a)$ on good 2. Can you think of any two goods for which this is true for you? For example, do you always put 25 per cent of your income towards your food budget and 20 per cent towards clothes?

2. What happens to your demands for the two goods if your income rises, when your preferences are either perfect substitutes or perfect complements or Cobb–Douglas? The demands rise proportionately with income. If, however, your preferences are Stone–Geary, this is not the case. Why not?

3. Can you draw a set of indifference curves for which the demand for one of the goods falls as income rises? Can you think of an example for which this might be the case for you?

4. Return to the case of a bad which was mentioned during the Review Questions for Chapter 6. Using the methods of this chapter, discover the amount of the bad that you buy.

5. Have you answered the question at the end of the Summary about how the demands with quasi-linear preferences vary? Consider, in particular, the demand for the good on the horizontal axis as a function of income. Note that it does not change. Why not? (Because the reservation prices are independent of income.)

(7.11) # Application:
how do we Infer Preferences?

This is a simple game which you could play with your fellow students of microeconomics. Although simple, it teaches a lot about how we can infer preferences from observations, and the most efficient way of so doing.

First split the tutorial group up into two teams and give to each team the following instructions.

There are two goods: good 1 and good 2. Good 2 is the *numeraire* good -- its price is unity. The price of good 1 is p. The income of your team is m. The quantities of the two goods demanded by your team are q_1 and q_2. Note that $pq_1 + q_2 = m$ is the implied budget constraint.

Your team should decide what your preferences concerning the two goods are. These preferences must be of one of the following three types:

- **Type 1: Perfect substitutes** with one unit of good 1 being always substitutable for or by a units of good 2. Hence the indifference curves are linear with common slope $-a$ ($0 < a <$ infinity).

- **Type 2: Perfect complements** with one unit of good 1 always needing to be complemented by a units of good 2. Hence the indifference curves are L-shaped with the corners being along a ray from the origin with slope a ($0 < a <$ infinity).

- **Type 3: Cobb–Douglas** with relative weights a and $(1 - a)$, that is, with indifference curves given by the equation: $q_1^a q_2^{(1-a)} =$ constant ($0 < a < 1$).

Illustrations of these three types were given in Chapter 5; details of the implications for the implied demands can be found in Chapters 5, 6 and 7.

Your team should choose one of these 3 types and a value for the parameter a. You should inform your tutor of these choices; he or she will act as the referee in what is to follow. You should, however, not tell the other team. It is their job to discover your preferences.

Each team knows its preferences – its type and the value of a. The purpose of the exercise is for each team to discover the preferences of the other team – that is, its type and the value of a. It must try to do this from answers to questions of the following form:

'What are your demands (q_1 and q_2) if the price of good 1 is p and your income is m?'

Only questions of this type are allowed, but the values of p and m can be any positive numbers.

To implement the game, both teams tell their tutor the type of preferences selected and the value of their parameter a. Ideally the teams should have decided these before the tutorial begins. The tutor then puts on the whiteboard two tables side by side, as in Table 7.1.

Table 7.1   Illustrative game showing demands for teams 1 and 2

Team 1's demands				Team 2's demands			
p	m	q_1	q_2	p	m	q_1	q_2

The game is played simultaneously by the two teams. First, both teams write up a question (a value of p and a value of m) in the appropriate table on the whiteboard; team 1 uses the first row in the table headed 'Team 2's demands' and Team 2 the table headed 'Team 1's demands'. Usually it takes some time for the teams to think up this initial question, but on reflection it becomes obvious that it does not really matter what the teams choose for p and m. Then the teams have to fill in their answers: the demands as given by their preferences to the values of p and m selected by the other team. This stage takes a bit of time unless the teams are really well prepared. I, as the referee, check that the answers are consistent with the preferences of the two teams. This is important as students frequently make mistakes.

At this point we have one complete row in each of the above tables. The teams are then invited to try and infer the preferences of the other team: their type and the value of the parameter a. I do not want to tell you too much at this point (otherwise it will spoil the point of the game), but only a certain amount can usually be inferred. Unless one of the q values is zero, in which case the type is clearly perfect substitutes, one cannot eliminate any type of preferences. However one can usually conclude something like the following: the preferences could be perfect substitutes, with a particular value of the parameter a (determined by the question and the answer); the preferences could be perfect complements, with a particular value of the parameter a (determined by the question and the answer); the preferences could be Cobb–Douglas, with a particular value of the parameter a (determined by the question and the answer).

Since nothing definite has been inferred by this stage, we repeat the procedure. The teams are invited to write up a second question (a value of p and a value of m) in the second row of the appropriate table on the whiteboard. The choice of p and m in this second question must be made carefully. Some teams will use the same value of p as in their first question, and change the value of m. After getting the other team's demands they realize that this question was stupid in that they have not, and could not have, learned anything from the answer. You should think why not; understanding this is an important part of learning from this game. The teams which have already realized this ask a question with the same value of m and a different value of p from their first question.

At this stage, if the second question has been formulated carefully, it should be possible to infer the type of preferences and, if the preferences are of type 2 (perfect complements) or type 3 (Cobb–Douglas), the value of the parameter a. If, however, the preferences are type 1 it is usually not possible to infer the value of the parameter a. I do not want to give too much away, but this case is difficult; normally you require lots of questions to pin down the value of a precisely.

The team that infers the preferences of the other team first is the winner.

Some hints are given in the appendix, but I would recommend that you do not read these hints until you have played the game. You will learn more if you work through the game yourselves.

You could, of course, make the game more interesting and more difficult by allowing further possible types of preferences. The obvious extension is to include Stone–Geary preferences. This makes it more difficult but more realistic. In practice we do not have a set of preferences from which to choose, so the set of possible preferences could be very large. There are other types of preferences that economists use, which are better approximations to actual preferences for certain people and certain goods, but discussing these would take us beyond the scope of this book.

7.12 Hints Appendix

This provides hints and comments on the game; you are recommended to read it AFTER you have played the game.

You should realise that the demands q_1 and q_2 depend upon p and m but also, and crucially, on the preferences of the individual. You should draw graphs of the relationship between q_1 and m for each of the three types of preferences; and similarly of the relationship between q_2 and m for each of the three types of preferences. What do you see? Nice neat linear relationships for each of the three types of preferences. So the shape of the relationship between demands and income, for the three preferences used in this tutorial, is not affected by the preferences. Why not? This is an interesting question; it tells you that there is no point in changing m when trying to determine the preferences of the other team. However, what do you notice if you draw graphs of the relationship between q_1 and p for each of the three types of preferences? And similarly, what do you notice if you draw graphs of the relationship between q_2 and p for each of the three types of preferences? The shape of the relationships is different for the three different types of preferences. You should work out what they look like. Hint:

● for perfect substitutes, as p rises from 0 then q_1 falls, while q_2 remains zero until p gets to a particular value (what value?), at which point q_1 drops to zero and stays there while q_2 becomes non-zero but constant;

● for perfect complements, as p rises q_1 and q_2 both fall, but in such a way that the ratio q_2/q_1 stays constant;

● for Cobb–Douglas, as p rises q_1 falls and q_2 stays constant, but in such a way that the ratio of expenditures q_2/pq_1 stays constant.

So the shape of the relationships between demands and price, and with more general preferences between demands and income, enables us to infer from demands what the underlying preferences are. Moreover the precise shape of the relationship enables us to detect the value of the parameter a. Note that, with perfect complements, the ratio of quantities demanded, q_2/q_1, is always equal to a; with Cobb–Douglas the ratio of expenditures, p_2q_2/p_1q_1, is always equal to $(1 - a)/a$. What can you say about perfect substitutes?

Exchange

8.1 Introduction

In many ways this chapter is the most important in the book. If you have time to study just one this is the one that you should study, even though it might be a bit difficult studying it on its own. It has a brilliant idea (the Edgeworth box), and it generates an exciting number of important results. It is used over and over again in the rest of the book.

It is exciting and insightful because it portrays, in a very simple way, the benefits that people get out of exchanging things. It shows what exchanges, if any, are possible; which are efficient and which are not; and what exchanges may take place under different institutions. It shows that what economists call perfect competition has some nice properties, while monopoly and monopsony have some less-than-nice properties.

8.2 Exchange

We consider a really simple story. We have an economy in which there are just two individuals and just two goods. Call the individuals A and B, and the goods 1 and 2. The economy is a simple pure-exchange economy – nothing is produced; the individuals wake up in the morning to find that they each have an endowment of each of the two goods. They could, if they wanted, simply consume their initial endowments, or they may find it mutually convenient to do some kind of trade or exchange between the two of them. The purpose of this chapter is to see whether it might be possible to have some mutually advantageous trade and, if so, whether we can offer some advice as to how it might be carried out.

Obviously the answers to these questions will depend upon the preferences of the individuals and their initial endowments. We shall start with a particular example and then try and generalize the results we have obtained. Later we shall present several more specific examples.

8.3 Individual A's Preferences and Endowments

Although we work with a particular example, you should pay attention to the general principles we are using. We start with a statement of the space in which we will be representing these preferences and endowments. This will be the same as we have been using for the last three chapters: with the quantity of good 1, denoted by q_1, along the horizontal axis and the quantity of good 2, denoted by q_2, along the vertical axis.

We now make a statement of individual A's preferences and endowments. We assume in this example that A has an initial endowment of 22 units of good 1 and 92 units of good 2. Further, we assume that A's preferences over these two goods are Cobb–Douglas with parameter $a = 0.7$. This enables us to draw A's indifference curves and endowment point in Fig. 8.1. Note that the endowment point is indicated by the letter E; it is at the point $(22, 92)$

You will note that we have drawn the indifference curve which passes through the initial endowment point (E). This enables us to answer the question:

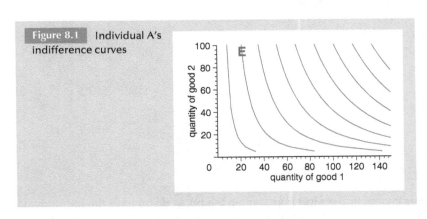

Figure 8.1 Individual A's indifference curves

to where in this space would individual A voluntarily move? The answer is simple: anywhere above and to the right of the indifference curve that passes through the point E.

8.4 Individual B's Preferences and Endowments

We now do the same for Individual B. Here we assume that he or she starts with an initial endowment of 128 units of good 1 and 8 units of good 2. We assume that B also has Cobb–Douglas preferences, but with a weight of just 0.6 on good 1. So B absolutely prefers good 1 but, relative to *A*, prefers good 2. B's indifference map and endowment point are in Fig. 8.2.

Note that B starts at $(128, 8)$. Fig. 8.2 shows the indifference curve passing through the initial point. B would be happy to move to any point above and to the right of this indifference curve.

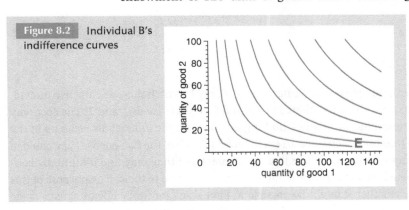

Figure 8.2 Individual B's indifference curves

8.5 The Edgeworth Box

We now do one of the clever things that Edgeworth did – first he turned individual B upside down! This gives us a picture of B's inverted indifference map in Fig. 8.3.

Let us consider carefully what this means. For B, his or her origin – the zero point – is at the top right hand corner of Fig. 8.3. The quantity of good 1 is measured from this top right hand corner leftwards, so the horizontal distance from the top right hand corner to the endowment point E is 128 units; this is the endowment that B has of good 1. In addition, the quantity of good 2 that B has is measured from the top right hand corner downwards, so the vertical distance from the corner to the endowment point E is 8 units – the endowment of good 2 that B has. Obviously the further to the left and the further down, the happier is individual B; B's happiness increases as he or she moves from the top right hand corner – the origin – down and to the left. In Fig. 8.3, lower indifference curves mean more happiness for individual B. It follows that B would be happy to move to any point in this space to the left of and below the indifference curve passing through the initial endowment point E.

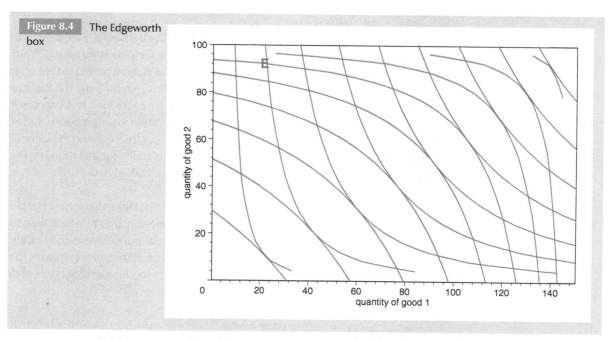

Figure 8.3 Individual B's indifference curves inverted

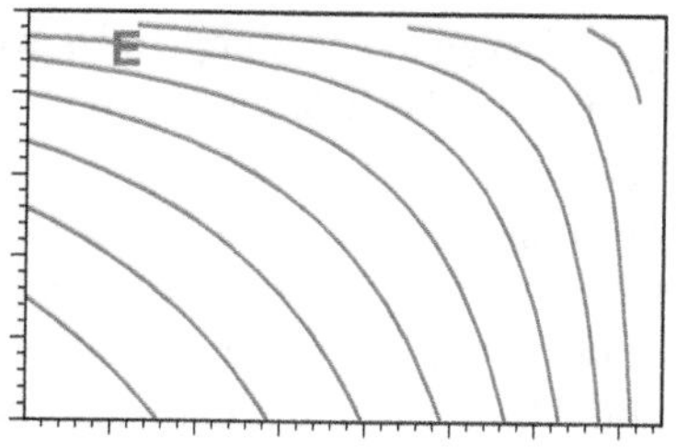

We note that A starts with 22 units of good 1 and 92 of good 2, while B starts with 128 units of good 1 and 8 of good 2. Between the two of them they have a grand total of 150 units of good 1 and 100 of good 2. The problem that we are going to discuss is the division of these 150 units of good 1 and 100 units of good 2 between the two of them given, of course, their initial allocation. To help us in this task we shall use a brilliant device, named the Edgeworth box after its originator.

We have already described one of the clever things that Edgeworth did – namely to turn B upside down; we now describe the second clever thing. He superimposed figure 8.3 on top of figure 8.1 in such a way that the initial endowment points coincided. This is done in Fig. 8.4.

Figure 8.4 The Edgeworth box

We note that the width of this box is the sum of the horizontal distance from A's origin to A's endowment of good 1 (22 units) plus the horizontal distance from B's origin to B's endowment of good 1 (128 units). Thus, the width of the box is the total amount of good 1 that the two individuals possess between them (150 units). We also note that the height of the box is the sum of the vertical distance from A's origin to A's endowment of good 2 (92 units), plus the vertical distance from B's origin to B's endowment of good 2 (8 units). That is, the height of the box is the total amount of good 2 that the two individuals possess between them (100 units). So the dimensions of the box are determined by the total amounts of the two goods that society (the two individuals together) has of the two goods. The width is the total amount of good 1; the height is the total amount of good 2.

Every point in the box represents a distribution of the goods between the two members of society. For example, point E is the initial distribution. The bottom origin (0, 0) represents a distribution in which A gets nothing and B gets everything. The top origin (150, 100) represents a distribution in which A gets everything and B gets nothing. The mid-point (75, 50) represents a distribution in which both A and B end up with 75 units of good 1 and 50 of good 2; they split the total evenly. And so on.

The question is: what happens? Are they happy to stay at point E? Or might they be better off moving to some other point in the space? We have already seen that A would be happy moving to any point to the right and above his or her indifference curve passing though E; similarly, B would be happy moving to any point to the left and below his or her indifference curve passing though E. A glance at Fig. 8.4 shows that there is quite a large region to which both of them would be happy to move. Can we narrow things down a bit?

8.6 The Contract Curve

If you examine Fig. 8.4 you will see that there are points of tangency between the indifference curves of A and those of B. If we join them up we get a very important curve, which is known as the *contract curve*[1]. As its name suggests, this curve indicates the points where some kind of contract – some kind of deal or exchange – might be made between A and B. Why? The contact curve itself is shown in Fig. 8.5

First of all, let us understand the curve's properties. Take any indifference curve of individual A and ask yourself: 'where on this indifference curve for A is B happiest?' Your answer should be: the point where there is an indifference curve of B tangential to that of A; this point, by definition, is on the contract curve. Now do the converse: take any indifference curve of individual B and ask yourself: 'where on this indifference curve for B is A happiest?' The answer? The point where there is an indifference curve of A that is tangential to that of B; and this point, by definition, is on the contract curve. So, the contract curve is the locus of points which are efficient in the sense that, for any given level of utility for individual A, the utility of B is maximized; and for any given level of utility for individual B, the utility of A is maximized.

It follows that points off the contract curve are inefficient. What does this mean? Simply that, from any point off the contract curve, there is always some direction in which we can move and increase the utility of at least one of the individuals without decreasing the utility of the other[2]. To show this, take any point off the contract curve and then move towards the contract curve by moving between an indifference curve of A and an indifference curve of B.

1. We should note that the contract curve is not necessarily the locus of tangency points. More generally, it is the locus of points for which A's utility is maximized given B's level of utility, and where B's utility is maximized given A's level of utility. When the indifference curves are strictly convex this is also the locus of tangency points. But we shall give examples in which the indifference curves are not strictly convex and we shall have to use the more general definition.
2. Actually we can usually say something stronger; that there is always some direction in which we can move and increase the utility of both the individuals.

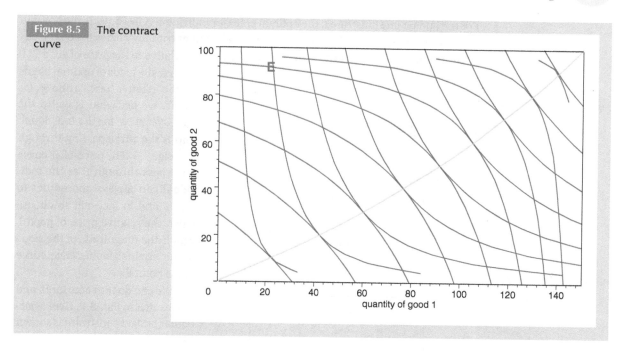

Figure 8.5 The contract curve

Starting at point E provides an obvious example: what happens if we move from E towards the contract curve by moving between A's original indifference curve and B's original indifference curve? The utility of both increases. This is true no matter where we start from, as long as it is off the contract curve. But once we are on the contract curve, we can no longer increase the utility of one individual without decreasing the utility of the other. Try it.

So the contract curve is the locus of efficient points. Points off the contract curve are inefficient in the sense that we can usually make both individuals better off by moving away from that point towards the contract curve. It seems reasonable to conclude that any contract between the two individuals should lie on the contract curve.

We have narrowed things down a lot. It seems we can conclude that any contract should be on the contract curve, between the point where A's original indifference curve intersects it and the point where B's original indifference curve intersects it (neither would accept a deal that made them worse off than at the initial point). Can we narrow things down even further?

One way we can narrow things down further is by imposing a particular trading institution and looking at the implications. An obvious choice, particularly in view of Chapter 2, is that institution called perfect competition. Essentially this is the imposition of a price, which both individuals take as given, such that demand and supply are equal. In the context of this chapter, it is the imposition of a price for which both individuals are happy to move to the same point in the box. If such a price exists, both will be happy to move to the same point and this point will be the chosen allocation. Does such a price exist?

8.7 Price-offer Curves

Let us first consider what individual A would want to do at different prices. A pair of prices – the price of good 1 and the price of good 2 – determines the budget constraint for A (and indeed for B), which has the usual properties; it passes through the initial endowment point E and has a slope equal to $-p_1/p_2$, as shown in Fig. 8.6.

For the budget line illustrated, the optimal point for individual A lies outside the box; but as we rotate the line around the point E, the optimal point eventually comes inside the box and then steadily moves leftward as the price of good 1 rises relative to the price of good 2. If we take the locus of optimal points as the relative price ratio p_1/p_2 varies, we get what is called the *price-offer curve* for the individual. This is the curve passing through E in Fig. 8.6. The price-offer curve must pass through E as the individual can always choose not to move, and in fact will so choose when the relative price of good 1 equals the magnitude of the slope of the original indifference curve at the point E.

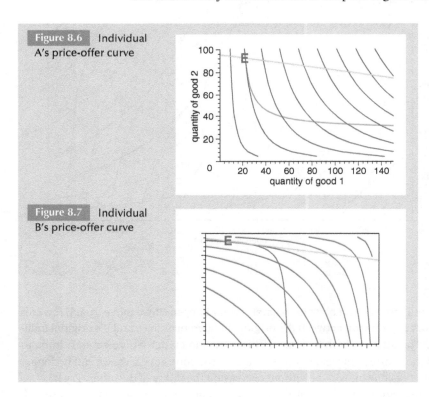

Figure 8.6   Individual A's price-offer curve

Figure 8.7   Individual B's price-offer curve

We can do the same for B, and the result is in Fig. 8.7. Here a particular budget constraint is shown (the straight line through E), and it is clear that the optimal point is on B's price-offer curve, (the curve through E). Once again, the price-offer curve passes through E as the individual can always choose not to move.

8.8   Competitive Equilibrium

We now put the two price-offer curves together and ask whether there is a point where they intersect. If there is, this is the competitive equilibrium which we have been looking for. Does it exist? Fig. 8.8 provides the answer.

There is such a point – and it is on the contract curve! That is interesting, and good news; but is it surprising? Let us call this competitive equilibrium point C; it is the intersection of the two price-offer curves. We know that C is on A's price-offer curve, which means that the budget constraint through the initial point pictured in Fig. 8.8 must be tangential to A's indifference curve at that point. Similarly, we know that C is on B's price-offer curve, which means that the budget constraint through the initial point pictured in the same figure must be tangential to B's indifference curve at that point. If the budget line is tangential to both A's and B's indifference curves, it must follow that A's indifference curve is tangential to B's at point C, and therefore C must be on the contract curve. It is not surprising. We thus have a really nice result; the competitive equilibrium must be on the contract curve and must therefore be efficient.

Let us note the implications of this. The initial point E provided A with 22 units of good 1 and 92 of good 2; and B with 128 units of good 1 and 8 of good 2. As you will see from Fig. 8.8, the competitive equilibrium is at the point (70, 36) when measured from the bottom left origin, and is at the point (80, 64) when measured from the top right origin. In this competitive equilibrium, A will have 70 units of good 1 and 36 of good 2, and B will

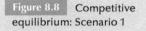

Figure 8.8 Competitive equilibrium: Scenario 1

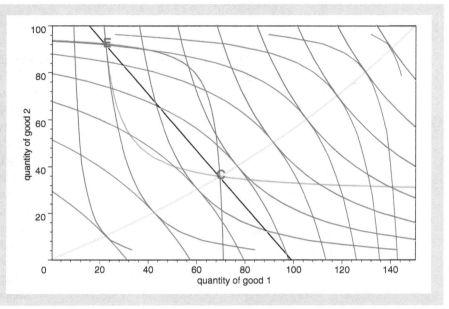

have 80 units of good 1 and 64 of good 2. It might be easier to see all this in a tabular form; see Table 8.1.

What has happened is that individual B has given 48 units of good 1 to A in exchange for 56 units of good 2 which individual A has given to B. The rate of exchange is 48 units of good 1 for 56 units of good 2. The slope of the line joining E and C in Fig. 8.8 determines the exchange rate; this slope equals $-56/48$ which of course is $-p_1/p_2$. So $p_1/p_2 = 56/48 = 1.167$. Good 1 is more expensive than good 2, in the sense that each unit of good 1 is exchanged for more than one unit of good 2.

Table 8.1 Changes between initial and competitive equilibrium allocations

	Individual A	Individual B	Society
Initial allocation			
Good 1	22	128	150
Good 2	92	8	100
Competitive equilibrium allocation			
Good 1	70	80	150
Good 2	36	64	100
Changes between the two allocations			
Good 1	+48	−48	0
Good 2	−56	+56	0

You might like to ask: why is the exchange the way it is – why does A give good 2 to B, and B give good 1 to A? You could simply say that A starts out with lots more of good 2 and B starts out with lots more of good 1. This is true, but it is more to do with where the initial point lies in relation to the contract curve. Indeed, you might like to ask why the contract curve is where it is: why is to the right and below the line joining the two origins? This is a consequence of the fact that the two individuals have different preferences, with B relatively (to A) preferring good 2. Note that both individuals absolutely prefer good 1 – their values of a are greater than 0.5 – but A's is 0.7 while B's is 0.6 so, relative to A, individual B prefers good 2. That is the reason why the contract curve is where it is.

8.9 Price-setting Equilibria

We have investigated one market institution – that of competitive equilibrium. Each agent takes the price as given and we ask whether there is a price at which both individuals want to move to the same point. If so, we have found a competitive equilibrium.

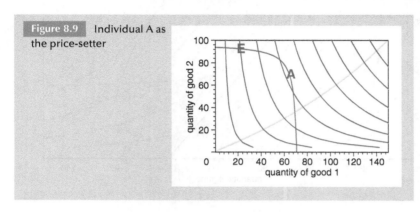

Figure 8.9 Individual A as the price-setter

Now we explore other trading institutions. In particular, we shall explore what happens if we give to one of the individuals the ability to choose the price (the exchange rate). The other individual simply takes the price as given and chooses the point to which he or she will move. This binds the first mover (the price setter) to accept that point. Suppose we give individual A the right to choose the price. He or she knows that individual B will choose the point to which he or she wants to move, and this binds them both. What does A do?

We can argue in this fashion. Given any choice of the price by A, individual B will respond by choosing the point on his or her price-offer curve. So, in essence, A is choosing a point on B's price-offer curve. What point does he or she choose? Consider Fig. 8.9. B's price-offer curve is the curve passing through point E. If A can choose any point on this curve, which point will he or she choose? Obviously, the best point on it relative to A's own indifference curves. Which is the highest position from that point of view? Point A: it is on the highest possible indifference curve of A.

So if A can choose the price, he or she will choose the budget line going from E through A. Given this budget line, B's best response is to choose point A, which is approximately (64, 72) as measured from the bottom left origin and (86, 28) as measured from the top right origin. Table 8.2 shows this information in tabular form.

Table 8.2   Changes between initial allocation and that determined by individual A setting the price

	Individual A	Individual B	Society
Initial allocation			
Good 1	22	128	150
Good 2	92	8	100
Allocation determined by A setting the price			
Good 1	64	86	150
Good 2	72	28	100
Changes between the two allocations			
Good 1	+42	−42	0
Good 2	−20	+20	0

Note what happens: in this allocation individual A gives 20 units of good 2 to B in exchange for 42 units of good 1. Compared to the competitive equilibrium, it is obviously a much better deal for A. This is hardly surprising: A chose it.

So it is better for A but worse for B. But there is something else. We see from Fig. 8.9 that the point chosen by individual A in setting the price – point A – is off the contract curve. It is inefficient! This means that there is some direction from point A in which the individuals can move which will make both of them better off. Why do they not do that? Simply because A is choosing the price, not the point. If A could choose a point then he or she would choose to be on the contract curve just below where it intersects B's original indifference curve. But choosing a price is not the same as choosing a point: choosing a price is choosing a direction to move from point E.

For completeness, we also present the case when B sets the price and A responds by choosing the point; you can probably anticipate the result. In this case B is effectively choosing a point on A's price-offer curve. Which point does he or she choose? Look at Fig. 8.10. B will choose the point on A's price-offer curve (the curve through the point E) which is best from B's point of view; he or she therefore chooses point B, by choosing the budget line going from E through B. What do we notice about point B? First, it implies the trades which are shown in Table 8.3.

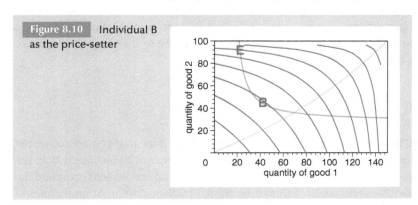

Figure 8.10 Individual B as the price-setter

Table 8.3   Changes between initial allocation and that determined by individual B setting the price

	Individual A	Individual B	Society
Initial allocation			
Good 1	22	128	150
Good 2	92	8	100
Allocation determined by B setting the price			
Good 1	42	108	150
Good 2	45	55	100
Changes between the two allocations			
Good 1	+20	−47	0
Good 2	−47	+20	0

In this exchange, individual A gives 47 units of good 2 to B in exchange for 20 units of good 1. Compared to the competitive equilibrium, it is obviously a much better deal for individual B, which is hardly surprising as it was chosen by B. But, like the point chosen by A, point B is off the contract curve; it is inefficient, and for the same reasons. So price-setting (monopoly or monopsony) by one of the two agents is inefficient, whereas perfect competition is efficient. That is why governments like competition.

8.10 Two Theorems of Welfare Economics

At this stage we can show two important theorems of what is called 'welfare economics'. Welfare economics is the study of the welfare of society and how it can be changed. For simplicity, in stating these theorems I assume that the indifference curves of the agents are everywhere smoothly convex, as in the example we have above. If the indifference curves are not everywhere smoothly convex then the theorems may not be true. You might like to think about this and perhaps provide some examples.

These theorems are an immediate and important implication of the result that we derived above – that the competitive equilibrium is necessarily on the contract curve. This result implies the first theorem of welfare economics, namely that 'whatever the initial allocation, price-taking trade takes us to a point on the contract curve and hence is Pareto efficient.' [3]. This is an important and interesting proposition. It implies that, if we have the market institution of competitive trading, the resulting outcome will be efficient. It is for this reason that governments like competition and encourage it. The second theorem of welfare economics is a sort of converse: it states that 'any point on the contract curve can be reached by competitive trading from some (in fact many) initial allocations.' This too is important, as it implies that a government can achieve any desired efficient point (one on the contract curve) by taxing people appropriately, and then leaving the rest to the competitive system. Precise planning is not required.

8.11 Alternative Scenarios

We have worked throughout with a particular example, but I hope that you are convinced that the results must be true in general. One thing which may not be obvious is how the competitive equilibrium allocation depends upon both the initial endowment point and the preferences of the two individuals. This can be shown mathematically (a mathematical derivation is provided in the mathematical appendix to this chapter), but I prefer to give you some further examples. This section, therefore, gives a number of further examples (I call them scenarios) in which endowments and/or preferences differ. From these you will be able to see how endowments and preferences affect the competitive equilibrium allocation. The results are not surprising: if one good becomes more abundant then its price falls; if one individual changes his or her preferences in such a way that they like a good more than before, the price of that good rises.

Let us turn to the second scenario. This differs from the first in that the preferences of individual B are changed; the Cobb–Douglas parameter is changed from 0.6 to 0.3. So individual B now absolutely prefers good 2 to good 1, and relative to A who has a parameter a equal to 0.7, B even more prefers good 2 to good 1 than in the first scenario. As a conse-

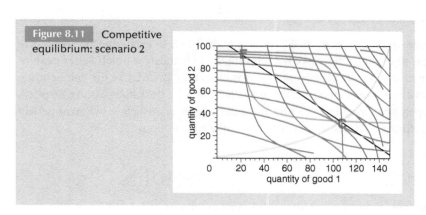

Figure 8.11   Competitive equilibrium: scenario 2

quence, the contract curve is even more convex and further away from the line that joins the two origins of the box. You will see in Fig. 8.11 where the competitive equilibrium lies. It is denoted it by C, as in scenario 1, and it remains at the intersection of the contract curve and the two price-offer curves.

In this competitive equilibrium, A ends up with more of good 1 than in scenario 1 (we

3. An allocation is said to be effective in the sense of Pareto if it is impossible to find another allocation at which one individual is strictly better off and the other no worse off than at the original point.

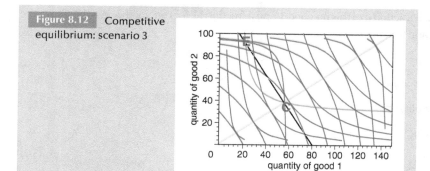

Figure 8.12 Competitive equilibrium: scenario 3

note that the budget line joining E and C is flatter) so that the equilibrium price of good 1 is lower. This occurs because B likes good 1 less than previously.

In scenario 3 we allow the two individuals to have identical tastes, but the same endowments as in scenario 1. It follows that the contract curve is the straight line joining the two origins. With Cobb–Douglas preferences this is always the case[4]. We thus have the situation pictured in Fig. 8.12.

The competitive equilibrium is on the line joining the two origins so individual A gets some 40 per cent of good 1 and 40 per cent of good 2, while B gets around 60 per cent of each. In this scenario individual A does relatively badly as he or she starts with rather little of good 1, which happens to be the good that both individuals prefer.

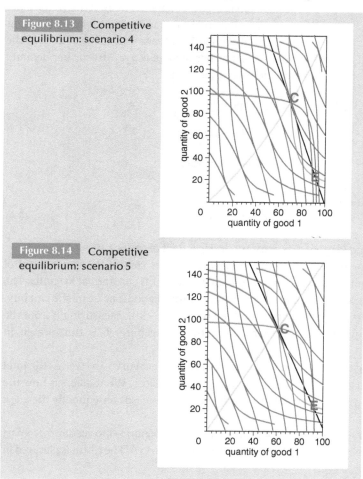

Figure 8.13 Competitive equilibrium: scenario 4

Figure 8.14 Competitive equilibrium: scenario 5

Scenario 4 is the same as scenario 1 in terms of preferences, but the endowments are rearranged so that A starts out with most of good 1 and B starts out with most of good 2; see Fig. 8.13. You will see that the competitive equilibrium more or less corrects this.

Scenario 5 has the same endowments as Scenario 4 but the two individuals have identical preferences, so the contract curve is the straight line joining the two origins. Once again, as Fig. 8.14 shows, the competitive equilibrium is on this line.

The next three scenarios are interesting in that we return to the totals in Scenario 1 (150 units of good 1 and 100 units of good 2), but we assume that individual A starts out with all 100 units of good 2 while B starts out with all 150 units of good 1. This is an interesting case in that the price-offer curve of A is horizontal, while that for B is vertical. Why is this?

Consider individual A: suppose the Cobb–Douglas parameter is a and he or she has an initial endowment of zero of good 1 and e_2 of good 2. Then the value of A's income is $p_2 e_2$, and we know that he or she

4. Indeed it is always true with identical *homothetic* preferences (though you do not need to know what homothetic preferences are). They are defined in the mathematical appendix.

wants to spend a fraction a of this on good 1 and a fraction $(1 - a)$ on good 2. We thus have the following demand functions.

$$q_1 = ap_2e_2/p_1$$
$$q_2 = (1 - a)p_2e_2/p_2 \qquad (8.1)$$

From (8.1) we obtain

$$q_1 = ap_2e_2/p_1$$
$$q_2 = (1 - a)e_2 \qquad (8.2)$$

Note what the second of these says: that the demand for good 2 is constant, independent of the prices, and is always equal to a fixed fraction of the initial endowment.

In Scenario 6, the value of A's parameter a is 0.7. Therefore A always wants to spend a fraction 30 per cent of his initial endowment on good 2; the initial endowment of good 2 is 100, so A always wants just 30 units of good 2. He or she sells the rest (70 units), and buys as many units as possible of good 1 with the proceeds. Hence the horizontal price-offer curve for individual A (see Fig. 8.15).

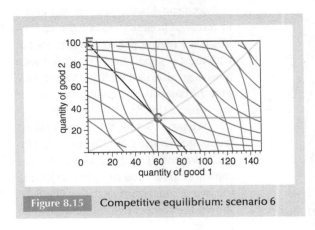

Figure 8.15   Competitive equilibrium: scenario 6

A similar argument applies for B. If the value of the parameter is a and he or she starts with an endowment of e_1 units of good 1 and zero units of good 2, then the value of his or her income is p_1e_1. His or her demand functions are therefore:

$$q_1 = ap_1e_1/p_1$$
$$q_2 = (1 - a)p_1e_1/p_2 \qquad (8.3)$$

From these we obtain

$$q_1 = ae_1$$
$$q_2 = (1 - a)p_1e_1/p_2 \qquad (8.4)$$

We note that the demand for good 1 is constant, independent of the prices.

In Scenario 6, a for B is 0.6 so he or she retains 60 per cent of the endowment of good 1; the endowment is 150 units; so the demand for good 1 is constant at 90 units. The remaining 60 units are sold in exchange for as many units of good 2 as he or she can buy. Thus the price-offer curve is vertical at the value 60 (= 150 − 90), measuring B from the top right origin. Taking all this together, the picture of scenario 6 is that drawn in Fig. 8.15.

We should note that the preferences – and hence the contract curve – as well as the total endowments of the two goods are the same as those in Scenario 1. What differs is how the endowments are initially allocated: we have a different allocation, so consequently there is a different competitive equilibrium.

The relationship of scenario 7 is to scenario 2 is that of scenario 6 to scenario 1, apart from the initial endowment, which is the same as that in scenario 6. The result is pictured in Fig. 8.16.

Similarly, the relationship of scenario 8 to scenario 3 is that of scenario 6 to scenario 1, again apart from the initial endowment which is the same as that in scenario 6. The situation is illustrated in Fig. 8.17. The two individuals have identical tastes, so the contract curve is the straight line joining the two origins.

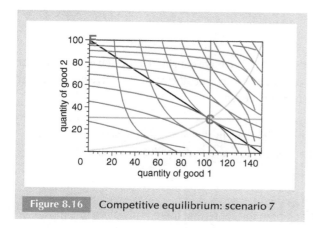

Figure 8.16 Competitive equilibrium: scenario 7

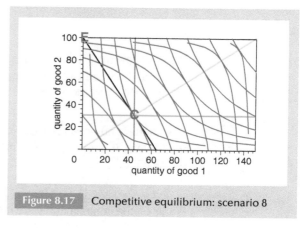

Figure 8.17 Competitive equilibrium: scenario 8

8.12 Comments

It should be clear that there are almost always possibilities for exchange. Only when the initial allocation point lies on the contract curve are such possibilities absent. Even when preferences are identical, so that the contract curve joins the two origins of the box, there will usually be the possibility of trade – unless the initial point is on the contract curve, for example when the endowments are identical so that we start at the middle point of the box. Even when the endowments are identical so that the initial point is in the centre of the box, there will usually be the possibility of trade unless the contract curve also passes through the centre of the box (as when preferences are identical). So, as long as *people are different*, we will generally have mutually advantageous trade.

This chapter paid particular attention to the competitive trading mechanism – showing that it is efficient and leads to trade on the contract curve. We also saw that price-setting (monopoly or monopsony) behaviour is inefficient. There are obviously other trading mechanisms and you might like to consider what their properties are.

8.13 Summary

We have covered a lot of ground in this chapter. We have considered the general problem of exchange between two individuals, and used the clever device of the Edgeworth box to examine this. We also discovered the contract curve.

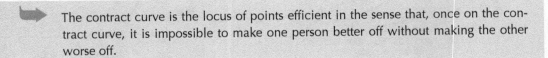 The contract curve is the locus of points efficient in the sense that, once on the contract curve, it is impossible to make one person better off without making the other worse off.

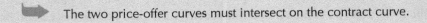 Points off the contract curve are inefficient in the sense that there is always some movement which makes at least one person better off without making the other worse off.

We have shown that the competitive equilibrium is on the contract curve.

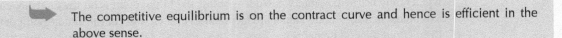 The two price-offer curves must intersect on the contract curve.

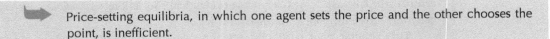 The competitive equilibrium is on the contract curve and hence is efficient in the above sense.

Price-setting equilibria, in which one agent sets the price and the other chooses the point, is inefficient.

Moreover, and very importantly, we have the condition.

The competitive equilibrium depends upon the preferences and the endowments.

8.14 Review Questions

1. What were the two clever things that Edgeworth did when constructing his box?

2. What determines the width of the box? What determines the height of the box?

3. Do the two individuals start at the same point in the box? (You should know that the answer to this is 'yes' because a point in the box represents a distribution of the resources available in the economy between the two individuals; the initial point represents the initial distribution.)

4. If the individuals start with the same endowments, where is the initial distribution or endowment point?

5. If the preferences are convex and identical, show that the contract curve must pass through the centre of the box. If the endowments are also identical, show that no trade is possible.

6. Is any other no-trade starting point possible?

8.15 Application: is Equality good? Is Planning good?

There are two propositions that many people consider self-evident: the first is that equality is a good thing and hence inequality is a bad thing; the second is that planning an economy is good for the people in the society, and hence leaving people open to market forces is bad. While these propositions may be true in some instances, we explore here whether there are situations in which they are not true. We use the apparatus of this chapter, and consider a very simple pure-exchange economy in which there are just two individuals; the individuals, crucially, are different.

There are two goods in this society, good 1 and good 2, and two individuals, A and B. We assume that there is available in the society a quantity of 100 units of good 1 and 100 units of good 2 to allocate between the two individuals. We ask whether the allocation of 50 units of each good to each individual, and the consequent consumption of these quantities, is a good thing or not. That is: is planning plus equality necessarily a Good Thing?

We assume that the individuals are different in their preferences; specifically, individual A has Cobb–Douglas preferences with parameter $a = 0.7$ (that is, a weight 0.7 on good 1 and a weight 0.3 on good 2), while B has Cobb–Douglas preferences with parameter $a = 0.3$ (a weight 0.3 on good 1 and 0.7 on good 2). So individual A relatively prefers good 1 while B relatively prefers good 2. Having a difference in the preferences is important and drives what follows. If the preferences were identical, the two propositions that we are examining become rather self-evident. But we know that, in the real world, *people are different.*

We use the apparatus of this chapter to investigate the allocation of the 100 units of good 1 and the 100 units of good 2 between the two individuals. We use an Edgeworth box of size 100 by 100, in which we measure individual A's consumption from the bottom left-hand origin and individual B's consumption from the top right-hand corner of the box. Every point within the box is an allocation of the 100 units of good 1 and 100 units of good 2 between the two individuals. Consider now a planned allocation, in which both individuals are given and consume 50 units each of each good. This allocation is point E at the centre of the Edgeworth box in Fig. 8.18.

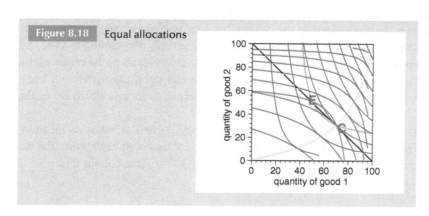

Figure 8.18 Equal allocations

The question is: are the two individuals happy to stay at this point, or would they prefer to be exposed to market forces? The answer depends on what these market forces are. If we have a competitive market, in which each individual takes the price as given, and we seek an equilibrium price at which both individuals would agree to a particular exchange, we can see that the answer must be 'yes'. The competitive equilibrium of this allocation problem is the point C in Fig. 8.18. It is on the contract curve, and is at the intersection of the two price-offer curves. At C, individual A consumes 70 of good 1 and 30 of good 2, while individual B consumes 30 of good 1 and 70 of good 2. In equilibrium the relative price of the two goods is one, and the slope of the line joining E with C is minus one. You might like to ask where these numbers (70 and 30, 30 and 70) come from; you should recall the preferences of the two individuals. We end up at an unequal allocation, having started at a planned equal allocation; and both individuals prefer the unequal allocation to the equal allocation. Inequality is not necessarily bad; market forces are not necessarily bad.

Indeed, you might like to argue that point C is in a sense the best allocation in the box; we started with an equal allocation and ended up, after trading at the competitive price, at a point they both prefer to the initial allocation. It is interesting to note that we could end up at this best point even if we have an initial allocation that is clearly not the same for the two individuals. For example, suppose we start with A having all 100 units of good 2, which he or she relatively dislikes, and B having all 100 units of good 1, which he or she relatively dislikes. See the situation shown in Fig. 8.19. Notice also that in both equilibria, the implicit

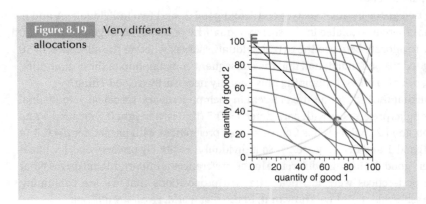

Figure 8.19 Very different allocations

prices of the two goods are equal; their relative price (minus the slope of the line joining the endowment point and the equilibrium point) is one.

Furthermore it is clear that it does not matter where we start as long as it is some point on the equilibrium budget constraint – the line joining the top left-hand corner of the box with the bottom right-hand corner. It is interesting to note that, at each point on this line, the values of the endowments of the two individuals are equal (at the equilibrium price ratio). So we could argue that this is truly a fair, though not necessarily equal (in terms of consumption) situation; start at any point on this equilibrium budget constraint and let the competitive market do the rest.

Obviously a planner could also find the point C if the preferences of the two individuals were known. Clearly point C depends on these preferences, and if the plan miscalculates them it will miscalculate the point C. One advantage of the market solution is that the government does not need to know the preferences of the individuals; it just needs to start them off on the equilibrium budget constraint. In a sense this is cheating since the equilibrium budget constraint is also dependent on the preferences; here we have chosen an example in which the equilibrium price ratio just happens to be one, but this does not have to be the case. Nevertheless the government can try and start the two individuals at the centre of the box and leave the competitive market to do the rest. We end up, if the individuals have different preferences, at a necessarily unequal consumption point; but one which we might argue is fair.

There are other qualifications which we should make; in particular, what we mean by market forces. If one of the two individuals can set the price, it may well be the case that we end up at an unsatisfactory equilibrium. Perhaps you would like to think about this.

8.16 Mathematical Appendix

Here we provide a solution to the general problem of competitive exchange between two individuals with Cobb–Douglas preferences. Let us denote the endowments (e_1, e_2) for individual A, and (f_1, f_2) for individual B. Let us suppose that A has Cobb–Douglas preferences with parameter a, and that B has Cobb–Douglas preferences with parameter b. Do recall that the parameter indicates the relative weight that the individual places on good 1, whilst the relative weight on good 2 is $(1 - a)$ or $(1 - b)$. From the material in Chapter 6 we know that A's gross demands for the two goods are as follows.

$$q_1 = a(p_1 e_1 + p_2 e_2/p_1$$
$$q_2 = (1 - a)(p_1 e_1 + p_2 e_2)/p_2 \qquad \text{(A8.1)}$$

B's gross demands are given in Eq. (A8.2)

$$q_1 = b(p_1 f_1 + p_2 f_2)/p_1$$
$$q_2 = (1 - b)(p_1 f_1 + p_2 f_2)/p_2 \qquad \text{(A8.2)}$$

From these we can calculate the aggregate gross demand for good 1 and impose the market-clearing equilibrium condition that aggregate gross demand should equal aggregate supply of good 1, which is $(e_1 + f_1)$. This gives us the following equilibrium condition.

$$a(p_1 e_1 + p_2 e_2)/p_1 + b(p_1 f_1 + p_2 f_2)/p_1 = e_1 + f_1 \qquad \text{(A8.3)}$$

This is an equation which can be solved for the price ratio p_2/p_1 which gives equilibrium in the market for good 1. Solving it yields:

$$p_2/p_1 = [(1 - a)e_1 + (1 - b)f_1]/(ae_2 + bf_2) \qquad \text{(A8.4)}$$

Before discussing the implications of this, let us derive the market-clearing condition for good 2. Imposing the same condition that aggregate gross demand for good 2 equals supply, from Eq. (A8.1) and Eq. (A8.2) we have the following equilibrium conditions, which are the equivalent to Eq. (A8.3).

$$(1 - a)(p_1 e_1 + p_2 e_2)/p_2 + (1 - b)(p_1 f_1 + p_2 f_2)/p_2 = e_2 + f_2 \qquad \text{(A8.5)}$$

If we solve (A8.5) for the implied equilibrium price ratio p_2/p_1 we get ... Eq. (A8.4)! Is this a surprise? Clearly not. If the market for good 1 is in equilibrium, so must be the market for good 2. You should check this out. Suppose the equilibrium in the market for good 1 has individual A giving x units to B, and B receiving x units from A; then it must be the case that individual A will receive y units of good 2 which individual B is giving in exchange, where $p_1 x = p_2 y$.

Now let us examine this equilibrium condition, after noticing that it is a condition on the relative prices of goods 1 and 2 (which determines the slope of the equilibrium budget constraint). From Eq. (A8.4) we see that

p_2/p_1 increases if either of e_1 or f_1 increases, and

p_2/p_1 decreases if any of e_2, f_2, a or b increases.

The first says that if good 1 becomes more plentiful its relative price decreases. The second says:

- if good 2 becomes more plentiful then its relative prices decreases;
- if good 1 becomes more preferred by either individual (either a or b increases), then the relative price of good 1 increases;
- if good 2 becomes more preferred by either individual (either a or b decreases), then the relative price of good 2 increases.

All of these accord with intuition.

Welfare

9.1 Introduction

Welfare economics is the treatment of welfare issues in economics. It concerns the appropriate allocation of resources within an economy and tries to answer the question: is there a 'best' allocation of resources? The importance of the chapter lies in the fact that it points out how far we can go in economics, and how much we have to rely on value judgements from others on distributional issues. As economists we can say more than many people would realize, but there are limits to what we can say without outside advice.

9.2 Aggregation of Preferences

We are discussing the appropriate allocation of resources within an economy. In Chapter 8 we were able to conclude that any contract between the two individuals ought to be on the contract curve because that is the locus of efficient points. Any point off the contract curve is inefficient and can be improved upon by some movement away from that point. But this does not define a unique point – because the contract curve is a set of points. The question which we address in this chapter is how society chooses between these various allocations along the contract curve.

When put in this stark way, particularly when we are dealing with an economy of two individuals, it may seem that there is no obvious answer unless we are prepared to say something about the relative merits of the two individuals. However we can show that there are special cases when we can say something, although there is a limit as to how far we can go; the rest is the job of politicians. But we need to be clear why this is so.

To economists, the nature of the problem with two individuals is obvious; there is a conflict of interest between the two agents; when one gets more the other gets less. But this conflict hides a more serious question: is there any way that we can derive the preferences of society from the preferences of the people that make up that society? Can we aggregate, in some sense, the preferences of individuals to obtain the preferences of society?

This is an important question and one that has occupied economists and philosophers and political scientists for some time in the past, and will doubtless continue to occupy them in the future. It seems to me that the only case where we can be sure that we can aggregate individual's preferences is when all individuals have the same preferences. In this case, society's preferences must coincide with those of every individual.

If different people have different preferences, it can be shown that there is no universally agreed way of aggregating those preferences into society's preferences. There is a well-known theorem – referred to as Arrow's impossibility theorem – which won Arrow a Nobel Prize in 1972 and which proves this very result. In essence, Arrow showed the following.

If we accept the axioms:
- if individual preferences exist, then so should Society's;
- if everyone prefers x to y, then so should Society;
- Society's preference between x and y should depend only on individual preferences between x and y;

then it follows that Society's ranking is that of one individual; in other words, we have dictatorship.

This is an important and influential result. Of course in practice societies adopt ways of aggregating preferences. These are embodied in the constitution of the society and determine how decisions are made. For example, some societies adopt a system of majority voting to determine what is decided.

But such mechanisms have flaws, which we can show with a particular example. Consider a majority voting system applied in a society where there are three individuals A, B and C, and in which there are three proposals: x, y and z. One and only one proposal is to be implemented. Suppose that the three individuals have the following preferences:

$$\begin{bmatrix} \text{A prefers } x \text{ to } y \text{ to } z \\ \text{B prefers } y \text{ to } z \text{ to } x \\ \text{C prefers } z \text{ to } x \text{ to } y \end{bmatrix}$$

What does the majority voting society choose or prefer?

We see there is a problem here: a majority of society (A and C) prefer x to y; a majority (A and B) prefer y to z; and a majority (B and C) prefer z to x. So what does society choose?

The problem is the aggregation rule. Arrow's theorem guarantees that, for any rule, we can find similarly odd examples.

9.3 Social Welfare Functions

The discussion above leads to the conclusion that there is in general no way that we can aggregate preferences to get an undisputed set of preferences for society. Perhaps this is an obvious implication of the fact that different people have different preferences, and that there will in general be a conflict between them. It also seems to accord with what we observe in society; if there was such an undisputed social welfare function such as a rule for aggregating individual preferences, then it would be embodied in the constitution of that society. In that case there would be no need for politicians!

But there are politicians. And what they disagree about is the way preferences should be aggregated. How they differ is precisely in how they approach this aggregation procedure. We could argue that this is the role of politicians – to define the social welfare function that they intend to use.

One way to do this is as follows: suppose that there are N people in society $n = 1, 2, ..., N$. Let us denote the utility of individual n by u_n. Then a social welfare function is simply a way of aggregating these individual utilities into society's function. In general, the welfare W of society is given by

$$W = f(u_1, u_2, ..., u_N) \tag{9.1}$$

In Eq. (9.1), f is some function increasing in its various arguments[1].

Different political parties will have different views as to the form of this function – and indeed this is precisely what distinguishes one political party from another. For example, a party which was exclusively concerned with the least well-off members of society might have the following function[2].

$$W = \min(u_1, u_2, ..., u_N) \tag{9.2}$$

One popular function is the 'classic utilitarian' form, which is Eq. (9.3).

$$W = u_1 + u_2 + \cdots + u_N \tag{9.3}$$

This form treats all individuals equally. By contrast, some parties think that different members of society ought to be given different weights, so for them a social welfare function would be:

$$W = a_1 u_1 + a_2 u_2 + \cdots + a_N u_N \tag{9.4}$$

In Eq. (9.4), a_n are positive weights reflecting the assumed importance of the members of the society.

Once we have a social welfare function we can choose the optimal allocation. This depends in part on the choices available to society. In the previous chapter we agreed that, whatever allocation is chosen, it should be on the contract curve[3]. As we moved along the contract curve, the utility of one individual increased while that of the other decreased. If we know the utility functions of the two individuals, we can calculate the utility of each individual at every point on the contract curve, and hence construct the *utility possibility frontier* available to society. In the example that follows, we specify the utility functions of A and B in Eq. (9.5).

A $U(q_1, q_2) = q_1^{0.56} q_2^{0.24}$

B $U(q_1, q_2) = q_1^{0.54} q_2^{0.36}.$ \hfill (9.5)

Fig. 9.1 shows the consumption levels of A and B and their indifference curves, all within an Edgeworth box. Individual A's consumption is measured from the bottom left origin, and that of individual B from the top right origin. Society has a total of 100 units of good 1 and 100 units of good 2. At the bottom left origin, A's utility is 0 and B's utility is $100^{0.54} \times 100^{0.36} = 100^{0.9} = 63.01$; at the top right origin, A's utility is $100^{0.56} \times 100^{0.24} = 100^{0.8} = 39.81$ and that of B is 0.

In Fig. 9.2 we draw society's utility possibility frontier with A's utility on the horizontal axis and B's on the vertical axis; this frontier goes from $(39.81, 0)$ to $(0, 63.01)$. In between, we can calculate the utility values at any point along the contract curve; one point is given in Fig. 9.1, with utility of 4.57 for A and 59.4 for B, and we can plot these against each other to give the frontier[4]. It is shown in Fig. 9.2.

---

1. An argument of a function is simply some variable which enters that function.
2. Called a Rawlsian welfare function after its originator, John Rawls.
3. Note that all the possible welfare functions that we have listed imply the result that the point chosen will be on the contract curve, since all the welfare functions are increasing (strictly, non-decreasing) in the utility of each member of society. Indeed it seems reasonable to argue that all reasonable social welfare functions must have this property, as it is one definition of 'reasonable'.
4. These figures are calculated by inserting the co-ordinates of the point on the contract curve into the two utility functions.

Figure 9.1   Along the contract curve

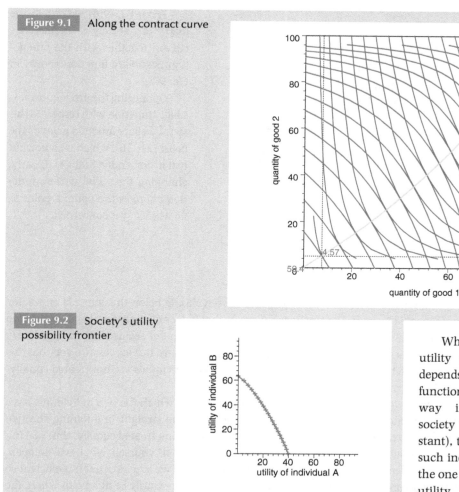

Figure 9.2   Society's utility possibility frontier

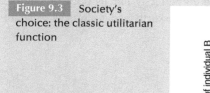

Where is the best point on the utility possibility frontier? This depends upon society's welfare function. If we define in the usual way indifference curves for society (defined by utility = constant), then we can draw a set of such indifference curves and find the one that is highest – given the utility possibility frontier in Fig. 9.2.

For example, suppose we work with the classic utilitarian form Eq. (9.3). For a society in which $N = 2$, the indifference curves are given by the formula $u_1 + u_2$ = constant. These are rather familiar; they form a set of straight lines with slope[5] equal to -1. The highest attainable one is illustrated in Fig. 9.3; the optimal point is around (5, 60). Individual B seems to do rather well in this society!

Figure 9.3   Society's choice: the classic utilitarian function

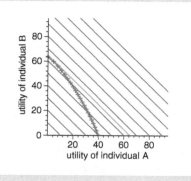

Obviously if we change the social welfare function, in general we shall change the welfare maximizing point. For example, working with the Nash welfare function appropriate for two people gives us the following function.

$$W = u_1 u_2 \qquad (9.6)$$

5. They should remind you of perfect 1:1 substitutes; this is effectively what classic utilitarianism is saying about different members of society – they are all equal.

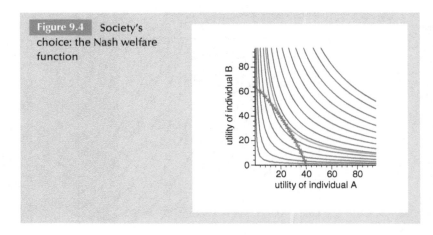

Figure 9.4 Society's choice: the Nash welfare function

From Eq. (9.6) we obtain the map of Society's indifference curves, together with the production possibility function shown in Fig. 9.4.

Optimizing the production possibility function with respect to this social welfare function gives us the point (21, 36), which is somewhat better for individual A. Clearly, changing the social welfare function changes the optimal point as far as society is concerned.

9.4 Is Inequality Bad?

The above discussion confirms that the point chosen should be on the contract curve, for otherwise it could be improved upon; and we note that it does not necessarily imply that the individuals should be treated equally. Perhaps this latter point seems a bit odd, and very dependent on the social welfare function adopted by politicians. But to reassure you that this is not the case, let us consider a situation in which the individuals are not treated equally, but are still happy nonetheless.

We take a two-person case and consider a situation in which the two individuals have different preferences, so that the contract curve is not the straight line joining the two corners of the box. Suppose we start with the individuals being treated equally, thus placing the initial endowment point at the centre of the box. Ask yourself what will happen. Obviously this depends upon the trading mechanism, but if we suppose that it is efficient so that we end up on the contract curve, it will clearly and necessarily be at a point where the two individuals are consuming different quantities of the two goods. One will be consuming more of good 1, and the other more of good 2. The reason is that we have assumed that they have different preferences.

Is this unequal outcome bad? Clearly not as both prefer it to the original position, which you could argue was fair because they were both given equal endowments. So the final outcome, while unequal, can be considered perfectly fair as both individuals prefer it to the original fair situation. Inequality is not necessarily bad, as long as *people are different*.

9.5 Measuring Utility

You might have noticed a problem with Section 9.3, though not Section 9.4: to make sense of it, we need utility to be measurable. Unfortunately we decided in Chapter 5 that, in general, this is not possible. While we could represent preferences with utility functions, such a representation was not unique. Indeed we decided that we could transform a utility function with any monotonically increasing function, and it would still represent the same preferences.

To implement the social welfare material discussed earlier, we (or, strictly speaking, politicians – for it is they who are implementing it) need to make preferences measurable and comparable. Or, perhaps simpler, we need to do something like making the social welfare function directly a function of consumption. Ultimately we need to be able to compare the happiness or utility (call it what you will) of different people. I do not really think that is something that economists can do; but at least we can make it explicit that that is what the politicians have to do, and do.

9.6 Summary

We have achieved a little, but it is still important. In particular we have concluded that something is not possible.

 Arrow's impossibility theorem shows that in general it is not possible to aggregate individual preferences into a society preference.

However the use of social welfare functions helps us to choose between allocations, although subject to the following condition:

 ... this requires that utility is measurable and comparable.

The allocation implied may be unequal, but we have shown that this is not necessarily unacceptable to members of society.

 An unequal allocation is not necessarily unfair.

9.7 Review Questions

① Why is it impossible to aggregate preferences if preferences differ?

② Why is it impossible for economists to decide whether particular distributions are fair?

③ In what sense, relative to the material of this chapter, do political parties differ?

④ If the social welfare function is not reasonable in the sense defined in this chapter (that is, is increasing in the utility of each member of society), why might the implied best allocation not be on the utility possibility frontier?

⑤ Why might an unequal distribution not be unfair? (Because *people are different*.)

9.8 Application: how can the Committee Chairman Manipulate the Outcome?

This is not really an application of economics, but rather a demonstration of the main result of the chapter; we cannot derive preferences for society solely from the preferences of the individuals within that society. We show this in an oblique way, by showing that, given some rules for deciding between possibilities, the person who decides the order in which decisions are taken can manipulate the outcome. Accordingly, that person becomes a dictator. We therefore have an indirect demonstration of the importance and relevance of Arrow's impossibility theorem.

Consider a society in which there are five individuals: A, B, C, D and E; and five possibilities: a, b, c, d and e, of which one must be chosen. Obviously if the five individuals have the same preferences over the five outcomes there is nothing to discuss. So, let us assume that preferences differ; specifically, let us assume that the individuals have the following preferences.

$$\begin{bmatrix} \text{A prefers } a \text{ to } b \text{ to } c \text{ to } d \text{ to } e \\ \text{B prefers } b \text{ to } c \text{ to } d \text{ to } e \text{ to } a \\ \text{C prefers } c \text{ to } d \text{ to } e \text{ to } a \text{ to } b \\ \text{D prefers } d \text{ to } e \text{ to } a \text{ to } b \text{ to } c \\ \text{E prefers } e \text{ to } a \text{ to } b \text{ to } c \text{ to } d \end{bmatrix}$$

You should note that a majority of the society prefers a to b; a majority prefers b to c; a majority prefers c to d; a majority prefers d to e; and a majority prefers e to a. You should note also that, if we rank each option from 1 for the most preferred to 5 for the least preferred in each individual's preferences, and count the average rank of each option, we find that all five options have an average rank of 3, and thus are ranked equally by society on this criterion.

You could do this exercise with a friend. The friend chooses the rule by which decisions are taken and you (as the committee chairman) choose the order in which decisions are taken. As committee chairman you have the power to make a casting vote if the outcome of the decision is a tie. Suppose you want option a to be chosen, can you choose an order to achieve your desired outcome? Or, alternatively, can your friend devise a set of rules that stops you from achieving your desired outcome?

This obviously depends upon the set of rules that your friend can choose. These rules must be generic and cannot relate to the specific problem under discussion. One such rule could be the following: decisions are taken sequentially between pairs of options; the option not chosen is rejected and not discussed further; decisions are by majority voting. This is a very common rule in practice.

What you should do as chairman in this case is clear. You organize the voting in the following order:

$$\begin{bmatrix} \text{between } d \text{ and } e; \\ \text{between } c \text{ and } d; \\ \text{between } b \text{ and } c; \\ \text{between } a \text{ and } b. \end{bmatrix}$$

Note what happens: d wins the first vote because a majority prefer it; c wins the second because a majority prefer it; b wins the third; and a wins the fourth and last. In the meantime, all the other options are excluded and your preferred option wins.

If your friend says that all options should be considered simultaneously and the decision taken by the average rank, then all options tie and you, as chairman, have the casting vote. Again, you get what you want.

Your friend could come up with other generic rules. The question for each of these is: can you choose the order of voting to get your way? Therefore, can a set of rules be drawn up to stop you manipulating the outcome? If it can in this instance, is it sufficiently robust regarding changes in the preferences?

part

2

Economies with Production

2.1 Summary

Part 2 stays in a competitive world but introduces production into the story, starting with a description of technology; that is, the relationship between inputs and outputs. We discuss a number of different types of technology, and then introduce the important concept of a cost function which tells us, for any given technology and any other constraints, the cheapest cost of producing any given output. This determines a firm's optimal demands for the inputs it uses. We show how this cost function is related to the technology of the firm, and hence that we can use this information to help us infer the technology of a firm from its cost function and, later, from its supply curve. This information helps us prescribe and predict. Having discussed the properties of the cost function and various other derived cost functions, we show how the optimal output of the firm is determined, and hence obtain its supply function. This allows us to confirm that the profit (surplus) of the firm is the area between the price received and the supply curve. Finally we move on to consider the production possibility frontier in an economy producing two goods with two factors of production.

2.2 Detail

This part adds production to the pure-exchange economy discussed in Part 1. Instead of simply exchanging goods, we allow production which permits the transformation of inputs into outputs. We could allow the one agent to do both the transforming and consuming, but here we assume that there exists division of labour; firms exist to transform inputs into outputs, while consumers or households consume outputs. At the same time households contribute one of the most important inputs into the production process, namely labour. Accordingly we tell the basic story of most capitalist economies: firms demand inputs and supply outputs; households supply labour inputs and demand outputs. In this part we show that the properties of supply functions relating to surplus carry over into the area of production. We also get an extra problem to solve; in addition to the efficient allocation of a given set of goods, we need to determine the efficient allocation of inputs to the production of goods, and also choose the set of goods to produce. We shall demonstrate this using Edgeworth boxes within production possibility frontiers.

Chapter 10 Firms and Technology: We discuss the concept of a firm: what it is and what it does; how it transforms inputs into outputs so that the set of goods available for exchange is enlarged. The chapter then concentrates on the process of transformation, and discusses it under the heading of the technology available. We describe technology through isoquants graphed in input space, and draw analogies with indifference curves. We present a number of different technologies, which vary according to the relationship of, and substitutability between, inputs. These include: perfect substitutes; perfect complements; Cobb–Douglas; and the constant elasticity of substitution form. We also introduce and illustrate the important concept of returns to scale.

Chapter 11 Cost Minimization and the Demand for Factors: We begin by arguing that the decision problems of a firm can be broken down into two components: the choice of the optimal output and, in a non-competitive world, the choice of the optimal implied price; and the choice of the optimal utilization of factors to produce that output. We begin this chapter with the second of these, and solve the firm's input decision problem. This is essentially that of choosing the input combinations in such a way that, whatever output is produced, it is produced in the cheapest possible way given input prices. We use various technologies and show that the technology determines the relationship between factor demands and factor prices. Once again we use this information to infer from observed factor demands the technology of the firm, which enables us to predict and prescribe.

Chapter 12 Cost Curves: From the analysis of the previous chapter we can derive the cost function of the firm which clearly depends upon the firm's technology. We introduce the concepts of marginal cost and average cost, and distinguish between the short and the long run. We spend some time exploring the relationship between the various cost curves, particularly that between long and short run total cost curves; hence the relationship between the long and short run marginal and average cost curves; and also the relationship between the marginal and total cost curves in both the long and the short run. Crucially, we derive the result that the area under the (long/short run) marginal cost curve is the (total/total variable) cost. We need this result for the next chapter in order to derive an important result about the profit (or surplus) of the firm.

Chapter 13 Firm Supply and Producer Surplus: This follows the previous analysis; in the long run the supply curve of the competitive firm is the marginal cost curve, and the area between the price paid and this supply curve is the firm's profit. We discuss one or two qualifications necessary in the long and short run.

Chapter 14 Production Possibility Frontiers: We now examine an entire economy, although one producing two goods only, and discuss the efficient production of these two goods with given factor resources for the economy as a whole. We start with the simple example of two inputs (two people), each of whom can produce both goods, and for whom the technology is linear. We then define the concept of the production possibility frontier for the economy and show that, in this economy with two linear technologies, the production possibility frontier for the economy as a whole is piecewise linear. Finally we generalize to an economy with two firms, each specializing in the production of one of the two goods and having the usual convex technology; we show that the production possibility frontier for this economy is concave.

Chapter 15 Production and Exchange: This chapter combines the Edgeworth box analysis of the penultimate chapter of Part I with the material in Chapter 14 on production possibility frontiers. We are then in a position to derive the overall optimality conditions of an economy with production.

Firms and Technology

10.1 Introduction

So far we have worked in a world without production; it is a pure-exchange world where people have initial endowments and might want to exchange them. We must now add production to the story. Production is essential in the real world. Production exists because people are aware that there are profits to be made by producing goods which people will want to buy.

Usually, but conventionally, we say that production is undertaken by firms which exist to produce. Indeed we can define a firm as an organization that buys certain inputs, does something to them, and sells the resulting product; a firm buys inputs and transforms them into output through some production process, and then sells the resulting output. Usually a firm produces several outputs using several inputs, but we will confine our analysis to a firm that uses two inputs to produce one output. All the results that we derive can be extended, but this (one output, two inputs) world is sufficiently simple to make the analysis relatively easy.

The purpose of this chapter is to explore and define the relationships between the output and the two inputs. In subsequent chapters we shall explore the implications of these relationships.

10.2 Production Functions

In this chapter a firm is defined as an organization that buys two inputs and transforms them into one output. Let us call the two inputs input 1 and input 2, and let us denote the quantities of each by q_1 and q_2. We will denote the quantity of output produced by y. We assume that both inputs are genuine inputs in the sense that the higher the quantity of each used, the larger the output of the firm.

Central to the firm is the production process which converts inputs into output. In general this can be described by a *production function*, which we can write as follows.

$$y = f(q_1, q_2) \tag{10.1}$$

We assume that the function is increasing in both its arguments. We will find it useful to describe this function in two ways as there are, in a sense, two dimensions to the description of the production process. The first is the relationship between the two inputs in the production process for a given scale of production; the second is the relationship between the scale of the inputs and the scale of the output.

To understand the relationship between the two inputs in the production process, it is useful to introduce the concept of an *isoquant*. This is a curve in (q_1, q_2) space, for which the level of output is constant. It is formally defined in the following manner.

$$f(q_1, q_2) = \text{constant} \tag{10.2}$$

We shall study this intensively later. In the meantime, to understand the relationship between the scale of inputs and the scale of output, we ask what happens when we change the scale of production. This implies moving from the point (q_1, q_2) to the point (sq_1, sq_2) where s is some scaling factor; that is, we multiply the quantity of both inputs by s. What happens?

Clearly output will change from $f(q_1, q_2)$ to $f(sq_1, sq_2)$. The interesting question is: will output be scaled up in the same proportion as inputs? In particular, is $f(sq_1, sq_2)$ greater than, equal to or less than $sf(q_1, q_2)$? That is, is the output multiplied by the same scaling factor as the two inputs?

Let us introduce some terminology. In the case when $f(sq_1, sq_2)$ is equal to $sf(q_1, q_2)$, we say that the production process exhibits *constant returns to scale*; multiplying the inputs by s causes output to be multiplied by s. In contrast when $f(sq_1, sq_2)$ is less than $sf(q_1, q_2)$, we say that the production process exhibits *decreasing returns to scale*; multiplying the inputs by s causes output to be multiplied by less than s. Finally, when $f(sq_1, sq_2)$ is more than $sf(q_1, q_2)$, we say that the production process exhibits *increasing returns to scale*; multiplying the inputs by s causes output to be multiplied by more than s.

It should be emphasized that these two dimensions – the shape of the isoquants and the returns to scale – exist independently of each other. We can have any shaped isoquant combined with different returns to scale; and we can have any kind of returns to scale combined with any shaped isoquant. We will therefore study them separately, beginning with different kinds of isoquant maps.

10.3 Isoquants

As we have already noted, an isoquant is the set of points in (q_1, q_2) space for which the level of output is constant, as defined in Eq. (10.2).

The shape of an isoquant depends upon the relationship between the two inputs in the production process. An isoquant is generally convex, reflecting the usual empirical fact that the two inputs are more efficient when used together. There is an isoquant through every point in (q_1, q_2) space. So the usual case is a family of isoquants with the form shown in Fig. 10.1.

Isoquants may well remind you of indifference curves, and indeed they do have much in common. You might like to reflect on the fact that the consumer in Chapters 3 to 7 buys goods and converts them into utility, while the firm in this chapter buys inputs and converts them into output. The analogy is almost complete; there is only one slight difference. Output is measurable, while utility is not. You might like to reflect on the implications of this.

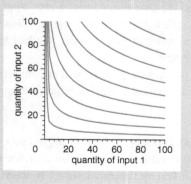

Figure 10.1 A possible family of isoquants

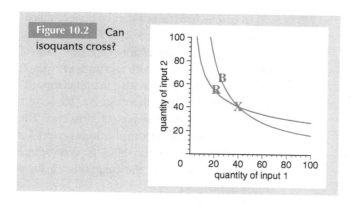

Figure 10.2 Can isoquants cross?

One thing which we never explicitly proved when describing indifference curves is that they cannot cross. The same is true for isoquants; perhaps it may be useful to prove this here. Consider the picture of two isoquants in (q_1, q_2) space in Fig. 10.2.

In Fig. 10.2, two isoquants are shown to cross at the point X. Is this possible? Consider first the isoquant which passes though the point B; according to this isoquant, the output at point X is the same as that at point B. Now consider the other isoquant which passes through the point R; according to this isoquant, the output at the point X is the same as at point R. It follows that the output at B must be the same as the output at R, which is contradictory to the assumption that both inputs are useful to the firm in the sense that more of either leads to increased output. At B there are more of both inputs than at R. We have a contradiction, and this proves that isoquants cannot cross.

The actual shape of isoquants is determined by the relationship between the two inputs in the production process. We can identify a number of different possibilities. The question as to which one is relevant in any particular instance is an empirical issue, which is determined by the nature of good being produced and the relationship between the two inputs.

One simple case occurs when the two inputs are perfect 1:1 substitutes. This means that they are identical and can be used interchangeably in the production process. The implied isoquants for this case are drawn in Fig. 10.3.

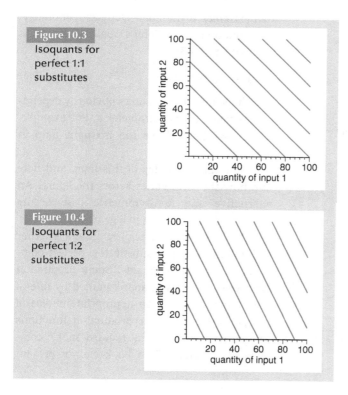

Figure 10.3
Isoquants for perfect 1:1 substitutes

Figure 10.4
Isoquants for perfect 1:2 substitutes

Consider any one of these – say the third, which goes from $(60, 0)$ to $(0, 60)$, This isoquant tells us that the same quantity of output can be produced with any combination of the two inputs along the line. So 60 units of input 1 and none of input 2 produce a given output; the same output can also be produced with 59 units of input 1 and one of input 2; or with 58 units of input 1 and two units of input 2; or ...; or with one unit of input 1 and 59 of input 2; or with no units of input 1 and 60 units of input 2. Every one unit less of input 1 needs to be substituted with an additional unit of input 2 to keep output constant; every unit less of input 2 needs to be substituted with an extra unit of input 1 to keep output constant. The slope of the isoquants is everywhere equal to −1; note also that the magnitude of the slope indicates the rate at which input 1 needs to be substituted with input 2 to keep output constant. This is given the name the marginal rate of substitution (MRS)[1]. For perfect 1:1 substitutes the MRS is everywhere equal to one.

1. Or sometimes the marginal *technical* rate of substitution.

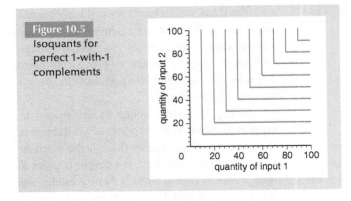

Figure 10.5
Isoquants for perfect 1-with-1 complements

Of course, two inputs can be perfect substitutes but not necessarily 1:1. For perfect 1:2 substitutes for which everywhere one unit of input 1 is substitutable with two units of input 2, and two units of input 2 with one unit of input 1, we have the isoquants shown in Fig. 10.4. Note that the MRS is everywhere equal to two. The general case for perfect substitutes is perfect 1:a substitutes in which the MRS is everywhere equal to a, and where the isoquants all have slopes equal to $-a$.

The polar extreme to perfect substitutes is perfect complements. These could be 1-with-1, where one unit of input 1 has always to be used with one unit if input 2 [2]. The isoquant map for this situation is in Fig. 10.5.

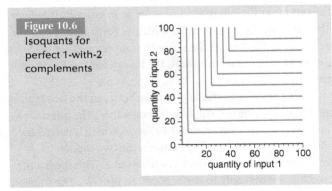

Figure 10.6
Isoquants for perfect 1-with-2 complements

Of course we can have other examples, for instance perfect 1-with-2 complements; the isoquant map for this is in Fig. 10.6.

More generally, we define perfect 1-with-a complements for which one unit of input 1 must always be combined with a units of input 2, and for which the corner points lie along the line $q_2 = aq_1$.

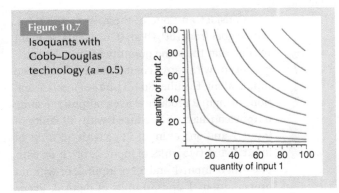

Figure 10.7
Isoquants with Cobb–Douglas technology ($a = 0.5$)

A case which is intermediate between these two extremes is the Cobb–Douglas technology. The equation for a Cobb–Douglas isoquant is given in Eq. (10.3).

$$q_1^a q_2^{(1-a)} = \text{constant} \qquad (10.3)$$

The shape this function takes obviously depends on the value of the parameter a. For example, when $a = 0.5$ we have the isoquant map in Fig. 10.7.

Note the symmetry of this map, and note also how the MRS varies across the figure. An alternative and non-symmetric case occurs when $a = 0.3$; the map is in Fig. 10.8.

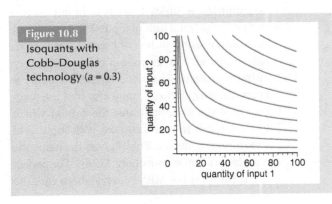

Figure 10.8
Isoquants with Cobb–Douglas technology ($a = 0.3$)

Obviously it is an empirical issue whether technology is perfect substitutes, perfect complements or Cobb–Douglas. Some production functions can be well approximated by one of these functions with an appropriate choice of the parameter a. Other production functions are more complex and require more complicated, formulae. This book cannot present

---

2. The classic example is men digging holes with spades. Every man needs a spade and every spade needs a man.

Figure 10.9

Isoquants with
constant elasticity
of substitution
technology
$(c_1 = 0.4, c_2 = 0.5,$
$\rho = 0.9$ and $s = 1.0)$

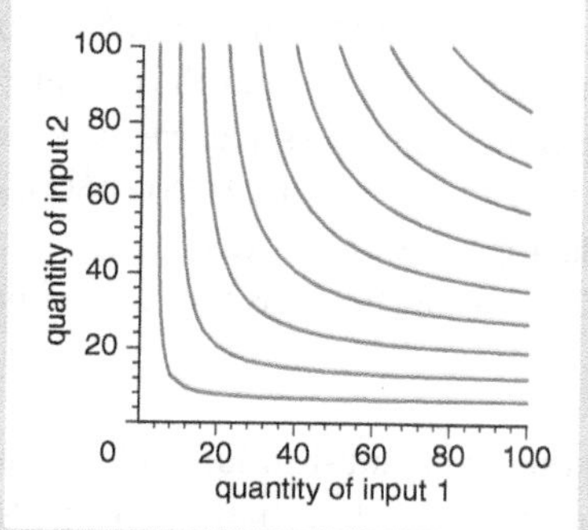

all the possibilities, but we should at least mention the constant elasticity of substitution (CES) case, which appears to have good empirical credentials. An example is in Fig. 10.9; the title gives values taken by the parameters – this will be more meaningful after we have considered the mathematical formula for the CES function in the following section.

10.4 Production Functions and Returns to Scale

The isoquant map determines the relationship between the two inputs in the production process; however it does not determine the returns to scale of the two inputs. This is given by the production function. We have already noted that there are two different dimensions in the production function. We need to be more specific.

Consider the case of perfect 1:1 substitutes defined by the isoquant map in Fig. 10.3. An isoquant is defined by the function.

$$q_1 + q_2 = \text{constant} \tag{10.4}$$

We note that this is consistent with different returns to scale. Consider, for example, the following production function.

$$y = f(q_1, q_2) = q_1 + q_2 \tag{10.5}$$

This has isoquants given by Eq. (10.4) and also displays constant returns to scale; if we multiply both inputs by s, then the output gets multiplied by s also.

A more complex production function is shown in Eq. (10.6).

$$y = f(q_1, q_2) = (q_1 + q_2)^{0.8} \tag{10.6}$$

This has isoquants given by $(q_1 + q_2)^{0.8} = \text{constant}$; that is, by $(q_1 + q_2) = \text{constant}$, which is Eq. (10.4). What about its returns to scale? If we multiply both inputs by s, output is multiplied by $s^{0.8}$, which means we have decreasing returns to scale.

More generally consider the following production function.

$$y = f(q_1, q_2) = (q_1 + q_2)^s \tag{10.7}$$

This displays perfect 1:1 substitute technology; it has increasing, constant or decreasing returns to scale depending upon whether the value taken by the parameter s is greater than, equal to or less than unity.

You need to be aware of what is happening. The technology determines the shape of the isoquants, but the returns to scale determine the output associated with each particular isoquant. With production function (10.4), the levels of output associated with the nine isoquants in Fig. 10.3 are 20, 40, 60, 80, 100, 120, 140, 160 and 180 respectively. You will see that every doubling in the scale of production doubles the implied output.

However if we take production function (10.6), which we have already established has decreasing returns to scale, we have levels of production associated with the nine isoquants in Fig. 10.3 equal to 10.99, 19.13, 26.46, 33.30, 39.81, 46.06, 52.11, 57.98 and 63.71 – doubling the scale of production less than doubles the level of output.

Finally, if we take the general form (10.7) and put the parameter s equal to two, giving perfect 1:1 substitutes with increasing returns to scale, we have levels of output associated with the nine isoquants in Fig. 10.3 equal to 400, 1600, 3600, 6400, 10 000, 14 400, 19 600, 25 600 and 32 400 – clear increasing returns to scale.

A quasi-general[3] case of perfect 1:a substitutes is the production function:

$$y = f(q_1, q_2) = (q_1 + q_2/a)^s \tag{10.8}$$

Here the parameter a determines the rate of substitution and the parameter s determines the returns to scale; s is greater than, equal to or less than one as the function displays increasing, constant or decreasing returns to scale. Note that the parameters a and s can be chosen quite independently of each other.

For perfect 1-with-1 complements, isoquants are given by:

$$\min(q_1, q_2) = \text{constant} \tag{10.9}$$

This is obviously consistent with the following production function.

$$y = f(q_1, q_2) = \min(q_1, q_2) \tag{10.10}$$

Eq. (10.10) displays constant returns to scale. But so also does the more general form in (10.11).

$$y = f(q_1, q_2) = [\min(q_1, q_2)]^s \tag{10.11}$$

This displays increasing, constant and decreasing returns to scale according to whether the parameter s is greater than, equal to or less than one.

For a quasi-general[4] case of perfect 1-with-a complements, the production function is given by

$$y = f(q_1, q_2) = [\min(q_1, q_2/a)]^s \tag{10.12}$$

Here the parameter a determines the rate of complementarity, and the parameter s determines the returns to scale; s is greater than, equal to or less than one as the function displays increasing, constant or decreasing returns to scale. The parameters a and s can be chosen independently of each other.

The Cobb–Douglas case is interesting. We have already noted that an isoquant has the following mathematical form

$$q_1^a q_2^{(1-a)} = \text{constant} \tag{10.3}$$

From this we obtain the general Cobb–Douglas production function

$$y = f(q_1, q_2) = A q_1^a q_2^b \tag{10.13}$$

The relative weights on input 1 and input 2 are $a/(a+b)$ and $b/(a+b)$ respectively; what determines the returns to scale is the sum $(a+b)$. To be specific, we make the following statement which you should check.

---

3. Obviously an even more general case of perfect substitutes is $y = f(q_1, q_2) = g(q_1 + q_2/a)$ where the function $g(.)$ is any increasing function.
4. Obviously an even more general case of perfect complements is $y = f(q_1, q_2) = g[\min(q_1, q_2/a)]$, where the function $g(.)$ is any monotonically increasing function.

> The general Cobb–Douglas production function has increasing, constant or decreasing returns to scale depending on whether $(a + b)$ is greater than, equal to or less than one.

We introduced the CES case on page 145. Its general production function takes the form set out in Eq. (10.14).

$$y = (c_1 q_1^{-\rho} + c_2 q_2^{-\rho})^{-s/\rho} \qquad (10.14)$$

We note that the parameter s determines the returns to scale, exactly as above, and the parameter ρ is the constant elasticity of substitution[5].

10.5 The Marginal Rate of Substitution and Marginal Products

For future reference, we conclude by defining the *marginal product* of each input. We can then relate the marginal rate of substitution to the two marginal products.

The marginal product of a particular input is simply the rate at which output increases when that input increases. If we were to draw a graph of output as a function of that particular input, with the quantity of the other output fixed, it would in general be an increasing function of that input and would generally be concave; as the units of input rise so does output, but less than proportionately[6]. At any point on the graph, the marginal product of that input is simply the rate at which the output rises when the input rises; it is the slope of the curve. Mathematically[7] the two marginal products are defined by:

marginal product of input 1 $= \partial y / \partial q_1 = \partial f(q_1, q_2) / \partial q_1$

marginal product of input 2 $= \partial y / \partial q_2 = \partial f(q_1, q_2) / \partial q_2 \qquad (10.15)$

We can now relate the marginal rate of substitution to these marginal products. The proof is given in the mathematical appendix and yields the following:

$$dq_2 / dq_1 = -[\partial f(q_1, q_2) / \partial q_1] / [\partial f(q_1, q_2) / \partial q_2] \qquad (10.16)$$

This says that the slope of an isoquant (dq_2 / dq_1) is equal to minus the ratio of the marginal product of input 1 to the marginal product of input 2. From this we get the important result.

> The marginal rate of substitution equals the ratio of the marginal product of input 1 to the marginal product of input 2

---

5. You might like to know that the elasticity of substitution is $d[\ln(q_2)]/d[\ln(q_1)]$ which is equal to $(dq_2/dq_1)/(q_2/q_1)$; this is the MRS divided by q_2/q_1. If the elasticity of substitution is constant, it follows that the MRS divided by q_2/q_1 is also constant; this implies that the MRS is proportional to q_2/q_1.
6. Obviously this is not always true, but it is generally; it is rare that we get increasing returns to a single input.
7. If y is a function of just one variable, we denote the derivative of y with respect to x by dy/dx; and if y is a function of several variables $x_1, x_2, \ldots$ then we denote the derivates of y with respect to $x_1, x_2, \ldots$ by $\partial y/\partial x_1, \partial y/\partial x_2, \ldots$

You might like to think about this. Perhaps it is simplest to take a particular example. Suppose we are at a point where the marginal product of input 1 is five and that of input 2 is two. This means that an increase of one unit of input 1 increases output by five units, and an increase of one unit of input 2 leads to an increase in output of two units. Now ask yourself: if we decrease the amount of good 1 by one unit, how much do we have to increase the amount of good 2 to keep output unchanged? Well, decreasing input 1 by one unit will lower output by five units as the marginal product of input 1 is five. To compensate, we need to increase the employment of input 2 by $2\frac{1}{2}$ units, as each increase of one unit of good 2 increases output by two. So to compensate for a fall in input 1 by one unit, we need to increase input 2 by $2\frac{1}{2}$ units. Hence the MRS is $2\frac{1}{2}$.

10.6　Concave and Convex Technology

Throughout this chapter we have implicitly assumed that the technology is convex, in the sense that the isoquants are convex. This is probably more common than the contrary case when the isoquants are concave; the latter is possible, but unlikely. But we include an example in Fig. 10.10 to show what concave isoquants look like.

What kind of technology does this imply? Remember that we are still assuming that both inputs are proper inputs, in that more of either implies more output. The technology implies that the two inputs are more efficiently employed separately rather than together. To see this, suppose that we have 100 units of input 1 and 100 units of input 2; and we are considering having two firms share these inputs. What is best: to have one firm use 100 of input 1 and none of input 2, and the other to use none of input 1 and 100 of input 2? Or to have both firms use 50 of input 1 and 50 of input 2? In which circumstance would total output be higher? The answer is: clearly in the first. We obtain the conclusion we stated above: that the inputs are better used separately rather than together. You might like to ask yourself whether this is likely to be empirically valid[8]. Let me note that, in practice, we usually observe firms in an industry all employing the same inputs rather than some firms using one input and other firms using others.

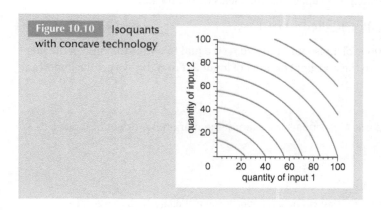

Figure 10.10　Isoquants with concave technology

8.　It creates no real problem to our subsequent analysis; in fact it almost trivializes it to such an extent that there is really no problem left to consider.

10.7 Summary

As you have been reading this chapter you probably had a feeling of *deja vu*. This is hardly surprising as much of what we have done is familiar from the material on the preferences of the individual in Chapter 5. There are strong parallels to which we have already alluded. The consumer buys goods and produces utility; the firm buys inputs and produces output. The mapping from goods to utility for the consumer is represented through indifference curves; the mapping from inputs to output for a firm is represented through isoquants. The main difference is that utility is not measurable; output is.

In this chapter we started with production functions which show the relationship between inputs and output. We then introduced the concept of an isoquant in (q_1, q_2) space.

➡️ Isoquants show the locus of input combinations for which output is constant.

➡️ Isoquants cannot cross.

➡️ The marginal rate of substitution measures the slope of an isoquant.

We then considered some special cases.

➡️ The isoquants for perfect substitutes are parallel straight lines.

➡️ The isoquants for perfect complements are in the form of an L.

We argued that convex technology is more common in practice than concave technology, and we gave two examples of convex technology which appear to have empirical validity: the Cobb–Douglas and the constant elasticity of substitution technologies.
Finally we defined returns to scale.

➡️ The technology has increasing, constant or decreasing returns to scale depending upon whether, when we increase the scale of inputs by *s*, the output goes up by more than, the same as, or less than the scale factor *s*.

We saw that the returns to scale and the type of technology (the shape of the isoquants) are completely independent attributes of the production function.

10.8 Review Questions

1   Try and think of examples in which the two inputs are perfect substitutes. Try and think of examples in which the two inputs are perfect complements.

2   Why are concave isoquants unlikely in practice?

3 Why do you think it is normally the case that isoquants are convex? What does this imply about the way that the marginal rate of substitution changes? (As the firm has less and less of one input, it needs increasing amounts of the other input to keep output constant when the first input decreases further.)

4 Suppose one of the two inputs is a bad in the sense that it interferes with the production process (like pollution from a factory affecting a farmer). What does this imply for the shape of the isoquants? Consider the two cases: when the firm is forced to use the bad input; when the firm can throw the bad input away costlessly.

10.9 Mathematical Appendix

We find the expression for the marginal rate of substitution, that is, the slope of an isoquant. Recall that the mathematical format of an isoquant is given by:

$$f(q_1, q_2) = \text{constant} \tag{10.2}$$

If we take the total derivative of this expression, we get

$$[\partial f(q_1, q_2)/\partial q_1]\,dq_1 + [\partial f(q_1, q_2)/\partial q_2]\,dq_2 = 0 \tag{A10.1}$$

From Eq. (A10.1) it follows that

$$dq_2/dq_1 = -[\partial f(q_1, q_2)/\partial q_1]/[\partial f(q_1, q_2)/\partial q_2] \tag{A10.2}$$

This is the result stated in the text.

Cost Minimization and the Demand for Factors

11

11.1 ## Introduction

We assume a very simple objective for firms – namely, that they want to maximize profits[1]. We will explore the implications of this statement in this chapter and the next two. We assume that the firm wants to choose its output and the quantity of the two inputs in such a way that profits are maximized. This problem can be considered in two parts: the choice of the optimal output; and, given that, the optimal choice of the two inputs to produce that output. We can split up the problem in this way because the two parts are independent; in particular, whatever choice of output is made the firm will want to produce that output in the most efficient way. To maximize its profits, the firm must minimize the cost of producing whatever output it chooses to produce.

This chapter considers the problem of choosing, for any given level of output, the cheapest way of producing that output. That is, we find in this chapter the cost-minimizing input combination for any particular level of output. This will enable us to identify the lowest cost of producing that output. For any given output y, we will denote this by $C(y)$ which will be referred to as the cost function of the firm. We shall study its properties in Chapter 12. Then, in Chapter 13, we shall use this cost function to find the profit maximizing output for the firm.

11.1 ## Isocost Curves

To help us find the cost-minimizing input combination for producing a given level of output, we introduce a useful expository and analytical device; *the isocost curve*. This is a curve in the space we used in Chapter 10 – (q_1, q_2) space – the space of input combinations. As you might anticipate, an isocost curve is a set of points in this space for which the cost of using a particular combination of inputs is constant. If we denote the price of input 1 by w_1 and that of input 2 by w_2, then the cost of purchasing the combination (q_1, q_2) is simply $w_1 q_1 + w_2 q_2$. An isocost curve is therefore defined by:

$$w_1 q_1 + w_2 q_2 = \text{constant} \tag{11.1}$$

1. For firms quoted on the stock exchange, this is equivalent to maximizing the value of the firm to the shareholders.

This is clearly a straight line in (q_1, q_2); space (it is linear in both q_1 and q_2). We rewrite the equation in the following form:

$$q_2 = \text{constant} - (w_1/w_2)q_1 \tag{11.2}$$

This has a slope equal to $-w_1/w_2$. So an isocost curve in (q_1, q_2) space is a straight line with slope equal to $-w_1/w_2$. Such an isocost curve passes through each point in the space, and we show some of these in Fig. 11.1.

In Fig. 11.1 it is assumed that $w_1 = w_2 = 1$, from which $-w_1/w_2$ is equal to -1, so that all the isocost curves have slopes equal to -1. For each isocost curve we can calculate the cost. For the lowest curve, that joining (20, 0) to (0, 20), the cost of each combination along the curve at prices $w_1 = w_2 = 1$ is obviously 20. So, 20 units of 1 and none of 2; 19 units of 1 and one of 2; 18 units of 1 and two of 2; ..., one unit of 1 and 19 of 2; no units of 1 and 20 of 2. For the second curve, the cost everywhere along it is 40; for the third curve, 60; and so on. The cost rises as we move outwards from the origin, and falls as we move inwards towards to the origin.

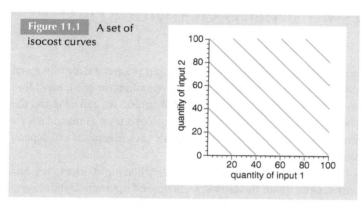

Figure 11.1 A set of isocost curves

If, instead of $w_1 = w_2 = 1$, the prices were $w_1 = w_2 = 2$, we would have exactly the same isocost curves, but the costs associated with them would differ; 40, 80, etc. instead of 20, 40, etc.

11.3 The Cheapest Input Combination

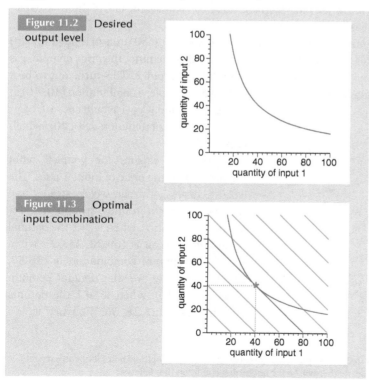

Figure 11.2 Desired output level

Figure 11.3 Optimal input combination

We can now proceed to find the cheapest way of producing any given level of output. Clearly the level of output that we want to produce has associated with it an isoquant. Suppose it is the one pictured in Fig. 11.2. Here I am assuming a symmetric Cobb–Douglas technology with a level of output equal to 40. So the equation of the curve is $q_1^{0.5}q_2^{0.5} = 40$ (the point (40, 40) is on this isoquant.)

We ask the question: which is the cheapest point on this isoquant? Obviously it is the one on the lowest isocost curve. Let us combine Figs. 11.1 and 11.2 to give Fig. 11.3.

Clearly the point indicated with the asterisk is on the lowest possible isocost curve consistent with producing the level of output indicated by the isoquant curve. We note in this example, which is a nice symmetrical example, that the optimal point is itself symmetrical with

40 units of each input and a cost of 80. There is no other point on the isoquant where the cost is lower.

You should note the optimizing condition[2]. If you look at the asterisked point, what do you see? At that point, the isocost line is tangential to the isoquant. It follows that the slope of the isocost line must be equal to the slope of the isoquant at the optimal point. But we know these two slopes; the first is simply minus the ratio of the input prices (w_1/w_2), and the second is minus the MRS. So the condition for the optimal input combination is:

$$w_1/w_2 = \text{MRS} \tag{11.3}$$

11.4 Input Demands as Functions of Input Prices and of Output

We have now solved the problem in principle; for any given input prices, and for any given level of output, we can now find the firm's cost-minimizing combination of inputs. More specifically, for any given input prices and for any given level of output, we can now find the firm's demand for the two factors. In the example above, with prices one and one and a level of output 40, the firm demands 40 units of each input. Obviously these demands will depend upon the technology, as we shall see.

We are also in a position to see how the input demands vary when input prices vary and when the desired output varies. Once again the answers will depend upon the technology.

Let us stay with the symmetric Cobb–Douglas technology for the moment. We will keep the desired level of output constant at 40 and the price of input 2 constant at $w_2 = 1$. But let us vary the price of input 1, w_1, starting at $\frac{1}{4}$, and then going to $\frac{1}{3}, \frac{1}{2}, 1, 2, 3$ and finally to 4. As you will no doubt anticipate, the slope of the isocost lines will vary; it will start at $-\frac{1}{4}$, then go to $-\frac{1}{3}, -\frac{1}{2}, -1, -2, -3$ and finally to -4. In Fig. 11.4 you will see the first of these cases pictured; the slope of all the isocost curves is $-\frac{1}{4}$.

In this case the optimal input combination is (80, 20), using 80 units of input 1 and 20 of input 2. The firm takes advantage of the fact that, in this scenario, the price of input 1 is low; consequently it buys lots of input 1 and very little of input 2. This turns out to be a cheaper way of producing the required output of 40. For example, a combination (40, 40) at prices $w_1 = \frac{1}{4}$ and $w_2 = 1$ would cost 50, compared to the combination (80, 20) which costs just 40.

You can explore for yourself what happens when the price of input 1 rises. The isocost curves get progressively steeper and the optimal point rotates around the isoquant. For instance, when $w_1 = \frac{1}{3}$ the optimal input combination is (69.28, 23.09); when $w_1 = \frac{1}{2}$ the optimal combination is (56.57, 28.28); when $w_1 = 1$ the optimal combination is (40, 40); when $w_1 = 2$ the optimal combination is (28.28, 56.57); when $w_1 = 3$

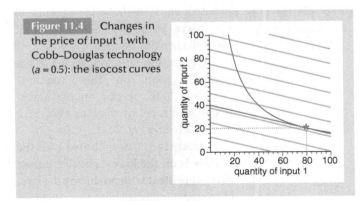

Figure 11.4 Changes in the price of input 1 with Cobb–Douglas technology ($a = 0.5$): the isocost curves

---

2. This condition assumes that the isoquant is smoothly convex and the optimal point it not an extreme point, if these are not true, neither will be the optimizing condition that follows.

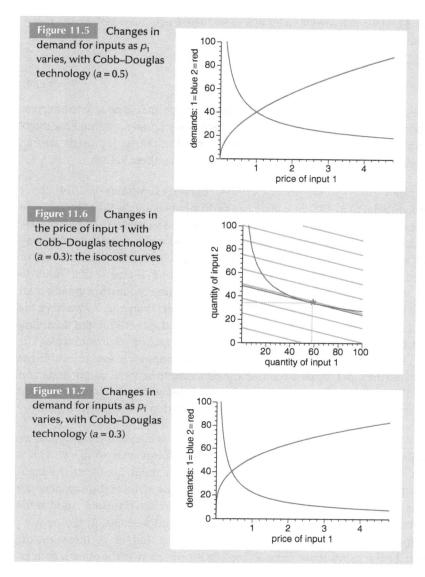

Figure 11.5 Changes in demand for inputs as p_1 varies, with Cobb–Douglas technology ($a = 0.5$)

Figure 11.6 Changes in the price of input 1 with Cobb–Douglas technology ($a = 0.3$): the isocost curves

Figure 11.7 Changes in demand for inputs as p_1 varies, with Cobb–Douglas technology ($a = 0.3$)

the optimal combination is (23.09, 69.28); and when $w_1 = 4$ the optimal combination is (20, 80). You may find it helpful to verify these results using Fig. 11.4.

If we now plot the optimal demands for inputs 1 and 2 against the price of input 1, we get the input demand functions as functions of the input price; these are shown in Fig. 11.5.

In Fig. 11.5 the price of input 1 is on the horizontal axis. The downward sloping curve represents the demand for input 1, and the upward sloping curve the demand for good 2. As the price of input 1 rises, the firm reduces its demand for input 1 and replaces it with an increased demand for input 2. The firm substitutes input 1 by input 2 as input 1 becomes more expensive.

These input demand functions depend upon the technology. If, instead of having a symmetric Cobb–Douglas technology we had a non-symmetric technology with weights 0.3 and 0.7 (for example), the problem to solve would be that drawn in Fig. 11.6 (note the different position of the isoquant). You will notice the different slopes of the isoquants in Fig. 11.6 compared to Fig.11.4. As before, the optimal point is marked by an asterisk. The graph of the demand curves for inputs 1 and 2 against changes in the price of input 1 are shown in Fig. 11.7; you should compare this figure with Fig. 11.5.

For reference purposes it may be useful to show the general formula for the optimal input demands in the general Cobb–Douglas case, the production function of which was given in Chapter 10:

$$y = f(q_1, q_2) = Aq_1^a q_2^b \tag{10.13}$$

The optimal input demands are found by minimizing the cost of producing output y, that is:

minimizing $(w_1 q_1 + w_2 q_2)$
with respect to $y = Aq_1^a q_2^b$

The proof can be found in the mathematical appendix. The resulting input demands are presented in Eq. (11.4). Be prepared for a bit of a shock! These equations look rather nasty, but we will explain what they mean.

$$q_1 = (y/A)^{1/(a+b)}[aw_2/(bw_1)]^{(b/(a+b))}$$
$$q_2 = (y/A)^{1/(a+b)}[bw_1/(aw_2)]^{(a/(a+b))}$$

(11.4)

It is not necessary for you to be able to derive these, but you should be able to interpret them. More importantly, you should understand the economic principles behind the interpretation. There are three variables that influence the demand for the two inputs: the desired level of output, and the prices of the two inputs. We will consider these in turn.

The effect of desired output on input demand In both expressions of (11.4), input demands are proportional to $y^{1/(a+b)}$; as y increases so do input demands. What is crucial to the way that these demands increase with y is the sum of the parameters $(a + b)$. But we already know what this sum indicates: the kinds of returns to scale which the technology exhibits. Recall from Chapter 10 that the technology exhibits increasing, constant or decreasing returns to scale according as to whether the sum $(a + b)$ is greater than, equal to or less than one. Now, the exponent on y is $1/(a + b)$; this is less than, equal to or greater than one according to whether $(a + b)$ is greater than, equal to or less than one. So we have the result that the input demands are concave, linear or convex in the desired output according to whether the technology shows increasing, constant or decreasing returns to scale. The constant returns to scale case is the simplest: to double the output we need to double the scale of the inputs, so the input demands double; the relationship between output and input demand is linear. When, instead, we have increasing (decreasing) returns to scale, we need to less (more) than double the input demands and the relationship is concave (convex).

The effect of w_1 on input demand If we look at the input demand functions (11.4) we see that, in the demand for input 1, the term w_1 appears with exponent $-b/(a + b)$. This is negative, which means that as w_1 increases the demand for input 1 falls; as the input becomes more expensive, less of it is bought. Note also that the value of the exponent lies between zero and one, so demand falls less and less as the price rises. If we look again at the input demand functions (11.4) and, in particular, the demand for input 2, the term w_1 appears with exponent $a/(a + b)$. This is positive which means that, as w_1 increases, the demand for input 2 rises; as one input becomes more expensive more of the other is bought. Since the value of the exponent lies between zero and one, demand rises less and less as the price rises. This is exactly what Fig. 11.7 shows.

The effect of w_2 on input demand Once again, look at the input demand functions (11.4). You will see that, in the demand for input 1, the term w_2 appears with exponent $b/(a + b)$. This is positive, which means that as w_2 increases then the demand for input 1 rises; as one input becomes more expensive more of the other is bought. The magnitude of the exponent is between zero and one, so demand rises less and less as the price rises. If we take a further look at the input demand functions (11.4), we see that the term w_2 appears with exponent $-a/(a + b)$ in the demand for input 2. This is negative, telling us that as w_2 increases the demand for input 2 falls; as the input becomes more expensive less of it is bought. As before, the exponent takes a value between zero and one so demand falls less and less as the price rises. These results are obviously just the converse of those discussed in the previous paragraph.

The effect of a and b on input demand You might like to think about the effect of a and b on input demands.

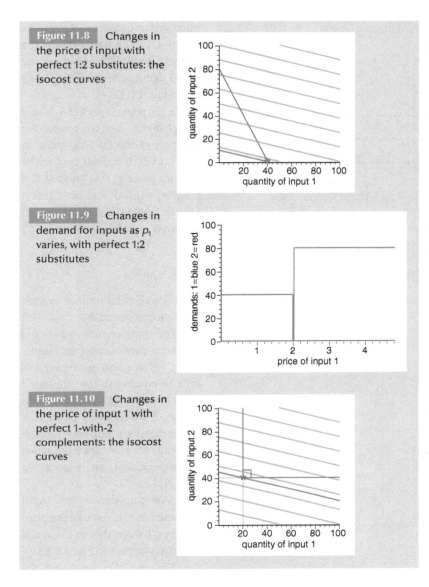

Figure 11.8 Changes in the price of input with perfect 1:2 substitutes: the isocost curves

Figure 11.9 Changes in demand for inputs as p_1 varies, with perfect 1:2 substitutes

Figure 11.10 Changes in the price of input 1 with perfect 1-with-2 complements: the isocost curves

The technology obviously influences the input demands. If we take a different technology we will have different demands. Consider, for example, perfect 1:2 substitutes. We begin with the usual isoquant/isocost analysis as in Fig. 11.8.

Here we have a price of input 2 equal to one and a price of input 1 equal to $\frac{1}{4}$. The desired output level is 40. I am assuming a production function of the form of Eq. (10.8) with $a = 2$ and $s = 1$. Clearly the optimal point is where the firm uses 40 units of input 1 and no units of input 2.

Now consider what happens when the price of input 1 rises from $\frac{1}{4}$ to $\frac{1}{3}$, $\frac{1}{2}$, 1, 2, 3 and finally 4. When the price is less than two it is obviously best for the firm to continue to buy 40 units of input 1 and none of input 2. When the price reaches 2 the isocost and the isoquant coincide, so any combination that produces the desired quantity of 40 is optimal. Above a price of two for input 1, it is best for the firm to buy only input 2 (80 units of it) and none of input 1. We thus have the demand functions drawn in Fig. 11.9.

The line which is horizontal at 40 until the price of two and then zero thereafter, is the demand for input 1; the other line which is zero until a price of two and horizontal at 80 thereafter is the demand for input 2. This case is perfect 1:2 substitutes, which is why the price of two for input 1 is critical (the price of input 2 is fixed at one.)

You might be able to verify the following demand functions for the general 1:a substitutes case, the production function for which was given by Eq. (10.8):

$$\text{if} \quad w_1 < aw_2, \quad \text{then,} \quad q_1 = y^{1/s} \quad \text{and} \quad q_2 = 0$$
$$\text{if} \quad w_1 > aw_2, \quad \text{then,} \quad q_1 = 0 \quad \text{and} \quad q_2 = (ya)^{1/s} \tag{11.5}$$

You might also like to reflect on the fact that, with the Cobb–Douglas technology the substitution from input 1 to input 2 is continuous, whereas with perfect substitutes it is all-or-nothing. The opposite extreme – that of no substitution – is found in the perfect complements case. An example, using perfect 1-with-2 complements, appears as Fig. 11.10.

Notice what happens when the isocost curves change their slope; the optimal combination is always at the asterisked point. So we get the following (rather boring) input demand

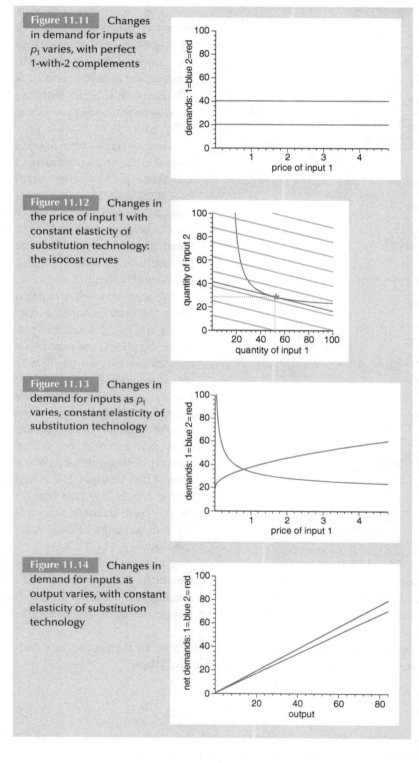

Figure 11.11 Changes in demand for inputs as p_1 varies, with perfect 1-with-2 complements

Figure 11.12 Changes in the price of input 1 with constant elasticity of substitution technology: the isocost curves

Figure 11.13 Changes in demand for inputs as p_1 varies, constant elasticity of substitution technology

Figure 11.14 Changes in demand for inputs as output varies, with constant elasticity of substitution technology

functions as functions of the price of input 1. The upper one is the demand for input 2; the lower one is the demand for input 1. They are in Fig. 11.11.

In the general perfect 1-with-a complements case, the production function of which was given in Eq. (10.12), it is clear that at the optimal point $q_2 = aq_1$ and at this point $q_1^s = (q_2/a)^s = y$; from this it follows that the optimal input demands must be given by:

$$q_1 = y^{1/s}$$
$$q_2 = ay^{1/s} \qquad (11.6)$$

Note the effect of returns to scale on the input demands.

For completeness we should include a case of constant elasticity of substitution technology, if only to emphasise that the input demands depend upon the technology. If we consider the effect of changing the input price on the demand, we start with the usual isocost/isoquant analysis, as in Fig. 11.12.

We can derive the input demands as functions of the price of input 1 from this in the usual way; they appear in Fig. 11.13.

We can also determine the effect of the desired output on input demands at fixed prices. This analysis is summarized in Fig. 11.14. The curves are linear. What can you infer about the returns to scale in the assumed technology? Yes – they are constant.

More generally, it can be shown that the input demand functions for the general constant elasticity of substitution case, the production function for which was given in Eq. (10.13), are given by the following expressions:

$$q_1^s = y(c_1/w_1)^{1/(1+\rho)}[(c_1 w_1^\rho)^{1/(1+\rho)} + (c_2 w_2^\rho)^{1/(1+\rho)}]$$
$$q_2^s = y(c_2/w_2)^{1/(1+\rho)}[(c_1 w_1^\rho)^{1/(1+\rho)} + (c_2 w_2^\rho)^{1/(1+\rho)}] \qquad (11.7)$$

It would be a useful exercise for you to think about the implied relationship between the input demands and the input prices. As far as the effect of output on the input demands is concerned, you should note that the relationship is increasing (obviously); and is concave, linear or convex depending on whether the technology exhibits increasing, constant or decreasing returns to scale.

11.5 Summary

We started by defining an isocost curve.

> An isocost curve is the locus of points in quantity space where the cost of producing that input combination is constant.

We then found, for technologies where the isoquants are smoothly convex, the following.

> The optimal input combination is (generally) where the MRS is equal to the ratio of the input prices.

Obviously for non-smoothly convex isoquants this may not be true, but we should always be able to find the point on the desired isoquant which is on the lowest possible isocost curve. In fact we did this for the cases of perfect substitutes and perfect complements.

> For perfect substitutes the cheapest input is used.

> For perfect complements both inputs are used.

We found in general an important result concerning optimal input demand.

> Input demands are a decreasing function of their own price and an increasing function of the price of the other input.

We also found that:

> Input demands rise with output – being concave, linear or convex if the technology displays everywhere increasing, constant or decreasing returns to scale.

11.6 Review Questions

1. Suppose the two inputs into the production process are perfect 1:*a* substitutes. What happens to the demand for input 1 when the price of input 1 rises with the output fixed and the price of input 2 is always equal to one? At what price does the demand for input 1 go to zero?

2. Suppose the two inputs into the production process are perfect 1-with-*a* complements. What happens to the demand for input 1 when the price of input 1 rises, with the output fixed and the price of input 2 always equal to one? Why is the demand constant? Why does the firm not substitute input 1 by input 2?

3. Argue intuitively that, with a Cobb–Douglas technology, the demand for either input must be a strictly decreasing function of its price, caused by the fact that the firm continually substitutes that good by the other.

11.7 Mathematical Appendix

We present the derivation of the input demand functions for the Cobb–Douglas case.

The problem is to find the combination (q_1, q_2) that minimizes the cost $(w_1 q_1 + w_2 q_2)$ subject to the condition that the desired output is produced; that is, subject to $y = A q_1^a q_2^b$. There are various ways to solve this but perhaps the simplest is to use the method of Lagrange and form the Lagrangian.

$$L = w_1 q_1 + w_2 q_2 + \lambda(y - A q_1^a q_2^b)$$ (A11.1)

We minimize the Lagrangian with respect to q_1, q_2 and λ. The optimality conditions are:

$$dL/dq_1 = w_1 - \lambda A a q_1^{a-1} q_2^b = 0$$
$$dL/dq_1 = w_2 - \lambda A b q_1^a q_2^{b-1} = 0$$
$$dL/d\lambda = y - A q_1^a q_2^b = 0$$ (A11.2)

Eliminating λ and solving these for q_1 and q_2 gives Eq. (11.4) in the text.

Cost Curves

12.1 Introduction

In Chapter 11 we found how to minimize the cost of producing any given level of output. This enables us to find the cheapest cost of producing any given level of output. This chapter studies this cheapest cost and explores its properties. In Chapter 13 we shall use these properties to find the profit-maximizing output of the firm.

Let us denote by y some level of output of the firm; we denote by $C(y)$ the minimum cost of producing that output. We call this function $C(.)$, the firm's *cost function*, and its graph a *cost curve*. We should note that this cost function depends upon various things, which we could include in the notation but we leave implicit. The key things that $C(.)$ depend upon are:

- the technology of the firm, and
- the prices of the two inputs.

We should also note that there may be different cost functions depending upon the constraints under which the firm is operating. Economists find it useful to distinguish between two scenarios, which determine the constraints under which the firm is operating and which are referred to as the *long run* and the *short run*. The long run is the familiar case in which the firm is free to vary the quantities of the two inputs. The short run is defined as a situation in which just one of the two inputs is freely variable while the other is fixed; we shall take input 1 to be freely variable in the short run while input 2 is fixed, its value q_2 equal to some fixed level Q_2. If it helps, you can imagine input 1 to be labour while input 2 is capital. In the short run the firm cannot change the level of its capital – only its labour; however in the long run it can vary both.

So we can have a long-run cost function and a short-run cost function. Obviously they are different – in the short run we have this additional constraint that input 2 is fixed. This implies that the short-run cost function differs from the long-run cost function; you should be able to work out that the short-run function can never be lower than the long-run function. (We are minimizing something; if we minimize something with a constraint, the minimum must be at least as large as the minimum without the constraint.) We will give examples during the chapter.

I should emphasise that $C(y)$ measures the minimum total cost of producing the output y. Later in the chapter we will derive two other cost functions from this total cost function: the *marginal cost* function, which measures the rate at which the total costs are increasing; and the *average cost function*, which measures the average cost of producing a particular output.

12.2 The Long Run Total Cost Curve

We start with the long run in which the firm can freely choose the level of both input 1 and input 2. I find it useful to start with a specific example which shows the important properties I want to discuss. Let us take the case of Cobb–Douglas technology. This has a production function given by

$$y = Aq_1^a q_2^b \tag{12.1}$$

In Chapter 11 we found the cost-minimizing input combinations for any given level of output. These were given in Eq. (11.4) and are:

$$q_1 = (y/A)^{1/(a+b)}[aw_2/(bw_1)]^{(b/(a+b))}$$
$$q_2 = (y/A)^{1/(a+b)}(bw_1/[aw_2])^{(a/(a+b))} \tag{12.2}$$

Now the cost of using the combination (q_1, q_2) is obviously $(w_1 q_1 + w_2 q_2)$, so the cheapest cost of producing output y in the long run is found by substituting the optimal input demands into the production function. This yields:

$$C(y) = (y/A)^{1/(a+b)}\{w_1[aw_2/(bw_1)]^{[b/(a+b)]} + w_2(y/A)^{1/(a+b)}[bw_1/(aw_2)]^{[a/(a+b)]}\} \tag{12.3}$$

This is the long run total cost function in the Cobb–Douglas case. It can be simplified to give the following function.

$$C(y) = (a+b)(y/A)^{1/(a+b)}(w_1/a)^{a/(a+b)}(w_2/b)^{b/(a+b)} \tag{12.4}$$

Let us take a numerical example. Let $A = 1$, $a = 0.3$ and $b = 0.5$. This technology exhibits decreasing returns to scale because $(a+b) = 0.8 < 1$. If we substitute these numbers in the expression above we get

$$C(y) = 1.938y^{1.25}w_1^{0.375}w_2^{0.625} \tag{12.5}$$

This is an increasing convex function of y, and an increasing concave function of the two input prices. If we graph the cost function against y we obtain the picture in Fig. 12.1.

Ensure that you understand the connection between the fact that the technology displays decreasing returns to scale and the fact that the cost function is convex; as output rises the scale has to rise proportionately faster, which makes the cost rise proportionately faster. Note that from Eq. (12.4) this is a general property. In fact we should write this as a result. It is very important.

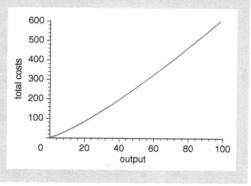

Figure 12.1 Long run total cost curve with decreasing returns to scale

 The total long run cost function is concave, linear or convex according to whether the technology displays increasing, constant or decreasing returns to scale.

12.3 The Short Run Total Cost Curve

Before we consider an example we should think a little about this curve. Let me remind you of the scenario. Input 2 is fixed at the level Q_2. The firm cannot change this in the short run; it can, however, vary input 1. It wants to continue to do what it has been doing in the past: for any given level of output it wants to find the cheapest way of producing that output, and thus it wants to find the cheapest cost of producing each level of output. Do you think that, with this additional constraint of being unable to vary the amount of input 2 in the short term, it can do better or worse than without it?

I hope the answer is immediate; with this additional constraint the firm is almost always doomed to do worse than before. Therefore the short run total cost function can never be lower than the long-run total cost function; if it were there would be a contradiction, because the long run function could not be minimizing costs in the long run. However, we could be lucky in the sense that the fixed quantity of input 2 might just be the right amount to minimize costs in the long run; in such a case the long and the short run costs would coincide.

Now let us take an example. Let us continue to use the Cobb–Douglas technology which we used in Section 12.2. Additionally we have $q_2 = Q_2$. So we have

$$y = Aq_1^a Q_2^b \tag{12.6}$$

On the right-hand side of Eq. (12.6) the only thing that is variable is q_1; as we vary q_1, output y varies. If we want to produce a particular level of output, it is clear that there is a unique value of q_1 for which this is possible – one that solves the above equation in terms of y. Solving it we obtain the following result.

$$q_1 = (y/A)^{1/a} Q_2^{-b/a} \tag{12.7}$$

To produce the output y, only this quantity of input 1 should be used; (rather obviously, it depends upon Q_2). It follows that the total cost of producing output y in the short run is given by $(w_1 q_1 + w_2 Q_2)$ where q_1 is given by the expression above. In this way we get the total short run cost function (12.8).

$$C(y) = w_1 (y/A)^{1/a} Q_2^{-b/a} + w_2 Q_2 \tag{12.8}$$

We note that it is an increasing convex function of y (if $0 < a < 1$), that it starts at the value $w_2 Q_2$ when y is zero (this is the cost of the fixed factor), and that it is increasing in both the input prices.

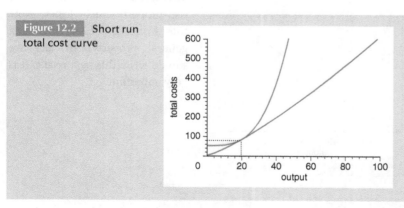

Figure 12.2 Short run total cost curve

Let us graph it. Obviously its position will depend upon the value of Q_2 – the value at which input 2 is fixed. I shall give several examples starting with $Q_2 = 50$. In the example that follows, as indeed in Fig. 12.1 I have taken $w_1 = w_2 = 1$, so the fixed cost[1] is 50. Hence the graph of total cost starts at 50. Thereafter it is an increasing convex function of y. It is the upper curve in Fig. 12.2.

---

1. The cost of the fixed input – namely $w_2 Q_2$.

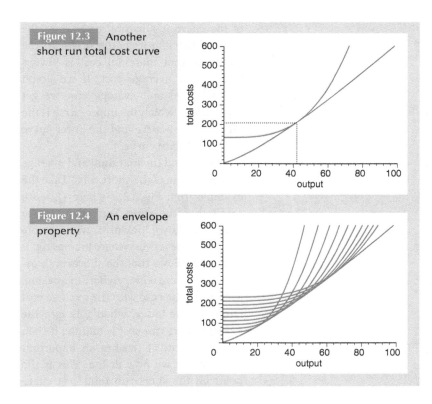

Figure 12.3 Another short run total cost curve

Figure 12.4 An envelope property

You will see that this is in agreement with our prior speculations. You will also see that there is a point at which the two curves coincide; indeed they are tangential at this point. This is at an output slightly below 20. What is the significance of this output? It is the output at which the employment of 50 units of input 2 would be optimal in the long run. So at that point the constraint is not really binding, and the firm does as well in the short run as it would in the long run.

If we take a different value of Q_2 we get a different short run total cost curve. For example, with $Q_2 = 130$ we get the picture in Fig. 12.3. The short-run total cost curve commences at 130 and is tangential to the long run curve at a higher level of output. Both short run curves have the same properties; they start positive (the fixed costs); they are increasing and convex, and are everywhere above the long run curves except at the point where they are tangential. We shall also note an important property of all the short run curves when they are put together. Here we just plot a selection in Fig. 12.4, but it should be clear what would happen if we plotted more. As mathematicians would say: the long run curve is the *envelope* of all the short run curves.

12.4 Marginal and Average Costs

So far we have been talking solely about total costs, both in the short run or the long. Now we want to introduce two new cost curves for both the long and the short run, which we can derive from the total cost curve and which will prove useful in the future. These are the marginal cost curve and the average cost curve.

The *marginal cost curve* tells us the rate at which total costs are increasing. Mathematically, marginal costs are the derivatives of the total cost function; that is, $dC(y)/dy$. Graphically, marginal costs are the slope of the total cost function.

The *average cost curve* measures the cost per unit produced. Mathematically, average costs are the ratio of total cost to output; that is, $C(y)/y$. Graphically – and this is a useful interpretation – average costs are the slope of the line joining the origin to the total cost curve at a particular level of output y.

We can derive marginal and average costs in both the long run and the short run. Let us start with the former. If we look at the graph of the total cost in the long run (Fig. 12.1) we see that the slope of the curve is everywhere increasing (it is a convex function); moreover the slope of the line from the origin to the curve is also increasing everywhere. It follows that both marginal cost and average cost are increasing everywhere. We also note that the slope

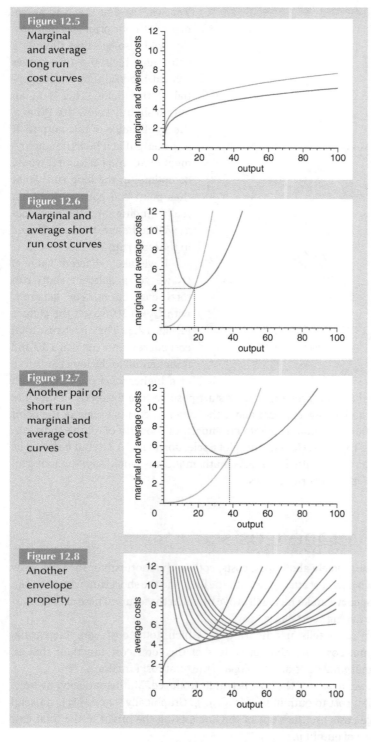

Figure 12.5
Marginal and average long run cost curves

Figure 12.6
Marginal and average short run cost curves

Figure 12.7
Another pair of short run marginal and average cost curves

Figure 12.8
Another envelope property

of the curve is always greater than the slope of the line from the origin to the curve, so that marginal cost is always larger than average cost. If we graph the marginal and average cost we get Fig. 12.5, in which the upper curve is the marginal cost curve and the lower curve the average cost curve.

Let us find the marginal and average curves for one of the short runs. Take the example from Fig. 12.2 where $Q_2 = 50$; recall that the short run curve is the upper one. If we look at it, we first note that the slope is everywhere increasing. It therefore follows that the short run marginal cost curve is everywhere increasing. This is not the case with the average cost curve. In the latter, when y is zero the average short run cost is infinite; it then decreases until it reaches an important point which we now define. This is the point on the short run total cost curve where the line from the origin is tangential to the curve. Clearly at this point marginal cost is equal to average cost. Moreover at this point average cost is at its minimum; up to this point average cost is decreasing – thereafter it is increasing. This is shown in Fig. 12.6.

The 'important point' is an output just below 18. At this output (in Fig. 12.2), a line from the origin to the curve is tangential to that curve at that point. Hence in Fig. 12.6, the marginal cost curve intersects the average cost curve and, moreover, the average cost curve reaches its minimum at that point. Obviously these properties are true for any short run; a proof is supplied in the mathematical appendix.

Fig. 12.7 shows the implied marginal and average cost curves for the second short-run (refer to Fig. 12.3). Note that, with a higher level of the fixed input, the minimum value of the average short run cost curve occurs at a higher output level, and also takes a higher minimum value.

Finally, we illustrate a second envelope property. We have already established that the long run total cost curve is the envelope of the short run cost curves. It follows that the long run average cost curve is the envelope of the short run average cost curves, as Fig. 12.8 shows.

12.5 Cost Curves with Increasing and Constant Returns to Scale

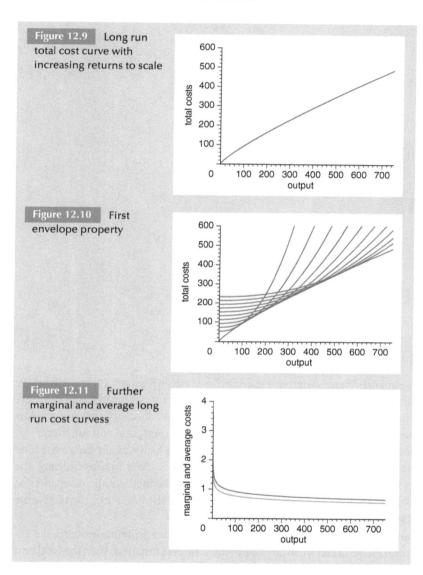

Figure 12.9 Long run total cost curve with increasing returns to scale

Figure 12.10 First envelope property

Figure 12.11 Further marginal and average long run cost curvess

Throughout the above analysis we have worked with a specific example in which the technology displayed decreasing returns to scale; however the results we have obtained apply also to increasing and constant returns to scale. The only thing that really differs is the shape of the long run total cost function; all the other properties concerning the relationship between the long and short run curves remain valid. We know that the long-run curve is concave, linear or convex according to whether the technology displays increasing, constant or decreasing returns to scale. Let us take an increasing returns example: Cobb–Douglas with parameters $a = 0.45$ and $b = 0.75$. The long run cost curve is depicted in Fig. 12.9.

In the short run we almost always have decreasing returns to the variable factor, so the short run total cost functions are convex[2]. We get the first envelope property, shown in Fig. 12.10.

Note that the long run curve is concave, but each of the short run curves are convex. This reflects increasing returns to scale in the long run, but decreasing returns to the variable factor in the short run. Because of the shape of the long run function, both the marginal and average long run cost curves are decreasing, with the marginal curve always below the average curve; this is illustrated in Fig. 12.11.

The short run marginal and average cost curves from this example are in Fig. 12.12. The usual second envelope of average cost curves is pictured in Fig. 12.13.

Obviously everything also works with constant returns to scale technology; the only thing that differs is that the long run total cost function is linear, and hence the long run average and marginal cost curves are horizontal and coincide.

---

2. In the case of Cobb–Douglas, if we put $0 < a < 1$ and $0 < b < 1$, this guarantees decreasing returns to each factor. In practice this is overwhelmingly the usual case.

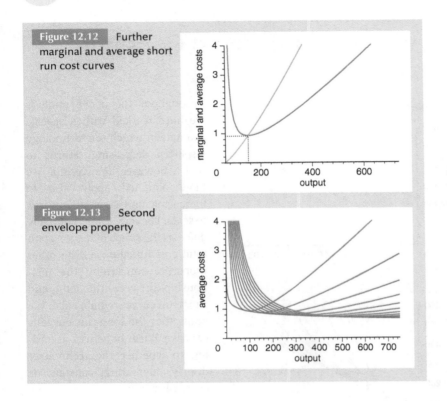

Figure 12.12 Further marginal and average short run cost curves

Figure 12.13 Second envelope property

12.6 From Marginal to Total

We have already explained how to derive a marginal cost curve from a total cost curve; we simply find the slope of the total cost curve. This tells us the rate at which total costs are increasing, and hence gives us marginal costs. To a mathematician, what we are doing is finding the derivative of the total cost function; this tells us the marginal cost function.

This final section asks how we might go the other way – how we might derive the total cost function from knowledge of the marginal cost function. To a mathematician, the reverse of finding the derivative is obtaining the integral (see the mathematical appendix to Chapter 1). So, if the marginal cost function is the derivative of the total, then the total is the integral of the marginal.

To a non-mathematician an integral is an area. So the above sentence is saying the following: if the marginal cost function is the slope of the total cost function, then the total cost function is the area underneath the marginal cost function; to get the total cost, we just add up all the marginal costs. More specifically, the total cost at a particular output level y is given by the area underneath the marginal cost function from 0 to y.

We provide an example which should help you verify this result. In Fig. 12.14 we show the long run total and marginal cost curves for the first example in this chapter. Rather obviously, the upper

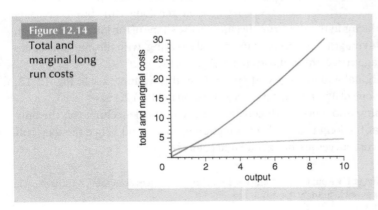

Figure 12.14 Total and marginal long run costs

curve is the total cost curve and the lower curve is the marginal cost curve. You should work both ways. First select an output level – say six. Draw a vertical line at this value, then calculate the slope of the upper line at the same point. Confirm that this is equal to the level of the marginal cost curve. Now do the opposite; work out the area between zero and six underneath the marginal cost curve. Confirm that this is equal to the level of the total cost curve.

The same works in the short run, with one slight difference. Consider Fig. 12.15, which shows total and marginal short run costs for the first of the short run examples we considered in this chapter. The top graph is the short run total cost curve; the lower one is the short run marginal cost curve. To go from the top curve to the bottom curve, we simply find the slope of the top curve. You should check this. To go the other way, we find the area beneath the bottom curve. However in this instance one thing missing: the fixed cost of 50. So the area under the bottom curve is the total short run cost excluding the fixed cost. You should check this.

Figure 12.15 Total and marginal short run costs

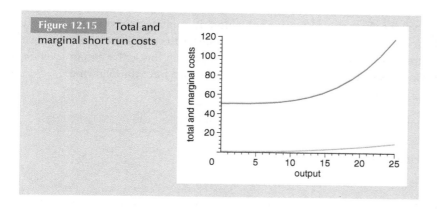

12.7 Summary

This chapter has provided some useful material for future chapters. You should remember and make sure that you understand the important results, which are summarized here.

We started by making a distinction between the long run and the short. In the long run the firm can freely chose the level of both inputs; in the short run, one of the two inputs is fixed. We started with the long run and used the results of Chapter 11 to find the cheapest way of producing any given level of output. We defined the total long run cost curve and found an important property of that curve.

 The long run curve shows the cheapest cost of producing each output. It is concave, linear or convex according to whether the technology shows increasing, constant or decreasing returns to scale.

We then examined the short run cost curve and found the relationship between the short and long run curves. In particular, we found that the short run curve is everywhere above the long run curve, except at one point where it is tangential; this is the output level for which the fixed input is at its optimal long term value. We then have the following.

 The long run total cost curve is the (lower) envelope of the short run total cost curves.

We next defined marginal and average costs.

 The marginal cost curve shows the rate at which total costs are increasing. It must be positive everywhere. In the long run it is decreasing, constant or increasing according to whether the technology shows increasing, constant or decreasing returns to scale. In the short run it is usually increasing everywhere as there are generally decreasing returns to the fixed factor.

 The average cost curve shows the cost per unit of output.

 The average cost curve and the marginal cost curve intersect at the minimum point of the average cost curve.

From the envelope result above it follows that:

 The long run average cost curve is the (lower) envelope of the short run average cost curves.

We define the fixed costs as those that are fixed in the short run and hence are the cost of producing zero output in the short run. Finally, we show how to go from the marginal cost curve to the total cost curve.

The area under the long run marginal cost curve is the long run total cost.

 The area under the short run marginal cost curve is the variable (total) cost.

12.8 Review Questions

1. Why must the total cost curve never be decreasing in output?

2. Why must any short-run total cost curve never be below the long-run total cost curve?

3. At what level of output does a short-run total cost curve touch the long-run total cost curve?

4. Argue that, if the marginal cost is below the average cost, then the average cost must be decreasing; and that, if the marginal cost curve is above the average cost, then the average cost must be rising. Use this to show that the marginal cost curve must intersect the average cost curve at its minimum point.

5. Verify graphically (by measuring slopes and areas) that the area underneath the long-run marginal cost curve is indeed the total cost. (Use one of the accurate graphs from the text).

6. We know that the total cost curve is concave, linear or convex according to whether the technology displays increasing, constant or decreasing returns to scale. Consider the implications for the short-run total cost curve. If there are always decreasing returns to one input (given a fixed level of the other), argue that the short-run total cost curves are everywhere convex. Do you think it reasonable to assume decreasing returns to scale for any one input?

12.9 Application: how do we Infer the Technology of a Firm?

This is a simple game that could be set as a tutorial exercise, and which you could play with your fellow students of microeconomics. It is very close in spirit to the exercise at the end of Chapter 7, though there is an added twist. Although simple, it teaches a lot about how we can infer technologies from observations, and the most efficient way of so doing.

This is how to organize the game. First, split the tutorial group into two teams, and give to each team the following instructions.

The objective is to discover the technology of a firm given observations on (minimum) costs of producing given outputs at given factor prices. Each team should imagine themselves as a firm with a given technology. The object of the rival team is to discover that technology. As in the exercise of Chapter 7, we make the task easier by restricting the set of possible technologies.

Underlying the technology are two factors (inputs): input 1 and input 2. Input 2 is the *numeraire* input – that is, its price is one. The price of input 1 is p; this price is constant, independent of the amount of the factors used.

Each team should decide what its technology is. Technology is restricted to one of the following:

Type 1: Perfect Substitutes with substitution ratio a – that is, one unit of input 1 can always be substituted by a units of input 2; and with returns to scale indicated by the parameter s – that is, q_1 units of input 1 and q_2 units of input 2 produces $(q_1 + q_2)^s$ units of output. So the production function is as given by Eq. (10.7), namely $y = f(q_1, q_2) = (q_1 + q_2)^s$.

Type 2: Perfect Complements with complementary ratio a; that is, if q_1 units of input 1 are employed, then output increases with units of input 2 until aq_1 units of input 2 are employed, after which no further increases in output are produced; and with returns to scale indicated by the parameter s – that is, q_1 units of input 1 combined with q_2 units of input 2 produce $[\min(q_1, q_2/a)]^s$ units of output. So the production function is that given by Eq. (10.12), namely $y = f(q_1, q_2) = [\min(q_1, q_2/a)]^s$.

Type 3: Cobb–Douglas with relative weights a and $(1 - a)$ on the two inputs, and with returns to scale indicated by the parameter s. So the production function is given by a slight variant on Eq. (10.13), namely $y = f(q_1, q_2) = [q_1^a q_2^{(1-a)}]^s$.

Each team should choose one of these three types, and suitable values for the parameters a and s. You should inform your tutor of these choices: he or she will act as a referee in what follows.

Both teams know their own technology, their type and their values of a and s. The purpose of the exercise is for each team to discover the technology of the other team; that is, its type and its values for a and s, by asking questions of the form: 'What is your minimum cost of producing y units of output when the price of input 1 is p?' Only questions of this type are allowed; however y and p can be any positive numbers.

The way to implement the game is as follows. First, both teams tell the tutor their type and the value of their parameters a and s. Ideally the teams will have decided these before the tutorial begins. Then put on the whiteboard two tables side by side as shown in Table 12.1.

Table 12.1	Illustrative game showing costs for teams 1 and 2				
Team 1's costs			Team 2's costs		
P	Y	C(y)	p	y	C(y)

The game is played simultaneously by the two teams. First both teams write up a question (a value of p and a value of y) in the appropriate table on the whiteboard. (Team 1 in the table headed 'Team 2's cost', and Team 2 in the table headed 'Team 1's costs'). Usually it takes some time for the teams to think up this initial question, but on reflection it becomes obvious that it does not really matter too much what the teams choose for p and y. Then the teams have to fill in their answers – the cost as given by their technologies at the p and y values selected by the other team. This stage takes a bit of time unless the teams are really well prepared. I, as the referee, check that the answers are consistent with the technologies of the two teams. This is important as students frequently make mistakes.

At this point we have one complete row in each of the above tables. The teams are then invited to try and infer the technologies of the other team: their type and the values of the parameters a and s. I do not want to tell you too much at this point otherwise it will spoil the point of the game, but only a certain amount can usually be inferred. Unless the cost is close to zero for a p value close to zero, one cannot eliminate any type of technology. However one can usually conclude something like the following: the technology could be perfect substitutes with particular values of the parameters a and s (determined by the question and the answer); the technology could be perfect complements with particular sets of values of the parameters a and s (determined by the question and the answer); the preferences could be Cobb–Douglas with particular sets of values of the parameters a and s (determined by the question and the answer).

Since nothing definite has been inferred by this stage we repeat the procedure. The teams are invited to write up a second question (a value of p and a value of y) in the appropriate table on the whiteboard. The choice of p and y in this second question must be done carefully. In this exercise it is quite clever to use the same value of p as in their first question and change the value of y. As is discussed in the hints appendix, you can use the information gained to determine the returns to scale parameter s. Once this is known it is quite easy to discover the type of technology and, though possibly less easily, the value of the parameter a.

This whole procedure is repeated until one team infers the type of the other and the values of the parameters a and s. Some hints are given below, but I recommend that you do not read these hints until you have played the game. You will learn more if you work through the game yourselves.

You could, of course, make the game more interesting and more difficult by allowing further possible types of technologies. One obvious extension is to include constant elasticity of substitution technology. This makes it more difficult but more realistic. In practice we do not have a set of technologies from which to choose, so the set of possible technologies could be very large. There are other types of technologies which are better approximations to real technologies used by actual firms, but discussing these would take us beyond the scope of this book.

12.10 Mathematical Appendix

We start with a proof of the result that the marginal cost curve intersects the average cost curve at the minimum point of the average cost curve. To do this we note that the average cost curve is simply given by the function.

$$AC(y) = C(y)/y \tag{A12.1}$$

To find the value of y where this is minimized, we need to find the point where $dAC(y)/dy = 0$; that is, the lowest point of the average cost curve. If we evaluate $dAC(y)/dy$ we obtain, using the quotient rule for derivatives which we noted in Chapter 1, the following function

$$dAC(y)/dy = [dC(y)/dy]/y - C(y)/y^2 \tag{A12.2}$$

Hence $dAC(y)/dy = 0$ where $[dC(y)/dy]/y - C(y)/y^2 = 0$, that is, where $dC(y)/dy = C(y)/y$; that is, where marginal cost is equal to the average cost. Hence our result.

12.11 Hints Appendix

Hints and comments – which you are recommended to read AFTER you have played the game.

This is quite a difficult, but very relevant, exercise. It is relevant because the whole point of this exercise is to show how we can infer technology from observations on costs. Once we have this information we can use it to predict the future behaviour of the firm. As for the difficulty of the exercise, it all depends on how you tackle it. Use the knowledge that is in your head and the text concerning the relation between the minimum production cost and the price p of the input and the output of the firm. Note that, in general, the form of these relationships depends upon the technology, although there is an important result that you can exploit. Consider changing the value of y without changing the value of p. The isocost curves keep the same slope. Given that the isoquants in all the technologies considered here have the property that they are radially parallel[3] (which means that, along any ray from the origin, the slope of every isoquant is the same), it follows that the quantities of both inputs increase in the same proportion. Suppose we multiply the output required by c and we find that the factor inputs are both multiplied by d. Then we have $y = f(q_1, q_2)$ and $cy = f(dq_1 dq_2)$. But, for all three technologies that we are considering (see Eqs (10.7), (10.12) and (10.13) above), it is true that $f(dq_1, dq_2) = d^s f(q_1, q_2)$, where s is the returns to scale parameter. Putting these equations together, we have $c = d^s$. Now we know c because we have specified it; and we know d because that is simply by how much the cost has been multiplied. So we can work out the returns to scale parameter s.

I do not want to say too much, but you should use your intuition. We have already used the relationship between the cost and y to infer the value of s. To find the technology and the value of the parameter a, we need to use our knowledge about the relationship between the cost and p. Consider, for example, type 1 – perfect substitutes. What do you we know? That the firm uses input 1, and only input 1, when it is cheap enough ($p < a$), and it uses input 2, and only input 2, when input 1 is too expensive ($p > a$). So if we plot the cost against p, it rises with p until p equals a, and thereafter it remains horizontal as a function of p. If this is what we find when we plot a graph of the cost against p, we can infer that the technology is type 1 and the value of a is the price at which the graph stops rising. Similar arguments – which I leave to you – apply to the other two types.

---

3.   Formally, this property is known as homotheticity of the isoquants.

Firm Supply and Producer Surplus

13.1 Introduction

The last two chapters have prepared the way for this chapter in which we find the optimal output of a price-taking (competitive) firm. We have all the apparatus that we need; in Chapter 11 we worked out the cheapest way to produce any given output, and we used this in Chapter 12 to work out the (lowest) cost of producing any output. We can now work out the profit from any output and hence find the output which maximizes the firm's profit.

In this chapter we assume that the firm takes the output price as given. This is termed competitive behaviour, and the assumption is usually justified by arguing that a single firm is so small relative to the market that it has no control over the price; it simply has to take it as given. Later we shall consider the opposite extreme, when the firm is the only one in the market and can thus choose the price; and we shall also consider cases in between. But, for the moment, we assume that the firm takes the price of its output as given.

13.2 Profit Maximization

We denote the output of the firm by y and the price by p. This price p is given and the firm cannot change it. What we are considering in this chapter is the optimal choice of y, by which I mean the choice of y which maximizes the profit of the firm.

We will plot a graph in which the choice variable y is on the horizontal axis, and revenue, costs and profits are on the vertical axis – so we can see easily where profits are maximized. Let us start with the firm's revenue, which is simply given by py. Recall that p is constant; then it is clear that revenue is simply a straight line through the origin with slope p. In Fig. 13.1 I have assumed a price of 30, so the slope of the revenue function is 30.

If we graph cost against output we know that the form depends upon the returns to scale in the technology. Let us start with decreasing returns to scale; later we shall look at constant and increasing returns. We know that, if the returns to scale are decreasing, then the cost function is increasing and convex; costs rise more than proportionately with output. We therefore get the situation depicted in Fig. 13.1.

The straight line is the revenue function and the convex curve is the cost function. The difference between revenue and costs – namely profits – is shown in the concave curve at the

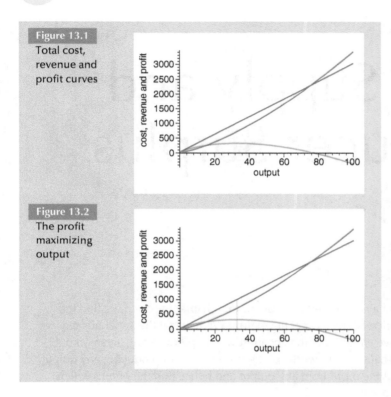

Figure 13.1
Total cost, revenue and profit curves

Figure 13.2
The profit maximizing output

bottom of the figure. Note that profits are zero at an output of zero (this must be the long run, as costs are zero at an output of zero); they are positive up to an output of around 76, after which they become negative. It is easy to see from this figure that there is a unique level of output at which profits are maximized. Indeed, it should be easy to see that this must always be the case, unless the cost curve is steeper at an output of zero than the revenue curve, in which case the best thing to do is to produce nothing. This profit-maximizing output is indicated in Fig. 13.2; the output is around 33.

Can we write down a condition to help us find the optimal output? If we look at Fig. 13.2, it is clear that profits are maximized when the vertical distance between the revenue curve and the cost curve is maximized. The condition for this is that the slope of the revenue curve must equal the slope of the cost curve. The former is simply the price p and the latter, by definition, is the marginal cost at the optimal output. The condition for maximizing profit is simply, for the price-taking firm:

$p = marginal\ cost$ (13.1)

We have found the profit-maximizing condition and output using the space[1] in Fig. 13.1, with output on the horizontal axis and total revenue, total cost and total profit on the vertical axis. This space is simple to use and easy to understand. However it is sometimes useful to do the analysis in a different space – again with output on the horizontal axis, but now with marginal revenue and marginal cost on the vertical axis. You will recall how to move from total cost to marginal cost; we simply find the slope of the total cost function. The same is true for marginal revenue; to obtain it from the total revenue function we simply find the slope of the total revenue function. But in this case we already know the slope; it is constant and equal to the price p of the good. So, for this competitive firm, the condition is that its marginal revenue is simply equal to the fixed price of the good; every extra unit which the firm sells provides it with an additional revenue equal to the price.

If we find the marginal revenue and marginal cost curves corresponding to the total curves in Fig. 13.2, we obtain the graphs in Fig. 13.3. Note that marginal cost (the slope of the total cost curve) is everywhere increasing[2].

In the analysis so far, a price $p = 30$ has been assumed so the marginal revenue curve is horizontal at 30. The same price 30 was assumed when drawing Fig. 13.2. In Fig. 13.3, we have indicated the profit-maximizing output where price equals marginal cost; notice that it

---

1. The term *space* was defined in Chapter 1. It merely defines the variables on the axes.
2. The fact that it is increasing at a decreasing rate – that is, the marginal cost curve is concave – comes from the fact, which is not immediately obvious, that the third derivative of the total cost function is negative.

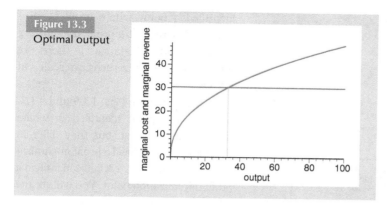

Figure 13.3
Optimal output

is around 33, exactly as before. Obviously it is the same point; all that differs is the graphical representation. You should see from Fig. 13.3 that, if the price changes, so will the optimal output. We shall explore the implications of this later.

13.3 Loss Minimization

We have to be a little careful in applying the profit-maximizing condition; it does not guarantee that the profit is positive, but merely that it is maximized. This is easy to see if we take the example above and add to the firm's costs some new fixed cost – perhaps a government tax – which is sufficiently large to make the profits everywhere negative. What happens? To the total revenue and hence marginal revenue curves, the answer is nothing. To the total cost curve, the new fixed cost shifts the entire cost curve up by a constant amount. To the marginal cost curve, nothing happens because shifting a curve vertically upwards by a constant amount does not change its slope at any point. So the addition of the fixed cost, while making profits negative everywhere, does not change Fig. 13.3; it looks exactly the same. Is the identified point still a profit-maximizing point? Well, yes; in the sense that it minimizes the losses which exist everywhere because of the fixed costs. But there is still a loss at that point. It may pay the firm to give up production altogether.

13.4 Increasing Returns to Scale

We also have to be a little careful when applying the condition that price should equal marginal cost, for we might have identified a point where the profits are minimized rather than maximized. Consider what happens if we have increasing returns to scale. In such a situation the cost function becomes concave and the total curves look like those drawn in Fig. 13.4.

We have also included in Fig. 13.4 the profits of the firm, and we have identified an output (around 18) at which the price (the slope of the revenue curve) equals the marginal cost (the slope of the cost curve). If we move into marginal space, as in Fig. 13.5, we can see this more clearly.

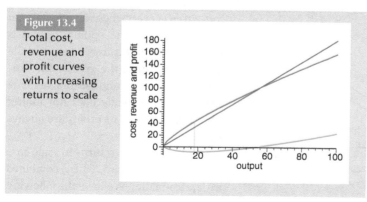

Figure 13.4
Total cost, revenue and profit curves with increasing returns to scale

In Fig. 13.5, the downward sloping curve is the marginal cost curve and the horizontal line is the constant marginal revenue (here assumed to be 1.8). If we compare Figs. 13.5 and 13.4, we see that the condition (price = marginal cost) has

Figure 13.5

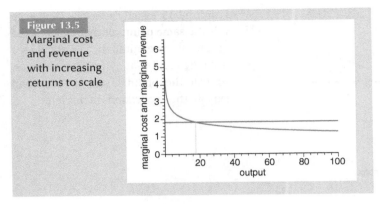

Marginal cost and revenue with increasing returns to scale

identified a point where profit is minimized. Where is the profit maximizing output? In this instance, if there are always increasing returns to scale, at infinity.

Let us compare Figs. 13.5 and 13.3. In both, the point identified is where price = marginal cost, but they differ in that Fig. 13.3 identified a profit maximization point whilst Fig. 13.5 has identified a profit minimization point. You will see the difference: in Fig. 13.3 the marginal cost curve intersects the price from below, in Fig. 13.5 the marginal cost curve intersects the price from above. We need to be sure that we have checked this second condition.

So, with increasing returns to scale the optimal output of the firm is infinite. This seems a bit unrealistic, and it alerts us to the fact that there must therefore be an incompatibility between increasing returns to scale and competition (price-taking behaviour). In practice the possibility of increasing returns to scale everywhere is highly remote, but even so this result indicates that, if an industry has increasing returns to scale over most realistic levels of output, then the industry cannot really be competitive (price-taking). We might expect a monopoly (one big firm exploiting the returns to scale) taking over the industry. Indeed that is what we see in practice in industries that are called 'natural monopolies'. We shall have more to say about this in Chapters 28 and 29.

13.5 Constant Returns to Scale

An interesting intermediate case is when the technology displays constant returns to scale. In this case the total cost curve is linear, as is the total revenue curve. What is the best course of action for the firm depends upon where these two curves are in relation to each other. We shall draw just one case; you should be able to envisage the others yourself.

This case is illustrated in Fig. 13.6, where the cost curve is everywhere below the total revenue curve – that is, when the constant marginal cost is everywhere smaller than the price. The top line is total revenue, the second total cost and the third total profit (the vertical difference between the first two). Where is the profit-maximizing point? If the returns to scale stay constant it is clear that profits will continue to increase, so the profit-maximizing point is at infinity.

Figure 13.6

Constant returns to scale (price > marginal cost)

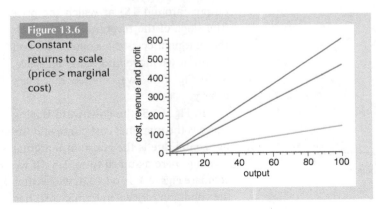

The opposite is the case if the total cost curve is everywhere above the total revenue curve – the optimal output is zero as any output causes a loss, and the greater the output the greater the loss. When the total cost and the total revenue coincide then it really does not matter what the firm does; its profits are always zero.

So the constant returns to scale case appears rather weird when combined with price-taking. We have the following results, where c denotes the constant marginal cost under constant returns:

$$\begin{bmatrix} \text{Optimal output} = \text{infinity if } p > c \\ \text{Optimal output} = \text{anything if } p = c \\ \text{Optimal output} = \text{zero if } p < c \end{bmatrix}$$

But there is an interesting implication of this case. Since output cannot be infinite in practice, the only way that constant returns to scale can co-exist with competitive (price-taking) behaviour is to have an industry in which the price is equal to the marginal cost, and the firms sharing the aggregate demand between them. Perhaps this is what is truly meant by a competitive industry.

13.6 The Supply Curve of the Firm

The supply curve tells us, for each output price, how much the firm would be willing to supply at that price. We know that the optimality condition is that the firm produces the quantity of output for which price = marginal cost. In Fig. 13.7 we examine the long run supply curve of the firm, so we draw its long run marginal cost curve. We take the example of the technology with which we started this chapter. Note that the variable along the horizontal axis is the quantity of output, and the variables on the vertical axis are the price and marginal cost.

For any given output price the firm will choose that level of output for which the price is equal to marginal cost. One case is shown in Fig. 13.7 where the price is ten. At this price the optimal output is about 2.5. If the price were to rise, then the optimal output would also rise along the marginal cost curve. Indeed, we can see that the marginal cost curve is the curve relating output to price, and hence is the supply curve of the firm. Of course, we should check that the profits are indeed positive at every point on the supply curve; as it happens this is true for the technology that we have assumed.

In the short run the principle is the same. We equate the price with the short run marginal cost. But we also ought to check whether the firm might not be better off simply closing down. We need to check that the profits, (while possibly negative) exceed the fixed costs. In Fig. 13.8, one of the short runs that we considered previously, this is always the case; so the firm's short run supply curve coincides with its short run marginal cost curve.

In Fig. 13.8 output is measured along the horizontal axis, and price and marginal cost on the vertical axis. The U-shaped curve is the short run average cost. The solid upward sloping curve is the short run marginal cost curve and

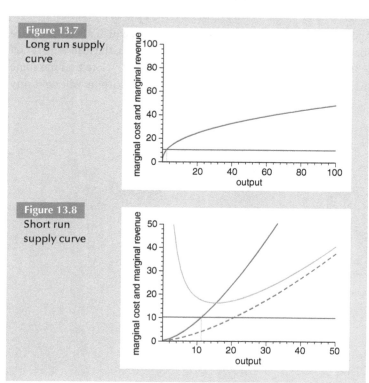

Figure 13.7
Long run supply curve

Figure 13.8
Short run supply curve

also the supply curve of the firm; and the dashed upward sloping curve is the short run average variable cost, excluding the fixed cost.

13.7 Producer Surplus

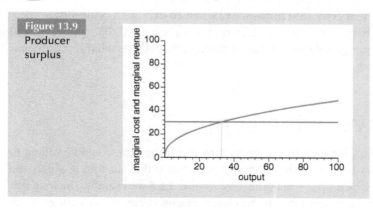

Figure 13.9
Producer surplus

We can prove a nice result about the producer surplus. You may like to anticipate it. Consider for some price (here 30) the optimal output decision; this is shown in Fig. 13.9.

The optimal output is about 33. Where in Fig. 13.9 is the firm's profit or surplus? The profit or surplus is the difference between revenue and costs. If the firm sells 33 units at a price of 30, its revenue is the product of the price (30) and the quantity (33); the revenue is precisely equal to the area of the rectangle bounded by the price and the quantity sold. The total cost of producing 33 units is given by the area below the marginal cost curve between zero and 33. The difference between these two areas is the firm's profit. It should be obvious that this difference is the area between the price and the marginal cost curve. But we know that the marginal cost curve is the firm's supply curve. So we get the nice result, which should be familiar, that:

 The surplus of the firm is the area between the price received and the supply curve.

This enables us to find immediately the effect of a policy change which affects the price that the firm receives. For example, if the price increases from 30 to 40, the firm is better off by the area between $p = 30$, $p = 40$ and the supply curve; see Fig. 3.10. Note that the same result is true in the short run, although the calculation of absolute surplus will omit any fixed cost.

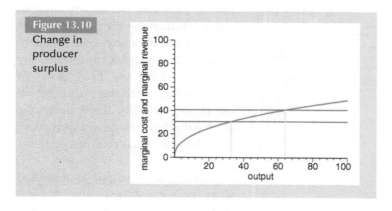

Figure 13.10
Change in producer surplus

13.8 Summary

We found in this chapter the optimal profit-maximizing output for the price-taking firm.

 The price-taking (competitive) firm produces up to the point where the price equals the marginal cost, at a point where marginal costs are increasing.

The implications of this condition are important.

 The supply curve of a competitive firm is upward sloping.

Most of this chapter assumed decreasing returns to scale. Indeed the combination of price-taking behaviour and constant or increasing returns was rather odd.

 With increasing returns to scale everywhere, the optimal output for a price-taking firm is infinite.

 With constant returns to scale, the optimal output is either infinite, indeterminate or zero.

Finally, we confirmed an important result that we have shown in another context.

 The surplus of the firm is the area between the supply curve and the price received.

13.9 Review Questions

1 Show that, if a firm has a technology which displays constant returns to scale in the long-run, its long-run supply curve (insofar as this has any meaning) is horizontal. What is the significance of the level at which it is horizontal?

2 In the short-run, the area below the marginal cost curve excludes any fixed costs. Show, nevertheless, that the change in profits when the output price changes is equal to the area between the two prices and the short-run marginal cost curve.

3 Use results concerning the relationship between the long-run and short-run marginal cost curves to see whether a firm benefits more or less from a price increase in the long-run than it does in the short-run.

Production Possibility Frontiers

14.1 Introduction

In Chapter 8 we considered the allocation of a given amount of goods in society. We saw that the final allocation depended upon the initial allocation. The obvious next question concerns the determination of this initial allocation; this obviously depends upon the choices open to society. It is to this question that we now turn: what determines the production possibilities open to a society?

We consider two different scenarios. In the first society consists of two individuals, each of whom can produce various combinations of two goods, using what we term a linear technology. We examine how the two individuals should divide up the work between them so that society (the two of them together) produces the maximum output possible. In the second scenario we have two firms, each producing one good with a fixed amount of inputs between them. We consider the optimal use of the two inputs so that, once again, output is maximized. In both scenarios we find the *production possibility frontier* available to society and discuss the factors which determine its shape.

14.2 Linear Technologies

We start with a nice simple story. The society consists of two individuals, A and B, and two goods, 1 and 2, which both A and B can produce. We tell a very simple story about each of their production capabilities. For each of the goods, there is a maximum amount that each individual can produce if he or she devotes all the time available to the production of that good – say m_1 for good 1 and m_2 for good 2 (these maximum amounts can differ from individual to individual, as we shall see). So, if an individual works all day on good 1, he or she can produce m_1 of good 1 and nothing of good 2; if the individual works all day on good 2 he or she can produce m_2 of good 2 and nothing of good 1. Moreover, let us assume that the working process is such that, if someone works for half a day on good 1 and half on good 2, he or she can produce $m_1/2$ of good 1 and $m_2/2$ of good 2. More generally, if he or she spends a fraction a of the day working on good 1 and a fraction $(1 - a)$ of the day working on good 2, he or she can produce a quantity am_1 of good 1 and a quantity $(1 - a)m_2$ of good 2. This is called a *linear technology*.

Now let us consider a specific example. We start with individual A and suppose that his or her maximum quantities are 120 units of good 1 and 60 units of good 2. Given what we have

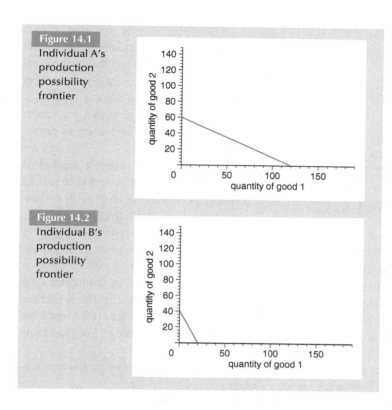

Figure 14.1
Individual A's
production
possibility
frontier

Figure 14.2
Individual B's
production
possibility
frontier

assumed above, individual A's production possibility frontier is shown in Fig. 14.1, which has the quantity of good 1 produced along the horizontal axis, and that of good 2 along the vertical axis.

The line indicates the possibilities open to individual A assuming that he or she works all day[1]. So, for example, the midpoint of the production possibility frontier represents what he or she would produce if half the day were spent on the production of each good.

We make the same kinds of assumptions about individual B, although we are assuming that he or she is less efficient than A in the production of both goods. We assume that, for individual B, the maximum quantities of goods 1 and 2 equal 20 and 40 respectively. We thus get the production possibility frontier for individual B in Fig. 14.2.

Working all day on good 1, B can produce 20 units of good 1 and none of good 2; working all day on good 2 he or she can produce 40 of good 2 and none of good 1. Working for half a day on each will lead to the production of 10 units of good 1 and 20 of good 2; and so on.

We note that B is absolutely worse than A in the production of both goods, although we can say that B is *relatively* better than A at producing good 2 and A is *relatively* better than B at producing good 1. How do we know this? We note that for individual A, for every extra unit of good 1 that is produced, 0.5 units less of good 2 are produced; whereas for B, for every extra unit of good 1 that is produced, two units less of good 2 are produced. So in terms of the cost of producing good 1, as measured by the amount of good 2 that is given up to produce the extra amount of good 1, it is relatively low for A. In this sense individual A is relatively better than B at producing good 1. We can reverse all this. For individual B, for every extra unit of good 2 that is produced 0.5 units less of good 1 are produced, whereas for A for every extra unit of good 2 that is produced two units less of good 1 are produced. So, in terms of the cost of producing good 2, as measured by the amount of good 1 that has to be given up to produce the extra amount of good 2, it is relatively low for B. In this sense then B is relatively better than A at producing good 2.

The issue that we now discuss is the maximum output of the two individuals combined. We want to find the highest production possibility of society. This depends on how A and B divide up the work between them.

The end points of society's production possibility frontier are easy to find: if society wants the maximum amount of good 1 then both individuals have to work all day to produce good 1, giving a total output of $(120 + 20) = 140$ units; if society wants the maximum of good 2, both individuals have to work all day on good 2 giving a total of $(60 + 40) = 100$ units. It is between these two extremes that the difficulties lie.

---

1. From now on we shall simply take this as given. If he or she works for less than a full day, then a point within the triangle will result.

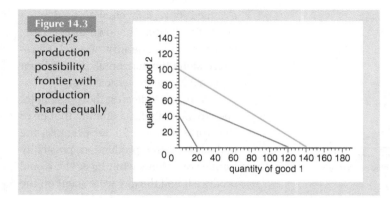

Figure 14.3

Society's production possibility frontier with production shared equally

One possibility is that they simply divide up the work equally in the following sense: if A works half the day on good 1, then so does B; more generally, if A works a fraction a of the day on good 1 then so does B. This gives us a production possibility frontier[2] for society as drawn in Fig. 14.3.

The top line is society's production possibility frontier if A and B share the work equally. The second line is A's production possibility frontier and the bottom line is B's. We have already discussed the extremes (140, 0) and (0, 100). Points in between are found by the 'sharing work equally' rule. For example, the point at the middle of society's frontier (70, 50) is reached by each working half the day on good 1 and half on good 2; so A produces 60 of good 1 and 30 of good 2, and B produces 10 of good 1 and 20 of good 2. A further example is the point a quarter of the way along (105, 25). This is reached by A working $\frac{3}{4}$ of the day on good 1 and $\frac{1}{4}$ on good 2, and producing 90 of good 1 and 15 of good 2; and by B working $\frac{3}{4}$ of the day on good 1 and $\frac{1}{4}$ on good 2, producing 15 of good 1 and 10 of good 2.

You might be asking yourself whether this is a particularly clever way for the two individuals to share the work. After all, we have already realized that A is relatively good at producing good 1 and B is relatively good at producing good 2. Might it not be better for each individual to specialize in the production of the good which they are relatively better at producing?

We can easily see that the answer to this question must be 'yes' by considering what happens at the point where each individual specializes in the good at which he or she is relatively good. If A works all day on good 1, he or she produces 120 of good 1 and 0 of good 2; if B works all day on good 2, then he or she produces 40 of good 2 and 0 of good 1. Between the two of them they produce 120 of good 1 and 40 of good 2, so society reaches the point (120, 40). What do you notice about the point (120, 40)? Yes; it lies outside the production possibility frontier for society which we have drawn above.

If we apply the principle that each individual specializes in the production of the good in which he or she has a relative advantage,

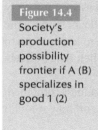

Figure 14.4

Society's production possibility frontier if A (B) specializes in good 1 (2)

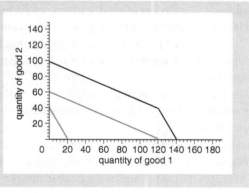

we get the society production possibility frontier shown in Fig. 14.4. We have already discussed the extremes, and also the point (120, 40) which is at the angle on society's frontier. This kink at (120, 40) point divides society's frontier into two regions – that above the kink and that below the kink. In the region above the kink, society is consuming more than 40 units of good 2; this is more than the amount of good 2 that can be produced by the expert in good 2 (individ-

2. As we shall show shortly, this is not the best production possibility frontier for society – just a possibility. We shall later reserve the term production possibility frontier for society to refer only to the *best* one.

ual B). So in the region above the kink, B spends all day on good 2 while A produces the rest. In the region below the kink, society consumes more than 120 units of good 1, that is, more of good 1 than the expert in good 1 (individual A) can produce. So in the region below the kink A will spend all day producing good 1 while B produces the rest. This way of dividing up the work between them is the most efficient possible in the sense that it leads to the highest possible production possibility frontier for society [3].

It is instructive to look at this frontier and see how it is derived. There is a part which corresponds to the frontier for A, shifted vertically upwards a distance 40 (corresponding to B specializing in good 2), and a part which corresponds to the frontier for B, shifted horizontally rightwards a distance 120 (corresponding to A specializing in good 1). You will notice that the frontier is concave; it must always be so if individuals specialize in what they are relatively good at producing.

You might now be able to work out what happens if a third individual enters the society. His or her impact on society's production possibility frontier clearly depends upon his or her own frontier. Let us suppose that it lies between A and B in terms of productive ability both absolutely and relatively, the frontier going from (50, 0) to (0.50) as in Fig. 14.5.

As before, society's frontier has a section corresponding to each individual, and is arranged in such a way that production is maximized. You should be able to verify this by examining society's production possibility frontier in Fig. 14.6.

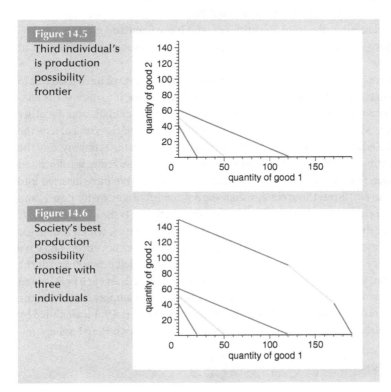

Figure 14.5
Third individual's is production possibility frontier

Figure 14.6
Society's best production possibility frontier with three individuals

You will note the following.

- if society wants a lot of good 1, both A and C will specialize in its production;
- if society wants a lot of good 2, both B and C will specialize in its production;
- in between, A specializes in good 1 and B specializes in good 2.

We see that the frontier remains concave; adding more individuals adds more segments (always one per individual), but the frontier remains concave. Note that the slope of any segment measures the marginal rate of substitution (MRS) between the two goods; and in each segment the MRS is that of some individual (which remains constant for any one individual).

---

3. Note that, at all levels of production A is relatively better than B in the production of good 1 and B is relatively better than A in the production of good 2. So A should produce as much of good 1 as possible, and B as much of good 2 as possible (although obviously this depends upon where one wants to be on society's frontier).

14.3   Non-linear Technologies

The interesting point about the material which we have discussed so far is that, although the individual technologies are linear in the sense that I have described, the frontier for society is concave. It is concave because of the specialization of the individuals.

In this section we also derive, under certain assumptions, a concave frontier for society, but we start from a different perspective. Here we make use of the material from Chapters 10 to 13. We assume that society consists of two firms, 1 and 2, each producing a particular good: firm 1 produces output 1 and firm 2 produces output 2. They produce the goods using two inputs, input 1 and input 2, the total quantities of which are fixed and given in society. The problem that society faces is the allocation of these two inputs in such a way that output is maximized.

To solve this problem it is useful to use an Edgeworth box. In the past we have used this to discuss the allocation of two goods between two individuals; here we use it to discuss the allocation of two inputs between two firms. We measure one firm from one origin and the other from the other. The horizontal axis indicates the quantity of input 1 and the vertical axis the quantity of input 2. The width of the box is the total quantity of input 1 in the economy, and the height is the total quantity of input 2 in the economy. A point in the box indicates an allocation of the two inputs between the two firms; this determines their outputs. We have inserted into the box isoquants for the two firms; those convex from the bottom left origin are for firm 1, and those convex from the top right origin are for firm 2. The Edgeworth box is shown in Fig. 14.7.

Now we know that the efficient points occur along the contract curve, which is inserted in Fig. 14.7; whatever society does, it should choose a point on the contract curve. Once we are on the contract curve there is a trade-off; moving from the bottom left origin towards the top right origin increases the output of firm 1 and decreases that of firm 2. At each point along the contract curve we can calculate the outputs of firms 1 and 2. An example is given in the figure; at this point the output of firm 1 is 5.94 and the output of firm 2 is 49.4 (calculated by inserting the co-ordinates of the point into the two production functions). Here I am assum-

Figure 14.7

Along the contract curve

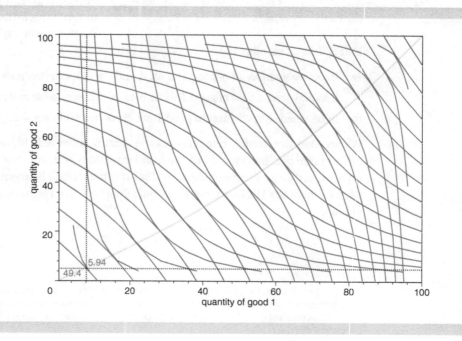

ing that the production function for firm 1 is Cobb–Douglas with parameters $a = 0.56$ and $b = 0.24$, and that for firm 2 is also Cobb–Douglas but with parameters $a = 0.48$ and $b = 0.32$. Note that both firms have decreasing returns to scale.

If we now plot the output of firm 2 against the output of firm 1 along the contract curve, we get society's production possibility frontier[4], as in Fig. 14.8.

We see that the frontier is concave. The reason is that the technology of each firm has decreasing returns to scale; as we move up the contract curve, the output of firm 1 rises, but at an increasingly slower rate, while that of firm 2 falls at an increasingly faster rate. Clearly the degree of the decreasing returns to scale will influence the concavity of the frontier. Suppose we replace $a = 0.56$ and $b = 0.24$ for firm 1 and $a = 0.48$ and $b = 0.32$ for firm 2 by $a = 0.49$ and $b = 0.21$ for firm 1 and $a = 0.42$ and $b = 0.24$ for firm 2 (notice that the ratio of a to b for each firm has not changed, so the isoquants look the same but their sum is smaller).

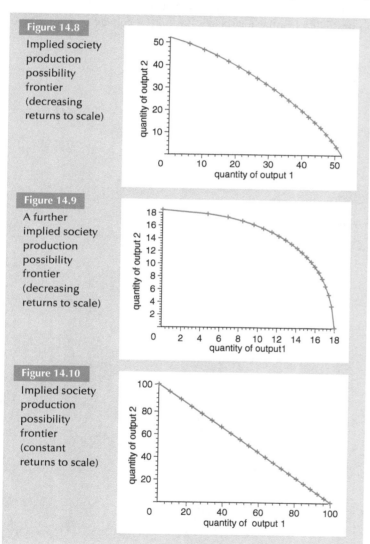

Figure 14.8

Implied society production possibility frontier (decreasing returns to scale)

Figure 14.9

A further implied society production possibility frontier (decreasing returns to scale)

Figure 14.10

Implied society production possibility frontier (constant returns to scale)

Then we have the production possibility frontier shown in Fig. 14.9; this is considerably more concave than that in Fig. 14.8.

It might be obvious now that, if both technologies had constant returns to scale, we would have a linear frontier; as we move along the contract curve from the bottom origin, the output of firm 1 rises linearly from zero while that of firm 2 falls linearly to zero. If we continue with this example and also replace $a = 0.56$ and $b = 0.24$ for firm 1 and $a = 0.48$ and $b = 0.32$ for firm 2 by $a = 0.7$ and $b = 0.3$ for firm 1 and $a = 0.6$ and $b = 0.4$ for firm 2 (notice that the ratio of a to b for each firm has not changed so the isoquants look the same but their sum is now unity), we get the production possibility frontier for society in Fig. 14.10. It is linear; the total quantities of the two inputs are 100 and 100 respectively, so if both inputs are fully used total output is 100.

You can probably anticipate what will happen if both firms have increasing returns to scale. As we move up the contract curve from the bottom left origin, the output of firm 1 rises at an increasingly faster rate while that firm 2 falls at an increasingly slower rate. We take the original example, but replace $a = 0.56$ and $b = 0.24$ for firm 1 and $a = 0.48$ and

---

4. This may all be very familiar. In fact, we did almost the same in Chapter 9 when deriving society's utility possibility frontier.

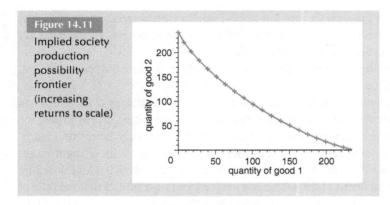

Figure 14.11

Implied society production possibility frontier (increasing returns to scale)

$b = 0.32$ for firm 2 by $a = 0.7/0.9$ and $b = 0.3/0.9$ for firm 1 and $a = 0.6/0.9$ and $b = 0.4/0.9$ for firm 2 (again, notice that the ratio of a to b for each firm has not changed so the isoquants look the same, but their sum is now greater than unity). We now have the production possibility frontier of society depicted in Fig. 14.11; it is convex.

Finally we can consider a sort of hybrid case; one in which firm 1 has increasing returns to scale while firm 2 has decreasing returns to scale. What do you think will happen? The answer is in Fig.14.12. Exactly – the production possibility frontier for society has both a convex and a concave section.

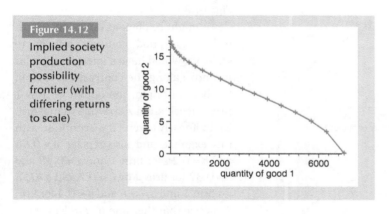

Figure 14.12

Implied society production possibility frontier (with differing returns to scale)

14.4 Summary

In this chapter we have constructed the production possibility frontier for society under different scenarios. The first scenario was when the production technology at the individual level was linear.

 In this economy society's production possibility frontier is piecewise linear and concave.

It is concave because everyone specializes in the production of the good in which they have a relative advantage.

We then moved on to consider what might be termed a more normal society, in which there are firms producing the output and they are competing for a fixed supply of inputs. On the assumption that the technology has convex isoquants, we showed the following important result.

 In an economy with increasing, constant or decreasing returns to scale everywhere, society's production possibility frontier is convex, linear or concave everywhere.

14.5 Review Questions

1. Construct examples of a linear society with three individuals and derive the production possibility frontier for society. Show that there is a linear segment of the society production possibility frontier corresponding to each individual.

2. Suppose a society consists of three individuals A, B and C. Suppose A has a comparative advantage over B, and B over C, in the production of good 1; and that C has a comparative advantage over B, and B over A, in the production of good 2. Suppose that, at the chosen point on society's production possibility frontier, B is working half time on the production of each good. Argue that A must be working full-time on good 1 and C full-time on good 2.

3. Does the addition of new individuals (however productive they are – as long as they are productive) always enlarge society's production possibility frontier.

14.6   Application: should Firms Choose the Same Technology?

If firms can choose their technology, should they choose the same as others or should they be different? The answer is that, if they are competing for scarce inputs they should be different. We will show this in the context of a simple example which can be generalized. The example also illustrates some of the key concepts that emerge from this chapter.

Consider a simple society in which there are two inputs into the production process, input 1 and input 2; suppose the quantities of these two inputs are fixed. Assume that there are two firms, firm A and firm B, which respectively produce good A and good B. Suppose the technology of firm A is fixed; it has a perfect 1-with-2 complements technology which displays constant returns to scale. Hence q units of input 1 combined with $2q$ units of input 2 to produce q units of good A.

Firm B has a choice of technology; both options display constant returns to scale and both are perfect complements: one is perfect 1-with-2 complements (like firm A); the other is perfect 2-with-1 complements. Which option should it use? We shall answer this by looking at the production possibilities open to the society under the two technologies. Intuitively you may think that, with limited input resources, firm B should use a different technology from firm A so the competition for resources is less. We shall show this formally, using a particular example in such a way that you should be able to generalize the result.

Suppose firm B uses the same technology as firm A. We can illustrate the output possibilities in an Edgeworth box which has input 1 on the horizontal axis and input 2 on the vertical axis. The width of the box is the total quantity of input 1 available in the economy; the height of the box is the total quantity of input 2 available in the economy. We assume that there 100 units of both inputs available. We measure the quantities used by firm A from the usual origin, and those used by firm B from the upper right-hand corner. Any point in the box represents an allocation of inputs to the two firms, and we can calculate the output of the two firms at any point in the box. Consider now Fig. 14.13.

The blue lines represent the isoquants of firm A for outputs of 1, 2, 3, 4, 5, and 6; they have angles at the points $(1, 2)$, $(2, 4)$, $(3, 6)$, $(4, 8)$ $(5, 10)$ and $(6, 12)$. The line marked AA joins up the corners of these isoquants. The output of firm A along the bottom and the left-hand sides of the box is zero. The red lines represent the isoquants of firm B for outputs of 1, 2, 3, 4, 5, and 6 (we measure the inputs going to firm B from the top right-hand corner); they have angles at the points $(11, 10)$, $(10, 8)$, $(9, 6)$, $(8, 4)$ $(7, 2)$ and $(6, 0)$. The line marked BB joins up the corners of these isoquants. Clearly the output of firm B along the top and the right-hand sides of the box is zero.

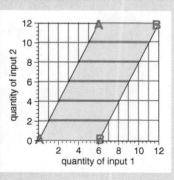

Figure 14.13

Deriving the production possibility frontier

Where is the contract curve in this society? The contract curve, remember, is the locus of efficient points in the sense that, on the contract curve, it is not possible to increase the output of one firm without decreasing the output of the other, while off the contract curve it is possible to increase the output of one firm without decreasing the output of the other. In this particular economy the 'contract curve' is an area – the area coloured yellow in Fig. 14.13. This is a consequence of the technologies we have assumed. The simplest way to show this is first to state what the production possibility frontier

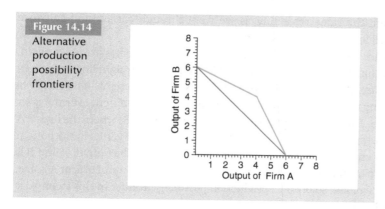

Figure 14.14

Alternative production possibility frontiers

is in this particular case, and then to relate it back to Fig. 14.13.

The production possibility frontier has the form of the lower straight line in Fig. 14.14. The end points are easy to explain. The point on the production possibility frontier in which the output of firm A is six and that of firm B is zero comes from the point (6, 12) in the Edgeworth box. The point on the production possibility frontier in which the output of firm A is zero and that of firm B is six comes from the point (0, 6) in the Edgeworth box. Actually this is slightly misleading: any point on the straight line between (6, 12) and (12, 12) in the Edgeworth box gives outputs of six for firm A and zero for firm B; and any point on the straight line between (0, 0) and (6, 0) gives outputs of zero for firm A and six for firm B. The crucial point is that, as we move along the straight line from (6, 12) to (12, 12), or along the straight line from (0, 0) to (6, 0), we are moving simultaneously along isoquants of firm A and of firm B; that is why the outputs of both firms remain constant. This gives us a clue as to why the 'contract curve' is the shaded area in the Edgeworth box. Once inside the shaded area, moving horizontally does not change the output of either firm; we are moving along their isoquants. However moving diagonally or vertically increases the output of one firm and decreases the output of the other. We cannot increase the output of both firms if we are inside the shaded area; all points inside the shaded area are efficient.

If we are outside the shaded area things are different. If we are to the left of it, moving rightwards increases the output of firm A but does not change that of firm B; while moving downwards increases the output of firm B but does not change that of firm A. If we are to the right of it, moving leftwards increases the output of firm B but does not change that of firm A, while moving upwards increases the output of Firm A but does not change that of firm B. So all points outside the shaded area are inefficient.

The production possibility frontier comes from the contract curve; you should be able to verify this. At all points where the output of firm A is one, the output of firm B is five; at all points where the output of firm A is two, the output of firm B is four; at all points where the output of firm A is three, the output of firm B is three; and so on. This verifies the linear production possibility frontier illustrated in Fig. 14.14. We shall discuss the green frontier shortly.

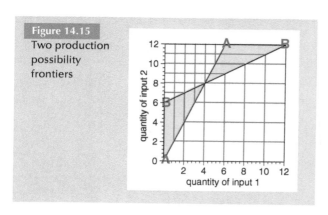

Figure 14.15

Two production possibility frontiers

Now we repeat the analysis with the alternative technique available to firm 2: perfect 2-with-1 complements. The Edgeworth box in Fig. 14.15 shows the appropriate analysis. The line AA is again the line joining the corners of the isoqants of firm A, and the line BB joins the corners of the isoquants of firm B. The latter is different from the earlier example because of the different technology used. Once again, the blue lines are the isoquants of firm A (zero output at the origin and then 1, 2, 3, 4, 5 and 6), and the red lines those of firm B (zero output at B's origin, and then 1, 2, 3, 4, 5 and 6). The contract curve is once again an area – that shaded yellow in Fig. 14.15.

You should go through the same reasoning as we went through earlier, and convince yourself that the shaded area is indeed the contract curve.

Let us now construct the production possibility frontier. The extremes are, once again, easy; at the bottom left-hand corner of the box and indeed along the straight line from (0, 0) to (0, 6), the output of firm A is zero and that of firm B is six; at the top right-hand corner of the box, and indeed along the straight line from (6, 12) to (12, 12), the output of firm A is six and that of firm B is zero. The middle point is also easy: at the point (4, 8) where the lines AA and BB intersect, the output of both firms is four. Other points you can verify: in the bottom triangle of the contract curve, whenever the output of firm A is two, the output of firm B is five, and so on; in the top triangle of the contract curve, whenever the output of firm A is five, the output of firm B is two, and so on. The production possibility frontier in this example is the kinked frontier in Fig. 14.14.

What do we notice? The production possibility frontier when firm B uses a different technology from that of firm A is everywhere further out than when both use the same technology. It is therefore unambiguously better for society that the two firms use different technologies. The reason is simple but important; the inputs in society are limited, and the less the competition for them, the better. To put it another way, the more efficiently they are used, the better for society.

Clearly this is a special case, but the important messages can be generalized. You should try to do this yourself. However other features of this special case do not generalize, although they are of interest. Let us go back to Fig. 14.15 and ask ourselves: where would competitive trading of the two inputs take us? We know, in general, that it will take us to the point on the contract curve where the two price-offer curves intersect. In the context of this example, the price-offer curve of firm A is the line AA, and that of firm B is the line BB. The competitive equilibrium is at the point (4, 8). This is a rather special point on the contract curve because, at that point and only at that point on the contract curve there is no waste of inputs. Everywhere else, some of one or other of the inputs are unused because their employment does not increase output. But at the competitive equilibrium no input resources are wasted. Do you think this is always the case?

Note there is no competitive equilibrium when the two firms have the same technology. You should re-examine Fig. 14.13 and ask yourself: where do the price-offer curves intersect? What is the answer? And why?

Production and Exchange

15.1 Introduction

We now put together the material from Chapter 8 on exchange with that of Chapter 14 on production possibilities to see if we can answer the question: what is the best output for society? This is a difficult question and, as we will see, this is a difficult chapter. A fully satisfactory answer to the question requires some mathematics at a level which is beyond the scope of this book. But I hope to be able to put across to you an intuitive feeling for the conclusions without losing you in the mathematics. I feel that intuition is important, and the message of the chapter can be understood with the aid of the various figures that we shall be presenting.

15.2 Production and Exchange

You will recall from Chapter 8 that we considered there the issue of the optimal allocation of some fixed bundle of goods. Specifically, we assumed a very simple economy consisting of two goods and two individuals. The total quantity of the two goods was assumed to be fixed, and we assumed some initial allocation of the two goods between the two individuals. We then examined whether some mutually advantageous trade might take place between the two individuals and, if so, what form it might take.

In Chapter 8 the initial quantity and the initial allocation of the two goods were fixed at some arbitrary levels, and it is this which we are examining in this chapter. More specifically, we assume here that society can choose this initial quantity (and, as we shall see, hence the initial allocation) and society can choose it from some production possibility frontier of the type that we studied in Chapter 14. What point should society choose?

The technique which we shall use in this chapter is to take a number of initial quantities and study the properties of the implied competitive equilibrium. We shall then see if we can compare these equilibria, with the intention of trying to find the best one.

15.3 A Linear Society

To make our analysis simple we work with a simple production possibility frontier, the properties and implications of which we know and understand. Specifically, we shall work with the simple linear society that we studied in Section 14.2. You will recall that in that society

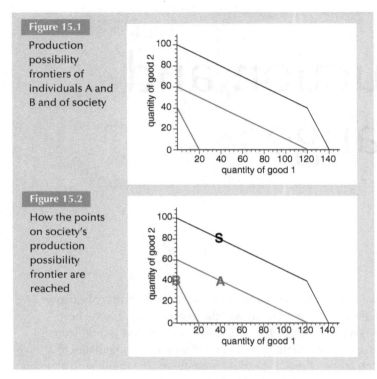

Figure 15.1

Production possibility frontiers of individuals A and B and of society

Figure 15.2

How the points on society's production possibility frontier are reached

there were just two individuals, A and B, who worked all day and were each subject to a linear technology. These assumptions are summarized in Fig. 15.1, which is identical to Fig. 14.4.

The bottom line is the production possibility frontier of B: if he or she works all day on good 1, 20 units of good 1 and none of good 2 will be produced; if he or she works all day on good 2, 40 units of good 2 and none of good 1 will be produced. If B works for half a day on good 1 and half on good 2, then the output will be 10 units of good 1 and 20 of good 2; and so on. The middle line is the production possibility frontier of A: working all day on good 1 will produce 120 units of good 1 and none of good 2; working all day on good 2 will produve 60 units of good 2 and none on good 1; working for half the day on good 1 and half the day on good 2 will produce 60 units of good 1 and 30 of good 2; and so on. The top curve, which is a piecewise linear function, is the production possibility frontier for society; it assumes that the two individuals specialize in the production of the good for which they have a comparative advantage (A in good 1 and B in good 2).

Note that to reach particular points on society's production possibility frontier requires that the two individuals are at particular points on theirs. In other words, the choice of a point on society's frontier implies that the individuals are at particular points on theirs. Let us use a specific example. If society wants to be at the point labelled S in Fig. 15.2, how does it achieve it? The answer is: by A being at point A and individual B at point B; there is no other way.

We can express this in tabular form. Scenario 1 in Table 15.1 shows the only way of attaining the point S (for society) in Fig. 15.2.

Table 15.1   Calculation of society's production possibility frontier: four scenarios

	Individual A	Individual B	Society
Scenario 1			
Good 1	40	0	40
Good 2	40	40	80
Scenario 2			
Good 1	80	0	80
Good 2	20	40	60
Scenario 3			
Good 1	120	0	120
Good 2	0	40	40
Scenario 4			
Good 1	120	10	130
Good 2	0	20	20

Point S yields 40 units of good 1 and 80 units of good 2. To produce this amount, individual A has to work $\frac{1}{3}$ of the day on good 1 and $\frac{2}{3}$ of the day on good 2, thereby producing 40 units of good 1 and 40 units of good 2; individual B must work all day producing 40 units of good 2 and none of good 1. What is crucial is that the point on society's frontier uniquely determines the production of the two goods by the two individuals; and hence it determines the initial allocation of the quantities of the two goods in society.

In what follows we shall study the properties of four scenarios; the one which we have just described and three others. The other three are as follows: scenario 2, like scenario 1, lies to the left of the kink on the production possibility frontier but further to the right than does scenario 1; scenario 3 is at the kink point; and scenario 4 is to the right of the kink point.

15.4   Competitive Trading

We are going to study these four scenarios in detail and, in particular, we shall examine the competitive equilibrium in each of these four cases. We will then compare them to see whether one equilibrium is better or worse than some other. Finally we shall see if we can determine some way of finding the 'best' of them.

We start with scenario 1. From Table 5.1 it can be seen that, if society chooses scenario 1, it will have 40 units of good 1 and 80 units of good 2. If we draw an Edgeworth box to analyse the distribution of these units, the box has width 40 units and height 80 units. The appropriate box appears in Fig. 15.3. We have deliberately drawn the Edgeworth box inside the production possibility frontier so that we can see where it has come from. Moreover it is obvious that the size of the box is determined by the point chosen on the frontier.

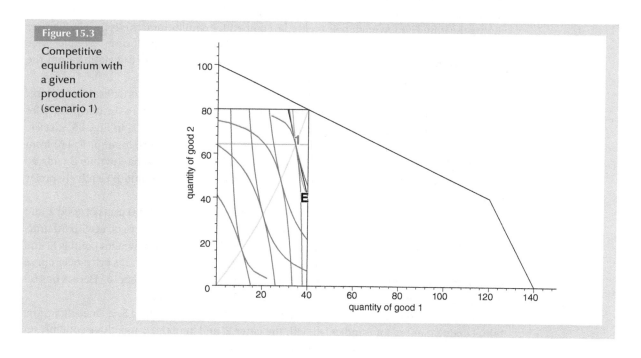

Figure 15.3

Competitive equilibrium with a given production (scenario 1)

Now it is clear from Section 15.3 that the selected point on the frontier determines the production of the two individuals, and therefore determines the initial allocation of the two goods. As can be seen from Table 15.1, individual A produces (and hence starts with) 40 units of good 1 and 40 units of good 2. In Fig. 15.3 we measure A's endowment and preferences from the bottom left corner of the box; so A starts at the point labelled E – the point (40, 40) as measured from the bottom left corner. Again from the table, we see that B starts with no units of good 1 and 40 units of good 2. We measure B's preferences and endowments from the top right corner of the box so his endowment point is also point E, as it obviously must be.

Now Fig. 15.3 is a little complicated so we should explain it. As we have already seen, A's preferences are measured from the bottom left corner, and we take it that A has nice convex indifference curves representing his or her preferences over the two goods. To be precise, I have assumed Cobb–Douglas preferences with weights 0.7 on good 1 and 0.3 on good 2 [1]. Therefore in Fig. 15.3 the convex curves represent A's preferences; as we move up the box and to the right, A becomes happier.

Now for individual B: his or her preferences are measured from the top right corner. We have again assumed nice smooth convex indifference curves and Cobb–Douglas preferences with weights 0.6 on good 1 and 0.4 on good 2. Therefore in Fig. 15.3 the curves, which are convex with respect to the top right origin, represent B's preferences; as we move down the box and to the left, B becomes happier.

It is clear that A and B have different preferences. It follows that the contract curve is not the line joining the two origins but the curve joining the two origins in Fig. 15.3. Two of the remaining three lines are the price-offer curves of the two individuals. The downward sloping line passing through point E is that for A. The horizontal line is that for B. You may wonder about this, but recall Chapter 8; there we showed that, with Cobb–Douglas preferences, if an individual is endowed with good 1 only then his or her price-offer curve is vertical; if he or she is endowed with good 2 only his or her price-offer curve is horizontal. In this example B is endowed with just good 2, therefore B's price-offer curve is horizontal at 40 per cent of the endowment of good 2 (since the weight on B's good 2 is 0.4). The final line is that joining the initial endowment point with the competitive equilibrium; this is the equilibrium budget constraint. The magnitude of its slope indicates the equilibrium relative price between good 1 and good 2 – the relative price which takes the two individuals from the initial endowment point E to the equilibrium point.

Let us suppose that society has competitive trading from whichever endowment point. We will therefore end up at the competitive equilibrium, which is where the two price-offer curves (and the contract curve) intersect. I have labelled this point '1' in Fig. 15.3, referring to scenario 1. This is the point (35, 64) from the bottom left origin, and (5, 16) from the top right origin; A ends up with 35 units of good 1 and 64 of good 2, while B ends up with five units of good 1 and 16 of good 2 (remember that both A and B relatively prefer good 1).

Fig. 15.4 repeats the above analysis for scenario 2. A starts with 80 units of good 1 and 20 of good 2; B starts with none of good 1 and 40 units of good 2. Society starts with 80 units of good 1 and 60 of good 2, so the size of the box is 80 by 60. The endowment point is E, and I have drawn the same curves in this figure as in Fig. 15.3. Once again B's price-offer curve is horizontal. The new competitive equilibrium is indicated by the number '2'. Here A has 65 units of good 1 and 44 of good 2; B has 15 of good 1 and 16 of good 2.

Let us finish off the four scenarios. The third is illustrated in Fig. 15.5. Once again the initial endowment point is indicated with the letter E, and here the competitive equilibrium is indicated with a '3'. In this scenario the price-offer curve of A is vertical as he or she starts with only good 1, and the price-offer curve of B is horizontal, as he or she starts with only good 2.

---

1. These details do not affect the principles that follow.

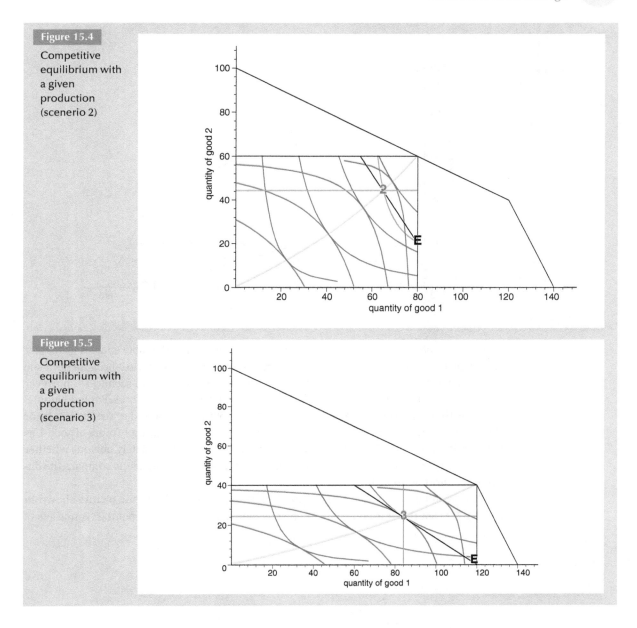

Figure 15.4

Competitive equilibrium with a given production (scenerio 2)

Figure 15.5

Competitive equilibrium with a given production (scenario 3)

Finally, in Fig. 15.6, we have scenario 4, where A starts with good 1 only, while B starts with both goods. The competitive equilibrium is indicated with a '4'.

It will be convenient to combine the results of these four scenarios into a single table (Table 15.2). This shows the consumption of goods 1 and 2 by individuals A and B at the

Table 15.2   Consumption of goods 1 and 2 by individuals A and B: four scenarios

	A's consumption1 of good 1	A's consumption of good 2	B's consumption of good 1	B's consumption of good 2
Scenario 1	35	64	5	16
Scenario 2	65	44	15	16
Scenario 3	84	24	36	16
Scenario 4	84	12	46	8

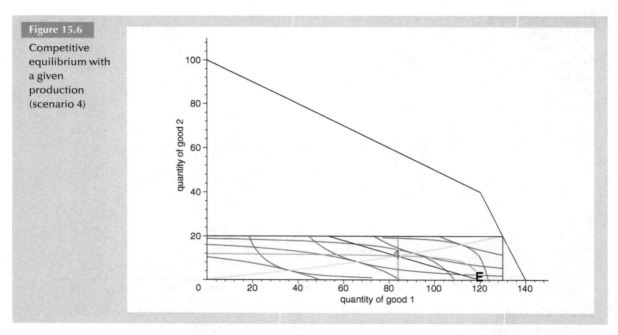

Figure 15.6

Competitive equilibrium with a given production (scenario 4)

equilibrium points of each of the four scenarios. Just looking at the table enables us to infer quite a lot. For example, it is obvious that A prefers scenario 3 to scenario 4 because he or she has the same amount of good 1 in both scenarios, but less of good 2 in scenario 4; however it is not immediately obvious which of scenarios 1, 2 or 3 is preferable for A. For individual B it is clear that scenario 3 is preferable to scenario 2, which is preferred to scenario 1; he or she has the same amount of good 2 in all three scenarios, but increasingly more of good 1 as B moves from scenario 1 to scenario 2 to scenario 3; it is not immediately obvious whether B prefers scenarios 3 or 4. To understand more of what is going on, let us compare the different scenarios graphically.

If we combine scenarios 1 and 2 in a single diagram we obtain the picture shown in Fig. 15.7. From this it is immediately obvious which is preferable. At point 2, A has less of

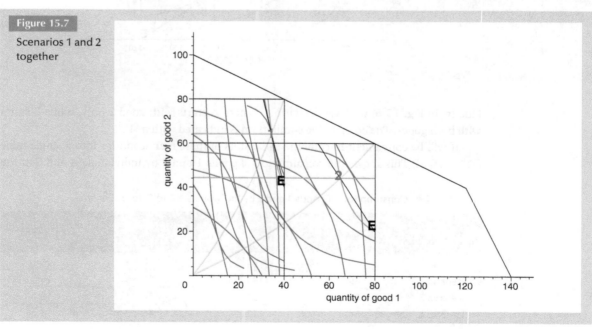

Figure 15.7

Scenarios 1 and 2 together

good 2 and more of good 1 than at point 1. This is potentially ambiguous. However the indifference curves of A tell us immediately and unambiguously that scenario 2 is better. Because A's indifference curves are all drawn from the same origin (the bottom left origin), they are the same indifference curves in the two boxes. Point 2 is higher than point 1 with respect to this indifference map and is hence preferred. We already know that B prefers scenario 2. So both A and B prefer scenario 2.

It is important to understand why. The answer lies in the various marginal rates of substitution. First, consider the slope of the production possibility frontiers at both the scenario 1 and scenario 2 equilibrium points; it is −0.5. So for each unit less of good 2 that society produces, society can produce two more units of good 1. Now consider the slope of the two individuals' indifference curves at competitive equilibrium 1. It is approximately minus four; each individual has a MRS of four. Clearly both individuals are more than happy to give up one unit of good 2 in exchange for two units of good 1, which is what a movement along the production possibility frontier offers them. The same is true at scenario 2; the MRS of each individual is approximately one (the magnitude of the slope of the indifference curves at the competitive equilibrium); this is still more than the MRS along the production possibility frontier. This suggests that a further move to the right might suit them both. To check this, let us compare scenarios 2 and 3 in Fig. 15.8. Here one would conclude that points 2 and 3 are on the same indifference curve for individual A. Given that B definitely prefers scenario 3, we may say that scenario 3 is preferable for society.

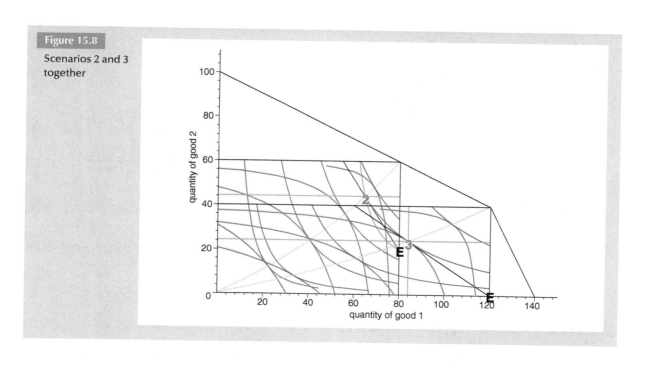

Figure 15.8

Scenarios 2 and 3 together

What about scenarios 3 and 4? We already know that A prefers scenario 3 to scenario 4. What about B? Well, it is clear that the figures we have been looking at cannot help because the point from which B's preferences are measured varies from box to box; the top right hand corners of the two boxes do not coincide as do the bottom left hand corners. However we can do something rather clever; we simply reverse A and B. Instead of measuring A from the bottom left and B from the top right, we measure B from the bottom left and A from the top right.

If we do this, we can compare scenarios 3 and 4 in the usual way, as shown in Fig. 15.9. Now all B's indifference curves are measured from the bottom left corner. Notice that the competitive equilibria are at the same points: (36, 16) for B and (84, 24) for A in scenario 3 and (46, 8) for B and (84, 12) for A in scenario 4. From Fig. 15.9 it is clear that B prefers scenario 3 to scenario 4. So both individuals prefer scenario 3. You may find it instructive to realise why. At the point on the frontier corresponding to scenario 4, the MRS is two: for each unit less of good 1 produced, society can have an extra two units of good 2. Now look at the competitive equilibrium in scenario 4. What do we note about each individual's MRS at the equilibrium? It is less than two (in fact it is about one). What does this mean? It means that each individual would be happy to give up one unit of good 1 in exchange for two units of good 2. That is, they would be happy with a move leftwards from scenario 4 to scenario 3.

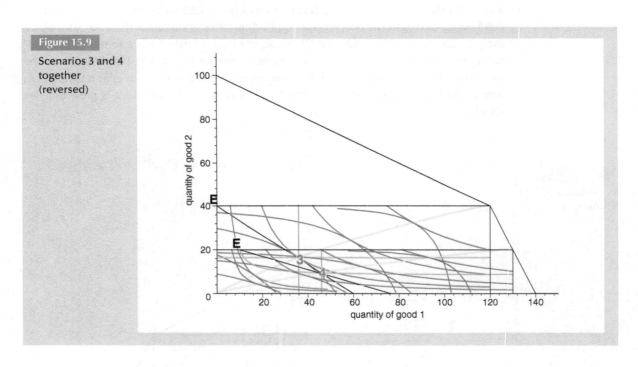

Figure 15.9

Scenarios 3 and 4 together (reversed)

We therefore conclude that, of the 4 scenarios considered here, both individuals – and hence society – prefers scenario 3. This is the kink point.

15.5 The Overall Optimum

In general, with a smoothly concave production possibility frontier for society there is no kink point. But even if there is, it is not necessarily true that the preferred point will be at the kink. Let us try and work out where the optimal point is in general. We might also wonder why both individuals agree on this.

The key is the fact that, at the competitive equilibrium, the MRS for the two individuals is identical; both are equal to the equilibrium relative price. This means that, if one of the two is happy to give up one unit of good 1 in exchange for a units of good 2, then so is the other.

If one of the two is happy to give up one unit of good 2 in exchange for *a* units of good 1, then so is the other. Now the slope of the production possibility frontier at the chosen point indicates the MRS in terms of production; it tells us how much of good 2 we can get by giving up units of good 1, and it tells us how much of good 1 we can get by giving up units of good 2. It tells us what is technically possible.

Let me tell you straight away what the optimality condition is (you might have anticipated this as I have been dropping quite a few hints). Unless the optimal point is at a kink point, it must have the property that the slope of the production possibility frontier (minus the technical MRS if you like) must be equal to the slope of the indifference curves at the competitive equilibrium.

Consider what must happen if this is not true. If they are not equal it must be the case that there is a direction along the frontier that they can move which implies that they give up one good for more units of the other that they need to keep them indifferent. In other words, if these MRS are not equal there must be a direction in which they can move which makes them both happier. We saw that in our example; moving from scenario 1 to scenario 2 makes them both better off because for every unit less of good 2 produced they get 2 more units of good 1 – and they are both happy with this exchange since they would happily accept less of good 1 as compensation. The same is true with the movement from scenario 4 to scenario 3.

Let us generalize the explanation. Suppose that, at the chosen point, the (technical) rate of substitution is not equal to the MRS of the two individuals. Specifically let us suppose that the former is *a* and the latter is *b*, and they are not equal. We need to consider two possibilities, one that *a > b* and the other that *b > a*.

Suppose that a > b. We use *a* to indicate the technical rate of substitution along the production possibility frontier. It indicates that, if the society were to give up one unit of good 1, it could have *a* more units of good 2; conversely, if society gave up one unit of good 2 it could have 1/*a* more units of good 1. Now *b* indicates the individuals' MRS at the competitive equilibrium; it implies that the individuals would be indifferent giving up one unit of good 1 in exchange for *b* units of good 2; or conversely, that they would be indifferent giving up one unit of good 2 in exchange for 1/*b* units more of good 1. The first of these implies that they would be better off exchanging one unit of good 1 for something more than *b* units of good 2. But that is exactly what a move along the production possibility frontier gives them; if they give up one unit of good 1 they can get *a* more units of good 2. By assumption this is greater than *b*, and it makes them strictly better off. So if *a > b*, they are both better off if society produces less of good 1 and more of good 2.

Suppose that a < b. We use *a* to indicate the technical rate of substitution along the production possibility frontier. It indicates that, if the society were to give up one unit of good 1 it could have *a* more units of good 2; conversely, if society gave up one unit of good 2 it could have 1/*a* more units of good 1. Now *b* indicates the individuals' MRS at the competitive equilibrium. It implies that the individuals would be indifferent giving up one unit of good 1 in exchange for *b* units of good 2; or conversely, that they would be indifferent giving up one unit of good 2 in exchange for 1/*b* units more of good 2. The second of these implies that they would be better off exchanging one unit of good 2 for something rather more than 1/*b* units of good 2. But that is exactly what a move along the production possibility frontier gives them; if they give up one unit of good 2 they can get 1/*a* extra units of good 1 which, from the above, makes them strictly better off. So if *a < b* they are both better off if the society produces less of good 2 and more of good 1.

If there is a kink point, this equality might not hold at the optimal point. At the kink, the technical MRS jumps from one number to another. The kink would be an equilibrium if the MRS of the two individuals at the competitive equilibrium corresponding to this kink point lies between these two numbers.

The mathematics behind the above result is too advanced to include in this book. In any case, it is more important that you understand the intuition that I have tried to explain.

15.6 Summary

We have covered some difficult ground in this chapter, but we have discovered an important rule for the choice of the optimal point on society's production possibility frontier.

> Overall optimality requires that the (technical) rate of substitution be equal to each individual's marginal rate of substitution (and they are equal in the competitive equilibrium).

15.7 Review Questions

1. If we compare two points on the production possibility frontier for society and find that the competitive equilibrium is preferred by both individuals at the first point, argue that society should choose the first point.

2. Suppose that at a point on the production possibility frontier the slope is two (that is, for each unit less of good 1 produced, society can produce two units more of good 2). Suppose also that, at the implied competitive equilibrium, the slopes of the indifference curves of the two individuals are both equal to one, then the two individuals would both prefer society to produce less of good 1 and more of good 2.

3. Use intuition to argue that the optimum point must have the property that the technical rate of substitution is equal to each individual's marginal rate of substitution.

Interlude

We now have a chapter of a different kind – not theory, but empirical applications of what we have done. The purpose of the chapter is to show that the theory with which this book is concerned has an empirical validity, and to demonstrate that it is useful for policy purposes.

Empirical Evidence on Demand, Supply and Surpluses

16.1 Introduction

This chapter shows that the theoretical material that we have been studying has empirical relevance. We apply the theory to the estimation of a demand and supply system for some commodity. We are searching for a specification that has both theoretical justification and which fits the facts; it is empirically relevant. It is quite possible to reproduce the kind of analysis which we have done here for other commodities.

I should warn you that this chapter assumes some basic familiarity with econometrics, particularly regression analysis. If you have not yet studied any econometrics, full understanding of this chapter may have to wait until later. I considered including some material on econometric pre-requisites, but decided against doing so on the grounds that such material would take up too much space. However there is a glossary of key terms at the end of the chapter. If you really have not done any basic regression analysis before, I would suggest that you might reserve this chapter for a later date, and take on faith the important message: that the theory we are presenting in this book does have empirical relevance and is useful. I should add that nothing in the remainder of this book relies on you understanding, or even having read, this chapter.

16.2 The Data to be Explained

We choose a commodity that is both important and interesting: the demand for and supply of food in the UK. We need to start with some data. We obtained these from the publication *Economic Trends Annual Supplement* (*ETAS*); actually the data were downloaded electronically from the UK Data Archive which is located at the University of Essex, but the data are also available in printed format in *ETAS*. If you look in that publication you will find two series for Household Expenditure on Food – one series in current prices (code name in *ETAS*: CCDW), and the other series in constant 1995 prices (code name: CCBM). The first of these is money expenditure, and the second corrects for price changes. So it is the latter which is the real indicator of the quantity of food purchased. We shall call this variable

RFOD – standing for **R**eal expenditure on **FOOD**. We shall call expenditure on food in current prices **NFOD** – standing for **N**ominal expenditure on **FOOD**. You will find these data in columns 5 and 6 in Table 16.1 at the end of the chapter.

From these two series we can derive the **Price** of **FOOD**, which we denote by **PFOD**; we do this by dividing the series **NFOD** (expenditure on food in current prices) by the series **RFOD** (expenditure on food in constant prices). Thus **PFOD = NFOD/RFOD**; these data are in column 8. Data are available from 1948 to 1999 – a total of 52 observations. If we draw a scatter diagram of price (**PFOD**) against quantity (**RFOD**) we obtain Fig. 16.1. We should note that these are annual data, and each cross represents the price and quantity of food purchased in a particular year. There are 52 observations and hence 52 crosses. The figure looks a little like a supply curve.

Note, however, that we have done something odd; since all prices are rising through time we ought to correct the price series for the general movement in prices. We do this by first obtaining data on overall prices. We take the series for the total household expenditure in current prices (code name: ABPB), which we shall call **NALL** (**N**ominal expenditure on **ALL** commodities). We divide this by the total household expenditure in constant prices (code name: ABPF), which we shall call **RALL** (**R**eal expenditure on **ALL** commodities). The data on these variables are in columns 3 and 4 of Table 16.1. Dividing **NALL** by **RALL** gives us **PALL** – the **P**rice of **ALL** commodities (column 8); thus **PALL = NALL/RALL**.

We can now obtain the relative price of food – **PFOD/PALL**. Graphed against the quantity of food purchased over the period 1948 to 1999, we obtain the scatter diagram shown in Fig. 16.2; again there are 52 crosses – one for each year.

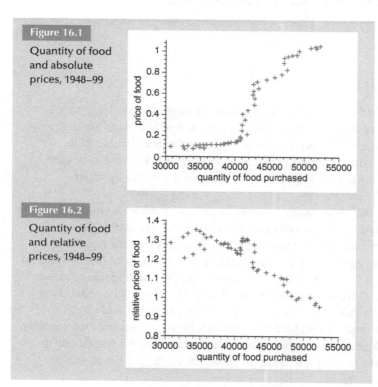

Figure 16.1

Quantity of food and absolute prices, 1948–99

Figure 16.2

Quantity of food and relative prices, 1948–99

16.3 The Demand for Food in the UK

Fig. 16.2 looks like a demand curve. It looks vaguely linear, and perhaps a linear demand curve might be a good fit. But we should think about the theory that we have been studying. Clearly we can reject the hypothesis that food is a perfect substitute for other commodities (ask yourself why), and that food is a perfect complement with other commodities (again, ask yourself why). So we will try Cobb–Douglas preferences. You will recall that this is particularly simple; it states that the amount spent on a commodity is a constant fraction of income. This means that **RFOD** should be a constant fraction of **NALL/PFOD**; in other words, real expenditure on food should be a constant fraction of the real income, or total real expenditure. For simplicity we are assuming that the decision taken by the consumer is how to allocate total consumption over the various commodities; we are excluding the saving decision which we have not yet studied. If we do a regression of **RFOD** against **NALL/PFOD** we obtain the following result:

$$\mathbf{RFOD} = 0.146 \ \mathbf{NALL/PFOD} + u$$
$$(21.0)$$
$$\text{log-likelihood} = -568.056 \tag{16.1}$$

This is the equation of the best-fitting straight line applied to the scatter produced by plotting **RFOD** against **NALL/PFOD**. These are not the data in Fig. 16.2, but you could draw a scatter diagram yourself using the data in the appendix, and insert the regression line calculated in Eq. 16.1.

The term in brackets under the coefficient is called the t-ratio; it tells us that the coefficient is significantly different from zero. The coefficient on **NALL/PFOD** indicates that consumers on average spend 14.6 per cent of total consumption expenditure on food. This is much higher than is actually the case; in 1999 the proportion was less than 10 per cent. This suggests that the specification is not particularly good. In fact a more direct test of the hypothesis that preferences are Cobb–Douglas can be found by simply looking at the proportion of total expenditure that is spent on food: this was almost 30 per cent in 1950, but less than 10 per cent in 1999. This is a clear rejection of the Cobb–Douglas specification.

The log-likelihood is a measure of the goodness of fit of the equation. It tells us that the fit is quite good. However it will become clear that other specifications fit the data better. One possible contender is the Stone–Geary utility function, which we already know (see Eq. (7.3)) leads to a demand function of the form shown in Eq. (16.2).

$$q_1 = s_1 + a(m - p_1 s_1 - p_2 s_2)/p_1 \tag{16.2}$$

In Eq. (16.2) good 1 is the good of interest – in this case food – and good 2 represents all other goods. Let us denote the price of all other goods by **QFOD**, which is simply given by (**NALL** – **NFOD**)/(**RALL** – **RFOD**). Then we can conclude that the Stone–Geary demand function for food is such that **RFOD** is a linear function of **NALL/PFOD** and **QFOD/PFOD**; that is, using the original notation, q_1 is a linear function of m/p_1 and p_2/p_1. If we fit the data to this function we get the result set out in Eq. (16.3).

$$\mathbf{RFOD} = 44\ 491 + 0.065 \ \mathbf{NALL/PFOD} - 23\ 426 \ \mathbf{QFOD/PFOD} + u$$
$$(11.4) \qquad (10.8) \qquad\qquad (3.6)$$
$$\text{log-likelihood} = -446.349 \quad R\text{-squared} = 0.943$$
$$\text{residual sum of squares} = 86\ 932\ 642 \tag{16.3}$$

The numbers in brackets under the coefficients are the corresponding t-ratios; they are clearly all significant. The implied subsistence level of expenditure on food is £44 491m – equivalent to around £800 per head per year in 1995 prices. The coefficient on the variable **NALL/PFOD** indicates that, once the subsistence levels of both food and other commodities have been bought, consumers on average spend 6.5 per cent of any extra income on food. This seems more reasonable. The log-likelihood of this equation is significantly higher than that for the Cobb–Douglas specification; and the R-squared indicates that 94.3 per cent of the variation in expenditure on food is explained by this Stone–Geary specification. This specification therefore seems reasonable on both econometric grounds[1] and on economic grounds.

---

1. We appreciate that econometricians would want to do some further tests of the specification. However such tests are beyond the scope of the book and would require us to bring in further econometric theory. The crucial point is that we have a specification that comes from economic theory, and is econometrically respectable.

16.4 Simultaneous Bias

At this stage we should recognize an important fact. The data we have of expenditure on food are not just demand data; they are generated by the simultaneous interaction of demand and supply. What effect does this have? We cannot give a full explanation here – it would require a course in econometrics – but we can explain the nature of the problem.

As we have already said, the data that we have reflect the interaction of demand with supply. If the demand and supply functions have remained stable throughout the observation period, that must mean that there is only one intersection point – and so we would observe just one value for **RFOD** and just one value for the price **PFOD**. As it happens we have lots of different observations; Figs. 16.1 and 16.2 make this clear. This must imply that one or both of the demand and supply schedules must have shifted during the observation period. Let us consider what might have happened.

Suppose just the demand schedule has shifted. We would have a situation something like that shown in Fig. 16.3. Notice where the intersection points lie; they are all along the supply curve! All we can observe from the data is the supply curve. We can deduce nothing about the demand curves (just consider a second family of demand curves with slopes different from those in Fig. 16.3).

However if it was just the supply curve that had moved, we would have something like that pictured in Fig. 16.4. Here we would be only able to observe the demand curve.

Now we know something from economic theory; we know that changes in income, or changes in the total expenditure, will shift the demand curve; and we know that changes in factor prices will shift the supply curve. If we look at the data on these variables over our observation period, we will see that all these variables have indeed changed. So both the demand and supply curve have shifted. If we ignore this information we are bound to get biases in our estimation. Going back to the demand curve estimated above, we should recognize that some of the movements must have resulted from shifts in the supply curve.

To explain how we eliminate these biases caused by the simultaneous determination of price and quantity takes us deep into econometrics and we cannot discuss these issues here. Suffice to say that, if we use a method of estimation called instrumental variables estimation, as distinct from ordinary least squares estimation which we used earlier, we can get rid of the bias.

Let us report the results of using instrumental variables estimation of the demand equation. This method takes into account the fact that the price variable on the right hand side of the equation is partly determined by the variables which enter the supply equation – namely

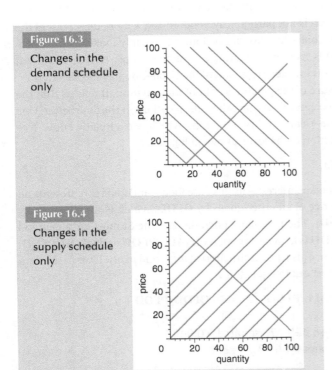

Figure 16.3

Changes in the demand schedule only

Figure 16.4

Changes in the supply schedule only

factor prices. Instrumental variables estimation using the factor prices (which we will discuss later) as instrumental variables yields the following estimate of the Stone–Geary demand function for food.

$$\textbf{RFOD} = 41\,962 + 0.049\,\textbf{NALL/PFOD} - 14\,210\,\textbf{QFOD/PFOD} + u$$
$$(8.5) \qquad (5.9) \qquad\qquad\qquad (1.6)$$
$$\text{residual sum of squares} = 4\,450\,094$$

$$(16.4)$$

The subsistence level of food expenditure is now £41 962m in 1995 prices. The proportion of extra income spent on food is 4.9 per cent. You will notice that changes have occurred to the estimates as a result of the elimination of simultaneous bias through the use of the instrumental variables. Given the fact that instrumental variables estimation is a consistent method of estimation while ordinary least squares is not (in the context of a simultaneous system), we take Eq. (16.4) as our estimate of the demand curve for food in the UK.

16.5 The Supply of Food in the UK

We assume a Cobb–Douglas production function, and also that the food production industry is competitive. We know from the chapters on cost curves that the cost function for a two-input Cobb–Douglas is proportional to the following: $y^{1/(a+b)} w_1^{a/(a+b)} w_2^{b/(a+b)}$. See Eq. (12.4) as the basis for this.

It follows that the marginal cost function for a firm or industry with decreasing returns to scale is proportional to $y^{(1-a-b)/(a+b)} w_1^{a/(a+b)} w_2^{b/(a+b)}$.

If we now use the profit maximizing condition that price should equal marginal cost, and if we solve that equation for the implied optimal output, we find that it is given by Eq. (16.5), in which k is some constant.

$$y = kp^{(a+b)/(1-a-b)} w_1^{-a/(1-a-b)} w_2^{-b/(1-a-b)}$$

$$(16.5)$$

This is the supply function for a two-input competitive industry with Cobb–Douglas technology. As most econometric packages prefer linear equations, we linearize Eq. (16.5) by taking logarithms; this gives us the logarithmic function Eq. (16.6).

$$\log(y) = \text{constant} + [(a+b)\log(p) - a\log(w_1) - b\log(w_2)]/(1-a-b)$$

$$(16.6)$$

Eq. (16.6) is a linear equation in the variables $\log(y)$, $\log(p)$, $\log(w_1)$ and $\log(w_2)$. You will notice that the price of food has a positive coefficient, while the input prices all have negative coefficients. Obviously if there are more than two factors of production, the equation can be generalized appropriately.

We now need some appropriate data. We already have the price of food; **PFOD**. We restrict ourselves to variables which can be easily found in *Economic Trends Annual Supplement*. There are three obvious factors of production: labour, capital, and raw materials and fuels. We take as our indicator of the wage rate the variable (code name: LNNK in *ETAS*) unit wage costs in the whole economy (there are no data specifically for the food-producing industry). We call this **PUW** and it is in column 10 of Table 16.1. As our indicator of the cost of capital, we take the interest rate on long-term government securities; this has the *ETAS* code AJLX and we call it **NLI** (the Nominal Long term rate of Interest); it is in column 2 of Table 16.1. Finally, recognising that the food industry has to buy materials and fuel as inputs, we take the price index for raw materials and fuels purchased by the manufacturing industry (again, there is no variable specifically for the food industry). This has the

ETAS code PLKW and we call it **PMAF** (see column 9 of Table 16.1). Our hypothesis is: that the log of **RFOD** is a linear function of the log of **PFOD**, the log of **PMAF**, the log of **NLI** and the log of **PUW**. If we carry out an instrumental variables estimation of this equation (again, to avoid simultaneous equation bias), we obtain the following estimate of the supply function of food.

$$\log(\textbf{RFOD}) = 13.68 + 0.761 \log(\textbf{PFOD}) - 0.0948 \log(\textbf{PMAF}) - 0.0934 \log(\textbf{NLI}) -$$
$$\quad (13.9) \quad (3.3) \qquad\qquad (1.2) \qquad\qquad\qquad (2.0)$$

$$0.485 \log(\textbf{PUW})$$
$$(2.1)$$

Residual sum of squares = 0.0102   (16.7)

Eq. (16.7) is our estimated supply equation. You will see that all the coefficients have the right signs and that they are all significant, except that on log(**PMAF**). We originally included this as the ordinary least squares estimation suggested that it was important; for the record, the ordinary least squares estimate is reported in Eq. (16.8).

$$\log(\textbf{RFOD}) = 11.98 + 0.348 \log(\textbf{PFOD}) - 0.148 \log(\textbf{PMAF}) - 0.0696 \log(\textbf{NLI}) -$$
$$\quad (23.5) \quad (3.1) \qquad\qquad (2.5) \qquad\qquad\qquad (2.0)$$

$$0.0786 \log(\textbf{PUW})$$
$$(0.6)$$

Residual sum of squares = 0.0056   (16.8)

You might like to disentangle the coefficients of the underlying Cobb–Douglas production function.

16.6 An Investigation of the Effect of a Tax on Food

At the moment food is exempt from VAT. Suppose the government were considering the imposition of VAT; let us examine what might happen.

The initial situation is given by the demand and supply equations (16.4) and (16.5). Let us take the position as in 1999 – the latest year for which data are available. In 1999 we have the following values for the exogenous variables:

NALL = 564 368	**NLI** = 4.7
PALL = 1.10043	**PUW** = 115
QFOD = 1.10621	**PMAF** = 83.7

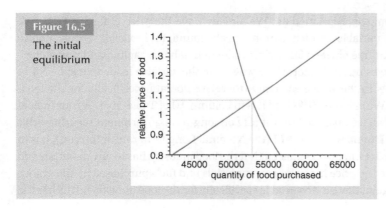

Figure 16.5

The initial equilibrium

If we substitute these values in the demand and supply equations and then graph the equations, the result is shown in Fig. 16.5.

You will see that the initial equilibrium – a value for **RFOD** of 52 832 and a value for **PFOD** of 1.076 – is very close to the 1999 outturn of a value for **RFOD** of 52 277 and a value for **PFOD** of 1.105. The reason that they are not exactly equal is simply that the estimated demand and supply curves do not fit exactly.

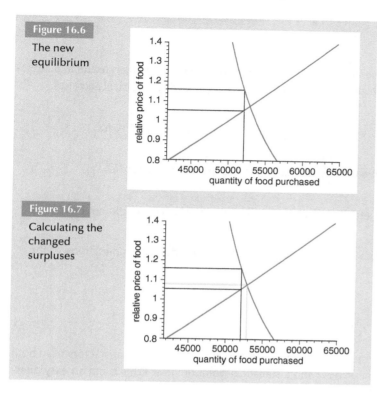

Figure 16.6

The new equilibrium

Figure 16.7

Calculating the changed surpluses

Now consider the introduction of a tax – let us say of 10 per cent. We will see in Chapter 27[2] that this drives a wedge, equal to 10 per cent of the selling price, between the demand and supply curves. The new equilibrium is shown in Fig. 16.6.

The new equilibrium price that the sellers receive is the lower price, which is 1.055; and the new equilibrium price paid by the buyers is the upper price, which is 1.160. This latter is 10 per cent higher than the former. The government takes the difference – 0.1055 – on each unit of the good sold. In this new equilibrium the quantity exchanged is 52 042, a reduction of some 1.5 per cent. This is a relatively modest fall because the demand is very insensitive to price changes, as one would expect with a commodity like food. For the same reason it is the buyers who largely pay the tax: the price they pay rises from 1.076 to 1.160, an increase of around 7.8 per cent. On the other hand the sellers see a fall in the price which they receive from 1.076 to 1.055; a fall of 1.98 per cent.

We can also calculate what happens to the surpluses of the buyers and sellers; consider Fig. 16.7. The buyers lose the surplus which was bounded by the old price, the new price and the demand curve (be careful: the graph does not go to zero at the left-hand axis). This area is approximately equal to (1.160–1.076) times (52 042 + 52 832)/2, which is 4405. We can calculate it exactly by finding the area by integration; the exact figure for the loss in consumer surplus is £4,423m. Assuming there are 55 million people in the UK, this is equivalent to £80 per head at 1995 prices.

The loss in producer surplus is the area bounded by the old price, the new price received by the sellers and the supply curve. This area is approximately equal to (1.076–1.055) times (52 042 + 52 832)/2, which is 1101. Again, we can calculate it exactly by integration; the exact figure for the loss in producer surplus is £1,106m in 1995 prices. Therefore the combined loss of surpluses is £5,529 at 1995 prices.

The government takes the tax – 0.0155 on each of the 52 042 units exchanged; this amounts to £5488 at 1995 prices. The difference between this figure and the combined loss of surpluses – £41m at 1995 prices – is the *deadweight loss of the tax*. This is a concept which we shall discuss in Chapter 27. It is equal to the little triangle bounded by the supply curve, the demand curve and the vertical line at the new quantity. The deadweight loss is relatively small because the demand curve is rather insensitive to the price.

2. This material anticipates somewhat the material of Chapter 27. You may find it helpful to have a quick glance at Chapter 27 before proceeding further with this chapter.

16.7 Summary

We have shown how the theoretical material we have been developing is useful in addressing practical policy problems. We have undertaken the following empirical exercises.

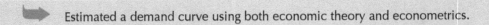 Estimated a demand curve using both economic theory and econometrics.

Estimated a supply curve using both economic theory and econometrics.

Mentioned the econometric problems that arise when we have a simultaneous system.

Used the estimated demand and supply system to work out the implications of the imposition of a new tax.

16.8 Review Questions

1   Consider why estimated supply and demand curves should be satisfactory from both an economic point of view and a statistical point of view. (This is not an easy question, and it requires you to understand some methodology of economic science. But it will do you no harm to consider such issues.)

2   Discuss the estimated coefficients of the demand curve of this chapter, and interpret them as parameters of the Stone–Geary preference function. Do you think that the parameter estimates are reasonable from an economic point of view?

3   Discuss the estimated coefficients of the supply curve of this chapter, and interpret them as parameters of the Cobb–Douglas production function. Do you think that the parameter estimates are reasonable from an economic point of view?

16.9 Glossary of Technical Terms

A complete treatment of the econometric issues involved in this chapter lies beyond the scope of this book. You may like to refer to some standard econometric text if you want further details. A good text which explains the key terms clearly is Kennedy, P. (1998) *A Guide to Econometrics*, 4th edn, Blackwell, Oxford. Here we provide a summary of some of the key terms used in this chapter.

We start with a scatter diagram, which is the type of graph illustrated in Figs. 16.1 and 16.2. This is simply a graph of one variable against another, where the points graphed are the observations on those variables. So, if we have 52 observations, we have 52 points – one for each observation. This is a two-dimensional scatter diagram.

The regression line fitted to this scatter diagram is the 'best-fitting' straight line which approximates the scatter. There are various definitions of what is meant by 'best-fitting'. In a simple ordinary least squares regression, the criterion of best-fitting used is the minimization of the sum of squared distances from the points to the line.

In general a regression line does not fit the observations exactly, unless the observations happen to lie exactly along a straight line, which is not the case with our scatter diagrams. It is useful to be able to report how closely the line fits the observations, or how well the line 'explains' the observations. There are various measures of goodness of fit; the most common one is called R^2, which measures the proportion of the variance of the data explained by the straight line. A value of $R^2 = 1$ means that the line 'explains' the data exactly, whilst a value of $R^2 = 0$ means that it does not 'explain' it at all[3]. The better the fit, the higher the value of R^2. An alternative measure is the log-likelihood, which we shall not explain here apart from noting that the higher the value of the log-likelihood, the better the fit.

The coefficients of the regression line are the estimates of the coefficients of the theoretical equation we are estimating: the coefficients are estimates of the theoretical coefficients. If the regression line does not fit the observations exactly the estimates will not equal the theoretical coefficients; there will be some margin of error associated with these estimates. The standard error of the estimate is a measure of this error. The smaller the standard error, the more precise is the estimate. We can use standard errors to test the proposition that the theoretical coefficients are zero. We do this by dividing the estimate by its standard error to form what is known as the t-ratio of that coefficient. If this t-ratio is big enough, we can reject the proposition that the theoretical coefficient is zero. What is meant by 'big enough' depends upon the context but, as a rough rule of thumb, a t-ratio larger than two is big enough. In this case we say that the estimated coefficient is significantly different from zero.

All this material can be generalized to the estimation of a function of more than one variable, although it is difficult to portray this graphically. In particular, we can generalize the idea of the best-fitting function to a function of more that one variable. The best-fitting criterion which we defined previously – minimizing the sum of squared distances from the points to the line – is defined as ordinary least squares. Under certain assumptions about the generating process, it can be shown that this is the best way of estimating the theoretical coefficients. In particular, these assumptions will be true if the independent variable(s) in the regression line are truly independent. If they are not, then the method of ordinary least squares may produce estimates that are biased; that is, they are not on average equal to the

---

3. We put the word 'explain' in quotation marks as this is merely a statistical – not a theoretical – explanation.

theoretical coefficients. They may even be inconsistent; that is, they do not approach the theoretical coefficients even with an infinite number of observations. In such cases other fitting methods may be better.

In the context of the demand and supply estimation that we have done, ordinary least squares fitting is appropriate if price (the independent variable) is truly independent. But we know that the price is the solution to the interaction of supply and demand, and therefore cannot be truly independent of demand. Thus some other method of fitting is appropriate; one that takes into account the fact that price is not independent. One such method is that of instrumental variables estimation, as used in this chapter. It uses truly independent variables to estimate the demand and supply equations. An explanation cannot be provided here; such issues occupy large parts of econometric texts. However Kennedy (cited above) provides a good explanation.

16.10 Appendix: Data and Data Sources

Table 16.1 Data

YEAR (1)	NLI (2)	NALL (3)	RALL (4)	RFOD (5)	NFOD (6)	PALL (7)	PFOD (8)	PMAF (9)	PUW (10)
1948		8 417	142 958	32 737	2 320	0.0589	0.0708		
1949		8 771	145 251	33 977	2 508	0.0604	0.0738		
1950		9 257	149 082	35 572	2 758	0.0621	0.0775		
1951		9 998	147 049	34 938	3 022	0.0680	0.0864		
1952		10 526	147 017	30 760	2 824	0.0716	0.0918		
1953		11 226	153 393	32 533	3 122	0.0732	0.0959		
1954		11 906	159 716	33 210	3 295	0.0745	0.0992		
1955		12 832	166 245	34 385	3 585	0.0772	0.1042		
1956		13 494	167 041	34 941	3 787	0.0808	0.1083		
1957		14 227	170 434	35 466	3 928	0.0834	0.1107		
1958		15 013	175 182	35 893	4 028	0.0856	0.1122		
1959		15 802	182 697	36 580	4 157	0.0864	0.1136		
1960		16 573	189 586	37 366	4 225	0.0874	0.1130		
1961		17 422	193 663	37 985	4 366	0.0899	0.1149		
1962		18 438	197 837	38 366	4 560	0.0931	0.1188		
1963	5.30	19 565	206 304	38 568	4 689	0.0948	0.1215		
1964	5.80	20 868	212 644	39 041	4 889	0.0981	0.1252		
1965	6.43	22 151	215 002	39 016	5 059	0.1030	0.1296		
1966	6.91	23 391	218 707	39 445	5 297	0.1069	0.1342		
1967	6.80	24 579	223 851	40 094	5 485	0.1098	0.1368		
1968	7.54	26 451	230 135	40 303	5 696	0.1149	0.1413		
1969	9.05	28 054	231 201	40 418	6 035	0.1213	0.1493		
1970	9.21	30 547	237 739	40 824	6 429	0.1284	0.1574		
1971	8.85	34 250	245 429	40 861	7 105	0.1395	0.1738		
1972	8.90	38 780	261 277	40 789	7 614	0.1484	0.1866		
1973	10.71	44 360	275 705	41 770	8 751	0.1608	0.2095		

Table A2.1   Continued

YEAR (1)	NLI (2)	NALL (3)	RALL (4)	RFOD (5)	NFOD (6)	PALL (7)	PFOD (8)	PMAF (9)	PUW (10)
1974	14.77	51 126	271 228	41 038	10 028	0.1884	0.2443	32.0	
1975	14.39	62 881	270 421	41 050	12 313	0.2325	0.2999	35.3	
1976	14.43	73 060	271 477	41 484	14 459	0.2691	0.3485	44.3	
1977	12.73	83 504	270 434	41 126	16 596	0.3087	0.4035	50.5	
1978	12.47	96 368	284 901	41 879	18 373	0.3382	0.4387	50.5	
1979	12.99	114 458	297 453	42 812	20 988	0.3847	0.4902	59.0	43.4
1980	13.78	132 663	297 256	42 866	23 655	0.4462	0.5518	69.3	53.0
1981	14.74	147 120	297 237	42 591	24 946	0.4949	0.5857	78.5	58.2
1982	12.88	160 997	299 810	42 694	26 490	0.5369	0.6204	83.4	66.7
1983	10.80	176 881	313 648	43 416	28 061	0.5639	0.6463	88.1	67.7
1984	10.69	189 244	319 357	42 676	29 274	0.5925	0.6859	96.6	70.0
1985	10.62	206 600	331 404	43 213	30 657	0.6234	0.7094	96.6	74.0
1986	9.87	228 848	353 831	44 572	32 574	0.6467	0.7308	81.0	76.9
1987	9.47	251 143	372 601	45 709	34 402	0.6740	0.7523	82.6	78.6
1988	9.36	283 425	400 427	46 745	36 491	0.7078	0.7806	84.5	80.8
1989	9.58	310 493	413 498	47 538	39 143	0.7508	0.8234	89.1	84.8
1990	11.08	336 492	415 788	47 055	41 817	0.8092	0.8886	88.5	90.4
1991	9.92	357 785	408 309	47 114	44 044	0.8762	0.9348	86.6	94.8
1992	9.12	377 147	410 026	47 664	45 193	0.9198	0.9481	86.3	95.0
1993	7.87	399 108	420 081	48 282	46 334	0.9500	0.9596	90.2	94.8
1994	8.05	419 262	431 462	48 931	47 122	0.9717	0.9630	91.9	95.3
1995	8.26	438 453	438 453	49 274	49 274	1.0000	1.0000	100.0	100.0
1996	8.10	467 841	454 686	50 931	52 513	1.0289	1.0310	98.8	105.4
1997	7.09	498 307	472 701	51 786	53 188	1.0541	1.0270	90.6	109.2
1998	5.45	530 851	491 378	51 627	53 789	1.0803	1.0418	82.5	114.6
1999	4.70	564 369	512 864	52 277	54 862	1.1004	1.0494	83.7	115.0

All data from *Economic Trends Annual Supplement*.

Raw Series

ABPB	Household Expenditure: Total Household Final Consumption Expenditure: CP	NALL
ABPF	Household Expenditure: Total Household Final Consumption Expenditure: KP95	RALL
CCBM	Household Expenditure: Household expenditure on food: KP95	RFOD
CCDW	Household Expenditure: Household expenditure on food: Current price	NFOD
AJLX	BGS: long-dated (20 years): Par yield – per cent per annum	NLI
LNNK	UWC: whole economy SA: Index 1995 = 100: UK	PUW
PLKW	PPI: 6 292 000 000: Materials and fuel purchased by manufacturing industry	PMAF

Derived Series

Price of Final Consumption Expenditure	NALL/RALL	PALL
Price of Food Expenditure	NFOD/RFOD	PFOD
Price of Non-Food Expenditure	(NALL-NFOD)/(RALL-RFOD)	QFOD

Values of Variables in 1999

NALL	564 369
PALL	1.10043
PMAF	83.7
NLI	4.7
PUW	115
PFOD	1.104945
RFOD	52 277
QFOD	1.106

Applications and Implications of the Basic Tools

3.1 Summary

This part continues within the competitive economy and considers a number of important implications, extensions and applications of the basic story presented in Parts 1 and 2. First we look at the aggregation problem and show how we can move from individual to aggregate supply and demand curves, and show that surpluses can be aggregated in a natural manner. We then look at one way of testing the basic assumptions underlying the theory of Parts 1 and 2 – namely that individuals have preferences with certain assumed properties, and that firms have technology with certain assumed properties. We then use the analysis to derive monetary measures (equivalent and compensating variations) of the welfare effects of price changes, and relate these to the basic concept of surplus that we have used extensively throughout the first two parts of the book. Finally we present three important applications of the core material: to inter-temporal choice (thus explaining, *inter alia*, saving decisions and the role of capital markets); to risky choice (explaining insurance decisions and the role of insurance markets amongst other matters); to the labour market (discussing when government intervention in the labour market might be beneficial, and other issues).

3.2 Detail

Chapter 17 *Aggregation:* Here we consider the aggregation problem; how we move from the individual analysis of Parts 1 and 2 to an aggregate economy consisting of many individuals. We discuss the aggregation of demand and supply curves, and the surpluses. We show that surpluses aggregate, which is an important result as it implies that, if we simply want to calculate aggregate surpluses, then all we need to know are the aggregate demand and supply schedules.

Chapter 18 *Revealed Preference and Revealed Technology:* This chapter is concerned with testing certain maintained assumptions of rationality which we have previously taken as given, namely that preferences and technology have particular properties. Clearly our analysis rests on these maintained hypotheses, so it is important that we know how to test for their empirical validity. (We also say a little about what might be the implications if these assumptions turn out not to be true.)

Chapter 19 *Compensating and Equivalent Variations:* This chapter looks more systematically at the question of getting a monetary measure of the welfare effects of a price change. Having a monetary measure facilitates many analyses which economists may need to do, such as measuring the welfare impact of a tax. We have already used the notion of surplus but we have seen that, for instance, with non-quasi-linear preferences there is a certain ambiguity about this measure. We therefore examine two alternative measures; the compensating variation and the equivalent variation of a price change. We show that these two measures are generally not the same, and that they usually bound the surplus. We also discuss the breakdown of the effect of a price change into two components – an income effect and a substitution effect; and we show that this breakdown can be done in two different ways.

Chapter 20 *Inter-temporal Choice:* This chapter uses the basic two-good framework to consider the allocation of resources through time. The two goods are interpreted as present consumption and future consumption. We define what might be meant by a perfect capital market (one which enables the trading of consumption through time), and explore its implications. Through this we can explain the determinants of borrowing and saving, and show how they depend upon the rate of interest.

Chapter 21 *The Discounted Utility Model:* This chapter takes a particular type of inter-temporal preferences (the discounted utility model), and discusses its assumptions and its predictions. This model is particularly important in the explanation of consumer behaviour, and appears to have strong empirical support.

Chapter 22 *Exchange in Capital Markets:* This chapter puts the material from the two chapters on inter-temporal choice into a market context, and explores its implications.

Chapter 23 *Choice under Risk:* This chapter uses the basic two-good framework to consider the allocation of resources in a risky world. For simplicity, we consider a world in which the risk is such that one of two states is possible *ex ante* (and just one *ex post*). The two goods are interpreted as consumption in these two states of the world. We define what might be meant by a perfect insurance market – one which enables the trading of consumption across different states of the world. In such a market we show that a risk-averse individual will always choose to fully insure.

Chapter 24 *The Expected Utility Model:* This chapter takes a particular type of preferences under risk (the expected utility model) and discusses its assumptions and predictions. This class of preferences is of particular importance because of its strong empirical properties.

Chapter 25 *Exchange in Insurance Markets:* This chapter puts the material from the two chapters on risky choice into a market context and explores its implications.

Chapter 26 *The Labour Market:* In many respects this has already been covered in Parts 1 and 2, but here we take the opportunity to spell out the implications, particularly concerning the effects of changes in the real wage on the demand for and supply of labour. Anticipating somewhat the material in the final part of the book, we also explore the effects of labour market legislation, particularly the introduction of a minimum wage on the labour market.

Aggregation

17.1 Introduction

This is a technical chapter in the sense that we need the results for future work. It contains very little new economics, and perhaps nothing that is not reasonably obvious after a little thought; but it is still important. The basic point concerns the aggregation of supply and demand. To date most of this book has been concerned with individuals, and individual demand and supply. To apply this material in the real world, where we are dealing with many individuals, we need to be able to move from the individual level to the aggregate level; we need to be able to aggregate the results we have obtained.

In essence there are two parts to this: one obvious, and one perhaps not so obvious. The first is the simple aggregation of the demand and supply functions with which we have been working. The second is the aggregation of the concept of surplus which we have been using. Regarding the first, we want to ask how we undertake the aggregation; we are also interested in whether the aggregate functions retain the properties of individual functions. With regard to the second, we want to know whether the surplus measured in aggregate functions is the aggregate of the surpluses as measured in the individual functions.

To simplify this chapter, I use just two individuals, A and B; if we can aggregate two individuals, it is an easy matter to aggregate more than two.

17.2 Aggregating Demand

We start with a familiar example: the demand for a discrete good. You will recall from Chapter 2 that the demand function for a discrete good takes the form of a step function with a step at every reservation price. You may be able to anticipate the results which follow. We work with a simple example.

Let us assume that individual A is prepared to buy up to three units of the good and has reservation prices equal to ten, five and one for the three units. So his or her demand function is that shown in Fig. 17.1.

For B we will assume that he or she would buy up to two units, with reservation prices of eight and four, as in the demand function in Fig. 17.2.

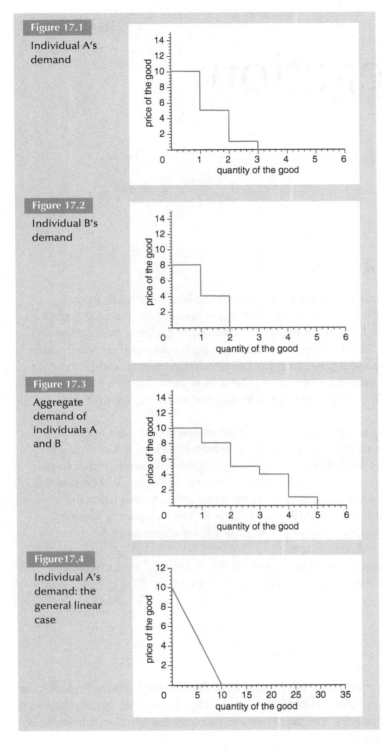

Figure 17.1

Individual A's demand

Figure 17.2

Individual B's demand

Figure 17.3

Aggregate demand of individuals A and B

Figure 17.4

Individual A's demand: the general linear case

The aggregation process is simple if we remind ourselves that we need to add up horizontally, because the quantity demanded is on the horizontal axis. The aggregation process is as follows: for each price we add together the demand of A and that of B. For example, at a price of five, A's demand is two and B's demand is one, so aggregate demand is three. Proceeding in this way we get Fig. 17.3.

Another way of thinking about this is through reservation prices. We know that the demand curve for a discrete good is a step function with a step at every reservation price. Now we already know that A has reservation prices of ten, five and one, and that B has reservation prices of eight and four. Taken together and put in order, the two individuals have reservation prices of ten, eight, five, four and one. Hence the aggregate function is as drawn in figure 17.3. You will notice that it has the same form as the individual functions; they are step functions and so is the aggregate.

This is not necessarily the case, although there are other examples where the aggregate function has the same form as the individual functions. One such example is when the individual demand functions are linear and all have the same intercept on the vertical axis. We will present this algebraically. Suppose A's demand function is $q_A = 10 - p$, so that A's demand becomes zero at a price of ten. Suppose that B's demand function is $q_B = 20 - 2p$, so that B's demand also becomes zero at the price of ten. Now find the aggregate demand. If Q denotes aggregate demand, then $Q = q_A + q_B = (10 - p) + (20 - 2p) = 30 - 3p$. The aggregate demand function is $Q = 30 - 3p$; you will see that it also

becomes zero at a price of ten. This is a second example where the aggregate function has the same form as the individual functions.

But it is not always the case. Consider the more general case of individual linear demand functions. We show this example graphically. We start with individual A, who has the demand function drawn in Fig. 17.4.

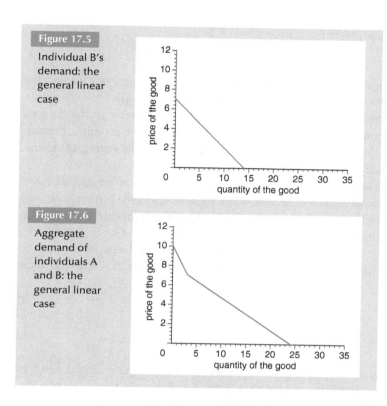

Figure 17.5

Individual B's demand: the general linear case

Figure 17.6

Aggregate demand of individuals A and B: the general linear case

We now graph individual B's demand function in Fig. 17.5.

When we aggregate we need to be careful. Remember that we are adding up horizontally. Note that A does not start buying until the price is below ten, whereas B does not start buying until the price is below seven. When looking at the aggregate, at any price between seven and ten only A is in the market and therefore the aggregate function in this price range is simply A's demand. For prices below seven, however, both A and B are in the market. We thus get the aggregate demand shown in Fig. 17.6[1].

Note the kink at the price of seven. This is the price at which B enters the market. You will see that, although the individual demand curves are linear, the aggregate demand curve is piecewise linear; it has a different form from the functions from which it was aggregated.

This is generally the case. Note moreover, that while aggregate demand is a function of the price of the good it will, in general, also be a function of *all* the individual incomes. Only in exceptional circumstances will aggregate demand be a function of the price of the good and aggregate income. To show this, let us do a little algebra. Suppose there are two goods, 1 and 2 with prices p_1 and p_2, and two individuals A and B with incomes m^A and m^B. We denote the demand of individual A for good 1 as q_1^A, and so on. In general we have the demand functions of A and B for good 1 as shown in Eq. (17.1)

$$q_1^A = f_1^A(p_1, p_2, m^A)$$
$$q_1^B = f_1^B(p_1, p_2, m^B)$$

(17.1)

There are similar demand functions for good 2, where $f_1(.)$ and $f_2(.)$ are functions whose form depends upon the preferences of the two individuals. It therefore follows that the aggregate demand for good 1 is given by

$$Q_1 = q_1^A + q_1^B = f_1(p_1, p_2, m^A) + f_2(p_1, p_2, m^B)$$

(17.2)

Only in very special circumstances can this be written with income aggregated, as has been done in Eq. (7.3).

$$Q_1 = f_1(p_1, p_2, m) \qquad \text{where} \quad m = m^A + m^B$$

(17.3)

One circumstance in which we can do this is when the individual functions are linear in the variables and the coefficient on income is the same for both individuals. We then have

$$q_1^A = a_0 + a_1 p_1 + a_2 p_2 + cm^A$$
$$q_1^B = b_0 + b_1 p_1 + b_2 p_2 + cm^B$$

(17.4)

---

1. Note that below a price of seven, A's demand is linear in price and so is B's. It follows that the sum of their demands must also be linear in price.

In this instance, aggregate demand is as set out in (17.5).

$$Q_1 = (a_0 + b_0) + (a_1 + b_1)p_1 + (a_2 + b_2)p_2 + cm \qquad (17.5)$$

In Eq. (17.5), the aggregate demand depends only on the prices and aggregate income; it is not affected by the distribution of income between the two individuals. The reason is simple: if we take money away from A and give it to B, then A reduces his or her demand for the good while B increases it by exactly the same amount. But if the coefficients on income in the individual equations differ, then aggregate demand depends not only on the aggregate income, but also on its distribution.

This latter point is important because it shows that, except in rather special cases, changing the distribution of income in society, while keeping aggregate income fixed, will change aggregate demand for a good or a service. This means that changing the distribution of income will change the demand. An obvious example is the demand for food; if we take money away from the rich and give it to the poor, the demand for food will rise because the rich will reduce their consumption of food by less than the poor will increase their consumption.

17.3 Aggregating Buyer Surplus

You may be wondering whether our previous result about the buyer's surplus survives aggregation. You may realize that we have already answered this question as far as a discrete good is concerned. Let us recall this point using the demand function from the previous section, taking a particular example. Suppose that A and B can both buy any amount they wish at a price of four. What are their individual demands and surpluses? Individual A demands two units and has a surplus of six on the first and a surplus of one on the second (A has reservation prices of ten, five and one); this gives a total surplus of seven at a price of four. B demands either one or two units, with a surplus of four on the first unit and zero on the second (since B's reservation prices are eight and four), giving a total surplus of four at a price four. So, the combined total surplus of the two individuals is eleven.

Let us now look at the surplus derived from the aggregate demand curve. Again we take a price of four. The aggregate demand curve is that of Fig. 17.3 and the surplus is measured in the usual way; it is the area between the price paid and the aggregate demand curve. This is illustrated in Fig. 17.7.

If we add up the areas they equal $(6 + 4 + 1 + 0) = 11$. This is exactly equal to the aggregate surplus which we measured earlier. When we think about it, clearly it must be so; we have a step at every reservation price, and the difference between the reservation price, and the price paid is the surplus or profit on that unit.

For those of you who know some mathematics, you will realize that this must always be the case, irrespective of the form of the demand curve. We are adding horizontally to obtain the aggregate demand curve, and it must be the case that the areas are also aggregated. Consider the linear demand curve example which we presented graphically in Fig. 17.6. Take a price of four. A's

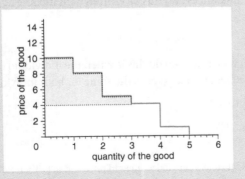

Figure 17.7

Aggregate surplus at a price of £4

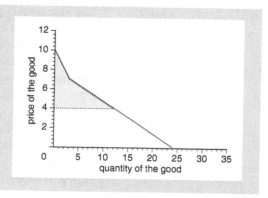

Figure 17.8

Aggregate surplus at a price of £4: the general linear case

surplus is the area between the price of four and A's demand curve as shown in Fig. 17.4. This area is a triangle with base six and height six, and the surplus is therefore 18. B's surplus is the area between the price of four and B's demand curve in Fig. 17.5. This area is a triangle with base six and height three, so the surplus is therefore nine. The total surplus is $(18 + 9) = 27$.

Now consider the aggregate demand curve from Fig. 17.6, to which a price line has been added at a price of four; this is shown in Fig. 17.8. To work out the area between the line at $p = 4$ and the demand curve, we divide the area into two triangles, formed by extending the upper segment of the demand curve until it reaches a price of four. The left hand triangle has a base of six and a height of six (is this familiar?), and the right hand triangle a base of six and height three (is this familiar?). The total area is thus $(\frac{1}{2} \times 6 \times 6) + (\frac{1}{2} \times 6 \times 3) = 27$; this is exactly as before. Indeed, for the reasons that we have already stated, this must always be the case. So we have the following important result.

 The surplus as measured from the aggregate demand curve in the usual way (by measuring the area between the price paid and the aggregate demand curve) is always equal to the aggregate surplus found by aggregating the individual surpluses.

This can be simplified as follows.

 The aggregate of the surpluses is always equal to the surplus of the aggregate.

This important result means that, if all we are interested in is the aggregate surplus and not its distribution, then all we need to know is the aggregate demand curve; we do not need to know the individual demand curves.

17.4 Aggregating Supply

This section does for supply what Section 17.2 did for demand. The methods are the same and the conclusions are the same.

As in Section 17.2, we start with a familiar example – one for the supply of a discrete good. You may recall that the supply function for a discrete good takes the form of a step function with a step at every reservation price. We work with a simple example. You should be able to anticipate the results that follow.

Assume that individual A will sell up to three units of the good, and has reservation prices equal to three, four and twelve for the three units; His or her supply function is in Fig. 17.9.

Individual B would be willing to sell up to two units with reservation prices of six and nine; this situation is graphed in Fig. 17.10.

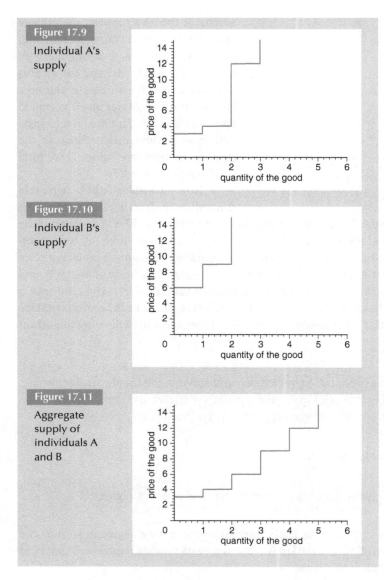

Figure 17.9

Individual A's supply

Figure 17.10

Individual B's supply

Figure 17.11

Aggregate supply of individuals A and B

The aggregation process is simple if we remind ourselves that we add up horizontally, because the quantity supplied is on the horizontal axis and we want to find the aggregate supply at any given price. So the aggregation process is the following: for each price we find the supply of A and that of B and then add them together. For example, at a price of seven A's supply is two and B's is one, so the aggregate supply is three. Proceeding in this way, we get Fig. 17.11.

Another way of thinking about this is through reservation prices. We know that the supply curve for a discrete good is a step function with a step at every reservation price. Now we know that A has reservation prices of three, four and twelve, and B has reservation prices of six and nine. Taken together and put in order, the two individuals have reservation prices of three, four, six, nine and twelve to give the aggregate function shown in Fig. 17.11. It has the same form as the individual functions, in that they are step functions and so is the aggregate.

This is not necessarily the case, although there are other examples where the aggregate function has the same form as the individual functions. One such example is when all individual supply functions are linear and have the same intercept on the vertical axis. We will present this algebraically. Suppose A's supply function is $q_A = p - 2$, so that A's supply becomes zero at a price of two. Suppose that B's supply function is $q_B = 2p - 4$ so that it also becomes zero at a price of two. Now find the aggregate. If Q denotes aggregate supply, then $Q = q_A + q_B = (p - 2) + (2p - 4) = 3p - 6$. You will see that the aggregate supply becomes zero at a price of two.

But this is not always the case. Consider the more general case of linear individual supply functions. We present this case graphically because it is clear from the graphs what is happening. We start with A, whose supply function is linear, and is given in Fig. 17.12, whilst that of individual B is in Fig. 17.13.

Figure 17.12

Individual A's supply: the general linear case

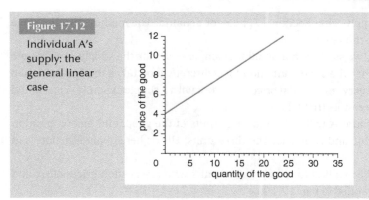

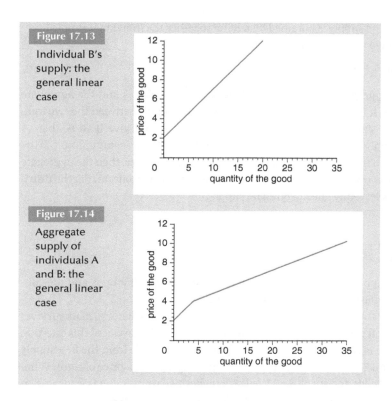

Figure 17.13

Individual B's supply: the general linear case

Figure 17.14

Aggregate supply of individuals A and B: the general linear case

We must be careful when we aggregate because we are adding up horizontally. Note that A does not start selling until the price is above four, while B starts selling when the price exceeds two. Therefore when the price is between two and four, only B is in the market and the aggregate function in this price range is just B's supply. For prices above four, however, both A and B are in the market. We thus get the aggregate supply of Fig. 17.14[2].

Note the kink at the price of four, which is the price at which A enters the market. As with demand, although the individual supply curves are linear, the aggregate supply curve is piecewise linear – it has a different form from the functions from which it was aggregated.

This will generally be the case. Note moreover that, while the aggregate supply is a function of the price of the good, it will, in general, also be a function of *all* the individual incomes. Only in exceptional circumstances will aggregate supply be a function of the price of the good and aggregate income.

To show this, let us do a little algebra. Suppose there are two goods, good 1 and good 2 with prices p_1 and p_2, and two individuals A and B with incomes m^A and m^B; we denote the supply for individual A for good 1 as q_1^A, and so on. In general supplies are given by Eq. (17.6) in the case of good 1.

$$q_1^A = f_1^A(p_1, p_2, m^A)$$
$$q_1^B = f_1^B(p_1, p_2, m^B) \tag{17.6}$$

Similar functions can be formulated for good 2, where $f_1(.)$ and $f_2(.)$ are two functions whose form depends upon the preferences of the individuals. The aggregate supply of good 1 is therefore given by:

$$Q_1 = q_1^A + q_1^B = f_1(p_1, p_2, m^A) + f_2(p_1, p_2, m^B) \tag{17.7}$$

Only in very exceptional circumstances may we write this in the following aggregate form:

$$Q_1 = f_1(p_1, p_2, m) \qquad \text{where} \quad m = m^A + m^B \tag{17.8}$$

One circumstance in which we can do this is when the individual functions are linear in the variables, and the coefficient on income is the same for both individuals. We then have

$$q_1^A = a_0 + a_1 p_1 + a_2 p_2 + cm^A$$
$$q_1^B = b_0 + b_1 p_1 + b_2 p_2 + cm^B \tag{17.9}$$

2. Above a price of four, A's supply is linear in the price and so is B's, so the aggregate supply curve must be linear in the price.

In this case aggregate supply is obtained by adding together the individual supply functions in Eq. (17.9) to give the aggregate function Eq. (17.10):

$$Q_1 = (a_0 + b_0) + (a_1 + b_1)p_1 + (a_2 + b_2)p_2 + cm \qquad (17.10)$$

In this example, aggregate supply is dependent only on the prices and the aggregate income; in other words it is not affected by the distribution of income between the two individuals. The reason is simple: if we take money away from A and give it to B, then A increases his or her supply of the good while B decreases it by exactly the same amount. If the coefficients on income in the individual equations are different, however, then the aggregate supply depends not only on the aggregate income but also on its distribution. So, the distribution of income in society may affect aggregate supply.

17.5 Aggregating Seller Surplus

This section does for supply what Section 17.3 did for demand. The methods and the conclusions are the same; these conclusions are important.

You should be able to deduce by now that our result about the seller's surplus survives aggregation. If you recall well, you will realize that we have already answered this question as far as a discrete good is concerned. Let us take a particular example from the first supply function. Suppose A and B can both sell any amount that they wish at a price of eight. What are their individual supplies and surpluses? Well, A supplies two units and has a surplus on the first unit of five and on the second of four (recall A's reservation prices are three, four and twelve); this gives A a total surplus of nine at a price of eight. B supplies one unit and his or her surplus is two (B's reservation prices are six and nine). The total surplus of the two individuals is eleven.

Let us look at the surplus as measured with respect to the aggregate supply curve (Fig. 17.11), taking a price of eight. The surplus is measured in the usual way – the area between the price paid and the aggregate supply curve; it is illustrated in Fig. 17.15.

If we add up the areas it is equal to $(5 + 4 + 2) = 11$. This is exactly equal to the aggregate surplus as calculated above. Indeed when we think about it it must be so; we have a step at every reservation price, and the difference between the reservation price and the price received is the surplus or profit on that unit.

If you know some mathematics you will realize that this must always be the case irrespective of the form of the supply curve. We are adding horizontally to get the aggregate supply curve, and it must be the case that the areas also aggregate.

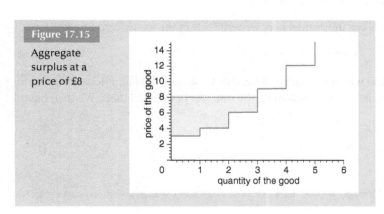

Figure 17.15

Aggregate surplus at a price of £8

Consider the linear supply curve example we presented graphically earlier. If the price received is eight, what is A's surplus? It is the area between the price eight and A's supply curve, as given in Fig. 17.12. This area is a triangle with base twelve and height four; the surplus therefore is 24. As for B's surplus, it is the area between the price received of eight and B's supply curve as given in Fig. 17.13. This area is a triangle with base twelve and height six – the surplus is therefore 36. The total surplus is $(24 + 36) = 60$.

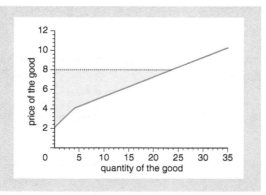

Figure 17.16

Aggregate surplus at a price of £8: the general linear case

Now consider the aggregate supply curve in Fig. 17.14 and work out the area between a price of eight and the supply curve; see Fig. 17.16.

What is this area? Well, we can chop it up into two triangles formed by extending the first linear segment of the supply curve until it reaches a price of eight. The left hand triangle has a base of twelve and a height of six (is this familiar?) and the right hand triangle a base of twelve and height four (is this familiar?). The total area is thus $(\frac{1}{2} \times 12 \times 6) + (\frac{1}{2} \times 12 \times 4) = 60$ – exactly as before. Indeed, for the reasons that we have already stated this must always be the case. So we have the important result that:

 The surplus as measured from the aggregate supply curve in the usual way (by measuring the area between the price received and the aggregate supply curve) is always equal to the aggregate surplus found by aggregating the individual surpluses.

This simplifies to:

 The aggregate of the surpluses is always equal to the surplus of the aggregate.

This result is very important because it means that, if all we are interested in is the aggregate surplus and not its distribution, then all we need to know is the aggregate supply curve; we do not need to know the individual supply curves.

17.6 Summary

This has been an important chapter. In particular it allows us to extend our key results on surpluses to aggregate functions.

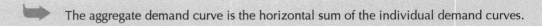 The aggregate demand curve is the horizontal sum of the individual demand curves.

The form of the aggregate demand curve may well be different from the form of the individual demand curves.

The aggregate consumer surplus, defined as the area between the aggregate demand curve and the price paid, is always exactly equal to the sum of the individual surpluses.

The aggregate supply curve is the horizontal sum of the individual supply curves.

The form of the aggregate supply curve may well be different from the form of the individual supply curves.

The aggregate seller surplus, defined as the area between the aggregate supply curve and the price received, is always exactly equal to the sum of the individual surpluses.

17.7 Review Questions

1 Construct a simple example of two linear demand curves with different intercepts and derive the aggregate demand curve. Then select any price and measure both the individual surpluses and the aggregate surplus; verify numerically the results of this chapter.

2 Construct a simple example of two linear supply curves with different intercepts and derive the aggregate supply curve. Then select any price and measure both the individual surpluses and the aggregate surplus; verify numerically the results of this chapter.

3 If you like mathematics you could show that the results concerning the aggregation of surpluses must be true however many individuals are aggregated.

Revealed Preference and Revealed Technology

18.1 Introduction

This chapter is in two parts: the first relates to preferences and the second to technology. Intellectually the material in the two parts is similar: first we discuss how we might use empirical observations to test the assumptions we have been making; then we discuss how we might use empirical observations to tell us something about preferences or about technology. In a sense we have done some of the second already; as we know, for example, how to distinguish between perfect substitutes, perfect complements or Cobb–Douglas preferences (or technology) on the basis of observations[1]. But it is important to be aware of the methods that we can use to test directly the assumptions we have been making. Some economists would argue that these assumptions are definitions of rational behaviour and must therefore be true; but empirical evidence suggests that we should be careful in jumping to such a conclusion.

The bulk of the material in this chapter relates to testing our assumptions, using observations on behaviour. We should be a little careful in using this material for two reasons:

- we know that any theory we use is empirically false, since any useful theory must be an approximation to reality;
- we know from countless experiments that human beings make mistakes when taking decisions.

In a sense these reasons are inter-related; given the fact that human beings make mistakes, any theory must be only approximately true unless we have some theory about how people make mistakes – which seems to be almost impossible by definition.

Be that as it may, the material in this chapter is useful as it tells us a little about what we might infer from observations. We begin with direct inferences, and then move on to indirect inferences.

---

1. Recall that, with perfect substitutes the demand for one of the two goods is usually zero; with perfect complements the ratio of the quantities purchased is constant; and with Cobb–Douglas the ratio of the amounts spent is constant.

18.2   Direct Inferences about Preferences

In this section we ask what we might infer about preferences on the basis of observations of demand. Let us start with a simple example in which we are given some information about an individual's demands in various scenarios. We suppose that we have two observations on the individual's behaviour: the first is when the individual has a money income of 80 and where the prices of goods 1 and 2 are two and one respectively; the second observation is when the individual has a money income of 80 and where the prices of goods 1 and 2 are one and two respectively.

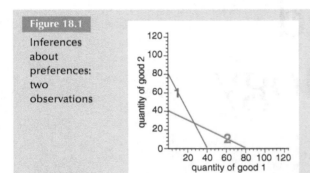

Figure 18.1

Inferences about preferences: two observations

Suppose we observe that the individual demands 10 units of good 1 and 60 units of good 2 in the first situation; and 60 units of good 1 and 10 units of good 2 in the second. We show all this in Fig. 18.1.

The first observation gives us a budget constraint going from (40, 0) to (0, 80); with an income of 80 and with prices two and one for goods 1 and 2, the individual can buy either 40 units of good 1 and none of good 2, or none of good 1 and 80 of good 2 (or any combination in between). This budget line is shown in Fig. 18.1, as is the observation (indicated by the point labelled 1) that the individual, faced with this budget constraint, bought 10 units of good 1 and 60 of good 2. The second observation gives a budget constraint from (80, 0) to (0, 40); with an income of 80 and prices equal to one and two for goods 1 and 2, the individual can buy either 80 units of good 1 and nothing of good 2, or none of good 1 and 40 units of good 2 (or any combination in between). This budget line is also shown in Fig. 18.1, as is the observation (indicated by the point labelled 2) that the individual, faced with this budget constraint, bought 60 units of good 1 and 10 of good 2.

Let us test the assumption that the preferences underlying these demands are represented by strictly convex indifference curves. If the assumption is true, what can we infer? More importantly, are the inferences that we can make consistent with each other? Or are they inconsistent with each other? If the latter, then we must conclude that our assumption about convex preferences must be false.

Given our assumption, what can we infer from the above observations? From observation 1 we can infer, given that the individual chose the point 1 when he or she could have chosen any point within the triangle defined by the vertices (0, 0), (40, 0) and (0, 80), that he or she strictly prefers point 1 to any other point in this triangle. Actually, when you think about it, this is quite a strong inference. It tells us that there must be a (smoothly convex) indifference curve tangential to the budget constraint at point 1. From observation 2 we can infer, given that the individual chose the point 2 when he or she could have chosen any point within the triangle defined by the vertices (0, 0), (80, 0) and (0, 40), that he or she strictly prefers point 2 to any other point in the triangle. Again, this is a strong inference; it tells us that there must be a (smoothly convex) indifference curve which is tangential to the budget constraint at the point 2.

So far so good. Are these inferences inconsistent with each other? Well, no; there is no contradiction between the two sets of inferences. One way to see this is to ask whether it is possible to draw a family of indifference curves that do not intersect and which are consistent with these observations. The answer is obviously yes. Moreover we can do this in various ways, so that point 1 is preferred to point 2 and *vice-versa*. Note that the observations do not tell us anything about the individual's preference between points 1 and 2. This is because when the individual chose point 1 the bundle 2 was not available (it was not within the budget constraint); and when the individual chose point 2 the bundle 1 was not available (it was not within the budget constraint).

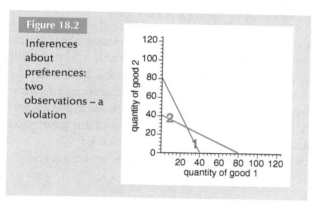

Figure 18.2

Inferences about preferences: two observations – a violation

Let us now consider a second individual. In the first observation he or she has an income of 80 and the prices of the two goods are two and one respectively. In the second observation the income is once again 80 and the prices are one and two respectively. Let us suppose that this individual is observed to buy 35 units of good 1 and 10 of good 2 in the first situation, and to buy 10 units of good 1 and 35 of good 2 in the second. These observations are shown in Fig. 18.2.

What can we infer? From the first observation, with the budget constraint from (40, 0) to (0, 80), he or she strictly prefers point 1 to all points within the triangle [(0, 0), (40, 0) (0, 80)]. Why? We know this because he or she chose point 1 when all the points within the triangle were available in the sense that they were all purchasable. But note that point 2 is also within this triangle. So we can infer from this first observation that point 1 is strictly preferred to point 2; point 1 was chosen when point 2 was available (purchasable).

The trouble is that, from the second observation, we can infer exactly the opposite. In this observation the individual chose point 2 when all the points within the triangle [(0, 0), (80, 0), (0, 40)] were available. But point 1 is within the triangle. So we can infer from this second observation that point 2 is strictly preferred to point 1; point 2 was chosen when point 1 was available (purchasable).

We have two inconsistent observations:

- from the first observation: that point 1 is strictly preferred to point 2;
- from the second observation: that point 2 is strictly preferred to point 1.

What do we conclude from this? We might be tempted to conclude that this individual is crazy – one moment preferring point 1 to point 2 and the next preferring point 2 to point 1. At the very least we conclude that this individual's behaviour is inconsistent with our assumption of smoothly convex indifference curves. You might note that it is impossible to draw smoothly convex indifference curves that do not cross, which leads to the observed choices[2].

This observed behaviour is a violation of the assumption that we have been using; it suggests that the individual is not predictable. Our assumption is that the individual is predictable in the sense that if he or she has a preference, then he or she has that preference. It seems to me that if we want to make economics a science which can predict behaviour, we need to make some such assumption.

Incidentally, and mainly for the record, I should note that the behaviour of our second individual is a violation of an assumption that economists call the *weak axiom of revealed*

2. If you try and draw one indifference curve through point 1 which is tangential to the first budget constraint, and a second indifference curve through point 2 which is tangential to the second budget constraint, and which are convex everywhere, they are doomed to cross, which we know is crazy. If we try to rationalize the observations with concave indifference curves, it fails because the individual would choose (almost) always an extreme point where either none of good 1 or none of good 2 was bought.

preference. This says that, if a bundle *X* is revealed as being directly[3] preferred to another bundle *Y*, it cannot be the case that *Y* is revealed as directly preferred to *X*.

18.3 Indirect Inferences about Preferences

In the previous section we discussed how we might make direct inferences about preferences. For example, from the first observation in Fig. 18.2 we could directly infer that point 1 was preferred to point 2 because 2 was available when 1 was chosen. If we make the assumption of *transitivity*, we can use a series of observations to make *indirect* inferences about preferences. Transitivity is the following assumption: if 1 is preferred to 2, and 2 is preferred to 3, then it must be true that 1 is preferred to 3. Some people regard this assumption as almost tautological, but it is an assumption. Consider how it might be used.

We will suppose that we have the following three observations on an individual's behaviour:

Observation 1: the individual has an income of 120 and faces prices three and one for goods 1 and 2; he demands 10 units of good 1 and 90 units of good 2.

Observation 2: the individual has an income of 80 and faces prices one and one for goods 1 and 2; he demands 20 units of good 1 and 60 units of good 2.

Observation 3: the individual has an income of 120 and faces prices one and three for goods 1 and 2; he demands 48 units of good 1 and 24 units of good 2.

The three observations are pictured in Fig. 18.3. What can we infer from them?

- From observation 1 we infer that point 1 (which was chosen) is preferred to all the points within the triangle [(0, 0), (40, 0), (0, 120)], including point 2 which is within that triangle and hence is available.

- From observation 2 we infer that point 2 (which was chosen) is preferred to all the points within the triangle [(0, 0), (80, 0), (0, 80)], including point 3 which is within that triangle and hence is available.

- From observation 3 we infer that point 3 (which was chosen) is preferred to all the points within the triangle [(0, 0), (120, 0), (0, 40)].

We have no direct evidence of the individual's preferences between point 1 and point 3 because, when point 1 was chosen 3 was not available, and when point 3 was chosen 1 was not available. However using observations 1 and 2, we know that point 1 is preferred to 2 and point 2 is preferred to 3, from which it follows (using transitivity) that point 1 must be preferred to point 3. This is an example of an *indirect* inference.

Figure 18.3
Inferences about preferences: three observations

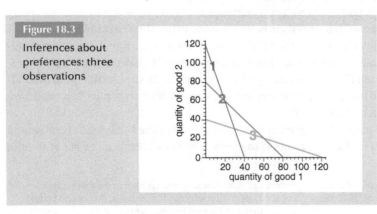

---

3. Through the kinds of observations that we have been discussing above.

Once again, for the record, we should note that implicit in what we have assumed (if we include transitivity as one of our assumptions) is a second assumption that economists call the *strong axiom of revealed preference*, which says that if a bundle X is revealed directly or indirectly preferred to another bundle Y, then it cannot be the case that Y is revealed directly or indirectly preferred to X. Of course, if this axiom is violated it simply means that the individual cannot have preferences of the type that we have assumed; in essence, the individual seems to be unaware of whether he or she prefers X to Y or *vice versa*.

18.4 Inferring Preferences

If the individual's behaviour does not violate either the weak or the strong axiom of revealed preference, it must be the case that we can draw indifference curves which are consistent with that behaviour. Obviously we cannot infer very much with just a few observations, but as the number of observations increases we can build up a clearer picture. This is one way to use observations to infer preferences.

However most economists prefer an alternative strategy. This assumes that preferences are part of a smallish set of possible preferences such as perfect $1{:}a$ substitutes, perfect 1-with-a complements or Cobb–Douglas with parameter a, and then use the observations to try and distinguish between these possibilities and estimate the parameter a. Of course there is almost certainly some degree of approximation involved as it is almost impossible that any one preference will fit the data exactly. A decision must be then taken to see if the approximation is good enough. If it is, then fine; if not, then the set of possible preferences must be widened in the search for a better approximation. We said a little about this in Chapter 16.

18.5 Direct Inferences about Technology

The material in this section is similar to that Section 18.2; the only difference is the context. In Section 18.2 we discussed how observations on the demand for goods by a consumer could be used to make inferences about his or her underlying preferences. We used this material to see how we might use such observations to test whether the individual's underlying preferences could be represented by smoothly convex indifference curves – as we have been assuming.

In this section we change the context to one of a firm buying inputs for its production process. Observations relate to the prices of the two inputs, the incurred costs of the firm and the actual demand by the firm for the two inputs. We want to infer from these observations whether the production process of the firm is consistent with our assumption that smoothly convex isoquants exist.

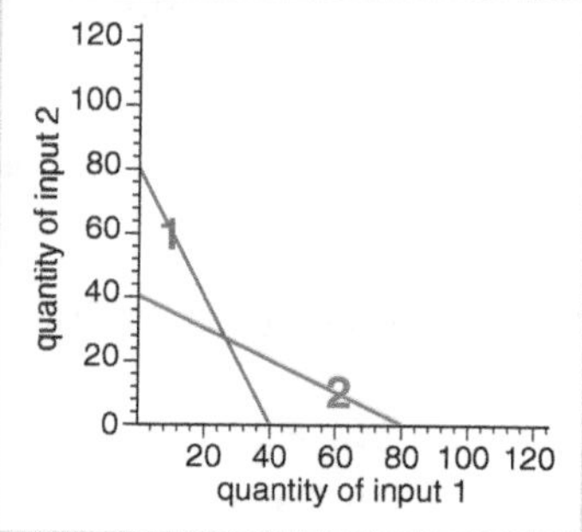

Consider the following two observations. The first is when the firm reports input costs of 80, and the prices of input 1 and input 2 are two and one respectively. The second observation is when the firm reports input costs of 80, and the prices of input 1 and input 2 are one and two respectively. Suppose we observe that the firm demands 10 units of input 1 and 60 units of input 2 in the first situation, and 60 units of input 1 and 10 units of input 2 in the second. We show all this in Fig. 18.4.

Figure 18.4

Inferences about technology: two observations

What can we infer from these observations? First, that input bundle 1 produces a greater level of output than all the bundles inside the triangle [(0, 0), (40, 0), (0, 80)] because bundle 1 was chosen while all the points inside the triangle were possible purchases. Second, that bundle 2 produces a greater level of output than all the bundles inside the triangle [(0, 0), (80, 0), (0, 40)] because bundle 2 was chosen while all the points inside the triangle were possible purchases. We might also ask what can we infer about the relative outputs of bundles 1 and 2. On the basis of what we know, we can infer very little. Consider the first situation. From Fig. 18.4 we see that when the firm chose bundle 1 it could not have bought bundle 2. So from this observation we cannot infer whether bundle 1 or bundle 2 produces a higher output. From Fig. 18.4 we also see that that when the firm chose bundle 2, it could not have bought bundle 1. So we cannot infer from this observation whether the output of the firm is greater with bundle 1 or bundle 2.

Consider now the following set of observations. Suppose we observe a firm facing the same set of prices and reporting the same costs. We observe that the firm buys 35 units of input 1 and 10 of input 2 in the first situation, and 10 units of input 1 and 35 of input 2 in the second. What can we infer? Consider Fig. 18.5.

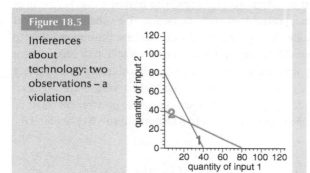

Figure 18.5

Inferences about technology: two observations – a violation

From the first observation we can see that bundle 1 leads to a higher output than all the points within the triangle [(0, 0), (40, 0), (0, 80)], including bundle 2; and from the second observation we can see that bundle 2 leads to a higher level of output than all the points inside the triangle [(0, 0), (80, 0), (0, 40)], including bundle 1. This is manifestly inconsistent with our assumptions about technology. The observations are telling us that, simultaneously, bundle 1 produces a higher output than bundle 2 and bundle 2 produces a higher output than bundle 1. It is a violation of our assumptions; we might even conclude that the firm is crazy. We could call this a violation of the weak axiom of revealed technology which asserts that this cannot happen. Another way of seeing this is to remember that it is impossible to draw isoquants which do not cross, which is implied by the choices made by the firm in the two situations. Try it![4]

18.6 Indirect Inferences about Technology

It should now be clear that we may be able to infer technologies from observations and check whether these technologies are consistent with our assumptions. Such inferences may be direct or indirect. Consider the following three observations.

Observation 1: costs 120 and input prices three and one: the firm demands 10 and 90 of inputs 1 and 2;

Observation 2: costs 80 and input prices one and one: the firm demands 20 and 60 of inputs 1 and 2;

Observation 3: costs 120 and input prices one and three: the firm demands 48 and 24 of inputs 1 and 2.

---

4. Note that concave technologies do not work because it is clear that, with such technologies, the firm would always choose a point on one of the two axes.

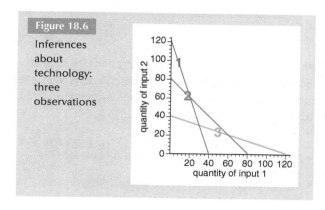

Figure 18.6

Inferences about technology: three observations

We show these observations in Fig. 18.6. Let us consider them one by one, in particular looking at the firm's revealed technology for the three bundles chosen.

With the first observation we can infer that bundle 1 produces a larger output than bundle 2, because bundle 1 was chosen when bundle 2 was available; but we can say nothing about the relative outputs of bundles 1 and 3, or of 2 and 3.

The second observation allows us to infer that bundle 2 produces a larger output than bundle 3, because 2 was chosen when 3 was available; but it tells us nothing about the relative outputs of 1 and 2, nor of 1 and 3.

The third observation does not tell us anything about the relative outputs of the three bundles.

If we combine the inferences from the first two observations, we can infer that bundle 1 must produce a larger output than bundle 3 because bundle 1 produces a larger output than bundle 2 and bundle 2 produces a larger output than bundle 3. The strong axiom of revealed technology says that we should not be able to find any inconsistency in inferred output, whether the inferences are direct or indirect.

18.7 Inferring Technology

If the firm's behaviour does not violate either the weak or the strong axiom of revealed technology, it must be the case that we can draw isoquants that are consistent with that behaviour. Obviously with just a few observations we cannot infer very much, but as the number of observations increases we can build up a clearer picture. This is one way to use observations to infer technology.

Most economists prefer an alternative strategy. They assume that the technology is one of a small set of possible technologies such as perfect 1:a substitutes, perfect 1-with-a complements, or Cobb–Douglas with parameter a. They then use the observations to try and distinguish between these possibilities and to estimate the parameter a. Of course there is almost certainly some degree of approximation involved; it is almost impossible that any one technology will fit the data exactly. A decision must be then taken to see if the approximation is good enough. If it is, fine; if not, then the set of possible technologies must be widened in the search for a better approximation. We said a little about this in Chapter 16.

18.8 Summary

This chapter has been concerned with what we can infer from observations, particularly whether the assumptions we have been using are consistent with the observations. We have seen how we might make direct or indirect inferences. One important assumption is that known as the weak axiom of revealed preference. This states that:

 If a bundle X is revealed directly preferred to another bundle Y, then it cannot be the case that Y is revealed directly preferred to X.

A second important axiom is the strong axiom of revealed preference which states:

 If a bundle X is revealed directly or indirectly preferred to another bundle Y, then it cannot be the case that Y is revealed directly or indirectly preferred to X.

There are similar axioms for revealed technology.

18.9 Review Questions

1. If an individual's behaviour violates the weak axiom of revealed preference, it must imply that the individual has indifference curves which cross. Argue that this must be incompatible with the idea that both goods are goods.

2. Suppose an individual consumes equal quantities of the two goods when their prices are both equal to one and the income is 100; and that the individual consumes more of good 1 than of good 2 when the price of good 1 rises to two while the price of good 2 stays at one, whilst income rises to 150. Is this behaviour consistent with the weak axiom of revealed preference? Draw a graph illustrating this case, and consider whether you can draw non-intersecting indifference curves for which this behaviour would be optimal.

3. Suppose an individual consumes equal quantities of the two goods when their prices are both equal to one and the income is 100; and that the individual consumes less of good 1 than of good 2 when the price of good 1 rises to two whilst the price of good 2 stays at one and income rises to 150. Is this behaviour consistent with the weak axiom of revealed preference? Draw a graph illustrating this case, and consider whether you can draw non-intersecting indifference curves for which this behaviour would be optimal.

chapter

Compensating and Equivalent Variations

19

19.1 Introduction

This chapter is both interesting and important, and it will help to answer a question you may well have been asking since we studied quasi-linear preferences at the beginning of the book. We saw then that, with quasi-linear preferences, we have an exact monetary measure of how much better off the individual is if he or she moves from one indifference curve to another (because the indifference curves are parallel). As a consequence, we saw that the area between the price paid and the demand curve (or the area between the price received and the supply curve) is an exact measure of the surplus or profit from trade.

You may have been asking: what happens if the preferences are not quasi-linear? The answer is that there is now no unique measure of how much better off an individual is. In that case, what exactly is that area between the price paid and the demand curve (or the area between the price received and the supply curve) measuring?

We will approach an answer rather obliquely. We do this by asking the question: suppose the price of some good changes, how can we measure how much better off or worse off the individual is as a consequence? We will see that there are at least two answers to this question, unless preferences are quasi-linear, and this leads us to realize that the search for a unique measure of 'how much better off' is bound to be fruitless.

19.2 The Effect on Behaviour of a Price Change

We start by looking at the effect on behaviour of a change in price. Then we look at how we might get a monetary measure of the welfare effects of this price change. Here we take a price increase, but we could do the whole analysis with a price decrease (although we would have to be slightly careful about the interpretations).

We return to the space which we used in Chapters 3 and 4. We are interested in some good; we therefore put the quantity of it on the horizontal axis. Having purchased the good, the individual has money left over to spend on other goods; we put the quantity of money to spend on other goods on the vertical axis. We assume that the individual has preferences over the quantity of the good and the quantity of money which can be represented by some indifference map. To begin with, let us assume that the indifference curves are smoothly convex; later we shall consider other cases.

We denote the price of good 1 by p. Rather naturally we take the price of the quantity of money available to spend on other goods to be one. We take the monetary income of the individual to be m; in the example that follows we let $m = 70$.

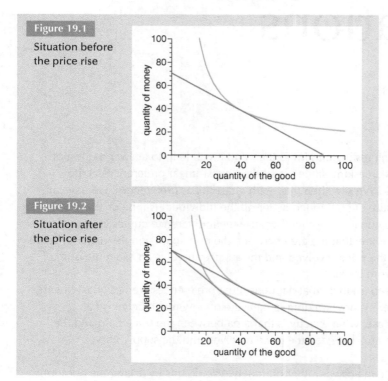

Figure 19.1

Situation before the price rise

Figure 19.2

Situation after the price rise

We start with the following position in which the price of the good is initially 0.8. So the budget line goes from 87.5 (m/p) on the horizontal axis to 70 (m) on the vertical axis. In Fig. 19.1 we have drawn this budget line, the highest attainable indifference curve and the optimal point.

We now suppose that the price of the good rises from 0.8 to 1.25. At this new price, the budget line goes from 56 (m/p) on the horizontal axis, to 70 (m) on the vertical axis. Fig. 19.2 shows the new budget line, the new highest attainable indifference curve and the new optimal point. Clearly the individual will change his or her behaviour as a consequence of the price rise; in this case by purchasing less of the good, and having less money left over to spend on other goods.

Let us look in greater detail at what has happened. Look at the the budget line. As you can see from Fig. 19.2, it has rotated around the point m on the vertical axis. So we can say that the slope of the budget line has changed and the size of the budget constraint has been reduced – from the triangle $[(0, 0), (87.5, 0), (0, 70)]$ to the triangle $[(0, 0), (56, 0), (0, 70)]$. In other words:

- the relative price of the good has changed; and

- the individual is worse off in that the value of his or her income has been reduced.

We call the first of these the *relative price effect*[1] and the second one the *income effect*.

We will find it extremely useful to separate these two effects. At the moment they are combined because the movement from the original budget line to the new budget line contains both effects; there is both a change in the slope and a change in the welfare of the individual. We can separate out these two effects by introducing an imaginary intermediary budget constraint which is illustrated in Fig. 19.3. It is very carefully positioned.

---

1. Some economists use the expression 'the substitution effect'.

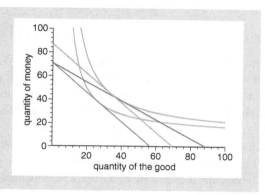

Figure 19.3

Compensating variation: smoothly convex indifference curves

This imaginary intermediate budget constraint is the dashed line in Fig. 19.3. Its position is determined by two considerations. First it is parallel to the new budget line and so reflects the new price. Secondly it is tangential[2] to the original indifference curve. This implies that the individual must be indifferent between the original budget constraint and the intermediate budget constraint. Why? Because with either budget constraint, the individual can reach the same indifference curve and is therefore just as well off. We can therefore say that, in moving from the original budget constraint to the intermediate budget constraint, the individual is no better or no worse off; his or her real income is the same in both situations.

We are now ready to separate out the two effects. We can consider the move from the original to the new budget constraint as equivalent (in terms of the final effect) to the following two moves:

● a move from the original budget constraint to the intermediate budget constraint; and

● a move from the intermediate budget constraint to the new budget constraint.

Why do we do this? Consider the first of these moves – from the original to the intermediate budget constraint. In this, the budget constraint rotates around the original indifference curve. The individual remains equally well off as he or she was originally, but the slope has changed from the original; this can be considered solely as the relative price effect, because there is no change in real income. Now consider the second of these two moves – from the intermediate to the new budget constraint. The budget line has the same slope before and after the move, but it has shifted parallel to itself. This move can be considered solely as the income effect; there is no change in price involved. To summarize – the move from the original to the new budget constraint can be decomposed into two moves: from the original to the intermediate; and from the intermediate to the new. The first captures the *relative price effect*; the second the *income effect*.

We can see from Fig. 19.3 that the effect of the move from the original to the intermediate budget constraint on the optimal behaviour of the individual is unambiguous; the individual will buy less of the good and has more money left over to spend on other goods. More importantly, you will see that it is bound to be unambiguous as it is the consequence of a rotation of the budget constraint around the original indifference curve. This cannot possibly increase the consumption of the good, and it will decrease if the indifference curve is smoothly convex[3]. So the relative price effect in unambiguous.

On the other hand the income effect may be ambiguous, although generally we expect that, for most goods that we consider normal, as income falls so does the demand for the good. In this case it does. But there are cases when the demand for the good rises as income falls; such a good is referred to as an inferior good. Real life examples are few and far between.

---

2. By which we mean that the intermediate budget constraint is a tangent to the original indifference curve.

3. It is possible that there is no change at all in the quantity purchased of the good if, for example, the preferences are perfect complements rather than smoothly convex; but the quantity purchased cannot increase.

19.3 The Effect on Welfare of the Price Change

So far we have considered the effect of the price change on behaviour. What about the effect on the welfare of the individual? We can easily see that the individual is worse off than originally, but by how much? There is one way we can find an answer to this question – by simply asking: 'how much money do we need to give to the individual to compensate him or her for this price rise?'. You may be able to answer this question. If we give money to the individual as compensation, we move the budget constraint parallel to itself (parallel to the new budget constraint) upwards and outwards. How far do we have to move it? Until it becomes tangential to the original indifference curve and the individual is just as well off as he or she was originally.

So, given the price rise and the fact that the budget constraint has shifted to a new position, to compensate the individual (take him or her back to the original position) we need to give enough money to the individual to shift the budget constraint back parallel to itself until it is tangential to the original indifference curve. That is, we have to move the budget constraint from the new position to the intermediate position which we have so carefully constructed.

Now if you look carefully at Fig. 19.3, you will see that the intermediate budget constraint has an intercept of a little over 86 on the vertical axis. Originally the income was 70. So this is telling us that, if we give a little over 16 (86 – 70) in money to the individual, this will compensate him or her for the effects of the price rise. It is a monetary measure of the welfare effects of the price rise[4] and is termed the *compensating variation*. It tells us how much money should be given to the individual to compensate him or her for the price rise.

An aside is necessary at this stage. If the price falls we can do all the above analysis. But the individual will still be better off. In this case the compensating variation is negative – the individual needs to give away money in order to compensate for the fact that he or she is better off than before.

19.4 An Alternative Decomposition

You may have noticed that the way we decomposed the overall effect of the price change into a price effect and an income effect was a little arbitrary. You may also have realized that there is another way. Consider Fig. 19.4 and compare it with Fig. 19.3.

Again we have drawn an imaginary intermediate budget constraint – the dotted line in Fig. 19.4. Notice how it is constructed. First, it is parallel to the original budget constraint and therefore reflects the original price; Second, it is tangential to the new indifference curve. This implies that the individual must be indifferent between the intermediate budget constraint and the new budget constraint. Why? Because, in moving from the intermediate budget constraint to the new budget constraint, the individual can reach the same indifference curve and is therefore just as well off as before; he or she is neither better or worse off, because real income is the same in both situations.

We are now ready once again to separate out the two effects. We can consider the move from the original to the new budget constraint as equivalent (in terms of the final effect) to the following two moves:

---

4. Recall that the variable on the vertical axis is money and that its price is unity.

● a move from the original budget constraint to the intermediate budget constraint; and

● a move from the intermediate budget constraint to the new budget constraint.

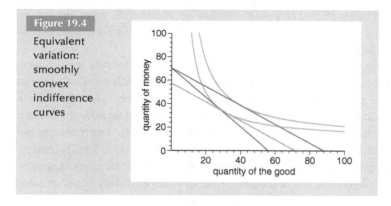

Figure 19.4

Equivalent variation: smoothly convex indifference curves

Why do we do this? For the same reason as before. Consider the first of these moves – from the original to the intermediate budget constraint. In this, the budget constraint moves parallel to the original budget constraint. This move can be considered as solely an income effect; there is no change in price involved. Now consider the second of these moves – from the intermediate to the new budget constraint; the budget line has rotated around the new indifference curve. The individual stays equally well off as he or she is with the new price, but the slope has changed from the original slope to the new slope. This move can be considered as solely the relative price effect; there is no change in real income involved.

Once again we see that the relative price effect is unambiguous; because the rotation is around the new indifference curve, the quantity of the good purchased must normally decrease[5]. On the other hand the income effect may be ambiguous, though generally we expect that; for most goods that we consider normal (as distinct from inferior goods as defined above), as income falls so does the demand for the good. In this case it does.

Once again we have considered the effect of the price change on behaviour. What about its effect on the welfare of the individual? We know that the individual is worse off than originally, but how much worse off? There is one way we can answer this question – by asking 'how much money would we have to take away from the individual at the original price to have the equivalent effect on his or her welfare?'. You may be able to answer this question. If we take money away from the individual at the original price, we move the budget constraint parallel to itself (and parallel to the original budget constraint) downwards and leftwards. We shall have to move it until it becomes tangential to the new indifference curve and the individual is just as well off as he or she is in the new position.

So, given the price rise and the fact that the budget constraint has shifted to the new position, to return to the original price (and instead take enough money away from the individual so that he or she ends up with the same welfare as in the new position) we need to take away enough money so that the budget constraint ends up parallel to the original budget constraint and tangential to the new indifference curve. That is, we have to move the budget constraint from the original position to the intermediate position that we have so carefully constructed in this section.

Now if you look carefully at Fig. 19.4 you will see that the intermediate budget constraint has an intercept of 57 on the vertical axis. Originally the income was 70. So this is telling us that, if we take away 13 (70 – 57) in money at the original price from the individual, this has the equivalent effect on his or her welfare as the price rises. It is a monetary measure of the welfare effects of the price rise[6], and is termed the *equivalent variation*. It tells

---

5. It is possible that there will be no change at all in the quantity of the good purchased if, for example, the preferences are perfect complements rather than smoothly convex, but the quantity purchased cannot increase.

6. Recall again that the variable on the vertical axis is money and that its price is unity.

us how much money should be taken away from the individual at the original price to have the equivalent effect on his or welfare as the price rises.

Again, an aside is necessary at this stage. If the price falls we can do all the above analysis. But the individual is better off. In this case the equivalent variation is negative because the individual needs to be given money at the original price to have the same effect on his or her welfare as the price falls.

So we have two monetary measures of the welfare effect of the price rise: the compensating variation and the equivalent variation. The first tells us how much we should give to the individual at the new price to compensate him or her for the price rise; the second tells us how much money we should take away from the individual at the original price to have the same effect on his or her welfare. You will see from this example that these two measures are different; the compensating variation is 16 and the equivalent variation is 13. The reason for this is that they are measuring things from different perspectives; the compensating variation is measured from the perspective of the new price, and the equivalent variation from the perspective of the original price. The compensating variation is larger than the equivalent variation because the price is lower with the original price – when the individual is better off. Note carefully in this example that demand increases with income; when the individual is better off, he or she buys more of the good. That is why the compensating variation is larger than the equivalent variation.

You may be able to work out that this is a property of the preferences that we have assumed. Indeed, if we had taken preferences for which the demand for the good falls as income rises, the compensating variation would have been smaller than the equivalent variation. Moreover, if the quantity purchased is independent of income, we would expect the two variations to be the same.

19.5 Quasi-linear Preferences

We know a case when the quantity purchased is independent of income – when the preferences are quasi-linear. In such a case, the compensating variation is as shown in Fig. 19.5.

The two indifference curves are parallel in a vertical direction. We see from Fig. 19.5 that the compensating variation is 8.5 (78.5 – 70) – that is, the intercept on the vertical axis of the intermediate budget constraint less the intercept of the original budget constraint. The equivalent variation is shown in Fig. 19.6.

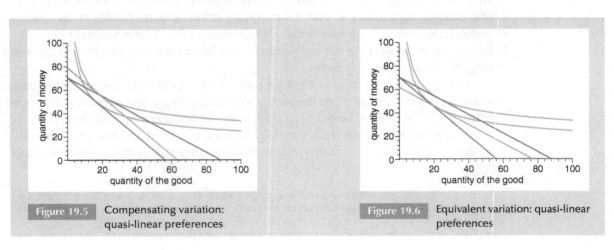

| **Figure 19.5** | Compensating variation: quasi-linear preferences |

| **Figure 19.6** | Equivalent variation: quasi-linear preferences |

Once again we see that the indifference curves are parallel. From Fig. 19.6 we can determine that the compensating variation is 8.5 (= 70 − 61.5) – that is, the intercept on the vertical axis of the original budget constraint minus the intercept of the intermediate budget constraint. The compensating and equivalent variations are equal; this is a consequence of the fact that the indifference curves are parallel. You should study and compare Figs. 19.5 and 19.6 to make sure you understand this.

19.6 Perfect Complement and Perfect Substitute Preferences

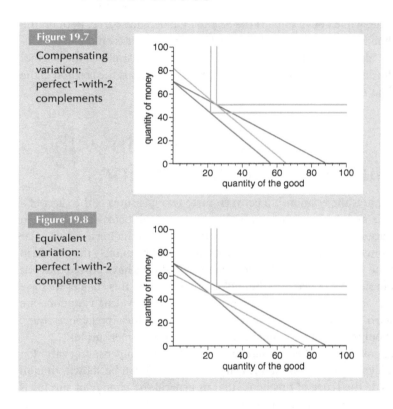

Figure 19.7

Compensating variation: perfect 1-with-2 complements

Figure 19.8

Equivalent variation: perfect 1-with-2 complements

It is interesting to consider some special cases – if only to see when the two effects are important and when they are not. Let us start with perfect complements, taking here the 1-with-2 case. The compensating variation is shown in Fig. 19.7 and the equivalent variation in Fig. 19.8.

In both these cases there is no relative price effect, in the sense that rotating the budget line around either the original or the new indifference curve has no effect. In a sense we could have anticipated this; with perfect complements there is no possibility for substitution. You will also notice that, once again, the compensating variation (about 11.5) is larger than the equivalent variation (about 9.5), because the demand for the good increases with income.

In the case of perfect 1:1 substitutes we have the compensating variation in Fig. 19.9 and the equivalent variation in Fig. 19.10.

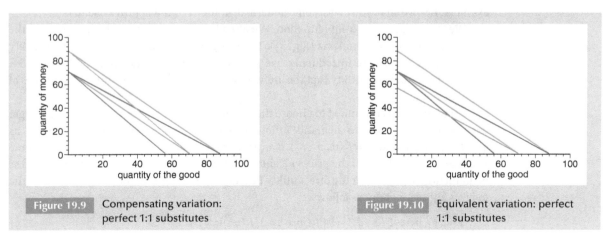

Figure 19.9 Compensating variation: perfect 1:1 substitutes

Figure 19.10 Equivalent variation: perfect 1:1 substitutes

Here the compensating variation is almost 18 and the equivalent variation 14; once again the latter is smaller because of the income effect on the demand for the good. In Fig. 19.9, from the intercept of 70 (the original income) on the vertical axis, we have three lines: the lowest is the new budget constraint; the next is the new indifference curve; and the top is the original budget line. Above these are two further lines: moving vertically, the next one is the intermediate budget line and the top one the original indifference curve. Both on the original budget line and on the intermediate budget line the optimal point is on the original indifference curve. You will also notice that the intermediate budget line is parallel to the new budget line.

In Fig. 19.10, from the intercept of 70 (the original income) on the vertical axis, we also have three lines: the lowest is the new budget line; the next is the new indifference curve; and the top one is the original budget line (as in Fig. 19.9). Below these three lines is the intermediate budget line, while above them is the original indifference curve. Both on the intermediate budget line and on the new budget line the optimal point is on the new indifference curve. You will also see that the intermediate budget line is parallel to the original budget line. In fact, the only thing that differs between the two figures is the position of the intermediate budget line.

19.7 Consumer Surplus and its Relationship with Compensating and Equivalent Variations

You may be asking: what is the relationship between these two measures of the effect of a price change on welfare, and the measure with which we started this book – the change in the surplus? We have argued that the surplus measures the gain from trading at a particular price. So if the price changes, and hence the surplus changes, then presumably the change in the surplus measures the welfare effect on the individual? Actually we have proved that this is true in the case of quasi-linear preferences, but not in other cases. In this chapter we have shown for quasi-linear preferences that the compensating and equivalent variations are equal. It is not too much of a jump to realize that, for the case of quasi-linear preferences, these two variations are not only equal, but are equal to the change in consumer surplus.

What about other preferences? Well, we already know that the compensating variation is not equal to the equivalent variation, and is generally larger. It can be shown, though using techniques outside the scope of this book, that in general the change in surplus is between the compensating and equivalent variations. We shall show this in a particular example. But we shall start with some general definitions that will prove useful later.

We introduce a new utility function. We already have a function which represents the preferences of the individual, viz $U(q_1, q_2)$. To distinguish this function from the new utility function that we will be introducing, we shall call the former the *direct* utility function because it measures the utility that the individual gets directly from consuming quantities of the two goods.

An individual is presumed to choose the optimal consumption bundle given the budget constraint. This leads to demand functions for the two goods which we write as $q_1 = f_1(m, p_1, p_2)$ and $q_2 = f_2(m, p_1, p_2)$. Note that these demands are functions of the income m of the individual and of the prices p_1 and p_2 of the two goods. If we now substitute these demand functions back in the direct utility function, we get a new utility function called the *indirect* utility function, as follows:

$$V(m, p_1, p_2) = U(q_1, q_2) = U(f_1(m, p_1, p_2), f_2(m, p_1, p_2)) \tag{19.1}$$

This tells us the utility of the individual when faced with prices p_1 and p_2 for the two goods and having income m, and when the individual chooses the optimal demands. In other words, it tells us the maximum utility of the individual when faced with prices p_1 and p_2 for the two goods and having income m. It is called the *indirect* utility function because the individual does not get utility directly from money and prices, but indirectly from the goods that they buy. Notice the arguments of $V(.)$ – the first is m, the second p_1 and the third p_2. The function is obviously increasing in m and decreasing in p_1 and p_2.

We can use this indirect utility function to calculate the utility that the individual gets for any given set of income and prices. We can thus use it to calculate the compensating and equivalent variations. Suppose the individual starts with an income m and faces prices p_1 and p_2. The individual has utility $V(m, p_1, p_2)$. Suppose now that the price of good 1 rises to P_1; the individual's utility is now $V(m, P_1, p_2)$. Since we have assumed that P_1 is greater than p_1, it follows that $V(m, P_1, p_2)$ is less than $V(m, p_1, p_2)$. To calculate the compensating variation, we need to find the increase in income necessary to restore the utility to its original level. If we denote the compensating variation by cv, it is defined by

$$V(m + cv, P_1, p_2) = V(m, p_1, p_2) \tag{19.2}$$

So, with compensation the individual has the same level of utility at the new price as he or she originally had at the old price. Similarly we can define the equivalent variation (ev) as

$$V(m, P_1, p_2) = V(m - ev, p_1, p_2) \tag{19.3}$$

Reducing income by ev at the old prices reduces the individual's utility to that implied by the new set of prices.

Let us give a particular example. This is the same example that we used in the previous sections. There the preferences were assumed to be symmetric Stone–Geary with the subsistence level of the good equal to five and the subsistence level of money equal to ten. From Chapter 5 we have the direct utility function

$$U(q_1, q_2) = (q_1 - 5)^{0.5}(q_2 - 10)^{0.5} \tag{19.4}$$

From Eq. (6.9) we have the optimal demands, where we denote the price of the good by p and we put the price of money equal to unity.

$$q_1 = 5 + (m - 5p - 10)/2p$$

$$q_2 = 10 + (m - 5p - 10)/2 \tag{19.5}$$

If we substitute these demand functions back into the direct utility functions, we obtain the indirect utility function shown in Eq. (19.6).

$$V(m, p) = (m - 5p - 10)/2p^{0.5} \tag{19.6}$$

In Eq. (19.6) we have suppressed the p_2 argument of the function because it is assumed to be constant.

Eq. (19.6) is the indirect utility function of an individual. It tells us the maximum utility of the individual for any price p and income m. We may use this to calculate the compensating and equivalent variations of any price change. We shall use the example considered in Section 19.2, we start with an income $m = 70$ and price $p = 0.8$. The individual's original utility level is $V(70, 0.8)$, which we calculate using Eq. (19.6) to be equal to 31.30.

Now suppose (following Section 19.2) that there is an increase in the price of the good p from 0.8 to 1.25. This causes a fall in the level of utility from $V(70, 0.8)$ to $V(70, 1.25)$, which we calculate, using Eq. (19.6), to be equal to 24.04. As a consequence of the price rise utility falls from 31.30 to 24.04. We note that these numbers are arbitrary as they depend upon the particular utility representation we have chosen; if we change the representation we change the numbers. However we are able to get some numbers that have more meaning if we calculate the compensating and equivalent variations.

Let us start with compensating variations, which we denote by cv. We know that this is the amount of money that we should give to the individual to compensate him or her for the price rise. So we know that the utility of the individual at the new price, but with income increased by cv, should provide exactly the same utility as the individual had originally. Now we know that the latter is 31.30, so cv satisfies the equation

$$V(70 + cv, 1.25) = 31.30 \tag{19.7}$$

Inserting this into Eq. (19.6) gives

$$(70 + cv - 5 \times 1.25 - 10)/2(1.25)^{0.5} = 31.30 \tag{19.8}$$

If we solve Eq. (19.8) for cv we find that it is 16.25; the compensation variation is 16.25 if, at the new price, we increase the individual's income by 16.25 then we return the individual back to his or her original level of utility. Note that this is almost equal to the approximate value (a little over 16) we obtained from the graphical analysis of Section 19.3.

We denote the equivalent variation by ev; this is the amount of money that we should take away from the individual at the original price to have the same effect on his or her utility as the price rises. So, we know that the utility of the individual at the original price but with his or her income decreased by ev should give exactly the same utility as the individual has in the new situation. We know that this latter is 24.04. So ev satisfies the equation

$$V(70 - ev, 0.8) = 24.04 \tag{19.9}$$

Using Eq. (19.6) again gives us the following result.

$$(70 - ev - 5 \times 0.8 - 10)/2(0.8))^{0.5} = 24.04 \tag{19.10}$$

If we solve this equation for ev we obtain ev = 13. The equivalent variation is 13 if, at the original price, we decrease the individual's income by 13 then there is the same effect on his or her welfare as the price rises. This is exactly the same figure as the one we obtained graphically in Section 19.4.

So far so good; we have calculated the compensating and equivalent variations and shown that the former is larger than the latter. There is actually quite a big difference between them, but that is because the price rise that we have considered is quite large.

What about the change in the surplus? Well, we know that the original surplus is the area between the price 0.8 and the demand curve for the good, while the new surplus is the area between the price of 1.25 and the demand curve for the good. So the change in the surplus is the area between the prices 0.8, 1.25 and the demand curve. See Fig. 19.11, which shows the demand curve for the good, which we know is given by

$$q_1 = 5 + (70 - 5p - 10)/2p \tag{19.11}$$

Note that, at a price of 0.8 demand equals 40, and at a price of 1.25 demand is 27.5.

The loss of surplus is the area between the two horizontal lines at prices 0.8 and 1.25 and the demand curve. Now demand at a price of 0.8 is 40, and at a price of 1.25 it is 27.5; so the area we need to calculate is somewhat less than a trapezium of height 0.45, base 40 and a top of 27.5. This trapezium has area 15.19, so the change in surplus is somewhat less than this. Of course we can always calculate the area precisely, either graphically or using calculus. With the latter we know that the area is equal to the integral with respect to p_1 of

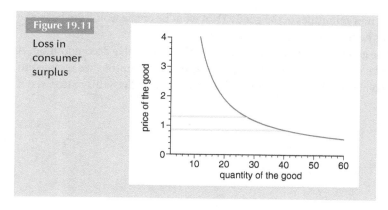

Figure 19.11

Loss in consumer surplus

the demand function $2.5 + 30/p$, between the values $p = 0.8$ and $p = 1.25$. This is equal to $2.5p + 30 \ln(p)$ evaluated between 0.8 and 1.25; solving this gives the solution 14.52, which represents the loss of surplus.

To summarize, we have for the effect of this price rise:

the compensating variation = 16.25

the loss in the surplus = 14.52

the equivalent variation = 13.00

We see that the change in the surplus is between the compensating and equivalent variations. This is a general result[7], which suggests that the change in the surplus might be a good compromise measure of the welfare effect of the price change. This is one reason why we have been advocating it so strongly. A second reason is that it is easy to calculate if we know the demand curve. In practice we often have a good estimate because we usually know more about demand than we do about preferences, if only because we can observe demand but not preferences.

19.8 Another Way of Doing the Decompositions

Before finishing this chapter we should note that you will find other authors who do the two decompositions which we have done in a different way[8]. In essence, when finding the intermediate budget constraint they consider it a rotation, either around the original optimal point or around the new optimal point, rather than around the original indifference curve or around the new indifference curve. I prefer not to do this particular decomposition for two reasons. In the first place, when we rotate the budget line around the original optimal point rather than around the original indifference curve, it is not true to say that the individual remains just as well off as before. Similarly, when we rotate the budget line around the new optimal point rather than around the new indifference curve, it is not true to say that the individual remains just as well off as in the new position. In fact a rotation around the optimal point is bound to make him or her better off[9]; I would call this an increase in his or her real income.

The second reason is that we recover two different monetary measures of the welfare effect of the price change from this decomposition. The appropriately equivalent compensating variation would tell us the amount of money that we need to give to the individual to enable him or her to purchase the original quantities of the goods. (Not, what he or she would do with that amount of money; he or she could buy different amounts and be better off than originally.) Similarly, the appropriately equivalent variation would tell us the amount of money that we should take away from the individual at the original price so that

---

7. Which we shall not prove here.
8. The way we have done the decomposition is usually attributed to the economist Hicks; the way we are describing it in this section is attributed to the economist Slutsky.
9. Try it! Draw any optimal point on any original budget constraint. Then rotate the budget line around this optimal point and ask yourself which the individual prefers – before or after the rotation. But ask yourself the same question about a rotation about the original indifference curve.

he or she could buy the new quantities of the goods. (Not what he or she would do; he or she would buy more and be better off than in the new situation.)

So there seems to be good intellectual reasons against this alternative decomposition. A practical reason in its favour is that it may be easier to use. But given that we are recommending that we use something even easier – the change in the surplus – this reason is not too overwhelming.

19.9 Summary

This chapter has clarified how we might get a monetary measure of a welfare effect of a price change with non-quasi-linear preferences. We also looked at the effect of the price change on behaviour.

 The effect of a price change on behaviour can be decomposed into a part that is due to the change in relative prices of the goods, and a part that is due to the change in the real income of the individual.

We saw that we can do this decomposition in two different ways. This leads us to realize that we can measure the welfare effect of a price change in two ways.

 ...the compensating variation, which is the amount of money that the individual would need to be paid at the new price to compensate him or her for the adverse effects of the price change;

 ...the equivalent variation, which is the amount of money that needs to be taken away at the original price to reduce the individual's welfare by the same amount as the price rise.

 In general, if the demand for the good increases with income, the compensating variation is larger than the equivalent variation and the change in consumer surplus lies between these two measures.

19.10 Review Questions

1. Take 1:1 perfect substitute preferences and decide whether the consumer is always worse off when the price of one of the goods rises.

2. Do the same for perfect 1-with-1 complements. Show that in this case the compensating variation is always equal to the increased cost of the original bundle of goods. Why is this the case? (Because with these preferences, no substitution is possible.)

3. Show that, if the indifference curves are strictly convex, the compensating variation is always less than the increased cost of the original bundle of goods. Why is this the case? (Because with these preferences, substitution is possible.)

4. What is the equivalent variation in the case of perfect 1-with-1 complements (the change in cost of the newly purchased bundle)? Why?

5. Show that, if the indifference curves are strictly convex, the equivalent variation is always less than the increased cost of the new bundle of goods. Why is this the case? (Because with these preferences, substitution is possible.)

19.11 Application: a Tool for Deciding whether Policies should be Implemented?

This chapter has demonstrated enormous potential, since it provides a way for deciding whether particular policies should be implemented or not. Some policies are straightforward; if they benefit a set of people and do not harm anyone else, then surely they should be implemented. But usually policies are not like this – they make some people better off and others worse off. How can decisions makers decide whether they should go ahead or not?

The chapter has shown a way of measuring, in monetary terms, how much better or worse off someone is if a price changes. Some policies affect only prices and we can therefore use the apparatus of this chapter to work out the effects on people. We will consider such a case here, though the method can be extended to other situations. This type of analysis is usually called cost-benefit analysis, since it compares the costs and benefits to the people affected by the policy change.

Consider a proposed policy that will increase the price of some good. Those people who buy the good would be worse off if the policy were implemented, while those who sell the good would be better off. We can measure and aggregate the costs to the buyers and the benefits to the sellers of the price change, using the methods of this chapter. Suppose there are I sellers, $i = 1, 2 ...I$, and J buyers, $j = 1, 2, ..., J$. For each of the buyers we can calculate the compensating variation – that is, the amount of money that we should give to a buyer to compensate him or her for the price rise. We denote this by c_j for buyer j. This can be considered the cost imposed on him or her by the policy implementation.

For each of the sellers, we can calculate the compensating variation or the amount of money that we should take away from the seller to 'compensate' him or her for the price rise – in this case, to reduce his or her welfare back to the level it was before he or she became better off as a consequence of the price rise. Denote this by b_i for seller i. This can be considered as a benefit he or she gets if the policy is implemented. An aggregate measure of the costs of the proposed policy is therefore $c = (c_1 + c_2 + \cdots + c_J)$; an aggregate measure of the benefits of the proposed policy is therefore $b = (b_1 + b_2 + \cdots + b_J)$. It could be argued that if $b > c$, then the policy should be implemented.

Why? Suppose that $c = ab$ where a is some fraction between 0 and 1. If the policy were implemented the sellers would be sufficiently better off, so they could all give a fraction a of their gain to the buyers; this collectively would be sufficient to compensate the buyers for being worse off. Thus, with the policy implemented, the sellers would be better off and the buyers no worse off than before. We are back to the simple type of policy that we discussed in the first paragraph of this section. Alternatively the sellers could all be charged their entire benefit and the total could be distributed appropriately among the buyers to make them better off than they were originally. The buyers would be better off and the sellers no worse off than before. Again, we are back to the simple type of policy. The reason is clear: in each case the benefits outweigh the costs. If this was not the case, that is, if $b < c$, we cannot argue in this way for the policy to be implemented; indeed one might think that it should not be implemented. But if the benefits outweigh the costs, that is if $b > c$, we could argue that the policy should be implemented because we can impose various payments from those who benefit to those who suffer, and everyone would be better off. Indeed, there are some economists who would argue that the policy should be implemented even if these payments are not made, for the total surplus to society is obviously higher even if its distribution is changed. Such a situation can be rectified by some appropriate taxation policy[10].

There is another way of looking at the problem. The above argument assumes that the *status quo* is the pre-policy implementation situation, and therefore the onus should be on those who want the policy implemented to show that it should be. But we could take the alternative perspective and argue that the *status quo* is the implementation of the policy. Starting from this position, we could then ask what would be the implications of dismantling it – that is, going back to the pre-policy implementation situation? Continuing our earlier example, it is clear that the buyers would be better off if the policy were dismantled and the sellers worse off. We know from the material of this chapter how to measure how much better off each buyer would be – by his of her equivalent variation of the original price rise. Denote this by B_j for a buyer j. This is the maximum that a buyer would pay to reverse the price rise. We also know how to measure how much worse off would be each seller – by his or her equivalent variation of the original price rise. Denote this by C_i for seller i. This is the minimum compensation that he or she would accept to reverse the price rise. So the total benefit from reversing the price rise (that is, from dismantling the policy) would be $B = B_1 + B_2 + \cdots + B_J$, and the total cost from reversing the price rise would be $C = C_1 + C_2 + \cdots + C_I$. We could argue, as before, that the policy should be dismantled if $B > C$. The story is the same. Suppose $B = AC$ where A is some fraction between 0 and 1. If this condition is satisfied, either

- each buyer pays a fraction AB_j of the benefits of reversing the policy and each seller receives his or her cost C_i from so doing;

- or all buyers pay B_j and the total is distributed among the sellers so that each receives at least their C_i;

- or something in between.

Under the first case, the buyers are all strictly better off if the policy is dismantled, and all the sellers are no worse off. Under the second, all the buyers are strictly better off and all the sellers are no worse off. Under the third, all buyers and sellers could be better off. The policy should be dismantled; it may be argued that the policy should not be implemented as there would be clear gains from its dismantlement.

So whether the policy should be implemented or not depends on the *status quo*, and upon whether either of the conditions $b > c$ or $B > C$ are satisfied. But these conditions are themselves interrelated. To focus our minds, consider the key case of quasi-linear preferences. We know that, in this case, the equivalent and compensating variations are equal. Thus we have $c_j = B_j$ for all j (the two variations are equal for each buyer), and $C_i = b_i$ for all i (the two variations are equal for each seller). It therefore follows that $c > b$ if and only if $C < B$; and that $c < b$ if and only if $C > B$. What does this mean? In the first case, the argument for the implementation of the policy says that it should not be implemented became the costs outweigh the benefits, and the argument for the dismantlement of the policy says that it should be dismantled as the benefits outweigh the costs. On either argument the policy should not be implemented. In the second case, the argument for the implementation of the policy says that it should be implemented because the benefits outweigh the costs, and the argument for

10. You probably realize that this is, in essence, the argument we have used for the superiority of competition over, for example, monopoly – namely that the total surplus is higher.

the dismantlement of the policy says that it should not be dismantled as the costs outweigh the benefits; on either argument the policy should be implemented. With quasi-linear preferences the policy advice is clear: implement the policy if $b > c$ (or equivalently if $C > B$), and do not implement it otherwise. Of course, we could instead use a comparison of the surpluses gained and lost, as we know with quasi-linear preferences these changes in surpluses are equal to the equivalent or compensating variation. This makes policy implementation simple: we simply need to calculate the changes in surplus, and to do this all we need to know are the relevant demand and supply schedules.

We can, of course, do the same with non-quasi-linear preferences, assuming the two arguments go the same way. If $b > c$ and $B < C$, then the policy should be implemented; if $b < c$ and $B > C$, the policy should not be implemented. In the first case the total increase in the surplus is positive; in the second it is negative. We can measure these surpluses from the appropriate demand and supply curves.

It is crucial to note that, since the surplus is between the equivalent and compensating variations when they are not equal, we may have cases in which the net surplus is positive but the two conditions $b > c$ and $B < C$ are not both met. Contrarywise, we can have cases in which the net surplus is negative but the two conditions $b < c$ and $B > C$ are not both met. These are interesting cases, and they leave us in a policy quandary.

Consider, for example, a situation in which $b > c$ but $B > C$. What does this imply? The first condition leads to the argument that the policy should be implemented; the second to the argument that, once implemented, it should be dismantled! We have a paradox. A similar paradox emerges if we have $b < c$ but $B < C$. This would imply that the policy should not be implemented but, if it is, it should not be dismantled. In these two paradoxical cases we have a real quandary as to what to do if we are to be guided solely by the arguments of this section. We leave it to the politicians to resolve this quandary. We should note, however, that such cases are likely to be rare. The more usual cases are where $b > c$ and $B < C$ and the net change in surplus is positive; and where $b < c$ and $B > C$ and the net change in surplus is negative. In the former the policy should be implemented; in the latter it should not.

Inter-temporal Choice

20.1 Introduction

We are now in a position to apply our methodology to a variety of contexts, including two particularly important ones – intertemporal choice and risky choice. As we shall see, we can use the apparatus we have constructed to analyse these interesting problems.

We start with intertemporal choice – that is, choice through time. Many of the important problems that we face are intertemporal choice problems including, possibly the most important, that of choosing an optimal consumption stream through time. We should emphasize the importance of these problems in economics. While our analysis so far has been static, many important decisions in life involve choices whose consequences will occur in the future. The most obvious is the decision how to allocate income through time: whether to save for retirement; whether to build up a pension fund; whether to save for a holiday. Equally important, though not specifically mentioned in this chapter, are problems faced by firms: whether to invest in new technology; whether to hold inventories; whether to borrow money in the capital market. This chapter discusses how such decisions might be taken, and emphasizes the important role played by the rate of interest in such decisions. A key variable, which is manipulated by governments or central banks, is the rate of interest. By lowering the rate they hope to encourage investment; by raising it they may hope to encourage saving. In this chapter we shall see how these things work.

In reality many of these problems involve many periods of time, but we can do all the analysis necessary with just two time periods, 1 and 2. There is no need for these periods to be the same size so, if you like, you can think of them as the present (extending a certain distance into the future) and the future (extending the rest of time). For the time being we do not want to get involved with problems of uncertainty (that is our next topic), so we will assume that there is no uncertainty involved with defining or thinking about these two periods.

Let us consider the problem of optimal consumption through time in this two-period world. We shall keep things simple and assume that the individual gets some income in each of these two periods, and has to decide when to consume that income. We shall assume that there exists a capital market in which the individual can borrow and save, so if the individual wants to consume more than his or her income in the first period, he or she may borrow money in this capital market and repay it, plus interest, in period 2. Alternatively if our individual wants to consume more than the income available in period 2, he or she invests part of the first period income in the capital market before realizing the proceeds and the interest in the second period.

We shall make things very simple by assuming a perfect capital market – one in which our individual can freely borrow and save at a constant and fixed rate of interest. In a concluding section we shall discuss how things change if the capital market is imperfect. This latter case is probably empirically more realistic, but the crucial parts of our analysis can be done by assuming a perfect capital market.

20.2 The Inter-temporal Budget Constraint

We denote by m_1 and m_2 the income of the individual in the two periods. We denote by c_1 and c_2 the consumption in the two periods. We assume that utility is a function of c_1 and c_2; later we will discuss what form this may take. As discussed above, we assume a perfect capital market with a constant interest rate[1] denoted by r. We operate in (c_1, c_2) space.

What is the budget constraint in this world? Well, it obviously passes through the point (m_1, m_2) as the individual can always choose simply to consume his or her income each period. But suppose the individual would prefer an alternative pattern of consumption, what possibilities are open to him or her? If the individual wanted to consume nothing in period 1, he or she could save the income m_1, investing it at the rate of interest r, earning interest rm_1 and thus having $m_1(1 + r)$ plus the income m_2 to spend in period 2. This would give a maximum consumption in period 2 of $m_1(1 + r) + m_2$. Alternatively, if our individual wanted to consume nothing in period 2, in period 1 he or she could spend the income of that period, m_1, plus what he or she could borrow on the strength of being able to pay back the income m_2 in period 2. Now the amount that could be borrowed on this basis is $m_2/(1 + r)$ since this would become m_2 with interest at r added by period 2. So the maximum consumption in period 1 would be $m_1 + m_2/(1 + r)$. More generally, if the person borrows an amount $c_1 - m_1$, he or she would have to pay this back plus interest in period 2 – an amount $(c_1 - m_1)(1 + r)$. The difference $m_2 - c_2$ would have to equal this amount. So the budget constraint is given by $(c_1 - m_1)(1 + r) = (m_2 - c_2)$, which we can write as

$$c_1(1 + r) + c_2 = m_1(1 + r) + m_2 \tag{20.1}$$

This says that the *future value* of the consumption stream must equal the future value of the income stream. Alternatively, dividing both sides by $(1 + r)$, we can write the budget constraint as follows:

$$c_1 + c_2/(1 + r) = m_1 + m_2/(1 + r) \tag{20.2}$$

Eq. (20.2) simply says that the *present value* of the consumption stream must equal the present value of the income stream.

We give an example in Fig. 20.1. We assume a rate of interest of 20 per cent ($r = 0.2$), and we take m_1 to be 30 and m_2 to be 50. We place consumption in period 1 (c_1) on the horizontal axis and consumption in period 2 (c_2) on the vertical axis; the figure is therefore in (c_1, c_2) space. The budget line is a straight line with slope equal to $-(1 + r)$; it passes through the initial point $(30, 50)$ – marked on Fig. 20.1 by X – as the individual can always chose to consume his or her initial incomes.

---

1. If the rate of interest is 10 per cent then $r = 0.1$; if the rate of interest if 20 per cent then $r = 0.2$; and so on.

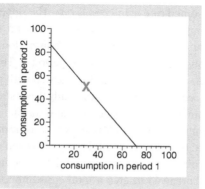

Figure 20.1   Inter-temporal choice: budget constraint with 20 per cent rate of interest

If the individual wanted to consume everything in period 1, he or she could consume 30 (the income of that period) plus $(50/1.2) = 41.66$. The latter is the maximum amount that he or she could borrow on the strength of paying it back, with interest at 20 per cent, with the income of 50 from period 2. Total consumption in period 1 is therefore 71.66, which is the intercept on the horizontal axis. By contrast, if our individual wanted to consume everything in period 2, he or she would consume the income from that period (50) plus the income from period 1 including interest at 20 per cent, which is $(30 \times 1.2) = 36$. So maximum consumption would be 86, which is the intercept on the vertical axis. The slope of the budget constraint is equal to $-86/71.66 = -1.2$ that is, minus one plus the rate of interest.

We will later find it useful to introduce some new terminology – the *rate of return* on an investment. This is simply one plus the rate of interest; it tells us how much money we get back in period 2 for every unit saved in period 1.

20.3 Optimal Inter-temporal Choice

We have found the intertemporal budget constraint. To find the optimal choice, we now need to consider the preferences of the individual over bundles of intertemporal consumption (c_1, c_2). In Chapter 21 we shall consider a particular type of preference which seems to have good empirical validity; in the meantime, we shall consider here some more general preferences.

Suppose we were trying to construct an indifference map in (c_1, c_2) space, what properties would it possess? First we would expect it to be convex: as consumption in period 2 decreased we would expect compensation required in period 1 to increase; as consumption in period 1 decreased we would expect compensation in period 2 to increase. You should be clear about this. Suppose that, with consumption of 50 in each of the two periods, the individual would be happy to give up one unit of consumption in period 1 if he or she were compensated with 1.2 extra units of consumption in period 2. We might expect that, when consumption is just 10 in period 1 but 90 in period 2, the individual would want more than 1.2 units of extra period 2 consumption to be compensated for giving up one of the 10 period 1 units.

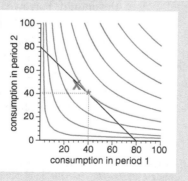

Figure 20.2   Effect of changes in the rate of interest: optimal consumption with symmetrical preferences

What else? Might we expect a symmetrical map? This depends on whether the individual treats the two periods symmetrically. If he or she did, we might get something like Fig. 20.2 – in which we can analyse the optimal choice as well as how that changes if the rate of interest changes. But symmetry is unlikely. Most people appear to have a preference for consumption in the present over consumption in the future.

In Fig. 20.2 the assumed rate of interest is zero; the slope of the budget line is −1. So for every unit less of consumption in period 1 the individual can, through lending, consume one more unit in period 2; and for every unit less of consumption in period 2 the individual can, through borrowing, consume one more unit in period 1. The initial endowment point (30 units in period 1 and 50 units in period 2) is indicated with an X. The optimal point on the highest indifference curve consistent with the budget constraint is indicated with an asterisk. Because of the symmetry of the preferences and the fact that the rate of interest is zero, this optimal point is symmetrical – with 40 units of consumption in period 1 and 40 units in period 2. The individual is using the capital market to even out his or her consumption. In period 1 he or she borrows 10 units in the capital market and consumes his or her income in period 1, plus that borrowed to give a total consumption of 40. In period 2 he or she pays back this 10 (with no interest because in this case the rate of interest is zero); he or she therefore consumes 10 less than the income in period 2. The individual in this situation is a borrower.

Now consider what happens when the rate of interest changes. The higher the rate, the steeper will be the budget line. As the rate of interest increases, the budget line will rotate in a clockwise manner around the initial income point X; it becomes steeper. If you compare the budget line in Fig. 20.2 with a zero rate of interest, with that in Fig. 20.1 with an interest rate of 20 per cent, this is clear. The budget line in Fig. 20.1 has a slope of −1.2 whilst that in Fig. 20.2 has a slope of −1; the former is steeper than the latter. Moreover the optimal point will move to the left when the rate of interest rises (X), as the individual will consume less in period 1 because the cost of borrowing has increased.

You might like to consider whether this individual might become a saver. The answer is 'yes', if the optimal point moves to the left of the initial point X. At what rate of interest will this happen? This depends upon the slope of the indifference curve at the point X. For reasons which will become clear, we will suppose that this slope[2] is $-(1 + s)$. The individual will switch from being a borrower to being a saver when the interest rate is higher[3] than s. So we have the nice result that this individual is a borrower at low rates of interest, reduces the extent of his or her borrowing as the interest rate rises, and becomes a saver at sufficiently high rates of interest. As you might expect, this is a fairly general result, although it obviously depends upon the preferences of the individual. For the particular preferences portrayed in Fig. 20.2, we have the relationship between saving and the rate of interest shown in Fig. 20.3.

The curve that starts out positive, becomes zero at a rate of return around 1.68 (rate of interest 0.68, that is, 68 per cent) and then becomes negative, is the net demand for consumption in period 1. If it is positive it is the amount borrowed in period 1; if it is negative it is the amount saved in period 1. The other curve is the net demand for consumption in period 2. If it is negative it is the amount repaid (including interest) in period 2; if it positive it is the total return from saving in the first period. Obviously these curves cross the axis at the same point. If the individual borrows in the first

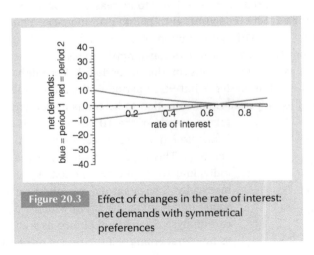

Figure 20.3   Effect of changes in the rate of interest: net demands with symmetrical preferences

---

2. For example if the slope there is −1.6 then $s = 0.6$ (that is, 60 per cent).
3. Recall that the slope of the budget line is $-(1 + r)$ so the budget line is tangential to the indifference curve passing through the point X at the point X if and only if $r = s$.

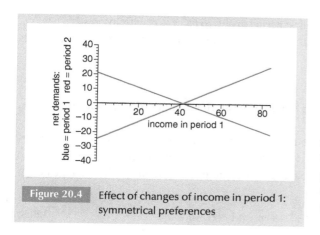

Figure 20.4 Effect of changes of income in period 1: symmetrical preferences

period, he or she has to repay in the second; if he or she saves in the first period, there is a positive return in the second.

The initial endowment point affects the behaviour of the individual. If, for example, one of the two incomes were to change, then the borrowing or saving behaviour would also change. For example, if the income in the first period were to increase we would get the relationship between the net demands and the first period income shown in Fig. 20.4; in this we keep the second period income fixed at 50 and the rate of interest fixed at 20 per cent.

The individual stops being a borrower and becomes a saver if his or her first period income becomes sufficiently high. The line which starts out positive and then becomes negative is the net demand for consumption in period 1; the other line is the net demand for consumption in period 2.

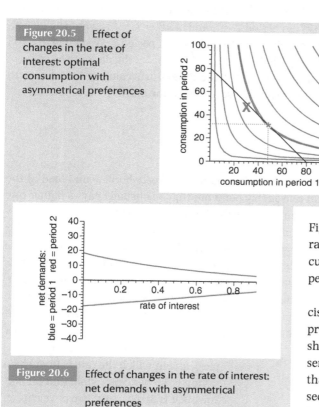

Figure 20.5 Effect of changes in the rate of interest: optimal consumption with asymmetrical preferences

Figure 20.6 Effect of changes in the rate of interest: net demands with asymmetrical preferences

The shape of these net demand curves depends upon the preferences of the individual. So far we have assumed symmetrical preferences, but it may be empirically more reasonable to assume asymmetrical preferences of a type where greater weight is put on present consumption. We shall discuss this in more detail in the next chapter, but in the meantime let us present a case with greater weight on present consumption, and compare it with the results presented earlier. Compare first Fig. 20.5 with Fig. 20.2. Fig. 20.5 shows the effect of changes in the rate of interest in the case of asymmetrical indifference curves, with increased weight on consumption in period 1.

If we carry out the same comparative static exercise that was portrayed in Fig. 20.3, but using the preferences from Fig. 20.5, we obtain the results shown in Fig. 20.6. Compared with the results presented in Fig. 20.3, we get much more borrowing than before. This is the – perhaps obvious – consequence of the greater weight placed on consumption in period 1.

20.4 Present and Future Values and Discounting

We shall assume that we are in a two-period world with incomes m_1 and m_2 in the two periods, and the rate of interest is r. In this case, the future value (fv) of this stream – that is, its value in period 2 – is given by Eq. (20.3)

$$fv = m_1(1+r) + m_2$$

(20.3)

This is because the income m_1 in the first period grows to $m_1(1 + r)$ with interest.

The present value (pv) of this future income stream – that is, its value in period 1 – is given by Eq. (20.4).

$$pv = m_1 + m_2/(1 + r) \qquad (20.4)$$

This is because $m_2/(1 + r)$ is what can be borrowed on the strength of being able to repay m_2 in period 2.

If we live in a T-period world with income m_t in period t ($t = 1, 2, ..., T$) then, with interest, m_1 in period 1 will grow to $m_1(1 + r)^{T-1}$ by period T; m_2 in period 2 will grow to $m_2(1 + r)^{T-2}$ by period T; and so on. So the future value of this stream – that is, its value in period T – is given by Eq. (20.5).

$$fv = m_1(1 + r)^{T-1} + m_2(1 + r)^{T-2} + \cdots + m_{T-1}(1 + r) + m_T \qquad (20.5)$$

The present value of the same income stream is given in Eq. (20.6).

$$pv = m_1 + m_2/(1 + r) + \cdots + m_{T-1}/(1 + r)^{T-2} + m_T/(1 + r)^{T-1} \qquad (20.6)$$

This is because $m_2/(1 + r)$ is what can be borrowed in period 1 on the strength of being able to repay m_2 in period 2, ...; $m_{T-1}/(1 + r)^{T-2}$ is what can be borrowed in period 1 on the strength of being able to repay m_{T-1} in period $T - 1$; and $m_T/(1 + r)^{T-1}$ is what can be borrowed in period 1 on the strength of being able to repay m_T in period T. We call $m_2/(1 + r)$ the *discounted value* of income m_2 in period 2; ..., $m_{T-1}/(1 + r)^{T-2})$ the discounted value of income m_{T-1} in period $T - 1$; and $m_T/(1 + r)^{T-1}$ the discounted value of income m_T in period T. We say that these incomes are being discounted at the market rate of interest r.

20.5 Imperfect Capital Markets

You may object to the assumption that the individual can freely borrow and lend at the market rate of interest. You might reasonably point out that one usually pays a higher rate of interest when borrowing than when saving. If this is the case, it is what we term an imperfect capital market. What does it imply for the budget constraint? When the individual is borrowing – that is, when he or she wants to move rightwards and downwards from the initial endowment point – the rate of interest is higher than when the individual is saving, or when he or she wants to move leftwards and upwards from the initial endowment point. This implies that the magnitude of the slope of the budget line is greater for movements to the right and down than for movements to the left and up; in other words, there is a kink at the initial endowment point. An example is given in Fig. 20.7, in which the initial incomes are 30 and 50 (as in the previous examples), and in which the rate of interest on saving is 10 per cent, while that on borrowing it is 50 per cent; (we have chosen a deliberately exaggerated example to obtain a figure which illustrates clearly the point we want to make).

The budget line now has a kink at the initial income point and two different slopes: −1.5 below the kink and −1.1 above it. The blue dotted line is the budget constraint that would exist in a

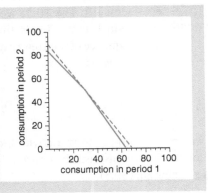

Figure 20.7 Budget constraint with an imperfect capital market

consumption in period 2

consumption in period 1

perfect capital market with a rate of interest of 30 per cent on both saving and borrowing. You might realize the possible impact of the kink on the individual's behaviour. It is quite likely that the optimal point will be at the kink point (if the MRS between period 1 and period 2 consumption lies between 1.0 and 1.4), so that the individual will neither borrow nor save.

20.6 Summary

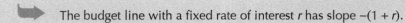 The budget line with a fixed rate of interest r has slope $-(1 + r)$.

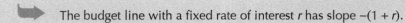 Whether the individual is a borrower or a lender depends on the individual's preferences, the initial endowment and the rate of interest.

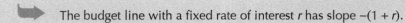 Increases in the rate of interest (usually) cause a borrower to reduce the level of borrowing.

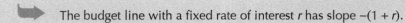 Decreases in the rate of interest (usually) cause a saver to reduce the level of saving.

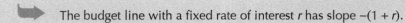 In an imperfect capital market there is a kink in the budget constraint at the endowment point, with a steeper section below the kink point and a flatter section above it.

20.7 Review Questions

1 Draw a diagram illustrating the budget constraint for an individual with incomes of 100 in each period facing (a) a zero rate of interest; and (b) a 10 per cent rate of interest. Show that, in the second case, the slope of the budget line is steeper than that in the first case.

2 Argue intuitively that a rise in the interest rate makes the individual better off if he or she is a saver between the two periods, and makes the individual worse off if he or she is a borrower. How does the individual respond to the interest rise in these two cases?

3 What is the slope of the budget line if the rate of interest is negative?

4 If purchasing power can be carried between the two periods in cash, and if there is no inflation between the two periods (that is, the value of money does not change), then the individual would never lend. Why not?

The Discounted Utility Model

21.1 Introduction

This chapter is important in that it introduces and explores the implications of an empirically relevant utility function representing intertemporal preferences. In fact it is not only empirically relevant, but it has the important normative property that individuals with such preferences are never dynamically inconsistent. This means that the relative evaluation of consumption in periods t and s remains constant through time; for instance, if today an individual regards £1000 in 2015 as equivalent to £1500 in 2017, that person will think the same way tomorrow, and in 2004, and so on. This means that it represents the kind of intertemporal preferences that people 'ought' to have if they want to be consistent in their intertemporal decision-making. These normative properties are not relevant in the two-period world which we have been analysing so far, but they become relevant in a world of more than two periods. We shall consider such a world after we have described the model and explored its implications in a two-period world.

21.2 The Discounted Utility Model in a Two-period World

This is a model of preferences over bundles of consumption (c_1, c_2), where c_1 denotes consumption in period 1 and c_2 denotes consumption in period 2. It is simply given as follows:

$$U(c_1, c_2) = u(c_1) + u(c_2)/(1 + \rho) \tag{21.1}$$

Note that there are two utility functions here. The first is U, which is defined over the consumption bundle (c_1, c_2) and which represents the utility of that bundle; the other is u, which is defined over a single period's consumption and which represents the utility gained from consuming a particular amount in a particular period. The discounted utility model states that the utility of a consumption bundle (c_1, c_2) is given by the utility gained from consuming the amount c_1 (in period 1), plus the utility gained from consuming the amount c_2 (in period 2) divided by $(1 + \rho)$. In this model, ρ is a parameter of the model, and usually varies from individual to individual. For most individuals the parameter ρ is positive, which means that $(1 + \rho)$ is greater than 1; this means that $u(c_2)/(1 + \rho)$ is smaller than $u(c_2)$, and hence a greater weight is attached to a particular level of consumption if it consumed in period 1 rather than in period 2.

Why is it called the discounted utility model? Because it discounts the utility gained from consumption in period 2 at the rate ρ. This parameter, for a particular individual, is called the individual's discount rate for the following reason. Consider the present value of the stream of income m_1 in period 1 and m_2 in period 2, when the market interest rate is r. Its present value (see Section 20.5) is given by

$$\rho v = m_1 + m_2/(1 + r) \tag{21.2}$$

As we have already seen in Chapter 20, as viewed from period 1 the future income m_2 is discounted by the market at the rate r because it will not be received for a period. Notice the similarity between this expression and that for the discounted utility model in Eq. (21.1). In the latter the individual discounts future utility, because it will not be received for a period. He or she discounts it at the rate ρ. We should emphasize that this discount factor is individual specific. Some individuals will have a high value for ρ, some a low value; it depends on how the individual regards the utility of consumption in period 2 relative to the utility of consumption in period 1. It may be the case that the individual regards them equally, in which case the parameter ρ will be zero; such an individual does not discount the future. However for most of us, it seems to be the case that we weight the present more highly than the future, in which case the value of the parameter ρ is positive. In addition, the more an individual regards the present relative to the future, the higher is ρ: alternatively, we can say the higher the individual regards the present relative to the future, the more the individual discounts the future. We should also point out that, as a parameter representing preferences, the value of ρ is independent of the value of the market discount rate r.

The parameter ρ captures the individual's preferences regarding the relative weighting of present and future consumption. To complete the specification of the discounted utility model we also need to specify the function u. This will also be individual specific. Normally we expect it to be a concave function – as consumption rises so does the utility gained from that consumption, but it rises less than proportionately. Or, in more casual terms, for every increase of one in consumption there is an increase in utility, but these increases get smaller as the amount consumed increases. In what follows we will assume that the function u is a square root function which is concave for positive consumption [1]. An alternative is that the u function is a logarithmic function which is also concave for positive consumption. With this function we get slightly different demand functions, but the important property concerning the relationship of r with ρ (which we shall prove shortly) is true for all concave u functions including the logarithmic function. In practice, of course, the form of the function depends upon the individual's preferences.

21.3 Indifference Curves with the Discounted Utility Model

We have now specified the discounted utility model. In the next section we shall explore its implications. But first, as we are going to use the framework for analysis developed in Chapter 20, we need to look at the properties of the indifference curves in (c_1, c_2) space implied by this model. There follows a little bit of mathematics; if you do not like maths, look away until we discuss the implications of the results.

---

1. It is difficult to conceive of negative consumption.

An indifference curve in (c_1, c_2) space is given, as ever, by

$$U(c_1, c_2) = \text{constant} \tag{21.3}$$

If we substitute the specification of the discounted utility model (21.1) into Eq. (21.3), we get the following equation for an indifference curve in (c_1, c_2) space.

$$u(c_1) + u(c_2)/(1 + \rho) = \text{constant} \tag{21.4}$$

From this we can find the slope of the indifference curve (a proof is provided in the mathematical appendix to this chapter); it is given by:

$$\text{slope of indifference curve} = -(1 + \rho)[du(c_1)/dc_1]/[du(c_2)/dc_2] \tag{21.5}$$

Here $du(c)/dc$ denotes the derivative of $u(c)$ with respect to c; that is, the rate at which utility is increasing with consumption.

The slope is negative so the indifference curves are downward sloping. Moreover if u is concave then, as we move down and rightwards along an indifference curve, c_1 is rising while c_2 is falling; hence $du(c_1)/dc_1$ is falling while $du(c_2)/dc_2$ is rising, and so the magnitude of the slope is falling. From this it follows that, if u is concave, the indifference curves are convex. However if u is linear, then both $du(c_1)/dc_1$ and $du(c_2)/dc_2$ are constant and the slope of the indifference curves are constant – that is, they are linear. If we continue this line of argument with a convex function u, we get the following result:

 If u is concave, linear or convex then the indifference curves in (c_1, c_2) space are convex, linear or concave.

As we have already argued, the concave u function is empirically more realistic; as people's consumption increases their utility rises, but at a decreasing rate.

One final result is of particular importance. If in Eq. (21.5) we put $c_1 = c_2$, we find the slope of an indifference curve is $-(1 + \rho)$. Calling the line $c_1 = c_2$ the 'equal consumption line', we get the important result that:

 Along the equal consumption line, the slope of every indifference curve of an individual with discounted utility model preferences is equal to $-(1 + \rho)$.

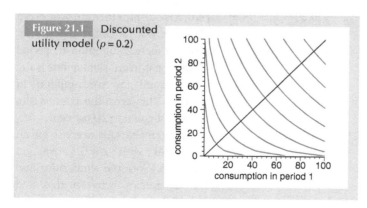

Figure 21.1 Discounted utility model ($\rho = 0.2$)

consumption in period 2

consumption in period 1

We illustrate this in Fig. 21.1. In this figure I have used the square root utility function for u, and I have put $\rho = 0.2$ (that is, the individual discounts the future at 20 per cent). In Fig. 21.1 I draw some of his or her indifference curves in (c_1, c_2) space. I have also inserted the equal consumption line. It can be seen that along this line the slope of every indifference curve is -1.2.

For an individual with a higher discount rate than 20 per cent, his or her indifference curves will everywhere be steeper along the equal consumption line.

21.4 The Implications in a Two-period World

You may be able to guess some of the implications. We know that along the equal income line the slope of the indifference curves are all $-(1 + \rho)$. It follows therefore that to the right of the equal income line the magnitude of the slope is everywhere less than $(1 + \rho)$, whilst to the left of the equal income line the magnitude of the slope is everywhere more than $(1 + \rho)$. Why is this important? Because we know that the magnitude of the slope of the budget line is $(1 + r)$, and we know that at the optimum point the magnitude of the slope of the budget line is equal to the magnitude of the slope of the indifference curve (because the budget line must be tangential to the indifference curve at the optimal point). So at the optimal point the slope of the indifference curve must be $-(1 + r)$.

There are three cases to consider. The simplest is when $r = \rho$. In this case the optimum point must lie somewhere along the equal consumption line for we know that the slopes of the indifference curves there are $-(1 + \rho)$; if this is equal to $-(1 + r)$ (because $r = \rho$), it follows that the optimum point, where the slopes of the indifference curve and the budget line are equal, must be along the equal consumption line. In this case the individual consumes the same amount in both periods, the reason being that the market discounts the future at exactly the same rate as the individual.

When $r > \rho$, we can argue that the optimal point must lie to the left of the equal consumption line so that the individual consumes more in the second period than the first. And when $r < \rho$, we can argue that the optimal point must lie to the right of the equal consumption line so that the individual consumes more in the first period than the second. What is crucial is whether the market discounts the future more heavily than the individual.

These properties are confirmed in the following example, in which we keep the initial incomes of 40 (in period 1) and 40 (in period 2) fixed, and vary the rate of interest from zero (which is shown in Fig. 21.2) upwards. We assume a value of ρ equal to 0.2 (20 per cent); that is, we use the preferences of Eq. (21.1). In Fig. 21.2 we show the optimal point (marked by an asterisk) in the case when the rate of interest is zero. You might like to verify that, when the market rate of interest reaches 20 per cent, the optimal point is on the equal consumption line.

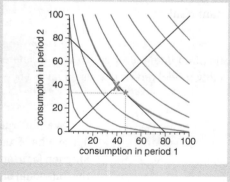

Figure 21.2 Effect of changes in the rate of interest: optimal consumption ($\rho = 0.2$)

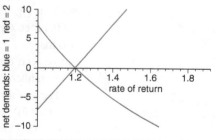

Figure 21.3 Effect of changes in the rate of interest: net demand ($\rho = 0.2$)

The implied borrowing and lending are pictured in Fig. 21.3. You should recall that the rate of return is one plus the rate of interest. The downward sloping line is the net demand for consumption in period 1, and the upward sloping line is the net demand for consumption in period 2. They cross the axis at a rate of interest equal to 20 per cent.

If we repeat this exercise for an individual with $\rho = 0.4$ we get Fig. 21.4. Note the similarities and the differences between this and Fig. 21.3.

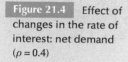

Figure 21.4 Effect of changes in the rate of interest: net demand ($\rho = 0.4$)

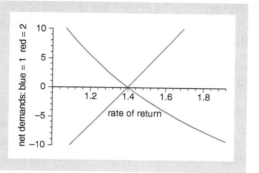

21.5 The Discounted Utility Model in a Many-period World

Although it lies a little outside the scope of this book, it is interesting to consider the extension of the discounted utility model to a many-period world. It is a natural extension of the discounting formula discussed in Section 20.4.

Suppose we are in a world which lasts T periods, where T may be finite, infinite or random. Suppose the individual has consumption c_1 in period 1, c_2 in period 2, ..., c_t in period t, ..., and c_T in period T. We consider his or her preferences for consumption bundles over these T periods – bundles which we denote by $(c_1, c_2, ..., c_t, ..., c_T)$. The discounted utility model states that preferences over these bundles are given by the following function

$$U(c_1, c_2, ..., c_t, ..., c_T) = u(c_1) + u(c_2)/(1+\rho)$$
$$+ \cdots + u(c_t)/(1+\rho)^{t-1} + \cdots + u(c_T)/(1+\rho)^{T-1} \tag{21.6}$$

Once again the model is specified by a discount rate ρ and a utility function u. The model is the natural extension of the two-period model. The utility of the bundle is the sum of the utilities of consumption in each period, discounted at the rate ρ. If ρ is positive the weight attached to future consumption declines with time from the present; period 1's consumption is given a weight of one; period 2's consumption is weighted by $1/(1+\rho)$; ...; period t's consumption by $1/(1+\rho)^{t-1}$; ...; and period T's by $1/(1+\rho)^{T-1}$. You may find it constructive to compare Eq. (21.6) with the formula in Section 20.4 giving the present value of an income stream; there, future incomes are discounted by the market at the rate r because they are received in the future. In the discounted utility model, future utilities are discounted by the individual at the rate ρ because they are experienced in the future.

Whether this is a good description of actual intertemporal preferences is obviously an empirical issue, but it may be instructive to give the normative reason why such preferences might be appropriate. In essence, the idea is that individuals with such preferences are dynamically consistent, in the sense that they carry out plans that they formulate. In a world with no uncertainty, there is no reason why one should ever want to change plans once formulated, so this property is an appealing one.

Let us discuss it in more detail. Suppose we start in period 1, and we know that the income stream is going to be m_1 in period 1, m_2 in period 2, ..., m_t in period t, ..., m_T in period T. Then the individual in period 1 formulates a plan for consumption $(c_1, c_2, ..., c_t, ..., c_T)$ through time on the basis of maximizing the utility (21.6), subject to both the income stream and the rate of interest which we are assuming is fixed and known. Accordingly, in period 1 the individual consumes the planned c_1. In period 2, what happens? Does the individual implement the planned consumption c_2? It depends. Suppose the individual re-plans at this stage. At this point in time he or she has a different objective function because period 1 has already been and gone. Now only periods 2 through T remain. If we update Eq. (21.6) to take account of this, the objective function now becomes that in Eq. (21.7).

$$U(c_2, ..., c_t, ..., c_T) = u(c_2) + u(c_3)/(1 + \rho)$$
$$+ \cdots + u(c_t)/(1 + \rho)^{t-2} + \cdots + u(c_T)/(1 + \rho)^{T-2} \tag{21.7}$$

Given the remaining stream of income, does the maximization of this lead to the same optimal values $c_2, ..., c_t, ..., c_T$ that were the optimal values in the original plan $c_1, c_2, ..., c_t, ..., c_T$, formulated at time period 1? The answer to this question is yes, though the reason for this may not be obvious. A proof is provided in the mathematical appendix, which shows that we can express the utility from period 1 onwards in the following form:

$$U(c_1, c_2, ..., c_t, ..., c_T) = u(c_1) + U(c_2, ..., c_t, ..., c_T)/(1 + \rho) \tag{21.8}$$

So the choice of the best values of $c_2, ..., c_t, ..., c_T$ – given the optimal value of c_1 from the maximization of utility as viewed from the first period with respect to the choice of $c_1, c_2, ..., c_T$ – leads to the same choice of $c_2, ..., c_t, ..., c_T$ as in the original choice of $c_1, c_2, ..., c_t, ..., c_T$ in the maximization of utility as viewed from the first period. The individual would not want to change the plans originally made.

In essence – and this should be clear from Eq. (21.7) – the reason is that, if we compare any two periods s and t, the relative weight attached to the utility of consumption in period s is always the same value $(1 + \rho)^{s-t}$, irrespective of which period we are viewing it from. This means that the individual never wishes to revise any plans that he or she has formulated. (Of course in a world were there was no uncertainty, there are no reasons why one should ever wish to revise any plans.) If, instead, the individual used a varying discount rate through time, then the individual might want to revise plans made earlier. In a sense this is because the individual, with a varying discount rate, is not just one individual but several – and they have conflicting views as to what is best to do. This is exactly the kind of person who resolves every morning not to drink in the evening – and then ends up doing so.

21.6 Summary

Most of this chapter has been concerned with the two-period discounted utility model, though the final section contained an extension to the many-period model in which we provided a normative justification for it. In the two-period case we showed the following.

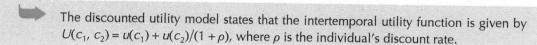 The discounted utility model states that the intertemporal utility function is given by $U(c_1, c_2) = u(c_1) + u(c_2)/(1 + \rho)$, where ρ is the individual's discount rate.

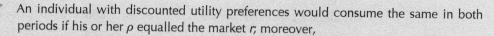 With the discounted utility model, the slope of all indifference curves along the equal-consumption line is $-(1 + \rho)$.

We recalled that the perfect capital market budget constraint has a slope of $-(1 + r)$ where r is the market interest rate. Combining these two results, we showed following.

An individual with discounted utility preferences would consume the same in both periods if his or her ρ equalled the market r; moreover,

- he or she will consume more in period 1 than in period 2 if $r < \rho$
- he or she will consume more in period 2 than in period 1 if $r > \rho$

We briefly extended the model to a many-period world, and showed that one attractive normative property of the model is that an agent with such preferences is never dynamically inconsistent.

21.7 Review Questions

1. If individual A has a higher discount rate than individual B, who cares relatively more about the future?

2. What is your discount rate? (See the next section.)

3. Do you think young people generally discount the future at a greater rate than middle-aged people? Or than old people?

4. How do you think the discount rate affects people's desire to save for a pension?

5. Do you think that you discount the future at a constant rate? (This is a difficult question; some light is shed on it in the next section.)

21.8 Application: at what Rate do you Discount the Future?

The discounted utility model incorporates the notion that individuals do not value consumption equally in all periods. In general it appears to be the case that individuals care more about the present than the future, although the extent to which they do this differs from individual to individual. Here you are invited to try and discover the extent to which *you* do this.

The model in a T-period world takes the form of Eq. (21.6), and in a 2-period world the form of Eq. (21.1). The latter says that a two-period bundle of consumption (c_1, c_2) is valued by the function

$$U(c_1, c_2) = u(c_1) + u(c_2)/(1 + \rho) \qquad (21.1)$$

In this function, $u(c)$ is the utility gained from consuming c in some period, and ρ is the individual's discount rate. Both of these are specific to the individual. Here we will concentrate on discovering your value of ρ assuming, of course, that your preferences are in accordance with the discounted utility model[2].

The method used is simple; we exploit the implications of the above equation, particularly those results that we have already derived concerning the slope of indifference curves. If we can find two points on the same indifference curve, then we can use these results to try to infer the value of ρ. Specifically, let us take Eq. (21.5):

$$\text{slope of indifference curve} = -(1 + \rho)[du(c_1)/dc_1]/[du(c_2)/dc_2] \qquad (21.5)$$

If we do not know the individual's utility function, then we start at a position where c_1 and c_2 are equal. This enables us to derive the result stated in the text:

 Along the equal consumption line the slope of every indifference curve of an individual with discounted utility model preferences is equal to $-(1 + \rho)$.

It follows that, if we start at a point where $c_1 = c_2 = c$ and we find a nearby point about which the individual feels the same (that is, on the same indifference curve), then we can infer the value of ρ. To fix ideas, suppose that the point $(c - a, c + b)$ is such a point; that is, the individual feels indifferent between the two-period consumption bundle (c, c) and the two-period consumption bundle $(c - a, c + b)$. Then the slope of the indifference curve is approximately equal to $-b/a$. This is an estimate of $-(1 + \rho)$. Hence we have an estimate that ρ is $b/a - 1 = (b - a)/a$. If the individual puts more weight on present than on future consumption, then b will be bigger than a because, to compensate the individual for consuming a less today, he or she will require more than a next period; and hence the estimate of ρ is positive.

Obviously the value of ρ depends upon the length of the period we are considering. Let us assume that the period is one year. You can now try and implement the above ideas, and hence find your yearly discount rate. You have to do the following introspection. Suppose you start from a position where you are consuming the same both this year and next year – for example, £5000 each year. Now suppose someone suggests that your consumption

---

2. If they are not, there is no ρ to discover.

this year will fall by (say) £100 to £4900, but that you will be given some extra consumption next year to compensate. You should ask yourself: what is the minimum compensation I would require? This is quite a difficult introspection, but you should attempt it. Try and narrow it down. Would £1 compensation be enough? Probably not. Would £1000 compensation be enough? Probably more than enough. Would £50 be enough? And so on.

The minimum compensation that you require gives an estimate of your discount rate ρ. Suppose this minimum compensation is £120. Then we have that $a = £100$ and $b = £120$, so that your ρ is 0.2 ($= (120 - 100)/100$). It should be clear that we can derive the following table of examples.

Table 21.1   Estimation of individual's discount rate

Minimum compensation required for a decrease in period 1 consumption of £100	Implied value of the discount rate ρ
£100	0.0
£110	0.1
£120	0.2
£130	0.3
£140	0.4

Note carefully that we are talking about changes in consumption and not about changes in money income. If it were the latter, and there was a perfect capital market in which you could freely borrow and lend at the constant rate of interest r, the answer to the question would have to be £100$(1 + r)$. We will not learn anything about your discount rate – only about the rate of interest in a perfect capital market!

Note the assumptions carefully:

● we start along the equal consumption line so that we do not have to worry about your utility function, which is difficult to infer;

● we consider a small reduction in period 1 consumption, otherwise we are moving around the indifference curve and its slope may change;

● you tell us honestly the minimum amount of compensation in terms of period 2 consumption you require.

If you do all this, you can find your discount rate.

If you are interested, you could explore the implications for a many-period world. In the extension to T periods, as given in Eq. (21.6), you will see that the discounted utility model assumes that the same discount rate is used throughout. This is obviously a strong assumption, but one that can be tested. Try one such test yourself. Suppose you have found that the minimum compensation you require, under the assumptions listed above, is £120. Then, starting from an equal consumption point, you regard having £100 less today as being compensative with an extra £120 in one year's time. Now repeat the exercise, but ask yourself what is the minimum compensation in two years' time for having £100 less today. Denote this minimum compensation by b, but remember that this will be consumed in two years' time. Repeating the argument that we used above, it follows that $-b/a$ is an estimate of $-(1 + \rho)^2$. To be consistent with the discounted utility model and with your previously derived estimate of ρ (which is 0.2), it must be the case that the minimum compensation you require in two years' time is £144, so that $b/a = (1 + \rho)^2$.

At first glance you may find this odd, or at least inconsistent with your introspection. Let us discover why the discounted utility model makes this prediction. We begin with your first introspection; you needed £120 in one year's time to compensate you for having £100 less today, that is, for each £1 less you receive today, you need £1.20 in compensation in one year's time. If this applies to consumption deferred for one year from today, it should also apply to consumption deferred for one year from next year. So, if you are to be compensated for having £100 less today, but will receive the compensation in two years' time, you can argue as follows: 'I would need £120 more in one year's time; and to defer each of these £120 for a further year, I shall need further compensation of £1.20 for each of those £120 – that is, a compensation of 1.2 times £120 = £144 in two year's time'. Was your introspection consistent with this?

You may be interested to know that there have been many experimental tests of the discounted model, and particularly its central assumption that the discount rate is constant[3]. The great strength of experimental economics is its central tenet that participants should be given appropriate incentives to behave in such a way that their behaviour reveals their preferences. In many areas it is easy to give appropriate incentives, as we shall see in the chapter on Game Theory, but in the area of intertemporal choice it is more difficult. We have already noted some strong assumptions that underlie the inferences we have made. These are difficult to enforce in the laboratory. The greatest problem, however, is that correct incentives in intertemporal choice experiments necessarily involve the passage of time. It may be difficult to ensure that participants and experimenters are still around after that passage of time.

---

3. Many of these studies suggest that the discount rate is not constant.

21.9 Mathematical Appendix

We first derive the proposition concerning the slope of the indifference curves implied by the discounted utility model.

As stated in the text, an indifference curve in (c_1, c_2) space is given by

$$U(c_1, c_2) = \text{constant} \tag{21.3}$$

If we substitute in the specification of the discounted utility model from Eq. (21.1), we get the following equation for an indifference curve in (c_1, c_2) space.

$$u(c_1) + u(c_2)/(1+\rho) = \text{constant} \tag{21.4}$$

To find the slope of the indifference curve we differentiate this totally to give the following.

$$u'(c_1)\, dc_1 + u'(c_2)\, dc_2/(1+\rho) = 0 \tag{21.5}$$

where $u'(c)$ denotes the derivative of $u(c)$ with respect to c. From this we get the slope of an indifference curve, equivalent to Eq. (21.5) in the text.

$$dc_2/dc_1 = -(1+\rho)u'(c_1)/u'(c_2) \tag{A21.1}$$

We now derive Eq. (21.8). Suppose the set $c^*_1, c^*_2, ..., c^*_t, ..., c^*_T$ maximizes the function

$$U(c_1, c_2, ..., c_t, ..., c_T) = u(c_1) + u(c_2)/(1+\rho) + \cdots + u(c_t)/(1+\rho)^{t-1}$$
$$+ \cdots + u(c_T)/(1+\rho)^{T-1} \tag{A21.2}$$

given an income stream $m_1, m_2, ..., m_t, ..., m_T$, and hence subject to the intertemporal budget constraint below:

$$m_1 + m_2/(1+r) + \cdots + m_{T-1}/(1+r)^{T-2} + m_T/(1+r)^{T-1}$$
$$= c_1 + c_2/(1+r) + \cdots + c_{T-1}/(1+r)^{T-2} + c_T/(1+r)^{T-1} \tag{A21.3}$$

It must be the case that the set $c^*_2, ..., c^*_t, ..., c^*_T$ maximizes

$$U(c_2, ..., c_t, ..., c_T) = u(c_2) + u(c_3)/(1+\rho) + \cdots + u(c_t)/(1+\rho)^{t-2}$$
$$+ \cdots + u(c_T)/(1+\rho)^{T-2} \tag{A21.4}$$

subject to the following constraint

$$m_1 + m_2/(1+r) + \cdots + m_{T-1}/(1+r)^{T-2} + m_T/(1+r)^{T-1}$$
$$= c^*_1 + c^*_2/(1+r) + \cdots + c^*_{T-1}/(1+r)^{T-2} + c^*_T/(1+r)^{T-1} \tag{A21.5}$$

because

$$U(c_1, c_2, ..., c_t, ..., c_T) = u(c_1) + U(c_2, ..., c_t, ..., c_T)/(1+\rho). \tag{A21.6}$$

Exchange in Capital Markets

22

22.1 Introduction

We are now in a position to examine trade in capital markets. We know that some people borrow and some people save. After a moment's reflection you will realize that the total amount borrowed must equal the total amount saved; if someone wants to borrow some money, there must be someone else willing to lend that money. In a capital market which is in equilibrium, the price of borrowing and saving must adjust so that borrowing and saving are equal. And what is this price? The rate of return $(1 + r)$ of course; for every £1 borrowed today £$(1 + r)$ must be repaid in one period's time; for every £1 saved there is a payoff of £$(1 + r)$ in one period's time. For the time being we are assuming there is no inflation[1]. We are also assuming, since we have the same rate of interest for borrowing and for saving, that financial institutions make no profit. This is obviously not true in practice, but it is a useful assumption for illustrative purposes.

This chapter looks at trade through time. We examine a capital market in which individuals can exchange money today for money in one period's time. This may be a bit confusing as what we put on the axes is consumption in the two periods; so we should explain a little more what it is that we are assuming.

We assume that the individuals get utility out of what they consume each period. 'Consumption' is an all-inclusive term, but it may simplify things a bit if we think of it as food. Individuals get utility out of consuming food each period. As we shall assume, they each get an endowment of food each period; when they wake up in period 1 there is an endowment of food waiting for them, and when they wake up in period 2 there is an endowment of food waiting for them. If they did no trading then they would simply consume the food with which they were endowed and that would be the end of it. However they might prefer to re-arrange their consumption, consuming more in one period and less in the other (for instance, if they were given lots of food in one period and very little in the other). Now suppose that food is perishable; if it is not consumed in period 1 it goes bad and cannot be consumed in the second period. If that is so, the only way to re-arrange consumption is to trade with someone else; A gives some food to B in period 1, for example, and B gives some food to A in period 2. Trade is thus essential if the endowment is in perishable food, if any kind of re-arrangement is to be implemented.

---

1. See later for the differences if there is inflation.

We now introduce money into the economy, and for the moment let us suppose that the price of consumption in both periods is one (we are assuming zero inflation). Then money and consumption are synonymous, and if we put 'consumption in period 1' on the horizontal axis it is just the same as if we had put 'money spent in period 1' on the horizontal axis. Similarly, if we put 'consumption in period 2' on the vertical axis it is the same as if we put 'money spent in period 2' on the vertical axis. Now, trade on this interpretation means exchanging 'money in period 1' for 'money in period 2'. So, for example, A gives some money to B in period 1 and, in exchange, B gives A some money in period 2; so far so good. The only problem with this interpretation is that, in a world with no inflation, money is not like perishable food; in fact £1 in period 1 remains £1 in period 2. It is therefore clear that no-one will accept an exchange which gives them less than £1 in period 2 for each £1 given in period 1. No-one will accept a negative rate of interest, as they can always guarantee themselves a zero rate of interest by simply saving the money under the bed. So we should be a little careful; if we use non-perishable money on the axes rather than perishable food or consumption, we should check that the equilibrium rate of interest is positive[2]. If it is not, then the lenders will choose not to lend and will save their money under the bed.

22.2 Trade in a Capital Market

We use the technique for analysing exchange that we introduced in Chapter 8 – that of the Edgeworth box. We assume a simple economy comprising just two people and two goods. The people are individuals A and B; the goods are consumption in period 1 and consumption in period 2. The individuals may or may not differ in their preferences over these two goods, and they may or may not differ in their endowments of the two goods.

Let us build up a specific example exactly as we did in Chapter 8. We start with individual A and assume that initially he or she has 100 units of consumption in period 1 and 25 units in period 2. This is rather an unbalanced endowment, and A may well be happy to trade to a more balanced consumption profile. We suppose that A has discounted utility preferences with a square root utility function which we used in Chapter 21, and a discount rate ρ equal to 0.3; A discounts the future at 30 per cent. We draw A's indifference curves and endowment point in Fig. 22.1; there are lots of points which A might prefer to the endowment point E.

We now turn to individual B. We assume that B initially has 50 units of consumption in period 1 and 75 units in period 2; this, too, is a somewhat unbalanced initial stock. As for preferences, let us assume that B has the same preferences as A – discounted utility model preferences with a square root utility function and a discount rate ρ equal to 0.3; so we can see whether trade is possible when the individuals have the same tastes. The map of B's indifference curves is shown in Fig. 22.2, measured from the usual origin; and again in Fig. 22.3, measured from the top right origin after inverting B's indifference map.

Figure 22.1

Capital market: individual A's indifference curves

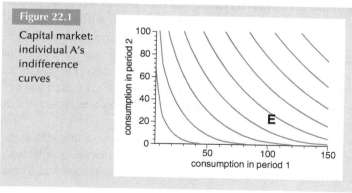

consumption in period 2

consumption in period 1

---

2. If there is inflation we should check that the equilibrium *real* rate of interest is positive.

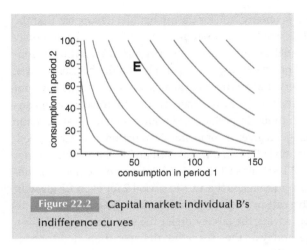

Figure 22.2   Capital market: individual B's indifference curves

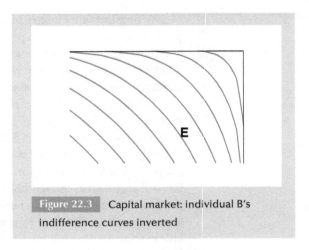

Figure 22.3   Capital market: individual B's indifference curves inverted

We now perform Edgeworth's clever trick. We place the inverted figure of B's indifference map on top of that of A (which is the correct way up), making sure that the two endowment points exactly coincide; and we get the Edgeworth box pictured in Fig. 22.4.

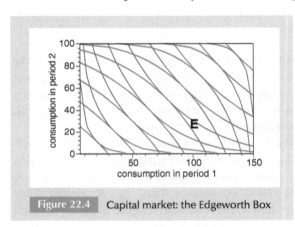

Figure 22.4   Capital market: the Edgeworth Box

The width of the box is the total initial stock of consumption in period 1, of which individual A has 100 units and B has 50, giving a total of 150 units. The height of the box is the total initial stock of consumption in period 2, of which individual A has 25 units and B has 75, making 100 in all. We ask ourselves whether trade is possible. The contract curve was not included in Fig. 22.4 but we have drawn it in Fig. 22.5; this will give us the answer.

The contract curve is the straight line joining the two origins because the two individuals' preferences are identical[3]. The contract curve has the same interpretation as in Chapter 8; it is the locus of efficient points in the space. Any point off the curve is inefficient, in the sense that there is always a direction to move in which both individuals are better off than before. However, once on the contract curve any movement is bound to make at least one of the two worse off. We might therefore expect that any contract entered into by A and B would be on the contract curve. A and B do not have identical endowments, and it is apparent from Fig. 22.5 that the initial endowment point E is not on the contract curve; accordingly, some trade ought to be possible. As before, let us investigate where competitive trading takes the two individuals. We have already noted that the price of 'consumption in period 1' relative to the price of 'consumption in period 2' is $(1 + r)$, where r is the rate of interest, for the simple reason that every pound consumed in period 1 costs $(1 + r)$ in terms of period 2 consumption – that is, what could be consumed in period 2 if the pound was not consumed in period 1. So the slope of a budget constraint is $-(1 + r)$. We already know this from the material in Chapter 20.

Now, for each rate of interest r we can draw the budget constraint – a line with slope $-(1 + r)$ passing through the point E – and hence find the optimal point for each individual. In this way we can find the price-offer (or interest-rate offer) curve for each individual. These

3. And, strictly speaking, because the preferences are homothetic, which is a mathematical concept outwith the scope of this book.

Figure 22.5

Capital market:
competitive
equilibrium
(scenario 1)

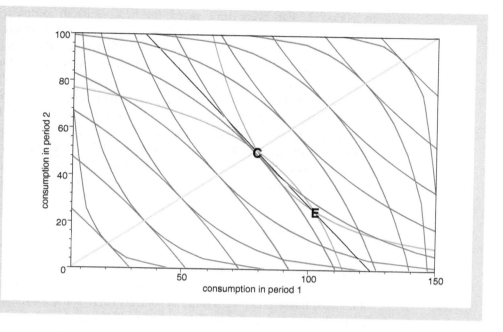

interest rate offer curves are also shown in Fig. 22.5. The convex curve passing through the endowment point E is the interest-rate offer curve for A, and the concave curve passing through E is the interest-rate offer curve for B. The straight line joining the two origins is the contract curve, and this passes through the point where the two interest-rate offer curves intersect. This is the competitive equilibrium, and the line joining it with the endowment point E is the equilibrium budget constraint.

Let us study carefully this competitive equilibrium, which is almost but not quite at the centre of the box. It is at the point (76.24, 50.83) as measured from the bottom left origin, and at the point (73.76, 49.17) when measured from the top right origin. In Table 22.1 we show, for individuals A and B separately and for society, the initial endowments in periods 1 and 2, the position at the competitive equilibrium, and the trade between the two.

Table 22.1   Capital markets: changes between initial and competitive equilibrium allocations

	Individual A	Individual B	Society
Initial Allocation			
Money/Consumption in period 1	100	50	150
Money/Consumption in period 2	25	75	100
Competitive Equilibrium Allocation			
Money/Consumption in period 1	76.24	73.76	150
Money/Consumption in period 2	50.83	49.17	100
Changes between the two			
Money/Consumption in period 1	−23.76	+23.76	0
Money/Consumption in period 2	+25.83	−25.83	0

We have the following exchange: A gives B 23.76 units of consumption in period 1, and B gives A 25.83 units of consumption in period 2. Consequently A forgoes 23.76 units of period 1 consumption but gets in return 25.83 units of period 2 consumption. Looking at it in terms of borrowing and saving, A lends 23.76 to B in period 1 and gets back from B 25.83

in period 2. For every unit saved (or lent to B) in period 1, A gets in return $25.83/23.76 = 1.087$ units in period 2; this represents a rate of return 1.087, and hence a rate of interest of 8.7 per cent. This is positive, which means that A is better off lending the money to B rather than keeping it under the bed. Note also that the slope of the equilibrium budget constraint, which is the line joining E and the competitive equilibrium, is -1.087.

In this equilibrium both individuals have re-arranged their consumption streams; A ends up consuming less than his income in period 1 (which was large), and in exchange gets more consumption in period 2. B increases his consumption in period 1, but has to pay (interest) for the privilege in terms of having a much lower second period consumption. The competitive equilibrium rate of interest is positive. You might like to ask yourself whether this will always be the case.

22.3 A Different Scenario

In this section we look at a different scenario, in which we assume identical endowments but different preferences. The first assumption means that the endowment point (E) is at the centre of the box; the second means that the contract curve is not a straight line joining the two origins. To be specific, we assume identical square root utility functions but different discount factors: $\rho = 0.1$ for A and $\rho = 0.5$ for B. Both discount the future, although B does so more heavily than A. For this reason the contract curve in scenario 2 is above and to the left of the line joining two origins – for any given division of period 2 consumption, B gets rather more than the equal share of consumption in period 1. Fig. 22.6 shows the picture for scenario 2.

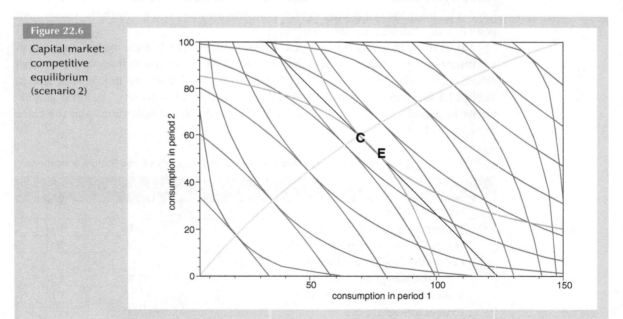

Figure 22.6

Capital market: competitive equilibrium (scenario 2)

Notice where the competitive equilibrium is. The equilibrium interest rate is 5 per cent (the slope of the line joining the endowment point and the competitive equilibrium is -1.05). Although the two individuals start out with the same endowment A is induced, by a positive rate of interest, to lend some money to individual B because, relative to A, B prefers to consume in the first period and is willing to pay interest for the privilege. As a consequence A ends up consuming more over the two periods combined.

22.4 Comments

You will realize that the analysis of this chapter is very similar to that of Chapter 8; indeed it is identical except for nomenclature: instead of two general goods we have consumption in periods 1 and 2, and trade takes place in the capital market where the individuals exchange 'money/consumption in period 1' for 'money/consumption in period 2'. The price of period 1 consumption in terms of period 2 consumption is one plus the rate of interest.

It follows that all the results of Chapter 8 are relevant including: the general possibility of trade except when the initial point is on the contract curve (which happens if endowments are identical and preferences are identical); the efficiency of trade along the contract curve; and the efficiency of the competitive equilibrium. Also relevant is the fact that the competitive equilibrium, and hence the equilibrium rate of interest, depends upon the initial endowments and the preferences.

22.5 Summary

We have shown that some kind of intertemporal trade is usually possible, although in a world with no inflation and with non-perishable money the competitive equilibrium may not be attainable because one of the agents may prefer to store his or her money under the bed rather than accept a negative rate of interest. Otherwise all the results from Chapter 8, which considered trade in general, remain valid. In a world with inflation, we simply correct the rate of interest for inflation and hence get a *real* rate of interest, which is equal to the nominal rate of interest minus the rate of inflation. We get the same kind of result; the equilibrium real rate of interest must be positive to induce both agents to engage in trade. We have also shown that the equilibrium (real) rate of interest depends upon the endowments and preferences of the individuals.

22.6 Review Questions

1. If we aggregate all the amounts borrowed in a particular country at a particular point in time, and we also aggregate all the amounts lent in a particular country at a particular point in time, which total is bigger?

2. Who supplies the mortgages of all the people borrowing from a building society? (The people who save with that building society.)

3. Why, in general but not always, are real interest rates positive?

4. What do you think happens to the totals of borrowing and saving when there is a rise in the interest rate?

5. Is there any way you can detect from interest rates whether people generally have a positive or a negative discount rate?

22.7 Application: how can Real Rates of Interest be Negative?

You may have noticed that, in certain periods of history, real interest rates have been negative. What do we mean by this? Simply that the rate of inflation exceeds the money rate of interest. Consider the following table, taken from statistics in the UK publication *Economic Trends Annual Supplement*:

Table 22.2   Inflation and money rates of interest 1973–76

Year	Retail Price index (1985 = 100)	Implied Rate of Inflation between current year and following year (%)	Interest Rate on Treasury Bills (%)
1973	25.1	9.1	12.52
1974	29.1	15.9	11.30
1975	36.1	24.1	10.93
1976	42.1	16.2	14.09
1977	48.8	n.a.	n.a.

Take 1974 for example: between then and 1975 the retail price index rose 15.9 per cent whilst the rate of interest on Treasury Bills was 11.30 per cent. This means that £100 invested in Treasury Bills in 1974 became worth £111.30 in 1975. Using the retail price index as a deflator, in 1975 £111.30 could buy 100/36.1 = 3.08 in goods, whereas in 1974 £100 could have bought 100/29.1 = 3.44 in goods. So, £100 invested in Treasury Bills was worth 10.4 per cent less in 1975 in terms of its buying power for goods than in 1974 – because of inflation. Prices rose 15.9 per cent while the interest rate was only 11.3 per cent, implying a negative real rate of interest. Money invested in the capital markets was worth less in 1975 than in 1974 in terms of its buying power over goods. You might well ask: how can this happen?

Let us use the analysis of this chapter. The key question is whether the equilibrium rate of interest can be negative. We have so far assumed zero inflation, and we will continue to do so for the moment and add inflation later. In Chapter 22 we assumed that both individuals put more weight on present consumption than on future consumption. It can be shown that, if this is true, the equilibrium rate of interest must be positive whatever the initial endowments. Hence, in order to get a case in which we have a negative rate of interest, we must suppose that one of the two individuals puts more weight on future consumption. Consider Fig. 22.7.

To produce this figure we have assumed that the rate of discount for individual A (whose consumption we measure from the bottom left-hand origin) is 0.4, and the rate of discount for individual B (whose consumption we measure from the top right-hand origin) is −0.4 (note the minus sign). So A puts a relative weight equal to 0.714 (= 1/(1 + 0.4)) on period 2 consumption, while B puts a relative weight of 1.667 (= 1/(1−0.4)) on period 2 consumption. Individual A cares more about period 1 consumption as we have assumed throughout our analysis; but B cares more about period 2 than period 1 consumption. There is nothing to say that this cannot happen; perhaps you know individuals who feel that way? Figure 22.7 shows the consequences.

Figure 22.7

Capital market:
negative
equilibrium rates
of interest

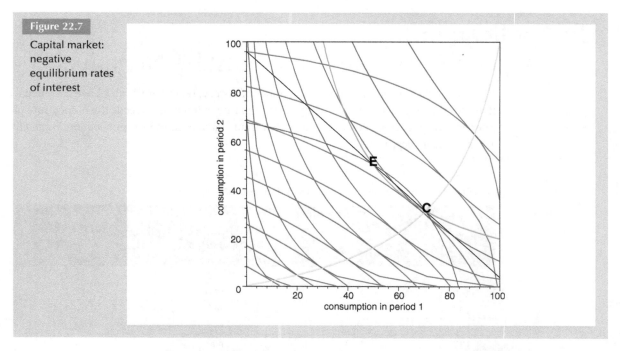

In Fig. 22.7 we assumed a perfectly symmetric endowment point – both individuals have 50 of each good in each period. The endowment point is indicated by the letter E, and the competitive equilibrium is at the point C where the two price-offer curves and the contract curve intersect, at approximately (71, 31). So in the equilibrium exchange, B gives 21 units of consumption in period 1 to A, and in exchange A gives 19 units of consumption in period 2 to B. The slope of the equilibrium budget constraint is thus $-19/21 = -0.904$. This, as we know, is equal to $-(1 + r)$ where r is the rate of interest. We therefore have an equilibrium rate of interest -0.096, that is -9.6 per cent. A is happy with this exchange as he or she prefers period 1 consumption; B is happy also as he or she prefers period 2 consumption. (Recall that the initial endowment point has equal consumption in both periods for both individuals.)

At this stage you could retort that B would not enter into this exchange because, rather than give up 21 units of period 1 consumption for just 19 of period 2 consumption, B would prefer to put the 21 units of period 1 consumption under the bed and consume it in period 2. If the good is perishable (food, for example) this is clearly not possible. But if it is money, could B not simply put the money under the bed?

This might work if money did not change its value during the period. But consider the possibility of inflation. Let the price of food be p_1 in period 1 and p_2 in period 2 . Suppose incomes are in food – both individuals have an endowment of 50 units of food in each period – and assume that food is perishable. Then individual B, in order to carry money over to next period, has to sell some of the endowment of food in period 1, and then buy back some more food in period 2. How does this change the analysis? Note that money *per se* has no value and cannot be consumed directly.

We repeat the analysis under this scenario and what do we find? There is an equilibrium price ratio between food in the two periods, which is clearly such that $p_1/p_2 = 19/21$ because the slope of the equilibrium budget line is $-19/21$. It follows therefore that the price in period 2 (p_2) is 21/19 times the price in period 1; there is inflation in the price of food between the two periods. So, putting the money under the bed makes no difference because it is worth less in period 2; indeed significantly less, such that if B put 21 in money under the bed in period 1, it would buy only 19 units of food in period 2 – exactly the same solution as if trade takes place between A and B! Of course, if there was some other asset which kept its value between the two periods (or which fell in value less than money), then B should buy that asset. Otherwise, he or she has to accept a negative rate of interest between the two periods, precisely because he or she values consumption more in period 2 than in period 1. This perhaps explains why we observe negative real rates of interest from time to time.

Choice under Risk

Introduction

We consider in this chapter optimal behaviour in conditions of risk. By this we mean that, when the individual takes a decision, he or she does not know with certainty what might happen. However we assume that the individual can list the various possible things that may happen, and can attach probabilities to them. For simplicity we assume that the set of possible outcomes contains only two[1] possibilities or states of the world, which we call state 1 and state 2. We denote by π_1 and π_2 the respective probabilities attached to these two states, and we assume that the decision maker knows these probabilities. Of course $\pi_1 + \pi_2 = 1$. So state 1 happens with probability π_1 and state 2 happens with probability π_2. Further, we assume that the income that the individual receives depends upon the state of the world that occurs; we use m_1 to denote the income the individual receives if state 1 occurs and m_2 the income if state 2 occurs. *Ex ante*, before the uncertainty is resolved the individual does not know which state will occur; *ex post*, one and only one of the two states will occur, and the individual will receive either an income of m_1 or an income of m_2. For simplicity in this chapter we will assume that the individual then consumes his or her income and thus gets utility directly from this income.

Now it may be the case that the individual is happy with this initial position – that is, is happy consuming m_1 if state 1 occurs and m_2 if state 2 occurs. But this is a position of *ex ante* risk if m_1 and m_2 are different. The individual might not like such a risky future; he or she may prefer an alternative scenario. For example, if the individual really dislikes risk he or she would want to re-arrange things so that the same income was received whichever state occurred.

The way an individual may be able to re-arrange the possibilities is through insurance. An insurance market specifically exists to re-arrange risk. For example, if you are worried that you may have an accident that would reduce your income, you might take out insurance so that, if an accident occurred, the insurance company would pay you money in compensation. This means that you pay money (the insurance premium) to the insurance company if the accident does not happen, and the company pays money to you if the accident does happen. We can think of this being done by buying and selling *contingent income* – income contingent on which state occurs. So, a

---

1. All the material can be generalized to more than two possibilities.

typical insurance contract involves you agreeing to give money to the insurance company if the accident does not occur, and the company agreeing to give you money if the accident does occur. Usually there is a relationship between the amount you give to the company if the accident does not occur and the amount that they give you if the accident does occur. This relationship is obviously affected by the probability of the accident occurring. We shall study this in more detail shortly.

23.2 The Budget Constraint

We define contingent income in a particular state of the world as the income you would get or pay if that state of the world occurred. It is a good or a commodity like any other, except that it is received or paid only if a particular state occurs. Let us denote the price of state 1 contingent income by p_1 and the price of state 2 contingent income by p_2. This means that, for each unit of state 1 income that you buy, the cost is p_1; and for each unit of state 2 income that you buy, the cost is p_2. Similarly, for each unit of state 1 income that you sell your revenue is p_1; and for each unit of state 2 income that you sell your revenue is p_2. You buy and sell state contingent income before you know whether state 1 or state 2 will occur. Nature then decides which state will occur, and you have the payoffs. If state 1 occurs, then, for each unit of state 1 contingent income that you have bought you receive a payment of one unit of money; for each unit of state 1 contingent income that you have sold you have to pay one unit of money. If state 2 occurs, then for each unit of state 2 contingent income that you have bought you receive a payment of one unit of money; for each unit of state 2 contingent income that you have sold you have to pay one unit of money. Note the sequence of events: *ex ante* you do not know whether state 1 or state 2 will occur (though you do know the respective probabilities): *ex ante*, you have to decide how much state contingent income to buy or sell; *ex post*, you are told which state has occurred, and then you receive or pay money depending which state has occurred and whether you have bought or sold income contingent on that state. For example suppose *ex ante* you have bought five units of state 1 contingent income (at a cost of $5p_1$), and you have sold ten units of state 2 contingent income (receiving a payment of $10p_2$); then, *ex post* if state 1 occurs you get paid five units of money, whereas if state 2 occurs you have to pay ten units of money.

With state contingent income you can change the riskiness of your position. Suppose, for example, that $m_1 = 40$ and $m_2 = 60$, that is, your *ex ante* income if state 1 were to occur is 40, and your *ex ante* income if state 2 were to occur is 60 (so you would be better off *ex post* if state 2 were to occur and worse off if state 1 were to occur). You could convert this into a position of *ex ante* certainty through state contingent income. Suppose for simplicity that $p_1 = p_2$. Then you simply buy ten units of state 1 contingent income and sell ten units of state 2 contingent income (the cost of the purchase of state 1 contingent income exactly equalling the revenue from the sale of state 2 contingent income). If 1 were to occur, your income would be 40 (your *ex ante* income in that state) plus 10 (the income from your ownership of 10 units of state 1 contingent income), making 50. If state 2 occurs your income would be 60 (your *ex ante* income in that state) minus 10 (the payment you have to make on the 10 units of state 2 contingent income that you have sold), which is 50. So, regardless of which state occurs, you always end up with an income of 50.

What is your budget constraint in this world? Suppose you start with income m_1 if state 1 occurs and income m_2 if state 2 occurs. Suppose you want to re-arrange things in such a way that you would have consumption c_1 if state 1 occurred and consumption c_2 if state 2 occurred. What constraints are you under at prices p_1 and p_2 for state contingent income? In fact it is simply the usual condition:

$$p_1 c_1 + p_2 c_2 = p_1 m_1 + p_2 m_2 \tag{23.1}$$

Why? Well, suppose you feel that your income if state 1 were to occur would be too low, and therefore you want to re-arrange things so that your consumption, if state 1 were to occur, would be c_1 where $m_1 < c_1$. Then you would have to buy $(c_1 - m_1)$ units of state 1 contingent income at a cost of $p_1(c_1 - m_1)$, and to finance this purchase you would have to sell a sufficient number of units of state 2 contingent income to pay for this. If you sell $(m_2 - c_2)$ units it would yield $p_2(m_2 - c_2)$ in revenue. So, in order to meet the budget constraint (23.1), you would have to have $p_2(m_2 - c_2) = p_1(c_1 - m_1)$.

Alternatively, suppose you feel that your income if state 2 were to occur would be too low, and therefore that you want to re-arrange things so that your consumption, if state 2 were to occur, would be c_2 where $m_2 < c_2$. Then you would have to buy $(c_2 - m_2)$ units of state 2 contingent income at a cost of $p_2(c_2 - m_2)$; to finance this you would need to sell a sufficient number of units of state 1 contingent income; if you sell $(m_1 - c_1)$ units it would yield $p_1(m_1 - c_1)$ in revenue. So you require $p_1(m_1 - c_1) = p_2(c_2 - m_2)$, which yields the budget constraint (23.1). Notice that plotted in (c_1, c_2) space, this is a straight line with slope $-p_1/p_2$ which passes through the initial income point (m_1, m_2). This all looks very familiar. Indeed it is very familiar; state contingent income is a commodity just like any other, except that it yields a payoff in only one state of the world.

23.3 A Fair Insurance Market

An insurance market is simply a market for buying and selling state contingent income. The prices of state contingent income obviously have some connection with the probability of that state occurring. For example if state 1 is very likely to occur, then the price of state 1 contingent income should be high, as there is a high chance of a payoff. Conversely if state 1 is very unlikely to occur, the price of state 1 contingent income should be low as there is a low chance of a payoff.

Let us see what the price should be in a particular type of insurance market – one we term a *fair* insurance market. What we mean is that, whether you are buying or selling state contingent income, you expect to break even on average. Some of the time you are paying out money and some of the time you are receiving money. It is fair if, on average, the amount you pay out equals the amount you receive.

Consider state 1 contingent income. A unit of this costs p_1. If state 1 actually does occur, each unit brings in one unit of money. If state 1 does not occur, each unit brings in nothing. These two events happen with probability π_1 and π_2 respectively. Thus a proportion π_1 of the time, one unit of state 1 contingent income brings in one unit of money; while a proportion π_2 of the time it brings in nothing. On average it brings in $(\pi_1 \times 1) + (\pi_2 \times 0) = \pi_1$ in money. For it to be fair this should equal the price of state 1 contingent income, which gives us the condition (23.2) for fair state 1 contingent income, or for fair insurance:

$$p_1 = \pi_1 \tag{23.2}$$

Similarly for state 2 contingent income:

$$p_2 = \pi_2 \tag{23.3}$$

For it to be a fair insurance market, the price for one unit of state contingent income should be equal to the probability of that state occurring. For a state that happens with probability 0.5, for example, the fair price for one unit of income contingent on that state should be $\frac{1}{2}$. Half the time it pays out one and half the time it pays out nothing; on average it pays out $\frac{1}{2}$ – hence its fair price.

The implication of a fair insurance market is that the insurance company breaks even on average; the premiums it receives are exactly equal to the claims it pays out. You may regard this as a bit unrealistic when you look at the profits that insurance companies make in practice, but you should note that a large part of an insurance company's business is in investing the premiums it receives; remember that it receives the premiums before it pays out any claims, and in the meantime it invests the premiums. Indeed it is not far from the truth to say that insurance companies make virtually all their profits from investment, and virtually none from insurance itself. If the market for insurance is fair, then they make no profits from insurance.

One implication of a fair market, in which insurance companies make zero profits from insurance itself, is that the insurance business is a simple redistribution. Those people who are lucky, in that they do not need to make any claims, pay through their premiums for those people who are unlucky and need to claim. Of course individuals could do some of this re-distribution themselves through time, but most prefer the insurance market to do it for them. The insurance market simply re-distributes the risk.

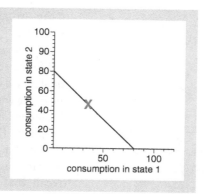

Figure 23.1 Choice under risk: budget constraint with prices 0.5 and 0.5

We present in Fig. 23.1 an example in which the two states of the world are equally likely, and in which we have fair insurance so that $p_1 = p_2 = 0.5$. In this example, the individual starts off with an income of 30 if state 1 occurs and 50 if state 2 occurs. The 'X' indicates the *ex ante* endowment point; note that the budget constraint must pass through this point. The budget constraint in this example has slope equal to -1. More generally it has slope of $-p_1/p_2$, or in a fair market $-\pi_1/\pi_2$ where π_1 and π_2 are the probabilities of states 1 and 2 respectively.

23.4 Preferences

Now let us think about preferences. First, one very important thing should be noticed. The space in which we are working is as follows: on the horizontal axis is the income/consumption (we assume these are the same) that the individual would have if state 1 occurred; and on the vertical axis is the income/consumption that the individual would have if state 2 occurred. *Ex ante*, the individual does not know which will occur; *ex post*, only one has occured. The individual will only get one of the two incomes, not both. This is a crucial difference compared to all our previous analyses. In the latter the individual received both goods on the two axes; in this chapter (and the following two) the individual receives only one of them. He or she has to decide in advance, before knowing which state will occur, on a point in this space. Then Nature will decide whether he or she gets the amount on the vertical axis or on the horizontal axis.

Someone who does not like *ex ante* risk will try and make the two possible incomes as close to each other as possible, so that whatever happens the income received is almost the same. Someone who likes risk may wish to gamble a bit. But, whatever the attitude to risk, we can represent the individual's preferences towards risk in this quantity space in the normal way, by using indifference curves. One thing we can say right away is that, if the individual is risk averse – that is, if he or she has an aversion to risk (a concept which we shall define more carefully shortly) – then his or her indifference curves must be convex. Why? Because the individual will want more and more compensation in terms of state 2 income for giving up units of state 1 income. Also we can say that the shape of the indifference curves will depend upon the two probabilities; if, for example, the probability of state 2 occurring is low, the individual would require higher compensation in terms of state 2 income for giving up state 1 income than if the probability of state 2 occurring is high. We will give more specific examples in the next chapter, but let us give one example here.

We start with a case where the individual is risk-averse and in which both probabilities are equal to 0.5; that is, the two states are equally likely. It seems reasonable in this case that the preferences are symmetric, as shown in Fig. 23.2. In this figure, the 45 degree line is the certainty line; along this the individual would receive the same income whichever of the two alternative states of the world occurred.

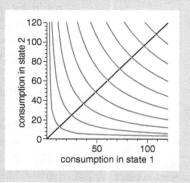

Figure 23.2   Risk-averse individual with probabilities 0.5 and 0.5

We have argued that, if the individual is risk-averse, he or she will have convex indifference curves in this space. Working the other way, we see from Fig. 23.2 that this individual prefers the point (50, 50) to the points (25, 75) and (0, 100), despite the fact that all three of these points have the same expected income – namely 50 (recall that the two states are equally likely). So the individual with the above preferences strictly prefers the certainty of 50 to any risky prospect with an expected income of 50. This is presumably what we mean by a risk-averse person.

What about a risk-neutral person? By this we presumably mean someone who simply ignores risk; it does not affect his or her preferences. Such a person cares only about the expected income from some point and does not worry about the risk. Can we specify such a person's indifference curves? Well, given some point (c_1, c_2) in this space, the expected consumption/income is $(\pi_1 c_1 + \pi_2 c_2)$.

The respective probabilities are π_1 and π_2, because the consumption/income is c_1 a proportion π_1 of the time, and the consumption/income is c_2 a proportion π_2 of the time. For a risk-neutral individual his or her utility (as we have just argued) is determined solely by the expected consumption/income, so an indifference curve for him or her is given by Eq. (23.4).

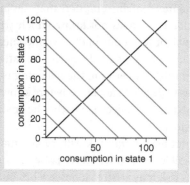

Figure 23.3   Risk-neutral individual with probabilities 0.5 and 0.5

$$\pi_1 c_1 + \pi_2 c_2 = \text{constant} \qquad (23.4)$$

This indifference curve is a straight line in (c_1, c_2) space with slope equal to $-\pi_1/\pi_2$. In the case of equally-likely states of the world, we get the indifference map for a risk-neutral individual shown in Fig. 23.3.

By comparison, for a risk-neutral individual when $\pi_1 = 0.4$ and $\pi_2 = 0.6$, we

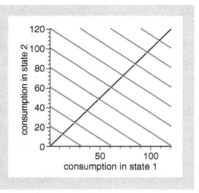

Figure 23.4   Risk-neutral individual with probabilities 0.4 and 0.6

have the situation shown in Fig. 23.4; note that the slope of the indifference curves depends upon the probabilities.

You should now be able to work out that someone who likes risk – a risk-lover – will have indifference curves that are concave; so for example, with equal probabilities such a person will strictly prefer $(100, 0)$ to $(50, 50)$, even though these two points have the same expected income 50. Accordingly we get the following nice result.

> In (c_1, c_2) space the indifference curves are convex, linear or concave according as to whether the individual is risk-averse, risk-neutral or risk-loving.

23.5 Optimal Choice

Apart from the interpretation, the analysis that we are doing should be familiar. Indeed we can find the optimal decision and see how it changes when the prices and the incomes change in the usual way. But there is one result which is of particular interest, and one which we shall explore in more detail and greater generality in Chapter 24; that concerns the amount of insurance that a risk-averse person buys. We consider here only the symmetric case as I need to appeal to your intuition, but we shall consider the more general case under a specific assumption about preferences in Chapter 24. I am assuming in what follows that the two states are equally likely, and therefore both have probabilities equal to 0.5.

It was asserted earlier that in the case of equal probabilities – both states being equally likely – then the indifference map should be symmetrical; therefore the case of a risk-averter should look like Fig. 23.2. The reason why intuition suggests symmetry is simply that there is no reason to treat the two states of the world any differently, given that they are equally likely. One particular implication of the assumption of symmetry concerns the slope of the indifference curves along the line $c_1 = c_2$, as drawn in Fig. 23.2. We rather naturally call this line the *certainty line*; along it the consumption/income of the individual is the same irrespective of which state of the world occurs. If the individual chooses to locate along that line, then we can say that he or she has chosen a position of *ex ante* certainty. In other words, he or she has chosen to be completely insured in the sense that the actual state of the world is irrelevant. Given our assumption of the symmetry of the indifference map, it follows that the slope of each indifference curve at any point on the certainty line must equal -1.

Let us now consider the optimal insurance decision of this individual if faced with fair insurance. This means that the prices are equal to the probabilities, and hence are both equal to 0.5, so the budget constraint has slope $-0.5/0.5 = -1$. We illustrate this in Fig. 23.5.

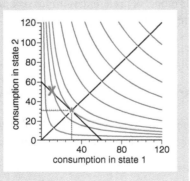

Figure 23.5   Optimal choice for a risk-averse individual with probabilities 0.5 and 0.5

The initial point is (30, 50); without insurance the individual would receive consumption/income equal to 30 if state 1 occurred and 50 if state 2 occurred. The optimal point is, as ever, the point on the budget constraint (the line through the original point X), on the highest possible indifference curve; we have indicated it with an asterisk.

We see that the optimal point is on the certainty line! It is there because the slope of the budget constraint is −1, which equals the slope of the indifference curves along the certainty line. So the individual chooses to be fully insured. *Ex ante*, the individual buys 10 units of state 1 contingent income and sells 10 units of state 2 contingent income, therefore moving from (30, 50) to (40, 40). Whichever state of the world occurs, the insured will receive consumption/income of 40; if state 1 occurs he or she will receive the income of 30 plus the income from the 10 units of state 1 contingent income purchased; if state 2 occurs he or she will get the income of 50 minus the cost of the 10 units of state 2 contingent income which were sold. If you like you can think of this as an insurance against state 1, the state in which the individual gets a low income. If this bad state occurs, because he or she gets a low income the insurance company pays 10; if the bad state does not occur, the individual pays 10 to the company.

Is this surprising? In a sense not, because we have assumed that the individual is risk averse and we have assumed fair insurance. And what does fair insurance do? It offers the chance to reduce the riskiness of future income without changing the expected income; and a risk-averse person, effectively by definition, will always prefer a less risky to a more risky prospect with the same expected value. But the result is nevertheless interesting.

The above discussion assumed fair insurance. What happens if we do not have fair insurance? Suppose we have more-than-fair insurance in the sense that $p_1 < \pi_1$. Consider Fig. 23.6, in which $p_1 = 0.2$. What does the individual do?

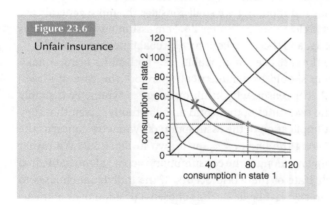

The individual will move from the initial point to the point marked by an asterisk point (77, 31), buying some 47 units of state 1 contingent income and selling some 19 units of state 2 contingent income. In the new position the individual will have an expected income of 54 – considerably above the initial expected income of 40. So this individual, despite being risk-averse, chooses to bet on state 1 happening and increases his expected income because he or she has been offered more-than-fair insurance. You might like to reflect what he or she would do if offered less-than-fair insurance for state 1; that is, a price $p_1 > \pi_1$.

We shall explore more of the implications of insurance markets in Chapter 24 where we introduce a particular model of preferences under risk. In the meantime you could consider what happens to the optimal decision if p_2 or either of the *ex ante* incomes m_1 and m_2 change.

23.6 Expected Values

We should formalize some definitions. If a variable X takes values x_1 and x_2 with probabilities π_1 and π_2 respectively, the expected value of X is given by

Expected value of $X = \pi_1 x_1 + \pi_2 x_2$ (23.5)

This is just a weighted average of the possible values of X weighted by the probabilities. It is called an expected value because, if we were to observe X a large number of times and calculate the average, this is the value we would expect x to take. We can generalize; if a variable X takes values $x_1, x_2, ..., x_i, ..., x_I$ with probabilities $\pi_1, \pi_2, ..., \pi_i, ..., \pi_I$ respectively, then the expected value of X is given by

$$\text{Expected value of } X = \pi_1 x_1 + \pi_2 x_2 + \cdots + \pi_i x_i + \cdots + \pi_I x_I \tag{23.6}$$

Once again, we take a weighted average of the possible values of X weighted by the probabilities.

23.7 Unfair Insurance

In this chapter we have assumed what we have called a perfect or fair market, where $p_1 = \pi_1$ and $p_2 = \pi_2$. An unfair market is one in which, if you want to buy state 1 income, the price at $p_1 > \pi_1$ is too high; and where, if you want to buy state 2 income, $p_2 > \pi_2$ is also too high. Notice what this does; it induces a kink in the budget constraint at the initial endowment point. Does this remind you of something?

23.8 Summary

We have looked at choice under risk where individuals do not know *ex ante* what is going to happen but can attach probabilities to the various possible outcomes.

We have argued that an insurance market enables the buying and selling of risk, and it does this through the buying and selling of state contingent income. One unit of income conditional on some state pays one unit of money if that state occurs, and pays nothing otherwise.

 We saw that, in a fair insurance market, the price of state contingent income should equal the probability of that state occurring.

As far as preferences were concerned we showed the following.

 An individual has convex, linear or concave indifference curves according to whether he or she is risk-averse, risk-neutral or risk-loving.

23.9 Review Questions

1 Suppose you take out insurance against the risk of your house burning down. If we define state 1 as the state in which your house does burn down and state 2 as the state in which your house does not burn down, and we suppose that the insurance premium is £100 per year and that the value of your house is £100,000, interpret the insurance contract as a contract involving state-contingent payments. (You pay so much to the insurance company if state 2 happens, and the insurance company pays you so much if state 1 happens.)

2 If the above premium is fair, calculate the probability of your house burning down.

3 Discuss the possibility that, if you are fully insured you have less incentive to take precautions against fire, and therefore that the true probability is more than the one that the insurance company used to calculate the fair premium.

4 In the light of the above, explain why insurance companies often charge lower premiums for fire insurance if you take precautions (such as installing smoke-detectors)?

5 Why are insurance premiums for young people more than those for middle-aged people?

The Expected Utility Model

24.1 Introduction

In this chapter we introduce an empirically-relevant model of preferences for representing behaviour under conditions of risk – the expected utility model. Like the discounted utility model which we used to describe intertemporal preferences, this model is not only a good empirical approximation to reality, but it also has compelling normative properties. These, as with the discounted utility model, refer to the consistency of the behaviour of an individual with such preferences, and to the potential inconsistency of the behaviour of individuals with preferences that do not satisfy the model.

We can easily illustrate the point with a discussion of a key axiom of the theory, known as the independence axiom. Let C and D be risky choices, and suppose we have an individual who prefers C to D. Let E be any other risky choice. The independence axiom states that he or she should also prefer the gamble (call it G) which yields C with a probability p and E with a probability $(1 - p)$, to another gamble (call it H) which yields D with a probability p and E with probability $(1 - p)$. Why? Because under G the individual gets either C or E, and with H the individual gets either D or E. Now it has been assumed that the individual prefers C to D – so he or she should prefer G to H. Depending on which is chosen, the person gets either C or D (and he or she prefers the first of these) or gets E (whichever was chosen). Does this seem reasonable? Why is it a criterion of consistency? Take for simplicity $p = 0.5$, and suppose that the G and H gambles are played out by tossing a fair coin; if it lands heads, our individual gets C or D depending on which of G and H he or she has chosen; and if it lands tails, he or she gets E.

Now consider an individual who does not obey the independence axiom and says that, while preferring C to D, H is preferred to G. He or she starts out preferring H to G and hence choosing H. Suppose we now toss the coin and it lands heads. Our individual now has D – which he or she prefers to C – but he or she would have had C if G had been chosen. At this point the individual would want to change the decision. The violation of the independence axiom implies a sort of built-in inconsistency in the preferences.

24.2 The Expected Utility Model

This is used to describe preferences under risk. We recall the decision situation and the notation from Chapter 23. We are considering a situation of risk in which the decision maker does not know *ex ante* which state of the world will occur. However he or she can list the various possibilities and can attach probabilities to them. For simplicity we assume two possible states of the world, state 1 and state 2, with respective probabilities π_1 and π_2. *Ex ante*, when choosing between various outcomes the decision maker does not know which of these states will occur. *Ex post*, one and only one of the states will occur.

We denote by c_1 the individual's consumption/income (we use these terms interchangeably) if state of the world 1 occurs, and by c_2 the individual's consumption/income if state of the world 2 occurs. The individual must choose *ex ante* between various uncertain bundles (c_1, c_2). *Ex post*, the individual gets one of c_1 or c_2 depending upon which state of the world has occurred. We want to describe preferences over *ex ante* risky consumption bundles (c_1, c_2). The expected utility model is specified as follows[1].

$$U(c_1, c_2) = \pi_1 u(c_1) + \pi_2 u(c_2) \tag{24.1}$$

The probabilities are given by the problem, so the only element that needs to be specified is the function $u(.)$. This is sometimes known as the Neumann–Morgenstern utility function, after a mathematician (von Neumann) and an economist (Morgenstern) who refined the theory. Given the function $u(.)$, which tells how much utility is obtained from some amount of consumption, the explanation of Eq. (24.1) is clear: with probability π_1, state 1 happens and the individual consumes c_1 from which he or she obtains utility $u(c_1)$; with probability π_2, state 2 happens and the individual consumes c_2 from which he or she obtains utility $u(c_2)$. So if we consider the utility that an individual expects to get from the *ex ante* risky bundle (c_1, c_2), it is clear that this is given by the right-hand side of Eq. (24.1). It seems reasonable to suppose that individuals choose between risky bundles on the basis of the utility that they expect to get from them; if they expect to get more utility from one bundle than from another, they should choose the first bundle rather than the second.

24.3 Indifference Curves with the Expected Utility Model

We have now specified the expected utility model; in the next section we explore its implications. But first, since we are going to use the framework for analysis developed in Chapter 23, we need to look at the properties of the indifference curves in (c_1, c_2) space implied by this model. To derive this result we need a little mathematics, which is provided in the mathematical appendix to this chapter. We start with the slope of an indifference curve.

$$\text{slope} = -\pi_1 \, du(c_1)/dc_1 [\pi_2 \, du(c_2)/dc_2] \tag{24.2}$$

In Eq. (24.2), $du(c)/dc$ indicates the slope of the function $u(c)$. The slope of an indifference curve is negative, so the indifference curves are downward sloping. Moreover if u is concave

---

1. It can be derived formally from a set of axioms which crucially include the independence axiom. A sketch of the proof is provided in the mathematical appendix to this chapter.

then, as we move down and rightwards along an indifference curve, c_1 is rising while c_2 is falling; hence $du(c_1)/dc_1$ is falling while $du(c_2)/dc_2$ is rising, and so the magnitude of the slope dc_2/dc_1 is falling. From this it follows that, if u is concave, then the indifference curves are convex. However if u is linear then both $du(c_1)/dc_1$ and $du(c_2)/dc_2$ are constant, and so the slope of the indifference curves are constant; that is they are linear. If we continue this line of argument with a convex function u, we get the following result.

If u is concave, linear or convex, then the indifference curves in (c_1, c_2) space are convex, linear or concave.

One final result is of particular importance. If we put $c_1 = c_2$ in Eq. (24.2), we get the slope of an indifference curve that is $-\pi_1/\pi_2$. Calling the line $c_1 = c_2$ the certainty line, we get the following important result.

Along the certainty line the slope of every indifference curve of an individual with expected utility model preferences is equal to $-\pi_1/\pi_2$.

We connect the result above – that the utility function u is concave, linear or convex according to whether the indifference curves are convex, linear or concave – with our interpretation in Chapter 23 of convex, linear and concave indifference curves. In Chapter 23, those were stated as representing persons who were risk-averse, risk-neutral and risk-loving respectively. It follows therefore that an individual with a concave, linear or convex utility function must be risk-averse, risk-neutral or risk-loving. We shall check this out in the next section.

24.4 Risk Aversion and Risk Premia

Consider an individual with a concave utility function u as drawn in Fig. 24.1. For those of you who wish to verify the detail algebraically, you might like to know that the utility function used here is given by

$$u(c) = (1 - e^{-0.03c})/(1 - e^{-3.3})$$

(24.3)

This is an example of what we call in Section 24.5 a *constant absolute risk averse utility function*. You do not need to use algebra, however, as all the information necessary is contained in Fig. 24.1.

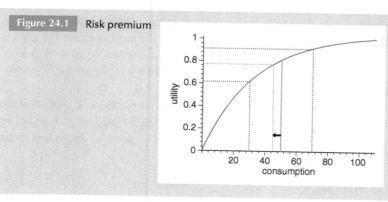

Figure 24.1   Risk premium

Suppose this individual is offered a 50 : 50 gamble between 30 and 70; that is, with probability 0.5 the individual will receive 30 and with probability 0.5 he or she will receive 70. How does this individual evaluate this risky bundle? We could say that the expected income from the risky bundle is 50 but we know that, if the individual has expected utility preferences, the evaluation is on the basis of expected utility rather than expected income. Now we know the utility function so we can calculate the expected utility of the risky prospect (30, 50). Consuming 30 gives utility approximately equal to 0.616, while consuming 70 gives utility approximately equal to 0.912. So this risky prospect gives utility 0.616 with probability 0.5 and utility 0.912 with probability 0.5. Hence the expected utility from this prospect is $(\frac{1}{2} \times 0.616 + \frac{1}{2} \times 0.912) = 0.764$. The three horizontal lines in Fig. 24.1 give these utilities: the bottom line is the utility of 30, the top line the utility of 70, and the middle line is the expected utility of the risky prospect (it is in the middle in this example because the two possibilities are equally likely).

Now we define the *certainty equivalent* of the risky prospect as the amount of money which, if received with certainty, the individual regards as equivalent to the risky prospect. Using our model of expected utility, the individual regards a sum of money as equivalent to a risky prospect if it gives the same expected utility as the prospect. Now obviously the expected utility of a certain amount is simply equal to the utility of that amount. So the certainty equivalent of the 50 : 50 risky prospect which gives 30 or 70, each with equal probability, is given by the following expression where *ce* denotes the certainty equivalent.

$$u(ce) = 0.5 \times u(30) + 0.5 \times u(70) = 0.764 \qquad (24.4)$$

From Fig. 24.1 we see that *ce* is approximately equal to 44.5, because the utility of 44.5 is 0.764. You will notice that the certainty equivalent of the risky prospect is less than the expected income from the risky prospect. This individual regards the risky prospect as being equivalent to having 44.5 with certainty, and regards having 50 with certainty as being preferable to having the risky prospect; the individual is clearly risk averse.

We now define another concept – the *risk premium* which the individual is willing to pay. This is defined as the difference between the certainty equivalent of the risky prospect and the expected income from the risky prospect. If we look at Fig. 24.1 we see that this risk premium is the distance indicated by an arrow. It is the difference between 50 (the expected income from the prospect) and 44.5 (the certainty equivalent of the prospect), which is 5.5. The vertical lines in Fig. 24.1 show these various monetary amounts; the left and right hand vertical lines are the two possible outcomes of the prospect; the line in the middle is the expected outcome of, or income from, the prospect; it is in the middle in this example because the two possible outcomes are equally likely. The line to the left of it is the certainty equivalent of the prospect. The difference indicated with an arrow is the risk premium.

What is the interpretation of this risk premium? If we took the risk away from the risky prospect we would have a certain return of 50 – the expected income from the prospect. So the risk premium is the maximum amount which the individual would pay to have the risk taken away from the prospect. It tells us how much, at most, the individual would pay to have certainty rather than risk. As you might anticipate, the risk premium depends upon the risky prospect itself and on the shape of the utility function. We will later show that it depends in particular on the concavity of the utility function; the more concave the greater the risk premium, and hence the more risk averse the individual. We shall study this in more detail shortly, but in the meantime let us generalize our definitions of the certainty equivalent and the risk premium.

Let us consider a general risky prospect (c_1, c_2) where the probability of c_1 is π_1 and the probability of c_2 is π_2. The certainty equivalent of this prospect, denoted by *ce*, is as before the amount of money received with certainty that the individual regards as equivalent to the risky prospect. It is given by Eq. (24.5).

$$u(ce) = \pi_1 u(c_1) + \pi_2 u(c_2) \qquad (24.5)$$

You need to be clear about this. It means that, if the individual is offered a choice between *ce* for sure and the risky prospect, he or she would claim to be indifferent, not minding which option he or she has or even whether someone else makes the choice. Furthermore, if offered a choice between some amount greater than *ce* for sure and the risky prospect our individual would take the certain amount; and if offered a choice between some amount less than *ce* for sure and the risky prospect, he or she would take the risky prospect.

The risk premium, denoted by *rp*, is defined in general in Eq. (24.6).

$$rp = (\pi_1 c_1 + \pi_2 c_2) - ce \tag{24.6}$$

In Eq. (24.6) *ce* is the certainty equivalent of the prospect as defined in Eq. (24.5). It is the difference between the expected income from the prospect and the certainty equivalent of the prospect. The risk premium is the maximum amount of money that the individual would pay to get rid of the riskiness of the prospect, and have it replaced by a certainty equal to its expected value.

In the next section we shall examine some particular utility functions, but in the meantime we note that the utility function which represents a particular set of preferences under risk is not unique. Indeed it can be shown that, if any function represents a set of preferences under risk, then so does any other function which is an arbitrary increasing linear transformation of that function. The reason is that if function *v* is an increasing linear function of function *u*, the expected value of *v* is the same linear function of the expected value of *u*. Specifically, if *u* represents the preferences of the individual, then so does *v* where *v* is defined by *v = a + bu*, *a* and *b* being arbitrary numbers though *b* must be positive. If the expected value of *u* represents preferences, then so does the expected value of *v*; if the expected value of *u* is higher with one gamble, then so must be the expected value of *v*. This means that the scale of the utility function is arbitrary[2].

24.5 Constant Absolute Risk Aversion

One popular, and empirically reasonable, utility function is that known as the *constant absolute risk aversion function*. It is given[3] by the following expression.

$$u(c) \text{ proportional to } - \exp(-rc) \tag{24.7}$$

In Eq. (24.7) *c* is the argument in the utility function; see Eq. (24.3). There is one parameter here – the parameter *r* – which is referred to as the *index of absolute risk aversion*. If *r* is positive the function (24.7) is concave and the individual is risk-averse; the greater the value of *r*, the greater the degree of concavity and the more risk averse is the individual. In the example at the beginning of Section 24.4, we used such a function with *r = 0.03*.

Why is it called the constant absolute risk aversion function? Because the risk premium that the individual is willing to pay is independent of the level of the prospect. For instance, taking the example we have already discussed and portrayed in Fig. 24.1, this function is of the constant absolute risk aversion form with the parameter *r* equal to 0.03. We have already calculated that an individual with this function, faced with the 50 : 50 prospect

2. If this worries you, think of temperature. Its scale is arbitrary; if you are told that the temperature is 80, that means nothing until you know what scale is being used; but we use temperatures all the time.
3. The words 'proportional to' simply reflect the fact that the scale is arbitrary.

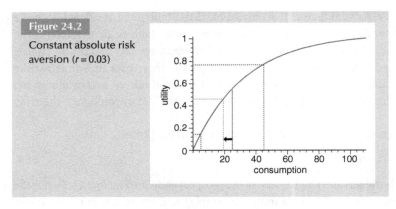

Figure 24.2

Constant absolute risk aversion (r = 0.03)

(30, 70), would pay a risk premium of 5.5. Now, consider the same individual faced with the 50 : 50 prospect (5, 45). How much would he or she pay as risk premium? Fig. 24.2 shows the answer: 5.5!

The same is true for the 50 : 50 prospect (55, 95). So this individual's risk premium for the 50 : 50 prospect (5, 45) is 5.5; for the 50 : 50 prospect (30, 70) it is 5.5; for the 50 : 50 prospect (55, 95) it is 5.5. And what is the difference between these three prospects? The expected income from the prospect is 25 or 50 or 75. But note very carefully that the riskiness of the prospects does not change; the two outcomes are always −20 or +20 with respect to the expected income. So the riskiness of these three prospects is the same, and that is why the risk premium for someone with constant absolute risk aversion remains unchanged.

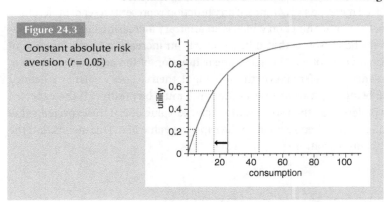

Figure 24.3

Constant absolute risk aversion (r = 0.05)

However if the riskiness of the prospect increases then the risk premium also increases. The risk premium is also larger for an individual with a more concave utility function, that is, one with a higher value of the parameter r. This can be seen clearly in Fig. 24.3, which shows the risk premium that an individual with r = 0.5 would be willing to pay for the 50 : 50 prospect (30, 70). You should compare this figure with Fig. 24.2.

24.6 Risk Neutrality

Risk neutrality is an important special case. In this the utility function u is linear. The risk premium is zero as the certainty equivalent of any risky prospect is equal to the expected income from the prospect. It is pictured in Fig. 24.4.

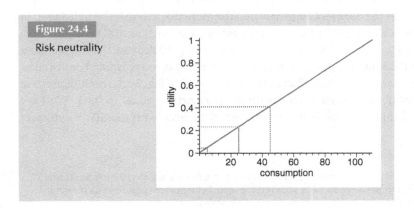

Figure 24.4

Risk neutrality

24.7 Constant Absolute Risk Loving

Here we have the function

$$u(c) \text{ proportional to } \exp(rc) \tag{24.8}$$

There is again one parameter – the parameter r – which is referred to as the *index of absolute risk loving*. If r is positive the function (24.8) is convex and the individual is risk-loving; the greater the value of r, the greater the degree of convexity and the more risk loving is the individual.

We can again define the certainty equivalent of any given risky prospect. For a risk-loving individual the certainty equivalent is greater than the expected income from the prospect. Fig. 24.5 illustrates this for the case when $r = 0.03$. Here the certainty equivalent of the 50 : 50 prospect *(30, 70)* is 53.5. We can, once again, define the risk premium as the difference between this and the expected income from the prospect; however in the case of a risk-lover, it is the minimum amount that he or she would be prepared pay to keep the risky prospect rather than have it replaced by the certainty of its expected value.

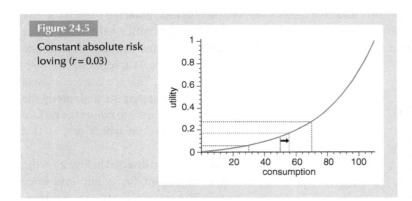

Figure 24.5

Constant absolute risk loving ($r = 0.03$)

If the function becomes more convex, the individual becomes more risk-loving and the risk premium rises; the individual is willing to pay more for the risk.

24.8 Constant Relative Risk Aversion and Loving

Some empirical evidence suggests that, for some individuals, their risk premium depends upon the level of their expected income; so the risk premium declines as the expected income rises. For such individuals the constant absolute risk averse utility function is not appropriate, and a better one may be the *constant relative risk aversion utility function*. This is specified as follows.

$$u(c) \text{ proportional to } c^{1-r} \tag{24.9}$$

Once again the parameter r indicates the level of risk-aversion or loving, and c is the argument of the utility function. If r takes the value zero, then u is linear and we have the risk-neutral case. If r is between zero and one, then the exponent of c in Eq. (24.9) is also between zero and one so that the function is concave and we have a risk-averse individual. Furthermore the closer is r to zero, the more concave is the function and the more risk-averse is the individual. If r is negative, the exponent of c in Eq. (24.9) is greater than one, so the function is convex and we have a risk-loving individual; furthermore the more negative is r, the more risk-loving the individual.

This utility function has a nice property. Let us denote by (x, y) a risky prospect which pays x with probability 0.5 and pays y with probability 0.5. Then with this utility function, the risk premium for *(5, 45)* is less than the risk premium for *(30, 70)*, which is less than the risk premium for *(55, 95)*. More generally the risk premium for *(a − b, a + b)* declines as *a* increases with *b* remaining constant.

You may be wondering why it is called the constant relative risk aversion function. This is because the risk premium for *[s(a − b), s(a + b)]* is proportional to the scale *s*. For example, the risk premium for *(15, 35)* is twice that for *(30, 70)* and three times that for *(45, 105)*.

24.9   Optimal Behaviour for an Individual with Expected Utility Preferences

We are now ready to work out what various individuals will do. Consider an example in which the two states of the world are equally likely and where the individual starts at the point *(30, 50)*; that is, without insurance the individual will get consumption/income of 30 if state 1 occurs, and consumption/income of 50 if state 2 occurs. This is the point marked X in Fig. 24.6 (and Figs. 26.7 and 26.8). Let us suppose that the individual has expected utility preferences and a constant absolute risk aversion utility function with *r = 0.03*. His or her indifference curves in (c_1, c_2) space are given in Fig. 24.6. Note that the slope of each and every indifference curve along the certainty line is −1. This is a consequence of the general result that the slope along the certainty line is equal to minus the ratio of the two probabilities which are, in this case, equal.

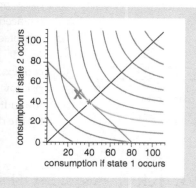

Figure 24.6   Optimal choice for a risk averter *(r = 0.03)*

We have also inserted in Fig. 24.6 the budget constraint for a fair insurance market. The prices of the two state contingent incomes are both $\frac{1}{2}$, so the budget constraint has a slope −1. It immediately follows that the optimal point lies on the certainty line at the point *(40, 40)* where the individual buys 10 units of state 1 contingent income and sells 10 units of state 2 contingent income. This is the point indicated by an asterisk in Fig. 24.6. Whichever state occurs, the individual ends up with 40 units of consumption/income; he or she chooses to be completely insured.

This must be true for any individual with expected utility preferences, as we know that the slope of each and every indifference curve along the certainty line is equal to $-\pi_1/\pi_2$, and we know that the fair insurance line has the same slope. For example, with $\pi_1 = 0.4$ and $\pi_2 = 0.6$ we have Fig. 24.7.

What about a risk-neutral individual? Well, we know that his or her indifference curves are parallel straight lines all with the slope $-\pi_1/\pi_2$, which is equal to the slope of the fair budget line. So we have Fig. 24.8 for the case of equal probabilities. The budget constraint coincides with an indifference curve, and the individual is therefore indifferent between all the

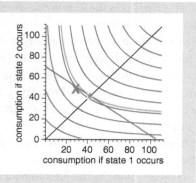

Figure 24.7   Optimal choice for a risk averter *($\pi_1 = 0.4, \pi_2 = 0.6$)*

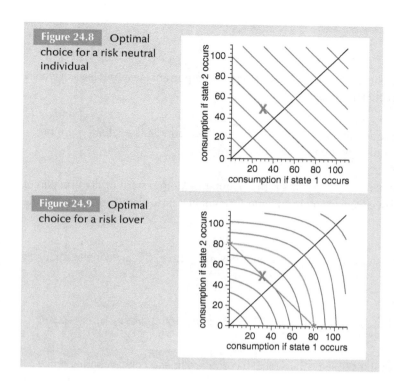

Figure 24.8 Optimal choice for a risk neutral individual

Figure 24.9 Optimal choice for a risk lover

points along it. Offered fair insurance, which changes the riskiness but not the expected income of his consumption/income, the risk-neutral individual is indifferent because he or she is indifferent to the risk.

What about a risk-loving individual? He or she has concave indifference curves, so his or her position is as in Fig. 24.9 for the equal probabilities case. The optimal point (the highest attainable indifference curve consistent with the budget constraint) is either at *(80, 0)* or at *(0, 80)*. The individual gambles either on state 1 happening or on state 2 happening. He or she uses the insurance market to do exactly the opposite of what you might think an insurance market is meant to do[4] – to create a riskier prospect which he or she prefers to the safer prospect.

---

4. In fact, many insurance companies ban this kind of deal, the reason being that the individual now has a strong incentive to try and change the probabilities of the two states.

24.10   Summary

This chapter has been a little difficult but it contains some important ideas, not least of which is the definition of expected utility preferences.

 The expected utility model postulates that an ex ante risky bundle is evaluated on the basis of the expected utility of the various outcomes.

A key component of these preferences is the Neumann–Morgenstern utility function of the individual defined over consumption/income. This enables us to identify the risk attitude of the individual.

 A risk-averse, risk-neutral, risk-loving individual has a concave, linear, convex utility function.

 From this we worked out the form of the individual's indifference curves in (c_1, c_2) space.

 A risk-averse, risk-neutral, risk-loving individual has convex, linear, concave indifference curves.

We introduced the important concepts of the certainty equivalence of a risky prospect and the risk premium.

 The certainty equivalent of a risky prospect is the amount of money received with certainty that the individual regards as equivalent to the risky prospect. The risk premium is the maximum amount of money that the individual would pay to exchange the risky prospect for a certainty with the same expected income.

As far as optimal insurance behaviour is concerned, we found some interesting results.

 Risk-averse individuals always choose to be fully insured in a fair market, while risk-neutral agents are indifferent and risk-loving agents use the market to take a risky gamble.

We also introduced two important special cases of Neumann–Morgenstern utility functions.

 The absolute risk premium paid by individuals with constant absolute risk averse utility functions is independent of the level of the risky prospect (adding a constant to all the outcomes does not change the risk premium).

 The relative risk premium paid by individuals with constant relative risk averse utility functions is independent of the scale of the risky prospect (multiplying by a constant all the outcomes multiplies the risk premium by the same constant).

24.10 Review Questions

1. Why does a risk-averter always choose to be fully insured if offered fair insurance?

2. How risk-averse are you? (See the next section).

3. Explain why it seems reasonable to obey the independence axiom of expected utility theory. Does your behaviour satisfy the theory?

4. Explain why an individual, who prefers the choice of a certain £300 to a gamble with an 80 per cent chance of £400 and a 20 per cent chance of £0, should also prefer a gamble with a 25 per cent chance of £300 and a 75 per cent chance of £0 to a gamble with a 20 per cent chance of £400 and an 80 per cent chance of £0. Is this true for you?

5. Suppose we know that an individual's utility function is such that $u(0) = 0$, $u(£100) = 0.5$, $u(£200) = 0.75$, $u(£300) = 0.875$ and $u(£400) = 1$. Predict what this individual would choose in the two choice problems of question (4).

6. Do you think that you are either constant absolute risk averse or constant relative risk averse?

24.12 Application: how Risk-averse are You?

Every year, either in Bari or York or both, depending on how I am feeling, I auction off to my students the right to play once with me the following game. 'You toss a fair coin once; if it comes down heads, I will give you £100; if it comes down tails; I will not give you anything.' I usually do a straightforward English-type auction. I start off at a price of £0 and ask all those who would be willing to pay that price to play the game with me to raise their hands. I then progressively raise the price and tell the students to put their hands down when the price gets to the maximum that they are willing to pay to play the game. I tell them that the last person who has his or her hand up will play the game with me, and that person has to pay the price at which the next-to-the-last person dropped out. I start at £0; usually all the students start with their hands up. By the time that the price has reached £10 quite a few have dropped out; more and more drop out as the price gets higher and higher; by the time it has reached £50 there are usually only a few left. Sometimes the penultimate person drops out at a price of more than £50. The last person in pays this price, and then he or she tosses the coin. If it lands heads I give him or her £100; if it lands tails, I do not give him or her anything; in either case I pocket the price that the individual has paid[5].

Why do I do this? To give the students some feel for how risk-averse they are, and to make them realize that people differ in their aversion to risk. Some are very risk-averse; they drop out of the auction at a very low price. Some are less risk-averse; they stay in somewhat longer. Some are risk-neutral; they stay in until the price gets to £50. Some are risk-loving; they will stay in above a price of £50. Amongst my students the vast majority are risk-averse, some very much so, and very few indeed are risk-loving.

At York, I follow up this auction with a tutorial exercise designed to shed more light on how risk-averse people are. The purpose of the exercise is to get students to discover their utility function for choice under risk – the utility function in the expected utility theory that we have been studying in this chapter. You can do the same; it is an amusing and instructive exercise. It is also a little difficult – not in a technical sense, but in that it asks you to introspect about yourself. This is something that is remarkably difficult to do.

Suppose your preferences concerning risky choice are in accordance with expected utility theory. Then there exists some underlying utility function which can be used to represent your choices in risky situations, in that you will always take that decision which maximizes the expected utility you get from the decision. The purpose of this exercise is to find your function. You should note that these functions are personal; your function represents how you behave. If *people are different*, then these functions are different.

We are going to find your function over some range of money. The method can be used over other arguments, but restricting it to money keeps the exposition simple. Let the range of money be from £0 to £100. Assuming that you prefer more money to less, it follows that having £100 is better than having any amount between £0 and £100 and that, in turn, is better than having £0[6]. In the terms of the mathematical appendix, £100 is the most preferred and £0 the least preferred. We will assign utilities of one and zero to these respectively. So we start with the following.

$$u(£100) = 1$$
$$u(£0) = 0 \tag{24.10}$$

These are two points on your utility function. You could start to draw a graph with money from £0 to £100 along the horizontal axis, and with utility from zero to one on the vertical axis. Insert the two points given by the equations above.

5. If you are interested, I can report that I have always had to pay out £100! Fate is obviously against me.
6. Of course, in addition to your present wealth; something we will take as given from now on.

To find other points on your utility function we use a simple procedure, combined with the expected utility theorem. We know that, if your preferences are in accordance with this theory, your choice is driven by expected utility. We will consider risky choices which have a particularly simple form: two outcomes are possible and they are equally likely. We will denote such a risky choice by (x, y), where the two outcomes are £x and £y. So (x, y) denotes a risky prospect in which the outcome could be £x with probability 0.5 or £y with probability 0.5.

Consider the risky choice *(0, 100)*; there is a 50 : 50 chance you will get £100 and a 50 : 50 chance you get nothing. It is the simple game that I auction off. You should ask yourself: at what price in this auction would you drop out? £10? £20? £23? At what price? This is a crucial introspection. It is not easy to do, but it determines your reservation price for playing the little game with me. At this reservation price you are indifferent between paying that price and playing the game with me, or not playing the game.

Let us denote this reservation price by x_1. Notice crucially that it varies from individual to individual. For you, you are indifferent between £x_1 for sure (for that is what you are giving up if you play the game with me) and the 50 : 50 risky gamble between £0 and £100. It follows therefore that the expected utility of £x_1 for sure must be equal (for you) to the expected utility of the 50 : 50 risky gamble between £0 and £100. The first of these (the expected utility of £x_1 for sure) is tautologically equal to the utility of £x_1, while the second of these (the expected utility of the 50 : 50 risky gamble between £0 and £100) is equal to $0.5u(£0) + 0.5u(£100)$, which is equal to 0.5 by virtue of the fact that we have put $u(£0) = 0$ and $u(£100) = 1$ – see Eq. (24.10). It immediately follows that

$$u(£x_1) = 0.5$$

(24.11)

We have therefore found a third point on your utility function. Insert it in your graph: the amount of money £x_1 for which you are indifferent between it and *(0, 100)* gives you utility 0.5.

To find other points we simply repeat the procedure. For example, to find the amount of money which gives you utility 0.25, we start with a gamble which we know gives you an expected utility 0.25, and ask you to tell us the amount of money which, received with certainty, makes you indifferent to that gamble. What gamble do we know gives you an expected utility 0.25? There are two that we know of; one is the 50 : 50 gamble between nothing and £x_1. Perhaps you would like to think what the other is. So one way to proceed is to ask you: what is the amount of money £x_2 which makes you indifferent between that amount of money and the risky choice $(0, x_1)$? The answer £x_2 is such that $u(£x_2) = 0.25$. This gives you a fourth point on your utility function. Other points can be found in the same way. You should check out the following.

$$\begin{bmatrix} \text{If you are indifferent between £}x_1 \text{ and } (0, 100), & \text{then } u(£x_1) = 0.5 \\ \text{If you are indifferent between £}x_2 \text{ and } (0, x_1), & \text{then } u(£x_2) = 0.25 \\ \text{If you are indifferent between £}x_3 \text{ and } (x_1, 100), & \text{then } u(£x_3) = 0.75 \\ \text{If you are indifferent between £}x_4 \text{ and } (0, x_2), & \text{then } u(£x_4) = 0.125 \end{bmatrix}$$

Clearly you can continue this way indefinitely, and hence build up a more and more accurate picture of your utility function. You should do this, along with your fellow-students, and then compare the functions you have obtained. If your function is linear everywhere, you are risk-neutral everywhere. If it is concave everywhere, you are risk-averse everywhere – the more concave, the more risk-averse. If it is convex everywhere, you are risk-loving everywhere – the more convex, the more risk-loving. Of course, you could have a utility function which is concave in some parts and convex in others – indicating that for certain gambles you are risk-averse whereas for other gambles you are risk-loving.

24.13 Mathematical Appendix

First we provide a sketch of the expected utility theorem. We should emphasize that it is only a sketch and many of the steps are omitted.

This theorem is based on axioms of rational behaviour. If the axioms are true, then so is the theorem. We consider risky gambles whose final outcome is one from a set $A_1, A_2, ..., A_I$ of payoffs. We first assume that the individual whose preferences we are describing can rank these final payoffs from best to worst, and can therefore define the best and the worst. Number the payoffs so that A_1 is the best (the most preferred by the individual), and A_I the worst (the least preferred).

The first axiom (*continuity*) is that for all A_i there is some probability u_i for which the individual is indifferent between A_i and a gamble between the best A_1 and the worst A_I with respective probabilities u_i and $(1 - u_i)$. Note, rather trivially, that u_1 must be one and u_I must be zero. Now define the utility of outcome A_i as u_i.

The second axiom (*dominance*) says that, in any two gambles involving only the best and the worst outcomes, the gamble which has the highest probability of the best outcome (and hence the lowest probability of the worst outcome) is preferred to the other. These first two axioms seem to be reasonable requirements of rational behaviour.

We now come to the key axiom, which we have already discussed in the text: the *Independence axiom*. Let us express it in a slightly different, but equivalent, form. Let C and D be risky choices, and suppose we have an individual who says that he or she is indifferent between C and D. Let E be any other risky choice. The independence axiom then states that he or she should also be indifferent between the gamble (call it G) which yields C with probability p and E with probability $(1 - p)$, and another gamble (call it H) which yields D with probability p and E with probability $(1 - p)$. This axiom is stronger than the first two, but seems to be an empirically reasonable description of much actual behaviour. We need it for the proof of the expected utility theroem. This we now show.

Consider two general gambles: C which yields outcomes $A_1, A_2, ..., A_I$ with probabilities $p_1, p_2, ..., p_I$; and D which yields outcomes $A_1, A_2, ..., A_I$ with probabilities $q_1, q_2, ..., q_I$. Using the independence axiom I times with each of C and D, we can argue that the individual should be indifferent between C and the two-stage gamble in which the outcomes $A_1, A_2, ..., A_I$ are replaced by the gambles between the best and the worst with which they said they were indifferent with the continuity axiom. We can argue the same for D. Now we invoke the reduction of compound gambles axiom, which states that the individual should be indifferent between a two-stage gamble and the equivalent single-stage gamble which results using the reduction of compound probabilities rule. This implies that the individual is indifferent between C and the gamble between the best and the worst, with respective probabilities $(p_1 u_1 + p_2 u_2 + \cdots + p_I u_I)$ and $[1 - (p_1 u_1 + p_2 u_2 + \cdots + p_I u_I)]$. Similarly, he or she should be indifferent between D and the gamble between the best and the worst with respective probabilities $(q_1 u_1 + q_2 u_2 + \cdots + q_I u_I)$ and $[1 - (q_1 u_1 + q_2 u_2 + \cdots + q_I u_I)]$.

Now examine these final two gambles, both involving just the best and worst outcomes. Which should the individual prefer? Using the dominance axiom, that with the highest probability of getting the best outcome. So we get the following result:

C is preferred to D if and only if $(p_1 u_1 + p_2 u_2 + \cdots + p_I u_I) > (q_1 u_1 + q_2 u_2 + \cdots + q_I u_I)$

Now note that $(p_1 u_1 + p_2 u_2 + \cdots + p_I u_I)$ is the expected utility from the gamble C, and $(q_1 u_1 + q_2 u_2 + \cdots + q_I u_I)$ is the expected utility from the gamble D because, using the continuity axiom, we have defined $u_1, u_2, ..., u_I$ as the respective utilities of the outcomes $A_1, A_2, ..., A_I$. Thus we have the expected utility theorem, which says that choice between risky gambles should be determined by the expected utility of the gambles: the higher the expected utility, the more preferred the gamble.

Second, we provide a derivation of the slope of an indifference curve implied by the expected utility model. An indifference curve in (c_1, c_2) space is given, as ever, by

$$U(c_1, c_2) = \text{constant} \tag{A24.1}$$

If we substitute in the specification of the expected utility model from Eq. (24.1), we get the following equation for an indifference curve in (c_1, c_2) space.

$$\pi_1 u(c_1) + \pi_2 u(c_2) = \text{constant} \tag{A24.2}$$

To find the slope of the indifference curve we differentiate this totally, getting:

$$\pi_1 du(c_1)/dc_1 \, dc_1 + \pi_2 du(c_2)/dc_2 \, dc_2 = 0 \tag{A24.3}$$

In Eq. (A24.3), $u'(c)$ denotes the derivative of $u(c)$ with respect to c. From this we get the slope of an indifference curve:

$$\text{the slope of an indifference curve is} = -\pi_1 du(c_1)/dc_1[\pi_2 \, du(c_2)/dc_2] \tag{24.2}$$

Exchange in Insurance Markets

25.1 Introduction

In this chapter we use the techniques that we have been developing in the previous two chapters to discuss the trade of risk. Insurance markets exist for that purpose. In particular we look at optimal risk-sharing between individuals and discuss how the trading of risk can make people better off. We use the techniques of Chapters 23 and 24, combined with the analysis of Chapter 8 where we discussed trade in general, to understand how the trading of risk works.

We use the framework of Chapter 8. We assume a very simple economy consisting of two individuals, A and B, and two possible states of the world, state 1 and state 2. *Ex ante*, when trading may take place it is not known which of the two states will occur, though their respective probabilities π_1 and π_2 are known. *Ex post*, one and only one of the two states will occur. The individuals start with some initial endowments of income/consumption, but they may be able to trade away from this initial point. We work throughout with a specific analysis, but the story can obviously be generalized. What is important is that you take away from this chapter an understanding of how insurance markets help to allocate risk efficiently.

25.2 An Edgeworth Box

We start with individual A. We assume that he or she would have an income of 75 if state 1 occurred and an income of 50 if state 2 occurred. We assume that the two states of the world are equally likely. As for preferences, we assume that A has expected utility preferences and we assume here a constant absolute risk aversion utility function with parameter $r = 0.01$. We picture A's preferences and endowment point in Fig. 25.1. The straight line is A's certainty line.

We now turn to individual B. We assume exactly the same initial endowment: an income of 75 if state 1 occurs and an income of 50 if state 2 occurs. However we assume that B is more risk averse than A, having a constant absolute risk aversion utility function with parameter $r = 0.03$. We portray B's preferences and endowment point the normal way up in Fig. 25.2, and upside down in Fig. 25.3. The straight line in Fig. 25.3 is B's certainty line.

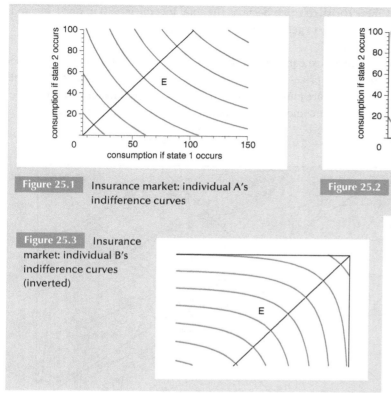

Figure 25.1 Insurance market: individual A's indifference curves

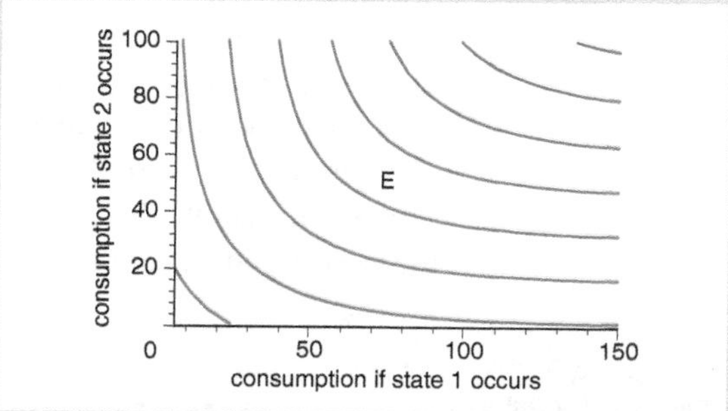

Figure 25.2 Insurance market: individual B's indifference curves

Figure 25.3 Insurance market: individual B's indifference curves (inverted)

Now we 'do an Edgeworth'. Superimpose B's upside down indifference map on top of A's in such a way that the endowment points coincide. We then get an Edgeworth box of dimension 150 (the total income/consumption if state 1 were to occur), times 100 (the total income/consumption if state 2 were to occur), with the endowment point exactly in the middle as their initial endowments are equal. You might like to think of state 2 as some kind of disaster in which society as a whole loses two-thirds of its income.

Inserted into Fig. 25.4 are the certainty lines of the individuals: the 45° line starting at the bottom left origin is that for A, and the 45° line starting at the top right origin is that for B. Note that the slopes of all the indifference curves for both the individuals along their respective certainty lines is −1; this equates the ratio of the probabilities of the two states.

If you study this figure you should be able to see where the contract curve is. In this case, where both individuals have constant absolute risk aversion utility functions, the contract curve is in an interesting position and has an interesting shape; it is a 45° line between the two certainty lines, but nearer to the certainty line of the more risk averse individual (B). This indicates the nature of efficient risk sharing. The contract curve is nearer to the certainty line for the more risk averse individual, which means that in any efficient contract B's position is less risky than that of A[1]. So A, the less risk-averse individual, bears more of the risk than the more risk-averse

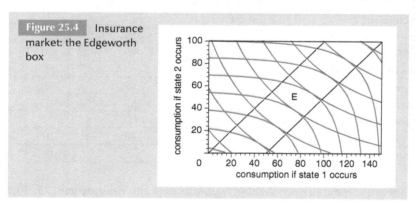

Figure 25.4 Insurance market: the Edgeworth box

---

1. Note that on a particular individual's certainty line there is no risk for that individual. As we move away – say at an angle of 90° – the riskiness increases, and the further away the greater the risk.

person. (Notice that there is risk to share because the total income is 150 in one state and 100 in the other; there is no way to get rid of the risk altogether, though the two individuals can change the way they share it.)

Let us look at the competitive equilibrium. It is the point marked C in Fig. 25.5. Also drawn in the figure are the two price-offer curves and the contract curve. The endowment point and the equilibrium point are joined together to indicate the equilibrium relative price (the price of state 1 contingent income relative to the price of state 2 contingent income).

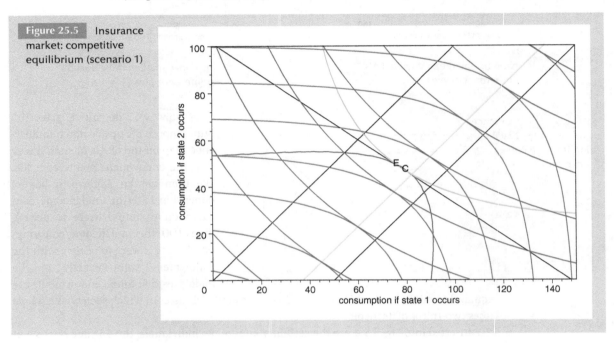

Figure 25.5   Insurance market: competitive equilibrium (scenario 1)

Let us summarize what happens in Table 25.1.

Table 22.1   Insurance markets: changes between initial and competitive equilibrium allocations (scenario 1)

	Individual A	Individual B	Society
Initial Allocation			
Consumption if state 1 occurs	75	75	150
Consumption if state 2 occurs	50	50	100
Competitive Equilibrium Allocation			
Consumption if state 1 occurs	83	67	150
Consumption if state 2 occurs	45	55	100
Changes between the two allocations			
Consumption if state 1 occurs	+8	−8	0
Consumption if state 2 occurs	−5	+5	0

Individual B is easy to understand. He or she starts out with an *ex ante* risky income (75, 50), by which we mean 75 if state 1 occurs and 50 if state 2 occurs. The expected income is 62.5 and the riskiness is ±12.5, meaning that the two values are 12.5 either side of the mean. After trading to the equilibrium point, B has an *ex ante* risky income of (67, 55). This has an expected value of 61 – which is lower than the expected income before trade – but the riskiness is now ±6. So individual B has reduced the riskiness of his or her *ex ante* income at the cost of having to accept a reduction in the expected income. But because B is rather risk-averse, he or she is happy to accept this reduction in the expected income in exchange for a reduction in risk. Note that at point C, individual B is on a higher indifference curve than he or she was at the equilibrium point E.

A, on the other hand, starts out with the same *ex ante* risky income (75, 50) which has an expected value of 62.5 and a riskiness of ±12.5. After the trade at the competitive equilibrium, A has an *ex ante* risky income of (83, 45). Note that this has an expected income of 64 and a riskiness of ±19. We see that A has accepted an increase in the riskiness of his or her position, but has also benefited by an increase in expected income. Despite the fact that A is moderately risk-averse, he or she is prepared to take a little bit of extra risk in return for a little bit of extra expected income. Individual A is on a higher indifference curve at C than at E.

We end up with more efficient risk-sharing than we had originally. In the original position they were both exposed to the same amount of risk; in the competitive equilibrium A (the relatively less risk-averse) has more of the risk than B (the relatively more risk-averse person), although A is rewarded with a higher expected income while B has to pay by accepting a lower expected income.

Incidentally this is not a fair insurance market because the relative price is clearly not equal to −1, which is the ratio of the probabilities. In fact the relative price is less than 1. You might like to ask yourself why.

25.3 Same Risk Attitudes but Different Endowments

Let us explore some other cases. We begin with a case in which the individuals have the same risk attitude but different endowments. We take constant absolute risk aversion functions with $r = 0.02$ for both individuals. You can probably guess where the contract curve is – yes, half way between the certainty lines of A and B. We assume different endowments in terms of riskiness, but the same expected values. Specifically, A starts with (100, 25) and B starts with (50, 75). Both have an expected value of 62.5; A's riskiness is ±37.5 while B's is ±12.5. The Edgeworth box is in Fig. 25.6. The various allocations are in Table 25.2.

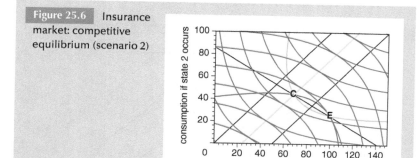

Figure 25.6 Insurance market: competitive equilibrium (scenario 2)

The competitive equilibrium is obviously on the contract curve, but it is closer to A's origin than to B's. As you will see, individual B does rather well out of the deal; starting with a risky income with expected value 62.5 and riskiness ±12.5, he or she ends up in the competitive equilibrium with (82, 56) which has expected value 69 and riskiness ±13. B accepts a little more riskiness and gets in exchange quite a big increase in expected value. A, on the other hand, starts out with expected value 62.5 and riskiness ±37.5 and ends up with (68, 44), which has expected value 56 and riskiness ±12. A accepts a big reduction in the riskiness in exchange for giving up quite a lot of expected value. But then A was initially exposed to a lot of risk.

Table 25.2 Insurance markets: changes between initial and competitive equilibrium allocations (scenario 2)

	Individual A	Individual B	Society
Initial Allocation			
Consumption if state 1 occurs	100	50	150
Consumption if state 2 occurs	25	75	100
Competitive Equilibrium Allocation			
Consumption if state 1 occurs	68	82	150
Consumption if state 2 occurs	44	56	100
Changes between the two allocations			
Consumption if state 1 occurs	−32	+32	0
Consumption if state 2 occurs	+19	−19	0

25.4 Similar Endowments but Different Preferences

An interesting case is when each individual gets income in just one state of the world: A in state 1 and B in state 2. What do they do? Consider the case when A's *ex ante* income is 100 in state 1 and zero in state 2, while B's is zero in state 1 and 100 in state 2. Between the two of them there is no uncertainty; their joint income is 100 whichever state occurs. So the Edgeworth box is of size 100 by 100 and the endowment point is at the bottom right hand corner.

Let us assume different preferences: A is constant absolute risk averse with parameter $r = 0.01$, while B is constant absolute risk averse with parameter $r = 0.03$. As before the contract curve lies between the two certainty lines – but in this case the certainty lines co-incide with the diagonal from the bottom left to the top right corners, and therefore so does the contract curve. Fig. 25.7 illustrates.

Figure 25.7 Insurance market: competitive equilibrium (scenario 3)

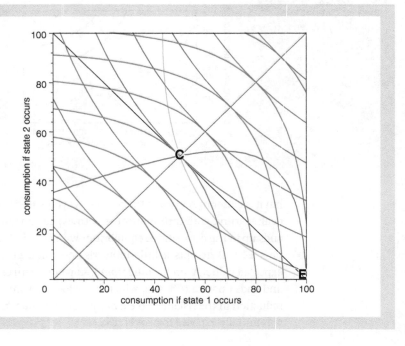

The two curves through the endowment point E are the price-offer curves. They are found in the usual way (see Chapter 8) by finding, for each possible budget line through the initial endowment point, the optimal choice of the individual. They intersect at the point C on the contract curve in the middle of the box. At the competitive equilibrium they are both at the point (50, 50) – whichever state of the world happens, both have an income of 50. This is an interesting case as, between the two of them, they manage to completely remove the risk that they both had originally. Note that the slope of the equilibrium budget constraint is −1 and also that we get this equilibrium, given the endowment, irrespective of the risk aversion of the two individuals. The contract curve is bound to be the main diagonal since this coincides with the certainty line for each of them; and so we know that the slopes of both their indifference curves are equal to −1 and hence are equal. Only at point C on the contract curve is the slope of the line joining E and that point on the contract curve also equal to −1. This is quite a reassuring result.

25.5 One Risk-Neutral Individual

When one of the individuals is risk neutral and the other is risk averse, we get a rather nice result. Let A be risk neutral and B risk averse. We have Fig. 25.8.

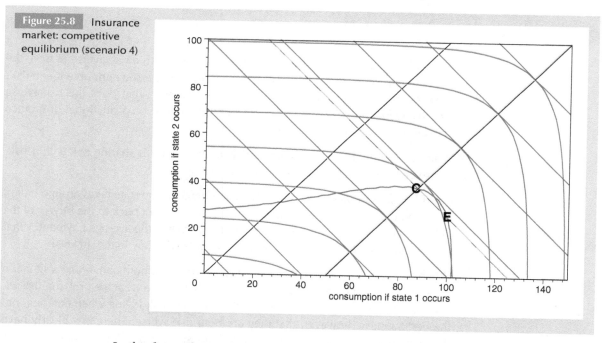

Figure 25.8   Insurance market: competitive equilibrium (scenario 4)

In this figure the contract curve coincides with the certainty line of individual B, so the competitive equilibrium is on B's certainty line; it is at the point C, given the endowment point E. So, wherever the endowment point is, the competitive equilibrium is a position of certainty for individual B; moreover, given that the slope of A's price-offer curve is −1 (equal to the slope of A's indifference curves), it follows that the expected income of B is the same at the competitive equilibrium as at the endowment point. B simply loses the risk. A gets all the risk, but does not care as he or she is risk neutral. This example is instructive as it shows that the presence of a risk-neutral individual removes the risk from elsewhere.

25.6 Summary

We showed that we could use the general exchange apparatus of Chapter 8 to examine the exchange of risk between two individuals. We saw that, in general, some exchange of risk is possible. In some cases we saw the individuals managing to completely eliminate the risk they faced. In others we saw that this was not possible, but some kind of efficient risk sharing was possible – usually with the less risk-averse person taking more of the risk.

 Insurance markets help to achieve an efficient sharing of the risk in society.

 In general, with an insurance market, the less risk-averse ends up taking more of the risk.

 In particular, if one individual is risk-neutral and the other risk-averse, the former ends up taking all of the risk.

25.7 Review Questions

1. Why is it that, if a risk-neutral person is sharing risk with a risk-averse person, the risk-neutral person takes all the risk and the risk-averse person ends up with no risk? What does the risk-neutral person gain by so doing? What does the risk-averse person pay for ending up with no risk? Does this remind you of anything? (Insurance markets where an unfair premium is charged.)

2. What do you think happens when a risk-loving person is sharing risk with a risk-averse person? (Assume a competitive equilibrium.)

3. Consider the National Lottery. This is clearly unfair as the state takes around half of the amount paid in (perhaps giving it to charities, but not back to the buyers of the lottery tickets). So the expected payout is around half of the average payment. What can you infer about the risk attitude of the people who buy lottery tickets?

4. When two people place a bet with each other, they are both converting a situation of certainty (not betting) into a gamble. If they both agree what the probabilities relevant to the bet are, we can conclude that both are risk-loving when entering into the bet. Suppose, however, that they are both risk-averse. Then they clearly have different perceptions of the relevant probabilities. Explain, using a simple example, where the bet is whether some event will happen or not.

25.8 Application: what if People are Not Different?

Throughout this book we have argued that, in general, if *people are different* then there will be an opportunity for mutually advantage exchange between them. Indeed we have shown that, if we have a simple society of two individuals who are different in either their preferences or their endowments, then mutually advantageous trade is possible as long as their initial position is not on the contract curve. In the examples given in the text, if the preferences are identical then the contract curve is a straight line joining the two origins, which passes through the mid-point of the box. It follows, therefore, that if the endowments are identical, we start at the mid-point of the box, on the contract curve, and mutually advantageous trade is not possible.

However in the examples considered so far we have assumed convex indifference curves. With such curves the proposition is true; if the individuals are identical in both their preferences and their endowments, then mutually advantageous trade is not possible. But in the context of risky choice, concave indifference curves are possible; they simply mean that the individual likes risk. Clearly there are such people in society: do you not know someone who plays the National Lottery?

Consider now two identical, risk-loving individuals. Possible indifference curves for them are illustrated in Fig. 25.9. The income/consumption of individual A is measured from the bottom left-hand origin and A's indifference curves are those which are concave

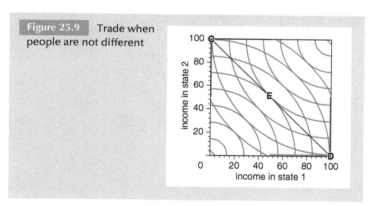

Figure 25.9 Trade when people are not different

with respect to that origin. The income/consumption of individual B is measured from the top right-hand origin; his or her indifference curves are those that are concave with respect to that origin, and are therefore convex with respect to the bottom left-hand origin. Note that both goods are still good, so moving upwards and rightwards in the box makes A better off and B worse off.

Where is the contract curve? We have to be careful. At first glance it would appear to be the line joining A's origin with B's origin, but a moment's reflection will make you realize that points along this line are not efficient. Indeed we can find a direction to move away from this diagonal and increase the welfare of both A and B. For example moving from the mid-point to either corner C or D makes both individuals better off; that is, it puts them both on higher indifference curves. In fact it can be shown that, in this case, the contract curve is the whole of the perimeter of the box; once we are on it we cannot make one individual better off without making the other worse off. If we are off it we can always find a direction to move and make both individuals better off. You should be aware that the contract curve is in an odd place in this example precisely because both individuals are risk-lovers. Around the perimeter they are both exposed to risk – which is what they like.

Now suppose the two start with identical endowments – the endowment point E at the centre of the box. Do they want to trade? Can we find a competitive equilibrium? Can we find the price-offer curves of the two individuals? These are the points to which they would move at given prices. That for A can be shown to be those parts of the perimeter of the box from (100, 0) to (100, 50) and the part from (0, 100) to (50 100); these parts are coloured blue in Fig. 25.9. Similarly we can find the price offer curve for B; those parts of the perimeter of the box from (50, 0) to (100, 0) and the part from (0, 50) to (0, 100); these are coloured red in Fig. 25.9. Notice that both individuals choose to move away from the certainty of the mid-point of the box to a risky point on the perimeter[2].

These two price-offer curves intersect at the points C and D – the upper left-hand and the lower right-hand corners of the box. Note that C and D are on the contract curve. We therefore have two competitive equilibria at points C and D with the same equilibrium budget constraint: the line joining C and D.

So we have trade, even though the two individuals have identical preferences and endowments. Note the nature of the trade; they start off in a completely safe situation, each getting income 50 in whatever state of the world happens. But they are risk-lovers, preferring risk to certainty. So they trade to a position in which one gets income 100 in one state of the world and nothing in the other, while it is the other way round for the other individual. It is just as if they agree to a bet; A pays to B 50 if something happens, and B pays 50 to A if it does not happen. They are both happier than they would be not having this bet, because points C and D are on higher indifference curves than point E for both of them. They are happier with the bet than without it. Do you not know people like that?

---

2. Though not any old point.

The Labour Market

26.1 Introduction

We now apply our various methodologies to a particularly important market – the labour market. We can use the methodology of Chapter 6 to find the supply of labour, by using the idea that individuals are endowed each day with leisure which either can be used as such or can be used to supply labour. This gives us one side of the market. The other side we have already done, when we studied the optimal input combination to produce a given level of output. We shall return to this theme and elaborate the implications.

26.2 The Supply of Labour

We envisage the suppliers of labour to be individuals who supply labour because they want to buy goods. We take the framework of Chapter 6. There the individual was endowed with income in the form of an endowment of each of two goods. In Chapter 6 the goods were general; here we specify particular goods. The good on the horizontal axis we take to be leisure, and that on the vertical axis money. Each day we suppose the individual gets an endowment of each of the two goods; obviously he or she gets each day an endowment of 24 hours of leisure, which can be used for any purpose whatsoever. There may also be an endowment of money. We use the space of Fig. 26.1, in which the variable on the horizontal axis is the number of hours of leisure available to the individual, and that on the vertical axis is the amount of money which the individual has to spend on other goods. We assume that his or her utility increases in respect of both the amount of money and the amount of leisure time that he or she has. We also assume that the price of money is unity.

Obviously the individual can work. If he or she does, the result

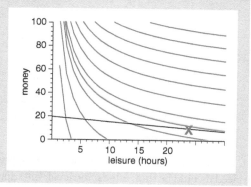

Figure 26.1 Labour market: changes in the wage rate

will be less leisure time but more money. This gives the individual a budget constraint in this space. If the wage rate per hour is denoted by w, then for each hour worked the individual has one hour less of leisure and w more in money. The budget constraint therefore has a slope equal to $-w$. It can be said that the cost of each hour of leisure is the wage rate w. If we denote l to represent the amount of leisure and m the amount of money, then the budget constraint is as shown in Eq. (26.1).

$$m = M + w(L - l) \qquad\qquad (26.1)$$

Here L denotes the initial endowment of leisure (24 hours) and M the initial endowment of money (which could be zero). The budget constraint passes through the initial endowment point (L, M) and has slope $-w$.

The individual's optimal point depends also on his or her preferences. In Fig. 26.1 we assume quasi-linear preferences. We also assume an initial endowment of 24 hours of leisure and 10 in money. The point X identifies the initial point. For each wage rate we have a budget constraint passing through X with slope $-w$. As the wage rate increases so does the slope of the budget constraint. In Fig. 26.1 we illustrate the case of $w = 0.4$. For this wage rate, if the individual takes 24 hours of leisure he will have just the initial 10 in money; if he or she takes no hours of leisure (working all day), then he or she will have the initial 10 plus wages of $0.4 \times 24 = 19.6$ in money; and so on.

Although the budget constraint in Fig. 26.1 continues to the right of the initial endowment point, it is clear that the individual cannot go there; the monetary endowment cannot be used to buy more leisure time! So, although for a wage rate of 0.4 it looks as if the optimal point is to the right of the initial point, it is clear that the individual cannot go there but must stay at the initial point. So, at a wage rate of 0.4 the individual takes 24 hours of leisure and does not work. The wage rate is too low, given the preferences.

As we increase the wage rate the optimal point moves to the left of the initial point. For example, at a wage rate of 2.0 the optimal point is at *(12.25, 33.4)*. This means that the individual wants 12.25 hours of leisure; he or she is willing to work $(24 - 12.25) = 11.75$ hours bringing in 23.5 in money at a wage rate of 2 giving a total of 33.5. It is the horizontal difference between the initial endowment point and the optimal point that gives the desired time spent working or the optimal supply of labour. We can repeat this exercise for other wage rates. Results are shown in Table 26.1, and you can check these.

Table 26.1   Demand for money and supply of labour as a function of the wage rate

Wage rate w	Optimal demand for leisure (hours)	Optimal demand for money	Optimal supply of labour (hours)
0.4	24.00	0	0
0.8	22.75	1	1.25
1.2	17.25	8	6.75
1.6	14.25	16	9.75
2.0	12.25	24	11.75
2.4	10.90	31	13.10
2.8	9.80	40	14.20
3.2	9.00	48	15.00
3.6	8.30	57	15.70
4.0	7.80	65	16.20

You will see that, as the wage rate increases so does the supply of labour. This is not necessarily the case. Indeed it could be that, after some level, the supply of labour falls as the wage

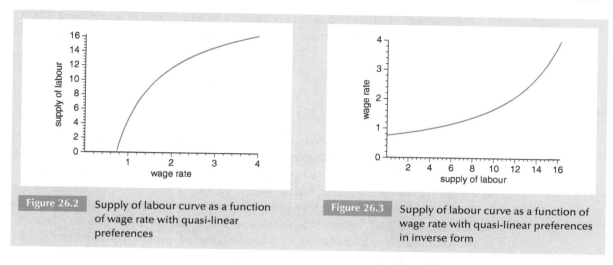

Figure 26.2 Supply of labour curve as a function of wage rate with quasi-linear preferences

Figure 26.3 Supply of labour curve as a function of wage rate with quasi-linear preferences in inverse form

rate increases; the reason for this is simple. A rise in the wage rate makes the individual better off; he or she may prefer to take advantage of this in the form of more leisure rather than more money; after all, he or she gets utility out of both.

We can graph the relationship between the supply of labour and the wage rate which is shown in the first and final columns of Table 26.1. We can do this in either the direct form with the wage rate on the horizontal axis (as shown in Fig. 26.2), or in inverse form with the wage rate on the vertical axis[1] (as in Fig. 26.3); it is obviously the same relationship. We shall see that the second proves useful later. You should note that, as ever, the area between the wage rate and the supply of labour curve measures the surplus of the individual, as measured by the vertical distance from the original indifference curve to the indifference curve at the optimal point.

It should be apparent that the form of the relationship depends upon the form of the preferences. For example, if we take Stone–Geary rather than quasi-linear preferences we obtain an alternative set of values to those in Table 26.1. The graphical representations of these are shown in Figs 26.4 and 26.5; you should compare these with Figs 26.2 and 26.3.

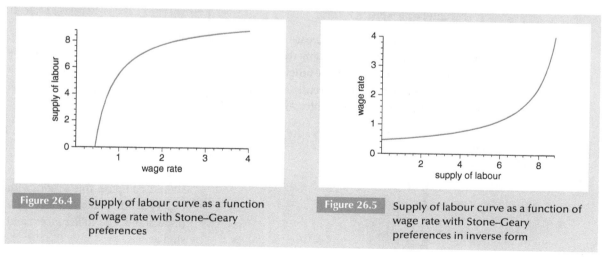

Figure 26.4 Supply of labour curve as a function of wage rate with Stone–Geary preferences

Figure 26.5 Supply of labour curve as a function of wage rate with Stone–Geary preferences in inverse form

1. If you are interested in the history of economic thought, you might like to know that the first of these is usually referred to as the 'Walrasian' form after the economist Walras; and the second the 'Marshallian' form after the economist Marshall.

Perhaps you would like to draw an example in which the supply of labour curve is backward-bending; that is, after a certain wage rate, the supply of labour decreases with further rises in the wage rate.

26.3 The Demand for Labour

Implicitly we have already considered this; in Chapter 11 we found the optimal labour input for any level of output, and in Chapter 13 we found the optimal level of output. We could simply put these together. However to make it clearer what we are doing, we adopt a simpler approach. We consider the short run decision in which the level of output, and hence the level of the labour input, is the only decision variable. To emphasize that we are interested in the demand for labour, we put that variable on the horizontal axis. Then we effectively reproduce the analysis from Chapter 13 when we graphed revenue, costs and profits, and later marginal revenue and marginal costs, on the vertical axis.

Let us start with the firm's costs as a function of the amount of labour it employs. In the short-run this is simple. If we continue to denote the price of labour by w, and let l denote the quantity that the firm employs, then costs are simply given by the expression in Eq. (26.2).

$$\text{costs} = wl + rK \tag{26.2}$$

Here r represents the price of the fixed factor and K the quantity of the fixed factor; you might like to think of this as capital, so rK represents the firm's fixed costs. As a graph with l on the horizontal axis, this is a straight line with intercept rK and slope w.

Total revenue as a function of the quantity of labour employed is a little more difficult. Recall that we are in the short run; we write the production function of the firm as follows:

$$y = f(l, K) \tag{26.3}$$

As previously, y denotes the output of the firm. If we let the price of the good equal p, then the firm's revenue is given by the following expression:

$$\text{revenue} = py = pf(l, K) \tag{26.4}$$

Now K is fixed, and as we increase l the output y increases and hence revenue increases. The rate at which y increases is, by definition, the marginal product of labour, and so this times p is the slope of the revenue function when plotted against the quantity of labour l. We almost always have decreasing returns to a single input, so the shape of the graph of revenue as a function of q is increasing and concave. Fig. 26.6 illustrates this.

The straight line (with a constant slope) is the total cost function, and the concave curve is the total revenue function. You should compare this graph with Fig. 13.2 and make sure that you understand the differences and similarities.

It will be noted that costs start out above revenues so that profits are negative; then there is a range (from about 0.5 to 7.0) in which

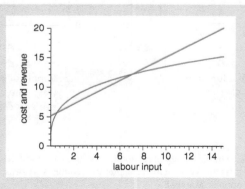

Figure 26.6 Cost and revenue as a function of labour input

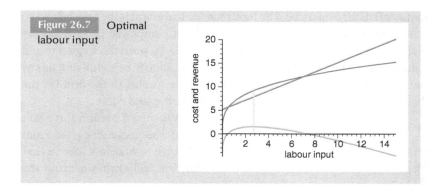

Figure 26.7 Optimal labour input

profits are positive; thereafter they are negative. Fig. 26.7 inserts the profit function, which is the difference between revenue and costs, and it indicates the point at which profits are maximized.

It will be seen that the profit-maximizing level of labour input is around 2.7. To identify exactly where it is in Fig. 26.7, we note that profits are maximized where the difference between revenue and costs is maximized, which occurs where the slope of the revenue function equals the slope of the cost function. Now we know these two slopes; the slope of the revenue function is equal to the price of output times the marginal product of labour; the slope of the cost function is equal to the price of labour (w). So the condition for profit maximization is simply[2] that

 Price of output times the marginal product of labour = price of labour = wage rate

Dividing both sides by the price p gives us the following profit-maximizing condition.

 Marginal product of labour = w/p = the real wage rate

Now we do as we did in Chapter 13; we move from a graph involving total revenue, total cost and total profit to a graph involving marginal revenue and marginal costs, by finding the slopes at each point. We know that the graph of total costs has a constant slope equal to the wage rate w, so the graph of marginal costs is constant at the level w. The slope of the total revenue function is decreasing everywhere and is equal to p times the marginal product of labour; so the marginal revenue function is decreasing everywhere and equals p times the marginal product of labour. Accordingly we get Fig. 26.8, in which I have taken the wage rate w to be unity (the same value as in the figures above).

Let us call p times the marginal product of labour the *value of the marginal product of labour*. Then the profit-maximizing level of labour, which is where the value of the marginal

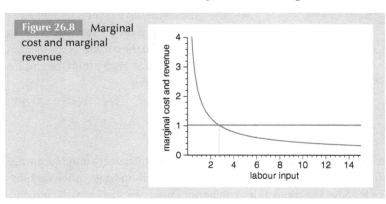

Figure 26.8 Marginal cost and marginal revenue

product of labour equals the wage rate, is around 2.7; this is obviously the same point as in the figures above.

We can find an interesting and familiar result concerning the firm's profit or surplus. If we examine Fig. 26.8, we see that the cost of buying the labour is simply the wage rate times the quantity of labour employed. So at the wage rate illustrated, the total labour cost is the area of the rectangle bounded by the wage

2. A mathematical proof can be found in the mathematical appendix to this chapter.

rate and the quantity of labour demanded. The total revenue to the firm is the area below the marginal product of labour curve, up to the quantity of labour employed (2.7). It follows that the profit is the difference between these, which is the area between the wage rate and the value of the marginal product of labour curve. As we shall shortly be identifying this as the labour demand curve, we get the familiar result that the surplus to the firm (as the demander of labour) is the area between the price paid and the demand curve.

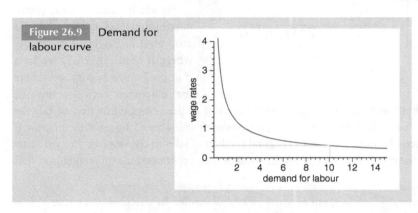

Figure 26.9 Demand for labour curve

We should confirm this result about the demand curve. From what we have seen it follows that the firm will always demand the quantity of labour for which the value of the marginal product of labour is equal to the wage rate. Therefore as the wage rate varies, the demand for labour will vary around the value of the marginal product of labour curve. It immediately follows that the value of the marginal product of labour curve is the demand curve for labour. Fig. 26.9 illustrates the demand for labour at a wage rate equal to 0.4; the profit or surplus at that rate is the area between the wage rate (0.4) and the demand curve.

26.4 The Labour Market

We are now in a position to put together the supply and demand curves in the labour market, and hence identify the competitive equilibrium. This is done in Fig 26.10.

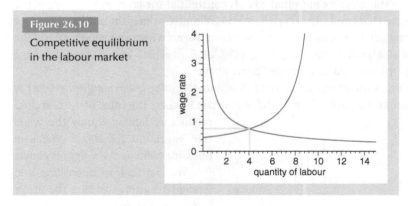

Figure 26.10

Competitive equilibrium in the labour market

We note, as usual, that in the competitive equilibrium total surplus (buyers plus sellers) is maximized. This result tells us that the competitive equilibrium is efficient in the sense of maximizing total surplus, but it tells us nothing about the distributive aspects and whether they are good or not; note that in Fig. 26.10 the surplus of the demanders is much bigger than the surplus of the sellers.

26.5 Minimum Wage Legislation

What happens in a competitive labour market if the government introduces minimum wage legislation? If the minimum wage is below the competitive equilibrium wage – then nothing. If the minimum wage is above the competitive equilibrium wage we shall witness: a reduction in employment (because the demand for labour at a higher wage is lower), a rise in the wages of those who remain employed, and an increase in unemployment. You might like to consider whether this is good or bad.

26.6 Summary

In this chapter we have built up a picture of the labour market using material from elsewhere in the book. We started with the supply of labour, and drew on our results from Chapter 6.

 The supply curve of labour depends upon the preferences of labour over leisure and consumption.

 The supply curve could be backward bending.

We then drew on results from the theory of the firm to derive the demand for labour.

 The demand curve for labour is the value of the marginal product of labour curve.

We then put everything together and looked at a competitive labour market where the wage rate is such that demand and supply are equal.

 In a competitive labour market, labour is paid its marginal product.

 Minimum wage legislation in a competitive labour market causes a loss of surplus and an increase in unemployment.

26.7 Review Questions

1. Do you think that increasing the wage rate will always increase the supply of labour? (We discuss this in the next section.)

2. Using the results of Chapter 11, discuss whether the demand for labour function is always a decreasing function of the wage rate.

3. In a competitive market, what do you think happens to the employment of labour if the government imposes a minimum wage above the competitive wage? And what happens if the minimum wage is below the competitive wage?

4. The condition for the optimal employment of labour is that the marginal product of labour should equal the real wage rate, which is the wage rate divided by the price of the output of the firm. What happens to profits if the firm employs more labour than this? Or if it employs less labour than this. (Assume that the wage rate is given and the firm cannot change it.)

5. What effect do you think paying overtime rates has on the supply of labour?

26.8 Application: does Lowering Income Tax Increase the Supply of Labour?

Mrs Thatcher, a long-serving Prime Minister in the UK, believed that lowering income tax rates would lead to an increased supply of labour because it would increase the real after tax-wage rate. Accordingly she cut income tax rates significantly during her term of office. However it was not clear that the tax cuts had the desired effect. We consider here what light economists can shed on her proposition.

We have already hinted at a possibility during this chapter; we will combine the analysis of this chapter with that done in Chapter 19. We know from both chapters that an increase in the real after-tax wage rate, which we shall call the wage rate from now on, has two effects; it changes the price of leisure relative to the price of the goods which are purchased with the labour income, and it increases the real income of the individual for any given supply of labour. The first of these – the relative price effect – unambiguously increases the supply of labour, provided the indifference curves between money and leisure have the usual downward-sloping convex shape. But the second of these – the real income effect – could have the opposite result. In other words, the individual might respond to the rise in the wage rate by simply taking more leisure; he or she uses the extra income to buy more leisure. In the chapter we asked you to consider whether this was possible, and if the income effect could be sufficiently strong to outweigh the relative price effect. Here we use Fig. 26.11 as an illustration.

Consider Fig. 26.11 which shows a set of downward-sloping convex indifference curves between money income and leisure. This is a possible set of preferences. We assume that the individual starts each day with 24 hours of leisure which could simply be consumed; alternatively he or she could convert some part into money through working at the going wage rate. We also assume that the individual gets some money income even if he or she is not

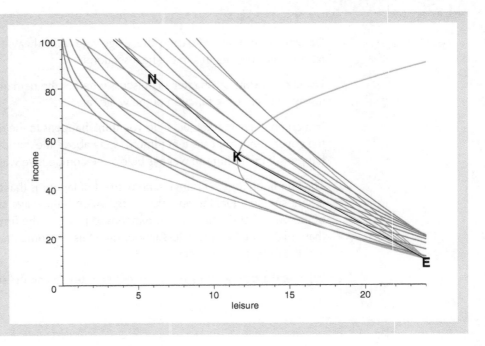

Figure 26.11

Consumption/leisure trade-off

working; you might like to think of this as unemployment benefit. In this example, we have assumed that this exogenous money income is 10 (£ per day). The endowment point is therefore the point labelled E in Fig 26.11. The budget line passes through point E and has a slope equal to the real wage rate (we are assuming that the price of money is one), which we denote by w. The actual position depends upon w, and in Fig. 26.11 we have drawn a total of nine possible budget lines, corresponding to w values 1.9, 2.3, 2.7, 3.1, 3.5, 3.9, 4.4, 5.0, 5.7 and 6.3 – all expressed as pounds per hour. We have also inserted the highest attainable indifference curve for each budget line, and we have joined these points together with the green curve; we could call this the wage expansion curve, as it shows the optimal point for each wage rate.

The crucial point about this wage expansion curve is that it is *backward-bending*. The optimal demand for leisure first decreases with the wage rate until we reach about the fifth budget line, with a wage rate of £3.50 per hour. After this, the optimal demand for leisure decreases with further increases in the wage rate. This implies that the supply of labour first increases with the wage rate, and then decreases. If we take the figures from the graph and plot them as a labour supply curve, we get the picture presented in Fig. 26.12. Note that Fig 26.11 showed the optimal demand for leisure – the implied supply of labour is the difference between the initial endowment of leisure (24 hours) and this optimal demand for leisure.

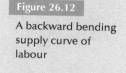

Figure 26.12

A backward bending supply curve of labour

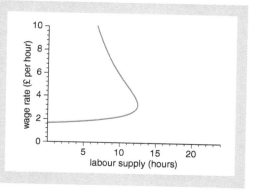

In Fig. 26.12, we have a backward-bending supply of labour curve; when the wage rate becomes sufficiently high (around £3.50 per hour), the supply of labour decreases with further increases in the wage rate. Obviously if this is possible at an individual level, it is also possible at aggregate levels including that of the economy. If the economy is currently in the downward sloping part of the curve, then cuts in income tax will simply reduce the supply of labour, rather than increase it as Mrs Thatcher wished.

Obviously it is an empirical question as to whether we are in the upward- or downward-sloping part of the curve, and we would need to do the kind of analysis that we did in Chapter 16 to determine the answer. But let us see what we can say if the Prime Minister is determined (perhaps for political reasons) to cut taxes, but would also like to see an increased supply of labour.

To focus our minds, suppose we find ourselves at the moment at the 'kink point', which we have labelled K in Fig. 26.11. If we reduce income taxes at this point, we will increase the slope of the budget line and an individual will respond by taking more leisure and working less. Indeed if the wage rate goes up from £3.50 per hour to £6.30 per hour (from the fifth to the ninth budget line), the supply of labour falls from around 12.5 hours per day to around 10 hours a day. The income tax cut has a 'perverse' effect. However you will see that the money income of the individual is higher (£68 per day) with the higher wage rate than it was with the lower (£53 per day).

But there is something that can be done. Suppose the Prime Minister reduces the tax rate on the part of income above that at the kink point K (£53 per day). Then there would be a kink in the budget constraint at the point K. We have inserted such a kinked budget constraint into Fig. 26.11, with a slope in the upper part equal to that of the ninth budget constraint (£6.30 per hour), and a slope equal to the fifth budget constraint (£3.50 per hour) in the lower part. What would our individual do? He or she would respond by working longer hours; the optimal point is now at the point N with labour supply of 18 hours a day.

There is a bit of a political problem with this unfortunately (taxing the rich proportionately less), and it would be difficult to implement. However it does allow us to demonstrate the potential of the analyses of this chapter. It should also get you thinking about the possible effects of different tax rates on different incomes. In practice, the tax rate goes up with income so we would not get the type of budget constraint illustrated above. But it would be kinked, with a kink at every change in the tax rate and, if the tax rate increased with income, it would be concave, rather than convex as in Fig. 26.11. What effect do you think that might have on the supply of labour?

We can also use this analysis to consider other possibilities, like changing the basic allowances of the tax system. This would have the effect of moving the endowment point vertically. How might this affect behaviour?

26.9 Mathematical Appendix

We provide a proof of the result concerning the firm's optimal demand for labour. We know that the profit of the firm is given by the following function.

$$\text{profit} = \text{revenue} - \text{costs} = py - (wl + rK) \tag{A26.1}$$

We also know that the output y of the firm depends upon the factor inputs through the production function (A26.2).

$$y = f(l, K) \tag{A26.2}$$

Substituting the production function in the expression for profits, we get the following expression for the firm's profits.

$$\text{profit} = p\, f(l, K) - (wl + rK) \tag{A26.3}$$

If we now apply the usual maximization condition ($d\,\text{profit}/dl = 0$) we obtain the function (A26.4)

$$pdf(l, K)/l = w \tag{A26.4}$$

Eq. (A26.4) can be expressed in the following manner:

$$df(l, K)/dl = w/p \tag{A26.5}$$

Eq. (A26.5) states that the firm will maximize its profit if it equates the marginal product of labour with the real wage rate.

Market
Inefficiencies of
Various Types

4.1   Summary

The first three parts of the book stay within a competitive world and, moreover, one in which technology and preferences have certain assumed properties. Some parts of the real world are not competitive, and there are certain markets in which the assumed properties do not hold. Accordingly Part 4 departs from this simple competitive world with the assumed properties and explores the implications. First, we see what happens if the government intervenes in a market in the form of taxation. We will find that surplus is lost as a consequence. We show this is also the case if monopoly or monopsony exist in a market, and we then discuss various ways of retrieving this lost surplus – one way being through discrimination. Next we look at a case part-way between competition and monopoly – duopoly – and explore its implications. The book concludes by examining three cases where the underlying assumptions of Parts 1 to 3 cannot hold: externalities, where one person's consumption or production affects another person's welfare; public goods, where one person's consumption of the good does not preclude someone else consuming it; and asymmetric information, where some people in a market have more information than others about the good being traded in the market. We show the problems that this raises for our previous analysis, and discuss possible solutions.

4.2   Detail

So far the book has looked at competitive outcomes in a world where certain key assumptions hold. This Part looks at the implications of both non-competitive behaviour and different underlying assumptions; included in the former is government intervention in a market via taxation.

Chapter 27 Taxation: We show how taxation disturbs the equilibrium in a competitive market and how there is a loss of surplus as a consequence; this is the deadweight loss of the tax. Its existence suggests that it may be inefficient to increase market prices through taxation.

Chapter 28 Monopoly and Monopsony: To a certain extent this has already been discussed implicitly, but now we examine it explicitly and ask what happens if there is a sole buyer or a sole seller in a market. We show that there is a loss of surplus, in the sense that the total surplus generated by the working of the market is lower, compared to the situation in a competitive market. There are obviously also distributional effects as well as effects on the quantity traded in the market.

Chapter 29 Natural Monopoly and Discrimination: This discusses whether the lost surplus of monopoly might be considered a good thing because of the existence of a natural monopoly, and also whether it might be possible to recover some of the lost surplus, caused by a non-competitive market, through discrimination of some form.

Chapter 30 Game Theory: This chapter introduces some basic concepts concerning rational behaviour in interactive and strategic situations. We introduce the idea of a Nash equilibrium, and give examples of games in which there are one, two or no Nash equilibria.

Chapter 31 Duopoly: The basic game theoretical concepts of Chapter 30 are applied to the problem of duopolistic behaviour. We show that, under certain conditions, in a quantity-setting game there is a unique Nash equilibrium, and the implied outcome is between (in a sense) that of the competitive and a monopolistic market. In a price-setting game, however, the Nash equilibrium coincides with that in a competitive market.

Chapter 32 Externalities: This chapter explores the implications of a situation in which one person's consumption influences the utility or profit of another person. Our previous assumptions assumed away this away problem. If it is true then previous results, particularly those concerning efficiency, may no longer hold. What might be done about it?

Chapter 33 Public Goods: Here we discuss a further instance when our earlier assumptions may not hold – the case of a public good. For such a good, lots of people can simultaneously consume the good. This changes our previous analysis; we discuss in what way and what might be done about it.

Chapter 34 Asymmetric Information: The chapters on behaviour under risk implicitly assumed that all agents had the same information. In this chapter we explore the implications of what happens when different people have different amounts of information. We look at this in the context of the insurance markets of Chapter 25.

Taxation

27.1 Introduction

We consider the effect of taxation on some good on the market for that good. We ask the questions: who pays the tax? What effect does it have on the equilibrium price and on the equilibrium quantity? What effect does it have on the surpluses? We shall see that taxation reduces the total surplus generated by the market; this loss caused by the tax is called the deadweight loss of the tax. It reduces the efficiency of the market by reducing the surplus generated by the market and, for that reason, might be considered 'a bad thing'. However it is important to remember that there are obvious offsetting advantages; for instance the government can use the revenue generated by the tax elsewhere in the economy. This 'good thing' might be worth the 'bad thing' caused by the reduction of the total surplus generated by the market in which the tax is collected.

In practice there are different kinds of taxes. The two most common are flat rate taxes and proportional taxes. The first are fixed taxes – taxes independent of the price of the good. The second are taxes such as value added tax which are levied at a rate proportional to the price of the good. The most common form of a tax is the proportional form; in many countries governments levy a value added tax. In the UK at present this is equal to 17.5 per cent of the (pre-tax) price of the good. However, there are also flat rate taxes; such was the case until recently with the vehicle registration licence. An even more famous example is the poll tax which Mrs Thatcher introduced on property ownership in the UK; the owner of any house, however big or small, had to pay the same amount of poll tax to the government. We shall examine both of these taxes in this chapter. However our methods can be applied to any kind of tax.

27.1 The Two Prices with a Tax

Whatever kind of tax we are examining, the crucial point is that, with a tax, there are two prices in the market: the price that buyers pay and the price that sellers receive. The difference between these two prices is the tax which the government takes. Only when there is no tax are these prices equal. Accordingly, when we use 'the price' as one of the variables in our analysis, we need to specify which price we mean. As we shall see, we can do our analysis with either price; we just have to be careful about which price it is.

27.3 The Pre-tax Position

Let us start with a situation in which there is no tax. We are going to work with a specific example initially; later we shall generalize. In the specific example we take simple linear demand and supply schedules so we can see exactly what is going on. This initial position is pictured in Fig. 27.1.

Figure 27.1

Original demand and supply curves

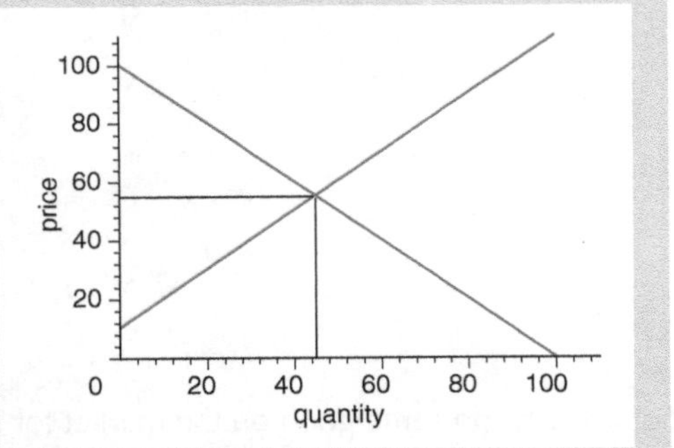

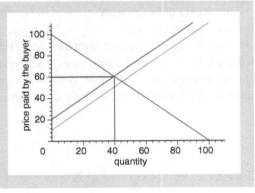

The equations for the demand and supply curves are presented in Eq. (27.1) and Eq. (27.2) respectively.

$$q_d = 100 - p_b \tag{27.1}$$

$$q_s = p_s - 10 \tag{27.2}$$

In these equations, q_d indicates the quantity demanded and q_s the quantity supplied. The price p_b is the price paid by the buyers, and p_s is the price received by the sellers. In this situation the two prices are identical as there is no tax, but when there is a tax they will differ. We see that the original equilibrium price is 55 and the original equilibrium quantity is 45.

27.4 A Flat Rate Tax

Let us now suppose that the government imposes a flat rate tax on the good at the rate 10 on every unit bought and sold; for every unit exchanged the government takes 10. What effect does this have? We look at the effect on the demand and supply schedules, and hence on the equilibrium.

Figure 27.2

Effect of a flat-rate tax when the price is the price paid by the buyers

Let us first do the analysis with the *price paid by the buyers* on the vertical axis. Since this is the relevant variable in the demand curve, the latter does not change from that drawn in Fig. 27.1. It is shown in Fig. 27.2.

What about the supply curve? Well, we cannot use Eq. (27.2) directly as the variable there is the price received by the sellers, which is not the price variable we are using in this analysis. We need to work out the new supply curve, using first a bit of algebra and then some numbers. The algebra is simple. Since the price paid by buyers differs from the price received by the sellers by the extent of the tax, we can relate the two prices as follows.

$$p_b = p_s + 10 \quad \text{or}$$

$$p_s = p_b - 10 \tag{27.3}$$

We can insert Eq. (27.3) into Eq. (27.2) to obtain the relationship between the quantity supplied (q_s) and the price paid by the buyers (p_b), which is shown in Eq. (27.4).

$$q_s = (p_b - 10) - 10 = (p_b - 20)$$

(27.4)

If we plot this in Fig. 27.2 we get the new supply curve, which is the upper line pictured in the figure.

In Fig. 27.2 the downward sloping line is the (new and old) demand curve; the thick upward sloping curve is the new supply curve, and the thin upward sloping line is the old supply curve. So the supply curve shifts upwards by the amount of the tax. Notice that the vertical distance between the two supply curves is everywhere equal to 10 – the amount of the tax.

An alternative way of seeing this is by working out some numbers. Consider table 27.1. The supply curve is illustrated in the first two columns, which show the relationship between the price received by the sellers and the quantity supplied; it is this relationship that defines the supply curve. We now derive the final column from the first, taking into account that the tax is 10 which makes the price paid by the buyers (p_b) always 10 higher than the price received by the sellers (p_s). In Fig. 27.2 we show the relationship between columns 2 and 3 in Table 27.1, because column 2 is the variable on the horizontal axis and column 3 is the variable on the vertical axis. This is the thick upward sloping line in Fig. 27.2.

The effect of the tax on the equilibrium can now be seen – it is at the intersection of the demand curve and the new supply curve, as indicated in the figure. The new equilibrium quantity is *40* and the new equilibrium price is 60. But let us be precise: the new equilibrium price paid by the buyers is 60; it follows that the new equilibrium price received by the sellers is 50.

Table 27.1	Supply as a function of the price received by sellers and the price paid by buyers (flat tax of 10 per cent)

Price received by the sellers	Supply	Price paid by the buyers
0	0	10
10	0	20
20	10	30
30	20	40
40	30	50
50	40	60
60	50	70
70	60	80
80	70	90
90	80	100
100	90	110

The price paid by the buyers is always 10 more than the price received by the sellers.

Before the tax 45 units were exchanged, with the buyers paying 55 for each unit and the sellers receiving 55 for each unit. With the tax, only 40 units are exchanged, with the buyers paying 60 for each unit, the sellers receiving 50 for each unit, and the government taking 10 in tax on each unit.

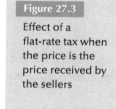

Figure 27.3

Effect of a flat-rate tax when the price is the price received by the sellers

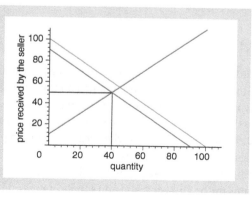

Let us repeat the analysis with the other price variable – the *price received by the sellers*. If this is the variable on the vertical axis then the supply curve is the same as it was originally because the price received by sellers is the variable which determines the supply. This is shown in Fig. 27.3.

What about the demand curve? Well, we cannot use Eq. (27.1) directly as the variable there is the price paid by the buyers (p_b), which is not the price variable which we are using in this analysis. We need to work out the new demand curve, using first a bit of algebra and then some numbers. Algebraically it is simple. The price paid by buyers differs from the price received by the sellers by the amount of the tax, and so we have Eq. (27.3) as before. If we insert this in Eq. (27.1), we obtain the relationship between the quantity demanded and the price received by the sellers.

$$q_d = 90 - p_s \qquad\qquad (27.5)$$

If we plot Eq. (27.5) in Fig. 27.3, we get the new demand curve pictured there.

In Fig. 27.3 the upward sloping line is the (new and old) supply curve; the thick downward sloping curve is the new demand curve and the thin one is the old demand curve. So the demand curve shifts downwards by the amount of the tax. The vertical distance between the two demand curves is everywhere equal to 10 – the amount of the tax.

An alternative way of seeing this is by working out some numbers, as in Table 27.2. The demand curve is illustrated in the first two columns, which show the relationship between the price paid by the buyers and the quantity demanded. It is this relationship that defines the demand curve. We derive the final column from the first, taking into the account that the tax is 10, making the price paid by the buyers always 10 more than the price received by the sellers. Fig. 27.3 shows the graph of the relationship between columns 2 and 3 of Table 27.2, because column 2 is the variable on the horizontal axis and column 3 (not column 1) that on the vertical axis. The new relationship is shown as the thick downward-sloping line in Fig. 27.3.

The effect of the tax on the equilibrium can now be seen; it is at the intersection of the new demand curve and the supply curve. The new equilibrium quantity is 40 and the new equilibrium price is 50. But let us be precise: the new equilibrium price received by the sellers is 50; the new equilibrium price paid by the buyers is 60.

Table 27.2 Demand as a function of the price received by sellers and the price paid by buyers (flat tax of 10 per cent)

Price payed by the buyers	Demand	Price receivedd by the sellers
0	100	0[3]
10	90	0
20	80	10
30	70	20
40	60	30
50	50	40
60	40	50
70	30	60
80	20	70
90	10	80
100	0	90

Always 10 less than the price paid by the buyers, except in the first row since a price of –10 received by the sellers would make no sense.

So we get exactly the same conclusions as before. Before the tax, 45 units are exchanged, with the buyers paying 55 for each unit and the sellers receiving 55 for each unit. With the tax, only 40 units are exchanged with the buyers paying 60 for each unit, the sellers receiving 50 for each unit, and the government taking 10 in tax on each unit.

27.5 The Effect on the Surpluses

We have seen that the tax has the effect of reducing the quantity exchanged in the market. In this section we investigate the effect that the tax has on the surpluses. First we note the surpluses before the introduction of the tax; they are shown in Fig. 27.4.

The buyer surplus is the area between the price paid and the demand curve – in this case $(0.5 \times 45 \times 45) = 1012.5$. The seller surplus is the area between the price received and the supply curve, which is also $(0.5 \times 45 \times 45) = 1012.5$.

To analyse the position with the tax we will find it useful to use a slightly different diagram; one that contains the original demand and supply curves and the new equilibrium.

Figure 27.4

Surpluses before
the tax

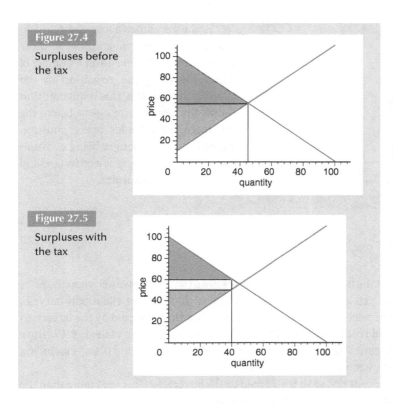

Figure 27.5

Surpluses with
the tax

We can do this by noting the properties of the new equilibrium: that the tax drives a wedge between the price that buyers pay and the price that sellers receive, and this wedge is exactly equal to the tax. We can think of the equilibrium quantity as the quantity at which the vertical distance between the demand and supply curves is exactly equal to the tax. Fig. 27.5 illustrates this, although you should be careful, if you are using this kind of diagram, to explain exactly what it is that you are illustrating.

The quantity indicated is the new equilibrium quantity. It is so because the vertical gap between the demand and supply curves at that quantity (note that it is unique) is exactly equal to the tax (10). The price given by the demand curve at the quantity 40 is the new equilibrium price paid by the buyers (p_b). The price given by the supply curve at the quantity of 40 is the new equilibrium price received by the sellers (p_s). The new buyer surplus is the area between the new price paid by the buyers and the demand curve, which is $(0.5 \times 40 \times 40) = 800$, giving a loss of surplus of 212.5. The new seller surplus is the area between the new price received by the sellers and the supply curve, which is $(0.5 \times 40 \times 40) = 800$, also giving a loss of surplus of 212.5.

The government raises money through the tax – this is the area bounded by the two prices (the price paid by the buyers and the price received by the sellers) and the quantity exchanged. In Fig. 27.5 the tax yield is the rectangle with area $(40 \times 10) = 400$. The government takes most of the reduction in the surpluses of the buyers and sellers.

But there is a bit of the original surpluses that no-one gets – not the buyers, not the sellers, not the government; it just disappears from the market because the quantity exchanged has fallen. This lost surplus is the triangular area illustrated in Fig. 27.6. In this example its magnitude is $(0.5 \times 5 \times 10) = 25$. This is called the *deadweight loss* of the tax.

If we check the arithmetic we shall obtain the following results

Original surpluses:	buyers	1012.2
	sellers	1012.5
	Total	**2025**
New surpluses:	buyers	800
	Sellers	800
	Government	400
	Total	**2000**
Deadweight loss of tax		**25**

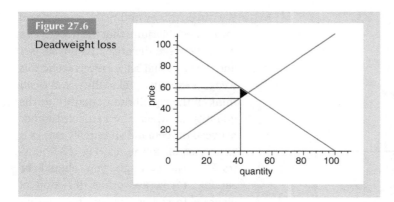

Figure 27.6

Deadweight loss

So the tax causes a loss of surplus. In this example the magnitude is quite small, but this will depend on a number of things including the reduction in the quantity traded. It is this reduction that causes the loss of surplus – as before the tax there were trades being consummated that are no longer being consummated. The tax causes fewer trades, and hence reduces the surplus.

27.6 A Proportional Tax

The crucial point is that the tax causes the demand curve to shift downwards when the price variable on the vertical axis is the price received by sellers; and it causes the supply curve to shift upwards when the price variable on the vertical axis is the price paid by the buyers; in both cases the magnitude of the vertical shift exactly equals the amount of the tax. We have showed that this is the case with a flat rate tax, but it is true with any kind of tax – including a proportional tax. Let us consider the latter case.

We assume a 20 per cent tax, so the price paid by the buyers is 20 per cent more than the price received by sellers, the difference being the tax. Let us consider the same case as before, so our starting position once again is Fig. 27.1. We again consider the analysis with the two different price variables, first starting where the price is that paid by the buyers. In this case, as we know, the supply curve will shift. We can find the impact of this shift either algebraically or numerically; algebraically we have

$$p_b = 1.2p_s \tag{27.6}$$

Buyers pay 20 per cent more than the sellers receive. Substituting Eq. (27.6) in the supply curve (27.2), gives us the new supply curve as a function of the price paid by buyers.

$$q_s = p_b/1.2 - 10 \tag{27.7}$$

Figure 27.7

Effect of a proportional tax when the price is the price paid by buyers

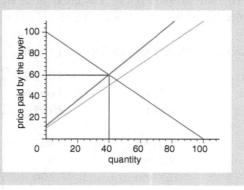

We show the graph of Eq. (27.7) in Fig. 27.7, where it is the steeper of the two supply curves.[1] Alternatively we can use numbers. Proceeding as before we create Table 27.3; we then draw a graph of the final two columns to get Fig. 27.7.

In Fig. 27.7 the downward-sloping line is the (new and old) demand curve. The thin upward-sloping line is the original supply curve and the thick upward-sloping line is the new supply curve. Notice that the vertical gap between the old and the new supply curves is exactly

---

1. Notice that the intercept of the supply curve is at a price of 24, which is 20 per cent higher than the original intercept.

Table 27.3 Demand as a function of the price received by sellers and the price paid by buyers (tax of 20 per cent)

Price received by the sellers	Supply	Price paid by the buyers
0	0	0
10	0	12
20	10	24
30	20	36
40	30	48
50	40	60
60	50	72
70	60	84
80	70	96
90	80	108
100	90	120

The price paid by the buyers is always 20 per cent more than that received by the sellers

the tax – the new curve is 20 per cent higher than the old even at the intercept. Why? Because, to produce a given quantity, the sellers need the buyers to pay 20 per cent more than they did originally – the 20 per cent which goes to the government in tax.

The new equilibrium is where the (new and old) demand curve intersects the new supply curve. As it happens this is at a quantity 40 and a price paid by the buyers of 60; this in turn implies a new price received by the sellers of 50; note that 50 plus 20 per cent equals 60. It is pure coincidence that the tax of 20 per cent has exactly the same effect as a tax of 10 per unit. In general, different taxes will have different effects.

Once again we can do all the analysis with the price received by sellers on the vertical axis. If we do, the supply curve is the original supply curve as the price relevant to the sellers is the price that they receive. But the demand curve shifts as the price relevant to the buyers is the price that they have to pay. To find the demand as a function of the price received by sellers, we need to substitute Eq. (27.6) into the demand curve (27.1); this gives us the following.

$$q_d = 100 - 1.2p_s \tag{27.8}$$

Fig. 27.8 shows the new demand curve, and also the new equilibrium point.

Alternatively we can use numbers. Proceeding as before we have Table 27.4, and when we graph the final two columns we get Fig. 27.8. We note that the first column is always 20 per cent more than the final column.

In Fig. 27.8 the upward-sloping line is the (new and old) supply curve. The thin downward-sloping line is the original demand curve and the thick downward-sloping line is the new demand curve. The vertical gap between the old and new is exactly the tax – the new

Table 27.4 Supply as a function of the price received by sellers and the price paid by buyers (tax of 20 per cent)

Price paid by the buyers	Demand	Price received by the sellers
0	100	0
10	90	$8\frac{1}{3}$
20	80	$16\frac{2}{3}$
30	70	25
40	60	$33\frac{1}{3}$
50	50	$41\frac{2}{3}$
60	40	50
70	30	$58\frac{1}{3}$
80	20	$66\frac{2}{3}$
90	10	75
100	0	$83\frac{1}{3}$

Always such that the price paid by the buyers is 20 per cent more than the price received by the sellers.

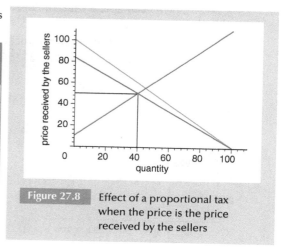

Figure 27.8 Effect of a proportional tax when the price is the price received by the sellers

curve is 20 per cent lower than the old curve, even at the intercept. Why? Because to buy a given quantity the buyers need the sellers to sell for 20 per cent less than they did originally; the 20 per cent which goes to the government in tax. The new equilibrium is where the (new and old) supply curve intersects the new demand curve. As before, this is at a quantity 40 and a price received by the sellers of 50 – this, in turn, implies a new price of 60 paid by the buyers. As before note that 50 plus 20 per cent equals 60.

Once again we notice that the tax drives a wedge between the price paid by the buyers and the price received by the sellers. In this instance, because the 20 per cent tax has exactly the same effect as the fixed-rate tax of 10 which we analysed earlier, and because we started in exactly the same position, the effect on the surpluses is exactly as it was before. In particular there is a deadweight loss of surplus caused by the tax.

27.7 Who Pays the Tax?

In the above example all the effects were nicely symmetrical; the price paid by the buyers went up by 5 and the price received by the sellers went down by 5. So the buyers paid half the tax of 10 and the sellers paid the other half. Moreover the effect on the surpluses was symmetrical – both buyers and sellers lost the same part of their surplus to the government and the same part to the deadweight loss. The reason for this symmetry is that the demand and supply curves were nicely symmetrical. If they were not, there is no reason why the effects should be symmetrical.

This section looks at asymmetrical cases and answers the question: who pays the tax?. As may be apparent in such cases, the answer depends upon the slope of the demand and supply curves. We examine four examples in which we consider three possibilities – flat, average and steep – where by average we mean a case between flat and steep:

● demand average, supply flat
● demand average, supply steep
● demand flat, supply average
● demand steep, supply average

In each case we take a flat-rate tax equal to 10. You may like to consider other examples yourself.

If the demand curve is of average steepness but the supply curve is very flat, we have the position pictured in Fig. 27.9. The original equilibrium had a quantity of 45 and a price of

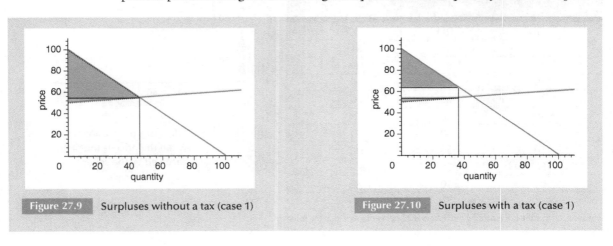

Figure 27.9   Surpluses without a tax (case 1)   **Figure 27.10**   Surpluses with a tax (case 1)

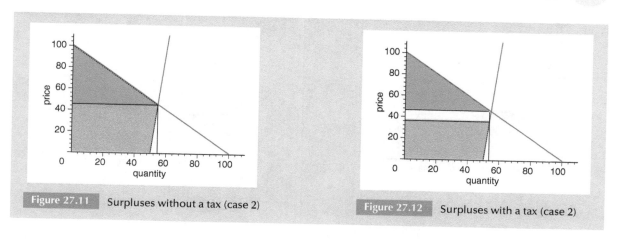

Figure 27.11 Surpluses without a tax (case 2)

Figure 27.12 Surpluses with a tax (case 2)

just under 55. The fact that the supply curve is very flat indicates that it is extremely sensitive to the price; a small increase in the price will lead to a large increase in the quantity supplied. You will see that originally the buyer surplus was very large and the seller surplus was very small. With the tax, the quantity exchanged falls to a little under 37, as indicated in Fig. 27.10.

The price paid by the buyers increases from just under 55 to almost 64 – a rise of almost 9. In contrast the price received by the sellers falls from just under 55 to just under 54 – a fall of just over 1. In this case, the tax of 10 is almost all paid for by the buyers, as they are less sensitive to the price than the sellers. Note that there is a large fall in the buyer surplus but only a modest fall in the seller surplus.

If the demand curve is of average steepness but the supply curve is very steep, we have the position shown in Fig. 27.11. The original equilibrium has a quantity of just over 54 and a price of around 45.5. The steepness of the supply curve indicates that it is not very responsive to changes in price. Notice that there are large buyer and seller surpluses.

The new equilibrium is shown in Fig. 27.12. In this position the quantity exchanged falls very little, to just under 54 (because the supply curve is steep). The price paid by the buyers rises from around 45.5 to around 46.5 – a rise of just 1. The price received by sellers, however, falls from around 45.5 to almost 36 – a fall of about 9, the reason being that the supply is not very sensitive to the price. The sellers pay the tax. There is a small fall in the buyer surplus but a large fall in the seller surplus. In this case the deadweight loss of the tax is very small because the quantity exchanged falls very little.

If the demand curve is very flat but the supply curve is of average slope, we have the position pictured in Fig. 27.13. The original equilibrium has a quantity of 36.5 and a price of just over 46. It will be seen that the buyer surplus is very small because the demand curve is flat, indicating that demand is very sensitive to price.

Figure 27.14 shows the impact of a tax on this situation. The tax causes a big reduction in the quantity exchanged because the demand is very sensitive to the price. For the same reason the price paid by the buyers rises very little – from just over 46 to around 47. In contrast the price received by the sellers falls a lot – from just over 46 to around 37, and there is a big fall in the seller surplus. In this case the sellers bear most of the burden of the tax. There is a large deadweight loss because the quantity exchanged falls considerably.

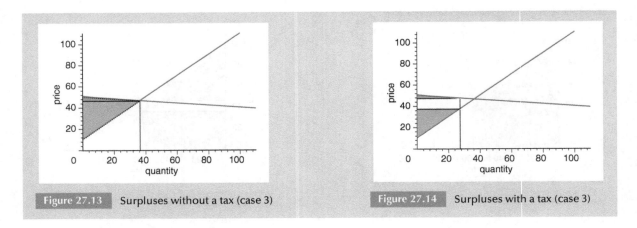

Figure 27.13   Surpluses without a tax (case 3)

Figure 27.14   Surpluses with a tax (case 3)

Finally, if the demand curve is very steep but the supply curve is of average slope, we have the position pictured in Fig. 27.15. The original equilibrium has a quantity of just under 45 and a price of just over 54. There are large buyer and seller surpluses.

The new position, taking into account the impact of the tax, is in Fig. 27.16. In the new equilibrium the quantity exchanged falls slightly from just below 45 to a little under 44. As a consequence the deadweight loss is rather small. The price paid by the buyers rises sharply from just over 54 to almost 64 – the reason being that the demand is rather insensitive to the price. In contrast there is just a small fall in the price received by the sellers, from just over 54 to just under 54. In this case the tax burden is almost all borne by the buyers because the demand is rather insensitive to the price.

The conclusion to be drawn is that the effects of the tax depend upon the form of the demand and supply schedules. If one of the two is relatively insensitive to the price, then that side of the market bears the burden of the tax. If one of the two is relatively sensitive to the price, the other side of the market bears the burden of the tax.

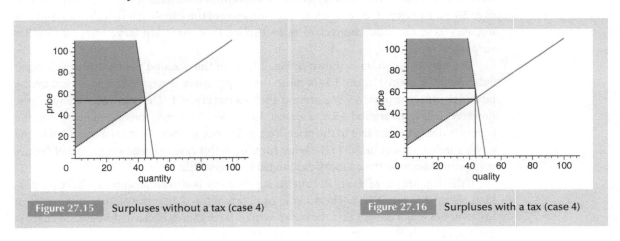

Figure 27.15   Surpluses without a tax (case 4)

Figure 27.16   Surpluses with a tax (case 4)

27.8 Summary

When analysing the effect of a tax on a market, the crucial point is that there are two prices when there is a tax: the price that buyers pay and the price that sellers receive.

 If the price variable is the price paid by the buyers, then the demand curve does not move but the supply curve moves up vertically by the amount of the tax.

 If the price variable is the price received by the sellers, then the supply curve does not move but the demand curve moves down vertically by the amount of the tax.

 A tax causes a reduction in the surpluses going to the buyers and sellers, and also causes an overall loss of surplus generated by the market – the deadweight loss of the tax.

 The shape of the demand and supply schedules determines the tax burden and the size of the deadweight loss. Generally, the less sensitive the schedule the greater the burden of the tax.

27.9 Review Questions

1. Who pays the tax on a product? (By this we do not mean who physically pays the tax, but on whom the tax burden falls.)

2. Is the tax burden higher when the tax is proportional or when it is flat-rate? (It depends upon the two tax rates.)

3. Why is it that the steepness of the demand and supply schedules determines the effect and incidence of the tax?

4. We have seen that a tax on the sale (and purchase) of a good causes a deadweight loss in that market. Does this mean that this form of a tax is necessarily bad? (We discuss this in the next section.)

5. Give examples of various kinds of tax on goods and services that we see in practice (VAT, excise duty, vehicle license duty), and discuss what kinds of tax they are. You may remember Mrs Thatcher's infamous poll tax which forced everyone to pay a fixed tax on his or her house, irrespective of its value. What kind of tax was this? (This latter is not an easy question.)

27.10 Application: Indirect or Direct Taxation?

Direct taxation is the term that economists use for taxes on income (in any form, including profits). Indirect taxation is the term used for taxes on expenditure – the kind of taxes that we have been considering in this chapter. One clear message from this chapter is that this form of taxation causes a deadweight loss; some of the surplus previously generated by the market disappears when taxation is introduced. The inference from this message might be that this form of taxation is therefore necessarily bad. Here we consider whether this is in fact the case.

We use a very simple story with linear demand and supply curves, like the one we have told in this chapter. Consider a market without tax where the demand and supply curves are as in Fig. 27.17. The equilibrium price is 50, the equilibrium quantity is 50, the buyer surplus is 1250 and the seller surplus is also 1250, giving a total surplus of 2500.

Now, suppose the government introduces a flat-rate tax of 20 on the good. The new equilibrium price paid by the buyers becomes 60, the equilibrium price received by the sellers is 40 (the difference between the two being the tax of 20). The surplus of the buyers becomes 800; the surplus of the sellers also becomes 800; the government gets 800 in tax; and there is a deadweight loss of 100. All this is shown in Fig. 27.18.

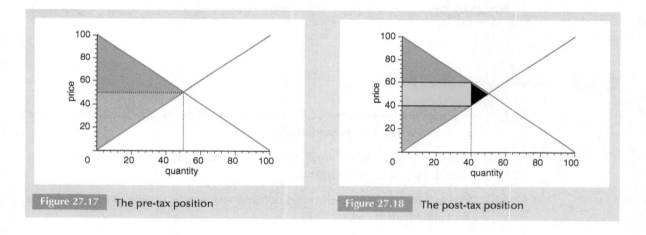

| Figure 27.17 | The pre-tax position |

| Figure 27.18 | The post-tax position |

Total surplus is now just 2400; the deadweight loss of 100 represents the loss of surplus generated in the market as a consequence of the introduction of the tax.

Critics might say that this is inefficient. A more efficient situation might be to levy the tax directly on the incomes of the agents involved. Let us see what happens if the government, instead of levying the tax indirectly, does so directly.

The analysis of one side of the market might be simple. If the suppliers consist of firms whose objective is to maximize profits, and if the direct tax introduced by the government is a tax on profits, then there is no shift in the supply curve. The quantity of output at which pre-tax profits are maximized must be the same quantity at which post-tax profits are maximized, if the tax simply takes a proportion of the profits. You should be clear about this. If we denote profits by π and output by q, and if we suppose that the government takes a proportion t of the profits in tax, then the without-tax optimization problem is to choose that q which maximizes π, while the with-tax optimization problem is to choose that q which maximizes $t\pi$. Clearly

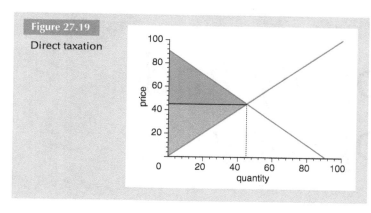

Figure 27.19

Direct taxation

the solution is the same. Multiplying the objective by a constant changes nothing[2].

So the supply curve might not shift. But the demand curve might, if the tax is on income and income affects demand. In general (that is, if the preferences are not quasi-linear), we would expect income to affect demand and we would therefore expect an increase in income tax to lower incomes and thus affect demand. In such a case we would expect that the demand curve would shift down. In general, it is not clear how much it would shift down, as this would depend on the amount of the tax and the responsiveness of demand to changes in income. One possibility is illustrated in Fig. 27.19, in which we have drawn an unchanged supply curve, and the demand curve has shifted downwards by 10.

In this example there is no indirect taxation. The equilibrium price is 45; the equilibrium quantity is 45, the surplus of the buyers 1012.5 and the surplus of the sellers is 1012.5. The government takes no indirect tax, but has revenue from the direct taxation. The total surplus is 2025, which is less than the original total surplus of 2500 before any tax was introduced. This last example is efficient in terms of the market, but less surplus is generated than initially. However there is, of course, the tax revenue raised by direct taxation.

We cannot conclude from this analysis whether one method of taxation is better than another, although we have shown the tools that economists can use to analyse the situation. But note: we have analysed only a part of the problem. The taxation will also have implications in other markets. There will be spillover effects elsewhere, affecting other prices and other quantities. To take into account all such effects we would need to do what is called *general equilibrium analysis*, which is beyond the scope of this book.

---

2. We should make one proviso. If the profits become negative then the firm may prefer to go out of business. If that happens we lose a bit of the supply. But if the tax is proportional and the pre-tax profit is positive, then so must be the post-tax profit.

Monopoly and Monopsony

28.1 Introduction

The previous chapter showed that if the government imposes a tax on some good there is a loss of surplus. We show a similar result in this chapter where we consider markets, on one side of which there is a single agent and, moreover, an agent that can choose the price in the market. Up to now we have been considering markets in which agents have to take the price as given; we called these price-taking or competitive markets, using the terms synonymously. There is clearly a bit of a hidden assumption here, namely that the number of agents in the market is too large for any one agent to choose the price. We gave some justification for this in Chapter 2, where we argued that in the competitive equilibrium there was no agent who could break the equilibrium price. In this chapter we consider a situation where this hidden assumption cannot possibly be true – namely a market in which there is just one agent on one side of the market; clearly that agent can set the price or, at a minimum, refuse to trade. Obviously if the agent can set the price then generally he or she will choose to do so, since by doing so will cause an increase in the profits or surplus (as we saw in Chapter 8). There are two possibilities – when the single agent is the single seller; and when the single agent is the single buyer. The first of these is called monopoly, the second monopsony. We consider the two in turn.

28.2 Profit Maximization for a Monopoly

We repeat the analysis of Chapter 13 with one difference. The firm can choose the price of the good as well as the quantity produced. Obviously the firm cannot choose these independently of each other; there is the constraint of the demand curve to consider. The higher the price that the firm selects, the lower the quantity it can sell; and the higher the quantity it wants to sell, the lower the price that it must charge. Otherwise it faces the same kind of problem as the price-taking firm; it must choose the output (and price) to maximize its profits.

The crucial point for a monopolist is that, when the firm increases its output, the lower is the price that it can charge. The constraint is the demand curve for the product, which we write in inverse form as

$$p = f(y) \tag{28.1}$$

In Eq. (28.1) y is the output produced and sold[1], and p is the price that the firm charges for the product. We expect the relationship to be a negative one; as the price rises, the quantity demanded, and hence sold, decreases.

Let us now do what we did in Chapter 13; we construct a graph with output along the horizontal axis and with total revenue, total cost and total profits on the vertical axis. The cost function is just as it was in Chapter 13; its shape will depend on the returns to scale that the firm has, and we shall discuss it shortly. In the meantime let us consider the shape of the total revenue function.

The revenue of the firm is simply the price multiplied by the output, that is:

$$revenue = py \tag{28.2}$$

For a competitive firm, for which the price is given and fixed, Eq. (28.2) is a linear function of y with slope equal to p. However for a monopolist, the price is not given and fixed, but depends upon the output that the firm produces and sells. If we combine Eqs (28.1) and (28.2), we find that the revenue of the firm is given by

$$revenue = py = f(y)y \tag{28.3}$$

Consider this as a function of y. There are two components: y and $f(y)$; the first increases with y, and the second decreases with y. The net effect depends upon the particular form of the demand function $f(.)$. Let us consider an important special case – a linear demand curve

$$p = \alpha - \beta y \tag{28.4}$$

In a graph with y on the horizontal axis and p on the vertical axis, this has an intercept on the vertical axis of α, a slope of $-\beta$, and an intercept on the horizontal axis of α/β.

Now consider the revenue of the firm. This is py; substituting Eq. (28.4) for p gives

$$revenue = py = \alpha y - \beta y^2 \tag{28.5}$$

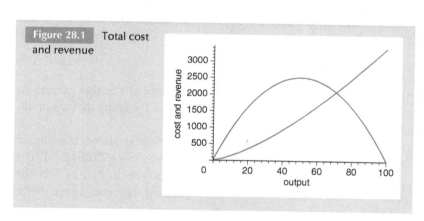

Figure 28.1 Total cost and revenue

Plotted in a graph with y on the horizontal axis and total revenue on the vertical axis, this is quadratic, starting at zero, rising at a decreasing rate until $y = \alpha/2\beta$, and then falling until $y = \alpha/\beta$ at which point the revenue is zero because the price is zero; beyond $y = \alpha/\beta$ the revenue is negative. This is shown in Fig. 28.1.

For future reference it will be found useful to find the slope of the revenue function, which is the rate at which revenue rises when the output rises. It is given the name of the marginal revenue function. From Eq. (28.5) we get

$$marginal\ revenue = d(revenue)/dy = \alpha - 2\beta y \tag{28.6}$$

The marginal revenue function is a straight line when plotted against y, with an intercept on the vertical axis of α, a slope of -2β, and an intercept on the horizontal axis of $\alpha/2\beta$.

1. There would be no point producing an output if it were not sold.

Note its relationship with the demand curve which we assumed to be linear; it has the same intercept on the vertical axis, and the intercept on the horizontal axis is half that of the demand curve. This intercept is where marginal revenue is zero, and it coincides with the output at which the revenue curve reaches its maximum.

Let us now return to our main theme. We draw a graph of total revenue, total cost and total profit as a function of output. We have already seen that, with a linear demand schedule the total revenue function is quadratic. We assume first that the firm has decreasing returns to scale so that its cost function is convex. Consider Fig. 28.2. In this the cost function is convex, the revenue function is quadratic and concave, and the profit function is also concave. It will be seen that profits are zero when the output is zero, and again when the output is just over 70. In between zero and 70 profits are positive; above an output of 70 they are negative.

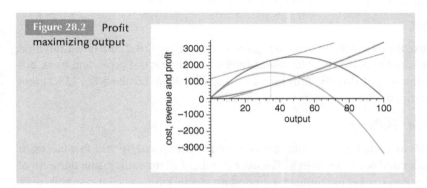

Figure 28.2 Profit maximizing output

The figure also shows the profit-maximizing output. This is where the profit function reaches its maximum or, alternatively, where the vertical distance between the revenue function and the cost function is maximized. It will be seen that this is where the slope of the revenue function equals the slope of the cost function (we have drawn the tangents to the two curves at this profit-maximizing point to make this clear).

Now we can interpret this condition. At the profit-maximizing point the slope of the revenue function must equal the slope of the cost function. Now we know what these two slopes are: the slope of the revenue function is the marginal revenue function; the slope of the cost function is the marginal cost function. So the profit-maximizing condition is that given in Eq. (28.7).

marginal revenue = marginal cost   (28.7)

A formal and general proof is provided in the mathematical appendix to this chapter. In the particular case that we are considering here, we can see from the graph that the profit-maximizing output is around 34.5.

As ever, we can translate everything from total curves to marginal curves. These are in Fig. 28.3. Let us assume that the demand curve (28.4) has the values $\alpha = 100$ and $\beta = 1$. The straight line in Fig. 28.3 is the marginal revenue curve, with intercept on the vertical axis at 100, a slope equal to -2, and an intercept on the horizontal axis of 50 (half that on the demand curve). The upward sloping curve is the marginal cost curve; we know that this is everywhere increasing if we have decreasing returns to scale. Where the two curves intersect is

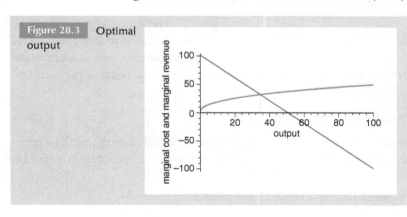

Figure 28.3 Optimal output

the profit-maximizing point at an output of around 34.5 – exactly the same as before. So we have the condition for the optimum output. The optimal price is given by the demand function.

28.3 Loss Minimization

We should be careful in applying the profit-maximizing condition; it does not guarantee a positive profit, but merely that profit is maximized. This is very easy to see if we take the above example and add to the firm's costs some new fixed cost – perhaps a government tax – which is sufficiently large to make the profits everywhere negative. What happens? The answer is, nothing to the total revenue and marginal revenue curves. The new fixed cost shifts the entire total cost curve up by a constant amount, but this has no impact on the marginal cost curve because shifting a curve vertically upwards by a constant amount does not change its slope at any point. So the addition of the fixed costs, while making profits everywhere negative, does not change Fig. 28.3; it looks exactly the same. Is the identified point still a profit-maximizing point? Well, yes, in the sense that it minimizes the losses which now exist everywhere as a result of the additional fixed costs. But even at that point there are losses; it may pay the firm to go out of business altogether.

28.4 Increasing Returns to Scale

You may recall that, for a competitive firm, the optimal output for a firm with increasing returns to scale is infinite. Let us see whether that is still the case for a monopoly. We repeat the analysis of Section 28.3, the only difference being that the cost curve is concave, and hence the marginal cost curve is everywhere decreasing. We construct Fig. 28.4, which shows total costs and revenues measured on the vertical axis.

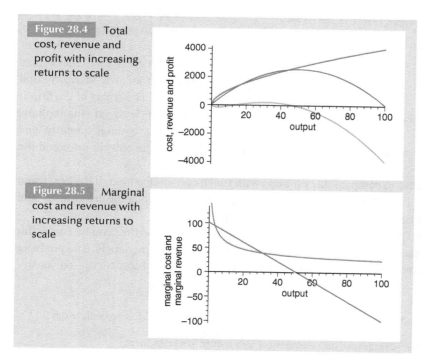

Figure 28.4 Total cost, revenue and profit with increasing returns to scale

Figure 28.5 Marginal cost and revenue with increasing returns to scale

The total cost curve is concave instead of convex as it was in Fig. 28.2. The total revenue and profit curves are also concave. We now derive the corresponding marginal curves (see Fig. 28.5).

From Fig. 28.5 we see that there are two points at which marginal revenue and marginal costs are equal – one at around an output of four and one around an output of 31. If we look back at Fig. 28.4, we see that the first of these is a (local) loss-maximizing point, while the second is a profit-maximizing point. If we examine Fig. 28.5 carefully, we can see that, for the first of these the marginal cost curve cuts the marginal revenue curve from above, while in the second the marginal cost curve cuts the marginal revenue curve from below. It is clear that we ought to supplement our condition for the profit-maximizing point in the following way[2]:

 profit maximization occurs when marginal revenue = marginal cost at a point where the marginal cost curve cuts the marginal revenue curve from below

28.5 The Supply Curve for a Monopolist

It should be clear that a supply curve for a monopolist does not exist, simply because the monopolist does not take the price as given but takes the demand curve as given.

28.6 Producer Surplus

What is the producer surplus under monopoly? Consider Fig. 28.6. In this figure we have inserted the demand curve – the downward sloping straight line from (100, 0) to (0, 100); the marginal revenue curve – the downward sloping straight line from (50, 0) to (0, 100); and the marginal cost curve – the upward sloping concave curve.

Optimal output is around 34.5, where the marginal revenue and marginal cost curves intersect. The optimal price is given by the demand curve and is shown in Fig. 28.6; it is around 65.5; (recall that the equation of the demand curve is given by $p = 100 - y$). The total revenue of the firm is the product of the quantity produced (34.5) and the price (64.5). It is the area of the rectangle bounded by the optimal quantity and the optimal price. The total costs of the firm to produce the output of 34.5 is the area under the marginal cost curve up to the optimal output. It follows, therefore, that the profit or surplus of the firm is the area between the optimal price, the optimal quantity and the marginal cost curve. The buyer surplus is the area between the optimal price and the demand curve.

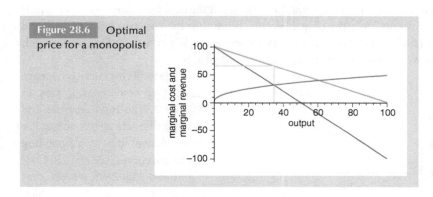

Figure 28.6   Optimal price for a monopolist

It is instructive to compare this situation with that under competition. If the firm was a price-taker and if an equilibrium price was charged, the output would be just over 61 and the price would be a little under 39, as shown in Fig. 28.7.

In this case, the buyer surplus is the area between the price and the demand curve; this is obviously bigger than the surplus which the buyers get under monopoly. The producer surplus is the area between the competitive price and the marginal cost curve – obviously[3]

---

2. This is the second-order condition which is proved formally in the mathematical appendix to this chapter.
3. You should make sure that you understand why I have written 'obviously' here.

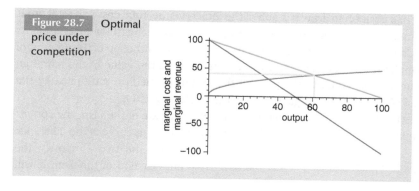

Figure 28.7 Optimal price under competition

smaller than the surplus the producer gets under monopoly. So there is a re-distribution of surplus; under monopoly the producer gets more surplus and the buyers get less. But there is also a reduction in the total surplus – the triangle between the monopoly output, the demand curve and the marginal cost curve is missing under monopoly. Monopoly is inefficient; it leads to a reduction in the total surplus because there is a reduction in the quantity traded.

28.7 Profit Maximization for a Monopsonist

We now build on the work that we did in Chapter 26 – the labour market. We considered there a firm demanding labour in the labour market, although we assumed there that the labour market was competitive and that the firm took the price of labour (the wage rate) as given. In this chapter we consider the situation in which the firm is the only buyer of labour; that is, we assume that the firm is a *monopsonist* in the labour market.

Recall the decision problem of the firm; to make things simple we assume that the firm is operating in the short run and it must decide the quantity of labour to employ. In Chapter 26 we assumed that the wage rate (the price of labour) w was fixed. If the firm is the only buyer in the labour market then it must take account of the supply curve of labour. If this is upward-sloping, then the more labour it employs the higher the wage rate that it must pay. Let us take a simple case and assume that the supply of labour curve is linear, specifically:

$$w = \gamma + \delta l \tag{28.8}$$

In Eq. (28.8) w is the wage rate and l the quantity of labour it employs. Now recall that the total cost to the firm of employing q units of labour at a wage rate w is given by

$$\text{total cost} = wl + rK \tag{28.9}$$

Here r is the price of the fixed input (we are in the short run) and K is the fixed quantity of the fixed input (capital if you like). For a competitive firm the value of w is fixed, but for a monopsonist it depends upon the quantity of labour purchased. As l rises so does w, and hence total cost rises more than proportionately. If we substitute Eq. (28.8) into the cost function Eq. (28.9), we can see how total costs depend on the employment of labour.

$$\text{total cost} = (\gamma + \delta l)l + rK \tag{28.10}$$

You will see that the total cost is a quadratic and convex function of l, since δ is positive.

For future reference it will be useful to define marginal cost as a function of l. This is the slope of the total cost function when graphed against l; it is given by the derivative of the total cost with respect to l.

$$\text{marginal cost} = \gamma + 2\delta l \tag{28.11}$$

You will see that it has the same intercept as the supply of labour curve and twice the slope. You should also note the parallels: the marginal revenue curve for a monopolist has the same intercept as the demand curve and twice the slope.

We are now in a position to draw a graph of the total revenue, total cost and total profit of the firm as a function of the amount of labour that it employs. Using the same arguments that we used in Chapter 26, the revenue function of the firm, as a function of the amount of labour that it employs, must be concave with a slope equal to the value of the marginal product of labour; that is, equal to the price of the output of the firm multiplied by the marginal product of labour. We thus get the picture drawn in Fig. 28.8.

In this figure the upper concave function is the total revenue of the firm, the convex (quadratic) function is the total cost of the firm, and the remaining curve is the difference between the two – namely the profit function of the firm. It will be seen that the profits reach a maximum where the gap between revenue and cost is maximized, which occurs where the slope of the revenue function is equal to the slope of the cost function. But we know these two slopes: the slope of the revenue function equals the value of the marginal product of labour; and the slope of the cost function is what we have called the marginal cost function. So the profit maximizing condition[4] is

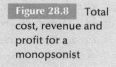

Figure 28.8 Total cost, revenue and profit for a monopsonist

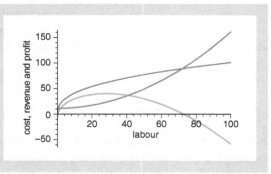

 Profit maximization occurs when the value of the marginal product of labour = the marginal cost of labour

Once again we can redraw all the total curves from Fig. 28.8 as curves involving the respective marginals, which are just the slopes of the total curves. We note that the slope of the total revenue curve is everywhere falling, and the slope of the total cost curve is everywhere rising. In the particular case that we are considering, we also know that the marginal cost curve in Eq. (28.11) is linear. We are therefore able to draw Fig. 28.9.

Figure 28.9 The profit maximizing output

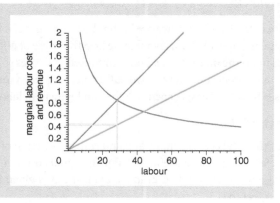

In Fig. 28.9, the downward-sloping line is the marginal revenue function, the lower upward-sloping line is the supply of labour function and the upper upward-sloping line (with twice the slope) is the marginal cost function. We can see that marginal cost equals marginal revenue (the value of the marginal product of labour) when around 28 units of labour are employed – exactly as we found earlier. This is the profit-maximizing condition for the firm. The wage rate that the firm pays is given by the supply of labour curve at the optimal quantity of labour; in this case a rate of just under 0.44.

---

4. A formal and general proof can be found in the mathematical appendix to this chapter.

We can now work out the various surpluses under monopsony. The workers get the area between the wage rate and the supply of labour curve. The firm gets the area bounded by the wage rate, the optimal employment and the marginal revenue curve[5].

What would happen under competition? The wage rate would be such that it equalled the value of the marginal product of labour – so optimal employment would be just under 44 and the wage rate would be around 0.65. Notice that monopsony reduces both the total employment and the wage rate. The latter seems obvious – a sole employer will pay less because it has the power to do so. At first the former seems less obvious, but it is the inevitable consequence of paying less; given the upward-sloping supply of labour curve, less labour is supplied at a lower wage.

Monopsony also changes the surpluses. Under competition the surplus going to labour is the area between the competitive wage and the supply of labour curve. The

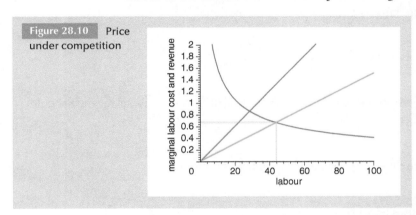

Figure 28.10 Price under competition

surplus going to the firm is the area between the competitive wage and the marginal revenue curve, which is the demand for labour curve under competition. So monopsony lowers the surplus going to labour and increases the surplus going to the firm[6]. But it also has the effect of reducing the total surplus – the triangular area between the monopsony price, the demand curve for labour and the supply curve of labour is now lost as a consequence of the lower quantity of labour employed. We get the familiar conclusion; monopsony is inefficient. It lowers the total quantity of surplus extracted from the market as the consequence of a lower quantity traded.

28.8 Minimum Wage Legislation

In this situation there is something that a government can do; it can introduce a legally-binding minimum wage. If it decides to do this, then the obvious thing to do is to set it exactly at the competitive wage level. In this way it forces the monopsonist to act as a competitive firm, and the surpluses are restored to what they would have been under competition. The amount of labour employed is also increased, although of course the monopsonist gets a lower profit under such legislation than if it was allowed to pay what it wanted.

---

5. The area underneath the marginal revenue curve is the total revenue, and the rectangular area bounded by the optimal wage rate and the optimal employment is the (short run) costs, so the difference is the profit (forgetting fixed costs).
6. Make sure you understand why this *must* be the case.

28.9 Summary

In this chapter we have considered two situations in which a single agent has the power to set the price: monopoly and monopsony. The first of these is when there is a single seller in a market; the second when there is single buyer.

➡ For a monopolist, profit maximization implies that marginal revenue should equal marginal cost at an output where the marginal cost curve intersects the marginal revenue curve from below.

➡ There is no such thing as a supply curve for a monopolist.

➡ Monopoly causes a loss of surplus.

➡ For a monopsonist, profit maximization implies that marginal labour revenue should equal marginal cost.

➡ There is no such thing as a demand curve for a monopsonist.

➡ Monopsony causes a loss of surplus.

➡ Minimum wage legislation helps restore the lost surplus.

You might like to ask whether maximum price legislation for a monopolist helps to replace the lost surplus.

28.10 Review Questions

1. Why do both monopoly and monopsony reduce the total surplus in a market? (Because the quantity exchanged is reduced.)

2. Show that, at the monopoly price, there are buyers who do not buy but who would be willing to buy at a price higher than the marginal cost of the monopolist. This is clearly inefficient. Can the monopolist do anything about it?

3. Discuss the effects of maximum price legislation in a market where there is a monopolist. What is the best maximum price for the government to set if it wants to maximize the total surplus in the market? Why might this create problems for a monopolist with an increasing-returns-to scale technology?

4. Discuss the effects of minimum wage legislation in a market where there is a monopsonist. What is the best minimum wage for the government to set if it wants to maximize the total surplus in the market?

28.11 Application: Monopoly and Monopsony in the Same Market

You may have been wondering what happens in a market where there is a single buyer and a single seller. We know what happens if we have a single seller and lots of buyers; the seller acts as a monopolist, takes a bigger surplus, and in so doing reduces the total surplus generated in the market. We also know what happens if we have a single buyer and lots of sellers; the buyer acts as a monopsonist, takes a bigger surplus, and in so doing reduces the total surplus generated in the market. You may be thinking: 'if there is a single seller and a single buyer, perhaps the two effects cancel out and we get back to the efficient case of perfect competition?'.

This seems a sensible conclusion, but it is difficult to justify. The problem is that we have not yet defined the rules of the trading game in such a market. In a market in which there is a single seller and lots of buyers, the obvious rule is easy to state: the seller posts a price and the buyers buy what they want at that price; the seller sells a quantity equal to aggregate demand at that price. In a market in which there is a single buyer and lots of sellers, the obvious rule is once again easy to state: the buyer posts a price and the sellers sell what they want to sell at that price; the buyer buys a quantity equal to the aggregate supply at that price.

However in a market with a single buyer and a single seller there is no such obvious rule. One possible theory is that the buyer and the seller indulge in some kind of bargaining process; they bargain over the price at which they will trade and the quantity which they want to exchange. Economists do have theories as to how bargaining is carried out, though a full discussion of such theories takes us way beyond the scope of this book. We can describe one such theory however, known as the cooperative bargaining solution. The term 'cooperative' may seem a bit odd in a bargaining situation – which is one of conflict – but we will describe what is meant by this. In essence it means that the two bargainers (the monopolist and the monopsonist in this example) agree to the rules governing the outcome to the bargaining process, and then ask someone to apply those rules. The rules must appear reasonable to both bargainers.

What might these rules be? One set was proposed by the brilliant mathematician and economist John Nash – the same man who proposed the Nash equilibrium concept in game theory, which we will discuss in Chapter 30, who won the Nobel Prize in Economics and about whom a book and a film, both called *A Beautiful Mind*, were made. These rules assume that the two bargainers obey the axioms of expected utility theory (see Chapter 24) so that they both have a cardinal utility function (invariant up to a positive linear transformation[7]) over the final outcome. Moreover there is assumed to be some disagreement outcome, which describes the utilities of the two bargainers if they fail to reach an agreement. In the context of the monopolist and the monopsonist, the disagreement point must simply be the situation in which they do not trade and therefore receive zero surpluses. The rules are the following:

- *efficiency*: the outcome must be efficient, in the sense that there is no other outcome which is better for one of the two bargainers and no worse for the other;

- *linear invariance*: if the utility function of one or other of the bargainers is linearly transformed into another function, then the outcome should be unchanged;

---

7. Which means that if the function $u(.)$ represents the preferences of one of the bargainers, then so does any other function $a + bu(.)$, where b is positive, and that no other function represents the preferences.

● *symmetry*: if the bargaining problem is symmetric (that is, the disagreement outcome is the same for both), then so should be the outcome;

● *independence of irrelevant alternatives*: if we have two bargaining problems (problem 1 and problem 2) with the same disagreement outcome, and for which the set of possible alternative outcomes in problem 1 is contained within the set of possible outcomes in problem 2, and if the chosen outcome in problem 2 is within the set of possible outcomes of problem 1, then the chosen outcome in problem 1 should be the same as that in problem 2.

The first assumption seems innocent, and so does the second; after all, the utility functions are unique only up to a linear transformation (changing the units of measurement of utility should not change the outcome). The third assumption is more subtle as it implies some kind of equality in the bargaining process. The final assumption looks difficult, but it can be stated more simply: it says that taking away possible outcomes that were not chosen should not change the chosen outcome. Stated in this form it appears innocuous. It is, however, quite important to what follows.

The idea is the following. These rules are presented to the bargainers; if they agree to them as general principles, then they should be happy with the implied outcome. What is the implied outcome? Nash showed something very clever; if these assumptions are accepted, then the implied outcome is that outcome which maximizes the product of the utility functions of the two bargainers[8]. To prove this result would take us beyond the scope of this book, but we can apply it. Let us do so in the context of the bargaining problem between the monopolist and the monopsonist. To make life easy, let us consider a very simple case; you can then try and extend it.

Consider a monopolist with the marginal cost schedule pictured in Fig. 28.11. This is the upward-sloping line, which would be the firm's supply function if it were a competitive firm. Suppose the monopsonist has the downward sloping marginal revenue curve in Fig. 28.11; this would be the firm's demand function if it were a competitive firm. If there was perfect competition, the equilibrium price would be 50 and the quantity exchanged would be 50.

The bargaining is over the price. Given the chosen price, the lesser of the demand and supply determines the quantity traded. Fig. 28.11 shows what would happen if the price agreed was 25. The monopolist would supply 25 units and this would be the amount traded. The monopsonist would have a surplus equal to the blue area – that is, 1562.5 – and the monopolist would have a surplus equal to the red area – that is, 312.5.

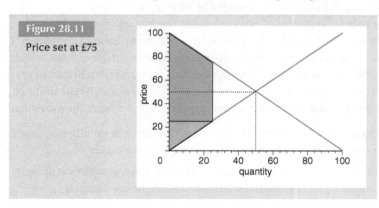

Figure 28.11

Price set at £75

Let us assume that both the bargainers are risk-neutral, and therefore their utilities are equal to their surpluses. At what price would the product of their surpluses (and hence the product of their utilities) be maximized? Take a price p above the equilibrium – as in Fig. 28.11. The quantity exchanged would be p (given by the supply curve), and the surplus of the seller would be $p^2/2$ (the area of the little triangle below the price). The surplus of the buyer

---

8. We mentioned this rule in Chapter 9.

would be the equivalent of the blue shaded area – namely $[p^2/2 + p(100 - 2p)]$. The product of the two surpluses would thus be

$$(p^2/2)[p^2/2 + p(100 - 2p)] = p^3(200 - 3p)/4 = 50p^3 - 3p^4/3. \tag{28.12}$$

If we maximize this with respect to p we find that the product-maximizing value of p is[9] ... 50. If we do the same with a price greater than 50, we get the same solution. Hence the outcome of the bargaining process, if the bargainers agree to the Nash bargaining solution, is the competitive price and hence the competitive outcome. Your intuition is confirmed!

This is a neat result and you should investigate how general it is. You can take different demand and supply schedules and repeat the analysis. You can probably guess that it is not general; we know that the competitive equilibrium is the outcome which maximizes the sum of the surpluses, while the Nash solution to the bargaining problem is the outcome which maximizes the product of the surpluses. These may be, but need not be, the same. But it is reassuring in this simple context that we get this neat result.

You should also note that the assumptions underlying the Nash solution are plausible, but not necessarily true. In addition, to apply the solution in practice requires the two bargainers to agree to the assumptions. You might like to ask if this is the procedure adopted when real bargaining takes place. In some instances it is; for example, when both sides to a bargaining dispute agree to hand over the problem to an independent tribunal which has agreed terms of reference. Independent pay review bodies are good examples of this kind of tribunal. But in other cases the bargaining breaks down without such a reference, and the two sides resort to industrial action of various kinds, such as strikes and lockouts. It would be interesting to examine such cases, but that would take us beyond the scope of this book.

---

9. If we denote the product by P, then $dP/dp = 150p^2 - 3p^3$ which, when equated to zero, gives $p = 50$ (and $p = 0$, which is a minimum).

28.12 Mathematical Appendix

We first provide a general proof of the profit-maximizing condition for a monopolist. This is short and simple. We first note that profits are the difference between revenue and costs, and both of these are functions of output. We denote revenue by $R(y)$ and hence get:

$$\text{Profit} = \pi = R(y) - C(y) \tag{A28.1}$$

Applying the usual condition for a maximum, that $d\pi/dy = 0$, we get

$$d\pi/dy = dR(y)/dy - dC(y)/dy = 0 \tag{A28.2}$$

Hence

$$dR(y)/dy = dC(y)/dy \tag{A28.3}$$

This simply says that marginal revenue should equal marginal cost – see Eq. (28.7).

We then invoke the second-order condition which says that the slope of π should be decreasing at the maximum; that is, that $d^2\pi/dy^2$ should be negative. This yields the condition that

$$d^2 R(y)/dy^2 < d^2 C(y)/dy^2 \tag{A28.4}$$

Eq. (A28.4) says that the marginal cost curve should cut the marginal revenue curve from below.

We now provide a general proof of the profit-maximizing condition for a monopsonist. This is also short and simple. Indeed it is almost identical to the derivation of the profit-maximizing condition for a monopolist. We first note that profits are the difference between revenue and costs, and that both of these are functions of the quantity of labour purchased. We denote revenue by $R(l)$ and costs by $C(l)$, and hence get:

$$\text{Profit} = \pi = R(l) - C(l) \tag{A28.5}$$

Applying the usual condition for a maximum, that $d\pi/dl = 0$, we obtain

$$d\pi/dl = dR(l)/dl - dC(l)/dl = 0 \tag{A28.6}$$

and hence

$$dR(l)/dl = dC(l)/dl \tag{A28.7}$$

This says that the value of the marginal product of labour (the marginal revenue from labour) should be equated with the marginal cost of labour, as stated in the text.

We then invoke the second-order condition which states that the slope of π should be decreasing at the maximum; that is, that $d^2\pi/dl^2$ should be negative. This yields the following condition:

$$d^2 R(l)/dl^2 < d^2 C(l)/dl^2 \tag{A28.8}$$

This requires that the marginal cost of labour curve should cut the value of the marginal product of labour curve from below.

Natural Monopoly and Discrimination

29.1 Introduction

This chapter discusses two things, both related to the fact that, in the presence of a monopoly, there is less surplus generated in the market because of the existence of the monopoly. You will recall that this was partly as a consequence of the monopolist choosing the price, but more the consequence of a lower quantity of the good being traded. The first thing we examine in this chapter is the issue of whether the lost surplus might be justifiable in some sense because the monopoly has access to a more efficient technology. The second is whether it might be possible to recover some of the lost surplus through discrimination of some form. After all, the reason why the monopolist cannot produce up to the point where the price is equal to the marginal cost is that, in the absence of discrimination, the monopolist has to charge the same price for everyone.

29.2 Natural Monopoly

One very obvious reason why a single large firm might be more appropriate in some industries is that a single large firm might have access to a more efficient technology than lots of small firms. This is plausible if centralization of the industry has consequences in terms of increased efficiency; on the contrary, if splitting it up into lots of little units causes losses of efficiency and increased bureaucratic costs. (You might consider if that is what happened when British Rail in the UK was split into several operating companies.) If this is the case then it may be better – in some sense which we will discuss shortly – to have a single large firm. Even if it behaves like a monopolist, and there is an associated deadweight loss as a consequence, the end product for both consumers and producer might be better.

The example that follows is extremely simple and is not meant to be realistic. The only point it makes is that output may be higher, and the price lower, with a monopoly that has access to a better technology than with a competitive industry with an inferior technology. We start by assuming a constant marginal cost function for both the industry when competitive and as a monopoly, the difference being that we assume a much lower (constant) marginal cost for the monopoly. We assume throughout a simple linear aggregate demand

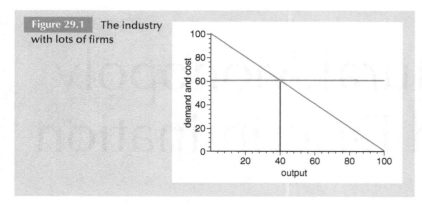

Figure 29.1 The industry with lots of firms

schedule in the industry. We start with the competitive industry, for which Fig. 29.1 shows the demand curve.

The demand curve has an intercept of 100 on both axes; the horizontal axis measures the aggregate quantity demanded and supplied, and the vertical axis the demand and the marginal cost. The horizontal line at 60 is the assumed constant marginal cost function: for all the firms in this competitive industry the marginal cost of producing an extra unit of output is 60.

In this competitive industry the aggregate output is where price equals marginal cost – that is, is where the marginal cost curve and the aggregate demand curve intersect. This is at an output of 40, and the price is equal to the marginal cost of 60. Fig. 29.2 shows the consumer surplus in the competitive equilibrium; there is no producer surplus.

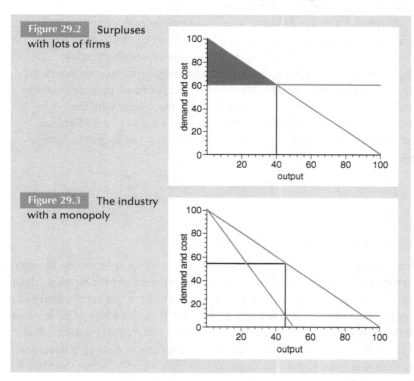

Figure 29.2 Surpluses with lots of firms

Figure 29.3 The industry with a monopoly

Now let us suppose that, if all the firms in the industry were merged into one big firm, the technology would be such that the marginal cost in the merged monopoly would be significantly reduced. Let us suppose that it could be reduced from 60 to 10. We then have Fig. 29.3.

In Fig. 29.3 we have inserted the marginal revenue schedule facing the firm; because there is a linear demand schedule with intercepts of 100 and 100 we know that the marginal revenue schedule is also linear, with the same intercept on the vertical axis and half the intercept on the horizontal axis. The horizontal line at the bottom is the monopolist's marginal cost curve. The monopolist's optimal output is at the point where marginal cost and marginal revenue are equal – as Fig. 29.3 shows, this occurs at an output of 45. The price that the monopolist will charge is given by the demand curve; as we see from Fig. 29.3 this is 55. We get the rather obvious result that, if the monopolist has a sufficiently lower marginal cost function, it can produce a higher quantity at a lower price than can the competitive industry.

It is instructive to look at the surpluses under this monopoly and compare them with the competitive case. These are shown in Fig. 29.4. The triangular area at the top left is the consumer surplus under monopoly – this is obviously larger than under competition because the quantity exchanged is higher and the price lower. The rectangular area is the

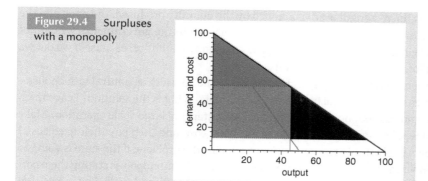

Figure 29.4 Surpluses with a monopoly

surplus going to the monopolist. The sum of these two surpluses is the total surplus generated by the monopoly. So with the more efficient monopolist, even if it chooses the price itself, we could have an industry in which the price is lower, the output higher, and the total surplus higher than if the firms were competitive. This kind of situation is what is usually meant by a natural monopoly.

But we can also identify a deadweight loss caused by the monopoly; this is the triangular area to the right of the figure. Why is this the deadweight loss caused by the monopoly? Well, if this industry behaved like a competitive industry in the sense that it set its output so that the price was equal to the marginal cost, then the output would be 90 and the price 10; the whole of the area above the marginal cost curve and under the demand curve would go to the consumers as their surplus.

So we have the following conclusion: with the more efficient monopoly replacing the competitive industry, the price is lower and the quantity is higher and everyone is happier. But if the monopolist could be made to behave as a competitive firm things could be even better, in the sense that the price could be lower still, the quantity higher still, and the aggregate surplus even larger.

So – you may be asking – why do we not recommend that the government imposes a maximum price in the market equal to the marginal cost of the monopolist? This would force the monopolist to produce the competitive output of 90, force it to charge a price of 10, and the consumers would get the surplus that they would have got under competition.

Indeed this is the best solution if the situation we have pictured is the long run and the surpluses are the true surpluses. This is often the situation in nationalized natural monopolies in many countries. But suppose that this is the short run situation. Suppose further that it masks the fact that the monopolist has to pay a fixed cost K. Let us add this into the analysis by inserting into the diagram a curve representing the average total costs of the firm. These are simply $K/y + 10$, where y is the output of the firm and the 10 is the marginal cost already portrayed in the figure. This average total cost function is obviously downward sloping, and is the convex curve in Fig. 29.5.

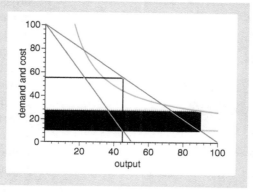

Figure 29.5 Loss caused to the monopoly with competitive pricing

What do we notice? At the monopoly output 45 and price 55, the price is quite clearly bigger than the average total cost, so the firm makes a positive profit. But at the competitive output 90 and price 10, the price is lower than the average total cost so the firm is making a loss. This is rather obvious for any fixed cost, because the price is covering only the marginal cost; indeed it is equal to the marginal cost! This loss is shown in Fig. 28.5; it is the rectangular area bounded by the quantity produced, the price and the average total cost. So the monopolist can legitimately say to the government: 'we cannot charge the marginal cost price and produce the competitive quantity, because if we did we would make a loss. We need to cover our fixed costs.'

This situation is typical of many industries we would consider as natural monopolies – the electricity, gas, water and rail industries, for example. What is the solution? Leave them as competitive and miss out on the technological advantages of large-scale operation? Make them state monopolies, force them to charge marginal cost, and then pay their fixed costs? This latter seems the best thing to do, but there remains the problem; if the state is going to pay the monopolist's fixed costs, how is the state sure that the monopoly is stating them correctly? There is a clear incentive for the monopoly to be lazy and inefficient. Does that remind you of anything?

29.3 Discrimination

At this point it may be useful to remind ourselves of why there is a deadweight loss with monopoly. Let us take a specific example, which we can then use to suggest a way of eliminating this deadweight loss through price discrimination. The example will use a discrete good but the point can also be made with a continuous good. Consider the aggregate demand curve in Fig. 29.6. Up to 10 units may be bought, with reservation prices 100, 90, 80, 70, 60, 50, 40, 30, 20 and 10.

Suppose the monopolist has a cost function such that the marginal cost of production is constant and equal to 36. If the monopolist is restricted to a unique price for every unit sold, what price should be chosen? A little calculation reveals that, if the monopolist's objective is to maximize profit, a price of 70 should be chosen. Fig. 29.7 illustrates this, and Table 29.1 gives more detail.

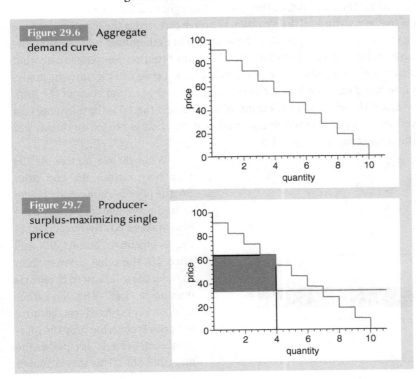

Figure 29.6 Aggregate demand curve

Figure 29.7 Producer-surplus-maximizing single price

I have assumed throughout that, if a potential buyer is indifferent between buying and not buying, he or she is classified as a buyer. Note that the consumer surplus is the area between the price line (70) and the demand curve, making a total of 60; and also that there is a deadweight loss of 42 caused by the monopoly, equal to the area between the monopoly quantity (4), the marginal cost and the demand curve. Under competition, the total surplus would be the entire area between the marginal cost and the demand curves – a total of 238; this would all go to the consumers. Table 29.1 gives a numerical picture of the same example. It also shows that the best price is 70.

Table 29.1 Producer-surplus-maximizing single price

Price	Surplus
100	64
90	108
80	132
70	136
60	120
50	84
40	28

Table 29.1 shows that, at a price of 70, buyers with reservation prices of 100, 90, 80 and 70 all buy, thus giving a total revenue of 280. Each unit costs the monopolist 36, thus costing 144 in total. This leads to a surplus of 280 minus 144, that is 136. But notice that the buyers with reservation prices 60, 50 and 40 do not buy, even though the monopolist could make a profit out of them given that the cost per unit is only 36. This raises an interesting question: why does the monopolist not sell to the buyers with reservation prices of 60, 50 and 40 at, say, a price of 40? The business would still make a profit of 12 out of them.

The problem is this: if the monopolist has to choose a unique price at which to sell all the units available for sale, it cannot charge a price of 70 to four of the buyers and a price of 40 to three of the buyers. It is obviously in the monopolist's interests to sell up to seven units because the first seven reservation prices are all greater than the cost of production. A price can be chosen for each unit which would make both the monopolist and the buyer happy, but if the monopolist charges a low price for the later units (in the absence of discrimination), then it has to charge a low price for the early units. The fact that the monopoly output falls short of the output at which marginal cost is equal to the price is not a consequence of the fact that the monopolist is a monopolist; it is a consequence of the fact that it charges a unique price for each unit of the good sold.

The obvious solution is for the monopolist to discriminate. The most efficient way is when the monopolist is allowed to discriminate completely, by charging a different price for each unit sold. In this example it is easy; the monopolist sells the first unit at a price of 100 to the buyer with a reservation price of 100, the second unit at a price of 90 to the buyer with a reservation price of 90, ..., the seventh unit at a price of 40 to the buyer with a reservation price of 40. In this way the monopolist gets a surplus or profit of $(100 - 36) + (90 - 36) + \cdots + (40 - 36) = 238$, which is the entire area between the marginal cost of 36 and the demand curve. If this were to happen there would be no deadweight loss and the whole surplus available under competition would be realized. The main difference, in this example, is that instead of it all going to the consumers, all the surplus now goes to the monopolist. This is not necessarily bad as the government can always tax it away. What is important is that the surplus is generated. As long as it is generated it can always be re-distributed. If it is not generated, there is nothing to re-distribute. For that reason, price discrimination might be a solution to the problem caused by the deadweight loss of monopoly.

The discrimination described above is called 'discrimination of the first degree'. It is complete discrimination in that, for each unit sold, there is a different price. So the monopolist discriminates, not only between individuals but also between different units bought by the same individual. For rather obvious reasons this kind of perfect discrimination might be difficult to implement[1] and enforce[2], and so in practice we observe less complete forms of discrimination.

Two kinds of discrimination can be observed in practice; one where there is discrimination of price depending upon the quantity purchased, and another where there is discrimination of price depending upon the purchaser. The first of these is called 'discrimination of the second degree' and the second 'discrimination of the third degree'.

1. The monopolist needs to know all the reservation prices.
2. The monopolist would have to somehow stop individuals with low reservation prices buying the good and then re-selling it to individuals with high reservation prices.

The most obvious example of discrimination of the second degree is when the monopolist offers discounts for bulk purchase; for example, supermarkets may give discounts if large quantities are bought. The most obvious discrimination of the third degree is when the monopolist offers different prices to different types of people; for example, train companies charge less to young people and to old people than to middle-aged people. The reason why they do this is to increase their surplus, otherwise they would not do it. In a sense these types of discrimination are somewhere between a situation of no discrimination and one of discrimination of the first degree: a situation in which all the surplus is extracted and a situation (as far as the extracted total is concerned, though not its distribution) under competition. Perhaps it is obvious that it is in the interests of the monopolist to extract and retain as much of this total surplus as possible. So the greater the degree of discrimination the better, as far as the extraction of the total surplus is concerned.

29.4 Summary

This chapter has been concerned with the deadweight loss caused by a monopoly. We have investigated whether it might be justified or eliminated.

> If a monopoly can take advantage of a more efficient technology, it may be the case that the price could be lower and the output higher under monopoly than under competition, and the total surplus higher (though there is still a deadweight loss caused by monopoly).

> A monopoly, forced by government legislation to charge a price equal to the marginal cost, may make a loss which could be covered by the government so as to maximize the surplus extracted from the market.

> Discrimination of price could reduce the deadweight loss, the extent of the reduction depending upon the extent of the discrimination.

29.5 Review Questions

1. Consider examples of natural monopolies that exist in practice. Does it matter whether these are run as nationalized industries or are privatized and subject to regulation by the government?

2. What problems are created for a monopolist with increasing-returns-to-scale technology if it is subjected to maximum price legislation with the price put equal to the competitive price? Can the problem be solved by the government subsidizing the monopoly? Is this what happens in practice? With what consequences?

3. Why do railways charge students less? Why do they have rail cards? Why do airlines charge less to those passengers who book early?

4. Give examples of discrimination in the real world.

29.6 Application: what kinds of Price Discrimination are there in the Real World?

There are innumerable examples of price discrimination in the real world. They are all illustrations of ways in which one side of the market tries to appropriate more of the surplus available in the market. In those markets in which the seller sets the price, such as most goods markets, the discrimination takes the form of different prices of the good sold to different people under different circumstances. In those markets in which the buyer sets the price, for example in most labour markets, the discrimination takes the form of different prices of the good bought from different people under different circumstances. The purpose of this simple application is merely to point out these numerous forms of discrimination in the real world.

The simplest form is discrimination over the quantity bought or sold. If the price per unit for a bulk purchase is less than the price per unit for a single purchase, we have this form of discrimination. Many sellers do this. At the moment my supermarket is full of offers of the form 'buy two, get the second at half-price'. They really annoy me! I end up with food that goes off in the fridge, or drinking too much beer (this is exactly what the supermarket wants).

Another type is when different people pay different prices for the same good or service. As the law in many countries is very hostile to certain forms of discrimination (for example, sex discrimination), it is rare to see different prices for men and for women (though note the habit of apparently the same garment being sold in the men's and women's section of a store at different prices). We often see, however, different prices for students, or for the elderly, or for the unemployed. This is clearly the sellers extracting more of the surplus than they would do in the absence of discrimination.

More subtle forms of discrimination exist: mobile phone companies charge a lower tariff to calls on the same network (ask yourself why); the new generation of cheap airlines charge lower prices to those people who book early (so a plane-load of people can show an enormous heterogeneity in the prices paid); clubs offer lower per-visit prices to members; the National Trust offers a free visit to those who join the Trust at the time of the visit; employers pay a higher salary to those who have been employed longer (though these could be more efficient workers); universities and other public sector employers have a pay scale such that their salary rises every year (though the workers could be getting more efficient). The list is almost endless. You could try to add to it yourself.

Game Theory

30.1 Introduction

We have now covered the two extremes – perfect competition and monopoly/monopsony. In the first, all agents are so small (or think that they are so small) that they cannot change the price; in the second, there is one agent so dominant that it can choose the price. More fundamentally, all the agents in these two extremes do not have to think about the behaviour of others, in the sense that they can predict what others will do. In this chapter and the next we consider an intermediate situation in which there are two or more agents, and each has to think about what the others might do when they are taking decisions. More specifically, the utility of each agent depends not only on what decision they take, but also on what decision the others take. To make the problem very clear, we assume in this chapter and the next that agents must take their decisions simultaneously and independently, without knowing what decision the other agents are taking.

This kind of problem is known as a *game*, and the purpose of this chapter is to analyse how people should play such games. We try to come up with some predictions which we can use in Chapter 31 when we study behaviour in a duopoly. A duopoly is a situation between competition and monopoly; we have a market in which there are just two firms selling the good.

30.2 A Simple Game

We shall consider games between two players: 1 and 2. We consider simultaneous play games in which the two players must take their decisions simultaneously and independently of each other. We consider games in which the payoffs to the individuals depend not only on their own decisions, but also on the decisions of the other. We give an example in Table 30.1

In this example and the ones that follow, we call player 1 the row player, in the sense that he or she must choose a row in the matrix. We call

Table 30.1 Example of a simple game

Game 1		Player 2	
		Choice A	Choice B
Player 1	Choice A	15, 15	10, 10
	Choice B	5, 5	0, 0

player 2 the column player, in that he or she must choose a column. In this example, player 1 has a choice between rows A and B; player 2 has a choice between columns A and B. The payoffs to the two players are given in pairs in the body of the matrix, the first number of the pair being the payoff to player 1 and the second number the payoff to player 2. As it is crucial that you are clear about this, we will explain all the payoffs in the above game.

- If player 1 chooses row A and player 2 chooses column A, the payoff to player 1 is 15 and the payoff to player 2 is 15.
- If player 1 chooses row A and player 2 chooses column B, the payoff to player 1 is 10 and the payoff to player 2 is 10.
- If player 1 chooses row B and player 2 chooses column A, the payoff to player 1 is 5 and the payoff to player 2 is 5.
- If player 1 chooses row B and player 2 chooses column B, the payoff to player 1 is 0 and the payoff to player 2 is 0.

What will the players do? Recall that they must choose simultaneously and independently; at the time of the choice, neither player knows what the other is choosing.

If you were player 1, what would you do? You might argue that what is best for you depends in principle on what player 2 is doing. You might then ask yourself: what is your best decision for each possible decision of player 2? If player 2 chooses column A, then your best decision is row A as 15 is a better payoff than 5. If player 2 chooses column B, then your best decision is row A as 10 is a better payoff than 0. So in this game, the best decision of player 1 is to play row A – independently of the choice of player 2. We say in this case that the choice of row A by player 1 is a *dominant strategy* for player 1, because it is best for player 1 irrespective of what player 2 does.

What about player 2? Does he or she have a dominant strategy? In this example, yes, because column A is also best for him or her, irrespective of what player 1 does. If player 1 chooses row A, the best decision for player 2 is column A since 15 is better than 10; if player 2 chooses row B, the best decision for player 2 is column A since 5 is better than 0. Player 2 also has a dominant strategy in this game – that of column A.

So in this game we seem to have a simple prediction: player 1 will play row A because it is a dominant strategy; and player 2 will play column A because it is a dominant strategy . The outcome of the game will be (A, A), and each player will get a payoff of 15.

30.3 Nash Equilibrium

As you might have anticipated, not all games are so simple. Consider game 2 in Table 30.2. Does either player have a dominant strategy? Let us check, starting with player 1.

- If player 2 chooses column A, the best decision for player 1 is row A.
- If player 2 chooses column B, the best decision for player 1 is row B.

So player 1 does not have a dominant strategy. What about player 2?

- If player 1 chooses row A, the best decision for player 2 is column A.
- If player 1 chooses row B, the best decision for player 2 is column A.

So player 2 does have a dominant strategy – that of choosing column A. This is best for player 2 irrespective of the decision which player 1 makes.

Let us go back to player 1. He or she does not have a dominant strategy. But player 1

Table 30.2 Game with a unique Nash equilibrium

Game 2		Player 2	
		Choice A	Choice B
Player 1	Choice A	15, 15	0, 10
	Choice B	10, 5	5, 0

may well be able to work out that player 2 does have a dominant strategy – that of choosing column A. Player 1 can then be confident that player 2 will choose column A, in response to which the best decision for player 1 is row A. So in this game it seems reasonable to argue that player 2 will choose column A, and having worked this out player 1 will choose row A. The outcome of the game will be (A, A) and both players will get a payoff of 15.

Moreover in this outcome, both players would be happy in the sense that neither would want to change their choices. Notice that this is not true at any other outcome. At (A, B) player 2 would want to change; at (B, A) player 1 would want to change; at (B, B) player 2 would want to change. Because of this property of the outcome (A, A), it is called a Nash[1] equilibrium. It is an equilibrium precisely in that sense; neither player would want to change their choice, given the choice of the other player.

You might ask at this point whether all games have a Nash equilibrium – clearly game 1 above has (also (A, A)). But what about the game in Table. 30.3?

This is a game which has two Nash equilibria (A, A) and (B, B)[2]. It might be argued that (A, A) is more likely to be the outcome in an actual game, but consider what would happen if the payoffs of 5 became large losses. If you were player 1 and were sure that player 2 would choose column A, there would be no problem; but suppose you were a bit worried about player 2 and thought that he or she might choose column B. In that case, playing row B might be safer for you as it avoids the possibility of incurring large losses.

Table 30.3 Game with two Nash equilibria

Game 3		Player 2	
		Choice A	Choice B
Player 1	Choice A	15, 15	5, 0
	Choice B	0, 5	10, 10

30.4 Mixed Strategies

Table 30.4 Game with no Nash equilibria (in pure strategies)

Game 4		Player 2	
		Choice A	Choice B
Player 1	Choice A	9, –9	–9, 9
	Choice B	–9, 9	9, –9

There are games with no Nash equilibria. Consider Table 30.4.

Let us check:

- (A, A) is not a Nash equilibrium because player 2 would want to change his or her decision.
- (A, B) is not a Nash equilibrium because player 1 would want to change his or her decision.
- (B, A) is not a Nash equilibrium because player 1 would want to change his or her decision.
- (B, B) is not a Nash equilibrium because player 2 would want to change his or her decision.

1. Named after the Nobel Prize winner, John Nash.
2. You should pause here and make sure you understand why. (A, A) is a Nash equilibrium because player 1 would not want to change his or her decision to play row A given that player 2 has chosen column A; and because player 2 would not want to change his or her decision to play column A given that player 1 has chosen row A. (B, B) is a Nash equilibrium because player 1 would not want to change his or her decision to play row B given that player 2 has chosen column B; and because player 2 would not want to change his or her decision to play column B given that player 1 has chosen row B.

In this kind of game we need to broaden the concept of a Nash equilibrium to other kinds of strategies. What do you think is the best strategy for each player to use? Obviously, a strategy that confuses the other player; if the other player knows what you are going to do, he or she can exploit that information. And the best way to confuse? By choosing A or B at random, and, in this case, with equal probabilities. This is what is known as a *mixed strategy*. In this game there is an equilibrium in these mixed strategies.

We will not consider such mixed strategy equilibria any further in this book, if only for the fact that we will not make use of them. But in more advanced economics they are heavily used. They are also intellectually quite exciting. It is a pity that we cannot study them further.

30.5   The Prisoner's Dilemma

This is a very famous and very important game which we shall meet again in Chapter 31. It is typical of many interesting economic problems, including duopoly and public goods problems. An example is presented in Table. 30.5.

Table 30.5   Example of the prisoner's dilemma

Game 5		Player 2	
		Choice A	Choice B
Player 1	Choice A	5, 5	99, 0
	Choice B	0, 99	96, 96

It may prove helpful to point out the structure of this game. First this game is symmetrical, though it does not need to be; this means that we can look at the payoffs to just one of the players. Let us take player 1. What is important is that in column A the payoff to player 1 is higher in row A, and in column B the payoff to player 1 is also higher in row A. But what is crucial is that the payoff to player 1 in the outcome (B, B) is higher than the payoff to player 1 in the outcome (A, A). Because of the symmetry of the game, this means that the outcome (B, B) Pareto-dominates the outcome (A, A). By this we mean that (B, B) is simply better for both players than (A, A). Remember this.

But what is our prediction? If we look to see if either player has a dominant strategy, we see that both have: for player 1 it is better to play row A irrespective of what player 2 chooses; for player 2 it is better to play column A irrespective of what player 1 does. The prediction that player 1 will play A and that player 2 will play A (because these are dominant strategies) seems to lead inexorably to the conclusion that the outcome of this game will be (A, A). This is the unique Nash equilibrium of the game.

The only problem is that (A, A) is Pareto-dominated by (B, B). However, despite this attractive feature, (B, B) is not a Nash equilibrium; on the contrary both players would want to change their decision if (B, B) was the outcome; note that, in this instance, A is better for player 1 and A is better for player 2.

This is the interestingly paradoxical feature of the prisoner's dilemma; we will look at the implications for economics in Chapters 31 and 33.

30.6   Nash Equilibrium when Choice is Continuous

In most interesting economic applications, the decision-maker usually has to choose the value of some variable, often from a continuum. For example, as we shall see in Chapter 31, in a duopoly problem each duopolist has to choose either the quantity to produce or the price to charge – and both of these can be any positive number. The ideas that have been discussed above are equally applicable to this case.

Let us be more specific. Let us denote the variable of choice by q and let us continue to denote the two players by 1 and 2. So q_1 denotes the decision of player 1 and q_2 denotes the decision of player 2.

The situation in which both players have a dominant strategy can easily be described. This is a situation in which the optimal decision of each player is the same irrespective of the decision of the other. We shall represent this graphically, with q_1 on the horizontal axis and q_2 on the vertical. For each player we draw a graph which represents the optimal choice of that player as a function of the decision of the other. In the case when both players have a dominant strategy, we have the kind of graph pictured in figure 30.1.

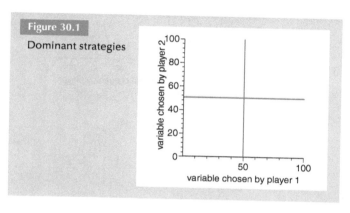

Figure 30.1

Dominant strategies

In Fig. 30.1 the vertical line is the optimal decision for player 1, as a function of the decision of player 2. You will see that it is vertical at the value 50, which implies that the choice of 50 is optimal for player 1, irrespective of the decision of player 2. Player 1 has a dominant strategy – to play 50 irrespective of what player 2 plays. The horizontal line is the optimal decision for player 2, as a function of the decision of player 1. The fact that it is horizontal at the value 50 means that it is optimal for player 2, irrespective of what player 1 chooses. Player 2 also has a dominant strategy. The outcome of this game should be clear; we will end up at the intersection of the two lines with both players choosing 50.

It might be useful to introduce some terminology to describe the relationship between the optimal decision of one player and the decision of the other. In economics this relationship is called the *reaction function* of the player. The vertical line in Fig. 30.1 is the reaction function of player 1, and the horizontal line is the the reaction function of player 2. It should be noted that this term is slightly misleading as it seems to suggest some kind of reaction; this is an irrelevant concept in a simultaneous play game, so you should remember what it means – simply the optimal decision of one player as a function of the decision of the other.

The reason why this is useful is that it helps us to find whether there is a Nash equilibrium in a game. Recall that a Nash equilibrium is an outcome for which neither player would want to change the decision, given the decision of the other. It should be clear that any Nash equilibrium must therefore be at the intersection of the two reaction functions. Consider figure 30.2.

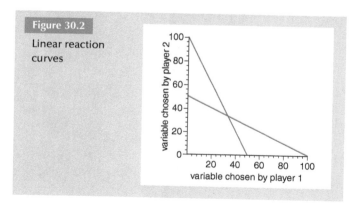

Figure 30.2

Linear reaction curves

This illustrates a case, which we will study in Chapter 31, when the reaction functions are linear. In this example the two functions intersect just once, at the point $(33\frac{1}{3}, 33\frac{1}{3})$. We can conclude that this point is the only possible Nash equilibrium in this game: at any point off the reaction function of player 1, player 1 would want to change his or her decision; similarly, at any point off the reaction function of player 2, player 2 would want to change his or her decision. Only when we are simultaneously on both reaction functions do we have an outcome where neither player would want to change his or her decision.

We might have games in which there are two Nash equilibria; an example is shown in Fig. 30.3. We might also have three (or more) Nash equilibria. An example is presented in Fig. 30.4. We provide some illustrations in Chapter 31.

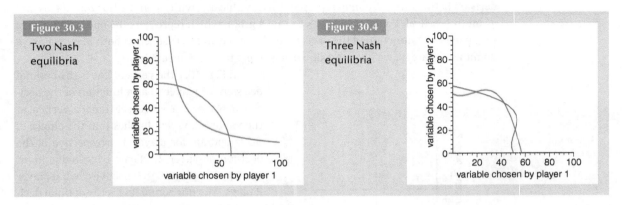

Figure 30.3

Two Nash equilibria

Figure 30.4

Three Nash equilibria

30.7 Summary

We have given a very brief overview of some aspects of game theory which will prove useful later. We have restricted ourselves to 2-player simultaneous play games in which each player must decide what to do at the same time as the other, and without knowing what the other player is choosing. We saw that some games might be simple, in that both players have a dominant strategy.

 A player has a dominant strategy (choice) if that choice is best irrespective of the choice of the other player.

Other games might be more complicated, and we introduced the important concept of a Nash equilibrium as a possible predictor of the outcome of the game.

 An outcome of a game is called a Nash equilibrium if neither player would want to change their choice given the choice of the other player.

 Games may have no Nash equilibrium (in pure strategies), a unique Nash equilibrium or multiple Nash equilibria.

We showed that such concepts were relevant for both games with a small number of possible decisions, and also those where the decision was from a continuum. For the latter we introduced the concept of a reaction function.

 A player's reaction function describes the optimal decision for a player as a function of the decision of the other.

 Any Nash equilibrium (in pure strategies) must be at the intersection of the players' reaction functions.

30.8 Review Questions

1. Construct examples of simple games with (a) one Nash equilibrium; (b) two off-diagonal Nash equilibria; (c) no Nash equilibria in pure strategies.

2. Why is randomizing the best strategy in game 4 (see Table 30.4)?

3. Do you think that letting the players discuss the game in advance of taking their decisions would help in resolving the prisoner's dilemma?

30.9 Playing Games

Game theory is perfect for testing in simple experiments. These are experiments that you can do with fellow students, though you are advised to have one person who keeps control of the situation (and perhaps supplies money to provide correct incentives). The games we have considered in this chapter have been simple two-person games and you are recommended to start with such games. You can always play these games with two teams and this is, in fact, what we do when we incorporate such games into a tutorial programme. Although the word 'game' suggests that they are not serious, that is not true; the purpose of these experiments is to test game theory, which has many important things to say about economic behaviour.

You can take virtually any game and experiment with it. In this chapter there are several examples and you can easily construct your own. The theory that we have been discussing in this chapter may make predictions about what will/should happen in such games, and it is therefore instructive to see if these predictions are correct. However in some games the theory that we have been discussing is agnostic; it predicts various possibilities, but does not say which of the various possibilities will emerge in practice. This happens, for example, when there are multiple Nash equilibria. In such games experiments are instructive in discovering which are the empirically realistic equilibria.

One game that is particularly instructive with which to start is the prisoner's dilemma. This is interesting as there is a unique Nash equilibrium which is supported by dominant strategies. However this Nash equilibrium is dominated by some other outcome, which unfortunately is not a Nash equilibrium. It seems odd that game theory should predict an outcome that is dominated by another outcome. You can see what happens in practice by running a simple experiment. Consider the following.

There are two players or teams. They are to play a simple simultaneous-move game in which team 1 has two choices (1 and 2), and in which team 2 has two choices (1 and 2). The payoffs to the teams are given in the following payoff matrix (Table 30.6). The amounts are in pounds[3]. The first number is the payoff to team 1; the second number is the payoff to team 2. So, for example, if team 1 plays 2 and team 2 plays 1, then team 1 will get a payoff of −£2 (yes, will lose £2), and team 2 will get a payoff of £20.

This has the classic structure of a prisoner's dilemma: for both teams, the choice of 1 (row or column) dominates the choice of 2; whatever the other team does, choosing 1 is better for either team. This is because £1 is better than −£2, and £20 is better than £6. As long as the game has this structure it is a prisoner's dilemma, and has the paradoxical prediction that both teams choose 1 and hence end up with £1, whereas they could have each ended up with £6 by both choosing 2.

The objective of the teams should be to make as much (real or hypothetical) money as possible[4] out of playing the game. You might think that the outcome of the game would depend on how it was implemented and, in particular, whether teams played it once or more than once. In fact there is a number of alternative scenarios or treatments you could try.

Table 30.6 Game: the prisoner's dilemma

Payoffs		Team 2's choice	
		1	2
Team 1's choice	1	£1, £1	£20, −£2
	2	−£2, £20	£6, £6

---

3. Ideally they should be in real pounds, and in many proper experiments they are real pounds; if you cannot find anyone to sponsor your experiment you should use hypothetical pounds, but try to act as you would if they were real.
4. In a real experiment with real money, the participants would be paid their payoffs in cash.

- (1) The game is played once;
- (2) The game is played n times, with lots of teams playing pairwise games in such a way that no two teams ever play each other more than once;
- (3) The game is played n times between the same two teams.

Treatment (2) is called (in the experimental literature) a 'strangers' treatment, and treatment (3) a 'partners' treatment. You might think that behaviour would be different in these three treatments: first between treatments (2) and (3), where strategic issues might force a difference; and second between treatment (1) and treatments (2) and (3), where learning may have an effect.

An additional factor may be whether or not communication is allowed. Perhaps if the teams could discuss the possibilities they might be able to get to the dominating outcome? Perhaps more important is whether binding commitments could be made and enforced. If so, the two teams might agree, after discussion, both to choose 2. But how could it be enforced? There would have to be some legally binding agreement, of a type recognized by courts of law, to ensure that any team which broke the agreement would end up worse off as a consequence. In some contexts it is difficult to imagine how this might be done. And, of course, there are legal costs to be incurred in drawing up a legally binding agreement.

In my tutorials I get the two teams to play the game four times without communication, and four times with communication. I refuse to police any agreements between the teams. What happens depends upon the teams: sometimes we get cooperation, occasionally of an oscillating nature (note that alternatively playing 1 and 2, and then 2 and 1, both teams can get an average payoff of £9 per play of the game), but often the cooperation breaks down, or does not even start.

You should see what happens, and also how sensitive is the outcome to the particular numbers in the payoff matrix.

Duopoly

31

31.1 Introduction

We now apply the game-theoretic ideas that we developed in Chapter 30 to the study of duopoly. This is a market in which there are just two sellers; it is a situation between competition and monopoly. In the former, the firms take the price as given; in the latter, the monopolist can set the price. In duopoly each firm has an influence on the price, but must take into account that the other firm also has an influence on the price. The profits of each firm depend on the decisions of both firms – and they must both take that into account when taking their decisions.

As we shall see, the outcome of the duopoly game depends upon its rules. In this chapter we consider two different sets of rules: the first we call the quantity-setting game, which is referred to as the Cournot model after the economist Cournot; and the second the price-setting game which is referred to as the Bertrand model after the economist Bertrand. In each of these we keep things as simple as possible by assuming that the firms are identical, both in their technology and in the good that they produce. We shall assume that both firms have constant returns to scale, with a cost function given by $C(q) = cq$, where q is the quantity produced and c is the constant marginal (and average) cost. Let us begin by considering the quantity-setting game (the Cournot model).

31.2 The Quantity-Setting Game

In this game the two duopolists, simultaneously and independently, choose the level of their output. Firm 1 chooses q_1 and firm 2 chooses q_2. Then the market decides the price of the product p through the following aggregate demand curve.

$$p = a - b(q_1 + q_2) \tag{31.1}$$

Note the implicit assumption here: that the good which the two firms produce is identical; and that the aggregate quantity determines the price at which it can be sold through the aggregate demand curve.

We shall see if there is a Nash equilibrium in this game. That is, we will see if there is a pair (q_1, q_2) for which each firm is happy with its decision (output), given the decision (output), of the other. As we know from Chapter 30, if such an equilibrium exists it must lie on the intersection of the two firms' reaction functions. We must therefore start by finding these two reaction functions and we commence by finding the optimal decision of each firm as a function of the decision of the other firm.

We work in (q_1, q_2) space, and we start by finding the reaction function of firm 1. To find this we introduce a new concept – that of an *iso-profit curve*. This, as you might anticipate, is a locus of points for which the profit is the same. Let us take firm 1 and write down an expression for its profits. Denoting the profits of firm 1 by π_1 and knowing that profits are revenue minus costs, we know that if the firm produces q_1 and sells this quantity at a price of p, then profits are given by the following function, where c represents the average costs of q_1.

$$\pi_1 = pq_1 - cq_1 \tag{31.2}$$

Now we must remember that the price is determined by the aggregate demand function (31.1); substituting this in Eq. (31.2) we obtain

$$\pi_1 = [a - b(q_1 + q_2)]q_1 - cq_1 \tag{31.3}$$

From Eq. (31.3) it follows that the profits of firm 1 are given by

$$\pi_1 = (a - c - bq_2)q_1 - bq_1^2 \tag{31.4}$$

You should note that this is a function of both q_1 and q_2. It is linear in q_2; indeed as q_2 increases the profits of firm 1 decrease because the coefficient on q_2 is negative. It is quadratic in q_1 with a negative coefficient; so as q_1 increases, first the profits of firm 1 increase and then they decrease.

An iso-profit curve for firm 1 is defined by $\pi_1 = $ constant, that is:

$$(a - c - bq_2)q_1 - bq_1^2 = \text{constant} \tag{31.5}$$

Plotted in (q_1, q_2) space, an iso-profit curve is quadratic. We give a particular example in which $a = 110$, $b = 1$ and $c = 10$ in Fig. 31.1.

We have already noted that the profits of firm 1 fall as q_2 rises. It follows from this that physically higher iso-profit curves correspond to lower profits. In fact in Fig. 31.1, the profits attached to the 10 iso-profit curves pictured, starting at the physically lowest, are 2300, 2000, 1700, 1400, 1100, 800, 500, 200 and −100 (yes, the top curve has a loss of 100).

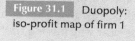
Figure 31.1   Duopoly: iso-profit map of firm 1

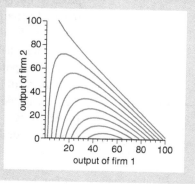

Now, to find the reaction function of firm 1 we need to find, for each level of output of firm 2, the optimal level of output of firm 1; by this we mean the profit-maximizing level of output. So, given some level of output of firm 2 (that is, given some horizontal line in Fig. 31.1), we want to find the point on it which lies on the iso-profit curve with the greatest level of output; that is, we want to find the physically-lowest iso-profit curve. It should be clear that this point must lie at the top of an iso-profit curve.

Joining all these points together we find the reaction function of firm 1, as shown in Fig. 31.2.

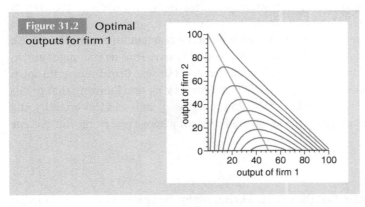

Figure 31.2   Optimal outputs for firm 1

We can also find the optimal output mathematically; the proof is in the mathematical appendix. It leads to the following reaction curve for firm 1.

$$q_1 = (a - c - bq_2)/(2b) \qquad (31.6)$$

In the case we are considering (where $a = 110$, $b = 1$ and $c = 10$), this gives $q_1 = (100 - q_2)/2$ which is the straight line in Fig. 31.2 joining the peaks of the iso-profit curves, as we showed on the previous page[1].

Let us examine the reaction function of firm 1. One point on it is where $q_2 = 0$; the optimal response is $q_1 = 50$. So, if firm 2 produces nothing, the best thing that firm 1 can do is to produce 50. A moment's thought should convince you that 50 must therefore be the monopoly output. A rather longer thought may be needed to interpret the other extreme of the reaction function, at which firm 2 produces 100 and the optimal response of firm 1 is to produce nothing. We shall later show that the output of 100 is what would be produced if the firms behaved competitively. In the meantime, you might like to ponder why.

Because we have identical firms we can easily work out the iso-profit map for firm 2 and its reaction function. We simply interchange q_1 and q_2, and re-do what we have already done; this gives us F.g 31.3.

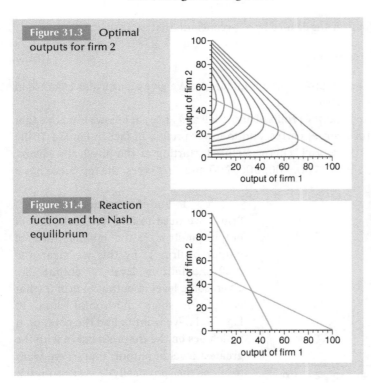

Figure 31.3   Optimal outputs for firm 2

The straight line in Fig. 31.3 is firm 2's reaction function. For example, if firm 1 produces nothing, firm 2 should produce 50; if firm 1 produces 100, firm 2 should produce nothing; if firm 1 produces 50 firm 2 should produce 25; and so on.

We can now answer the question as to whether there is a Nash equilibrium in the game. In Fig. 31.4 we put the two reaction curves together.

There is a unique intersection at the point $(33\frac{1}{3}, 33\frac{1}{3})$, so this must be the unique Nash equilibrium of the game. Game theory predicts that each firm will produce $33\frac{1}{3}$ and the total output will be $66\frac{2}{3}$, giving a price of $43\frac{1}{3}$. You should be clear why this is a Nash equilibrium; if firm 2 produces $33\frac{1}{3}$, then the optimal output for firm 1 (given by its reaction function) is $33\frac{1}{3}$; and if firm 1 produces $33\frac{1}{3}$, then the optimal output for firm 2 (given by its reaction function) is $33\frac{1}{3}$. So in this Nash equilibrium both firms are happy

Figure 31.4   Reaction fuction and the Nash equilibrium

1. Be careful when trying to interpret this as it gives q_1 as a function of q_2.

with their decision, given the decision of the other. You should note that at no other point in the graph is this true.

31.3 Collusion?

You may have realized that it might be better for the two firms to try and collude, rather than choose their outputs independently of each other. We can see the possibilities for collusion if we combine Figs. 31.2 and 31.3. This gives Fig. 31.5, into which I have inserted a curve which one might tentatively call the contract curve between the two duopolists,

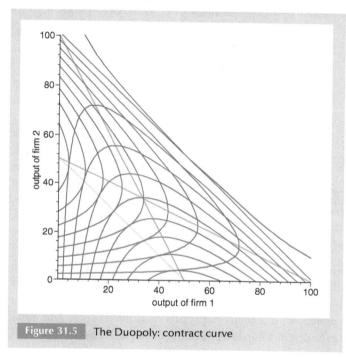

Figure 31.5 The Duopoly: contract curve

Why might we call this line the contract curve? Because it is the locus of points efficient in the sense of the profits of the two firms: given any level of profit of firm 1, then firm 2's profit is highest on the contract curve; given any level of profit of firm 2, then firm 1's profit is highest on the contract curve. You might find it interesting to note that the equation of this contract curve is given by

$$q + q_2 = 50 \qquad (31.7)$$

In other words, it states that the joint output of the two firms is 50. Does this 50 remind you of anything? Yes – the monopoly output. So we get the conclusion that the two firms are behaving efficiently if they are acting as if they are monopolists. This is a nice conclusion, though a rather obvious one.

However, to be on the contract curve they have to collude. Moreover each firm has a natural incentive to cheat on any collusive agreement. Why? Simply because none of the points on the contract curve are on either firm's reaction function, so neither firm is behaving optimally given the output decision of the other. This tells us that there are natural incentives why any collusive agreement may break down, and we end up at the Nash equilibrium.

We can see this more clearly by working out the profits of the firms at the Nash equilibrium, and at the symmetrical joint profit maximizing situation. These are shown in Table 31.1, where we have rounded the profits to the nearest whole number.

You might recognise the structure of this game; it is that of a classic prisoner's dilemma. Note that there is a unique Nash equilibrium (which we have already identified), and there is another outcome – the joint profit maximizing outcome – which is better for both of them but which is not a Nash equilibrium. Both firms have an incentive to renege on any agreement to produce 25 units. Collusion is not a Nash equilibrium in this game.

Table 31.1 The Nash equilibrium

	$q_2 = 33\frac{1}{3}$	$q_2 = 2.5$
$q_1 = 33\frac{1}{3}$	1111, 1111	1389, 1041
$q_1 = 25$	1041, 1389	1250, 1250

31.4 Sequential Play

You may well be asking whether the outcome would be different or better if we changed the rules of the game; for example, by letting the players play sequentially rather than simultaneously. This situation is referred to as the Stackelberg model after the economist Stackelberg. Let us see what happens. Consider the situation where firm 1 chooses first and then announces the decision to firm 2, which then takes its decision. What does firm 1 do? We have already considered this type of situation in Chapter 8. Firm 1 will reason that, whatever output firm 1 chooses, firm 2 will respond with the appropriate output from its (that is, firm 2's) reaction function; after all, that gives the optimal response by firm 2 to any output decision of firm 1. Now we know the reaction function of firm 2; it is the line shown in Fig. 31.6.

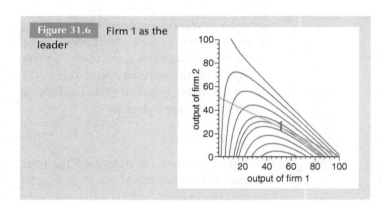

Figure 31.6   Firm 1 as the leader

Firm 1 knows that, whatever value of q_1 it chooses, firm 2 will choose the corresponding point on its reaction function. So essentially firm 1 is choosing a point on the reaction function. Which is the best point on it from firm 1's point of view? Presumably it is the point on the highest (in terms of profit) iso-profit curve; that is, on the physically lowest curve in the figure. This optimal point is labelled 1 in Fig. 31.6. It is where $q_1 = 50$ and $q_2 = 25$, and where the profits of firm 1 are 1250. The profits of firm 2 in this situation are just 625.

Using symmetry, the outcome when firm 2 moves first is $q_1 = 25$ and $q_2 = 50$, with respective profits of 625 and 1250. Clearly firm 1 will prefer to move first; it will then prefer simultaneous play; and will least prefer firm 2 to move first. For firm 2 the opposite is true; it prefers to move first; it then prefers simultaneous play; and it least prefers firm 1 to move first. In this case it is clear that the first mover has an advantage. Do you think that is always the case?

31.5 Monopoly, Duopoly and Competition Compared

We have already worked out what will happen in this specific example: under monopoly we have an output of 50; under duopoly a total output of $66\frac{2}{3}$; and under competition a total output of 100. Correspondingly, the price under monopoly is 60; under duopoly it is $43\frac{1}{3}$; and under competition it is 10 (the marginal cost). We can generalize these results.

We know the reaction functions of the firms; that of firm 1 is $q_1 = (a - c - bq_2)/(2b)$ (Eq. (31.6)). We can conclude that the monopoly output is found by putting $q_2 = 0$, giving us the following.

monopoly output $= (a - c)/(2b)$ (31.8)

The total duopoly output is given by the sum of the values of q_1 and q_2 at the intersection of the two reaction functions $q_1 = (a - c - bq_2)/(2b)$ and $q_2 = (a - c - bq_1)/(2b)$. Hence

$$q_1 = q_2 = (a - c)/(3b) \tag{31.9}$$

Hence also:

$$\text{total duopoly output} = 2(a - c)/(3b) \tag{31.10}$$

The total competitive output can be found in two ways. First, it is where the price is equal to the marginal cost; that is, where

$$p = a - b(q_1 + q_2) \text{ (the demand curve)} = c \text{ (the marginal cost)} \tag{31.11}$$

This solves to give

$$\text{total competitive output} = (a - c)/(b) \tag{31.12}$$

The second way is to argue that, if one firm produces so much that the other firm's optimal output is zero, then the first firm is producing the competitive outcome. This gives the same output as Eq. (31.12) (put $q_1 = 0$ in firm 1's reaction function and solve for q_2).

It is interesting to note that the duopoly output lies between the monopoly output and the competitive output. Even more interesting is the generalized result that you could try to prove (although the proof requires the generalization of the concept of a Nash equilibrium to a game with n players). This generalized result says that the total output in an *oligopoly* situation with n identical firms playing the same rules is given by

$$\text{total oligopoly output} = n(a - c)/[(n + 1)b] \tag{31.13}$$

You will see that as n approaches infinity this approaches the competitive output. This is a reassuring result.

You may like to work out for yourself the implication for the price of the product in the various situations. For the record, the price is lowest under competition, highest under monopoly, and in between in an oligopoly with n firms (with the price approaching the competitive price as n approaches infinity).

31.6 A Price-Setting Game

A completely different scenario emerges when we change the rules of the game. Suppose we now make it a *price-setting* game; that is each firm, independently and simultaneously, chooses the price for its product. If we continue to assume that the firms produce an identical product, and if we make the rather important assumption that both firms can satisfy any demand that is forthcoming, then it is clear that, if one firm is charging less than the other it will get all the demand. So the reaction functions of the two firms are easy to work out. Given any price charged by the other firm, the optimal price for a firm is a fraction less than that of the other firm, as long as the price is not lower than the marginal (average) cost. So both firms will undercut each other until they both have prices equal to the marginal cost. This is the unique Nash equilibrium.

This is an interesting case as the outcome is exactly that of competition; the price is equal to marginal cost. If this is what the world looks like, we do not need regulatory bodies to control duopolies or oligopolies.

31.7   Summary

We have studied duopoly behaviour under a variety of assumptions. In particular, we have studied a quantity-setting game and a price-setting game.

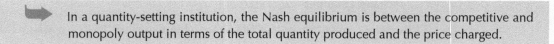 In a quantity-setting institution, the Nash equilibrium is between the competitive and monopoly output in terms of the total quantity produced and the price charged.

Collusive situation is better for both – but not a Nash equilibrium.

Both firms would prefer that they were the leader.

In a price-setting institution, the Nash equilibrium implies marginal cost pricing (so duopoly looks like competition).

31.8   Review Questions

1. In a graph with the price of firm 10 on the horizontal axis and the price of firm 2 on the vertical axis, draw the reaction curves of the two duopolists playing the price-setting game of Section 31.6 (that of firm 2 is horizontal at its marginal cost until it hits the 45-degree line, and then lies just below the 45-degree line; that of firm 1 is symmetrically placed). Hence show that the Nash equilibrium is when both firms charge the marginal cost.

2. Do you think that some pre-decision discussion can help duopolists achieve the monopoly outcome?

3. Can you prove the generalization stated in Section 31.5? (A difficult question.)

31.9 Can Duopolists Co-operate?

This exercise is a good follow-up to the game theory experiment of the previous chapter. In essence it is the same exercise but the context differs. Again it can be played with two teams, which play two duopolists competing in a market for some good which they both produce. The structure of the exercise is as follows.

The two duopolists produce an identical product. Each duopolist has constant marginal and average costs of 10p per unit. The aggregate demand curve for the duopolists' product is

$$p = 100 - (q_1 + q_2) \tag{31.14}$$

In Eq. (31.14) p is the market price (in pence), and q_1 and q_2 are the outputs of teams 1 and 2 respectively. Teams must decide on their q's; the tutor or person keeping control works out p using the above formula.

For example, if $q_1 = 20$ and $q_2 = 30$ then $p = 50$, and the revenues to teams 1 and 2 are respectively $50 \times 20 = 1000(= £10)$, and $50 \times 30 = 1500(= £15)$. Costs are respectively $10 \times 20 = 200(= £2)$ and $10 \times 30 = 300(= £3)$, so profits are £8 and £12 for team 1 and team 2 respectively.

As in the game theory experiment, I suggest that the teams play this simple duopoly problem eight times. During the first four times no communication will be allowed between the two teams; for the last four times communication will be allowed, but no physical threats and no enforcement of contracts by the tutor/referee.

This is a little more complicated, as it is not immediately clear what are the payoffs to the various decisions that the teams may take. In fact there are not just two choices as in the game theory experiment, but a whole continuum; the two quantities can be any positive numbers, though numbers greater than 100 would be a bit silly as they would imply negative prices and negative profits. Interestingly, though, it has the same structure; there is a unique Nash equilibrium (can you find it?) that is dominated by an outcome in which the two duopolists collude and collectively produce the monopoly output. The interesting question is whether that collusive outcome can be sustained – obviously without legal support as the law in most countries is strongly against collusive monopoly-type agreements, and usually without communication as the law also forbids that. What do you find?

31.10 Mathematical Appendix

We find the reaction function for firm 1. To do this we need to find, for each level of output of firm 2, the optimal output of firm 1. We can find this by differentiating π_1 with respect to q_1 (for a given level of q_2), putting this expression equal to zero, and then solving for q_1 as a function of q_2.

From (31.4) we get

$$d\pi_1/dq_1 = (a - c - bq_2) - 2bq_1 \qquad\qquad \text{(A31.1)}$$

Setting $d\pi_1/dq_1 = 0$ implies that

$$q_1 = (a - c - bq_2)/(2b) \qquad\qquad \text{(A31.2)}$$

This is Eq. (31.6).

Externalities

32.1 Introduction

This chapter considers situations in which the actions of one individual affect the utility of some other individual; this occurs without the individual being affected choosing to be so affected, in the sense of entering some market and either buying or selling some good. In fact, the basic problem in this chapter is the involuntary consumption of some good without any market being involved.

We consider in this chapter externalities in consumption and externalities in production. Externalities in consumption occur when one person's consumption of a good directly affects the utility of some other person; such externalities can be positive or negative – positive when utility is increased, negative when it is decreased. Externalities in production occur when some person's production of some good affects directly the utility of some other person; such externalities can be positive or negative – positive when the utility is increased, negative when it is decreased.

Examples are easier to come by than general definitions. Let us start with negative consumption externalities. These occur when a person's consumption of some good has a harmful effect on someone else. Examples include that irritating businessman on the train whose mobile phone calls annoy others; that youngster with his scooter with the deliberately sabotaged silencer, so that every time he or she revs up the whole neighbourhood shakes; the students in the flat opposite who have loud parties at three o'clock in the morning and wake up all the little old ladies; those tourists who will insist on eating food in pubs when you are trying to have a peaceful cigarette; the Minster bells at eleven o'clock on a Sunday morning after you have had a tiring and emotional Saturday night; the football fans who think that everyone else should celebrate their team's victory (or defeat). In each of these cases someone is getting pleasure out of something, but there is someone else who is suffering as a result. And the key thing is that there is no market for this something. I should note that these things are obviously personal; what may be a negative consumption externality to one person may not be so to another.

Positive consumption externalities are also very common although, for obvious reasons, we are less likely to complain about them. Examples include that extremely pretty young man or woman who gives immense pleasure to everyone just walking down the street; that beautiful garden in that council flat; that wonderful opera that those really cultivated students across the street play at just the right volume on Sunday afternoons; that really stupid businessman with his mobile phone on the train about whom you can laugh with your friends later that night; an Italian beach on a weekday not in August; the smells from your local Indian restaurant which is right next to your flat. Note again that these may be personal – what may be a positive externality to one person could be negative to another. ('That extremely pretty young man makes me so jealous because he is so pretty.')

Production externalities are when the production of something affects someone else. They could be positive or negative. It could be utility that is affected or the production of some other good. An example of a negative production externality that affects utility (have you ever been to Stockton-on-Tees?) is pollution from some factory which pollutes the air breathed by the people who live nearby. An example of a negative production externality that affects production is pollution which damages the crops on nearby farms. Positive production externalities are also possible, like the warm water that a firm produces and in which people can swim; but these are rarer.

This chapter can only look briefly at the problems caused by externalities, but by the time you finish the chapter you should be aware of what an externality is; why it creates a problem for the operation and efficiency of markets; what might be done about it; and why it might be difficult to do anything about it.

32.2 Consumption Externalities

It might make our life simpler – and it will certainly make the issues we want to discuss clearer – if we work throughout this section with a particular example of a negative consumption externality: that of loud music. Right at the beginning I should point out that I really dislike music played too loud, and I particularly dislike other people playing their music too loud. I rent a flat in the centre of Bari; one year one of my neighbours (who now seems to have moved on, thank goodness) thought that it would be great fun if he or she played the same pieces of easy-listening Italian music over and over again at high volume all afternoon and every afternoon. It was so loud that it was impossible to think or work or sleep or eat or to watch telly or even drink lots of beer. And I wanted to do all of these. I tried everything to get them to stop; I appealed to them in my impeccable Italian to turn the music down just a little, please (I had to do this in the gaps in the music as I could not even hear myself shouting at them when the music was on); I appealed to the locals to help me; I went to the carabinieri (who went with me to the people concerned, who told the comandante from the carabinieri where to go to, and who told me to go back to Naples: 'you foreigner').

Now while I am tempted to think that the easy-music-lovers turned on their music and then went to the beach, I suspect that the truth is they belonged to a frighteningly large set of people who simply like loud music – the louder the better, up to a point (even they have some limit). They obtained utility out of loud music. (Perhaps it helped them escape from something, perhaps themselves?) In contrast, I get disutility out of loud music; the louder, the worse. The problem is that, despite the fact that they closed their windows (and the mind boggles as to how loud the music must have been inside their flat) their consumption of loud music imposed an externality on me. And note: there was no market for this music.

You will note that one of the things that I did was to go the carabinieri. I thought that they would know the law. John Hey: 'Surely they are not allowed to play music this loud at this time of the day?' Comandante: 'Well, ...'.

Clearly this is one solution: that the law says what is permissible and what is not. There are problems with this though. Can the law specify, for every possible externality, what is allowable and what is not? Can the law specify this sufficiently precisely so as to pre-empt endless disputes about the interpretation? Is the law enforceable in the sense that it is worth bringing cases to court for every possible externality? Is this kind of law efficient?

These questions open an enormous Pandora's box, and we cannot hope to begin to answer most of the questions. But perhaps we ought to consider the final question; after all, we are economists. Would it be efficient simply to ban the playing of any music, however loud, just because one bad-tempered foreign academic does not like it? Would it be efficient to do the contrary – to let anyone who likes loud music play it whenever they want and at whatever volume? Note the problem: that some people like loud music while others dislike it. Is that any different from the fact that some people want to sell some good while other people want to buy the same good? After all, *people are different*.

Part of the problem is that there is no market for loud music. But it might be interesting to consider what would happen if there was; or at least to consider the background to such a market. Participants in it would be me and my neighbours in Bari. Let us assume that we would be the only participants. (I should note that when I asked my other neighbours whether they liked the loud music or not, they used to reply – after my asking several times as they were having trouble hearing what I was saying – 'what loud music?') We would be involved in a process of exchange. In analysing such a process we can use the apparatus of Chapter 8 and construct an Edgeworth box. I begin with my neighbours, and shall refer to them from now on as 'the young person'; I shall refer to myself as the 'older person'.

The key components of the story are loud music and money, which I would have been willing to pay to get the noise reduced if it was indeed the case that they had the right to play such loud music. I shall make the assumption that the young person has preferences over loud music and money – preferences of the usual kind. To the young person, money is a good and so is loud music; indeed one could measure the quantity of the good 'loud music' by the loudness of it. The young person is happier the louder is the music – up to a certain level which is, I suppose, the level at which he or she played it (except when shouting at the comandante from the carabinieri). Obviously I did not have the opportunity to measure precisely the utility function of the young person over money and loud music, but we can do our analysis in principle with some general specifications. Let us assume that these preferences have the usual form, as pictured in Fig. 32.1.

In Fig. 32.1 the quantity of money which the young person has is measured along the horizontal axis, and the volume of the music to which he or she is listening is measured up the vertical axis. The louder the music, the higher up the axis and the happier the young person. I am assuming the usual situation in which the indifference curves are convex; the less money the individual has, the less he or she is willing to pay to have an increase in the volume of noise. You will notice one rather special feature of this indifference map – the indifference curves become vertical when the volume of noise reaches 100. This means that even the young person has enough noise when the volume becomes that high; this represents his or her limit.

What about me? Well I consider loud music a 'bad'; the louder it is the less happy I am. What I regard as a good is the opposite; I will call this 'peace and

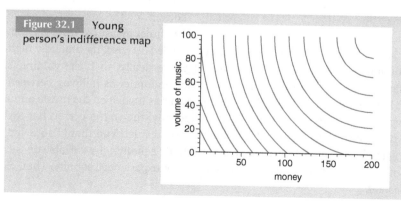

Figure 32.1 Young person's indifference map

quiet', but this is not a particularly good description as it sounds like an all or nothing situation. What I mean by this is the following: as 'peace and quiet' increases, then the volume of music played by the neighbours decreases. What would be bliss to me is total silence, which is measured 100 on the peace and quiet scale. The other extreme – when the neighbour's music is blasting out at the limit – gives me nought on the peace and quiet scale. In between, as the amount of peace and quiet increases I get happier and happier. My preferences between the two goods 'peace and quiet' and money are as illustrated in Fig. 32.2.

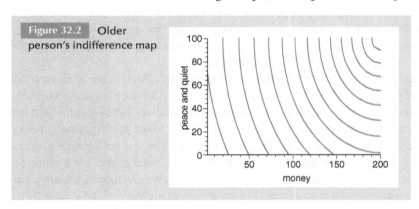

Figure 32.2 Older person's indifference map

Note that my indifference curves become vertical when 'peace and quiet' reaches 100; as I have already explained, this is when there is total silence and I am 100 per cent happy (as far as noise is concerned). My preferences between the two goods, 'peace and quiet' and money, have the usual convex shape.

Now put the pair of us together – after first turning me upside down – to form an Edgeworth box. Notice that we can do this as 'peace and quiet' is the opposite to the volume of loud music. You might want to know what the initial endowments are – so let us assume that both I and the young person have 100 in money. As far as the initial endowment of the variable on the vertical axis is concerned, this is something we shall have to discuss, but we can leave the height of the box equal to the joint limits of 100. If the young person plays loud music at a certain volume, I have (100 minus that) as far as my 'peace and quiet' variable is concerned. We get the Edgeworth box pictured in Fig. 32.3.

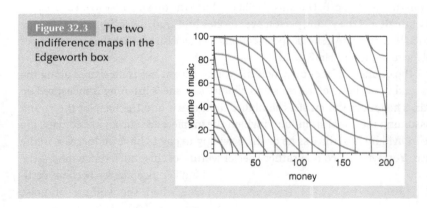

Figure 32.3 The two indifference maps in the Edgeworth box

We should be careful about the interpretation of this. Along the horizontal axis is money, measured from the left the amount that the young person has, and measured from the right the amount that I have. Initially we each have 100, so we start in the middle horizontally. Along the vertical axis is the volume of the music measured from the bottom, or the amount of peace and quiet measured from the top.

Any point in the box indicates how the 200 in money is divided between us, and how high the volume of the music is being played. If we are at 50 vertically, then the volume is halfway to the limit, while I regard the amount of peace and quiet as halfway between heaven and hell. If we are at 0 vertically, the young person has turned off the music and I have 100 per cent peace and quiet. If we are at 100 vertically, the young person has the music as loud as he or she can bear it and I have zero peace and quiet. You should note that the variable along the horizontal axis is to be shared (initially equally); the variable on the vertical axis is not to be shared in the usual sense, but is to be experienced equally. That, of course, is the problem.

An economist looking at the above figure would conclude that any sensible arrangement would be along the contract curve, the position of which is obvious from the figure. Any point off the contract curve is inefficient, in the sense that we would both be better off by moving away from that point towards the contract curve. But where do we start? This is part of the problem, and it takes us back to the law and the carabinieri. My young neighbour clearly thought that a person was entitled to make as much noise as he or she cared to make; so I presume that my neighbour felt that the initial endowment point was that labelled E in Fig. 32.4.

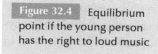

Figure 32.4 Equilibrium point if the young person has the right to loud music

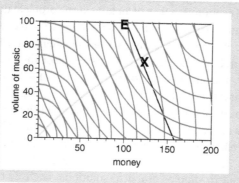

The economist would then say that, with competitive trading, we would end up at an efficient point – namely that labelled X in Fig. 32.4. Given the endowment point (which I obviously do not like, but have to accept if that is indeed the law) I pay some money to the young person to turn the volume down a bit. This happens, and the music is not as loud as it would be if it were unconstrained; he or she is compensated with a little extra money to buy some more CDs. I am happier than I would be if the volume was not turned down. However I obviously think differently about the endowment point; I think I am entitled to complete peace and quiet. I think we should start from the point labelled F in Fig. 32.5.

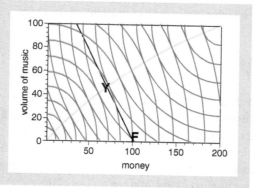

Figure 32.5 Equilibrium point if the older person has the right to peace and quiet

The economist would say that, with competitive trading, we would end up at an efficient point – namely that labelled Y in Fig. 32.5. I would accept a little bit of noise in return for some money (with which I buy earplugs), and the young person is happy to pay a little money in return for being allowed to play his music loud.

Notice what would happen if trading were not allowed and there was a clear statement of the law – which was enforced perfectly. We would end up at either point E (if the younger person had the right to noise) or at point F (if I had the right to silence). Neither of these points are efficient; they are both off the contract curve. The economist's contribution is that competitive trading would take us to a point on the contract curve, and the inefficiency caused by the externality would be eliminated. We should note that the externality itself cannot be eliminated; it exists because I and the young person have different tastes.

The problem of course is the 'competitive trading' part of this story. There was a problem in the first place because there was no market for noise. To implement the economist's approach, we need somehow to create a market in which competitive trading can take place. You can probably see other problems: even if my neighbour understood and accepted all of the above, he or she might think that there should be some relationship between the assignment of property rights (do I have the right to silence, or does my neighbour have the right to noise?) and the operation of the market. My neighbour might well think that, if he or she has the property right – the right to noise – that confers on him or her the right to set the price in the market. And we already know that this institution leads to a point off the contract curve, and hence is inefficient. Indeed I might well prefer the point E to the point that would be chosen by my neighbour. Similarly he or she might prefer point F to the point that I would choose if I had the property right (the right to silence) and could set the price. More generally, it is not clear how competitive trading could be enforced if the law relating to the original problem was itself not enforceable.

Anyhow, the economist's way of looking at the problem does enable us to see where efficient outcomes may lie. An alternative way to get to one of these outcomes is for the government to impose a tax on the imposer of the externality. But again, this requires us to define the imposer. If it is the young person, then he or she could be taxed proportionately to the volume of the music. This would imply a budget line for the young person through the endowment point if the level of the tax was chosen correctly, forcing the young person to choose a point on the contract curve. The proceeds of the tax would be paid to me and this would create the market (but the tax would not necessarily be paid to me if we were interested only in the efficiency of the market). But there remain problems – not least the enforcement of the tax. In practice this would prove both difficult and complicated. Indeed such complications lead to simpler practical solutions, such as the banning of loud music at certain times of the day, coupled with legal enforcement through paying fines for those caught violating the ban. In fact, if you think of the myriad externalities that we are subjected to in everyday life, when the law intervenes it is usually in such a form. Examples include: the banning of smoking in public places; limits on emissions of carbon dioxide from car exhausts; and offences such as 'drunk and disorderly'. When the externalities are too minor to make legal intervention worthwhile, there are usually appeals to 'public spirit': 'please use your mobile phones with consideration to others ... '.

32.3   Production Externalities

Perhaps because production externalities are generally larger, they tend to be taken more seriously. An example which we can analyse, using the same apparatus as above, is that of two firms where the production activities of one firm influence the output possibilities of the other. The classic example is that of a steel producer and a fishery; the former is located (rather unfortunately but necessarily for an externality to exist) upstream from the latter. The steel producer produces steel, and makes use of the river water that flows downstream to the fishery. This fact, coupled with the steel manufacturing process, means that the steel producer pollutes the water in the river; this affects the output of the fishery.

Let us be more precise. We assume that the output of the steel producer is steel, and that its inputs are labour and pollution. This latter may appear a bit strange in the sense that pollution is normally considered an output, but we should think in the following way; at any level of labour input, the producer can produce steel, the quantity of which is also dependent on the amount of pollution it produces; the greater the level of pollution, the greater the level of output. Alternatively the steel producer can reduce the quantity of pollution which it produces, but only at the expense of some of the steel produced. We can therefore think of labour and pollution as the inputs, and steel as the output. We can represent all of this in an isoquant map; the shape of this will depend on the firm's technology, but it will have the general shape illustrated in Fig. 32.6.

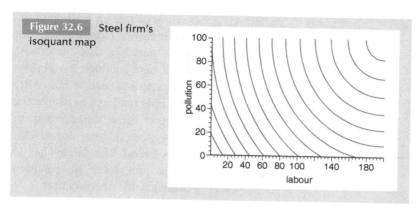

Figure 32.6 Steel firm's isoquant map

Along the horizontal axis is the amount of labour that the firm uses; up the vertical axis is the amount of pollution produced. The curves are isoquants; as we move up and to the right, the quantity of steel produced increases. For any given level of labour, output increases as pollution increases. You should note that I have drawn the isoquants becoming vertical at a level of pollution of 100; this is presumed to be the maximum pollution that the firm is capable of producing. Note that, if the firm does not have to pay for the input pollution, it will choose[1] some point along the top of this figure where the level of pollution is equal to 100.

Let us now think about the downstream fishery. It produces fish, and uses labour and the river to produce the fish. What it wants is clean water – the cleaner the better in the sense that the cleaner the river water, the larger the catch of fish for any given level of labour employment. We can portray the technology of the fishery using isoquants in the usual way; this is done in Fig. 32.7.

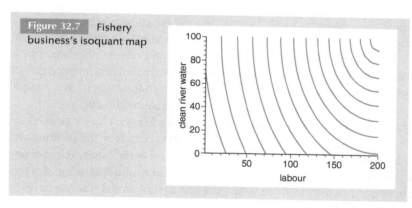

Figure 32.7 Fishery business's isoquant map

We have the labour input along the horizontal axis. On the vertical axis is the cleanliness of the water: at zero, the water is maximally polluted; at 100, the water is super-clean. In between it is in-between; as we move up the vertical axis, the water becomes cleaner. The curves are isoquant curves for the fishery; as we move up and to the right, the quantity of fish caught increases. As is clear from the isoquant map, for any given quantity of labour employed, the cleaner the water, the larger the fish harvest. Notice that the isoquants become vertical when the cleanliness of water reaches 100 – its cleanliness limit.

We once again form an Edgeworth box in Fig. 32.8, very much like the one we produced in Section 32.2. We assume that the total quantity of labour in this mini-society is fixed at 200 and we make the box of that width. The variable on the vertical axis is pollution as measured from the bottom, and cleanliness as measured from the top. These are the same, and both the steel producer and the fishery experience the same level of this variable; it is not a variable to be divided between them, but one to be experienced equally. We make the height of the box equal to the distance between super-polluted and super-clean[2].

1. If the price of pollution is zero, then the isocost curves are vertical and hence parallel to an isoquant when the level of pollution is 100 (and when the isoquants are vertical).
2. You will note that this box, except for the labelling and interpretation, looks exactly like the box in Fig. 32.3. For this reason we do not reproduce all the intermediate figures.

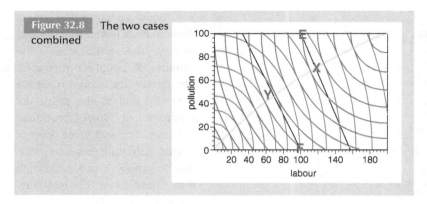

Figure 32.8 The two cases combined

For any given division of the labour between the two firms, if it is the steel firm that can choose the level of pollution it will obviously choose a level of 100. After all it does not have to pay for the pollution (until the government intervenes), as there is no market for pollution. The fishery has to accept the level of pollution chosen by the steel producer.

But this is obviously inefficient; a point along the top of the box lies off the contract curve and could be improved upon. How? The economist would say: by competitive trading. From where? Well, this depends upon the assignment of property rights. If the steel firm has the right to pollute as much as it wants, we start at the point E and competitive trading takes us to point X. If the fishery has the right to clean water, then we start at the point F and competitive trading takes us to point Y. Clearly the steel firm prefers to be at point X and the fishery at point Y, but both prefer to be at X rather than at E and both prefer to be at Y rather than at F. So, the economist concludes, if we have a clear assignation of the property rights and if we have competitive trading, we can eliminate the inefficiencies caused by the externality, though obviously we cannot eliminate the externality itself [3]. Notice that the assignment of property rights does not affect the efficiency of the outcome, although it does affect the distribution of the surpluses. Note also that the assignment of property rights plus the establishment of a market is bound to be better (more efficient) than either the assignment of property rights to the steel producer ('you can pollute as much as you like'), or to the fishery ('you cannot pollute at all') – since both these solutions lead to points off the contract curve.

Having got this far, it is clear that there are other ways of reaching an efficient point – any point on the contract curve – for example through the imposition of a tax by the government. The tax could be imposed on the steel firm and the proceeds paid to the fishery (but not necessarily so if we are interested only in the efficiency of the market we are discussing). But the tax would have to be computed correctly to guarantee that a point on the contract curve is reached; also the level of pollution would have to be measured correctly. This introduces extra costs into the whole procedure, as indeed does any process which involves the law.

Alternatively we could leave everything to the market. As long as the two firms remain distinct, the sum of their profits can never be higher than if the two firms merged into one, because generally they would not be on the contract curve. But what would happen if the two firms merged? The combined management would choose a point on the contract curve and increase the combined profits of the combined firm. So there is a natural incentive for the two firms to merge and hence internalize the externality.

32.4 Markets for Permits

One thing that a market appears to be able to do efficiently is to allocate a fixed number of permits for pollution. Suppose the government is able to measure the amount of pollution

---

3. You might be tempted to suggest that the government simply bans the pollution. But there is a cost to society of so doing, unless the steel firm can somehow costlessly eliminate the link between pollution and output.

that firms emit, and desires to restrict the total amount of pollution in a particular industry. It can do what is practiced in America and elsewhere; that is, to distribute to firms in industry a number of permits equal to the desired level of pollution, and allow firms in the industry to trade those permits. It can be shown that the competitive trading of permits leads to an efficient allocation of those permits. We can use the same kind of analysis as before, but with two changes. We consider an industry composed of two firms and we draw, as before, an Edgeworth box in which the variable on the horizontal axis is labour, and that on the vertical axis permits. The height of the box is determined by the total number of permits that the government allocates. One of the two firms in the industry is measured from the bottom left corner, and the other from the top right, as illustrated in Fig. 32.9. Any point in the box represents an allocation of labour and permits between the two firms.

Suppose the firms start with an equal endowment of labour. In that case the initial allocation point is somewhere along the vertical line in the centre of the box. We already know, from wherever we start, that competitive trading of permits between the two firms will take us to a point on the contract curve which is included in Fig. 32.9. Clearly the initial allocation of permits affects the distribution of the resulting surpluses, but competitive trading eliminates any inefficiency in the market.

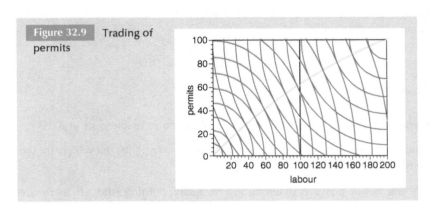

Figure 32.9 Trading of permits

32.5 Over-fishing

I am not sure whether this is a public goods/bads problem, which we will discuss in Chapter 33, or whether it is an externality problem. I suspect that it is a bit of each because public goods problems seem to involve a specific type of externality. In any case, let me briefly discuss it now.

Cod – a fish caught for hundreds of years around Britain – is in serious danger of disappearing. In fact the situation is so severe that there has been at times a total ban on the fishing of cod in the North Sea around the UK. The reason is because it has been over-fished in the past, and the reason for this is that there is some kind of externality imposed when a new fisherman starts fishing for cod. When a potential new cod fisherman is considering whether or not to take up fishing, he considers only his own and his family's costs and benefits, and fails to take into account the effect of his activities on the fishermen already in the market. His entrance into the market inevitably imposes a cost – an externality – on those other fisherman, because it makes it more difficult for them to catch fish. But as there is no organization to control entry, people will make individual decisions based solely in their own interests. The consequence is inevitable: over-entry and over-fishing. To correct this externality requires potential entrants to be charged the costs imposed on the others. But who is to do this?

32.6 Summary

We have made a lot of progress in this chapter, although we have also identified some limits on what economists can say. We have identified what is meant by an externality and have shown that, if a market does not exist and if property rights are not defined or enforced, the externality will cause a loss of efficiency. The clear assignment of property rights, coupled with the enforcement of some kind of trading mechanism, can eliminate the inefficiency, but there are problems attached. We have seen that in practice a more legalistic approach is usually adopted, but this does not eliminate the inefficiency. When the externalities are small and badly defined, an economic solution to the problem is often impracticable. However when the externalities are large and there are ways of measuring them accurately, an economic solution is possible. In the case of production externalities, they may be eliminated by market forces operating through profits and the stock market, which lead to the internalization of the externality.

32.7 Review Questions

1. What do you think that I should have done about my noisy neighbours in Bari?

2. Give examples of laws which are designed to give property rights, but which are too expensive to enforce.

3. What happens about positive externalities? (Usually nothing, though there are examples such as when beautiful film stars take steps to preserve their privacy and then sell their stories to glossy magazines.) What should happen? (The answer depends, partly, on whether it is costly for those providing the positive externality.)

4. Why is that some countries are peaceful and quiet while others are noisy?

Public Goods

chapter

33

33.1 Introduction

Some people regard the message of this chapter – that there are problems with the private provision of public goods – as surprising or depressing. But the message is important nonetheless. As we shall see, the chapter suggests ways of resolving these difficulties.

33.2 A Simple Public Goods Experiment

I do this experiment from time to time in my lectures. It is potentially costly to me, but I have sufficient faith in economics and in human nature. You should get your lecturer to run it in his or her lecture. You could suggest that real money is used; I do that from time to time.

All the students in the lecture room are invited to contribute £10 to a public fund. A collecting box will be passed round the room; each student will be asked to put in the box either a £10 note out of his or her own pocket, or an identically-sized piece of paper on which is written 'I do not contribute' which I have distributed earlier. The point is that no-one, other than each student, knows whether he or she has contributed £10 or not. After the box has been round the room and all the students have either put in a £10 note or the slip of paper, it comes to the front of the room and is publicly opened. The £10 notes are separated from the slips of paper and counted. I then take out of my own pocket an identical number of £10 notes and add them to the pile of £10 notes contributed by the students. This constitutes the public fund. I then divide up the resulting public fund equally amongst all the students in the lecture, and distribute the proceeds equally. End of experiment.

Consider, for example, a lecture with 100 students. Suppose 63 of them contribute a £10 note while the remaining 37 contribute a worthless piece of paper. When the box is opened and counted a total of £630 is there. I add another £630 from my own pocket, so we have a grand total of £1260 in the public fund. This is divided up equally amongst all 100 students present in the lecture, so each students get £12.60.

It is important that you understand what is going on, so let me give two further examples. In both we have the same 100 students. In this second example, 35 students contribute a £10 note while the remaining 65 contribute a worthless piece of paper. When the box is opened and counted a total of £350 is there. I add another £350 from my own pocket, so we have a grand total of £700 in the public fund. This is divided up equally so each student gets £7.00. In the third example 88 students contribute £10, while the remainder each contributes a worthless piece of paper. When the box is opened there is a total of £880, to which I add another £880 so we have a grand total of £1760 in the public fund. This is divided up equally amongst all the 100 students present in the lecture, so each student gets £17.60. What would you contribute? £10 or nothing?

By now you might be starting to think in economic terms. You might argue: 'Well, no one knows what I am contributing, so I cannot affect what others are contributing; I might as well take as fixed what others are contributing. Let me suppose that x of the 99 others are contributing while the rest are not. Then the total from the others is x times £10, and if I contribute this will become $(x + 1)$ times £10. Both of these totals will be doubled before they are divided equally between all 100 students. Let me consider my options:

- If I contribute, I will have to pay £10 and I will get back $20(x + 1)/100$ – a net return of $20(x + 1)/100 - 10$;

- If I do not contribute, I pay nothing and I get back $20x/100$ – a net return of $20x/100$.'

Which is bigger? $[20(x + 1)/100 - 10]$ or $20x/100$? Obviously the second of these, for the first is equal to $[20x/100 + (20/100 - 10)]$, and $(20/100 - 10)$ is clearly negative. The difference between the two is $20/100 - 10 = -£9.80$. So contributing the £10 causes you to lose £9.80, in the sense that you would be £9.80 better off if you did not contribute irrespective of what anyone else is contributing.

The moral of the story is really simple, and is perhaps hidden by this bit of maths; if you contribute £10 then you are already £10 down. What do you get back from this contribution? Obviously the contribution doubled divided by the number of students in the lecture, which is obviously 20p; you are down on the deal by £9.80. What do you contribute? £10 or nothing?

If you agree with the above reasoning, you contribute nothing. You are happy to take your share of the public fund, but realize that you are down on the deal if you yourself make a contribution. If you contribute, then you end up £9.80 worse off than you would do if you did not contribute, irrespective of what the other students do. To use the terminology of Chapter 30, for you not contributing is a dominant strategy; it is better for you, irrespective of what anyone else does.

At the same time you may realize that, if everyone thinks and acts the same way as you do, it will be worse for everyone. If everyone contributed to the public fund, everyone would be better off than if everyone played their dominant strategy. Let us compare these two extremes: if everyone plays the dominant strategy then no-one contributes anything and the public fund is zero, to which I add zero; every one receives zero. However, if everyone contributes a £10 note we have a total of £1000 in the public fund; I add £1000 making a total public fund of £2000. When distributed equally everyone (except me) walks away with £10 more than they had at the start of the lecture – the £20 share minus the £10 which they contributed.

All this is very interesting, but it does not solve your problem. Suppose you are trying to decide whether to contribute or not. Consider the two extremes for the other students. We get the following payoff matrix for you. The entries in the matrix are your payoffs.

In each column, the difference between the two rows is £9.80. This confirms what we have already seen,

Table 33.1   A payoff matrix

	All the others contribute nothing	All the others contribute £10
You contribute nothing	£0	£19.80
You contribute £10	−£9.80	£10

that you are £9.80 worse off if you contribute than if you do not. But notice also that there is a minus sign in the bottom left hand cell – you will actually walk away from the lecture £9.80 worse off if you do contribute when the others do not. Moreover, as the top right-hand cell tells us, you will walk away from the lecture with £19.80 extra in your pocket if you do not contribute while the others do. You are under overwhelming pressure not to contribute.

This is the public good problem. A public good is one that every member of the public (the lecture) can enjoy (if they want – they can always refuse to accept the payout). In this experiment the public good is the share of the public fund, and everyone gets it whether they have contributed to it or not. And the problem is clear; when invited to contribute anonymously to the public good, every one has a strong incentive not to contribute; to free-ride on the contributions of others.

You might argue that we should precede the actual decision by a period of discussion in which you point out to the other students the mutual benefits of contributing. You might also want to include a sort of 'public declaration' of what everyone intends to do. But if the actual contributions are anonymous, this does not change the fact that everyone has a very strong incentive to free-ride by not contributing when it comes to the time of actually contributing. You could institute some kind of written declaration of intentions to try to forestall free-riding, but there remain problems with implementing and verifying such written agreements, particularly when contributions are anonymous.

Perhaps this suggests that the intervention of the state in some form is needed, which seems an eminently sensible suggestion. While one can think of various public goods that are financed privately, it does seem that in practice most public goods are provided publicly. The usual examples include all sorts of local amenities like street lighting, police, public parks and libraries, street cleaning facilities, plus all sorts of national amenities, particularly defence. While some of these may in practice be undertaken by private firms, the financing is usually through local and national taxes.

33.3   All-or-nothing Public Goods

The example in Section 33.2 was of a public good which could be provided in differing amounts, but in which private contributions were either nothing or some fixed amount. There are other types of public good; a more familiar concept, perhaps, is an all-or-nothing public good. This is one which is either provided or it is not. Let us clarify in what sense it is a public good. The usual definition is that it is nonrival and nonexclusive. Nonrival means that providing it for one person provides it for all (in the appropriately defined society); nonexclusive means that no-one can be excluded from consuming it (unless they want to be excluded).

With this kind of public good there are two issues: should it be provided; and who should pay for it? Perhaps economists can say a little on these two issues. We can analyse the key points with a very simple society in which there are just two individuals, A and B. Let us suppose that, if the public good is provided, both individuals can consume it; it is nonrival and nonexclusive. We assume that it costs an amount c to provide it. Whether it should be provided or not will depend upon how the two individuals evaluate it; we can use the concept of the reservation price to decide this. Let us suppose that individual A's reservation price for the public good is r_A and that of individual B is r_B. These are the maximum amounts that the two individuals would pay to consume the good. In general these reservation prices will depend upon the incomes of the two individuals, but here we will just take them as given. There is a number of cases to consider:

$$
\begin{bmatrix}
(1) & r_A > c & \text{and} & r_B > c & & & & \\
(2) & r_A > c & \text{and} & r_B < c & \text{or} & r_A < c & \text{and} & r_B > c \\
(3) & r_A < c & \text{and} & r_B < c & \text{and} & (r_A + r_B) > c & & \\
(4) & r_A < c & \text{and} & r_B < c & \text{and} & (r_A + r_B) < c & &
\end{bmatrix}
$$

We can dismiss case (4) immediately; neither individual would be willing to buy the public good on their own, and jointly they do not value it sufficiently to cover its cost. In this case it would clearly be inefficient to provide the public good.

The other cases are more interesting, and in each of these the provision of the public good could be a Pareto-improvement[1] on its non-provision, depending upon how the cost is divided between the two individuals. In each of these three cases, a division of the cost into a part paid by individual A (c_A) and a part paid by individual B (c_B) would be possible; this would require that $(c = c_A + c_B)$, such that each individual pays an amount less than their respective reservation values – that is, $c_A < r_A$ and $c_B < r_B$. In these cases the provision of the public good would be a Pareto-improvement; both individuals would be better off with the good than without it, in the sense that they are both paying an amount less than their reservation values.

So, in cases (1) to (3) the provision of the public good could be a Pareto-improvement. The problem is in dividing up the cost in an acceptable way, and this depends on what is known about the reservation values. If both individuals know not only their own reservation value but also that of the other person there are several possibilities, perhaps relating the cost contributions to the reservation values[2]. But it is clear that, in some of these cases, the individuals have an incentive to lie about their reservation values.

For example, in the first of the two possible cases under (2), if individual B knows that individual A values the public good more than its cost, it is obviously in B's interest to pretend that his or her reservation value is zero – so that B ends up paying nothing while A pays the full cost, in which case B will enjoy the public good for nothing; he or she free-rides on A.

In case (3), which we could regard as the most empirically relevant case, particularly when generalized to a society of more than two people, both individuals have an incentive to lie about their reservation prices (on condition that the good is provided, of course).

So the problem, both of deciding whether the public good should be provided and who should pay for it, reduces to finding out the reservation prices of the members of society. This could prove difficult as there is no market in which the reservation prices could be revealed and, as we have already argued, individuals have a strong incentive to lie about their reservation prices. The issue then is whether some scheme could be devised which forces individuals to reveal their true reservation values.

One scheme, which we can predict will probably not work, is the following. The potential public good is announced, and all members of society are asked to specify an amount of money which they are willing to pay towards it. These amounts are added up and, if the total exceeds the cost, the good will be provided and all members of society will be sent a bill, in which the cost is proportional to the amount of money that they specified (so that everyone pays an amount less than or equal to the amount of money they specified). If the total falls short of the cost of providing the public good, it is not provided and no-one is billed.

---

1. Pareto efficiency was defined in a footnote on page 117.
2. It is difficult for economists to recommend a scheme, as the various schemes obviously differ in their distributional implications.

The trouble with this scheme is that the cost an individual would pay depends upon the amount of money specified. If the good is to be provided anyhow, and the sum of the amounts specified by the other members of society already exceeds the cost, then an individual has an incentive to reduce to zero the amount of money which he or she specifies; in this way the person ends up with the good and pays nothing. In the case when the individual is pivotal in the decision – that is, when the sum of the amounts specified by the other members of society falls short of the cost, but would exceed it if his reservation price were added to the contributions of others – the individual still has an incentive to reduce the amount specified to the exact difference between the cost and the sum of the amounts specified by the others. It seems that in all cases there is an incentive to understate the reservation price and to free-ride.

There are schemes which provide appropriate incentives to state the correct reservation prices but they, too, have their drawbacks. For example, the scheme known as the Clarkes–Grove mechanism (after the two economists who invented it) gets everyone to reveal their reservation prices, but it taxes (perhaps rather heavily, and certainly unfairly) the individuals who are pivotal in the decision-making process; that is, those whose reservation values change the decision from no provision to provision or *vice versa*. As a consequence these schemes, while they might be good in terms of efficiency, have drawbacks in terms of distributional aspects. Indeed they seem politically unattractive. It is interesting to note that it is difficult to find examples of their application in the real world. In practice, the decision as whether or not to provide public goods and how they should be financed seems to be essentially political.

33.4 Variable-level Public Goods

In contrast to the all-or-nothing public goods which we discussed in Section 33.3, other public goods are variable level, in the sense that it is the level of the provision which must be decided. This is obviously a generalization of the previous case. In a sense the all-or-nothing case is simple, as the question of its provision revolves around the reservation values of the members of society though, as we have seen, even this case involves difficulties in implementation. The variable-level case is more complicated. Let us try and shed some light on it, using the tools at our disposal.

Let us stay with the simple case of a society of just two individuals, each of whom will have his or her own preferences concerning the public good. Remember that the crucial feature of a public good is that, if it is provided at a certain level, both members of society can consume it at that level. So the amount of the public good that both members of society can consume is the sum of the amounts bought by the two individuals.

Consider the analysis of Fig. 33.1, in which we do a standard indifference curve analysis of the optimal choice of the individual. We take a situation in which the individual has to allocate a fixed monetary income – in this example equal to 50 – between a private good (which only he or she consumes) and a public good (which both individuals can consume, and to which they can both contribute). Both goods have a price of one in this example. I assume that the preferences over the two goods are Cobb–Douglas.

There are two alternative situations to consider: the first, which is pictured in Fig. 33.1, is where the other individual will contribute nothing to the provision of the public good; and the second, which is pictured in Fig. 33.2, is where the other individual is prepared to contribute 20 to the public good. In both graphs the variable on the horizontal axis is the quantity of the public good consumed by (our) individual, and that on the vertical axis is the quantity of the private good consumed.

Figure 33.1 Optimal choice if the other contributes nothing to the public good (Cobb–Douglas preferences)

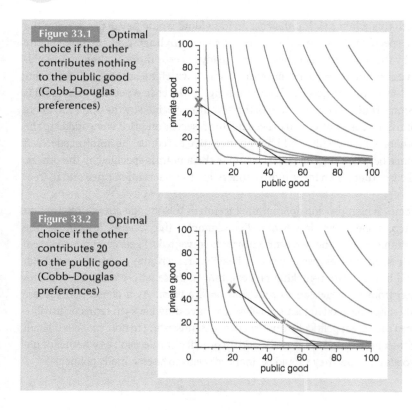

Figure 33.2 Optimal choice if the other contributes 20 to the public good (Cobb–Douglas preferences)

Notice the difference between the two graphs. The large X indicates the individual's endowment point. If the other individual contributes nothing to the public good, then our individual has a budget constraint which goes through the point (0, 50) and has a slope equal to −1, that is, minus the relative prices of the two goods. This is the budget constraint in Fig. 33.1. But if the other individual contributes 20 to the public good, the budget constraint of our individual starts at the point (20, 50) and has a slope of −1. This is the budget constraint in Fig. 33.2; it starts at the point (20, 50) because our individual, if he or she wanted, could consume the 20 units of the public good that the other individual has supplied and buy 50 units of the private good with his or her own income. Obviously the budget line in Fig. 33.2 does not go to the left of the point X because our individual cannot sell the public good contribution of the other individual.

If we check to see what our individual does in the two situations, we find that in the first case, when the other individual contributes zero, our individual spends 35 on the public good and 15 on the private good[3]. In the second case, when the other individual contributes 20 to the public good, our individual spends 29 on the public good and 21 on the private good. Note carefully that, in this second case, our individual consumes 49 of the public good, of which 20 is contributed by the other individual and 29 personally[4]. Thus when the contribution of the other goes up from zero to 20, the contribution of our individual goes down from 35 to 29. This is free-riding to a certain extent; the contribution goes down by 6 when that of the other goes up by 20.

You can probably anticipate the case of complete free-riding, when every increase of one in the contribution of the other causes a decrease in contribution of one by our individual; yes – when the preferences are quasi-linear. We have the same two alternatives here as we had in the case of Cobb–Douglas preferences, and the treatment is similar. Fig. 33.3 shows the situation where the other individual contributes nothing. Figure 33.4 shows the alternative picture – that in which the other individual contributes 20 to the provision of the public good. In both cases, our individual consumes a total of 50 of the public good.

Since our individual always consumes 50 of the public good, any increase in the contribution of the other is invariably met by an equivalent decrease in our individual's con-

---

3. The Cobb–Douglas utility function that I have used has weights 0.7 on the public good and 0.3 on the private good.
4. In the second case we consider the income of the individual to be 70 – his or her own 50 plus the 20 contribution of the other.

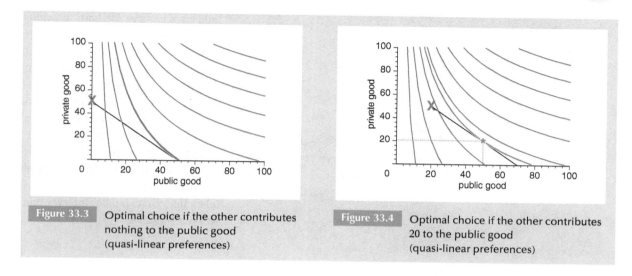

Figure 33.3 Optimal choice if the other contributes nothing to the public good (quasi-linear preferences)

Figure 33.4 Optimal choice if the other contributes 20 to the public good (quasi-linear preferences)

tribution. In fact, if we draw a graph of the contribution of our individual *vis-à-vis* the contribution of the other, we obtain Fig. 33.5, which is perhaps the best illustration of free-riding behaviour.

We might be tempted to ask whether there is a Nash equilibrium in this situation. If we assume that the two individuals are identical, it is clear that a Nash equilibrium exists where each contributes 25 to the public good. This is the intersection of the two reaction curves, of which that of our individual is shown in Fig. 33.3.

But is this an efficient outcome? We can begin to answer this by pursuing a different line of argument. Suppose that each individual agrees, on the grounds that they are both identical, to do the same as the other. We may call this the 'do as you would be done by' case. In this alternative, the budget line changes to that portrayed in Fig. 33.6.

We want to find the optimum point in this 'do as you would be done by' situation. It is shown in Fig. 33.7 as the point to the right, marked by an asterisk. Fig. 33.7 has the same indifference curves and budget line as Fig. 33.6, but includes additional information. This point, marked by an asterisk, would be chosen if each individual worked on the assumption that the other would contribute the same as he or she contributes. We can compare this with the Nash equilibrium which is illustrated in Fig. 33.7 at the point (50, 25). Which is better? It is obviously the 'do as you would be done by' outcome, because it leads to a higher

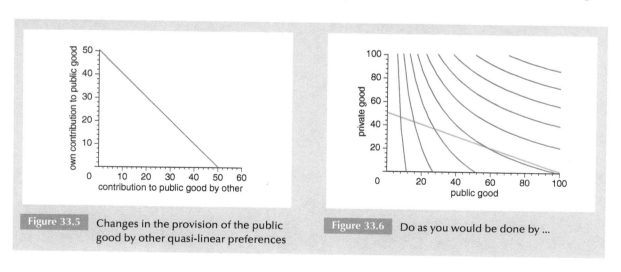

Figure 33.5 Changes in the provision of the public good by other quasi-linear preferences

Figure 33.6 Do as you would be done by ...

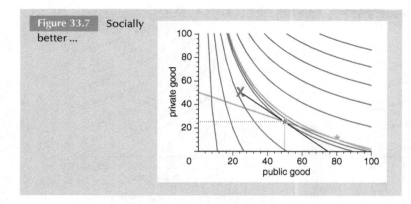

Figure 33.7   Socially better ...

indifference curve for both individuals. But, what is the problem with this socially better outcome? Yes, it is not located on the individuals' reaction curves, and is therefore not an equilibrium. Does this remind you of anything? It is the prisoner's dilemma once again. It seems that private optimizing in this particular public good situation does not lead to a social optimum; once again, it seems inevitable that public intervention will be necessary.

33.5 Summary

 A public good is one that can be consumed simultaneously by more than one person – that is, it is nonrival and nonexclusive.

This chapter points out that there are problems with the private provision of public goods. There are obvious private incentives for individuals to try and free-ride on the contribution of others.

 With all-or-nothing public goods, a necessary and sufficient condition for the optimality of the provision of the public good is that the sum of the individual reservation values exceeds the cost of the provision of the public good.

But we saw that there are problems with getting individuals to reveal their true reservation values. There are mechanisms which might improve things, but these have distributional difficulties.

 In general with public goods there are clear private incentives for individuals to free ride on the contributions of others.

 The Nash equilibrium in a variable-level public good game is clearly Pareto inferior to the social optimum.

 Public good provision seems to require political intervention.

This latter conclusion should not surprise us.

33.6 Review Questions

1. Give examples as to how the provision of public goods is solved in practice.

2. Why do people give to charities? Is this a public good problem? (No, but the financing problem is similar.)

3. What about the lifeboat service in the UK? (It is a private institution maintained by private contributions.

33.7 How can an Experiment Help to Understand the Public Goods Problem?

This is a simple experiment which helps us understand the nature of the public goods problem. To implement it requires a small group of people and some people – 'the experimenters' – who can control the running of the experiment. The instructions are as follows.

The experimenters should organize and implement this public good allocation experiment a predetermined number of times, which the group as a whole should decide in advance. Each time the following should be implemented.

All members of society are given an initial endowment of 100 tokens. Each member of society must individually and simultaneously decide how many of their 100 tokens to 'put into account A' and how many to 'put into account B', the sum of these two numbers being less than or equal to 100. All will declare their decisions individually and simultaneously; the experimenters should decide how they will collect this information. Everyone will then be told the sum of the amounts put into account B; denote this sum by X. As a consequence of these decisions, each member of society will get paid (in hypothetical money, though all should imagine it to be real) the amount (in pence) they themselves put into account A, plus the value of X divided by two.

So, imagine that your society consists of six people and suppose they put the following amounts into their accounts A:

[Accounts A: 0   100   50   20   80   50]

This implies that they put respectively the following into account B:

[Account B: 100   0   50   80   20   50]

The total put into account B was 300; half of this is 150. Thus the payments received would be (in pence)

[Received: 150   250   200   170   230   200]

Payments received are based on half the total of 300 put into account B (150), plus the sum deposited into individuals' account A. As far as each member of society is concerned, they should imagine that they are taking part in an experiment from which they will take away their earnings over the predetermined number of repetitions of the experiment. The object is not to beat other persons, but to make as much money as possible.

After playing the experiment, the group should answer the following questions:

● What has the above experiment to do with public goods?
● Which is the public good and which is the private good?
● What is the Nash equilibrium in this game?
● What is the (best) Pareto efficient outcome of this game?
● What was the outcome in the experiment? Why?

I do not want to give too much away at this stage, but you should note that it is 'best' collectively to put all 100 tokens into account B, whereas if everyone does what it is best for them personally (given what the others are doing), everyone will put nothing into account B. If all six people do the collectively optimal thing, they will each end up with 300 pence; whereas if all six do what is best for them individually, they will each end up with just 100 pence. There seems a contradiction here which you should try and understand. This, of course, is the nature of the public goods problem.

Asymmetric Information

34.1 Introduction

So far we have assumed that all agents in the market have the same information about the good being traded. In this final chapter we consider the problems which arise if some agents have more information than others. The usual case is that the seller knows more about the product being traded than the buyer; an obvious example is the used car market with which we shall start. However the situation can be the other way round; for example, in the insurance market the buyers of insurance usually know more about their risks than does the insurance company which is selling them insurance. This is the second case we shall consider. A final example, with which you will be familiar, is the labour market; when trying to sell your labour (get a job) you know much more about how good you are than do the potential employers; you have to convince them that you are good. I hope this book helps you to do so.

34.2 The Market for Used Cars

We start with an extremely simple and unrealistic example and then generalize it. We consider the market for used cars (known as the 'market for lemons' through the title of an article written by the Nobel Prize winning economist, Akerlof). As you know, it is extremely difficult to tell the difference between a used car that is in good condition and one that is in bad condition. In practice there is a variety of devices that are used to help us distinguish the two, such as the appearance of the car and of the people selling it, the existence or otherwise of a guarantee with the car, and so on; but we consider here an extremely simple scenario in which there is absolutely nothing to help a potential buyer decide whether the car is of good quality or not. To keep things really simple, let us assume that there are just two possibilities – the car is either good or bad, but the potential buyer cannot determine *ex ante* which it is. We assume that the seller knows, however, and we investigate in this section the implications of this asymmetry of information.

The willingness of the seller to sell, as expressed in his or her reservation price for the car, obviously depends on whether the car is good or bad. Let us assume that the reservation price is £10 000 if the car is good and £5000 if it is bad. However the seller of a bad car obviously has no incentive to reveal that it is bad; if he or she can pass it off as good and sell it at a higher price as a consequence, so much the better.

Similarly the willingness of a buyer to buy – as expressed in his or her reservation price for a car – obviously depends upon whether the car is good or bad. Let us assume that the reservation price is £12 000 if it is good and £6000 if it is bad. But recall that the buyer does not know whether the car he or she is looking at is good or bad. Suppose, however, that half the sellers are selling good cars and half are selling bad cars; and everyone knows that.

If a buyer is risk neutral, then the most that he or she would be willing to pay for a used car is his or her *expected* reservation price – that is, £($\frac{1}{2}$ × 12 000 + $\frac{1}{2}$ × 6000) = £9000. But if the buyer knows the reservation prices of the seller he or she will be able to work out that, at that price, only the sellers of bad cars will be willing to sell them, because £9000 is below the reservation price of the seller of a good car. So the buyer is able to work out that all the cars on offer must be bad cars, and is therefore willing to pay only up to £6000 for a car. In such a market only the bad cars will be traded – at a price between £5000 and £6000 – and none of the good cars will be exchanged.

This is obviously inefficient; the market has half collapsed. Only the bad cars get traded – no good cars are traded; and the reason is asymmetry of the information. The sellers know the quality of the cars being traded but the buyers do not. Notice that it is difficult to find a way round the collapse of the market using just price information. You might argue that the sellers of the good cars just need to ask a price between £10 000 and £12 000, and that doing so will signal that the cars they are selling are of high quality; but the problem with this is that the sellers of bad cars have an even greater incentive to try and sell their cars between £10 000 and £12 000. So a high price tag on a car does not guarantee that the car is good.

This example suggests that the asymmetry of information causes the market to half collapse. In practice we can clearly see some markets which have collapsed like this, but usually ways are found to get around this asymmetry of information. These usually involve the passage of time in some way: by car sellers establishing reputations[1], and offering guarantees of some form[2]. We shall consider other such devices later in the chapter.

In the meantime let us slightly generalize this example. In it there were just two qualities. In practice there is a range of qualities. Let us make the natural assumption that the reservation price of the sellers increases with the quality, so that supply is an increasing function of the price, and also that the average quality of the goods on offer increases as the prices increases. This two-fold effect of the price on supply and quality means that the effect of price on demand is two-fold. First we have the usual price effect; as price rises the demand falls. Second, we have the quality effect; as the price rises so does the average quality, and hence the demand. These two effects counteract each other, and the net impact depends upon the relative strengths of the two effects. It seems reasonable that, as the price increases, demand initially increases but then falls. The demand and supply schedules might then look like those in Fig. 34.1.

If this happens we have a unique equilibrium where the two curves intersect. We note that, because the quality increases with the price, the lowest quality cars are sold but not those of the highest quality. In a sense this is a generalization of our earlier result; the asymmetry of information could lead to a market in which the high quality goods do not get traded.

---

1. Note that 'fly-by-night' sellers usually sell at very low prices, while your established car showroom asks high prices. What can you infer about the quality of the goods they respectively sell?
2. It is interesting to note that guarantees are usually not perfect; and that is because the sellers are not sure about the quality of the goods they are selling.

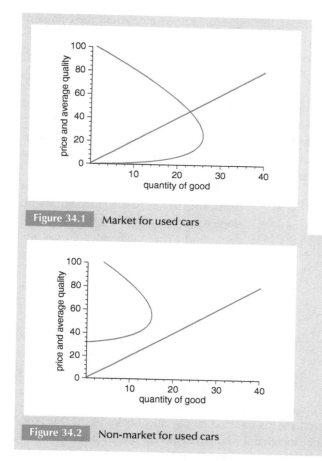

Figure 34.1   Market for used cars

Things could be worse, however. Consider the possibilities below, both of which are consistent with the above story. In Fig. 34.2 the adverse price effect outweighs the positive quality effect 'too soon', so that the demand curve fails to intersect the supply curve. In this market there is no equilibrium – no trade takes place.

In Fig. 34.3, the demand curve is such that it intersects twice with the supply curve and we have two intersections – one at a low price and one at a higher price.

This case is interesting and you might ask whether one of the two equilibria is more realistic

Figure 34.2   Non-market for used cars

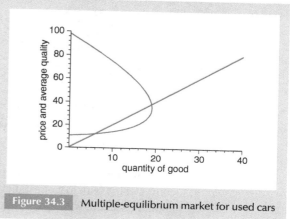

Figure 34.3   Multiple-equilibrium market for used cars

than the other. One might be tempted to answer this by adding some kind of *ad hoc* story to explain how the market adjusts when it is not in equilibrium. We have not explained how this happens, or even how an equilibrium can be attained[3]. But if the price is not an equilibrium price then, if demand exceeds supply the price rises; and if supply exceeds demand the price falls. This could be justified by noting that, if there is excess demand, then the unsatisfied buyers have an incentive to bid the price up; and if there is excess supply, the unsatisfied sellers have an incentive to bid the price down.

Suppose we accept this; can we describe what would happen in the market pictured in Fig. 34.3? If the price is above the higher-price equilibrium, there is excess supply and the price will fall; if the price is between the lower-price equilibrium and the higher-price equilibrium, there is excess demand and the price will rise; if the price is below the lower-price equilibrium, there is excess supply and the price will fall. Taken together, these suggest that either the price will fall to zero (and the market will cease to exist), or the price will move towards the higher-price equilibrium. Even at this equilibrium only the lower quality goods are traded. Whatever happens, the high quality goods are not traded.

34.3 The Market for Insurance

Let us now consider a market in which it is the buyers who have more information about the quality of the good being traded – the market for insurance. Here, when the insurance

---

3. Because it is difficult to formulate a convincing theory of the adjustment of a market out of equilibrium.

company sells insurance to an individual, the individual knows more than the company about the risks which he or she is buying insurance against.

We have already studied the case of the market for insurance with symmetrical information in Chapter 25. Let me begin by reminding you of the story. We assume that there are two possible states of the world, state 1 and state 2. We assume initially that the probabilities of these two states are 0.4 and 0.6 respectively, and that both the insurance company and the individual taking out the insurance know these probabilities. This is the symmetric information case. We assume a perfect (fair) insurance market and a risk-averse individual who has expected utility preferences. We assume that the individual has initially an *ex ante* risky income of 10 if state 1 occurs and 70 if state 2 occurs. We then get Fig. 34.4.

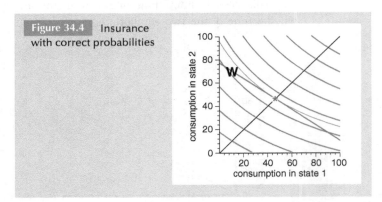

Figure 34.4   Insurance with correct probabilities

Here the point W is the endowment point, and the line passing through it with slope equal to $-0.4/0.6$ is the fair insurance line[4]. The indifference curves are convex and have a slope equal to $-0.4/0.6$ (minus the ratio of the probabilities) along the certainty line, because the individual has expected utility preferences. It follows that the optimal point for the individual is the asterisked point: as we already know, the individual chooses to be completely insured and chooses a point on the certainty line.

Now there are two possible problems of asymmetric information that may arise in this context. First with just one individual, the insurance company may not know the true probabilities. Second, with more than one individual who have different probabilities, the insurance company may not be able to distinguish between them. Let us consider these in turn.

The first problem may be caused by the presence of the insurance itself. It may be the case that the individual, because he or she is completely covered, is not so worried about whether state 1 happens or not (note that, at the chosen point, the individual is insuring against state 1). In this case it is possible that the probability of state 1 happening goes up, unbeknown to the insurance company. Suppose that it rises from 0.4 to 0.5, but the insurance company continues to think that it is 0.4. Then we get Fig. 34.5.

In this figure, point W remains the endowment point, and the line passing through that point with a slope equal to $-0.4/0.6$ is what the insurance company *thinks* is the fair insurance line, because it continues to think that the true probabilities are 0.4 and 0.6. But the individual knows that the true probabilities are 0.5 and 0.5, and hence the indifference curves have a slope equal to $-0.5/0.5$ along the certainty line. The individual would choose the asterisked point in Fig. 34.5; because the company is offering him more than fair insurance for state 1, he or she now

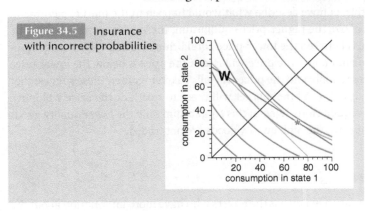

Figure 34.5   Insurance with incorrect probabilities

---

4. Recall that the slope of the fair insurance line is minus the ratio of the probability of state 1 to the probability of state 2.

chooses to gamble on state 1 happening. And the insurance company? It loses money, because the fair insurance line is the straight line through W with slope −0.5/0.5.

This is the problem known as *moral hazard*. The very existence of the insurance contract makes the individual less careful, and changes the probabilities of the two states occurring. The insurance company loses money if it is not aware that this has happened. This is the reason why, in practice, insurance companies take measures to prevent moral hazard; by requiring that householders install burglar alarms and smoke detectors, for example.

The second problem of asymmetric information occurs when there are different potential buyers of insurance who differ in their riskiness, but whom the company finds it difficult to distinguish between. This is called the problem of *adverse selection*, a term which will become clearer shortly.

Suppose that in an insurance market there are two kinds of potential buyers of insurance, whom we call high-risk and low-risk. For the high-risk people the probability of state 1 happening is 0.5; for the low risk it is 0.4. We assume that all individuals have the same initial endowment point (10, 70) as point W above. We have the situation pictured in Fig. 34.6.

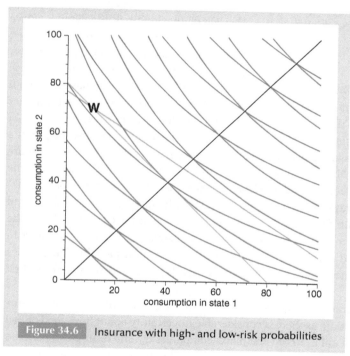

Figure 34.6   Insurance with high- and low-risk probabilities

Here the point W is the endowment point for both high-risk and low-risk persons. The straight lines through W are the two fair insurance lines for the two groups: the flatter line with slope −0.4/0.6 is appropriate for the low-risk group; and the steeper line with slope −0.5/0.5 is appropriate for the high-risk group. The convex curves are the indifference curves of the two groups. Those with slope −0.4/0.6 along the certainty line are the indifference curves of the low-risk group; and those with slope −0.5/0.5 along the certainty line are the indifference curves of the high-risk group. If the insurance company can tell the two groups apart, then the solution is simple. The company offers the low-risk budget line to the low-risk group and it offers the high-risk budget line to the high-risk group. Every one gets full insurance. The company breaks even.

But what happens if the company cannot distinguish between the two groups and has to offer both budget lines to everyone? As we have seen, the low-risk group will choose the low-risk line and chose to be fully insured; with this group the insurance company breaks even. However the high-risk group will also choose the low-risk line, and will choose to bet on state 1 happening for the reasons we have discussed above. With the high-risk group the insurance company loses money. Unless the company can do something clever, it will decide that, in order not to lose money, it can only offer the high-risk line. The high-risk group will completely insure, while the low risk group may take out a little insurance (though not complete because the price is unfair to them). This is called a pooling equilibrium. Notice that it has the same implications as the market for used cars; the high risk (low quality) drives out the low risk (high quality) participants in the market.

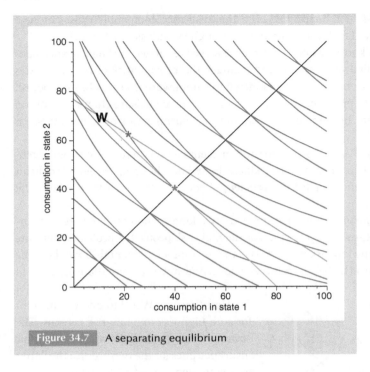

Figure 34.7   A separating equilibrium

But is there something 'clever' that the insurance company can do? Well yes, to an extent. It can get the two types to reveal their types. How does it do this? By offering two insurance contracts – one that it knows the low-risk type will accept, and the other one that it knows that the high-risk type will accept. The key to this is re-defining a contract. Instead of defining a contract by a budget line, we define it by a point. Consider Fig. 34.7 and, in particular, the two asterisked points. These are two contracts which the insurance company offers. One of the two contracts is on the certainty line and on the fair insurance line for the high-risk group; this is the contract accepted by the high-risk group. The other contract is on the fair insurance line for the low-risk group, and is just to the left of the high-risk indifference curve that passes through the high-risk contract; this is the contract accepted by the low-risk group. It is not accepted by the high-risk group because is it is 'just to the left of the high-risk indifference curve that passes through the high-risk contract'. But it is accepted by the low-risk group because it is on a higher low-risk indifference curve than both the point W and the high-risk contract.

This is called a *separating equilibrium* because it separates the two groups. *Ex post* the company can identify the two groups. The company breaks even because both contracts are on the correct fair insurance line. The only problem is that it does not offer full insurance to the low-risk group. So we still get a residual problem in the presence of asymmetric information.

In practice there are ways round these problems. Many involve the passage of time and reflect the fact that the contract is repeated many times. You might like to think that, if the above story is repeated more than once, the company can exploit the fact that the choice in the above problem reveals the type. But note the individuals can anticipate this. If the choice is to be repeated several times, it may not be in their interests to reveal their type on the first repetition.

If you look at actual practice, you will see what insurance companies do. Motor insurance is particularly interesting, as there is considerable uncertainty about how good or bad a driver a particular individual is. In the first place, companies try and distinguish between people on the basis of observable characteristics, which are known to be connected with the probability of having an accident – age, sex, etc. In the second place, many companies use no claim bonus schemes so that there is an incentive not to have an accident and a reward for not having had one. There are also reductions in premiums for non-smokers and for people who take precautions of various kinds.

34.4   The Labour Market

As you may have already realized, the labour market suffers from problems of asymmetric information. When you come to sell your labour, you have to convince potential employers that you are better than the next person; and potential employers have to find ways to distinguish between applicants. As far as the second of these is concerned you may be familiar with some of the devices used; interviews, various tests, perhaps even a period of trial employment with some promise of permanent employment.

As to what you can do to convince employees, the usual way is through sending signals of various types. You may include in your CV that you have certain interesting hobbies which make you more employable; that you do certain kinds of voluntary work; and so on. But probably the most important signals that employers look for, and which you can offer, are your qualifications of various kinds – particularly a degree. There is a high chance that you are currently studying for a degree. Obviously the better the degree that you obtain, the better the signal you will end out to potential employers. What is crucial, however, is that employers know that there is value in the signal. They need to know that a first-class mark signals that the student is better than a student with a second-class mark, and so on. Good universities make sure this is the case by making it more difficult to get a first-class mark than a second-class mark. Indeed, so it should be. To get a first-class mark you really have to understand the material – not just memorize it – and be good at using it.

I hope that this book helps you understand the material. At the same time you have to help yourself by working through the book – not just reading it. You have to work through the examples I have provided, and then make sure that you understand the examples and are able to generalize them. Remembering particular examples will not help you; you have to understand the underlying principles and then be able to apply them in other contexts. The exam questions which I set test these underlying principles, rather than whether students are able to memorize the text. Often students ask me 'where is the answer to this question? We cannot find the answer in any text.' I respond by saying, 'Of course not; if the answer was in the text it would not be a good question. The answer is in your brain.' I hope this book helps you develop your brain so that you become a good economist – and can put out good signals.

34.5 Summary

We have shown in this chapter that asymmetric information causes problems in markets.

 Asymmetric information may cause a market to collapse (disappear completely), or partially collapse (with fewer trades than would be the case with complete information).

We saw that there are some ways around these problems.

 There may be the possibility of a separating equilibrium in which information is revealed by the behaviour of agents in the market.

 Agents may acquire signals which accurately reveal the information.

In a dynamic world there are other ways round the problems which we have alluded to, but which are too complex to cover in this book.

 In practice we see guarantees and reputations which reveal the information.

34.6 Review Question

1　Why is it that prices in tourist resorts are higher than elsewhere?

2　Why do doctors form themselves into professional organizations (helped and supported by the law)?

3　Why do some garages offer guarantees? And why do some garages offer better guarantees than others?

4　Why do car insurance policies have a no-claims discount feature?

5　Why do insurance companies charge more to first-time drivers?

6　Why does SAGA (an insurance company for the over-50s) charge lower insurance premiums than those companies who sell to everyone?

7　Why are you doing a degree?

34.7   Do Lemons always have to Drive Out Plums?

This is a simple experiment on the problem of asymmetric information. You can try it yourself with a group of fellow students. One or more of you should act as 'the experimenter(s)'; the rest of you (make this an even number) should act as the members of a particular market. The experimenters should organize and implement this asymmetric information experiment a predetermined number of times, which the group as a whole should decide in advance. Each time the following should be implemented.

Half the market members will be designated as (potential) buyers, half as (potential) sellers. Each wants to buy or sell at most one unit. There are two kinds of sellers in the market, but only themselves and the experimenters know which type they are. Indeed the experimenters should find a way of determining (without anyone except the individual seller knowing) whether each seller is one type or the other. The probability of any one seller being one or other of the two types is 0.5, so the experimenters could (in the vision of only the seller) toss a coin to decide what type he or she is.

The two types are 'sellers of a lemon' and 'sellers of a plum'. You should first run the experiment with the type of each seller being randomly chosen each round of the experiment. This means that no-one can infer anything from the fact that a particular seller was the seller of a plum in one round of the experiment, as to whether he or she will be the seller of a plum or a lemon in succeeding rounds of the experiment.

The following incentive scheme should be put in place by the experimenters, using either real or hypothetical money (in this latter case, the subjects should imagine that it is real money).

- A buyer who buys a plum will be paid £24, but has to pay the agreed price;
- A buyer who buys a lemon will be paid £12, but has to pay the agreed price;
- A seller of a plum who sells it will be charged £20, but receives the agreed price;
- A seller of a lemon who sells it will be charged £10, but receives the agreed price;
- Sellers who do not sell will not be charged, and buyers who do not buy will not be paid.

Sellers make money by selling at a price above the amount they will be charged, whilst buyers make money by buying at a price less than the amount they will be paid. For example, if a buyer buys a plum from a seller at a price of £22.50, the seller makes a profit of £2.50 from the exchange, whilst the buyer makes a profit of £1.50. If a buyer buys a lemon from a seller at a price of £10.50, the seller makes a profit of £0.50 whilst the buyer makes a profit of £1.50. Of course losses can be made: for example, if a buyer buys a lemon from a seller at a price of £15, then the seller makes a profit of £3 whilst the buyer makes a loss of £5.

The problem is that buyers do not know who are the sellers of lemons or who are the sellers of plums. Furthermore only the individual sellers themselves, and the experimenters (who won't tell anyone), know what type they are.

Now let trade take place, by whatever mechanism you as a group have decided: it could be a double auction; it could be shifting bilateral negotiations; etc. It is up to you to decide. Then play the game the predetermined number of times and work out how much each person has earned. Participants should, as before, try and earn as much as possible.

After playing the experiment, the group should answer the following questions:

- What has this got to do with asymmetric information?
- What is the complete information outcome?

- Did the lemons drive out the plums?
- Were the sellers of plums able to convince buyers that they were the sellers of plums?
- Were the sellers of lemons able to convince buyers that they were the sellers of plums?
- Did things get better with repetition?

There are various 'variations on a theme' that you could try, and which are informative and interesting. Whatever you do, it must be made explicit that buyers are not able to draw any inferences about what type a seller is – selling lemons or plums – from what he or she sold in the previous round. The type of seller must vary randomly from round to round. But clearly, in this obviously non-anonymous experiment, people may be able to infer something about the honesty of a particular seller by observing his or her behaviour throughout the experiment. A more realistic variant of this game is when the seller of plums remains a seller of plums throughout all the rounds of the experiment, and a seller of lemons remains a seller of lemons throughout all rounds of the experiment. In this case, a seller has more to lose by being revealed as dishonest; reputation effects become more important, and it may be the case that these allow the market to function efficiently in that plums are sold for higher prices than lemons.

You might then like to explore other devices which help the market operate efficiently, like offering enforceable guarantees by sellers or the introduction of sustainable legal systems which punish sellers selling lemons at high prices. The ultimate objective of the experiment is to see how the problem of asymmetric information may be overcome by sustainable market mechanisms.

Farewell

I hope you have enjoyed this book, and have learned as much from reading it as I have from writing it. I have discovered a lot. In particular, I found the fundamental truth – economic activity exists because *people are different*. I hope you are different after having read the book.

Exam Questions

Preamble

These are a subset of the examination questions that I have set over the years in the Universities of York and of Bari. As a general rule I try to make all questions unique, and difficult to answer through memory alone. Indeed, if anything is needed to answer the question which requires memory, I usually give the information. A good examination should not be a test of memory, but a test of understanding.

You will see that not all the questions are unique; there are overlaps between one question and another. There is a limit to my ingenuity. Occasionally the questions can be answered rather too easily from the text alone. However there is usually some unique element in every question, and usually some part which requires original thought based on true understanding.

Students often ask me where the answers to the questions are. With everything else on an Internet site, one can understand them expecting (hoping?) that the answers are there too. But I refuse to do this. I am only too familiar with those students who will mis-use answers provided for them; they look at the answers before they have tried to solve the problem for themselves. If they do this, then they learn nothing from the examination questions. If the questions are to be used to learn and to understand, then it is vital that students attempt the questions themselves. Only in this way will true understanding come. Also, as you will see when you tackle the questions yourself, all the questions have answers which are 'obvious once you see them'. This, I feel, is the key to a good examination question – *ex post* it should be obvious; *ex ante* it should be new. None of the examination questions are tests of memory or of mathematics; they are all tests of understanding. Once you 'see' the answer, you know it is right. There is no real need to check whether your answer is right or wrong.

Enjoy!

1   The Market Chapter 2

1.1   Consider a market for a good in which there are ten potential sellers each of whom wants to sell one unit of the good, and ten potential buyers each of whom wants to buy one unit of the good. Suppose that the reservation prices of the ten sellers are £1, £2, £3, £4, £5, £6, £7, £8, £9 and £10 – that is, one seller would sell at £1, one seller would sell at £2, and so on. Suppose that the reservation prices of the buyers are £11, £10, £9, £8, £7, £6, £5, £4, £3 and £2 – that is, one buyer would pay £11, one buyer would pay £10, and so on.

(a)   Draw the demand and supply curves in this market.   [6]

(b)   Find the competitive equilibrium price. Is it unique? Find the competitive equilibrium quantity. Is it unique?   [3]

(c)   Calculate the buyer and the seller surpluses in the competitive equilibrium.   [3]

(d)   Show that the number of trades is not maximized in the competitive equilibrium. What is the maximum possible number of trades? Calculate the total surplus with this number. Which situation is best?   [6]

1.2   Consider a market for a good in which there is one potential seller who wants to sell up to ten units of the good, and ten potential buyers each of whom wants to buy one unit of the good. Suppose that the reservation prices of the buyers are £11, £10, £9, £8, £7, £6, £5, £4, £3 and £2 – that is, one buyer would pay £11, one buyer would pay £10, and so on. Suppose that the reservation prices of the seller are £1 for the first unit, £2 for the second unit, and so on, up to £10 for the tenth unit – that is, the seller would accept £1 for the first unit, £2 for the second unit, and so on.

(a)   Draw the demand and supply curves in this market.   [6]

(b)   Find the competitive equilibrium price. Is it unique? Find the competitive equilibrium quantity. Is it unique?   [3]

(c)   Calculate the buyer and the seller surpluses in the competitive equilibrium.   [3]

(d)   Suppose now that the seller can determine a unique price at which he or she would sell. What price would the seller choose? Would the seller prefer to sell each unit at a different price?   [6]

1.3   Consider a market for some good in which there are five potential sellers, each of whom wants to sell one unit of the good, and ten potential buyers, each of whom wants to buy one unit of the good. Suppose that each seller would accept any price for the good. Suppose that the reservation prices of the ten buyers are £10, £9, £8, £7, £6, £5, £4, £3, £2 and £1 – that is, one buyer would pay £10, one buyer would pay £9, and so on.

(a) Draw the demand and supply curves in this market.   [5]

(b) Find the competitive equilibrium price. Is it unique? Find the competitive equilibrium quantity. Is it unique? Calculate the buyer surplus and the seller surplus in the competitive equilibrium.   [5]

(c) Suppose now that the sellers can choose a unique price. What price would they choose? Might they prefer to sell each unit at a different price?   [4]

(d) Show that, if the buyers could choose a unique price, they would choose a price of zero. But now there would be a problem of the allocation of the five units amongst the ten buyers. How might this be resolved?   [4]

1.4   Consider a market for some good in which there are two potential sellers, seller 1 and seller 2, each of whom wants to sell one unit of the good; and two potential buyers, buyer 1 and buyer 2, each of whom wants to buy one unit of the good. Suppose that the reservation price of seller 1 is £2 and that the reservation price of seller 2 is £6; that is seller 1 would sell at £2, and seller 2 at £6. Suppose that the reservation price of buyer 1 is £10 and that the reservation price of buyer 2 is £6; that is buyer 1 would pay £10 and buyer £6.

(a) Draw the demand and supply curves in this market.   [4]

(b) Find the competitive equilibrium price. Is it unique? Find the competitive equilibrium quantity. Is it unique? Find also the surplus of each buyer, the surplus of each seller, and the total surplus in the competitive equilibrium.   [5]

(c) Now suppose that buyer 1 buys one unit from seller 2 at a price of £8, and buyer 2 buys one unit from seller 1 at a price of £4. Calculate the surplus of every buyer and of every seller, and the total surplus. Is this equilibrium more efficient or more fair than the competitive equilibrium?   [4]

(d) Finally, suppose that the two sellers can choose together a unique price. What price would they choose? Calculate the deadweight loss caused by this situation of 'monopoly'. Explain this loss.   [5]

1.5   Consider a market for some good in which there are five potential sellers, each of whom wants to sell one unit of the good, and ten potential buyers, each of whom wants to buy one unit of the good. Suppose that the reservation price of each seller is £5 – that is, each seller would sell at a price of £5. Suppose that the reservation price of each buyer is £10 – that is, each buyer would pay up to £10.

(a) Draw the demand and supply curves in this market.   [5]

(b) Find the competitive equilibrium price. Is it unique? Find the competitive equilibrium quantity. Is it unique? Calculate the buyer surplus and the seller surplus in the competitive equilibrium.   [5]

(c) Suppose that the sellers could choose a unique price. What price would they choose? Explain the difference between the surpluses in this case and in the case of perfect competition. [4]

(d) Suppose that the buyers could choose a unique price. What price would they choose? Explain the difference between the surpluses in this case and in the case of perfect competition. [4]

2 Demand and Supply Chapters 3–7

2.1 (a) Consider an individual (individual A) with preferences over a good and money such that he considers the good and money perfect 1-with-1 complements. The individual has an initial endowment of ten units of money and zero units of the good. Draw in a graph (with the quantity of the good on the horizontal axis and the quantity of money on the vertical axis) the endowment point of the individual and his indifference curves through the points $(2, 2)$, $(4, 4)$, $(5, 5)$, $(6, 6)$, $(8, 8)$ and $(10, 10)$. [4]

(b) Suppose that the price of the good is p and that of money unity. Graphically or otherwise, show that the individual demands ten units of the good at a price $p = 0$, eight units of the good at a price $p = \frac{1}{4}$, five units of the good at a price $p = 1$, and two units of the good at a price $p = 4$. Show that these values are consistent with a demand function $q = 10/(p + 1)$. [5]

(c) Individual B, instead, considers the good and money perfect 1:1 substitutes, and starts with an endowment of five units of the good and zero units of money. Draw in a graph (with the quantity of the good on the horizontal axis and the quantity of money on the vertical axis) the endowment point of the individual and his indifference curves through the points $(0, 1)$, $(0, 2)$, $(0, 3)$, $(0, 4)$ and $(0, 5)$. Show that the supply of individual B of the good is zero up to a price $p = 1$, after which the supply is equal to five units. [5]

(d) In a graph with p from 0 to 4 on the vertical axis and q (the quantity of the good) from 0 to 10 on the horizontal axis, draw the demand curve of individual A and the supply curve of individual B. Find the price and quantity in the competitive equilibrium, and show that the surplus of individual B is zero. Indicate on the graph the surplus of individual A. [4]

2.2 (a) Consider an individual (individual A) with preferences over a good and money such that he considers the good and money perfect 1-with-1 complements. The individual has an initial endowment of zero units of money and ten units of the good. Draw on a graph (with the quantity of the good on the horizontal axis and the quantity of money on the vertical axis) the endowment point of the individual and his indifference curves through the points $(2, 2)$, $(4, 4)$, $(5, 5)$, $(6, 6)$, $(8, 8)$ and $(10, 10)$. [4]

(b) Suppose that the price of the good is p and that of money is one. Graphically or otherwise, show that the individual would sell ten units of the good at a price $p = 0$, eight units of the good at a price $p = \frac{1}{4}$, five units of the good at a price $p = 1$, and two units of the good at a price $p = 4$. Show that these values are consistent with a supply curve $q = 10 - 10p/(p + 1)$ for individual A.   [5]

(c) Individual B, instead, considers the good and money perfect 1:1 substitutes, and starts with an endowment of zero units of the good and five units of money. Draw in a graph (with the quantity of the good on the horizontal axis and the quantity of money on the vertical axis) the endowment point of the individual and his indifference curves through the points (0, 1), (0, 2), (0, 3), (0, 4) and (0, 5). Show that the demand of individual B of the good is $5/p$ up to a price $p = 1$, after which the demand is equal to zero.   [5]

(d) In a graph, with p from 0 to 4 on the vertical axis and q (the quantity of the good) from 0 to 10 on the horizontal axis, draw the supply curve of individual A and the demand curve of individual B. Find the price and quantity in the competitive equilibrium, and show that the surplus of individual B is zero. Indicate in the graph the surplus of individual A.   [4]

. . . .

2.3   A daily ticket to enter a sports club costs, respectively, £5 for members and £10 for non-members. The membership fee is £M per year.

(a) Use X to indicate the number of yearly entrances to the sports club and Y the money remaining (in £10), and suppose that your preferences between X and Y are representable by strictly convex indifference curves. Show graphically the maximum value of M that makes it convenient to have an annual subscription to the sports club. Suppose that your annual income is equal to £1,000.   [4]

(b) Under the assumptions listed above, does an annual subscription to the club induce more or less attendances?   [4]

(c) Now suppose instead that your preferences are such that you regard X and Y as perfect 1-with-1 complements. How does your answer to parts (a) and (b) change?   [5]

(d) Finally, suppose instead that you regard X and Y as perfect 1:1 substitutes. How does your answer to parts (a) and (b) change?   [5]

. . . .

2.4   The following question refers to a discrete good – that is, one that can be bought and sold only in integer amounts.

(a) Individual A has quasi-linear preferences relative to the number of units of a good that he or she possesses and the amount of money that he or she has to spend on other goods. In the following graph, on the horizontal axis is indicated the number of units of the good that the individual possesses; and on the vertical axis the amount of money that he or she has

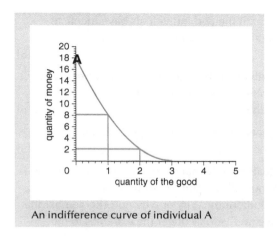

An indifference curve of individual A

left over to spend on other goods. Individual A has an initial endowment zero units of the good and 18 units of money, the price of which is equal to unity. The graph shows the indifference curve of individual A that passes through the endowment point. Obviously the individual can only buy the good. Argue that his or her reservation price for the first unit of the good is ten, for the second unit six and for the third unit two.   [4]

Draw the demand curve of individual A in a graph, putting the quantity of the good on the horizontal axis and the price of the good on the vertical axis.

(b)   Individual B also has quasi-linear preferences over the number of units of the good and the amount of money left over to spend on other goods. In the adjacent graph, on the horizontal axis is indicated the number of units of the good, and on the vertical axis the amount of money to spend on other goods. Individual B has an initial endowment of four units of the good and no units of money, the price of which is equal to unity. The graph shows the indifference curve of the individual B passing through the endowment point. Obviously individual B can only sell the good. Argue that his or her reservation price for the first unit of the good is one, for the second three, for the third five and for the fourth seven.   [4]

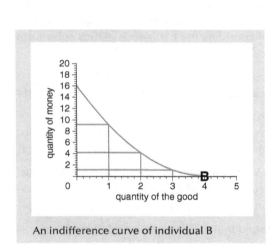

An indifference curve of individual B

Draw the supply curve of individual B in a graph (the same graph in which you have drawn the demand curve of individual A), putting the quantity of the good on the horizontal axis and the price of the good on the vertical axis.

(c)   Now argue that in the competitive equilibrium, two units of the good will be exchanged. What is the equilibrium price? Is it unique? If it is unique, calculate the surplus of each individual at this price; if it is not unique, calculate the surplus of each individual at the average equilibrium price.   [5]

(d)   Show the surpluses of the two individuals in the first two graphs in this question, and explain their economic significance.   [5]

3   The Edgeworth Box   Chapter 8

3.1   Consider an economy without production (only exchange), with two individuals and two goods.

(a) In an Edgeworth box show that, if the two individuals have identical convex preferences, the contract curve must pass through the centre point of the box.   [3]

(b) Now suppose that the two individuals have identical endowments as well as having identical convex preferences. Is it true that mutually advantageous trade is impossible?   [4]

(c) Is it true that, if the endowments are not identical, then mutually advantageous trade must be possible?   [5]

(d) Show that, if the two individuals have identical concave preferences and identical endowments, then mutually advantageous trade is possible. Is there a unique competitive equilibrium? Why or why not? (Remember that, when preferences are concave, individuals prefer the extremes to the average.)   [6]

3.2   Consider a pure-exchange economy with two individuals, A and B, and two goods, 1 and 2. Suppose that individual A considers the two goods perfect substitutes 1:2, while individual B considers the two goods perfect substitutes 2:1. The total quantity of each good in this economy is equal to ten.

(a) In an Edgeworth box corresponding to this economy, draw the indifference curves of both individuals and the contract curve.   [6]

(b) Suppose that individual A starts with all ten units of good 2, and that individual B starts with all ten units of good 1. Find the relative price ratio (p_1/p_2) and the final allocation in the competitive equilibrium.   [4]

(c) Now suppose that individual A starts with all ten units of good 1, and that individual B starts with all ten units of good 2. Find the relative price ratio (p_1/p_2) and the final allocation in the competitive equilibrium.   [4]

(d) Compare the two equilibria found in parts (b) and (c), and discuss why they have the characteristics that they do.   [4]

3.3   Consider a pure-exchange economy, without production, with two individuals, individual A and individual B, and with two goods, good 1 and good 2. The economy has ten units of good 1 and ten units of good 2. For individual A the two goods are perfect complements 1-with-1, thus $U = \min(x_1, x_2)$; while for individual B what matters is the total quantity consumed, and hence B thinks of the two goods as perfect 1 : 1 substitutes.

(a) Draw the indifference curves of the two individuals in an Edgeworth box.   [4]

(b) Derive the contract curve in this economy.   [5]

(c) Suppose now that individual A has as initial endowment all ten units of good 1 and that individual B has all ten units of good 2. Suppose too that the economy is perfectly competitive. Find the relative price (between good 1 and good 2), and the quantity exchanged in the competitive equilibrium.   [5]

(d) Suppose now that individual A has, as initial endowment, all ten units of good 2, and that individual B has all ten units of good 1. How does the equilibrium price change from that in (c)? [4]

3.4 Consider a pure-exchange economy with two individuals, A and B, and two goods, 1 and 2. Suppose that the two individuals have identical symmetrical Cobb–Douglas preferences, that is with parameter $a = 0.5$. Suppose further that they have identical endowments of five units each of each of the two goods.

(a) In an Edgeworth box corresponding to this economy, draw the contract curve. [4]

(b) Now find the relative price (p_1/p_2) and the quantities exchanged in the competitive equilibrium. What characteristics has this equilibrium? Why? [4]

(c) Now find the relative price (p_1/p_2) and the quantities exchanged in the equilibrium when individual B chooses the (relative) price at which trade takes place. [5]

(d) Compare the equilibrium allocations in the two equilibria described in (b) and (c), and explain why they have the particular characteristics that they do. [5]

4 Cost Curves Chapters 10–12

4.1 Consider a firm which produces an output with two inputs (input 1 and input 2) with fixed prices w and one respectively. Suppose that the technology has constant returns to scale and that both of the inputs are variable.

(a) Describe the relationship between the cost of producing some output y and y itself. [3]

(b) In a graph with the cost of production on the vertical axis and w (the price of input 1 on the horizontal axis, show the relationship between the cost and w (at a fixed level of output) in the case in which the two inputs are perfect 1:a substitutes (one unit of input 1 can be substituted with a units of input 2, and either produces one unit of output). [5]

(c) In a graph with the cost of production on the vertical axis and w (the price of input 1 on the horizontal axis, show the relationship between the cost and w (at a fixed level of output) in the case in which the two inputs are perfect 1-with-a complements (one unit of input 1 must be combined with a units of input 2, and this combination produces one unit of output). [5]

(d) How many observations are necessary to discover whether the two inputs are perfect substitutes or perfect complements? How many observations are necessary to discover the value of a? [5]

4.2   Consider a market with two identical firms. Each firm produces an output with two inputs: input 1 and input 2. Suppose that input 2 is fixed in the short run but variable in the long run, but input 1 is variable in both the short and the long run. Suppose that in the long run the technology has constant returns to scale. Suppose also that the two inputs are perfect 1:1 substitutes, such that one unit of input 1 can always be substituted with one unit of input 2. Suppose finally that one unit of input 1 (or one unit of input 2) produces one unit of output. Let us denote the fixed quantity of input 2 (in the short run) by k, and the prices of the two inputs by w_1 and w_2 respectively.

(a)   Derive, graphically or otherwise, the short run cost function (a) when $w_1 < w_2$, (b) when $w_1 > w_2$. Hence show that the marginal cost is zero up to $y = k$, and w_1 after $y = k$.   [6]

(b)   Derive, graphically or otherwise, the long run cost function (a) when $w_1 < w_2$, (b) when $w_1 > w_2$. Hence show that the marginal cost is $\min(w_1, w_2)$.   [3]

Now suppose that the aggregate demand for the good produced by the two firms is given by $p = 1 - (y_1 + y_2)$, where p is the price of the output. Suppose too that the two firms are price-takers.

(c)   Consider first the short period and consider the three cases: (a) $p < w_1$, (b) $p = w_1$, (c) $p > w_1$. In each case find the optimal output for the two firms and check whether the price can be an equilibrium price. (Substitute the optimal outputs in the demand function and check if the implied price is equal to the assumed price.)   [6]

(d)   Would the form of your answer to part (c) be different in the long run?   [3]

. . . .

4.3   Consider a firm which produces an output with two inputs (input 1 and input 2) with fixed prices w and one respectively. Suppose that the technology has constant returns to scale and both the inputs are variable. We use the expression 'the cost' to indicate the minimum total cost to produce a given level of output, given the price of input 1.

(a)   What is the form of the relationship between the cost of producing an output y, and y itself?   [3]

(b)   In a graph with the cost of production on the vertical axis and w (the price of input 1) on the horizontal axis, draw the relationship between the cost and w (with the output constant) in the case in which the two inputs are perfect 1:1 substitutes (one unit of input 1 can be substituted by one unit of input 2, and produces one unit of output).   [5]

(c)   In a graph with the cost of production on the vertical axis and w (the price of input 1) on the horizontal axis, draw the relationship between the cost and w (with the output constant) in the case in which the two inputs are perfect 1-with-1 complements (one unit of input 1 must be combined with one unit of input 2, and this combination produces one unit of output). [5]

(d) Finally, consider the case in which the isoquants are strictly convex – a case in between perfect substitutes and perfect complements. Describe the form of the relationship between the cost and w (with the output constant).   [5]

5 Production Possibility Frontiers Chapter 14

5.1 Consider an economy with production and with two firms and two inputs. The quantity of each input is fixed: ten units of input 1 and ten units of input 2. Suppose that each firm has a technology with constant returns to scale, and in which the two inputs are perfect 1-with-1 complements such that each firm can produce one unit of output using one unit of input 1 and one unit of input 2.

(a) Draw an Edgeworth box with width ten and height ten, and draw in this box the isoquants of the two firms.   [3]

(b) Derive and draw in the box the locus of efficient points in the sense of the use of the two inputs.   [6]

(c) Hence derive and draw the production possibility frontier for the society.   [7]

(d) Is there an optimal point on this frontier?   [2]

5.2 Consider an economy with production and with two individuals (individual A and individual B) who produce two goods.

(a) Draw two linear production possibility lines (one for each individual) in such a way that each individual has an absolute advantage in the production of one of the two goods.   [4]

(b) Draw the production possibility frontier for the society (which consists of the two individuals).   [4]

(c) Now suppose that a third individual (individual C) would like to enter into this society, but suppose that both individuals A and B have an absolute advantage in the production of both goods relative to individual C. Show that, nonetheless, individuals A and B would welcome the entrance of individual C into the society, in the sense that the production possibility frontier with individual C is bigger than that without individual C. Draw the production possibility frontier for the society that consists of the three individuals.   [6]

(d) Suppose that individual C enters into the society, and in the consequent equilibrium individual A produces only one of the two goods while individual C uses half the time on the production of each of the two goods. What does individual B produce?   [4]

5.3   Consider an economy with production with two firms and with two inputs. The quantity of each input is fixed: a quantity 20 of input 1 and a quantity 10 of input 2. Suppose that each firm has a technology with constant returns to scale, and in which the two inputs are perfect substitutes – but the rates of substitution are different for the two firms.

(a)   Draw an Edgeworth box with width 20 and height 10, and draw in this box the isoquants of the two firms.   [3]

(b)   Derive and draw in the box the locus of points efficient in the sense of the use of the two inputs.   [6]

(c)   Hence derive and draw the production possibility frontier for the economy.   [7]

(d)   Is there an optimal point on this frontier?   [2]

6 Revealed Preference Chapter 18

6.1   There are two goods, good 1 and good 2, with respective prices p_1 and p_2. The money income is denoted by m, whereas the quantities consumed are denoted by q_1 and q_2. Suppose that the following table shows observations of an individual on his or her quantities consumed for various price-income combinations.

Observation number	p_1	p_2	m	q_1	q_2
1	1	1	150	75	75
2	1	1	300	150	150
3	1	2	150	50	50
4	1	2	300	100	100

(a)   Which preferences can rationalize the behaviour of the individual as regards consumption of the two goods?   [5]

(b)   In two separate graphs, draw the budget constraint, the highest indifference curve attained and the optimal point for the four observations reported in the table. In a first graph show observations 1 and 3, and in a second graph show observations 2 and 4.   [4]

(c)   Now consider the first observation and find the value of the income, denoted by m_1, for which the optimal point is on the same indifference curve as the third observation. Analogously, consider the second observation and find the value of income, denoted by m_2, for which the optimal point is on the same indifference curve as the fourth observation. Explain the significance of the results that you have obtained.   [5]

(d) Now consider the third observation and find the value of income, denoted by m_3, for which the optimal point is on the same indifference curve as the first observation. Analogously, consider the fourth observation and find the value of income, denoted by m_4, for which the optimal point is on the same indifference curve as the second observation. Explain the significance of the results that you have obtained. [4]

6.2 Consider an individual who is deciding how to distribute his or her given income between two goods.

(a) State the weak axiom of revealed preference (WARP), and give an example in which it is violated. [3]

(b) Consider the following observations on some individual:
  ● Buys four units of good 1 and two units of good 2 when his or her income is equal to ten, the price of good 1 is two and the price of good 2 is one;
  ● Buys two units of good 1 and three units of good 2 when his or her income is equal to eight, the price of good 1 is one and the price of good 2 is two.

  Is this behaviour consistent with WARP? [5]

(c) State the strong axiom of revealed preference (SARP). [3]

(d) Suppose now that we have a third observation on the behaviour of the above individual:
  ● Buys three units of good 1 and four units of good 2 when his or her income is equal to nine, the price of good 1 is one and the price of good 2 is 1.5.

  Are these three observations consistent with WARP and/or SARP? [7]

7 Compensating and Equivalent Variations Chapter 19

7.1 Consider an individual who is deciding how to distribute a given income m between two goods, the quantities of which are denoted by x_1 and x_2. The individual considers that the two goods are perfect 1-with-2 complements – one unit of good 1 with two units of good 2. Therefore the indifference curves of the individual are given by $\min(2x_1, x_2) = $ constant. Let us denote the prices of the two goods by p_1 and p_2 respectively.

(a) Put $p_1 = p_2 = 1$ and $m = 300$. Draw the budget constraint facing the individual in a graph, with x_1 on the horizontal axis and x_2 on the vertical axis. Indicate the optimal point and draw the highest indifference curve that the individual can reach. [5]

(b) Repeat (a) in the case when $p_1 = 2$, $p_2 = 1$ and $m = 300$. [4]

(c)   Now return to the case $p_1 = p_2 = 1$. Derive an expression to determine the value of m (call this value m_1) for which the optimal point is on the same indifference curve as in (b). Finally consider and the case $p_1 = 2$ and $p_2 = 1$. Derive an expression to determine the value of m (call this value m_2) for which the optimal point is on the same indifference curve as in (a).   [6]

(d)   Which of $(300 - m_1)$ or $(m_2 - 300)$ is the better measure of the effect of the price rise of good 1 from one to two) on the welfare of the individual?   [3]

....

7.2   Consider an individual who is deciding how to spend a given income m between two goods, the quantities of which are denoted by x_1 and x_2. The preferences of the individual are given by the Cobb–Douglas indifference curve: $x_1^2 x_2 = $ constant. Let us denote the prices of the two goods by p_1 and p_2 respectively.

(a)   The demand curves implied by the above preferences are: $x_1 = 2m/(3p_1)$ and $x_2 = m/(3p_2)$. Put $p_1 = p_2 = 1$ and $m = 30$. Draw the budget constraint facing the individual in a graph, with x_1 on the horizontal axis and x_2 on the vertical axis. Indicate the optimal point and draw the highest indifference curve that the individual can reach.   [4]

(b)   Repeat (a) in the case $p_1 = 2$, $p_2 = 1$ and $m = 30$.   [4]

(c)   Now return to the case $p_1 = p_2 = 1$. Derive an expression which determines the value of m for which the optimal point is on the same indifference curve as in (b). What is the economic significance of the difference between this value and the original value of income m (30)?   [5]

(d)   Finally consider the case $p_1 = 2$ and $p_2 = 1$. Derive an expression which determines the value of m for which the optimal point is on the same indifference curve as in (a). What is the economic significance of the difference between this value and the original value of income m (30)?   [5]

....

7.3   Consider an individual who is deciding how to spend a given income m between two goods, the quantities of which are denoted by x_1 and x_2. The preferences of the individual are given by the Cobb–Douglas indifference curve $x_1 x_2 = $ constant. Let us denote the prices of the two goods by p_1 and p_2 respectively.

(a)   The demands curve implied by the above preferences are: $x_1 = m/2p_1$ and $x_2 = m/2p_2$. Put $p_1 = p_2 = 2$ and $m = 100$. Draw the budget constraint facing the individual in a graph with x_1 on the horizontal axis and x_2 on the vertical axis. Indicate the optimal point and draw the highest indifference curve that the individual can reach.   [5]

(b)   Repeat (a) when $p_1 = 2$, $p_2 = 1$ and $m = 100$.   [4]

(c)   Find an approximate value for the increase in consumer surplus caused by the fall in the price of good 2 from two to one.   [6]

(d)   Discuss alternative possible ways of measuring the welfare effect of the price fall. (There is no need to do any calculations.)   [3]

8   Discounted Utility Model   Chapters 20–22

8.1   Consider an individual who distributes his intertemporal consumption on the basis of discounted utility: the higher the value of discounted utility, the happier the individual. Hence in a world with two periods, if the individual consumes C_1 in period 1 and C_2 in period 2, then the utility of the individual is given by $U(C_1, C_2) = u(C_1) + u(C_2)/(1 + \rho)$ where $u(.)$ is the utility function of the individual, given by $u(C) = \sqrt{C}$.

(a)   Suppose that the individual is indifferent between the intertemporal bundle (36, 49) and the intertemporal bundle (49, 36). Show that the value of the parameter ρ must be equal to 0. Discuss the economic significance of this result.   [4]

(b)   Now suppose that the individual has an income in the first period of zero and an income in the second period of 100, and that the rate of interest is equal to zero. Determine the individual's optimal consumption in each period.   [5]

(c)   If, instead, the rate of interest is positive, is the optimal consumption in the first period greater or less than that in the second?   [4]

(d)   As in parts (b) and (c), continue to assume that the income of the individual is zero in the first period and 100 in the second. Show that this individual is indifferent between this situation and a situation in which his or her income is 25 in each period. Argue that the rate of interest implicit in an exchange from (0, 100) to (25, 25) is 200 per cent – that is, the individual would borrow 25 in the first period and repay 75 in the second. Show that the individual would not choose the bundle (25, 25) if the rate of interest was 200 per cent. Why not?   [5]

8.2   Consider two individuals, A and B. Suppose that each individual decides on his or her intertemporal consumption on the basis of discounted utility: the higher the value of discounted utility, the happier is the individual. Therefore, in a world with two periods, if the individual consumes C_1 in period 1 and C_2 in period 2, the utility of the individual is $U(C_1, C_2) = u(C_1) + \rho u(C_2)$ where $u(.)$ is the utility function of the individual. Suppose that the two individuals have the same utility function $u(C) = \sqrt{C}$, but their values of ρ are different: for individual A $\rho = 0.5$, while for individual B $\rho = 1.0$.

(a)   For each individual draw in (C_1, C_2) space (with C_1 from 0 to 200 on the horizontal axis and C_2 from 0 to 200 on the vertical axis), the indifference curve which passes through the point (100, 100). (Draw the curves at the points $C_2 = 64$, $C_2 = 100$ and $C_2 = 144$.)   [6]

(b)   Show that the curve of individual A is above the curve of individual B to the left of the point (100, 100), and is below the curve of individual B to the right of the point (100, 100). Explain the economic significance of this fact.   [3]

(c)   Suppose now that each individual has an income of 100 in period 1 and an income 100 in period 2. Suppose too that there is no market to exchange income in the two periods – any exchange must be done between the two individuals. In an Edgeworth box, or otherwise, show that mutually advantageous trade between the two individuals is possible. Hint: consider individual A at the point (121, 64) and individual B at the point (79, 136).

[6]

(d)   Why, in this trade, does individual A consume more than his or her income in period 1 and less than it in period 2? What is the implicit rate of interest in this trade? Could this implicit rate of interest be negative?

[3]

....

8.3   Consider two individuals, individual A and individual B, with identical discounted utility model preferences regarding their intertemporal consumption, such that their preferences with respect to the intertemporal consumption bundle (c_1, c_2) are given by the function $U(c_1, c_2) = u(c_1) + u(c_2)$ where c_1 and c_2 are, respectively, consumption in periods 1 and 2. Let us suppose that the utility function over consumption in any period is given by $u(c) = \sqrt{C}$, as shown in the following figure.

(a)   Show that each individual is indifferent between consuming 25 in each period and consuming zero in one period and 100 in the other. Explain the economic significance of this fact.

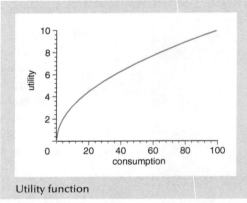

Utility function

[4]

(b)   Suppose that initially the total joint income of the two individuals is equal to 100 in each period. Consider the Edgeworth box below, which has height and width equal to 100, the total joint income in the two periods. The indifference curves of individual A are drawn from the origin at the bottom left and are the dashed curves. The indifference curves of individual B are drawn from the origin at the top right and are the dotted

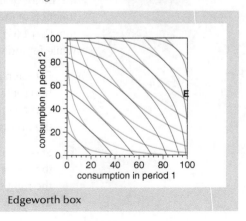

Edgeworth box

curves. Explain the economic significance of the fact that these curves are convex with respect to their respective origins. What is the relationship between the convexity of the indifference curves and the form of the utility function graphed in (a)?   [4]

(c)   Draw in the contract curve and explain what it means.   [5]

(d)   Suppose, finally, that the total joint income of the two individuals is divided as follows: individual A has 100 in period 1 and 50 in period 2; individual B has zero in period 1 and 50 in period 2. This means that the initial endowment point is the point E in the graph in (b). Determine whether (a) there does not exist a competitive equilibrium; (b) there exists a unique competitive equilibrium; and (c) there exist two competitive equilibria. If one or more competitive equilibria exist, find the implicit interest rate and the exchange that follows. If no equilibrium exists, explain why not.   [5]

9 Expected Utility Model Chapters 23–25

9.1   Consider an individual who chooses between risky prospects on the basis of expected utility: the higher is the expected utility, the happier the individual. Therefore, if a prospect yields C_1 with probability p and yields C_2 with probability $(1 - p)$, its value to the individual is given by the value of the expression $pu(C_1) + (1 - p)u(C_2)$ where $u(.)$ is the utility function of the individual.

(a)   Suppose that $u(C) = C$ (that is, the utility of consumption C is equal to C; for example, if C is four the utility is four, if C is five the utility is five, and so on). Draw this utility function in a graph and discuss its economic meaning.   [4]

(b)   Now suppose that there are two states of the world: S_1 and S_2, with probabilities p and $(1 - p)$ respectively. If the individual is indifferent between (a) a risky prospect which yields four if S_1 happens and six if S_2 happens and (b) a risky prospect which yields ten if S_1 happens and zero if S_2 happens, show that the value of p is $\frac{1}{2}$.   [4]

(c)   Draw in (C_1, C_2) space the indifference curve of the individual which passes through the point $(4, 6)$. Does this indifference curve pass through the point $(10, 0)$? Argue that the slope of the curve is -1 where $C_1 = C_2$. (You can quote standard results.)   [5]

(d)   Suppose now that the individual has an *ex ante* risky income $(4, 6)$ (which means that his or her income would be four if S_1 happens and would be six if S_2 happens); and also has the possibility of buying insurance in a fair insurance market (remember that the probability of each state is $\frac{1}{2}$). What quantity of insurance would the individual buy?   [5]

9.2   Consider an individual who chooses between risky prospects on the basis of expected utility: the higher the expected utility, the happier is the individual. Therefore, if a prospect yields C_1 with probability p and yields C_2 with probability $(1 - p)$, its value to the individual is given by the value of the expression $pu(C_1) + (1 - p)u(C_2)$ where $u(.)$ is the utility function of the individual.

(a) Suppose that $u(C) = \sqrt{C}$ (that is, the utility of consumption C is equal to the square root of C; for example, if C is 16 the utility is four; if C is 25 the utility is five; and so on). Draw this utility function in a graph and discuss its economic meaning.   [3]

(b) Now suppose that there are two states of the world, S_1 and S_2, with probabilities p and $(1 - p)$ respectively. If the individual is indifferent between (a) a risky prospect which yields 36 if S_1 happens and 49 if S_2 happens, and (b) a risky prospect which yields 49 if S_1 happens and 25 if S_2 happens, show that the value of p is $\frac{2}{3}$.   [4]

(c) Draw in (C_1, C_2) space the indifference curve of the individual which passes through the point (36, 49), or describe the form of this curve. Does this curve pass through the point (49, 25)? Argue that the slope of this indifference curve is −2 where $C_1 = C_2$. (You can quote standard results.)   [5]

(d) Now suppose that the individual has an *ex ante* risky income (M_1, M_2) – M_1 if S_1 happens and M_2 if S_2 happens – and can also buy insurance at the price P – which means that the company pays to the individual the sum x if S_1 happens, and the individual pays to the company the sum Px if S_2 happens (where x is any amount – positive or negative – that the individual can choose *ex ante*). At what price P would the individual choose complete insurance? (Complete insurance exists when the individual ends up with the same income, after the payment to or from the company, in either state of the world.)   [6]

9.3   Consider an individual who chooses between risky prospects on the basis of expected utility: the higher the expected utility, the happier the individual. Therefore, if a prospect yields C_1 with probability p and yields C_2 with probability $(1 - p)$, its value to the individual is given by the value of the expression $pu(C_1) + (1 - p)u(C_2)$ where $u(.)$ is the utility function of the individual.

(a) Suppose that $u(C) = C^2$ (that is, the utility of consumption C is equal to C^2 – for example, if C is four the utility is 16, if C is five the utility is 25, and so on). Graph this utility function and discuss its economic meaning.   [4]

(b) Now suppose that there are two states of the world, S_1 and S_2, with probabilities p and $(1 - p)$ respectively. If the individual is indifferent between (a) a risky prospect which yields two if S_1 happens and three if S_2 happens, and (b) a risky prospect which yields three if S_1 happens and one if S_2 happens, show that the value of p is $\frac{8}{13}$.   [4]

(c) Draw in (C_1, C_2) space the indifference curve that passes through the point $(2, 3)$, or describe the form of this curve. Does this curve pass through the point $(3, 1)$? Show that the slope of the curve where $C_1 = C_2$ is $-\frac{8}{5}$. (You can quote standard results.)

[5]

(d) Suppose now that the individual has an *ex ante* risky income $(2, 3)$ (which means that his or her income would be two if S_1 happens and three if S_2 happens), and can also buy insurance at the price P, which means that the company pays to the individual the sum x if S_1 happens and the individual pays to the company the sum Px if S_2 happens (where x is any amount – positive or negative – that the individual can choose *ex ante*). At what price P would the individual choose complete insurance? (Complete insurance exists when the individual ends up with the same income, after the payment to or from the company, in either state of the world.) [5]

....

9.4 Consider two individuals, individual A and individual B, with identical expected utility preferences for decision making under risk. Specifically, their preferences over the *ex ante* risky prospects (c_1, c_2) are given by the function
$U(c_1, c_2) = \pi_1 u(c_1) + \pi_2 u(c_2)$
where π_1 and π_2 are respectively the probability of c_1 and c_2, and where utility $\pi_1 + \pi_2 = 1$. Suppose also that their utility function over consumption is given by $u(c) = c^2$, which is shown in the graph.

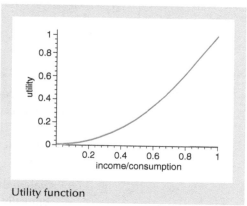

Utility function

(a) Show that the certainty equivalent (which obviously is the same for both individuals) of a risky prospect which yields income zero with probability 0.5 and yields one with probability 0.5, is 0.71. Explain the significance of the fact that this certainty equivalent is larger than the expected value (0.5) of the risky prospect.

[4]

(b) Now suppose that there are two possible states of the world, each with probability 0.5. Suppose too that the total income of the two individuals in each of the two states of the world is equal to one. Consider the Edgeworth box at the right, which is constructed to have both a height and width equal

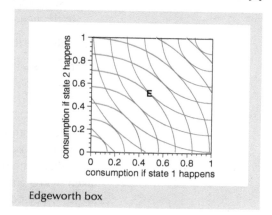

Edgeworth box

to one, the total income of the two individuals in each state of the world. The indifference curves of individual A are drawn from the bottom left origin and are the dashed curves in the box. The indifference curves of individual B are drawn from the top right origin and are the dotted lines in the box. What is the economic significance of the fact that the indifference curves are concave with respect to their respective origins. What is the connection between this characteristic and the form of the utility function $u(c)$? [4]

(c) Now draw the contract curve in the above graph. Explain its economic significance and why it takes that particular shape. [5]

(d) Suppose that the initial income is divided equally between the two individuals. This implies that the initial endowment point is the point marked E in the Edgeworth box. Argue that there are two competitive equilibria – each with the same relative price. Describe the exchange which takes place between the two individuals in these two equilibria, and explain why there is mutually advantageous trade even through the two individuals have identical preferences and identical endowments. [5]

10 Taxation Chapter 27

10.1 Consider a competitive market for some good. Suppose that at the moment there is no tax on the good, but the government is considering introducing a 100 per cent tax. This would mean that, if the price received by the sellers is p, then the price paid by the buyers would be $2p$ and the tax taken by the government would be p.

(a) Analyse the effect of the tax on the equilibrium price and quantity in the competitive equilibrium (graphically or otherwise). In this part you should assume that the demand curve is horizontal and that the supply curve is vertical. [4]

(b) Analyse the effect of the tax on the equilibrium price and quantity in the competitive equilibrium (graphically or otherwise). In this part you should assume that the demand curve is vertical and that the supply curve is horizontal. [4]

(c) Calculate the change in the buyer and seller surpluses in the two cases. [5]

(d) Calculate the deadweight loss of the tax in the two cases. Who pays the tax? [5]

10.2 Consider a competitive market for some good. Suppose that at present the government imposes a tax of 100 per cent on the good. This means that if the price received by the sellers is p, then the price paid by the buyers is $2p$ and the tax taken by the government is p. Now the government is thinking of reducing the tax from 100 per cent to zero.

(a) Using the price received by the sellers as the price variable in your analysis, analyse the effect of the abolition of the tax on the equilibrium price and quantity in the market (graphically or otherwise). You may suppose that both the demand and supply curves are linear. You can assume any specific forms for these two curves, as long as the demand curve is downward-sloping and the supply curve upward-sloping. You are advised to use forms that will make your analysis simple. [7]

(b) Now repeat the analysis, with the same demand and supply curves, using the price paid by the buyers as the price variable in your analysis. [5]

(c) Show that the two analyses give the same results (concerning the effect of the abolition of the tax on the equilibrium price and quantity). [6]

(d) Show that the total surplus (the sum of the buyer surplus and the seller surplus) is higher after the abolition of the tax than before. Is this a good reason for its abolition? [7]

10.3 Consider a competitive market for some good. Suppose that at the moment there is no tax on the good, but the government is thinking of introducing a tax at a flat-rate t on the good. This means that, if the price received by the sellers is p, then the price paid by the buyers is $(p+t)$ and the tax collected by the government is t.

(a) Derive the equilibrium price and the equilibrium quantity before the introduction of the tax (graphically or otherwise). You should suppose that the demand and supply curves are linear. You can assume any specific forms for these two curves, as long as the demand curve is downward-sloping and the supply curve upward-sloping. You are advised to take forms that will make your analysis simple. Show the buyer and seller surpluses. [4]

(b) Analyse the effect of the tax on the equilibrium price and quantity (graphically or otherwise). [6]

(c) Find the changes in the buyer and seller surpluses. How much tax does the government receive? [5]

(d) Is there a deadweight loss caused by the tax? Discuss the effect of the tax on the market. [3]

11 Monopoly Chapter 28

11.1 Consider the market for a good when there is a single seller in the market – a monopolist. Suppose that the aggregate demand for the good is given by $p = 100 - q$, where p denotes the price of the good and q the aggregate demand. Suppose that the monopolist has a technology with constant returns to scale, and that the total cost to produce an output q is given by $C(q) = 50q$

(a) Argue that the marginal cost of the monopolist is constant and equal to 50. [3]

(b) Draw in a graph (with the price from 0 to 100 on the vertical axis and the quantity from 0 to 100 on the horizontal axis) the demand curve in the market and the marginal cost curve of the monopolist. Find the optimal output for the monopolist. What price does the monopolist charge?   [5]

(c) Calculate the profit of the monopolist, the buyer surplus and the deadweight loss caused by the existence of the monopolist in the market.   [5]

(d) Suppose now that the government wants to eliminate the deadweight loss caused by the monopolist. Therefore the government decides to introduce a maximum price in the market. What maximum price should the government choose if it wishes to minimize the deadweight loss? What happens to the various surpluses and to the deadweight loss if it does this?   [5]

....

11.2   Consider an industry in which the aggregate demand is given by $Q = 100(2 - p)$, or in inverse form by $p = 2 - 0.01Q$, where p is the price of the good and Q is the aggregate quantity.

(a) Suppose that initially the industry is competitive and consists of 60 identical firms, all with a marginal cost function given by marginal cost $= q$ where q is the output of an individual firm. Show that the supply curve of each firm is given by $q = p$, and hence that the aggregate supply curve is given by $Q = 60p$.   [3]

(b) Hence show that the equilibrium price is $p^* = 1.25$ and the equilibrium quantity is $Q^* = 75$. Calculate the buyer surplus and the seller surplus in this equilibrium.   [4]

(c) Suppose now that the government is thinking of replacing the 60 small firms with one large firm which has a more efficient technology, such that its marginal cost is always equal to 0.5. Use the fact that the marginal revenue curve in this industry is given by marginal revenue $= 2 - 0.02Q$ and show that, if the single large firm acts as a monopolist, it will produce a quantity $Q^* = 75$ and charge a price $p^* = 1.25$. Calculate the buyer and seller surplus in this situation.   [5]

(d) In what sense is this second situation better or worse that the initial situation? Might it be better in the second situation if the government introduced maximum price legislation?   [6]

....

11.3   Consider a market in which there is a single firm supplying the good. Suppose that the aggregate demand curve for the good has an intercept equal to 100 and a slope equal to −1. To produce one litre of the good, the firm requires to use exactly one litre of petrol and one hour of labour input, which have fixed prices of €20 per litre and €10 per hour respectively.

(a) Draw the demand curve in this market, the marginal revenue curve, and the marginal and average cost curves (in a graph with the quantity of the output produced and sold on the horizontal axis).   [4]

(b) In the same graph show the price charged by the monopolist and the output produced and sold to maximize the firm's profit.   [4]

(c) Now suppose that the production of the output causes the emission of fumes dangerous to the workers, and the government insists that all workers are protected through the use of protective masks. These cost €10 per hour. What effect does this government regulation have on the price and output of the monopolist?.   [5]

(d) Who pays for the protective masks?   [5]

11.4 The bar PUZ is the only place where it is possible to eat in the University and, as a consequence, behaves like a monopolist. The clients of the bar PUZ are equal numbers of economics students and law students. They have different habits: the economics students always pay in cash, while the law students always pay with the ITALIAN EXPRESS credit card. As a consequence, the cost of a sandwich at the bar is £1 for the economics students and £2 for the law students (the difference being the commission that ITALIAN EXPRESS charges). For simplicity assume that the demand curves for these two groups of students are identical and are linear.

(a) Show graphically the behaviour of the bar PUZ in the case when it can charge what it wants to the two groups of students.   [5]

(b) Suppose now that the government introduces legislation which says that the bar must charge the same price to both groups of students. What does the bar do now?   [5]

(c) What are the advantages and disadvantages of the government legislation?   [5]

(d) Continuing to assume that the government legislation is in force, what difference would it make if the bar PUZ operated as a price taker?   [3]

11.5 The technology of a monopolist is Cobb–Douglas and is given by production function $y = q_1 q_2$, where y is the output of the monopolist and q_1 and q_2 are the quantities of the two inputs used by the firm.

(a) Five of the isoquants implied by this technology are shown in the figure. In order, the levels of output associated with the isoquants are 1, 4, 9, 16 and 25. Discuss the economies of scale that the firm possesses.

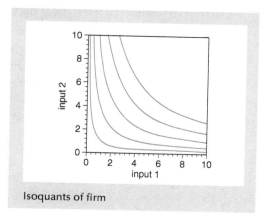

Isoquants of firm

[4]

(b) Assume now that the prices of the two inputs are both equal to one. Show, graphically or otherwise, that the most efficient way to produce nine units of output is to use three units of each input, Hence it follows that the minimum cost of producing nine units of output is six. In an analogous fashion, show that the minimum cost of producing one unit of output is two, and that for producing 25 units of output is ten. Generalizing, argue that the form of the cost function is such that the cost is proportional to the square root of the quantity, that is $C(y) = 2\sqrt{y}$.   [5]

(c) If the cost function has this form, then it can be shown that the marginal cost function is given by $MC = 1/\sqrt{y}$ (you do not have to prove this). This marginal cost function is drawn in the adjoining graph. Discuss the economic significance of the fact that this marginal cost function is negatively sloped.

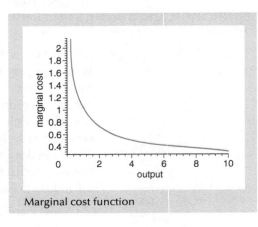

Marginal cost function

[3]

(d) Let us suppose, finally, that the demand curve facing the monopolist is given (in inverse form) by $p = 2 - 0.2y$. Draw this curve in the preceding graph, and insert the marginal revenue curve of the monopolist. What is the optimal price and output for the monopolist?   [6]

· ·

11.6   The technology of a perfectly competitive firm takes the Cobb–Douglas form $y = 2q_1^{.25}q_2^{.25}$, where y is the output of the firm and q_1 and q_2 are the quantities of the two inputs used by the firm.

(a) In the graph are shown five isoquants from the above technology. In order, the levels of output associated with the five isoquants are 6, 7, 8, 9 and 10. Discuss the returns to scale associated with the technology of the firm.

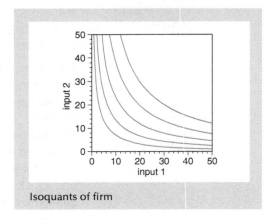

Isoquants of firm

[4]

(b) Now assume that the prices of each of the two inputs are fixed at one. Show, graphically or otherwise, that the most efficient way to produce eight units of output is to use 16 units of each input, and hence that the minimum cost of eight units of output is 32. Argue in a similar way that the cheapest cost of producing six units of output is 18, and the cheapest cost of producing ten units of output is 50. Generalizing, argue that the cost function is quadratic, in particular $C(y) = y^2/2$. [4]

(c) If the cost function is quadratic, as in part (b) above, it can be shown that the marginal cost function is linear, and in this case is given by the function: marginal cost = y (you do not need to prove this). Use the graph, or some other means, to argue that the supply curve of the firm is given by $y = p$, where y is the price of the output of the firm (taken as given by the firm).

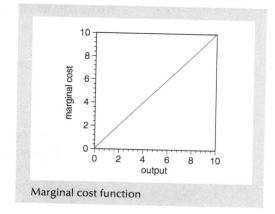

Marginal cost function

[5]

(d) Now consider a particular price, let us say $p = 5$. Show that the optimal output is five and hence that total revenue is 25. Use the total cost function of the firm to show that the cost of producing an output of five is 12.5, and hence that the profits of the firm are $(25 - 12.5) = 12.5$. Show this result as an area in the graph above. [5]

12 Game Theory and Duopoly Chapters 30–31

12.1 Consider a simultaneous play game with two players.

(a) Explain the concept of a Nash equilibrium in such a game, and discuss whether it could be generalized to a game with more than two players. [4]

(b) Give a numerical example of a game in which both players have two choices and in which there are two Nash equilibria – one of which is Pareto-superior to the other.

		Player B	
		Choice 1	Choice 2
Player A	Choice 1		
	Choice 2		

[5]

(c) Do you think that the Pareto-superior outcome will be the actual outcome in practice?   [3]

(d) Consider a duopoly. Argue that the situation described in part (b) is unlikely in a game between two duopolists.   [6]

12.2 Consider a duopoly with two identical firms. Suppose that the aggregate demand is a linear function of price; the two firms have constant returns to scale; the two firms choose their outputs simultaneously; and the demand curve determines the price of their product. Under these conditions, the reaction curves of the two firms are linear:

$$\begin{bmatrix} \text{firm 1: } x_1 = a - 0.5x_2 \\ \text{firm 2: } x_2 = a - 0.5x_1 \end{bmatrix}$$

where x_1 and x_2 are the outputs of firms 1 and 2 respectively.

(a) Draw in a graph in (x_1, x_2) space these two reaction curves. Denote with x_c the aggregate output that the firms would produce in a competitive market; and denote with x_m the aggregate output that the two firms would produce if they merged together and acted like a monopolist. Argue that $x_c = 2a$ and $x_m = a$.   [5]

(b) Note that the reaction curves intersect at the point $(2a/3, 2a/3)$. Consider three values of output: $a/3$, $2a/3$ and a. In the following table give an example of the profits of the two firms at these three values. (Suppose that at the outputs $x_1 = x_2 = 2a/3$, the profits are 50 and 50.)

	$x_2 = a/3$	$x_2 = 2a/3$	$x_2 = a$
$x_1 = a/3$			
$x_1 = 2a/3$		50, 50	
$x_1 = a$			

Show that $(x_1 = x_2 = 2a/3)$ is a Nash equilibrium in the game represented by the table.   [5]

(c) Suppose now that the reaction functions are not linear. In (x_1, x_2) space draw the reaction curves of the two firms in such a way that there are three Nash equilibria – at the points $(x_1, x_2) = (a/3, a)$, $(2a/3, 2a/3)$ and $(a, a/3)$. Also show, in the following table, profits for the two firms that are consistent with the notion that there are three Nash equilibria in the game between the two firms.   [6]

	$x_2 = a/3$	$x_2 = 2a/3$	$x_2 = a$
$x_1 = a/3$			
$x_1 = 2a/3$			
$x_1 = a$			

(d) Which of these three Nash equilibria is the most plausible?   [3]

12.3 Consider a market for a good in which there are two sellers, firm 1 and firm 2. The aggregate demand for the identical good that they produce is given by $p = 100 - (q_1 + q_2)$, where q_1 is the output of firm 1 and q_2 is the output of firm 2.

(a) Argue that the demand for the output of firm 1, if firm 2 supplies a quantity $q_2 = Q_2$, is given by $p = (100 - Q_2) - q_1$, and hence that the marginal revenue of firm 1, given a certain level of output of firm $2 = Q_2$, is given by marginal revenue $= (100 - Q_2) - 2q_1$. (You can use standard results concerning the relationship between a linear demand curve and the implied marginal revenue curve.) [5]

(b) Assume that neither firm incurs any production costs. Using the condition for the optimal output for a monopolist, argue that the optimal output for firm 1, given a level of output for firm $2 = Q_2$, is given by the solution to the equation $(100 - Q_2) - 2q_1 = 0$; and hence is given by $q_1 = (100 - Q_2)/2$. In a similar way, argue that the optimal output for firm 2, given a level of output for firm 1 (Q_1), is given by $q_2 = (100 - Q_1)/2$ [5]

(c) Now consider a simultaneous game between the two firms in which each firm must choose – at the same time and without knowing what the other firm is choosing – their output. What are the outputs of the two firms in the Nash equilibrium of this game? What is the price of the good in this Nash equilibrium? [5]

(d) What would be the price in this market if both firms were price-takers? [3]

Index